THE LOEB CLASSICAL LIBRARY

FOUNDED BY JAMES LOEB, LL.D.

EDITED BY

†T. E. PAGE, c.h., litt.d.

E. CAPPS, ph.d., ll.d.   W. H. D. ROUSE, litt.d.

L. A. POST, m.a.   E. H. WARMINGTON, m.a.

PLINY

NATURAL HISTORY

II

LIBRI III-VII

PLINY

'NATURAL HISTORY'

WITH AN ENGLISH TRANSLATION
IN TEN VOLUMES

VOLUME II
LIBRI III–VII

BY

H. RACKHAM, M.A.
FELLOW OF CHRIST'S COLLEGE, CAMBRIDGE

CAMBRIDGE, MASSACHUSETTS
HARVARD UNIVERSITY PRESS
LONDON
WILLIAM HEINEMANN LTD
MCMXLVII

First printed 1942
Reprinted 1947

PREFATORY NOTE

Tнɪꜱ translation is designed to afford assistance to the student of the Latin text; it is not primarily intended to supply the English reader with a substitute for the Latin.

CONTENTS

INTRODUCTION

THIS volume contains Books III–VII of Pliny's *Naturalis Historia*.

The detailed contents will be found in Pliny's own outline of his work, which, with lists of the authorities used for each Book, constitutes Book I; for Books III–VII see Volume I, pp. 28–41, of this edition.

The subject of Books III–VI is the geography, physical, political and historical, of the ancient world.

Book III: Southern Spain; Southern Gaul; Italy; the Western Mediterranean and Ionian and Adriatic Islands; the countries round the north of the Adriatic.

Book IV: Greece and the rest of the Balkan Peninsula; the islands of the Eastern Mediterranean; the Black Sea and the countries west of it; Northern Europe.

Book V: North Africa; the Eastern Mediterranean and Asia Minor.

Book VI: Countries from the Black Sea to India; Persia; Arabia; Ethiopia; the Nile valley.

The subject of Book VII is the human race—its biology, physiology and psychology.

PLINY:
NATURAL HISTORY

PLINII NATURALIS HISTORIA

LIBER III

1 I. Hactenus de situ et miraculis terrae aquarumque et siderum ac ratione universitatis atque mensura.

Nunc de partibus, quamquam infinitum id quoque existimatur nec temere sine aliqua reprehensione tractatum, haut ullo in genere venia iustiore, si modo minime mirum est hominem genitum non omnia humana novisse. quapropter auctorem neminem unum sequar, sed ut quemque verissimum in quaque parte arbitror, quoniam commune ferme omnibus fuit ut eos quisque diligentissime situs diceret in 2 quibus ipse prodebat.[1] ideo nec culpabo aut coarguam quemquam. locorum nuda nomina et quanta dabitur brevitate ponentur, claritate causisque dilatis in suas partes; nunc [2] enim sermo de toto est. quare sic accipi velim ut si vidua fama sua nomina qualia fuere primordio ante ullas res gestas nuncu-

---

[1] V.l. prodibat.   [2] V.l. nec.

PLINY: NATURAL HISTORY

BOOK III

I. So much as to the situation and the marvels of land and water and of the stars, and the plan and dimensions of the universe.

Now to describe its parts, although this also is *Geography* considered an endless task, not lightly undertaken *of the world.* without some adverse criticism, though in no field does enquiry more fairly claim indulgence, only granting it to be by no means wonderful that one born a human being should not possess all human knowledge. For this reason I shall not follow any single authority, but such as I shall judge most reliable in their several departments, since I have found it a characteristic common to virtually all of them that each gave the most careful description of the particular region in which he personally was writing. Accordingly I shall neither blame nor criticise anyone. The bare names of places will be set down, and with the greatest brevity available, their celebrity and its reasons being deferred to their proper sections; for my topic now is the world as a whole. Therefore I should like it to be understood that I specify the bare names of the places without their record, as they were in the beginning before they had achieved

pentur, et sit quaedam in his nomenclatura quidem, sed mundi rerumque naturae.

3 Terrarum orbis universus in tres dividitur partes, Europam Asiam Africam. origo ab occasu solis et Gaditano freto, qua inrumpens oceanus Atlanticus in maria interiora diffunditur. hinc intranti dextera Africa est, laeva Europa, inter has Asia; termini amnes Tanais et Nilus. xv p. in longitudinem quas diximus fauces oceani patent, v in latitudinem, a vico Mellaria Hispaniae ad promunturium Africae

4 Album, auctore Turranio Gracile iuxta genito; T. Livius ac Nepos Cornelius latitudinis tradiderunt minimum [1] vii p., ubi vero plurimum, x: tam modico ore tam inmensa aequorum vastitas panditur. nec profunda altitudo miraculum minuit: frequentes quippe taeniae candicantis vadi carinas territant; qua de causa limen interni maris multi eum locum appellavere. proximis autem faucibus utrimque impositi montes coercent claustra, Abyla Africae, Europae Calpe, laborum Herculis metae, quam ob causam indigenae columnas eius dei vocant, creduntque perfossas exclusa antea admisisse maria et rerum naturae mutasse faciem.

5 Primum ergo de Europa altrice victoris omnium gentium populi longeque terrarum pulcherrima, quam plerique merito non tertiam portionem fecere verum

---

[1] *Edd.*: minus.

---

any history, and that though their names are mentioned, it is only as forming a portion of the world and of the natural universe.

The whole circuit of the earth is divided into three *Three* parts, Europe, Asia and Africa. The starting point *continents.* is in the west, at the Straits of Gibraltar, where the *Gibraltar.* Atlantic Ocean bursts in and spreads out into the inland seas. On the right as you enter from the ocean is Africa and on the left Europe, with Asia between them; the boundaries are the river Don and the river Nile. The ocean straits mentioned are fifteen miles long and five miles broad, from the village of Mellaria*a* in Spain to the White Cape*b* in Africa, as given by Turranius Gracilis, a native of the neighbourhood, while Livy and Cornelius Nepos state the breadth at the narrowest point as seven miles and at the widest as ten miles: so narrow is the mouth through which pours so boundless an expanse of water. Nor is it of any great depth, so as to lessen the marvel, for recurring streaks of whitening shoal-water terrify passing keels, and consequently many have called this place the threshold of the Mediterranean. At the narrowest part of the Straits stand mountains on either side, enclosing the channel, Ximiera in Africa and Gibraltar in Europe; these were the limits of the labours of Hercules, and consequently the inhabitants call them the Pillars of that deity, and believe that he cut the channel through them and thereby let in the sea which had hitherto been shut out, so altering the face of nature.

To begin then with Europe, nurse of the race that *Europe: its* has conquered all the nations, and by far the loveliest *four gulfs.* portion of the earth, which most authorities, not without reason, have reckoned to be not a third part but a

5

aequam, in duas partes ab amne Tanai ad Gaditanum fretum universo orbe diviso. oceanus a
quo dictum est spatio Atlanticum mare infundens
et avido meatu terras quaecunque venientem ex-
pavere demergens resistentis quoque flexuoso litorum anfractu lambit, Europam vel maxime recessibus
crebris excavans, sed in quattuor praecipuos sinus,
quorum primus a Calpe Hispaniae extimo (ut dictum
est) monte Locros, Bruttium usque promunturium,
inmenso ambitu flectitur.

6   In eo prima Hispania terrarum est Ulterior appellata, eadem Baetica, mox a fine Murgitano Citerior
eademque Tarraconensis ad Pyrenaei iuga.   Ulterior
in duas per longitudinem provincias dividitur, siquidem Baeticae latere septentrionali praetenditur
Lusitania amne Ana discreta. ortus hic in Lamini-
tano agro Citerioris Hispaniae et modo in stagna se
fundens modo in angustias resorbens aut in totum
cuniculis condens et saepius nasci gaudens in Atlanticum oceanum effunditur. Tarraconensis autem ad-
fixa Pyrenaeo totoque eius a latere decurrens et
simul ad Gallicum oceanum Hiberico a mari transversa se pandens Solorio monte et Oretanis iugis
Carpentanisque et Asturum a Baetica atque Lusitania
distinguitur.

7   Baetica a flumine eam mediam secante cognominata

ᵃ Nearly the present Andalusia; named from the river
Baetis, the Guadalquivir.
ᵇ Portugal, excluding the part between the Douro and the
Minho.
ᶜ The Guadiana (Arabic *wadi*, ' river ').
ᵈ Perhaps Alhambra.
ᵉ *i.e.* from the Balearic Channel to the Bay of Biscay.

half of the world, dividing the whole circle into two portions by a line drawn from the river Don to the Straits of Gibraltar. The ocean, pouring the Atlantic sea through the passage I have described, and in its eager progress overwhelming all the lands that shrank in awe before its coming, washes also those that offer resistance with a winding and broken coast-line: Europe especially it hollows out with a succession of bays, but into four chief gulfs, of which the first bends in a vast curve from the Rock of Gibraltar, which, as I have said, is the extremity of Spain, right to Locri on Cape Spartivento. *Western Mediterranean.*

The first land situated on this gulf is called Further Spain or Baetica,[a] and then, from the frontier at Mujacar, Hither Spain or the Department of Tarragon, extending to the chain of the Pyrenees. Further Spain is divided lengthwise into two provinces, Lusitania[b] extending along the north side of Baetica and separated from it by the river Anas.[c] This rises in Hither Spain, in the territory of Laminium,[d] and now spreading out into meres, now contracting into narrows, or burrowing entirely underground and gaily emerging again several times over, discharges itself into the Atlantic Ocean. The Department of Tarragon adjoins the Pyrenees, running down along the whole of one side of the chain and also extending across from the Iberian Sea to the Gallic Ocean,[e] and is separated from Baetica and Lusitania by Mount Solorius[f] and by the ranges of the Oretani and Carpentani and of the Astures.[g] *The Spanish Peninsula.* *Physical geography.*

Baetica, named after the river Baetis which *Andalusia.*

[f] The Sierra Nevada.
[g] The Sierra Morena, Mont de Toledo and Sierra de las Asturias.

7

cunctas provinciarum divite cultu et quodam fertili
ac peculiari nitore praecedit. iuridici conventus ei
IV, Gaditanus Cordubensis Astigitanus Hispalensis.
oppida omnia numero CLXXV, in iis coloniae IX, muni-
cipia c. R. X, Latio antiquitus donata XXVII, libertate
VI, foedere III, stipendiaria CXX. ex his digna
memoratu aut Latino sermone dictu facilia, a
flumine Ana, litore oceani, oppidum Ossonoba,
Aestuaria cognominatum, inter confluentes [1] Luxiam
et Urium, Hareni montes, Baetis fluvius, litus
Curense inflexo sinu, cuius ex adverso Gadis inter
insulas dicendae, promunturium Iunonis, portus
Vaesippo, oppidum Baelo, Mellaria, fretum ex
Atlantico mari, Carteia Tartesos a Graecis dicta,
8 mons Calpe. dein litore interno oppidum Barbesula
cum fluvio, item Salduba, oppidum Suel, Malaca
cum fluvio, foederatorum. dein Maenuba cum fluvio,
Sexi cognomine Firmum Iulium, Sel, Abdara, Murgi
Baeticae finis. oram eam in universum originis
Poenorum existimavit M. Agrippa; ab Ana autem
Atlantico oceano obversa Bastulorum Turdulorumque
est. in universam Hispaniam M. Varro pervenisse
Hiberos et Persas et Phoenicas Celtasque et Poenos
tradit; lusum enim Liberi patris aut lyssam cum eo

---

[1] *Detlefsen.*: inter fluentes.

---

[a] Probably the Tinto.   [b] IV. 119.

[c] Cape Trafalgar.

divides it in two, stands first among the whole of the
provinces in the richness of its cultivation and in a
sort of peculiar fertility and brilliance of vegetation.
It comprises four jurisdictions, those of Cadiz,
Cordova, Ecija and Seville. Its towns number in
all 175, of which 9 are colonies, 10 municipalities of
Roman citizens, 27 towns granted early Latin
rights, 6 free towns, 3 bound by treaty to Rome and
120 paying tribute. Worthy of mention in this
district, or easily expressed in Latin, are: on the
ocean coast beginning at the river Guadiana, the
town Ossonoba, surnamed Aestuaria, at the confluence of the Luxia and the Urium *a*; the Hareni
Mountains; the river Guadalquivir; the winding
bay of the Coast of Curum, opposite to which is
Cadiz, to be described *b* among the islands; the
Promontory of Juno *c*; Port Vaesippo; the town of
Baelo; Mellaria, the strait entering from the
Atlantic; Carteia, called by the Greeks Tartesos;
Gibraltar. Next, on the coast inside the straits,
are: the town of Barbesula with its river; ditto
Salduba; the town of Suel; Malaga with its river,
one of the treaty towns. Then comes Maenuba
with its river; Firmum Julium surnamed Sexum;
Sel; Abdara; Murgi, which is the boundary of
Baetica. The whole of this coast was thought by
Marcus Agrippa to be of Carthaginian origin; but
beyond the Guadiana and facing the Atlantic Ocean
is the territory of the Bastuli and Turduli. Marcus
Varro records that the whole of Spain was penetrated by invasions of Hiberi, Persians, Phoenicians,
Celts and Carthaginians; for he says that it was the
sport (*lusus*) of Father Liber, or the frenzy (λύσσα)
of those who revelled with him, that gave its name to

bacchantium nomen dedisse Lusitaniae, et Pana praefectum eius universae. at quae de Hercule ac Pyrene vel Saturno traduntur fabulosa in primis arbitror.

9 Baetis in Tarraconensis provinciae non, ut aliqui dixere, Mentesa oppido sed Tugiensi exoriens saltu (iuxta quem Tader fluvius qui Carthaginiensem agrum rigat) Ilorci refugit Scipionis rogum, versusque in occasum oceanum Atlanticum provinciam adoptans petit, modicus primo, sed multorum fluminum capax quibus ipse famam aquasque aufert. Baeticae primum ab Ossigetania infusus amoeno blandus alveo crebris dextra laevaque accolitur oppidis.

10 Celeberrima inter hunc et oceani oram in mediterraneo Segida quae Augurina cognominatur, Iulia quae Fidentia, Urgao quae Alba, Ebura quae Cerialis, Iliberri quod Liberini, Ilipula quae Laus, Artigi quod Iulienses, Vesci quod Faventia, Singili, Ategua, Arialdunum, Agla Minor, Baebro, Castra Vinaria, Cisimbrium, Hippo Nova, Illurco, Osca, Oscua, Sucaelo, Unditanum, Tucci Vetus—omnia Bastetaniae vergentis ad mare. conventus vero Cordubensis circa flumen ipsum Ossigi quod cognominatur Latonium, Iliturgi quod Forum Iulium, Ipra, Isturgi quod Triumphale, Sucia, et XVII p. remotum in mediterraneo Obulco quod Pontificense appellatur, mox Ripa, Epora foederatorum, Sacili Martialium, Onuba et dextra Corduba colonia Patricia cognomine, inde primum navigabili Baete, oppida Carbula, Decuma, fluvius Singilis, eodem Baetis latere incidens.

Lusitania, and that Pan was the governor of the whole of it. The stories related of Hercules, Pyrene or Saturn I regard as absolutely mythical.

The Guadalquivir rises in the province of Tarragon, not at the town of Mentesa, as some authorities have said, but in the Tugiensian Forest bordered by the river Segura that waters the territory of Cartagena; at Lorea it avoids the Sepolcro de Scipion and, turning westward, makes for the Atlantic Ocean, giving its name to the province; it is first of moderate size, but it receives many tributaries, from which it takes their glory as well as their waters. It first enters Baetica at Ossigetania, gliding gently in a picturesque channel past a series of towns situated on both its banks.

The river Guadalquivir.

Between this river and the Ocean coast the most famous places inland are : Segida surnamed Augurina ; Julia or Fidentia ; Urgao or Alba ; Ebura or Cerialis ; Iliberri or Liberini ; Ilipula or Laus ; Artigi or Julienses ; Vesci or Faventia ; Singili, Ategua, Arialdunum, Agla Minor, Baebro, Castra Vinaria, Cisimbrium, New Hippo, Illurco, Osca, Oscua, Sucaelo, Unditanum, Old Tucci—all of which are places in that part of Bastetania which stretches towards the sea. In the jurisdiction of Cordova in the neighbourhood of the actual river are Ossigi surnamed Latonium, Iliturgi or Forum Julium, Ipra, Isturgi or Triumphale, Sucia, and 17 miles inland Obulco or Pontificense, then Ripa, Epora (a treaty town), Sacili Martialium, Onuba, and on the right bank the colony of Cordova surnamed Patricia. At this point the Guadalquivir first becomes navigable, and there are the towns of Carbula and Detunda, the river Xenil flowing into the Guadalquivir on the same side.

11

11 Oppida Hispalensis conventus Celti, Axati, Arua,
Canama, Evia, Ilipa cognomine Ilpa Italica, et a
laeva Hispal colonia cognomine Romulensis, ex
adverso oppidum Osset quod cognominatur Iulia
Constantia, Vergentum quod Iuli Genius, Orippo,
Caura, Siarum, fluvius Maenuba Baeti et ipse a
dextro latere infusus. at inter aestuaria Baetis oppidum Nabrissa cognomine Veneria et Colobana,
coloniae Hasta quae Regia dicitur et in mediterraneo
Asido quae Caesarina.

12 Singilis fluvius in Baetim quo dictum est ordine
inrumpens, Astigitanam coloniam adluit cognomine
Augustam Firmam, ab ea navigabilis. huius conventus sunt reliquae coloniae inmunes Tucci quae
cognominatur Augusta Gemella, Iptuci quae Virtus
Iulia, Ucubi quae Claritas Iulia, Urso quae Genetiva
Urbanorum; inter quae fuit Munda cum Pompeio filio
rapta. oppida libera Astigi Vetus, Ostippo, stipendiaria Callet, Callicula, Castra Gemina, Ilipula Minor,
Marruca, Sacrana, Obulcula, Oningis, Sabora, Ventippo. Maenubam amnem et ipsum navigabilem
haut procul accolunt Olontigi, Laelia, Lastigi.

13 Quae autem regio a Baete ad fluvium Anam tendit
extra praedicta Baeturia appellatur in duas divisa
partes totidemque gentes, Celticos qui Lusitaniam
attingunt, Hispalensis conventus, Turdulos qui Lusitaniam et Tarraconensem accolunt, iura Cordubam

---

a Gnaeus the eldest son of Pompeius Magnus was defeated
at Munda (possibly near Cordova) 45 B.C., and soon afterwards
captured and killed; the town was destroyed.

The towns of the jurisdiction of Hispalis are Celti, Axati, Arua, Canama, Evia, Ilipa surnamed Ilpa Italica; on the left bank is the colony Hispal surnamed Romulensis, while on the opposite side are the towns Osset surnamed Julia Constantia, Vergentum or Juli Genius, Orippo, Caura, Siarum, and the river Maenuba, a tributary of the Guadalquivir on its right. Between the estuaries of the Guadalquivir are the towns of Nabrissa, surnamed Veneria, and Colobana, with two colonies, Hasta, which is called Regia, and inland Asido, which is called Caesarina.

The river Xenil, joining the Guadalquivir at the *The Xenil.* place in the list already mentioned, washes the colony of Astigi, surnamed Augusta Firma, from which point it becomes navigable. The other colonies in this jurisdiction exempt from tribute are Tucci, surnamed Augusta Gemella, Iptuci or Virtus Julia, Ucubi or Claritas Julia, Urso or Genetiva Urbanorum; and among these once was Munda, which was taken with the younger Pompey.[a] The free towns are Old Astigi and Ostippo, with the tributary towns of Callet, Callicula, Castra Gemina, Ilipula Minor, Marruca, Sacrana, Obulcula, Oningis, Sabora and Ventippo. At no great distance, on the Maenuba, another navigable river, are the settlements of Olontigi, Laelia and Lastigi.

The region stretching from the Guadalquivir to the river Guadiana beyond the places already mentioned is called Baeturia, and is divided into two parts and the same number of races, the Celtici bordering on Lusitania, of the jurisdiction of Seville, and the Turduli, who dwell on the borders of Lusitania and the Tarragon territory, but are in the jurisdiction of

petunt. Celticos a Celtiberis ex Lusitania advenisse
manifestum est sacris, lingua, oppidorum vocabulis
14 quae cognominibus in Baetica distinguntur: Seriae
adicitur Fama Iulia, Nertobrigae Concordia Iulia,
Segidae Restituta Iulia, Contributa Iulia Ugultuniae
(cum qua et Curiga nunc est), Lacimurgae Constantia
Iulia, Steresibus Fortunales et Callensibus Aeneanici.
praeter haec in Celtica Acinipo, Arunda, Arunci,
Turobriga, Lastigi, Salpesa, Saepone, Serippo. altera
Baeturia, quam diximus Turdulorum et conventus
Cordubensis, habet oppida non ignobilia Arsam, Mel-
lariam, Mirobrigam Reginam, Sosintigi, Sisaponem.
15 Gaditani conventus civium Romanorum Regina,
Latinorum Laepia Regia, Carisa cognomine Aurelia,
Urgia cognominata Castrum Iulium, item Caesaris
Salutariensis; stipendiaria Besaro, Belippo, Barbesula, Blacippo, Baesippo, Callet, Cappacum, Oleastro,
Iptuci, Ibrona, Lascuta, Saguntia, Saudo, Usaepo.
16 Longitudinem universam eius prodidit M. Agrippa
$\overline{\text{CCCCLXXV}}$ p., latitudinem $\overline{\text{CCLVIII}}$, sed cum termini
Carthaginem usque procederent: quae causa magnos
errores conputatione mensurae saepius parit, alibi
mutato provinciarum modo alibi itinerum auctis aut
diminutis passibus. incubuere maria tam longo aevo,
alibi processere litora, torsere se fluminum aut

14

Cordova. That the Celtici came from the Celtiberi
in Lusitania is proved by their religion, their language,
and the names of their towns, which in Baetica are
distinguished by surnames: Seria has the additional
name of Fama Julia, Nertobriga that of Concordia
Julia, Segida that of Restituta Julia, Ugultunia that
of Contributa Julia (in which now is also included
the town of Curiga), Lacimurga that of Constantia
Julia, and Stereses the surname of Fortunales and
Callenses that of Aeneanici. Besides these places
there are in Celtica Acinipo, Arunda, Arunci,
Turobriga, Lastigi, Salpesa, Saepone, Serippo. The
other part of Baeturia, which we have said belongs
to the Turduli and to the jurisdiction of Cordova,
contains the not undistinguished towns of Arsa,
Mellaria, Mirobriga Regina, Sosintigi and Sisapo. To
the jurisdiction of Cadiz belong Regina, with Roman
citizens, Laepia Regia with Latin citizens, Carisa
surnamed Aurelia, Urgia surnamed Castrum Julium,
and also Caesaris Salutariensis; the tributary towns
of Besaro, Belippo, Barbesula, Blacippo, Baesippo,
Callet, Cappacum, Oleastro, Iptuci, Ibrona, Lascuta,
Saguntia, Saudo, Usaepo.

The total length of Baetica according to Marcus *Dimensions*
Agrippa is 475 miles, and its breadth 258 miles, but *of Baetica.*
this was when its bounds extended as far as Cartagena: such extensions comparatively often give
rise to great errors in the measurements of distances,
as they sometimes cause alterations in the boundary
of provinces and sometimes an increase or reduction
of the mileage of roads. During so long a period of
time the seas have been encroaching on the land or
the shores have been moving forward, and rivers have
formed curves or have straightened out their wind-

15

correxere flexus. praeterea aliunde aliis exordium
mensurae est et alia meatus: ita fit ut nulli duo con-
cinant.

17   II. Baeticae longitudo nunc a Castulonis oppidi
fine Gadis $\overline{\text{CCL}}$ et a Murgi maritima ora $\overline{\text{XXV}}$ p. amplior,
latitudo a Carteia Anam ora $\overline{\text{CCXXXIV}}$ p. Agrippam
quidem in tanta viri diligentia praeterque in hoc
opere cura, cum orbem terrarum urbi[1] spectandum
propositurus esset, errasse quis credat et cum eo
divum Augustum? is namque conplexam eum
porticum ex destinatione et commentariis M.
Agrippae a sorore eius inchoatam peregit.

18   III. Citerioris Hispaniae sicut conplurium provinciarum aliquantum vetus forma mutata est,
utpote cum Pompeius Magnus tropaeis suis quae
statuebat in Pyrenaeo DCCCLXXVI oppida ab Alpibus
ad fines Hispaniae ulterioris in dicionem ab se
redacta testatus sit. nunc universa provincia dividitur in conventus septem, Carthaginiensem Tarraconensem Caesaraugustanum Cluniensem Asturum
Lucensem Bracarum. accedunt insulae quarum
mentione seposita civitates provincia ipsa praeter
contributas aliis CCXCIII continet oppida CLXXXIX, in
iis colonias XII, oppida civium Romanorum XIII, Latinorum veterum XVIII, foederatum unum, stipendiaria
CXXXV.

19   Primi in ora Bastuli, post eos quo dicentur[2]
ordine intus recedentes Mentesani, Oretani et ad

---

[1] *Edd.*: orbi.
[2] *Rackham*: dicitur.

---

[a] The Porticus Octaviae, between the Circus Flaminius and
the Theatre of Marcellus.

ings. Moreover different persons take different starting-points for their measurements and follow different lines; and the consequence is that no two authorities agree.

II. At present the length of Baetica from the frontier of the town of Cazlona to Cadiz is 250 miles, and from the sea-front of Murgi 25 miles more; its breadth from Carteia along the coast to the Guadiana is 234 miles. Agrippa was a very painstaking man, and also a very careful geographer; who therefore could believe that when intending to set before the eyes of Rome a survey of the world he made a mistake, and with him the late lamented Augustus? for it was Augustus who completed the portico ^a containing a plan of the world that had been begun by his sister in accordance with the design and memoranda of Marcus Agrippa.

III. The old shape of Hither Spain has been considerably altered, as has been that of several provinces, in as much as Pompey the Great on his trophies which he set up in the Pyrenees testified that he had brought into subjection 876 towns between the Alps and the borders of Further Spain. Today the whole province is divided into seven jurisdictions, namely those of Cartagena, Tarragon, Saragossa, Clunia, Astorga, Lugo, Braga. In addition there are the islands which will be mentioned separately, but the province itself contains, besides 293 states dependent on others, 189 towns, of which 12 are colonies, 13 are towns of Roman citizens, 18 have the old Latin rights, one is a treaty town and 135 are tributary.

Western Spain.

The first people, on the coast, are the Bastuli, and after them in the following order proceeding inland come the Mentesani, the Oretani, the Carpetani

Districts.

17

Tagum Carpetani, iuxta eos Vaccaei, Vettones et
Celtiberi Arevaci. oppida orae proxima Urci,
adscriptumque Baeticae Barea, regio Bastitania,
mox deinde Contestania, Carthago Nova colonia,
cuius a promunturio quod Saturni vocatur Caesaream
Mauretaniae urbem C̄LXXXXVII p. traiectus. reliqua
in ora flumen Tader, colonia inmunis Ilici, unde
Ilicitanus sinus; in eam contribuuntur Icositani.
20 mox Latinorum Lucentum, Dianium stipendiarium,
Sucro fluvius et quondam oppidum, Contestaniae
finis. regio Edetania amoeno praetendente se
stagno, ad Celtiberos recedens. Valentia colonia
III p. a mari remota, flumen Turium, et tantundem
a mari Saguntum civium Romanorum oppidum
21 fide nobile, flumen Udiva. regio Ilergaonum,
Hiberus amnis navigabili commercio dives, ortus
in Cantabris haut procul oppido Iuliobrica, per
C̄CCCL p. fluens, navium per C̄CLX a Vareia oppido
capax, quem propter universam Hispaniam Graeci
appellavere Hiberiam. regio Cessetania, flumen
Subi, colonia Tarracon, Scipionum opus, sicut
Carthago Poenorum. regio Ilergetum, oppidum
Subur, flumen Rubricatum, a quo Laeetani et
22 Indigetes. post eos quo dicetur ordine intus recedentes radice Pyrenaei Ausetani, Iacetani perque

---

ᵃ Rather than surrender to Hannibal, the Saguntines set
fire to their town and perished in the flames, 219 B.C. The
town was rebuilt eight years later.

on the Tagus, and next to them the Vaccaei, the
Vettones and the Celtiberian Arevaci. The towns
nearest the coast are Urci and Barea that belongs to
Baetica, then the district of Bastitania, next after
which comes Contestania and the colony of New
Carthage, from the promontory of which, called the
Cape of Saturn, the crossing to Caesarea, a city of
Mauretania, is 197 miles. There remain to be
mentioned on the coast the river Tader and the
tax-free colony of Ilici, from which the Ilicitan Gulf
takes its name; to this colony the Icositani are
subordinate. Next come Lucentum, with Latin
rights, Dianium, a tributary town, the river Sucro
and in former days a town of the same name, forming
the boundary of Contestania. The district of Edetania comes next, with a lovely expanse of lake in
front of it, and reaching back to Celtiberia. The
colony of Valencia three miles from the sea, the river
Turium, Saguntum, also three miles from the sea,
a town with Roman citizenship, famous for its loyalty,[a]
and the river Udiva. The district of the Ilergaones,
the river Ebro, rich in ship-borne trade, rising in the
district of the Cantabri not far from the town of
Juliobrica, with a course of 450 miles, for 260 of which
from the town of Vareia it is navigable for ships, and
because of it the Greeks have called the whole of
Spain by the name of Iberia. Next the district of
Cessetania, the river Subi, the colony Tarragon,
which was founded by the Scipios, as Cartagena was
by the Carthaginians. The district of the Ilergetes
comes next, the town of Subur and the river Rubricatum, after which begin the Laeetani and the Indigetes. After them in the following order proceeding
inland from the foot of the Pyrenees are the Ausetani,

Pyrenaeum Cerretani, dein Vascones. in ora autem
colonia Barcino cognomine Faventia, oppida civium
Romanorum Baetulo, Iluro, flumen Arnum, Blandae,
flumen Alba, Emporiae, geminum hoc veterum
incolarum et Graecorum qui Phocaeensium fuere
suboles, flumen Ticer. ab eo Pyrenaea Venus in
latere promunturi altero x̄l̄.

23 Nunc per singulos conventus reddentur insignia
praeter supra dicta. Tarracone disceptant populi
xlii, quorum celeberrimi civium Romanorum Derto-
sani, Bisgargitani, Latinorum Ausetani, Cerretani
qui Iuliani cognominantur et qui Augustani, Edetani,
Gerundenses, Gessorienses, Teari qui Iulienses,
stipendiariorum Aquicaldenses, Aesonenses, Baeculonenses.

24 Caesaraugusta colonia immunis amne Hibero
adfusa ubi oppidum antea vocabatur Salduba,
regionis Edetaniae, recipit populos lv, ex his
civium Romanorum Bilbilitanos, Celsenses ex colonia,
Calagurritanos qui Nasici cognominantur, Ilerdenses
Surdaonum gentis iuxta quos Sicoris fluvius, Oscenses
regionis Suessetaniae, Turiassonenses; Latinorum
veterum Cascantenses, Ergavicenses, Graccurritanos,
Leonicenses, Osicerdenses; foederatos Tarracenses;
stipendiarios Arcobrigenses, Andelonenses, Arace-
litanos, Bursaonenses, Calagurritanos qui Fibula-

the Jacetani, the Cerretani along the Pyrenees, and then the Vascones. On the coast is the colony of Barcelona, surnamed Faventia, the Roman towns of Badalona and Iluro, the River Arnum, Blandae, the river Alba, Amporias, one part of which is inhabited by the original natives and the other by Greeks descended from the Phocaeans, and the river Ticer. From it Cabo de Cruz on the other side of the promontory is 40 miles distant.

We will now take the jurisdictions in order and give *Administrative* noteworthy facts about them in addition to those *divisions.* mentioned above. Forty-two peoples are subject to the jurisdiction of the courts of Tarragona; of them the best known are—with the rights of Roman citizens, the people of Tortosa and the Bisgargitani; with Latin rights, the Ausetani, the Cerretani surnamed Juliani, and those surnamed Augustani, the Edetani, Gerundenses, Gessorienses, and Teari or Julienses; tributaries, the Aquicaldenses, Aesonenses and Baeculonenses.

Caesaraugusta, a colony that pays no taxes, is *Saragossa.* washed by the river Ebro; its site was once occupied by a town called Salduba, belonging to the district of Edetania. It is the centre for 55 peoples; of these with the rights of Roman citizens are the Bilbilitani, the Celsenses (once a colony), the Calagurritani (surnamed Nasici), the Ilerdenses belonging to the race of the Surdaones next to the river Sicoris, the Oscenses of the district of Suessetania, and the Turiassonenses; with the old Latin rights are the Cascantenses, Ergavicenses, Graccurritani, Leonicenses and Osicerdenses; bound by treaty are the Tarracenses; tributary are the Arcobrigenses, Andelonenses, Aracelitani, Bursaonenses, Calagurri-

renses cognominantur, Conplutenses, Carenses, Cincienses, Cortonenses, Damanitanos, Ispallenses, Ilursenses, Iluberitanos, Iacetanos, Libienses, Pompelonenses, Segienses.

25 Carthaginem conveniunt populi LXV exceptis insularum incolis : ex colonia Accitana Gemellense, ex Libisosana cognomine Foroaugustana, quibus duabus ius Italiae datum, ex colonia Salariense, oppidani Latii veteris Castulonenses qui Caesarii Iuvenales appellantur, Saetabitani qui Augustani, Valerienses. stipendiariorum autem celeberrimi Alabanenses, Bastitani, Consaburrenses, Dianenses, Egelestani, Ilorcitani, Laminitani, Mentesani qui et Oretani, Mentesani qui et Bastuli, Oretani qui et Germani cognominantur, caputque Celtiberiae Segobrigenses, Carpetaniae Toletani Tago flumini inpositi, dein Viatienses et Virgilienses.

26 In Cluniensem conventum Varduli ducunt populos XIV, ex quibus Alabanenses tantum nominare libeat, Turmogidi IV, in quibus Segisamonenses et Segisamaiulienses. in eundem conventum Carietes et Vennenses V civitatibus vadunt, quarum sunt Velienses. eodem Pelendones Celtiberum IV populis, quorum Numantini fuere clari, sicut in Vaccaeorum XVII civitatibus Intercatienses, Palantini, Lacobri-
27 genses, Caucenses. iam[1] in Cantabricis VII populis Iuliobriga sola memoretur, in Autrigonum X civitatibus Tritium et Virovesca. Arevacis nomen dedit

---

[1] *Rackham* : nam.

tani surnamed Fibularenses, Conplutenses, Carenses, Cincienses, Cortonenses, Damanitani, Ispallenses, Ilursenses, Iluberitani, Jacetani, Libienses, Pompelonenses and Segienses.

At Cartagena assemble sixty-five peoples, not *Cartagena.* including inhabitants of islands: from the colony of Accitana Gemellensis and from Libisosana named Foroaugustana, to both of which Italic rights have been given, from the colony of Salaria; townsmen with the rights of old Latium, the Castulonenses, also called Caesarii Juvenales, the Saetabitani or Augustani, and the Valerienses. Of the tributary peoples the best known are the Alabanenses, Bastitani, Consaburrenses, Dianenses, Egelestani, Ilorcitani, Laminitani, Mentesani or Oretani, Mentesani or Bastuli, the Oretani surnamed Germani, and the people of Segobriga, capital of Celtiberia, the people of Toletum on the Tagus, the capital of Carpetania, and then the Viatienses and the Virgilienses.

To the jurisdiction of Corunna the Varduli bring *Corunna.* fourteen peoples, of whom we would mention only the Alabanenses, and the Turmogidi bring four, including the Segisamonenses and the Segisamajulienses. To the same jurisdiction go the Carietes and the Vennenses with five states, of whom the Velienses form one. Thither too go the Pelendones of the Celtiberians with four peoples, of whom the Numantines were once famous, as among the seventeen states of the Vaccaei were the Intercatienses, Palantini, Lacobrigenses and Caucenses. Then among the Cantabrici, seven peoples, one state only, Juliobriga, need be mentioned, and Tritium and Virovesca among the ten states of the Autrigones. The Arevaci got their name from the river Areva; to

fluvius Areva; horum VI oppida, Secontia et Uxama,
quae nomina crebro aliis in locis usurpantur, praeterea Segovia et Nova Augusta, Termes ipsaque
Clunia Celtiberiae finis. ad oceanum reliqua ver-
gunt Vardulique ex praedictis et Cantabri.

28 Iunguntur iis Asturum XXII populi divisi in Augus-
tanos et Transmontanos, Asturica urbe magnifica;
in his sunt Gigurri, Pescii, Lancienses, Zoelae.
numerus omnis multitudinis ad C̄C̄XL liberorum
capitum.

Lucensis conventus populorum est XV, praeter
Celticos et Lemavos ignobilium ac barbarae appella-
tionis sed liberorum capitum ferme C̄LXVI.

Simili modo Bracarum XXIV civitates C̄C̄LXXXV
capitum, ex quibus praeter ipsos Bracaros Biballi,
Coelerni, Callaeci, Equaesi, Limici, Querquerni
citra fastidium nominentur.

29 Longitudo citeriori Hispaniae est ad finem Castulonis a Pyrenaeo D̄C̄VII p. et ora paulo amplius,
latitudo a Tarracone ad litus Olarsonis C̄C̄C̄VII, e
radicibus Pyrenaei, ubi cuneatur angustiis inter
duo maria; paulatim deinde se pandens, qua contingit ulteriorem Hispaniam tantundem et amplius
latitudini adicit.

30 Metallis plumbi ferri aeris argenti auri tota ferme
Hispania scatet, citerior et specularis lapidis, Baetica
et minio. sunt et marmorum lapicidinae. universae
Hispaniae Vespasianus imperator Augustus iactatum

them belong six towns, Secontia and Uxama, common names in other regions, also Segovia and Nova Augusta, with Termes and Corunna itself, the end of Celtiberia. The rest of the country stretches towards the ocean, and here are the Varduli of those already mentioned and the Cantabri.

Adjoining these are twenty-two peoples of the Astures, divided into the Augustani and the Transmontani, with the splendid city of Asturica; these include the Gigurri, Pescii, Lancienses and Zoelae. The total number of the population amounts to 240,000 free persons.

The jurisdiction of Lucus contains 15 peoples, *Lugo.* unimportant and bearing outlandish names, excepting the Celtici and Lemavi, but with a free population amounting to about 166,000.

In a similar way the twenty-four states of Braga *Braga.* contain 285,000 persons, of whom besides the Bracari themselves may be mentioned, without wearying the reader, the Biballi, Coelerni, Callaeci, Equaesi, Limici and Querquerni.

The length of Hither Spain from the Pyrenees to *Dimensions* the frontier of Cazlona is 607 miles, and a little more *of (Hither)* *Spain.* along the coast; its breadth from Tarragon to the shore of Olarson is 307 miles, starting from the foot of the Pyrenees, where the country forms the shape of a wedge between the two seas; then gradually it widens out, and where it touches Further Spain it adds more than as much again to its breadth.

Nearly the whole of Spain is covered with mines of *Minerals* lead, iron, copper, silver and gold, Hither Spain *of the* *Peninsula.* with muscovite mines also; Baetica abounds in cinnabar as well. There are besides quarries of marble. His Majesty the Emperor Vespasian be-

25

procellis rei publicae Latium tribuit. Pyrenaei montes Hispanias Galliasque disterminant promunturiis in duo diversa maria proiectis.

31 IV. Narbonensis provincia appellatur pars Galliarum quae interno mari adluitur, Bracata antea dicta, amne Varo ab Italia discreta Alpiumque vel saluberrimis Romano imperio iugis, a reliqua vero Gallia latere septentrionali montibus Cebenna et Iuribus, agrorum cultu, virorum morumque dignatione, amplitudine opum nulli provinciarum postferenda breviterque Italia verius quam provincia.

32 in ora regio Sordonum intusque Consuaranorum, flumina Tetum, Vernodubrum, oppida Illiberis, magnae quondam urbis tenue vestigium, Ruscino Latinorum, flumen Atax e Pyrenaeo Rubrensem permeans lacum, Narbo Martius decumanorum colonia XII p. a mari distans, flumina Araris, Liria.

33 oppida de cetero rara praeiacentibus stagnis. Agatha quondam Massiliensium et regio Volcarum Tectosagum atque ubi Rhoda Rhodiorum fuit, unde dictus multo Galliarum fertilissimus Rhodanus amnis ex Alpibus se rapiens per Lemannum lacum segnemque deferens Ararem nec minus se ipso torrentes Isaram et Druantiam. Libica appellantur duo eius ora

---

^a From the linen breeches worn by the natives.
^b L'Étang de Sigéan.

stowed the rights of Latium on the whole of Spain when it had been storm-tossed by civil disorders. The frontier between the Spanish and the Gallic provinces is formed by the mountains of the Pyrenees, with headlands projecting into the two seas on either side.

IV. The part of the Gauls washed by the Mediterranean is entitled the province of Narbonne, having previously had the name of Bracata.[a] It is divided from Italy by the river Var, and by the ranges of the Alps, a very secure protection for the Roman Empire, and from the rest of Gaul on the north by the Cevennes and Jura mountains. Its agriculture, the high repute of its men and manners and the vastness of its wealth make it the equal of any other province : it is, in a word, not so much a province as a part of Italy. On the coast there is the district of the Sordones, and more inland that of the Consuarani ; the rivers are the Tech and the Verdouble, and the towns Elne, the mere shadow of what was once a mighty city, and Castel Roussillon, which has Latin rights. Then come the river Aude, which flows from the Pyrenees through the lake Rubrensis,[b] Narbonne, a colony of the tenth legion twelve miles from the sea, and the rivers Hérault and Lez. Apart from those mentioned there are but few towns, owing to the marshes that fringe the coast. There is Agde, formerly belonging to Marseilles, the district of the Volcae Tectosages, and the former site of Rhoda, a colony of Rhodes, that has given its name to the Rhone, the most fertile river of the two Gauls, which rushes from the Alps through the Lake of Geneva, bringing along the sluggish Saône and the Isère and Durance which are as rapid as itself. Of its mouths the two smaller are called Libica,

Southern Gaul : its geography, cities and tribes.

27

modica, ex his alterum Hispaniense alterum Metapinum, tertium idemque amplissimum Massalioticum. sunt auctores et Heracleam oppidum in ostio Rhodani fuisse. ultra fossae ex Rhodano C. Mari opere et nomine insignes, stagnum Mastromela, oppidum Maritima Avaticorum, superque Campi Lapidei, Herculis proeliorum memoria, regio Anatiliorum et intus Dexivatium Cavarumque; rursus a mari Tricorium et intus Tritollorum Vocontiorumque et Segovellaunorum, mox Allobrogum. at in ora Massilia Graecorum Phocaeensium foederata, promunturium Zao, Citharista portus, regio Camactulicorum, dein Suelteri supraque Verucini. in ora autem Athenopolis Massiliensium, Forum Iuli octavanorum colonia quae Pacensis appellatur et Classica, amnis nomine Argenteus, regio Oxubiorum Ligaunorumque, super quos Suebri, Quariates, Adunicates. at in ora oppidum Latinum Antipolis, regio Deciatium, amnis Varus ex Alpium monte Caenia profusus.

36   In mediterraneo coloniae Arelate sextanorum, Baeterrae septimanorum, Arausio secundanorum, in agro Cavarum Valentia, Vienna Allobrogum. oppida Latina Aquae Sextiae Salluviorum, Avennio Cavarum, Apta Iulia Vulgientium, Alaebaece Reiorum Apollinarium, Alba Helvorum, Augusta Tricastinorum, Anatilia, Aetea, Bormani, Comani, Cabellio,

one the Spanish, the other the Metapinian; the third
and largest is the Massaliotic. Some authorities
state that at the mouth of the Rhone there was once
a town called Heraclea. Beyond are the canals
leading out of the Rhone, famous as the work of
Gaius Marius whose distinguished name they bear,
Lake Mastromela and the town of Maritima of the
Avatici, and above are the Stony Plains, where
tradition says that Hercules fought battles, the
district of the Anatilii, and inland those of the
Dexivates and Cavares. Returning to the sea we
have the districts of the Tricores and inland those of
the Tritolli, Vocontii and Segovellauni, and after them
the Allobroges. On the coast is Marseilles, founded
by the Greeks of Phocaea and now a confederate
city, then the promontory of Zao, the harbour of
Citharista, the district of the Camactulici, then the
Suelteri and above them the Verucini. On the coast
too are Athenopolis of the Massilians, Fréjus, a
colony of the eighth legion, called Pacensis and
Classica, a river named Argenteus, the district of
the Oxubii and Ligauni, beyond whom come the
Suebri, Quariates and Adunicates. On the coast is
the town of Antibes with Latin rights, the district
of the Deciates and the river Var, which rises in
Mont Cenis in the Alps.

The colonies in the interior are: Arles, the station
of the sixth legion, Béziers of the seventh, Orange of
the second, Valence in the territory of the Cavares,
and Vienne in that of the Allobroges. The towns with
Latin rights are Aix in the territory of the Salluvii,
Avignon of the Cavares, Apt of the Vulgientes, Riez
of the Reii Apollinares, Alba of the Helvi, Augusta
of the Tricastini, Anatilia, Aetea, the Bormani, the

Carcasum Volcarum Tectosagum, Cessero, Carpen-
toracte Meminorum, Caenicenses, Cambolectri qui
37 Atlantici cognominantur, Forum Voconi, Glanum
Libii, Lutevani qui et Foroneronienses, Nemausum
Arecomicorum, Piscinae, Ruteni, Samnagenses, Tolosani Tectosagum Aquitaniae contermini, Tasgoduni,
Tarusconienses, Umbranici, Vocontiorum civitatis
foederatae duo capita Vasio et Lucus Augusti,
oppida vero ignobilia xix sicut xxiv Nemausensibus
adtributa. adiecit formulae Galba imperator ex
Inalpinis Avanticos atque Bodionticos, quorum
oppidum Dinia. longitudinem provinciae Narbo-
nensis $\overline{\text{CCCLXX}}$ p. Agrippa tradit, latitudinem $\overline{\text{CCXLVIII}}$.
38   V. Italia dehinc primique eius Ligures, mox
Etruria, Umbria, Latium, ubi Tiberina ostia et Roma
terrarum caput, $\overline{\text{XVI}}$ p. intervallo a mari. Volscum
postea litus et Campaniae, Picentinum inde ac
Lucanum Bruttiumque, quo longissime in meridiem
ab Alpium paene lunatis iugis in maria excurrit
Italia. ab eo Graeciae ora, mox Sallentini, Paediculi,[1] Apuli, Paeligni, Frentani, Marrucini, Vestini,
Sabini, Picentes, Galli, Umbri, Tusci, Veneti, Carni,
39 Iapudes, Histri, Liburni. nec ignoro ingrati ac
segnis animi existimari posse merito si obiter atque
in transcursu ad hunc modum dicatur terra omnium
terrarum alumna eadem et parens, numine deum
electa quae caelum ipsum clarius faceret, sparsa

---

[1] *Rackham* (cf. 102) : Pediculi, Poediculi.

---

[a] Now Toulouse.
[b] Now Tarascon.
[c] Perhaps Vabres.
[d] See § 102 n.

Comani, Cavaillon, Carcassonne of the Volcae
Tectosages, Cessero, Carpentras of the Memini, the
Caenicenses, the Cambolectri surnamed Atlantici,
Forum Voconi, Glanum Libii, the Lutevani also
called Foroneronienses, Nîmes of the Arecomici,
Pézenas, the Ruteni, the Samnagenses, the Tolosani *a*
of the Tectosages on the border of Aquitania, the
Tasgoduni, the Tarusconienses,*b* the Umbranici,*c* the
two capitals of the confederate state of the Vocontii,
Vasio and Lucus Augusti; and also unimportant
towns to the number of 19, as well as 24 assigned to
the people of Nîmes. The Emperor Galba added
to the list two peoples dwelling in the Alps, the people
of Avançon and the Bodiontici, whose town is Digne.
According to Agrippa the length of the province of
Narbonne is 370 miles and the breadth 248.

V. After this comes Italy, the first people of it *Italy: its*
being the Ligurians, after whom come Etruria, *races.*
Umbria and Latium, where are the mouths of the
Tiber and Rome, the capital of the world, sixteen
miles from the sea. Afterwards come the coast of
the Volsci and of Campania, then of Picenum
and Lucania and the Bruttii, the southernmost point
to which Italy juts out into the sea from the almost
crescent-shaped chain of the Alps. After the Bruttii
comes the coast of Magna Graecia, followed by the
Sallentini, Paediculi,*d* Apuli, Paeligni, Frentani,
Marrucini, Vestini, Sabini, Picentes, Gauls, Umbrians,
Tuscans, Venetians, Carni, Iapudes, Histri and Liburni. I am well aware that I may with justice be
considered ungrateful and lazy if I describe in this
casual and cursory manner a land which is at once
the nursling and the mother of all other lands, chosen
by the providence of the gods to make heaven itself

congregaret imperia ritusque molliret et tot populorum discordes ferasque linguas sermonis com_
mercio contraheret ad colloquia et humanitatem
homini daret, breviterque una cunctarum gentium
40 in toto orbe patria fieret. sed quid agam? tanta
nobilitas omnium locorum,—quos quis attigerit?—
tanta rerum singularum populorumque claritas tenet.
urbs Roma vel sola in ea . . .[1] et digna iam tam
festa cervice facies, quo tandem narrari debet opere!
qualiter Campaniae ora per se felixque illa ac beata
amoenitas, ut palam sit uno in loco gaudentis opus
41 esse naturae! iam vero tanta ea vitalis ac perennis
salubritas, talis caeli temperies, tam fertiles campi,
tam aprici colles, tam innoxii saltus, tam opaca
nemora, tam munifica silvarum genera, tot montium
adflatus, tanta frugum vitiumque et olearum fertilitas,
tam nobilia pecudi vellera, tam opima tauris colla,
tot lacus, tot amnium fontiumque ubertas totam
eam perfundens, tot maria, portus, gremiumque
terrarum commercio patens undique et tamquam
iuvandos ad mortales ipsa avide in maria procurrens.
42 neque ingenia ritusque ac viros et lingua manuque
superatas commemoro gentes. ipsi de ea iudicavere
Grai, genus in gloriam suam effusissimum, quotam
partem ex ea appellando Graeciam Magnam!

---

[1] *Lacunam Mayhoff.*

more glorious, to unite scattered empires, to make manners gentle, to draw together in converse by community of language the jarring and uncouth tongues of so many nations, to give mankind civilisation, and in a word to become throughout the world the single fatherland of all the races. But what am I to do? The great fame of all its places—who could touch upon them all?—and the great renown of the various things and peoples in it give me pause. In that list even the city of Rome alone, a . . . countenance and one worthy of so glorious a neck, what elaborate description it merits! In what terms to describe the coast of Campania taken by itself, with its blissful and heavenly loveliness, so as to manifest that there is one region where nature has been at work in her joyous mood! And then again all that invigorating healthfulness all the year round, the climate so temperate, the plains so fertile, the hills so sunny, the glades so secure, the groves so shady! Such wealth of various forests, the breezes from so many mountains, the great fertility of its corn and vines and olives, the glorious fleeces of its sheep, the sturdy necks of its bulls, the many lakes, the rich supply of rivers and springs flowing over all its surface, its many seas and harbours and the bosom of its lands offering on all sides a welcome to commerce, the country itself eagerly running out into the seas as it were to aid mankind. I do not speak of the character and customs of its people, its men, the nations that its language and its might have conquered. The Greeks themselves, a people most prone to gushing self-praise, have pronounced sentence on the land by conferring on but a very small part of it the name of Great Greece! The truth is that in this part of my

Rome.

Physical geography and climate of Italy.

33

nimirum id quod in caeli mentione fecimus hac
quoque in parte faciendum est, ut notas quasdam
et pauca sidera attingamus. legentes tantum
quaeso meminerint ad singula toto orbe edissertanda
festinari.

43   Est ergo folio maxume querno adsimilata, multo
proceritate amplior quam latitudine, in laevam se
flectens cacumine et Amazonicae figura desinens
parmae, ubi a medio excursu Cocynthos vocatur,
per sinus lunatos duo cornua emittens, Leucopetram
dextra, Lacinium sinistra. patet longitudine ab
Inalpino fine Praetoriae Augustae per urbem Ca-
puamque cursu meante Regium oppidum in umero
eius situm, a quo veluti cervicis incipit flexus, decies
centena et viginti milia passuum, multoque amplior
mensura fieret Lacinium usque, ni talis obliquitas
44 in latus degredi videretur. latitudo eius varia est,
quadringentorum decem milium inter duo maria
inferum et superum amnesque Varum atque Arsiam,
media autem ferme circa urbem Romam ab ostio
Aterni amnis in Hadriaticum mare influentis ad
Tiberina ostia c̅x̅x̅x̅v̅i̅, et paulo minus a Castro Novo
Hadriatici maris Alsium ad Tuscum aequor, haud
ullo in loco c̅c̅ latitudinem excedens. universae
autem ambitus a Varo ad Arsiam |x̅x̅| x̅l̅i̅x̅ p. efficit.
45 abest a circumdatis terris Histria ac Liburnia quibusdam locis centena milia, ab Epiro et Illyrico
quinquaginta, ab Africa minus ducenta, ut auctor
est M. Varro, ab Sardinia centum viginti milia, ab

ᵃ Shaped like a crescent but with two curves and a projection between them on the inner side.

ᵇ The three projections named are now Punta di Stilo, Capo
delle Colonne and Capo dell' Armi.

subject also I must do what I did when I spoke about
the heavens—touch upon particular points and only a
few of the stars.   I merely ask my readers to remem-
ber that I am hastening on for the purpose of setting
forth in detail all the contents of the entire world.

In shape, then, Italy much resembles an oak leaf, *Geography*
being far longer than it is broad, bending towards the *of Italy.*
left at its top and ending in the shape of an Amazon's
shield,[a] the projection in the centre being called
Cocynthos, while it sends out two horns along bays
of crescent shape, Leucopetra on the right and
Lacinium on the left.[b]   Its length extends for 1020
miles, beginning from Aosta at the foot of the Alps
and passing through Rome and Capua in a winding
course to the town of Reggio situated on its shoulder,
where begins the curve, as it were, of the neck.   The
measure would be much greater if the line were
carried on to Lacinium, but with that bend the line
would seem to diverge to one side.   The breadth
varies, being four hundred and ten miles between
the rivers Var and Arsa where they flow into the
Mediterranean and the Adriatic, but about at the
middle, in the neighbourhood of the city of Rome,
from the mouth of the river Pescara, which flows into
the Adriatic Sea, to the mouths of the Tiber, its
breadth is 136 miles, and a little less from Castrum
Novum on the Adriatic Sea to Palo on the Tuscan
Sea, in no place exceeding a width of 200 miles.
The circuit of the entire coast from the Var round to
the Arsa is 2049 miles. Its distances from the
countries that surround it are as follows: from Istria
and Liburnia in certain places 100 miles, from Epirus
and Illyricum, 50 miles, from Africa, according to
Marcus Varro, less than 200, from Sardinia 120, from

35

Sicilia MD, a Corcyra minus L̄XXX, ab Issa L̄.[a] incedit
per maria caeli regione ad meridiem quidem, sed,
si quis id diligenti subtilitate exigat, inter sextam
horam primamque brumalem.[b]

46 Nunc ambitum eius urbesque enumerabimus, qua
in re praefari necessarium est auctorem nos divum
Augustum secuturos, discriptionemque ab eo factam
Italiae totius in regiones XI, sed ordine eo qui litorum
tractu fiet; urbium quidem vicinitates oratione
utique praepropera servari non posse, itaque interiore
exin parte digestionem in litteras eiusdem nos
secuturos, coloniarum mentione signata quas ille
in eo prodidit numero. nec situs originesque
persequi facile est Ingaunis Liguribus—ut ceteri
omittantur—agro tricies dato.

47 Igitur ab amne Varo Nicaea a Massiliensibus
conditum, fluvius Palo, Alpes populique Inalpini
multis nominibus, sed maxime Capillati; oppidum
Vediantiorum civitatis Cemenilo, portus Herculis
Monoeci, Ligustina ora. Ligurum celeberrimi ultra
Alpes Sallui, Deciates, Oxubi, citra Veneni, Turri,
Soti, Vagienni, Statielli, Binbelli, Maielli, Cuburriates,
Casmonates, Velleiates et quorum oppida in ora
48 proxime dicemus. flumen Rutuba, oppidum Album
Intimilium, flumen Merula, oppidum Album In-
gaunum, portus Vadorum Sabatium, flumen Porcifera,

---

[a] Now Lissa, an island in the Adriatic.
[b] About S.E., so the line meant is S.S.E.

Sicily 1½, from Corcyra less than 80, from Issa *a* 50.
It stretches through the seas in a southerly direction,
but a more careful and accurate calculation would
place it between due south and sunrise *b* at midwinter.

We will now give an account of a circuit of *Administra-tive districts* Italy, and of its cities. Herein it is necessary to *and cities.* premise that we intend to follow the authority of his
late Majesty Augustus, and to adopt the division that
he made of the whole of Italy into eleven regions,
but to take them in the order that will be suggested
by the coast-line, it being indeed impossible, at all
events in a very cursory account, to keep the neighbouring cities together; and so in going on to deal
with the inland districts we shall follow the
Emperor's alphabetical arrangement, adopting the
enumeration of the colonies that he set out in that
list. Nor is it easy to trace their sites and origins,
the Ligurian Ingauni, for example—not to mention
the other peoples—having received grants of land
on thirty occasions.

Therefore starting from the river Var we have Nice, *Liguria.* founded by the people of Marseilles, the river Pag-
lione, the Alps and the Alpine tribes with many
names, of which the chief is the Long-haired; Cimiez,
the town of the state of the Vediantii, the port of
Hercules of Monaco, and the Ligurian coast. Of
the Ligurians beyond the Alps the most famous are
the Sallui, Deciates and Oxubi; on this side, the
Veneni, Turri, Soti, Vagienni, Statielli, Binbelli,
Maielli, Cuburriates, Casmonates, Velleiates, and
the tribes whose towns on the coast we shall mention
next. The river Royas, the town of Ventimiglia,
the river Merula, the town of Albenga, the port of
Vaï or Savona, the river Bisagna, the town of Genoa,

oppidum Genua, fluvius Fertor, portus Delphini,
Tigulia intus et Segesta Tigulliorum, flumen Macra,
Liguriae finis. a tergo autem supra dictorum
omnium Appenninus mons Italiae amplissimus
perpetuis iugis ab Alpibus tendens ad Siculum
49 fretum. ab altero eius latere ad Padum amnem
Italiae ditissimum omnia nobilibus oppidis nitent,
Libarna, Dertona colonia, Iria, Vardacate, Industria,
Pollentia, Correa quod Potentia cognominatur,
Foro Fulvi quod Valentinum, Augusta Bagien-
norum, Alba Pompeia, Hasta, Aquis Statiellorum.
haec regio ex discriptione Augusti nona est. patet
ora Liguriae inter amnes Varum et Macram $\overline{\text{ccxi}}$ p.
50 Adnectitur septima, in qua Etruria est ab amne
Macra, ipsa mutatis saepe nominibus. Umbros
inde exegere antiquitus Pelasgi, hos Lydi, a quorum
rege Tyrreni, mox a sacrifico ritu lingua Graecorum
Tusci [1] sunt cognominati. primum Etruriae oppidum Luna, portu nobile, colonia Luca a mari recedens
propiorque Pisae inter amnes Auserem et Arnum
ortae a Pelopidis sive a Teutanis, Graeca gente,
vada Volaterrana, fluvius Caecina, Populonium,
51 Etruscorum quondam hoc tantum in litore. hinc
amnes Prile, mox Umbro navigiorum capax, et ab
eo tractus Umbriae portusque Telamo, Cosa Volcien-
tium a populo Romano deducta, Graviscae, Castrum
Novum, Pyrgi, Caeretanus amnis et ipsum Caere
intus m. p. VII Agylla a Pelasgis conditoribus dictum,

[1] Thusci *edd.*

---

[a] Θυοσκόοι, from θύειν (Dion. Hal. Ant. *Rom.* I. 30).
[b] Now the Serchio, a tributary of the Arno.
[c] Now the village of Vadi.
[d] Now the Vaccina.

the river Fertor, Porto Fino, Tigulia inland, Sestri di
Levante, and the river Magra, which is the boundary
of Liguria. Behind all the above-mentioned lie the
Apennines, the largest range of mountains in Italy,
extending in an unbroken chain from the Alps to the
Straits of Messina. On one side of the range, along
the Po, the richest river of Italy, the whole country
is studded with famous and flourishing towns:
Libarna, the colony of Dertona, Iria, Vardacas,
Industria, Pollenza, Correa surnamed Potentia,
Forum Fulvi or Valenza, Augusta of the Bagienni,
Alba Pompeia, Aste, Acqui. Under the partition of
Augustus this is the ninth region. The coast of Liguria
extends 211 miles between the rivers Var and Magra.

The adjoining region is the seventh, in which is *Etruria.*
Etruria, beginning at the river Magra, a district that
has often changed its name. From it in ancient
times the Umbri were driven out by the Pelasgi, and
these by the Lydians, who after a king of theirs were
styled Tyrrheni, but later in the Greek language
Tusci,[a] from their ritual of offering sacrifice. The
first town in Etruria is Luni, famous for its harbour;
then the colony of Lucca, some way from the sea and
nearer to Pisa, between the rivers Auser[b] and Arno,
which owes its origin to the Pelopidae or to the
Greek tribe of the Teutani; then come the Marshes
of Volterra,[c] the river Cecina and Piombino, once
the only Etruscan town on the coast. After these
is the river Prile, and then the navigable river
Ombrone, at which begins the district of Umbria,
the port of Telamone, Cosa of the Volcientes, founded
by the Roman people, Graviscae, Castrum Novum,
Pyrgi, the river[d] and the town of Caere, seven
miles inland, called Agylla by the Pelasgians who

39

Alsium, Fregenae, Tiberis amnis a Macra $\overline{\text{CCLXXXIV}}$ p.
Intus coloniae Falisca Argis orta (ut auctor est Cato)
quae cognominatur Etruscorum, Lucus Feroniae,
52 Rusellana, Seniensis, Sutrina. de cetero Arretini
Veteres, Arretini Fidentiores, Arretini Iulienses,
Amitinenses, Aquenses cognomine Taurini, Blerani,
Cortonenses, Capenates, Clusini Novi, Clusini Veteres,
Florentini praefluenti Arno adpositi, Faesulae,
Ferentinum, Fescennia, Hortanum, Herbanum, Ne-
peta, Novem Pagi, Praefectura Claudia Foroclodi,
Pistorium, Perusia, Suanenses, Saturnini qui antea
Aurini vocabantur, Subertani, Statonenses, Tarquinienses, Tuscanienses, Vetulonienses, Veientani,
Vesentini, Volaterrani, Volcentani cognomine Etrusci,
Volsinienses. in eadem parte oppidorum veterum
nomina retinent agri Crustuminus, Caletranus.
53 Tiberis antea Thybris appellatus et prius Albula
e media fere longitudine Appennini finibus Arre-
tinorum profluit, tenuis primo nec nisi piscinis
corrivatus emissusque navigabilis, sicuti Tinia et
Glanis influentes in eum, novenorum ita conceptu
dierum, si non adiuvent imbres. sed Tiberis propter
aspera et confragosa ne sic quidem praeterquam
trabibus verius quam ratibus longe meabilis, fertur
per $\overline{\text{CL}}$ p., non procul Tiferno Perusiaque et Ocriculo,
Etruriam ab Umbris ac Sabinis, mox citra $\overline{\text{XVI}}$ p.

---

[a] Now Arezzo.	[b] Cortona.
[c] Chiusi.	[d] Florence.
[e] Fiesole.	[f] Volterra.

Bolsena.

founded it, Alsium, Fregenae, and the river Tiber,
284 miles from the Magra. Inland are the colonies
of Falisca, founded according to Cato by the Argives
and surnamed Falisca of the Etruscans, Lucus
Feroniae, Rusellana, Siena and Sutria. The remain-
ing people are the Arretini ^a Veteres, Arretini
Fidentiores, Arretini Julienses, Amitinenses,
Aquenses surnamed Taurini, Blerani, Cortonenses,^b
Capenates, Clusini ^c Novi, Clusini Veteres, the
Florentini ^d on the bank of the Arno that flows
by, Faesulae,^e Ferentinum, Fescennia, Hortanum,
Herbanum, Nepi, Nine Villages, the Claudian
Prefecture of Foroclodium, Pistorium, Perugia, the
Suanenses, the Saturnini formerly called the Aurini,
the Subertani, Statonenses, Tarquinienses, Tus-
canienses, Vetulonienses, Veientani, Vesentini,
Volaterrani,^f the Volcentani surnamed Etrusci, and
Volsinienses.^g In the same district the territories of
Crustumium and Caletra still keep the names of the
ancient towns.

The Tiber, the former name of which was Thybris, *The river*
and before that Albula, rises in about the middle of *Tiber.*
the Apennine chain in the territory of Arezzo. At first
it is a narrow stream, only navigable when its water
is dammed by sluices and then discharged, in the
same way as its tributaries, the Tinia and the Chiana,
the waters of which must be so collected for nine days,
unless augmented by showers of rain. But the Tiber,
owing to its rugged and uneven channel, is even so
not navigable for a long distance, except for rafts,
or rather logs of wood; in a course of 150 miles
it divides Etruria from the Umbrians and Sabines,
passing not far from Tifernum, Perugia and Ocri-
culum, and then, less than 16 miles from Rome,

41

54 urbis Veientem agrum a Crustumino, dein Fidenatem
Latinumque a Vaticano dirimens, sed infra Arretinum
Glanim duobus et quadraginta fluviis auctus, praeci-
puis autem Nare et Aniene, qui et ipse navigabilis
Latium includit a tergo, nec minus tamen aquis
ac tot fontibus in urbem perductis, et ideo quamlibet magnarum navium ex Italo mari capax, rerum
in toto orbe nascentium mercator placidissimus,
pluribus prope solus quam ceteri in omnibus terris
55 amnes accolitur adspiciturque villis. nullique fluvio-
rum minus licet inclusis utrimque lateribus; nec
tamen ipse pugnat, quamquam creber ac subitus
incrementis et nusquam magis aquis quam in ipsa
urbe stagnantibus. quin immo vates intellegitur
potius ac monitor, auctu semper religiosus verius
quam saevus.

56   Latium Antiquum a Tiberi Cerceios servatum est
m. p. L longitudine: tam tenues primordio imperi
fuere radices. colonis saepe mutatis tenuere alii aliis
temporibus, Aborigines, Pelasgi, Arcades, Siculi,
Aurunci, Rutuli, et ultra Cerceios Volsci, Osci,
Ausones, unde nomen Lati processit ad Lirim
amnem. in principio est Ostia colonia a Romano
rege deducta, oppidum Laurentum, lucus Iovis
Indigetis, amnis Numicius, Ardea a Danae Persei

42

separates the territory of Veii from that of Crustumium, and afterwards that of Fidenae and Latium from Vaticanum. But below the confluence of the Chiana from Arezzo it is augmented by forty-two tributaries, the chief being the Nera and the Severone (which latter is itself navigable, and encloses Latium in the rear), while it is equally increased by the aqueducts and the numerous springs carried through to the city; and consequently it is navigable for vessels of whatever size from the Mediterranean, and is a most tranquil trafficker in the produce of all the earth, with perhaps more villas on its banks and overlooking it than all the other rivers in the whole world. And no river is more circumscribed and shut in on either side; yet of itself it offers no resistance, though it is subject to frequent sudden floods, the inundations being nowhere greater than in the city itself. But in truth it is looked upon rather as a prophet of warning, its rise being always construed rather as a call to religion than as a threat of disaster.

Old Latium has preserved the original limits, *Latium.* extending from the Tiber to Cerceii, a distance of 50 miles; so exiguous at the beginning were the roots of the Empire. Its inhabitants have often changed: at various times it has been occupied by various peoples—the Aborigines, the Pelasgi, the Arcades, the Siculi, the Aurunci, the Rutuli, and beyond Circello the Volsci, Osci and Ausones, owing to which the name of Latium came to be extended as far as the river Garigliano. To begin with there is Ostia, a colony founded by a Roman king, the town of Laurentum, the grove of Jupiter Indiges, the river Numicius, and Ardea, founded by Danaë the mother

57 matre condita. dein quondam Aphrodisium, Antium colonia, Astura flumen et insula, fluvius Nymphaeus, Clostra Romana, Cercei quondam insula
inmenso quidem mari circumdata, ut creditur Homero, et nunc planitie. mirum est quod hac de
re tradere hominum notitiae possumus. Theophrastus, qui primus externorum aliqua de Romanis
diligentius scripsit—nam Theopompus, ante quem
nemo mentionem habuit, urbem dumtaxat a Gallis
captam dixit, Clitarchus ab eo proximus legationem
tantum ad Alexandrum missam—hic iam plus quam
58 ex fama Cerceiorum insulae et mensuram posuit
stadia LXXX in eo volumine quod scripsit Nicodoro
Atheniensium magistratu qui fuit urbis nostrae
CCCCXL anno. quicquid ergo terrarum est praeter
x̄ p. ambitus adnexum insulae post eum annum ac-
59 cessit Italiae. aliud miraculum a Cerceis palus
Pomptina est, quem locum XXIV urbium fuisse
Mucianus ter consul prodidit. dein flumen Aufentum, supra quod Tarracina oppidum lingua Vols-
corum Anxur dictum, et ubi fuere Amyclae sive
Amynclae a serpentibus deletae, dein locus Spelun-
cae, lacus Fundanus, Caieta portus, oppidum Formiae
Hormiae dictum, ut existimavere, antiqua Laestry-
gonum sedes. ultra fuit oppidum Pirae, est colonia
Minturnae Liri amne divisa Clani olim[1] appellato,

1 *Mayhoff*: Glanico.

---

[a] This was inferred from the identification of the name with
Homer's Circe.

of Perseus. Then comes the site of what was once Aphrodisium, the colony of Antium, the river and island called Astura, the river Ninfa, the Roman Bulwarks, Circello, once an island surrounded by a boundless sea,[a] if we are to believe Homer, but now surrounded by a plain. The facts that we are able to publish for the information of the world on this matter are remarkable. Theophrastus, the first foreigner to write with special care about the Romans —for Theopompus, before whom nobody mentioned them, merely states that Rome was taken by the Gauls, and Clitarchus, the next after him, only that an embassy was sent to Alexander—Theophrastus, I say, relying on more than rumour, has actually given the measurement of the island of Circello as 80 furlongs in the volume that he wrote in the archonship of Nicodorus at Athens, which was the 440th year[b] of our city. Whatever land therefore has been joined to the island beyond the circumference of 10 miles was added to Italy after that year. Another marvel not far from Circello is the Pomptine Marsh, a place which Mucianus, who was three times consul, has reported to be the site of 24 cities. Then comes the river Aufentum, above which is the town of Tarracina, called Anxur in the dialect of the Volsci, and the site of Amyclae, or Amynclae, the town destroyed by serpents, then the place called the Grottoes, Lake Fundanus, the port of Gaeta, the town of Formiae, called also Hormiae, the ancient abode, it has been thought, of the Laestrygones. Beyond this formerly stood the town of Pirae, and still exists the colony of Minturnae, through which runs the river Liris, once called Clanis; and

[b] 314 B.C.

45

Sinuessa, extremum in Adiecto Latio, quam quidam
Sinopen dixere vocitatam.

60 Hinc felix illa Campania est, ab hoc sinu incipiunt
vitiferi colles et temulentia nobilis suco per omnis
terras incluto, atque (ut veteres dixere) summum
Liberi Patris cum Cerere certamen. hinc Setini et
Caecubi protenduntur agri; his iunguntur Falerni,
Caleni. dein consurgunt Massici, Gaurani Surrentini-
que montes. ibi Leborini campi sternuntur et in
delicias alicae politur messis. haec litora fontibus
calidis rigantur, praeterque cetera in toto mari
conchylio et pisce nobili adnotantur. nusquam
generosior oleae liquor est,[1] hoc quoque certamen
humanae voluptatis. tenuere Osci, Graeci, Umbri,
61 Tusci, Campani. in ora Savo fluvius, Volturnum
oppidum cum amne, Liternum, Cumae Chalcidensium,
Misenum, portus Baiarum, Bauli, lacus Lucrinus et
Avernus, iuxta quem Cimmerium oppidum quondam,
dein Puteoli colonia Dicaearchea dicti, postque
Phlegraei campi, Acherusia palus Cumis vicina.
62 litore autem Neapolis Chalcidensium et ipsa, Parthenope a tumulo Sirenis appellata, Herculaneum,
Pompei haud procul spectato monte Vesuvio,
adluente vero Sarno amne, ager Nucerinus et $\overline{\text{ix}}$ p.
a mari ipsa Nuceria, Surrentum cum promunturio

[1] *Mayhoff*: et.

Sinuessa, the last town in the Extension of Latium, and stated by some authorities to have been once styled Sinope.

Then comes the favoured country of Campania; Campania. in this valley begin those vine-clad hills with their glorious wine and wassail, famous all the world over, and (as old writers have said) the scene of the severest competition between Father Liber and Ceres. From this point stretch the territories of Sezza and Caecubum, with which march the Falernian and those of Calvi. Then rise up Monte Massico, Monte Barbaro and the hills of Sorrento. Here spread the plains of Leborium, where the spelt crop is sedulously tended to produce delicious frumity. These shores are watered by hot springs, and are noted beyond all others throughout the whole of the sea for their famous shell and other fish. Nowhere is there nobler olive oil—another competition to gratify man's pleasure. Its occupants have been Oscans, Greeks, Umbrians, Tuscans and Campanians. On the coast are the river Saove, the town of Volturno with the river of the same name, Liternum, the Chalcidian colony of Cumae, Miseno, the port of Baiae, Bacolo, the Lucrine lake, Lake Averno near which formerly stood the town of Cimmerium, then Pozzuoli, formerly called the Colony of Dicaearchus; after which come the plains of Salpatara and the Lago di Fusaro near Cumae. On the coast stands Naples, itself also a colony of the Chalcidians, named Parthenope from the tomb of one of the Sirens, Herculaneum, Pompei with Mount Vesuvius in view not far off and watered by the river Sarno, the Nucerian territory and nine miles from the sea Nocera itself, and Sorrento with the promontory of Minerva that once was the abode

Minervae Sirenum quondam sede. navigatio a
63 Cerceis $\overline{\text{II}}$ de $\overline{\text{LXXX}}$ patet. regio ea a Tiberi prima
Italiae servatur ex discriptione Augusti.

Intus coloniae Capua ab $\overline{\text{XL}}$ p. campo dicta, Aqui-
num, Suessa, Venafrum, Sora, Teanum Sidicinum
cognomine, Nola; oppida Abellinum, Aricia, Alba
Longa, Acerrani, Allifani, Atinates, Aletrinates,
Anagnini, Atellani, Aefulani, Arpinates, Auximates,
Abellani, Alfaterni (et qui ex agro Latino item
Hernico item Labicano cognominantur), Bovillae,
Caiatiae, Casinum, Calenum, Capitulum Hernicum,
Cereatini qui Mariani cognominantur, Corani a
Dardano Troiano orti, Cubulterini, Castrimoenienses,
64 Cingulani, Fabienses in monte Albano, Foropopulien-
ses ex Falerno, Frusinates, Ferentinates, Freginates,
Fabraterni Veteres, Fabraterni Novi, Ficolenses,
Fregellani, Forum Appi, Forentani, Gabini, Interam-
nates Sucasini qui et Lirenates vocantur, Ilionenses,
Lanivini, Norbani, Nomentani, Praenestini urbe
quondam Stephane dicta, Privernates, Setini, Signini,
Suessulani, Telesini, Trebulani cognomine Ballienses,
65 Trebani, Tusculani, Verulani, Veliterni, Ulubrenses,
Urbanates, superque Roma ipsa, cuius nomen
alterum dicere nisi [1] arcanis caerimoniarum nefas
habetur, optimaque et salutari fide abolitum enun-
tiavit Valerius Soranus, luitque mox poenas. non

---

[1] nisi *add. Mommsen coll. C.I.L.*

of the Sirens. From this place the distance by sea from Cerceii is 78 miles. This region, beginning from the Tiber, under the partition made by Augustus is regarded as the first region of Italy.

Inland are the following colonies: Capua, so named from its forty miles of plain (*campus*), Aquino, Suessa, Venafro, Sora, Teano surnamed Sidicinum, and Nola; and the towns of Abellinum, Aricia, Alba Longa, the Acerrani, the Allifani, the Atinates, the Aletrinates, the Anagnini, the Atellani, the Aefulani, the Arpinates, the Auximates, the Abellani, the Alfaterni (both those that take their surname from the Latin territory, and from the Hernican, and from the Labican), Bovillae, Caiatiae, Casinum, Calenum, Capitulum of the Hernici, the Cereatini who have the surname of Mariani, the Corani descended from the Trojan Dardanus, the Cubulterini, the Castrimoenienses, the Cingulani, the Fabienses on Mount Albanus, the Foropopulienses from the Falernian district, the Frusinates, the Ferentinates, the Freginates, the Old Fabraterni, the New Fabraterni, the Ficolenses, the Fregellani, Forum Appi, the Forentani, the Gabini, the Interamnates Sucasini, also called the Lirenates, the Ilionenses, the Lanivini, the Norbani, the Nomentani, the Praenestini with their city once called Stephane, the Privernates, the Setini, the Signini, the Suessulani, the Telesini, the Trebulani surnamed Ballienses, the Trebani, the Tusculani, the Verulani, the Veliterni, the Ulubrenses, the Urbanates; and besides all these Rome itself, whose other name it is held to be a sin to utter except at the ceremonies of the mysteries, and when Valerius Soranus divulged the secret religiously kept for the weal of the state, he soon paid the penalty. It seems

alienum videtur inserere hoc loco exemplum religionis
antiquae ob hoc maxime silentium institutae: namque diva Angerona, cui sacrificatur a. d. XII kal. Ian.,
ore obligato obsignatoque simulacrum habet.

66   Urbem III portas habentem Romulus reliquit, ut
plurimas tradentibus credamus, IV. moenia eius
collegere ambitu imperatoribus censoribusque Ves-
pasianis anno conditae DCCCXXVI m. p. XIII·CC, con-
plexa montes septem. ipsa dividitur in regiones
quattuordecim, compita Larum CCLXV. eiusdem
spatium mensura currente a miliario in capite
Romani fori statuto ad singulas portas, quae sunt
hodie numero XXXVII ita ut Duodecim semel nume-
rentur praetereanturque ex veteribus VII quae esse
desierunt, efficit passuum per directum XX.M.DCCLXV.

67   ad extrema vero tectorum cum castris praetoriis ab
eodem miliario per vicos omnium viarum mensura
colligit paulo amplius LX p.; quod si quis altitudinem
tectorum addat, dignam profecto aestimationem con-
cipiat, fateaturque nullius urbis magnitudinem in
toto orbe potuisse ei comparari. clauditur ab oriente
aggere Tarquini Superbi inter prima opere mirabili;
namque eum muris aequavit qua maxime patebat
aditu plano. cetero munita erat praecelsis muris

---

   ^a *I.e.* Vespasian and Titus, who was saluted Emperor after
the siege of Jerusalem, and was associated with his father in
the government, and shared the duties of the censorship.
   ^b A.D. 73.
   ^c Chapels of the Lares Compitales stood at places where
two or more streets crossed.
   ^d These were double gates.

pertinent to add at this point an instance of old religion established especially to inculcate this silence: the goddess Angerona, to whom sacrifice is offered on December 21, is represented in her statue with a sealed bandage over her mouth.

Romulus left Rome possessing three or, to accept *Topography* the statement of the authorities putting the number *of Rome.* highest, four gates. The area surrounded by its walls at the time of the principate and censorship of the Vespasians,[a] in the 826th year[b] of its foundation, measured 13 miles and 200 yards in circumference, embracing seven hills. It is itself divided into fourteen regions, with 265 crossways with their guardian Lares.[c] If a straight line is drawn from the milestone standing at the head of the Roman Forum to each of the gates, which to-day number thirty-seven (provided that the Twelve Gates [d] be counted only as one each and the seven of the old gates that exist no longer be omitted), the result is a total of 20 miles 765 yards in a straight line. But the total length of all the ways through the districts from the same milestone to the extreme edge of the buildings, taking in the Praetorians' Camp, amounts to a little more than 60 miles. If one were further to take into account the height of the buildings, a very fair estimate would be formed, that would bring us to admit that there has been no city in the whole world that could be compared to Rome in magnitude. On the east it is bounded by the Dyke of Tarquinius Superbus, a work among the leading wonders of the world, for he made it as high as the walls where the approach was flat and the city lay most open to attack. In other directions it had the protection of lofty walls or else of precipi-

aut abruptis montibus, nisi quod exspatiantia tecta
multas addidere urbes.

68 In prima regione praeterea fuere in Latio clara
oppida Satricum, Pometia, Scaptia, Politorium,
Tellena, Tifata, Caenina, Ficana, Crustumerium,
Ameriola, Medullum, Corniculum, Saturnia ubi
nunc Roma est, Antipolis quod nunc Ianiculum in
parte Romae, Antemnae, Camerium, Collatia, Ami-
69 tinum, Norbe, Sulmo; et cum iis carnem in monte
Albano soliti accipere populi Albenses, Albani,
Aesolani, Accienses, Abolani, Bubetani, Bolani,
Cusuetani, Coriolani, Fidenates, Foreti, Hortenses,
Latinienses, Longulani, Manates, Macrales, Mu-
nienses, Numinienses, Olliculani, Octulani, Pedani,
Polluscini, Querquetulani, Sicani, Sisolenses, Toleri-
enses, Tutienses, Vimitellari, Velienses, Venetulani,
70 Vitellenses. ita ex antiquo Latio LIII populi interiere
sine vestigiis.

In Campano autem agro Stabiae oppidum fuere
usque ad Cn. Pompeium L. Catonem coss. pr. kal.
Mai., quo die L. Sulla legatus bello sociali id delevit
quod nunc in villam abiit. intercidit ibi et Taurania;
sunt morientes Casilini reliquiae. praeterea auctor
est Antias oppidum Latinorum Apiolas captum a
L. Tarquinio rege, ex cuius praeda Capitolium is
inchoaverit. a Surrentino ad Silerum amnem XXX
m. p. ager Picentinus fuit Tuscorum, templo Iunonis

---

a The reference is to Tibur, Aricia and other places
absorbed in the spreading suburbs.
b I.e. to share in sacrifices.
c An old town between Pompei and Sorrento.
d 89 B.C.

tous hills, except for the fact that the increasing spread of buildings has added a number of cities to it.[a]

The first region formerly included the following *Latium.* celebrated towns of Latium besides those mentioned: Satricum, Pometia, Scaptia, Politorium, Tellena, Tifata, Caenina, Ficana, Crustumerium, Ameriola, Medullum, Corniculum, Saturnia on the site of the present Rome, Antipolis, which to-day is Janiculum and a part of Rome, Antemnae, Camerium, Collatia, Amitinum, Norbe, Sulmo; and together with these the Alban peoples who were accustomed to 'receive flesh'[b] on the Alban Hill, namely the Albani, Aesolani, Accienses, Abolani, Bubetani, Bolani, Cusuetani, Coriolani, Fidenates, Foreti, Hortenses, Latinienses, Longulani, Manates, Macrales, Muni-enses, Numinienses, Olliculani, Octulani, Pedani, Polluscini, Querquetulani, Sicani, Sisolenses, Toleri-enses, Tutienses, Vimitellari, Velienses, Venetulani, Vitellenses. Thus 53 peoples of Old Latium have perished without leaving a trace.

In the Campanian territory the town of Stabiae[c] *Campania.* existed right down to April 29 in the consulship[d] of Gnaeus Pompeius and Lucius Cato, when Lieu-tenant-General Lucius Sulla in the Allies' War destroyed the place that has now been reduced to a farmhouse. Here also was Taurania, which has now perished; and the remains of Casilinum are in process of disappearance. Furthermore, Antias records that the Latin town of Apiolae was captured by King Lucius Tarquinius, who used the spoils of it to begin building the Capitol. The 30 miles of Picentine territory between the district of Sorrento and the river Silaro belonged to the Etruscans; it

Argivae ab Iasone condito insignis. intus oppidum Salerni, Picentia.

71 A Silero regio tertia et ager Lucanus Bruttiusque incipit, nec ibi rara incolarum mutatione. tenuerunt eum Pelasgi, Oenotri, Itali, Morgetes, Siculi, Graeciae maxime populi, novissime Lucani a Samnitibus orti duce Lucio. oppidum Paestum Graecis Posidonia appellatum, sinus Paestanus, oppidum Elea quae nunc Velia, promunturium Palinurum, a quo sinu recedente traiectus ad Columnam Regiam c

72 m. p.; proximum autem flumen Melpes, oppidum Buxentum Graeciae Pyxus, Laus amnis—fuit et oppidum eodem nomine. ab eo Bruttium litus, oppidum Blanda, flumen Baletum, portus Parthenius Phocensium, sinus Vibonensis, locus Clampetiae, oppidum Tempsa a Graecis Temese dictum et Crotoniensium Terina sinusque ingens Terinaeus.

73 oppidum Consentia intus. in peninsula fluvius Acheron, a quo oppidani Acherontini; Hippo, quod nunc Vibonem Valentiam appellamus; portus Herculis, Metaurus amnis, Tauroentum oppidum, portus Orestis et Medma; oppidum Scyllaeum, Crataeis fluvius, mater (ut dixere) Scyllae; dein Columna Regia, Siculum fretum ac duo adversa promunturia, ex Italia Caenus, e Sicilia Pelorum, xii stadiorum

74 intervallo; unde Rhegium xciii. Inde Appennini

---

[a] The modern Reggio, see § 86 note.
[b] Now the Arconte.
[c] Perhaps Punta del Pezzo.
[d] Capo di Faro.

was famous for the temple of Argive Juno founded by
Jason. Further inland was Picentia, a town of Salerno.

At the Silaro begins the third region, the Lucanian *The toe of*
and Bruttian territory; in this too there have been *Italy.*
frequent changes of population. It has been
occupied by Pelasgi, Oenotri, Itali, Morgetes, Siculi,
and mostly by peoples of Greece, and most
recently by the Lucani, Samnite in origin, whose
leader was Lucius. The town of Paestum (called
Posidonia by the Greeks), the bay of Paestum,
the town of Elea, now Velia, Cape Palinuro, from
which across the bay that here stretches inland the
distance to the Royal Pillar[a] is 100 miles. Next
is the river Melpes, the town of Buxentum (the
Greek name of which is Pyxus) and the river Laus—
there was once a town also of the same name. Here
begins the coast of the Bruttii, with the town of Blanda,
the river Baletum, the port of Parthenius, founded
by the Phocians, the Bay of Vibo, the site of Clam-
petia, the town of Tempsa (the Greek name of which
is Temese), and Terina, founded by the people of
Croton, and the extensive Bay of Terina; and inland
the town of Cosenza. On a peninsula is the river
Acheron,[b] which gives its name to the township
of the Acherontians; Hippo, which we now call
Vibo Valentia; the Port of Hercules, the river
Metaurus, the town of Tauroentum, the Port of
Orestes, and Medma; the town of Scyllaeum and
the river Crataeis, known in legend as the Mother
of Scylla; then the Royal Pillar, the Straits of
Messina and the two opposing headlands, Caenus[c]
on the Italian and Pelorum[d] on the Sicilian side, the
distance between them being 1½ miles; Reggio is
11½ miles away. Next comes the Apennine forest

55

silva Sila, promunturium Leucopetra $\overline{\text{xv}}$ p. ab ea,
$\overline{\text{LI}}$ Locri, cognominati a promunturio Zephyrio;
absunt a Silaro $\overline{\text{cccIII}}$. et includitur Europae sinus
primus.

In eo maria nuncupantur: unde inrumpit, Atlanticum, ab aliis Magnum; qua intrat, Porthmos a
Graecis, a nobis Gaditanum fretum; cum intravit,
Hispanum quatenus Hispanias adluit, ab aliis Hibericum aut Baliaricum; mox Gallicum ante Narbonensem
75 provinciam, hinc Ligusticum; ab eo ad Siciliam
insulam Tuscum, quod ex Graecis alii Notium alii
Tyrrenum, e nostris plurumi Inferum vocant. ultra
Siciliam quod est ad Sallentinos Ausonium Polybius
appellat, Eratosthenes autem inter ostium oceani
et Sardiniam quicquid est Sardoum, inde ad Siciliam
Tyrrenum, ab hac Cretam usque Siculum, ab ea
Creticum.

76 Insulae per haec maria primae omnium Pityussae
Graecis dictae a frutice pineo, nunc Ebusus vocatur
utraque, civitate foederata, angusto freto inter-
fluente. patent $\overline{\text{XLVI}}$, absunt ab Dianio DCC stadia,
totidem Dianium per continentem a Carthagine
nova, tantundem a Pityussis in altum Baliares
77 duae et Sucronem versus Colubraria. Baliares

---

of Sila, and the promontory of Leucopetra 15 miles from it, and Epizephyrian Locri (called after the promontory of Zephyrium) 51 miles; it is 303 miles from the river Silaro. And this rounds off the first gulf *a* of Europe.

The names of the seas that it contains are as follows: that from which it makes its entrance is the Atlantic, or as others call it, the Great Sea; the strait by which it enters is called by the Greeks Porthmos and by us the Straits of Cadiz; after it has entered, as far as it washes the coast of the Spains it is called the Spanish Sea, or by others the Iberian or the Balearic Sea; then the Gallic Sea as far as the Province of Narbonne, and afterwards the Ligurian Sea; from that point to the Island of Sicily the Tuscan Sea, which some of the Greeks call the Southern Sea and others the Tyrrhenian, but most of our own people the Lower Sea. Beyond Sicily, as far as the south-eastern point of Italy Polybius calls it the Ausonian Sea, but Eratosthenes calls all the part between the ocean inlet and Sardinia the Sardoan Sea, from Sardinia to Sicily the Tyrrhenian, from Sicily to Crete the Sicilian, and beyond Crete the Cretan.

Divisions of the Western Mediterranean.

The first of all the islands scattered over these seas are called with the Greeks the Pityussae, from the pinetrees *b* that grow on them; each of these islands is now named Ebusus,*c* and in treaty with Rome, the channel between them being narrow. Their area is 46 miles, and their distance from Denia 87½ miles, which is the distance by land from Denia to New Carthage, while at the same distance from the Pityussae out to sea are the two Balearic islands, and opposite the River Xucar lies Colubraria. The

Sixty-four islands, including the Balearics.

funda bellicosas Graeci Gymnasias dixere. maior
c̄ p. est longitudine, circuitu vero c̄c̄c̄c̄l̄x̄x̄v̄ m.; oppida
habet civium Romanorum Palmam et Pollentiam,
Latina Cinium et Tucim, et foederatum Bocchorum
fuit. ab ea x̄x̄x̄ distat minor, longitudine x̄l̄, circuitu
c̄l̄; civitates habet Iamonem, Saniseram, Magonem.
78 a maiore x̄ī ī in altum abest Capraria insidiosa
naufragiis, et e regione Palmae urbis Menariae ac
Tiquadra et parva Hannibalis.

Ebusi terra serpentes fugat, Colubrariae parit,
ideo infesta omnibus nisi Ebusitanam terram in-
ferentibus; Graeci Ophiussam dixere. nec cunicolos
79 Ebusus gignit populantis Baliarium messes. sunt
aliae viginti ferme parvae mari vadoso, Galliae
autem ora in Rhodani ostio Metina, mox quae
Blascorum vocatur, et tres Stoechades a vicinis
Massiliensibus dictae propter ordinem quo sitae
sunt. nomina singulis Prote, Mese quae et Pomponiana vocatur, tertia Hypaea; ab his Iturium,
Phoenice, Phila, Lero et Lerina adversum Antipolim,
in qua Berconi oppidi memoria.
80 VI. In Ligustico mari est Corsica quam Graeci
Cyrnon appellavere, sed Tusco propior, a septen-

---

a Their slingers served as mercenaries under the Carthaginians, and later for Rome.
b The Iles d'Hyères.
c Sainte Marguerite de Lérins.
d Saint Honorat de Lérins.

Balearic islands, formidable in warfare with the sling,[a] have been designated by the Greeks the Gymnasiae. The larger island, Majorca, is 100 miles in length and 475 in circumference. It contains towns of Roman citizen colonists, Palma and Pollenza, towns with Latin rights, Sineu and Tucis; a treaty town of the Bocchi, no longer existing. The smaller island, Minorca, is 30 miles away from Majorca; its length is 40 miles and its circumference 150; it contains the states of Iamo, Sanisera and Port Mahon. Twelve miles out to sea from Majorca is Cabrera, treacherous for shipwrecks, and right off the city of Palma lie the Malgrates and Dragonera and the small island of El Torre.

The soil of Iviza drives away snakes, but that of Colubraria breeds snakes, and consequently that island is dangerous to all people except those who bring earth from Iviza; the Greeks called it Snake Island. Iviza does not breed rabbits either, which ravage the crops of the Balearics. The sea is full of shoals, and there are about twenty other small islands; off the coast of Gaul at the mouth of the Rhone is Metina, and then the island named Brescon, and the three [b] which the neighbouring people of Marseilles call the Row of Islands because of their arrangement, their Greek names being First Island, Middle Island, also called Pomponiana, and the third Hypaea; next to these are Iturium, Phoenica, Lero,[c] and opposite Antibes Lerina,[d] on which according to local tradition there was once a town called Berconum.

VI. In the Ligurian Sea, but adjoining the Tuscan, is the island of Corsica, the Greek name of which is Cyrnos; it lies in a line from north to south, and is *Corsica and other islands.*

59

trione in meridiem proiecta, longa passuum C̅L̅, lata
maiore ex parte L̅, circuitu C̅C̅C̅X̅X̅V̅; abest a Vadis
Volaterranis L̅X̅I̅I̅. civitates habet X̅X̅X̅I̅I̅ et colonias
Marianam a C. Mario deductam, Aleriam a dictatore
Sulla. citra est Oglasa, intra vero, et L̅X̅ p. a Corsica,
Planasia a specie dicta, aequalis freto ideoque
81 navigiis fallax. amplior Urgo et Capraria, quam
Graeci Aegilion dixere, item Igilium et Dianium
quam Artemisiam, ambae contra Cosanum litus, et
Barpana, Menaria, Columbaria, Venaria, Ilva cum
ferri metallis, circuitus C̅, a Populonio X̅, a Graecis
Aethalia dicta; ab ea Planasia X̅X̅V̅I̅I̅I̅. ab his ultra
Tiberina ostia in Antiano Astura, mox Palmaria,
82 Sinonia, adversum Formias Pontiae. in Puteolano
autem sinu Pandateria, Prochyta, non ab Aeneae
nutrice sed quia profusa ab Aenaria erat, Aenaria
a statione navium Aeneae, Homero Inarime dicta,
Pithecusa, non a simiarum multitudine (ut aliqui
existimavere) sed a figlinis doliorum. inter Pausily-
pum et Neapolim Megaris, mox a Surrento V̅I̅I̅I̅
distantes Tiberi principis arce nobiles Capreae
83 circuitu XI m., Leucothea, extraque conspectum,
pelagus Africum attingens, Sardinia minus V̅I̅I̅I̅ p.
a Corsicae extremis, etiamnum angustias eas artanti-
bus insulis parvis quae Cuniculariae appellantur

---

a The distance is really about 90 miles.
b In Etruria, now Torre di Vada.
c Now Ventotiene.
d Il. II. 783, where however the more probable reading is
εἰν Ἀρίμοις—Arima is said to be a volcanic region in Cilicia
or elsewhere. Virgil like Pliny, read Εἰναρίμοις, as he calls
the island Inarime, Aen. IX. 716; it is the modern Ischia.
e πίθηκοι.
f πίθος, πιθάκνη, a jar.
g Now Castel del Ovo.

150 miles long and at most points 50 miles broad:
its circumference measures 325 miles; it is 62 [a]
miles from the Shallows of Volterra.[b] It contains
32 states, and the colonies of Mariana founded by
Gaius Marius and Aleria founded by Sulla when
Dictator. Nearer the mainland is Oglasa, and inside
that, and 60 miles from Corsica, Pianosa, so named
from its appearance, as it is level with the sea and
consequently treacherous to vessels. Then La
Gorgona, a larger island, and Capraia, the Greek
name of which is Aegilion, and also Giglio and
Gianuto, in Greek Artemisia, both opposite the coast
at Cosa, and Barpana, Menaria, Columbaria, Venaria,
Elba with its iron mines, an island 100 miles round
and 10 miles from Populonium, called by the Greeks
Aethalia; the distance between Elba and Pianosa
is 28 miles. After these beyond the mouths of the
Tiber and off the coast of Antium is Astura, then
Palmarola, Senone, and opposite to Formiae Ponza.
In the gulf of Pozzuoli are Pandateria,[c] Prochyta
(so called not after Aeneas's nurse but because it was
formed of soil deposited by the current from Aenaria),
Aenaria (named from having given anchorage
to the fleet of Aeneas but called Inarime in Homer[d])
and Pithecusa (named not from its multitude of
monkeys,[e] as some people have supposed, but from
its pottery[f] factories). Between Posilippo and Naples
is Megaris[g]; then, 8 miles from Sorrento, Capri,
celebrated for the Emperor Tiberius's castle—the
island is 11 miles round; Leucothea; and out
of sight, being on the edge of the African Sea,
Sardinia, which is less than 8 miles from the end of
Corsica, and moreover the channel is narrowed by
the small islands called the Rabbit Warrens, and also

itemque Phintonis et Fossae, a quibus fretum ipsum Taphros nominatur.

84 VII. Sardinia ab oriente patens $\overline{\text{CLXXXVIII}}$ p., ab occidente $\overline{\text{CLXXV}}$, a meridie $\overline{\text{LXXVII}}$, a septentrione $\overline{\text{CXXV}}$, circuitu $\overline{\text{DLXV}}$, abest ab Africa Caralitano promunturio $\overline{\text{CC}}$, a Gadibus $\overline{|\text{XIV}|}$. habet et a Gorditano promunturio duas insulas quae vocantur Herculis, a

85 Sulcensi Enosim, a Caralitano Ficariam. quidam haut procul ab ea et Berelida ponunt et Callodem et quam vocant Heras Lutra. celeberrimi in ea populorum Ilienses, Balari, Corsi oppidorum XVIII, Sulcitani, Valentini, Neapolitani, Vitenses, Caralitani civium R., et Norenses, colonia autem una quae vocatur Ad Turrem Libisonis. Sardiniam ipsam Timaeus Sandaliotim appellavit ab effigie soleae, Myrsilus Ichnusam a similitudine vestigi. contra Paestanum sinum Leucasia est a Sirene ibi sepulta appellata, contra Veliam Pontia et Isacia, utraeque uno nomine Oenotrides, argumentum possessae ab Oenotris Italiae, contra Vibonem parvae quae vocantur Ithacesiae ab Ulixis specula.

86 VIII. Verum ante omnes claritate Sicilia, Sicania a Thucydide dicta, Trinacria a pluribus aut Trinacia a triangula specie, circuitu patens, ut auctor est

---

^a Perhaps Isola Rossa.
^b The Straits of Bonifaccio, Fretum Gallicum.
^c One of these islands now has the name of Torricella.

by the islands of Caprera, and Fossa,[a] from which comes the Greek name of the Straits [b] themselves, Taphros.

VII. The east coast of Sardinia is 188 miles long, *Sardinia.* the west coast 175, the south coast 77 and the north coast 125; its circumference is 565 miles; and at Cape Carbonara its distance from Africa is 200 miles and from Cadiz 1400. It also has two islands off Capo Falcone called the Islands of Hercules, one off La Punta dell'Alga called Santo Antiocho, and one off Cape Carbonara called Coltelalzo. Near it some authorities also place the island sof Berelis, Callodes and the one called the Baths of Hera. The best-known peoples in Sardinia are the Ilienses, Balari, Corsi (who occupy 18 towns), Sulcitani, Valentini, Neapolitani, Vitenses, Caralitani (who have the Roman citizenship), and the Norenses; and one colony called At Libiso's Tower. Sardinia itself was called by Timaeus Sandaliotis, from the similarity of its shape to the sole of a shoe, and by Myrsilus Ichnusa, from its resemblance to a footprint. Opposite to the Bay of Paestum is La Licosa, called after the Siren buried there; and opposite Velia are Pontia and Isacia, both included under the one name of the Oenotrides, which is evidence that Italy was once in the possession of the Oenotri; and opposite to Vibo are the small islands called the Isles of Ithaca, from the watch-tower [c] of Ulysses that stands there.

VIII. But before all the islands of the Mediter- *Sicily:* ranean in renown stands Sicily, called by Thucydides *physical* Sicania and by a good many authors Trinacria or *geography;* Trinacia from its triangular shape. The measurement of its circumference, according to Agrippa, is

63

Agrippa, $\overline{\text{DXXVIII}}$ p., quondam Bruttio agro cohaerens, mox interfuso mari avulsa $\overline{\text{XV}}$ in longitudinem freto, in latitudinem autem MD p. iuxta Columnam Regiam: ab hoc dehiscendi argumento Rhegium Graeci

87 nomen dedere oppido in margine Italiae sito. in eo freto est scopulus Scylla, item Charybdis mare verticosum, ambo clara saevitia. ipsius triquetrae, ut diximus, promunturium Pelorum vocatur adversus Scyllam vergens in Italiam, Pachynum in Graeciam, $\overline{\text{CCCCXL}}$ ab eo distante Peloponneso, Lilybaeum in Africam $\overline{\text{CLXXX}}$ intervallo a Mercuri promunturio et a Caralitano Sardiniae CXC m. inter se autem haec promunturia ac latera distant his spatiis: terreno itinere a Peloro Pachynum $\overline{\text{CLXXXVI}}$, inde Lilybaeum $\overline{\text{CC}}$, inde Pelorum $\overline{\text{CXLII}}$.

88 Coloniae ibi v, urbes ac civitates LXIII. a Peloro mare Ionium ora spectante oppidum Messana civium R. qui Mamertini vocantur, promunturium Drepanum, colonia Tauromenium quae antea Naxos, flumen Asines, mons Aetna nocturnis mirus incendiis: crater eius patet ambitu stadia viginti, favilla Tauromenium et Catinam usque pervenit fervens, fragor

89 vero ad Maroneum et Gemellos colles. scopuli tres Cyclopum, portus Ulixis, colonia Catina, flumina Symaethum, Terias. intus Laestrygoni campi. op-

---

^a Now Reggio; to the Greek ear it suggests 'Breach' as if from ῥήγνυμι.
^b § 73.   ^c Now Capo di Passaro.
^d Now Cape Bon, really only 78 miles from the Capo di Boco Marsala in Sicily.

528 miles. In former times it was attached to the
southern part of Italy, but later it was separated
from it by an overflow of the sea, forming a strait
15 miles long and 1½ miles wide at the Royal
Pillar: this monument of the formation of the gap
is the origin of the Greek name of the town situated
on the Italian coast, Rhegium.[a] In these Straits
is the rock of Scylla and also the whirlpool of
Charybdis, both notoriously treacherous. Sicily
itself is triangular in shape, its points being the
promontory mentioned before[b] named Pelorum,
pointing towards Italy, opposite Scylla, Pachynum[c]
towards Greece, the Morea being 440 miles away,
and Lilybaeum towards Africa, at a distance of 180
miles from the Promontory of Mercury[d] and 190
from Cape Carbonara in Sardinia. The following are
the distances of these promontories from one another
and the length of the coast lines: from Pelorum
to Pachynum by land is 186 miles, from Pachynum
to Lilybaeum 200 miles, and from Lilybaeum to
Pelorum 142 miles.

Sicily contains five colonies and sixty-three cities *circuit of*
and states. Starting from Pelorum, on the coast facing *coast;*
the Ionian Sea is the town of Messina, whose denizens
called Mamertines have the Roman citizenship,
the promontory of Trapani, the colony of Taormina,
formerly Naxos, the river Alcantara, and Mount
Etna with its wonderful displays of fire at night:
the circuit of its crater measures 2½ miles; the
hot ashes reach as far as Taormina and Catania,
and the noise to Madonia and Monte di Mele.
Then come the three Rocks of the Cyclopes, the
Harbour of Ulysses, the colony of Catania, and the
rivers Symaethum and Terias. Inland are the

pida Leontini, Megaris, amnis Pantacyes, colonia
Syracusae cum fonte Arethusa (quamquam et
Temenitis et Archidemia et Magea et Cyane et
Milichie fontes in Syracusano potantur agro), portus
Naustathmus, flumen Elorum, promunturium Pachy-
num, a qua fronte Siciliae flumen Hyrminum, oppidum
Camarina; fluvius Gelas, oppidum Acragas quod
90 Agrigentum nostri dixere; Thermae colonia; amnes
Achates, Mazara, Hypsa, Selinuus; oppidum Lily-
baeum, ab eo promunturium; Drepana, mons Eryx,
oppida Panhormum, Soluus, Himera cum fluvio,
Cephaloedis, Aluntium, Agathyrnum, Tyndaris colonia, oppidum Mylae et unde coepimus Pelorias.
91 Intus autem Latinae condicionis Centuripini,
Netini, Segestani, stipendiarii Assorini, Aetnenses,
Agyrini, Acestaei, Acrenses, Bidini, Cetarini, Dre-
panitani, Ergetini, Echetlienses, Erycini, Entellini,
Enini, Egguini, Gelani, Galateni, Halesini, Hennen-
ses, Hyblenses, Herbitenses, Herbessenses, Herbulen-
ses, Halicuenses, Hadranitani, Imacarenses, Ipanen-
ses, Ietenses, Mutustratini, Magellini, Murgentini,
Mutycenses, Menanini, Naxi, Noini, Petrini, Paro-
pini, Phintienses, Semelitani, Scherini, Selinunti,
Symaethii, Talarenses, Tissinenses, Triocalini, Tyra-
cinenses, Zanclaei Messeniorum in Siculo freto
sunt.
92 Insulae ad Africam versae Gaulos, Melita a
Camerina L̄X̄X̄X̄V̄Ī, a Lilybaeo C̄X̄V̄Ī, Cossyra, Hieron-
nesos, Caene, Galata, Lepadusa, Aethusa quam alii

---

a Now Girgenti.
b ' Hot springs,' now Termini.
c Now San Juliano.
d The identification is uncertain, but Tauromenium was
said to be a colony from Naxos.

Laestrygonian Plains. Then there are the towns of Lentini, Megaris, the river Porcaro, the colony of Syracuse with the Spring of Arethusa (although the territory of Syracuse is also supplied with water by the springs of Temenitis, Archidemia, Magea, Cyane and Milichie), the harbour of Naustathmus, the river Elorum, the promontory of Pachynum. On this side of Sicily are the river Hyrminus, the town of Camarina, the river Gelas; the town of Acragas, called Agrigentum [a] in our language; the colony of Thermae; [b] the rivers Achates, Mazara, Hypsa and Selinus; the town of Lilybaeum and the promontory to which it gives its name; Trapani, Mount Eryx, [c] the towns of Palermo, Solunto, Himera with its river, Cephaloedis, Aluntium, Agathyrnum; the colony of Tindari, the town of Melazzo, and the district of Pelorum from which we began.

In the interior the towns having Latin rights are *interior;* those of the Centuripini, Netini and Segestani; tributaries are Asaro, Nicolosi, Argiro, the Acestaei, the Acrenses, the Bidini, the peoples of Cassaro, Trapani, Ergetium, Orchula, Eryx, Entella, Castro Giovanni, Gangi, Gela, Galata, Tisa, Hermae, Hybla, Nicosia, Pantalica, Herbitenses, Saleni, Aderno, Imacara, Ipana, Iato, Mistretta, Magella, Mandri, Modica, Mineo, Taormina, [d] Noara, Petra, Colisano, Alicata, Semelita, Scheria, Selinunte, Symaethus, Talaria, Randazza, Troccoli, Tyracinum and Zancle, a Messenian settlement on the Straits of Sicily.

The islands on the side towards Africa are Gozo, *adjacent islands* Malta (which is 87 miles from Camerina and 113 from Lilybaeum), Pantellaria, Maretino, Limosa, Calata, Lampedosa, Aethusa (written by others

Aegusam scripserunt, Bucion et a Solunte $\overline{\text{LXXV}}$
Osteodes, contraque Paropinos Ustica. citra vero
Siciliam ex adverso Metauri amnis $\overline{\text{XXV}}$ ferme p. ab
Italia septem Aeoliae appellatae, eaedem Liparaeo-
rum, Hephaestiades a Graecis, a nostris Volcaniae,
Aeoliae, quod Aeolus Iliacis temporibus ibi regnavit.

93   IX. Lipara cum civium Romanorum oppido, dicta
a Liparo rege qui successit Aeolo, antea Milogonis
vel Meligunis vocitata, abest $\overline{\text{XXV}}$ ab Italia, ipsa
circuitu paulo minor v m. inter hanc et Siciliam
altera, antea Therasia appellata, nunc Hiera quia
sacra Volcano est colle in ea nocturnas evomente
94 flammas. tertia Strongyle a Lipara $\overline{\text{VI}}$[1] p. ad
exortum solis vergens, in qua regnavit Aeolus, quae
a Lipara liquidiore tantum flamma differt; a cuius
fumo quinam flaturi sint venti in triduum praedicere
incolae traduntur, unde ventos Aeolo paruisse existimatum. quarta Didyme minor quam Lipara;
quinta Eriphusa, sexta Phoenicusa pabulo proximarum
relictae; novissima eademque minima Euonymos.
hactenus de primo Europae sinu.

95   X. A Locris Italiae frons incipit Magna Graecia
appellata, in tris sinus recedens Ausonii maris,
quoniam Ausones tenuere primi. patet $\overline{\text{LXXXVI}}$, ut
auctor est Varro; plerique $\overline{\text{LXXV}}$ fecere. in ea ora

---

[1] $\overline{\text{VI}}$ add. *Detlefsen.*

---

[a] Its modern name is Volcano.

Aegusa), Levanzo, Alicus (75 miles from Solunto), and Ustica opposite to Paropus. On the Italian side of Sicily facing the river Metaurus, at a distance of nearly 25 miles from Italy, are the seven islands called the Aeolian and also the Liparean: their Greek name is the Hephaestiades, and the Roman Vulcan's Islands; they are called Aeolian from King Aeolus who reigned there in the Homeric period.

IX. Lipari, with a town possessing rights of Roman citizenship, takes its name from King Liparus, who succeeded Aeolus—it was previously called Milogonis or Meligunis; it is 25 miles from Italy, and its circumference measures a little less than 5 miles. Between it and Sicily is another island formerly called Therasia, and now Holy Island *a* because it is sacred to Vulcan, on it being a hill that vomits out flames in the night. The third island is Stromboli, six *volcanoes.* miles to the east of Lipari; here Aeolus reigned. It differs from Lipari only in the fact that its flame is more liquid; the local population are reported to be able to foretell from its smoke three days ahead what winds are going to blow, and this is the source of the belief that the winds obeyed the orders of Aeolus. The fourth of the islands, Didyme, is smaller than Lipari. The fifth, Eriphusa, and the sixth, Phoenicusa, are left to provide pasture for the flocks of the neighbouring islands; the last and also the smallest is Euonymus. So far as to the first gulf of Europe.

X. At Locri begins the projection of Italy called *Magna* Magna Graecia, retiring into the three bays of the *Graecia.* Ausonian Sea, so called from its first inhabitants the Ausones. According to Varro its length is 86 miles, but most authorities have made it 75. On this

69

flumina innumera, sed memoratu digna a Locris
Sagra et vestigia oppidi Caulonis, Mustiae, Consilinum castrum, Cocynthum quod esse longissimum
Italiae promunturium aliqui existumant, dein sinus
et urbs Scolagium, Scylletium Atheniensibus cum
conderent dictum; quem locum occurrens Terinaeus
sinus peninsulam efficit, et in ea portus qui vocatur
Castra Hannibalis, nusquam angustiore Italia: $\overline{XX}$
p. latitudo est. itaque Dionysius maior intercisam
96 eo loco adicere Siciliae voluit. amnes ibi navigabiles
Carcinus, Crotalus, Semirus, Arogas, Thagines,
oppidum intus Petilia, mons Clibanus, promunturium Lacinium, cuius ante oram insula $\overline{x}$ a terra
Dioscoron, altera Calypsus quam Ogygiam appellasse
Homerus existimatur, praeterea Tyris, Eranusa,
Meloessa. ipsum a Caulone abesse $\overline{LXX}$ prodit
Agrippa.
97　XI. A Lacinio promunturio secundus Europae
sinus incipit magno ambitu flexus et Acroceraunio
Epiri finitus promunturio, a quo abest $\overline{LXXV}$. oppidum Croto, amnis Neaethus, oppidum Thurii inter
duos amnes Crathim et Sybarim, ubi fuit urbs
eodem nomine. similiter est inter Sirim et Acirim
Heraclea aliquando Siris vocitata. flumina Aca-
landrum, Casuentum, oppidum Metapontum, quo
98 tertia Italiae regio finitur. mediterranei Bruttio-

---

coast are rivers beyond count; but the places worthy
of mention, beginning at Locri, are the Sagriano
and the ruins of the town of Caulon, Monasteraci,
Camp Consilinum, Punta di Stilo (thought by some
to be the longest promontory in Italy), then the gulf
and city of Squillace, called by the Athenians when
founding it Scylletium. This part of the country
is made into a peninsula by the Gulf of Santa Eufemia
which runs up to it, and on it is the harbour called
Hannibal's Camp. It is the narrowest part of Italy,
which is here 20 miles across, and consequently
the elder Dionysius wanted to cut a canal across the
peninsula in this place, and annex it to Sicily. The
navigable rivers in this district are the Corace, Alli,
Simari, Crocchio and Tacina; it contains the inland
town of Strongolo, the range of Monte Monacello,
and the promontory of Lacinium,[a] off the coast of
which ten miles out lies the Island of the Sons of
Zeus [b] and another called Calypso's Island, which is
thought to be Homer's island of Ogygia, and also
Tyris, Eranusa and Meloessa. According to Agrippa
the distance of the promontory of Lacinium from
Caulon is 70 miles.

XI. At the promontory of Lacinium begins the
second Gulf of Europe; it curves round in a large
bay and ends in Acroceraunium,[c] a promontory of
Epirus; the distance from cape to cape is 75 miles.[d]
Here are the town of Crotona, the river Neto, and
the town of Turi between the river Crati and the
river Sibari, on which once stood the city of the same
name.[e] Likewise Heraclea, once called Siris, lies
between the Siris and the Aciris. Then the rivers
Salandra and Bassiento, and the town of Torre di
Mare, at which the third region of Italy ends. The

rum Aprustani tantum, Lucanorum autem Atinates,
Bantini, Eburini, Grumentini, Potentini, Sontini,
Sirini, Tergilani, Ursentini, Volcentani, quibus
Numestrani iunguntur. praeterea interiisse Thebas
Lucanas Cato auctor est, et Mardoniam Lucanorum
urbem fuisse Theopompus, in qua Alexander Epirotes
occubuerit.

99   Conectitur secunda regio amplexa Hirpinos, Calabriam, Apuliam, Sallentinos $\overline{\text{CCL}}$ sinu qui Tarentinus
appellatur ab oppido Laconum (in recessu hoc intimo
situm, contributa eo maritima colonia quae ibi fuerat,
abest $\overline{\text{CXXXVI}}$ a Lacinio promunturio) adversam ei
Calabriam in peninsulam emittens. Graeci Messa-
piam a duce appellavere et ante Peucetiam a Peucetio
Oenotri fratre in Sallentino agro. inter promunturia
$\overline{\text{C}}$ intersunt; latitudo peninsulae a Tarento Brundisium terreno itinere $\overline{\text{XXXV}}$ patet, multoque brevius
100 a portu Sasine. oppida per continentem a Tarento
Uria, cui cognomen ob Apulam Messapiae,[1]
Sarmadium, in ora vero Senum, Callipolis, quae
nunc est Anxa, $\overline{\text{LXXV}}$ a Tarento. inde $\overline{\text{XXXIII}}$ promunturium quod Acran Iapygiam vocant, quo
longissime in maria excurrit Italia. ab eo Basta
oppidum et Hydruntum decem ac novem milia
passuum, ad discrimen Ioni et Hadriatici maris, qua

[1] *Mayhoff*: cognomen Apulae Messapia.

---

[a] Capo di S. Maria di Luca.

only inland community of the Bruttii are the Aprustani, but in the interior of Lucania are the Atinates, Bantini, Eburini, Grumentini, Potentini, Sontini, Sirini, Tergilani, Ursentini and Volcentani adjoining whom are the Numestrani. Moreover it is stated by Cato that the town of Thebes in Lucania has disappeared and Theopompus says that there was once a city of the Lucanians named Mardonia, in which Alexander of Epirus died.

Adjoining this district is the second region of Italy, embracing the Hirpini, Calabria, Apulia and the Sallentini with the 250-mile bay named after the Laconian town of Taranto (this is situated in the innermost recess of the bay and has had attached to it the sea-board colony that had settled there, and it is 136 miles distant from the promontory of Lacinium),—throwing out Calabria which is opposite to Lacinium to form a peninsula. The Greeks called it Messapia from their leader Messapus, and previously Peucetia from Peucetius the brother of Oenotrius, and it was in the Sallentine territory. The distance between the two headlands is 100 miles; and the breadth of the peninsula overland from Taranto to Brindisi is 35 miles, and considerably less if measured from the port of Sasine. The towns inland from Taranto are Uria, which has the surname of Messapia to distinguish it from Uria in Apulia, and Sarmadium; on the coast are Senum and Gallipoli, the present Anxa, 75 miles from Taranto. Next, 33 miles farther, the promontory called the Iapygian Point,[a] where Italy projects farthest into the sea. Nineteen miles from this point are the towns of Vaste and Otranto, at the boundary between the Ionian Sea and the Adriatic, where is the shortest

The heel of Italy, and the Adriatic coast of Italy.

73

in Graeciam brevissimus transitus, ex adverso
Apolloniatum oppidi latitudine intercurrentis freti
101 ⊥ non amplius. hoc intervallum pedestri continuare
transitu pontibus iactis primum Pyrrus Epiri rex
cogitavit, post eum M. Varro, cum classibus Pompei
piratico bello praeesset; utrumque aliae impedivere
curae. ab Hydrunte Soletum desertum, dein Fratuertium, portus Tarentinus, statio Miltopes, Lupia,
Balesium, Caelia, Brundisium ⊥ p. ab Hydrunte in
primis Italiae portu nobile ac velut certiore transitu
sicuti longiore, excipiente Illyrici urbe Durrachio
c̄c̄xxv traiectu.

102 Brundisio conterminus Paediculorum[1] ager; novem
adulescentes totidemque virgines ab Illyriis xii
populos genuere. Paediculorum[1] oppida Rudiae,
Egnatia, Barium, amnes Iapyx a Daedali filio rege,
a quo et Iapygia Acra, Pactius, Aufidus ex Hirpinis
montibus Canusium praefluens.

103 Hinc Apulia Dauniorum cognomine a duce Diomedis socero, in qua oppidum Salapia Hannibalis
meretricio amore inclutum, Sipontum, Uria, amnis
Cerbalus Dauniorum finis, portus Aggasus, promunturium montis Gargani a Sallentino sive Iapygio
c̄c̄xxxiv ambitu Gargani, portus Garnae, lacus

---

[1] *Rackham* (*cf.* 38): Poediculorum, Pediculorum.

[a] In Illyria.
[b] Straits of Otranto.
[c] A bastard formation from παῖς.

74

crossing to Greece, opposite to the town of Apollonia,[a] separated by an arm of the sea[b] not more
than 50 miles wide. King Pyrrhus of Epirus first
conceived the plan of carrying a causeway over
this gap by throwing bridges across it, and after
him Marcus Varro had the same idea when command-
ing the fleets of Pompey in the Pirate War; but both
were prevented by other commitments. After
Otranto comes the deserted site of Soletum, then
Fratuertium, the harbour of Taranto, the roadstead
of Miltope, Lecce, Baleso, Cavallo, and then Brindisi,
50 miles from Otranto, one of the most famous places
in Italy for its harbour and as offering a more certain
crossing albeit a longer one, ending at the city of
Durazzo in Illyria, a passage of 225 miles.

Adjacent to Brindisi is the territory of the
Paediculi,[c] whose twelve tribes were the descendants
of nine youths and nine maidens from the Illyrians.
The towns of the Paediculi are Ruvo, Agnazzo and
Bari; their rivers are the Iapyx, named from the son
of Daedalus, the king who also gives his name to the
Iapygian Point, the Pactius and the Aufidus, which
runs down from the Hirpini mountains and past
Canossa.

Here begins Apulia, called Apulia of the Daunii, *Apulia.*
who were named after their chief, the father-in-law
of Diomede; in Apulia is the town of Salpi, famous
as the scene of Hannibal's amour with a courtezan,
Sipontum, Uria, the river Cervaro marking the
boundary of the Daunii, the harbour of Porto
Greco, the promontory of Monte Gargano (the
distance round Gargano from the promontory of
Sallentinum or Iapygia being 234 miles), the port of
Varano, the lake of Lesina, the river Frento which

75

Pantanus, flumen portuosum Fertor, Teanum Apulorum itemque Larinum, Cliternia, Tifernus amnis;
104 inde regio Frentana. ita Apulorum genera tria:
Teani a duce e Grais; Lucani subacti a Calchante,
quae nunc loca tenent Atinates; Dauniorum praeter
supra dicta coloniae Luceria, Venusia, oppida Canusium, Arpi aliquando Argos Hippium Diomede
condente, mox Argyripa dictum. Diomedes ibi
delevit gentes Monadorum Dardorumque et urbes
duas quae in proverbi ludicrum vertere, Apinam
105 et Tricam. cetera intus in secunda regione Hirpinorum colonia una Beneventum auspicatius mutato
nomine quae quondam appellata Maleventum,
Ausculani, Aquiloni, Abellinates cognomine Protropi,
Compsani, Caudini, Ligures qui cognominantur
Corneliani et qui Baebiani, Vescellani, Aeclani,
Aletrini, Abellinates cognominati Marsi, Atrani,
Aecani, Alfellani, Atinates, Arpani, Borcani, Collatini,
Corinenses et nobiles clade Romana Cannenses,
Dirini, Forentani, Genusini, Herdonienses, Irini,
Larinates cognomine Frentani, Merinates ex Gargano, Mateolani, Neretini, Natini, Rubustini, Silvini,
Strapellini, Turnantini, Vibinates, Venusini, Ulurtini.
Calabrorum mediterranei Aegetini, Apamestini,
Argentini, Butuntinenses, Deciani, Grumbestini,
Norbanenses, Palionenses, Stulnini, Tutini. Sallen-

---

[a] *Apinae Tricaeque*, 'Châteaux en Espagne.' Martial
14. 1 7; *tricae* ' trifles ' or ' tricks,' is probably a word of different
origin.
[b] The accusative of the Greek Μαλόεις when Latinized
suggested to the Roman ear ' ill come.'
[c] By Hannibal, 216 B.C.
[d] Forenza.
[e] Ginosa; and among the following are the modern Noja,

forms a harbour, Teanum of the Apuli and Larinum
of the Apuli, Cliternia, and the river Biferno, at
which begins the district of the Frentani. Thus the
Apulians comprise three different races: the Teani,
so called from their chief, of Graian descent; the
Lucanians who were subdued by Calchas and who
occupied the places that now belong to the Atinates;
and the Daunians, including, beside the places
mentioned above, the colonies of Lucera and Venosa
and the towns of Canossa and Arpa, formerly called
Argos Hippium when founded by Diomede, and
afterwards Argyripa. Here Diomede destroyed
the tribes of the Monadi and Dardi and two cities
whose names have passed into a proverbial joke,
Apina and Trica.[a] Besides these there are in the
interior of the second region one colony of the
Hirpini formerly called Maleventum [b] and now more
auspiciously, by a change of name, Beneventum,
the Ausculani, Aquiloni, Abellinates surnamed Protropi, Compsani, Caudini, Ligurians with the surnames
of Corneliani and Baebiani, Vescellani, Aeclani,
Aletrini, Abellinates surnamed Marsi, Atrani,
Aecani, Alfellani, Atinates, Arpani, Borcani, Collatini,
Corinenses, Cannae celebrated for the Roman
defeat,[c] Dirini, Forentani,[d] Genusini,[e] Herdonienses,
Irini, Larinates surnamed Frentani, the Merinates
from Monte Gargano, Mateolani, Neretini, Natini,
Rubustini, Silvini, Strapellini, Turnantini, Vibinates,
Venusini, Ulurtini. Inland Calabrian peoples are
the Aegetini, Apamestini, Argentini, Bututinenses,
Deciani, Grumbestini, Norbanenses, Palionenses,
Stulnini and Tutini; inland Sallentini are the

Savigliano, Rapolla, Bovino and Bitonto; others are now
Ostuni, Veste, San Verato.

tinorum Aletini, Basterbini, Neretini, Uzentini,
Veretini.

106   XII. Sequitur regio quarta gentium vel fortissi-
marum Italiae. in ora Frentanorum a Tiferno
flumen Trinium portuosum, oppida Histonium,
Buca, Hortona, Aternus amnis. intus Anxani
cognomine Frentani, Caretini Supernates et In-
fernates, Lanuenses; Marrucinorum Teatini; Pae-
lignorum Corfinienses, Superaequani, Sulmonenses;
Marsorum Anxatini, Antinates, Fucentes, Lucenses,
Marruvini; Albensium Alba ad Fucinum lacum;
107 Aequiculanorum Cliternini, Carseolani; Vestinorum
Angulani, Pennenses, Peltuinates quibus iunguntur
Aufinates Cismontani; Samnitium quos Sabellos
et Graeci Saunitas dixere, colonia Bovianum Vetus
et alterum cognomine Undecumanorum, Aufide-
nates, Aesernini, Fagifulani, Ficolenses, Saepinates,
Tereventinates; Sabinorum Amiternini, Curenses,
Forum Deci, Forum Novum, Fidenates, Interamnates, Nursini, Nomentani, Reatini, Trebulani qui
cognominantur Mutuesci et qui Suffenates, Tiburtes,
108 Tarinates. in hoc situ ex Aequicolis interiere Comini,
Tadiates, Caedici, Alfaterni. Gellianus auctor est
lacu Fucino haustum Marsorum oppidum Archippe
conditum a Marsya duce Lydorum, item Vidici-
norum in Piceno deletum a Romanis Valerianus.
Sabini, ut quidam existimavere, a religione et deum
cultu Sebini appellati, Velinos accolunt lacus roscidis

---

    a Now the Pescara.
    b Now Pelino.
    c I.e. ' Sabini ' was originally ' Sebini ' from σέβας.

Aletini, Basterbini, Neretini, Uzentini and Veretini.

XII. There follows the fourth region, which in- *Frentani and*
cludes the very bravest races in Italy. On the coast, *Samnium.*
in the territory of the Frentani, after Tifernum are the
river Trigno, affording a harbour, and the towns of
Histonium, Buca and Hortona and the river Aternus.[a]
Inward are the Anxani surnamed Frentani, the Upper
and Lower Caretini and the Lanuenses; and in the
Marrucine territory Chieti; in the Paelignian, the
people of Corfinium,[b] Subequo and Sulmona; in the
Marsian, those of Lanciano, Atina, Fucino, Lucca
and Muria; in the Albensian region the town of
Alba on Lake Fucino; in the Aequiculan, Cliternia
and Carsoli; in the Vestinian, Sant' Angelo, Pinna
and Peltuina, adjoining which is Ofena South of the
Mountain; in the region of the Samnites, who once
were called Sabelli and by the Greeks Saunitae, the
colony of Old Bojano and the other Bojano that
bears the name of the Eleventh Legion, Alfidena,
Isernia, Fagifulani, Ficolea, Supino, and Terevento;
in the Sabine, Amiternum, Correse, Market of Decius,
New Market, Fidenae, Ferano, Norcia, La Mentana,
Rieti, Trebula Mutuesca, Trebula Suffena, Tivoli,
Tarano. In this district, of the tribes of the Aequicoli
the Comini, Tadiates, Caedici and Alfaterni have disappeared. It is stated by Gellianus that a Marsian
town of Archippe, founded by the Lydian commander Marsyas, has been submerged in Lake
Fucino, and also Valerian says that the town of the
Vidicini in Picenum was destroyed by the Romans.
The Sabines (according to some opinions called Sebini
from their religious beliefs and ritual[c]) live on the
lush dewy hills by the Lakes of Velino. Those

109 collibus. Nar amnis exhaurit illos sulpureis aquis
Tiberim ex his petens, replet e monte Fiscello
Avens[1] iuxta Vacunae nemora et Reate in eosdem
conditus. at ex alia parte Anio in monte Trebanorum
ortus lacus tris amoenitate nobilis qui nomen dedere
Sublaqueo defert in Tiberim. in agro Reatino
Cutiliae lacum, in quo fluctuetur insula, Italiae
umbilicum esse M. Varro tradit. infra Sabinos
Latium est, a latere Picenum, a tergo Umbria,
Appennini iugis Sabinos utrimque vallantibus.

110 XIII. Quinta regio Piceni est, quondam uberrimae
multitudinis: $\overline{\text{CCCLX}}$ Picentium in fidem p. R. venere.
orti sunt a Sabinis voto vere sacro. tenuere ab
Aterno amne, ubi nunc ager Hadrianus et Hadria
colonia a mari $\overline{\text{VI}}$ p., flumen Vomanum, ager Praetu-
tianus Palmensisque, item Castrum Novum, flumen
Batinum, Truentum cum amne, quod solum Liburnorum in Italia relicum est, flumina Albula, Tessuinum, Helvinum quo finitur Praetutiana regio et
111 Picentium incipit; Cupra oppidum, Castellum Firma-
norum, et super id colonia Asculum, Piceni nobilissima.
intus Novana; in ora Cluana, Potentia, Numana a
Siculis condita, ab iisdem colonia Ancona adposita
promunturio Cunero in ipso flectentis se orae cubito,
a Gargano $\overline{\text{CLXXXIII}}$. intus Auximates, Beregrani,

---

[1] *Codd.* aves *aut* labens.

---

[a] 299 B.C.
[b] In time of danger the produce of the next spring was
vowed to the gods; the children then born in early times
perhaps were sacrificed, but later were allowed to grow up
and then driven across the frontier to settle wherever Providence might lead them.

lakes drain into the river Nera, which from these derives the river Tiber with its sulphurous waters, and they are replenished by the Avens which runs down from Monte Fiscello near the Groves of Vacuna and Rieti and loses itself in the lakes in question. In another direction the Teverone rising in Mount Trevi drains into the Tiber three lakes famous for their beauty, from which Subiaco takes its name. In the district of Rieti is the lake of Cutilia, which is said by Marcus Varro to be the central point of Italy, and to contain a floating island. Below the Sabine territory lies Latium, on one side of it Picenum, and behind it Umbria, while the ranges of the Apennines fence it in on either side.

XIII. The fifth region is that of Picenum, which formerly was very densely populated: 360,000 Picentines took the oath of allegiance to Rome.[a] They derived their origin from the Sabines, who had made a vow to celebrate a Holy Spring.[b] The territory that they took possession of began at the river Aterno, where are now the district and colony of Adria, 6 miles from the sea. Here is the river Vomanus, the territories of Praetutia and Palma, also the New Camp, the river Batinus, Tronto with its river, the only Liburnian settlement left in Italy, the river Albula, Tessuinum, and Helvinum where the region of the Praetutii ends and that of Picenum begins; the town of Cupra, Porto di Fermo, and above it the colony of Ascoli, the most famous in Picenum. Inland is Novana, and on the coast Cluana, Potentia, Numana founded by the Sicilians, and Ancona, a colony founded by the same people on the promontory of Cunerus just at the elbow of the coast where it bends round, 183 miles from Monte Gargano.

Picenum (Abbruzzo).

Cingulani, Cuprenses cognomine Montani,Falarienses,
Pausulani, Planinenses, Ricinenses, Septempedani,
Tollentinates, Treienses, Urbesalvia Pollentini.

112   XIV. Iungetur his sexta regio Umbriam con-
plexa agrumque Gallicum citra Ariminum. ab
Ancona Gallica ora incipit Togatae Galliae cognomine. Siculi et Liburni plurima eius tractus tenuere,
in primis Palmensem, Praetutianum Hadrianumque
agrum. Umbri eos expulere, hos Etruria, hanc
Galli. Umbrorum gens antiquissima Italiae existimatur, ut quos Ombrios a Graecis putent dictos
quod in [1] inundatione terrarum imbribus super-
113 fuissent. trecenta eorum oppida Tusci debellasse
reperiuntur. nunc in ora flumen Aesis, Senagallia,
Metaurus fluvius, coloniae Fanum Fortunae, Pisau-
rum cum amne, et intus Hispellum, Tuder. de
cetero Amerini, Attidiates, Asisinates, Arnates,
Aesinates, Camertes, Casuentillani, Carsulani, Dolates cognomine Sallentini, Fulginiates, Foroflami-
nienses, Foroiulienses cognomine Concupienses, Fo-
robrentani, Forosempronienses, Iguini, Interamnates
cognomine Nartes, Mevanates, Mevanionenses, Mati-
licates, Narnienses, quod oppidum Nequinum antea
114 vocitatum est, Nucerini cognomine Favonienses et
Camellani, Otriculani, Ostrani, Pitulani cognomine
Pisuertes et alii Mergentini, Plestini, Sentinates,
Sassinates, Spoletini, Suasani, Sestinates, Suillates,
Tadinates, Trebiates, Tuficani, Tifernates cognomine Tiberini et alii Metaurenses, Vesinicates,

---

[1] in add. *Mayhoff*: *an* inundationi? *Rackham.*

---

[a] From ὄμβρος, a storm of rain.

Inland are Osimo, Beregra, Cingula, Cupra surnamed
Montana, Falerona, Pausula, Plalina, Ricinum, Sep-
tempedum, Tollentinum, Treia, and the people from
Pollentia settled at Urbisaglia.

XIV. Adjoining to this will come the sixth region, *Umbria (The*
embracing Umbria and the Gallic territory this side *Marches).*
Rimini. At Ancona begins the Gallic coast named
Gallia Togata. The largest part of this district was
occupied by Sicilians and Liburnians, especially the
territories of Palma, Praetutia and Adria. They
were expelled by the Umbrians, and these by
Etruria, and Etruria by the Gauls. The Umbrians
are believed to be the oldest race of Italy, being
thought to be the people designated as Ombrii *a* by
the Greeks on the ground of their having survived
the rains after the flood. We find that 300 of their
towns were conquered by the Etruscans. On this
coast at the present time are the river Esino, Sini-
gaglia, the river Meturo and the colonies of Fano
and Pesaro with the river of the same name and
inland those of Spello and Todi. Besides these there
are the peoples of Amelia, Attiglio, Assisi, Arna,
Iesi, Camerino, Casuentillum, Carsulae; the Dolates
surnamed Sallentini; Foligno, Market of Flaminius,
Market of Julius, surnamed Concupium, Market
Brenta, Fossombrone, Gubbio, Terni on the Nera,
Bevagna, Mevanio, Matilica, Narni (the town formerly
called Nequinum); the people of Nocera surnamed
Favonienses and those surnamed Camellani; Otricoli,
Ostra; the Pitulani surnamed Pisuertes and others
surnamed Mergentini; the Plestini; Sentinum,
Sassina, Spoleto, Suasa, Sestino, Sigello, Tadina,
Trevi, Tuficum, Tifernum on the Tiber, Tifernum on
the Meturo; Vesinica, Urbino on the Meturo and

83

Urbanates cognomine Metaurenses et alii Hortenses, Vettonenses, Vindinates, Visuentani. in hoc situ interiere Felignates, et qui Clusiolum tenuere supra Interamnam, et Sarranates cum oppidis Acerris quae Vafriae cognominabantur, Turocaelo quod Vettiolum, item Solinates, Suriates, Falinates, Sappinates. interiere et Arinates cum Crinivolo et Usidicani et Plangenses, Paesinates, Caelestini. Ameriam supra scriptam Cato ante Persei bellum conditam annis DCCCCLXIII prodit.

115 XV. Octava regio determinatur Arimino, Pado, Appennino. in ora fluvius Crustumium, Ariminum colonia cum amnibus Arimino et Aprusa, fluvius Rubico, quondam finis Italiae. ab eo Sapis et Vitis et Anemo, Ravenna Sabinorum oppidum cum amne Bedese, ab Ancona $\overline{cv}$ p. nec procul a mari Umbrorum Butrium. intus coloniae Bononia, Felsina vocitata tum[1] cum princeps Etruriae esset, Brixillum, Mutina, Parma, Placentia; oppida Caesena, Claterna,

116 Foro Clodi, Livi, Popili, Truentinorum, Corneli, Licini, Faventini, Fidentini, Otesini, Padinates, Regienses a Lepido, Solonates, Saltusque Galliani qui cognominantur Aquinates, Tannetani, Veleiates cognomine veteri Regiates, Urbanates. in hoc tractu interierunt Boi quorum tribus CXII fuisse auctor est Cato, item Senones qui ceperunt Romam.

---

[1] *Mayhoff*: vocitatum.

---

a 171–167 B.C.

b Probably the Pisatello.

c A Gallic tribe who settled South of the Alps, and were conquered by Scipio Nasica in 191 B.C. They migrated to Bohemia, which takes its name from them.

Urbino of the Garden, Bettona, the Vindinates and the Visuentani. Peoples that have disappeared in this district are the Felignates and the inhabitants of Clusiolum above Interamna, and the Sarranates, together with the towns of Acerrae surnamed Vafriae and Turocaelum surnamed Vettiolum; also the Solinates, Suriates, Falinates and Sappinates. There have also disappeared the Arinates with the town of Crinivolum and the Usidicani and Plangenses, the Paesinates, the Caelestini. Ameria above-mentioned is stated by Cato to have been founded 963 years before the war [a] with Perseus.

XV. The boundaries of the eighth region are marked by Rimini, the Po and the Apennines. On its coast are the river Conca, the colony of Rimini with the rivers Ariminum and Aprusa, and the river Rubicon,[b] once the frontier of Italy. Then there are the Savio, the Bevano and the Roneone; the Sabine town of Ravenna with the river Montone, and the Umbrian town of Butrium 105 miles from Ancona and not far from the sea. Inland are the colonies of Bologna (which at the time when it was the chief place in Etruria was called Felsina), Brescello, Modena, Parma, Piacenza, and the towns of Cesena, Quaderna, Fornocchia, Forli, Forli Piccolo, Bertinoro, Cornelius Market, Incino, Faenza, Fidentia, Otesini, Castel Bondino, Reggio named from Lepidus, Città di Sole, Groves of Gallius surnamed Aquinates, Tenedo, Villac in old days surnamed Regias, Urbana. Peoples no longer existing in this region are the Boii,[c] said by Cato to have comprised 112 tribes, and also the Senones who captured Rome.[d]

Gallia Cispadana (Emilia).

[d] 390 B.C. : their city Agedincum is now Sens.

117 XVI. Padus e gremio Vesuli montis celsissimum
in cacumen Alpium elati finibus Ligurum Vagien-
norum visendo fonte profluens condensque se cuniculo et in Forovibiensium agro iterum exoriens,
nullo amnium claritate inferior, Graecis dictus
Eridanus ac poena Phaethontis inlustratus, augetur
ad canis ortus liquatis nivibus, agris quam navigiis
torrentior, nihil tamen ex rapto sibi vindicans
118 atque, ubi liquit, ubertate largitor.[1] c̄c̄c̄ p. a fonte
addens meatu duo de LXXXX, nec amnes tantum
Appenninos Alpinosque navigabiles capiens sed
lacus quoque inmensos in eum sese exonerantes, omni
numero XXX flumina in mare Hadriaticum defert,
celeberrima ex iis Appennini latere Iactum, Tanarum,
Trebiam Placentinum, Tarum, Inciam, Gabellum,
Scultennam, Rhenum, Alpium vero Sturam, Orgum,
Durias duas, Sesitem, Ticinum, Lambrum, Adduam,
119 Ollium, Mincium. nec alius amnium tam brevi
spatio maioris incrementi est; urguetur quippe
aquarum mole et in profundum agitur gravis terrae,
quamquam diductus in flumina et fossas inter
Ravennam Altinumque per c̄xx̄, tamen qua largius
vomit Septem Maria dictus facere.

Augusta fossa Ravennam trahitur, ubi Padusa

---

[1] *V.l.* linquit ubertatem largitur.

---

[a] Phaethon when driving the chariot of his father the Sun
lost control of the horses, and was struck down by Jupiter to
prevent his setting the earth on fire; Ovid, *Met.* II. 47 ff. makes
him fall into the Padus.

XVI. The source of the Po, which well deserves a The river
Po : its
sources,
tributaries
and mouths. visit, is a spring in the heart of Monte Viso, an extremely lofty Alpine peak in the territory of the Ligurian Vagienni; the stream burrows underground and emerges again in the district of Vibius Market. It rivals all other rivers in celebrity; its Greek name was Eridanus, and it is famous as the scene of the punishment of Phaethon.[a] The melting of the snows at the rising of the Dogstar causes it to swell in volume; but though its flooding does more damage to the fields adjacent than to vessels, nevertheless it claims no part of its plunder for itself, and where it deposits its spoil it bestows bounteous fertility. Its length from its source is 300 miles, to which it adds 88 by its windings, and it not only receives navigable rivers from the Apennines and the Alps, but also immense lakes that discharge themselves into it, and it carries down to the Adriatic Sea as many as 30 streams in all. Among these the best-known are: flowing from the Apennine range, the Jactum, the Tanaro, the Trebbia (on which is Piacenza), the Taro, the Enza, the Secchia, the Panaro and the Reno; flowing from the Alps, the Stura, Orco, two Doras, Sesia, Ticino, Lambra, Adda, Oglio and Mincio. Nor does any other river increase so much in volume in so short a distance; in fact, the vast body of water drives it on and scoops out its bed with disaster to the land, although it is diverted into streams and canals between Ravenna and Altino over a length of 120 miles; nevertheless where it discharges its water more widely it forms what are called the Seven Seas.

The Po is carried to Ravenna by the Canal of Augustus; this part of the river is called the Padusa,

vocatur quondam Messanicus appellatus. proximum inde ostium magnitudinem portus habet qui Vatreni dicitur, qua Claudius Caesar e Britannia triumphans praegrandi illa domo verius quam nave
120 intravit Hadriam. hoc ante Eridanum ostium dictum est, ab aliis Spineticum ab urbe Spina quae fuit iuxta, praevalens, ut Delphicis creditum est thesauris, condita a Diomede. auget ibi Padum Vatrenus amnis ex Forocorneliensi agro.

Proximum inde ostium Caprasiae, dein Sagis, dein Volane quod ante Olane vocabatur, omnia ea fossa Flavia quam primi a Sagi fecere Tusci egesto amnis impetu per transversum in Atrianorum paludes quae Septem Maria appellantur, nobili portu oppidi Tuscorum Atriae a quo Atriaticum mare ante
121 appellabatur quod nunc Hadriaticum. inde ostia plena Carbonaria, ac [1] Fossiones Philistinae,[2] quod alii Tartarum vocant, omnia ex Philistinae fossae abundatione nascentia, accedentibus Atesi ex Tridentinis Alpibus et Togisono ex Patavinorum agris. pars eorum et proximum portum facit Brundulum, sicut Aedronem Meduaci duo ac fossa Clodia. his se Padus miscet ac per haec effunditur, plerisque, ut in Aegypto Nilus quod vocant Delta, triquetram

[1] ac *hic edd.*: *post* Fossiones *aut om. codd.*
[2] *Edd.*: Philistina.

its name previously being Messanicus. The mouth
nearest to Ravenna forms the large basin called the
Harbour of the Santerno; it was here that Claudius
Caesar sailed out into the Adriatic, in what was a
vast palace rather than a ship, when celebrating his
triumph over Britain. This mouth was formerly
called the Eridanus, and by others the Spineticus
from the city of Spina that formerly stood near it,
and that was believed on the evidence of its treasures
deposited at Delphi to have been a very powerful
place; it was founded by Diomede. At this point
the Po is augmented by the river Santerno from the
territory of Cornelius Market.

The next mouth to this is the Caprasian mouth,
then that of Sagis, and then Volane, formerly called
Olane; all of these form the Flavian Canal, which was
first made from the Sagis by the Tuscans, thus discharging the flow of the river across into the marshes
of the Atriani called the Seven Seas, with the famous
harbour of the Tuscan town of Atria which formerly
gave the name of Atriatic to the sea now called the
Adriatic. Next come the deep-water mouths of
Carbonaria and the Fosses of Philistina, called by
others Tartarus, all of which originate from the
overflow of the Philistina Canal, with the addition
of the Adige from the Trentino Alps and of the
Bacchiglione from the district of Padua. A part of
these streams also forms the neighbouring harbour
of Brondolo, as likewise that of Chioggia is formed
by the Brenta and Brentella and the Clodian Canal.
With these streams the Po unites and flows through
them into the sea, according to most authorities
forming between the Alps and the sea-coast the figure
of a triangle, like what is called the Delta formed

figuram inter Alpes atque oram maris facere proditus,
122 stadiorum π̄[1] circuitu. pudet a Graecis Italiae
rationem mutuari, Metrodorus tamen Scepsius dicit,
quoniam circa fontem arbor multa sit picea, quales
Gallice vocentur padi, hoc nomen accepisse, Ligurum
quidem lingua amnem ipsum Bodincum vocari,
quod significet fundo carentem. cui argumento
adest oppidum iuxta Industria[2] vetusto nomine
Bodincomagum, ubi praecipua altitudo incipit.

123   XVII. Transpadana appellatur ab eo regio unde-
cima, tota in mediterraneo, cui marina[3] cuncta
fructuoso alveo inportat. oppida Vibi Forum,
Segusio, coloniae ab Alpium radicibus Augusta
Taurinorum, inde navigabili Pado, antiqua Ligurum
stirpe, dein Salassorum Augusta Praetoria iuxta
geminas Alpium fores, Graias atque Poeninas,—his
Poenos, Grais Herculem transisse memorant,—
oppidum Eporedia Sibyllinis a populo Romano
conditum iussis,—eporedias Galli bonos equorum
124 domitores vocant,—Vercellae Libiciorum ex Salluis
ortae, Novaria ex Vertamacoris, Vocontiorum hodieque pago, non (ut Cato existimat) Ligurum, ex quibus
Laevi et Marici condidere Ticinum non procul a
Pado, sicut Boi Transalpibus profecti Laudem
Pompeiam, Insubres Mediolanum.   Orumbiviorum

---

[1] *Edd.*: v̄.   [2] *V.l.* Industriam.   [3] *Mayhoff*: maria.

[a] Now Monte di Po.
[b] Now the Little and Great St. Bernard passes: the name
of the former survives in the 'Graian Alps.'
[c] Now Pavia.

by the Nile in Egypt; the triangle measures 250 miles in circumference. One is ashamed to borrow an account of Italy from the Greeks; nevertheless, Metrodorus of Scepsis says that the river has received the name of Padus because in the neighbourhood of its source there are a quantity of pine-trees of the kind called in the Gallic dialect *padi*, while in fact the Ligurian name for the actual river is Bodincus, a word that means 'bottomless.' This theory is supported by the fact that the neighbouring town of Industria,[a] where the river begins to be particularly deep, had the old name of Bodincomagum.

XVII. The eleventh region receives from the river the name of Transpadana; it is situated entirely inland, but the river carries to it on its bounteous channel the products of all the seas. Its towns are Seluzzo and Susa, and the colony of Turin at the roots of the Alps (here the Po becomes navigable), sprung from an ancient Ligurian stock, and next that of Aosta Praetoria of the Salassi, near the twin gateways of the Alps, the Graian pass and the Pennine,[b]—history says that the latter was the pass crossed by the Carthaginians and the former by Hercules—and the town of Ivrea, founded by the Roman nation by order of the Sibylline Books—the name comes from the Gallic word for a man good at breaking horses—, Vercelli, the town of the Libicii, founded from the Sallui, and Novara founded from Vertamacori, a place belonging to the Vocontii and now-a-days a village, not (as Cato thinks) belonging to the Ligurians; from whom the Laevi and Marici founded Ticinum [c] not far from the Po, just as the Boians, coming from the tribes across the Alps, founded Lodi and the Insubrians Milan. According to Cato, Como,

Gallia Transpadana.

stirpis esse Comum atque Bergomum et Licini
Forum aliquotque circa populos auctor est Cato,
sed originem gentis ignorare se fatetur, quam
docet Cornelius Alexander ortam a Graecia interpretatione etiam nominis vitam in montibus degen-
125 tium. in hoc situ interiit oppidum Orumbiviorum
Parra, unde Bergomates Cato dixit ortos, etiamnum prodente se altius quam fortunatius situm.
interiere et Caturiges Insubrum exsules et Spina
supra dicta, item Melpum opulentia praecipuum,
quod ab Insubribus et Bois et Senonibus deletum eo
die quo Camillus Veios ceperit Nepos Cornelius
tradidit.
126   XVIII. Sequitur decima regio Italiae Hadriatico
mari adposita, cuius Venetia, fluvius Silis ex montibus Tarvisanis, oppidum Altinum, flumen Liquentia
ex montibus Opiterginis et portus eodem nomine,
colonia Concordia, flumina et portus Reatinum,
Tiliaventum Maius Minusque, Anaxum quo Varanus
defluit, Alsa, Natiso cum Turro, praefluente Aquileiam
127 coloniam $\overline{xv}$ p. a mari sitam. Carnorum haec regio
iunctaque Iapudum, amnis Timavos, castellum
nobile vino Pucinum, Tergestinus sinus, colonia
Tergeste, $\overline{xxxiii}$ ab Aquileia. ultra quam sex
milia p. Formio amnis, ab Ravenna $\overline{clxxxix}$, anticus
auctae Italiae terminus, nunc vero Histriae; quam

---

^a *I.e.* ' Orumbivii' is understood to come from ὄρος and βίος.
^b In 396 B.C.
^c The inhabitants in the 5th c. A.D., to escape from Attila
and the Huns, fled to the adjoining islands, and founded
Venice.
^d Perhaps the Risano.
^e In the time of Augustus, before Istria was added to
Italy.

Bergamo, Incino and some surrounding peoples are
of the Orumbivian stock, but he confesses that he
does not know the origin of that race; whereas
Cornelius Alexander states that it originated from
Greece, arguing merely by the name, which he
renders 'those who pass their lives in mountains.' [a]
In this locality a town of the Orumbivii named
Parra, said by Cato to be the original home of the
people of Bergamo, has perished, its remains still
showing its site to have been more lofty than advantageous. Other communities that have perished
are the Caturiges, an exiled section of the Insubrians,
and the above-mentioned Spina, and also the excep- § 120.
tionally wealthy town of Melpum, which is stated by
Cornelius Nepos to have been destroyed by the
Insubrians, Boii and Senones on the day [b] on which
Camillus took Veii.

XVIII. Next comes the tenth region of Italy, *Venetia.*
on the coast of the Adriatic Sea. In it are Venetia,[c]
the river Silo that rises in the mountains of Treviso,
the town of Altino, the river Liquenzo rising in the
mountains of Oderzo, and the port of the same name,
the colony of Concordia, the river and port of Rieti,
the Greater and Lesser Tagliamento, the Stella,
into which flows the Revonchi, the Alsa, the Natisone,
with the Torre that flows past the colony of Aquileia
situated 15 miles from the sea. This is the region
of the Carni, and adjoining it is that of the Iapudes,
the river Timavo, Castel Duino, famous for its wine,
the Gulf of Trieste, and the colony of the same
name, 33 miles from Aquileia. Six miles beyond
Trieste is the river Formio,[d] 189 miles from Ravenna,
the old frontier [e] of the enlarged Italy and now the
boundary of Istria. It has been stated by many

93

cognominatam a flumine Histro in Hadriam effluente
e Danuvio amne eodemque Histro exadversum
Padi fauces, contrario eorum percussu mari interiecto
dulcescente, plerique dixere falso, et Nepos etiam
128 Padi accola; nullus enim ex Danuvio amnis in mare
Hadriaticum effunditur. deceptos credo quoniam
Argo navis flumine in mare Hadriaticum descendit[1]
non procul Tergeste, nec iam constat quo flumine.
umeris travectam Alpes diligentiores tradunt, subisse
autem Histro, dein Savo, dein Nauporto, cui nomen
ex ea causa est, inter Aemonam Alpesque exorienti.
129 XIX. Histria ut peninsula excurrit. latitudinem
eius $\overline{XL}$, circuitum $\overline{CXXV}$ prodidere quidam, item
adhaerentis Liburniae et Flanatici sinus, alii $\overline{CCXXV}$,
alii Liburniae $\overline{CLXXX}$. nonnulli in Flanaticum sinum
Iapudiam promovere a tergo Histriae $\overline{CXXX}$, dein
Liburniam $\overline{CL}$ fecere. Tuditanus qui domuit Histros
in statua sua ibi inscripsit: Ab Aquileia ad Tityum
flumen stadia MM.[2] oppida Histriae civium Romanorum Aegida, Parentium, colonia Pola quae nunc
Pietas Iulia, quondam a Colchis condita; abest a
Tergeste $\overline{CV}$. mox oppidum Nesactium et nunc

----

[1] descenderit? *Rackham.*
[2] MM *Detlefsen*: M.

----

[a] Ship's Harbour (doubtless suggesting also the portage).
Emona on its banks later became a Roman colony, Julia
Augusta, and is the modern Laibach, which is also the name
of the river.
[b] Now the Golfo di Quarnaro.
[c] C. Sempronius, consul 129 B.C.
[d] *I.e.* 250 miles; the MSS. give 1000 stades, *i.e.* 125 Roman
miles. The Roman mile was a little shorter than the English.
[e] Perhaps Capo d'Istria.
[f] Believed to be Castel Nuovo.

authors, even including Nepos, who lived on the banks of the Po, that Istria takes its name from the stream called Ister flowing out of the river Danube (which also has the name of Ister) into the Adriatic, opposite the mouths of the Po, and that their currents, colliding from contrary directions, turn the intervening sea into a pool of fresh water; but these statements are erroneous, for no river flows out of the Danube into the Adriatic. I believe that they have been misled by the fact that the ship Argo came down a river into the Adriatic not far from Trieste, but it has not hitherto been decided what river this was. More careful writers say that the Argo was portaged on men's shoulders across the Alps, but that she had come up the Ister and then the Save and then the Nauportus,[a] a stream rising between Emona and the Alps, that has got its name from this occurrence.

XIX. Istria projects in the form of a peninsula. *Istria.* Some authorities have given its breadth as 40 miles and its circuit as 125 miles, and the same dimensions for the adjoining territory of Liburnia and the Flanatic Gulf;[b] others make it 225 miles, and others give the circuit of Liburnia as 180 miles. Some carry Iapudia, at the back of Istria, as far as the Flanatic Gulf, a distance of 130 miles, and then make the circuit of Liburnia 150 miles. Tuditanus,[c] who conquered the Istrians, inscribed the following statement on his statue there: *From Aquileia to the river Keriko* 2000 *furlongs.*[d] Towns in Istria with the Roman citizenship are Aegida,[e] Parenzo and the colony of Pola, the present Pietas Julia, originally founded by the Colchians, and 105 miles from Trieste. Then comes the town of Nesactium,[f] and the river Arsa, now the frontier of

finis Italiae fluvius Arsia.   Polam ab Ancona traiectus
$\overline{\text{CXX}}$ p. est.

130   In mediterraneo regionis decimae coloniae Cremona, Brixia Cenomanorum agro, Venetorum autem
Ateste et oppida Acelum, Patavium, Opitergium,
Velunum, Vicetia, Mantua Tuscorum trans Padum
sola reliqua.   Venetos Troiana stirpe ortos auctor est
Cato, Cenomanos iuxta Massiliam habitasse in
Volcis.   Feltini et Tridentini et Beruenses Raetica
oppida, Raetorum et Euganeorum Verona, Iulienses
Carnorum;   dein, quos scrupulosius dicere non
attineat, Alutrenses, Asseriates, Flamonienses Vanienses et alii cognomine Curici, Foroiulienses cognomine Transpadani, Foretani, Nedinates, Quarqueni,
131 Tarvisani, Togienses, Varvari.   in hoc situ interiere
per oram Irmene, Pellaon, Palsicium, ex Venetis
Atina et Caelina, Carnis Segesta et Ocra, Tauriscis
Noreia.   et ab Aquileia ad XII lapidem deletum
oppidum etiam invito senatu a M. Claudio Marcello
L. Piso auctor est.

In hac regione et XI lacus incluti sunt amnesque
eorum partus, aut alumni si modo acceptos reddunt,
ut Adduam Larius, Ticinum Verbannus, Mincium

---

^a The town of Flagogna.   ^b Friuli.
^c Nadin.   ^d Quero.

Italy. The distance across from Ancona to Pola
is 120 miles.

In the interior of the tenth region are the colonies *Gallia*
of Cremona and Brescia in the territory of the *Cisalpina.*
Cenomani, and Este in that of the Veneti, and the
towns of Asolo, Padua, Oderzo, Belluno, Vicenza
and Mantua, the only remaining Tuscan town across
the Po. According to Cato, the Veneti are descended
from a Trojan stock, and the Cenomani lived among
the Volcae in the neighbourhood of Marseilles.
There are also the Rhaetic towns of Feltre, Trent
and Berua, Verona which belongs to the Rhaeti and
Euganei jointly, and Zuglio which belongs to the
Carni; then peoples that we need not be concerned
to designate with more particularity, the Alutrenses,
Asseriates, Flamonienses *a* Vanienses and other
Flamonienses surnamed Curici, the Forojulienses *b*
surnamed Transpadani, Foretani, Nedinates,*c* Quarqueni,*d* Tarvisani,*e* Togienses, Varvari. In this district
there have disappeared, on the coast-line, Irmene,
Pellaon, Palsicium, Atina and Caelina belonging
to the Veneti, Segesta and Ocra to the Carni,
Noreia to the Taurisci. Also Lucius Piso states
that a town 12 miles from Aquileia was destroyed
by Marcus Claudius Marcellus, although against
the wish of the Senate.

This region also contains eleven famous lakes and *The Italian*
the rivers of which they are the source, or which, *Lakes.*
in the case of those that after entering the lakes
leave them again, are augmented by them—for
instance the Adda that flows through Lake Como,
the Ticino through Maggiore, the Mincio through
Garda, the Seo through the Lago di Seo, and the

e Treviso.

Benacus, Ollium Sebinnus, Lambrum Eupilis, omnes incolas Padi.

132 Alpis in longitudinem x̄ p. patere a supero mari ad inferum Caelius tradit, Timagenes x̄x̄v̄ p. deductis, in latitudinem autem Cornelius Nepos c̄, T. Livius īīī stadiorum, uterque diversis in locis; namque et centum milia excedunt aliquando, ubi Germaniam ab Italia submovent, nec l̄x̄x̄ inplent reliqua sui parte graciles, veluti naturae providentia. latitudo Italiae subter radices earum a Varo per Vada Sabatia, Taurinos, Comum, Brixiam, Veronam, Vicetiam, Opitergium, Aquileiam, Tergeste, Polam, ad ¹ Arsiam D̄C̄C̄x̄L̄v̄ colligit.

133 XX. Incolae Alpium multi populi, sed inlustres a Pola ad Tergestis regionem Fecusses, Subocrini, Catali, Menoncaleni, iuxtaque Carnos quondam Taurisci appellati, nunc Norici; his contermini Raeti et Vindelici, omnes in multas civitates divisi. Raetos Tuscorum prolem arbitrantur a Gallis pulsos duce Raeto. verso deinde in ² Italiam pectore Alpium Latini iuris Euganeae gentes, quarum

134 oppida xxxiv enumerat Cato. ex his Triumpilini, venalis cum agris suis populus, dein Camunni conpluresque similes finitimis adtributi municipiis. Lepontios et Salassos Tauriscae gentis idem Cato

---

¹ ad add. *Rackham.*   ² in add. *Dalecampius.*

ᵃ The stade or furlong was ⅛ of a Roman mile. But it looks as if the text were wrong, as what follows seems to show that 100 miles should be the higher figure, and the estimate of 3000 stades attributed to Livy is improbably large.

ᵇ The name survives in Val Trompia.

ᶜ Presumably they accepted membership of the Roman Empire for a pecuniary consideration.

ᵈ Val Camonica.   ᵉ Val Leventina.   Val d'Aosta.

Lambro through Lago di Pusiano—all of these
streams being tributaries of the Po.

The length of the Alps from the Adriatic to the *The range*
Mediterranean is given by Caelius as 1000 miles; *of the Alps.*
Timagenes puts it at 25 miles less. Their breadth
is given by Cornelius Nepos as 100 miles, by Livy
as 375 miles,[a] but they take their measurements
at different points; for occasionally the Alps exceed
even 100 miles in breadth, where they divide Germany
from Italy, while in the remaining part they are as
it were providentially narrow and do not cover 70
miles. The breadth of Italy at the roots of the Alps,
measured from the river Var through Vado, the
port of Savo, Turin, Como, Brescia, Verona, Vicenza,
Oderzo, Aquileia, Trieste and Pola, to the river Arsa,
amounts to 745 miles.

XX. The Alps are inhabited by a great many *Alpine*
nations, but the notable ones, between Pola and the *races.*
district of Trieste, are the Fecusses, Subocrini, Catali
and Menoncaleni, and next to the Carni the peoples
formerly called Taurisci and now Norici; adjoining
these are the Raeti and Vindelici. All are divided
into a number of states. The Raeti are believed
to be people of Tuscan race driven out by the Gauls;
their leader was named Raetus. Then, on the side
of the Alps towards Italy, are the Euganean races
having the Latin rights, whose towns listed by Cato
number 34. Among these are the Triumpilini,[b]
a people that sold themselves[c] together with their
lands, and then the Camunni[d] and a number of
similar peoples, assigned to the jurisdiction of the
neighbouring municipal towns. Cato before mentioned considers the Lepontii[e] and Salassi[f] to be
of Tauriscan origin, but almost all other authors give

99

arbitratur; ceteri fere Lepontios relictos ex comitatu Herculis interpretatione Graeci nominis credunt
praeustis in transitu Alpium nive membris; eiusdem
exercitus et Graios fuisse Graiarum Alpium incolas
praestantesque genere Euganeos, inde tracto no-
135 mine; caput eorum Stoenos. Raetorum Vennonen-
ses Sarunetesque ortus Rheni amnis accolunt,
Lepontiorum qui Uberi vocantur fontem Rhodani
eodem Alpium tractu. sunt praeterea Latio donati
incolae, ut Octodurenses et finitimi Centrones,
Cottianae civitates et Turi Liguribus orti, Vagienni
Ligures et qui Montani vocantur, Capillatorumque
plura genera ad confinium Ligustici maris.
136   Non alienum videtur hoc loco subicere inscrip-
tionem e tropaeo Alpium, quae talis est:

> Imp. Caesari divi filio Aug. pont. max., imp. XIV,
> tr. pot. XVII, S. P. Q. R., quod eius ductu auspiciisque
> gentes Alpinae omnes quae a mari supero ad inferum
> pertinebant sub imperium p. R. sunt redactae. Gentes
> Alpinae devictae Triumpilini, Camunni, Venostes,

ᵃ 'Lipontius,' from λείπω.

ᵇ The Little St. Bernard, under Mont Blanc; see p. 90,
note b.

ᶜ From εὐγένειοι or εὐγενεῖς.

ᵈ In Cantons Valais and Vaud.

ᵉ Centron in Savoy.

ᶠ Near Mont Cenis.

ᵍ An arch with a portion of this inscription remaining stood
in fairly recent times near Nicaea in Albania.

ʰ Adopted son of his great-uncle Julius Caesar.

ⁱ 17 B.C.

ʲ Some of these are identifiable in the modern place-names:
Venostes, Val Venosco; Isarchi, Val de Sarcho; Breuni,
Val Bregna; Genaunes, Val d'Agno; Focunates, Vogogna;
Licates, Augsburg on the Lech; Brixentes, Brixen; Seduni,
Sion; Medulli, Maurienne; Ucenni, Bourg d'Oysans; Caturiges,

a Greek interpretation to their name and believe
that the Lepontii are descended from companions
of Hercules 'left behind' [a] because their limbs had
been frostbitten in crossing the Alps; and that the
inhabitants of the Graian [b] Alps were also Grai
from the same band, and that the Euganei were of
specially distinguished family, and took their name
from that fact; [c] and that the head of these are
the Stoeni. The Raetian tribes Vennones and
Sarunetes live near the sources of the river Rhine,
and the Lepontian tribe called the Uberi at the source
of the Rhone in the same district of the Alps. There
are also other native tribes that have received Latin
rights; for instance, the Octodurenses [d] and their
neighbours the Centrones,[e] the Cottian states [f] and
the Turi of Ligurian descent, the Ligurian Vagienni
and those called the Mountain Ligurians, and several
tribes of Long-haired Ligurians on the borders of the
Ligurian Sea.

It seems not out of place to append here the in- *Arch of*
scription from the triumphal arch [g] erected in the *Nicaea.*
Alps, which runs as follows:

> *To the Emperor Caesar, son [h] of the late lamented
> Augustus, Supreme Pontiff, in his fourteenth year of
> office as Commander-in-chief and seventeenth year [i]
> of Tribunitial Authority—erected by the Senate and
> People of Rome, to commemorate that under his
> leadership and auspices all the Alpine races stretching
> from the Adriatic Sea to the Mediterranean were
> brought under the dominion of the Roman people.
> Alpine races [j] conquered—the Triumpilini, Camunni,*

Chorges; Brigiani, Briançon; Nemaloni, Miolans; Eguituri,
Guillaumes; Velauni, Bueil.

137   *Vennonetes, Isarchi, Breuni, Genaunes, Focunates,*
Vindelicorum gentes quattuor, Cosuanetes, Rucinates,
Licates, Catenates, Ambisontes, Rugusci, Suanetes,
Calucones, Brixentes, Leponti, Uberi, Nantuates,
Seduni, Varagri, Salassi, Acitavones, Medulli, Ucenni,
Caturiges, Brigiani, Sobionti, Brodionti, Nemaloni,
Edenates, Vesubiani, Veamini, Gallitae, Triullati,
Ecdini, Vergunni, Eguituri, Nematuri, Oratelli,
Nerusi, Velauni, Suetri.

138   Non sunt adiectae Cottianae civitates xv quae non
fuerant hostiles, item adtributae municipiis lege
Pompeia.

  Haec est Italia dis sacra, hae gentes eius, haec
oppida populorum; super haec Italia quae L.
Aemilio Papo,[1] C. Atilio Regulo coss. nuntiato
Gallico tumultu sola sine externis ullis auxiliis atque
etiam tunc sine Transpadanis equitum l̄xxx̄, peditum
d̄cc̄ armavit. metallorum omnium fertilitate nullis
cedit terris; sed interdictum id vetere consulto
patrum Italiae parci iubentium.

139   XXI. Arsiae gens Liburnorum iungitur usque ad
flumen Tityum. pars eius fuere Mentores, Himani,
Encheleae, Buni et quos Callimachus Peucetios
appellat, nunc totum uno nomine Illyricum vocatur
generatim. populorum pauca effatu digna aut facilia
nomina. conventum Scardonitanum petunt Iapudes

---

[1] *Edd.*: Paulo.

---

[a] 225 B.C. Regulus fell in action.

Venostes, Vennonetes, Isarchi, Breuni, Genaunes,
Focunates, four tribes of the Vindelici, the Cosuanetes,
Rucinates, Licates, Catenates, Ambisontes, Rugusci,
Suanetes, Calucones, Brixentes, Leponti, Uberi, Nan-
tuates, Seduni, Varagri, Salassi, Acitavones, Medulli,
Ucenni, Caturiges, Brigiani, Sobionti, Brodionti,
Nemaloni, Edenates, Vesubiani, Veamini, Gallitae,
Triullati, Ecdini, Vergunni, Eguituri, Nematuri,
Oratelli, Nerusi, Velauni, Suetri.

This list does not include the 15 states of the
Cottiani which had not shown hostility, nor those that
were placed by the law of Pompeius under the
jurisdiction of the municipal towns.

This then is Italy, a land sacred to the gods, and
these are the races and towns of its peoples. Moreover this is that Italy which, in the consulship [a]
of Lucius Aemilius Papus and Gaius Atilius Regulus,
on receipt of news of a rising in Gaul, single-handed
and without any alien auxiliaries, and moreover at
that date without aid from Gaul north of the Po,
equipped an army of 80,000 horse and 700,000 foot.
She is inferior to no country in abundance of mineral
products of every kind; but mining is prohibited
by an old resolution of the Senate forbidding the
exploitation of Italy.

XXI. The race of the Liburni stretches from the *N.E. coast*
Arsa to the river Tityus. Sections of it were the *of Adriatic.*
Mentores, Himani, Encheleae, Buni, and the people
called by Callimachus the Peucetii, all of whom are
now designated collectively by the one name of
Illyrians. Few of the peoples are worthy of mention,
nor are their names easy to pronounce. To the
jurisdiction of Scardona resort the Iapudes and the

103

et Liburnorum civitates XIV, ex quibus Lacinienses,
Stulpinos, Burnistas, Olbonenses nominare non
pigeat. ius Italicum habent eo conventu Alutae,
Flanates a quibus sinus nominatur, Lopsi, Varvarini,
inmunesque Asseriates, et ex insulis Fertinates,
140 Currictae. Cetero per oram oppida a Nesactio
Alvona, Flanona, Tarsatica, Senia, Lopsica, Ortoplinia, Vegium, Argyruntum, Corinium, Aenona,
civitas Pasini, flumen Tedanium quo finitur Iapudia.
insulae eius sinus cum oppidis praeter supra signifi-
catas Absortium, Arba, Crexi, Gissa, Portunata.
rursus in continente colonia Iader quae a Pola $\overline{\text{CLX}}$
abest, inde $\overline{\text{XXX}}$ Colentum insula, $\overline{\text{XVIII}}$ ostium Titii
fluminis.

141   XXII. Liburniae finis et initium Delmatiae Scardona in amne eo $\overline{\text{XII}}$ passuum a mari. dein Tario-
tarum antiqua regio et castellum Tariona, promunturium Diomedis vel, ut alii, paeninsula Hyllis
circuitu $\overline{\text{c}}$, Tragurium civium Romanorum marmore
notum, Siculi in quem locum divus Claudius veteranos
142 misit, Salona colonia ab Iader $\overline{\text{CXII}}$. petunt in eam
iura viribus discriptis in decurias CCCXLII Delmataei
XXV Deuri, CCXXXIX Ditiones, CCLXIX Maezaei, LII
Sardeates. in hoc tractu sunt Burnum, Andetrium,
Tribulium, nobilitata proeliis castella. petunt et
ex insulis Issaei, Colentini, Separi, Epetini. ab his

---

14 communities of the Liburni, of which it may not be tedious to name the Lacinienses, Stulpini, Burnistae and Olbonenses. In this jurisdiction states having Italic rights are the Alutae, the Flanates from whom the gulf[a] takes its name, the Lopsi, the Varvarini, the Asseriates who are exempt from tribute, and of the islands Berwitch and Karek. Moreover along the coast starting from Nesactium are Albona, Fianona, Tersact, Segna, Lopsico, Ortoplinia, Viza, Argyruntum, Carin, Nona, the city of the Pasini and the river Zermagna, at which Iapudia terminates. The islands of the gulf with their towns are, besides the above specified, Absortium, Arba, Cherso, Gissa, Portunata. Again on the mainland is the colony of Zara, 160 miles from Pola, and 30 miles from it the island of Mortero, and 18 miles from it the mouth of the river Kerka.

XXII. At the city of Scardona on the Kerka, 12 *Dalmatia.* miles from the sea, Liburnia ends and Dalmatia begins. Then comes the ancient region of the Tariotares and the fortress of Tariona, the Promontory of Diomede,[b] or as others name it the Peninsula of Hyllis, measuring 100 miles round, Tragurium, a place possessing Roman citizenship and famous for its marble, Siculi where the late lamented Claudius sent a colony of ex-service men; and the colony of Spalato, 112 miles from Zara. Spalato is the centre for jurisdiction of the Delmataei whose forces are divided into 342 tithings, Deuri into 25 tithings, Ditiones into 239, Maezaei 269, Sardeates 52. In this district are Burnum, Andetrium and Tribulium, fortresses that are famous for battles. Island peoples also belonging to the same jurisdiction are the Issaeans, Colentini, Separi and Epetini.

castella Peguntium, Nareste, Onium, Narona colonia
tertii conventus a Salona L̄XXXV p., adposita cogno-
minis sui fluvio a mari X̄X p. M. Varro LXXXIX civitates
143 eo ventitasse auctor est; nunc soli prope noscuntur
Cerauni decuriis XXIV, Daursi XVII, Desitiates CIII,
Docleates XXXIII, Deretini XIV, Deraemestae XXX,
Dindari XXXIII, Glinditiones XLIV, Melcumani XXIV,
Naresi CII, Scirtari LXXII, Siculotae XXIV, popula-
toresque quondam Italiae Vardaei non amplius quam
XX decuriis. praeter hos tenuere tractum eum
Ozuaei, Partheni, Hemasini, Arthitae, Armistae.
144 a Narone amne C̄ p. abest Epidaurum colonia. ab
Epidauro sunt oppida civium Romanorum Rhizinium,
Acruium, Butuanum, Olcinium quod antea Col-
chinium dictum est a Colchis conditum, amnis
Drino superque eum oppidum civium Romanorum
Scodra a mari X̄VĪII; praeterea multorum Graeciae
oppidorum deficiens memoria nec non et civitatium
validarum: eo namque tractu fuere Labeatae,
Endirudini, Sasaei, Grabaei; proprieque dicti Illyri
et Taulanti et Pyraei. retinet[1] nomen in ora Nymphaeum promunturium. Lissum oppidum civium
Romanorum ab Epidauro C̄ p.
145 XXIII. A Lisso Macedonia provincia. gentes
Partheni et a tergo eorum Dassaretae, montes
Candaviae a Dyrrachio L̄XXVĪII p., in ora vero Denda
civium Romanorum, Epidamnum colonia propter

---

[1] *V.l.* retinent.

---

[a] Now Almissa. [b] Now Mucarisea.
[c] Now Ragusa Vecchia. [d] Capo Rodoni.

After these come the fortresses of Peguntium,[a] Nareste[b] and Onium, and the colony of Narenta, the seat of the third centre, 85 miles from Spalato, situated on the river also called Narenta 20 miles from the sea. According to Marcus Varro 89 states used to resort to it, but now nearly the only ones known are the Cerauni with 24 tithings, the Daursi with 17, Desitiates 103, Docleates 33, Deretini 14, Deraemestae 30, Dindari 33, Glinditiones 44, Melcumani 24, Naresi 102, Scirtari 72, Siculotae 24, and the Vardaei, once the ravagers of Italy, with not more than 20 tithings. Besides these this district was occupied by the Ozuaei, Partheni, Hemasini, Arthitae and Armistae. The colony of Epidaurum[c] is 100 miles distant from the river Naron. After Epidaurum come the following towns with Roman citizenship—Risine, Cattaro, Budua, Dulcigno, formerly called Colchinium because it was founded by the Colchians; the river Drino, and upon it Scutari, a town with the Roman citizenship, 18 miles from the sea; and also a number of Greek towns and also powerful cities of which the memory is fading away, this district having contained the Labeatae, Endirudini, Sasaei and Grabaei; and the Taulanti and the Pyraei, both properly styled Illyrians. The promontory of Nymphaeum[d] on the coast still retains its name. Lissum, a town having the Roman citizenship, is 100 miles from Epidaurum.

XXIII. At Lissum begins the Province of Macedonia. Its races are the Partheni and in their rear the Dassaretae. The mountains of Candavia are 78 miles from Durazzo, and on the coast is Denda, a town with Roman citizenship, the colony of Epi- *West coast of Macedonia.*

inauspicatum nomen a Romanis Dyrrachium appellata,
flumen Aous a quibusdam Aeas nominatum, Apollonia quondam Corinthiorum colonia IV p. a mari
recedens, cuius in finibus celebre Nymphaeum
accolunt barbari Amantes et Buliones. at in ora
oppidum Oricum a Colchis conditum. inde initium
Epiri, montes Acroceraunia quibus hunc Europae
determinavimus sinum. Oricum a Salentino Italiae
promunturio distat $\overline{\text{LXXX}}$.

146 XXIV. A tergo Carnorum et Iapudum, qua se
fert magnus Hister, Raetis iunguntur Norici; oppida
eorum Virunum, Celeia, Teurnia, Aguntum, Iuvavum,
Vianiomina, Claudia, Flavium Solvense. Noricis
iunguntur lacus Peiso, deserta Boiorum; iam tamen
colonia divi Claudi Sabaria et oppido Scarabantia
Iulia habitantur.

147 XXV. Inde glandifera Pannoniae, qua mitescentia
Alpium iuga per medium Illyricum a septentrione ad
meridiem versa molli in dextra ac laeva devexitate
considunt. quae pars ad mare Hadriaticum spectat
appellatur Delmatia et Illyricum supra dictum; ad
septentriones Pannonia vergit: finitur inde Danuvio.
in ea coloniae Aemona, Siscia. amnes clari et
navigabiles in Danuvium defluunt Draus e Noricis

---

a Now Durazzo.   b The Voioussa.
c Now Pollina.   d In § 97.
e Promunturium Iapygium.
Perhaps the Neusiedler See near Vienna.

damnum which, on account of the ill-omened sound of that name, has been renamed Dyrrachium *a* by the Romans, the river Aous,*b* called by some Aeas, and the former Corinthian colony of Apollonia *c* 4 miles distant from the sea, in the territory of which is the famous Shrine of the Nymphs, with the neighbouring native tribes of the Amantes and Buliones. Actually on the coast is the town of Ericho, founded by the Colchians. Here begins Epirus, with the *Epirus.* Acroceraunian mountains, at which we fixed *d* the boundary of this Gulf of Europe. The distance between Ericho and Cape Leuca *e* in Italy is 80 miles.

XXIV. Behind the Carni and Iapudes, along the *The Upper Danube.* course of the mighty Danube, the Raetians are adjoined by the Norici; their towns are Wolk-Markt, Cilley, Lurnfelde, Innichen, Juvavum, Vienna, Clausen, Solfeld. Adjoining the Norici is Lake Peiso,*f* and the Unoccupied Lands of the Boii, now however inhabited by the people of Sarvar, a colony of his late Majesty Claudius, and the town of Sopron Julia.

XXV. Then come the acorn-producing lands of *Pannonia.* the province of Pannonia, where the chain of the Alps gradually becomes less formidable, and slopes to the right and left hand with gentle contours as it traverses the middle of Illyria from north to south. The part looking towards the Adriatic is called Dalmatia and Illyria mentioned above, while § 139 the part stretching northward is Pannonia, terminating in that direction at the Danube. In it are the colonies of Aemona and Siscia. Famous navigable rivers flowing into the Danube are the Drave from Noricum, a rather violent stream, and the Save

109

violentior, Saus ex Alpibus Carnicis placidior, $\overline{\text{cxx}}$ intervallo, Draus per Serretes, Sirapillos, Iasos, 148 Andizetes, Saus per Colapianos Breucosque. populorum haec capita; praeterea Arviates, Azali, Amantini, Belgites, Catari, Cornacates, Eravisci, Hercuniates, Latovici, Oseriates, Varciani, mons Claudius, cuius in fronte Scordisci, in tergo Taurisci. insula in Savo Metubarbis, amnicarum maxima. praeterea amnes memorandi Colapis in Saum influens iuxta Sisciam gemino alveo insulam ibi efficit quae Segestica appellatur, alter amnis Bacuntius in Saum Sirmio oppido influit, ubi civitas Sirmiensium et Amantinorum. inde $\overline{\text{xlv}}$ Taurunum, ubi Danuvio miscetur Saus; supra influunt Valdasus, Urpanus, et ipsi non ignobiles.

149   XXVI. Pannoniae iungitur provincia quae Moesia appellatur, ad Pontum usque cum Danuvio decurrens; incipit a confluente supra dicto. in ea Dardani, Celegeri, Triballi, Timachi, Moesi, Thraces Pontoque contermini Scythae. flumina clara e Dardanis Margus, Pingus, Timachus, ex Rhodope Oescus, ex Haemo Utus, Asamus, Ieterus.

150   Illyrici latitudo qua maxima est $\overline{\text{cccxxv}}$ p. colligit, longitudo a flumine Arsia ad flumen Drinium $\overline{\text{dxxx}}$; a Drinio ad promunturium Acroceraunium clxxv Agrippa prodidit, universum autem sinum Italiae

---

[a] Despoto Dagh in the Balkan chain.
[b] The Great Balkan.

from the Carnian Alps which is more gentle, there being a space of 120 miles between them; the Drave flows through the Serretes, Sirapilli, Iasi and Andizetes; the Save through the Colapiani and Breuci. These are the principal peoples; and there are besides the Arviates, Azali, Amantini, Belgites, Catari, Cornacates, Eravisci, Hercuniates, Latovici, Oseriates and Varciani, and Mount Claudius, in front of which are the Scordisci and behind it the Taurisci. In the Save is the island of Zagrabia, the largest known island formed by a river. Other noteworthy rivers are the Culpa, which flows into the Save near Siscia, where its channel divides and forms the island called Segestica, and another river the Bossut, flowing into the Save at the town of Sirmich, the capital of the Sirmienses and Amantini. From Sirmich it is 45 miles to Tzeruinka, where the Save joins the Danube; tributaries flowing into the Danube higher up are the Walpo and the Verbas, themselves also not inconsiderable streams.

XXVI. Adjoining Pannonia is the province called *The lower* Moesia, which runs with the course of the Danube *Danube.* right down to the Black Sea, beginning at the confluence of the Danube and the Save mentioned above. Moesia contains the Dardani, Celegeri, Triballi, Timachi, Moesi, Thracians and Scythians adjacent to the Black Sea. Its famous rivers are the Morava, Bek and Timoch rising in the territory of the Dardani, the Iscar in Mount Rhodope [a] and the Vid, Osma and Jantra in Mount Haemus.[b]

Illyria covers 325 miles in width at its widest point, *S.E. coast of* and 530 miles in length from the river Arsa to the *Adriatic:* river Drin; its length from the Drin to the Promontory of Glossa is given by Agrippa as 175 miles, and

et Illyrici ambitu |xvii|. in eo duo maria quo distinximus fine, Ionium in prima parte, interius Hadriaticum quod Superum vocant.

151 Insulae in Ausonio mari praeter iam dictas memoratu dignae nullae, in Ionio paucae, Calabro litore ante Brundisium quarum obiectu portus efficitur, contra Apulum litus Diomedia conspicua monumento Diomedis et altera eodem nomine a quibusdam Teutria appellata.

Illyrici ora mille amplius insulis frequentatur, natura vadoso mari aestuariisque tenui alveo intercursantibus. clarae ante ostia Timavi calidorum fontium cum aestu maris crescentium, iuxta Histrorum agrum Cissa, Pullaria et Absyrtides Grais dictae a fratre Medeae ibi interfecto Absyrto.

152 iuxta eas Electridas vocavere in quibus proveniret sucinum quod illi electrum appellant, vanitatis Graecae certissimum documentum, adeo ut quas earum designent haut umquam constiterit. contra Iader est Lissa et quae appellatae, contra Liburnos Crateae aliquot nec pauciores Liburnicae, Celadussae, contra Surium Bavo et capris laudata Brattia, Issa civium Romanorum et cum oppido Pharia.

---

^a *I.e.* the sea south of the Straits of Otranto, between the south of Italy and Greece.
^b South of the toe of Italy and east of Sicily.
^c Now Tremiti.
^d Now Caprara.
^e Bagni di Monte Falcone.

the entire circuit of the Italian and Illyrian Gulf as
1700 miles. This gulf, delimited as we described § 100.
it, contains two seas, in the first part the Ionian [a]
and more inland the Adriatic, called the Upper
Sea.

There are no islands deserving mention in the *Islands S. of*
Ausonian Sea [b] besides those already specified, and *Italy and in*
only a few in the Ionian—those lying on the coast *atic.*
S.E. Adri-
of Calabria off Brindisi and by their position forming
a harbour, and Diomede's Island [c] off the coast of
Apulia, marked by the monument of Diomede,
and another island [d] of the same name but by some
called Teutria.

On the coast of Illyricum is a cluster of more than
1000 islands, the sea being of a shoaly nature and
divided into a network of estuaries with narrow
channels. The notable islands are those off the
mouth of the Timavo, fed by hot springs [e] that rise
with the tide of the sea; Cissa near the territory
of the Histri; and Pullaria and those called by the
Greeks the Absyrtides, from Medea's brother
Absyrtus who was killed there. Islands near these
the Greeks have designated the Electrides, because
amber, the Greek for which is *electrum,* was said to
be found there; this is a very clear proof of Greek
unreliability, seeing that it has never been ascertained which of the islands they mean. Opposite
to the Zara are Lissa and the islands already
mentioned; opposite the Liburni are several called § 140.
the Crateae, and an equal number called the Liburnicae and Celadussae; opposite Surium Bavo and
Brattia, the latter celebrated for its goats, Issa with
the rights of Roman citizenship and Pharia, on which
there is a town. Twenty-five miles from Issa is the

ab Issa Corcyra Melaena cognominata cum Cni-
diorum oppido distat $\overline{xxv}$, inter quam et Illyricum
Melite, unde catulos Melitaeos appellari Callimachus auctor est. $\overline{xv}$ ab ea VII Elaphites. in Ionio
autem mari ab Orico $\overline{xii}$[1] p. Sasonis piratica statione
nota.

[1] *Brotier*: MM.

---

[a] Now Curzola or Karkas; the Greek name 'Black Corcyra'
is due to its pine forests.
[b] More usually derived from the better-known Melite, Malta.

island called Corcyra Melaena,[a] with a town founded
from Cnidos, and between Corcyra Melaena and
Illyricum is Meleda, from which according to Callimachus Maltese terriers get their name.[b] Fifteen
miles from Meleda are the seven Stag Islands,[c] and
in the Ionian Sea twelve [d] miles from Oricum is
Sasena, notorious as a harbour for pirates.

[c] So called from their combined outlines, Giupan forming
the head, Ruda the neck, Mezzo the body, Calemotta the
haunches and Grebini or Petini the tail.
[d] The MSS. give 'two.'

BOOK IV

E

LIBER IV

1   I. Tertius Europae sinus Acrocerauniis incipit
montibus, finitur Hellesponto, amplectitur praeter
minores sinus $\overline{\text{xix}}$ $\overline{\text{xxv}}$ passuum. in eo Epiros, Acarnania, Aetolia, Phocis, Locris, Achaia, Messenia,
Laconia, Argolis, Megaris, Attica, Boeotia, iterumque ab alio mari eadem Phocis et Locris, Doris,
Phthiotis, Thessalia, Magnesia, Macedonia, Thracia.
omnis Graeciae fabulositas sicut et litterarum
claritas ex hoc primum sinu effulsit, quapropter
paululum in eo commorabimur.

2   Epiros in universum appellata a Cerauniis incipit
montibus. in ea primi Chaones a quibus Chaonia,
dein Thesproti, Antigonenses, locus Aornos et
pestifera avibus exhalatio, Cestrini, Perrhaebi quorum
mons Pindus, Cassiopaei, Dryopes, Selloe, Hellopes,
Molossi apud quos Dodonaei Iovis templum oraculo
inlustre, Talarus mons centum fontibus circa radices

3 Theopompo celebratus. Epiros ipsa ad Magnesiam
Macedoniamque tendens a tergo suo Dassaretas
supra dictos, liberam gentem, mox feram Dardanos
habet. Dardanis laevo Triballi praetenduntur latere

---

    a The first half of this description enumerates the coastal
countries of Greece beginning at the N.W. and going round the
Peloponnese and up the E. coast as far as the Straits of
Euripus between Euboea and the mainland; the second half
of the list goes N. from that point and round the N. coast of the
Aegean to the Dardanelles.'
    b Άορνος, 'without birds.'

118

BOOK IV

I. THE third gulf of Europe begins at the Mountains of Khimarra and ends at the Dardanelles. Its coast-line measures 1925 miles not including smaller bays. It contains Epirus, Acarnania, Aetolia, Phocis, Locris, Achaia, Messenia, Laconia, Argolis, Megaris, Attica and Boeotia; and again, on the side of the other sea, Phocis and Locris before-mentioned and Doris, Phthiotis, Thessaly, Magnesia, Macedonia and Thrace.[a] All the legendary lore of Greece and likewise its glorous literature first shone forth from this gulf; and consequently we will briefly dwell upon it.

Epirus in the wide sense of the term begins at the Mountains of Khimarra. The peoples that it contains are first the Chaones who give their name to Chaonia, and then the Thesproti and Antigonenses; then comes the place called Aornos[b] with exhalations that are noxious to birds, the Cestrini, the Perrhaebi to whom belongs Mount Pindus, the Cassiopaei, the Dryopes, the Selloi, the Hellopes, the Molossi in whose territory is the temple of Zeus of Dodona, famous for its oracle, and Mount Talarus, celebrated by Theopompus, with a hundred springs at its foot. Epirus proper stretches to Magnesia and Macedonia, and has at its back the Dassaretae above mentioned, a free race, and then the savage tribe of the Dardani. On the left side of the Dardani stretch the Triballi

et Moesicae gentes, a fronte iunguntur Medi ac
Denseletae, quibus Threces ad Pontum usque
pertinentes. ita succincta Rhodopes, mox et Haemi,
4 vallatur excelsitas. in Epiri ora castellum in Acrocerauniis Chimera, sub eo Aquae Regiae fons,
oppida Maeandria, Cestria, flumen Thesprotiae
Thyamis, colonia Buthrotum, maximeque nobilitatus
Ambracius sinus, D passuum faucibus spatiosum
aequor accipiens, longitudinis $\overline{\text{xxxvii}}$, latitudinis $\overline{\text{xv}}$.
in eum defertur amnis Acheron e lacu Thesprotiae
Acherusia profluens $\overline{\text{xxxv}}$ passuum inde et mille
pedum ponte mirabilis omnia sua mirantibus. in
sinu oppidum Ambracia, Molossorum flumina Aphas,
Aratthus, civitas Anactorica, locus Pandosiae.
5   Acarnaniae, quae antea Curetis vocabatur, oppida
Heraclia, Echinus, et in ore ipso colonia Augusti
Actium cum templo Apollinis nobili ac civitate
libera Nicopolitana. egressos sinu Ambracio in
Ionium excipit Leucadium litus, promunturium
Leucates, dein sinus et Leucadia ipsa paeninsula
quondam Neritis appellata, opere accolarum abscisa
continenti ac reddita ventorum flatu congeriem
harenae adtumulantium, qui locus vocatur Dioryctos
stadiorum longitudine trium; oppidum in ea Leucas,
quondam Neritum dictum.   deinde Acarnanum urbes

---

^a This now gives its name to the range.
^b Now the Calama.
^c Now an island, Santa Maura.

and the Moesic races, and joining them in front are
the Medi and the Denseletae, and joining these the
Thracians who extend all the way to the Black Sea.
Such is the girdle that walls in the lofty heights of
Despoto Dagh and then of the Great Balkan. On the
coast of Epirus is the fortress of Khimarra *a* on the
Acroceraunians, and below it the spring named the
Royal Water and the towns of Maeandria and Cestria,
the Thesprotian river Thyamis,*b* the colony of Butrinto,
and the very celebrated Gulf of Arta, whose inlet,
half a mile wide, admits an extensive sheet of water,
37 miles long and 15 miles broad. Into it discharges
the river Acheron flowing from the Acherusian Lake
in Thesprotia, a course of 35 miles, and remarkable
in the eyes of people who admire all the achievements of their own race for its 1000-foot bridge.
On the gulf lies the town of Ambracia, and there are
the Molossian rivers Aphas and Arta, the city of
Anactoria and the place where Pandosia stood.

The towns of Acarnania, which was previously
called Curetis, are Heraclia, Echinus, and, on the
actual coast, the colony founded by Augustus, Actium, with the famous temple of Apollo, and the free
city of Nicopolis. Passing from the Gulf of Ambracia
into the Ionian Sea we come to the coast of Leucadia
and Capo Ducato, and then to the gulf and the
actual peninsula *c* of Leucadia, formerly called
Neritis, which by the industry of its inhabitants was
once cut off from the mainland and which has been
restored to it by the mass of sand piled up against it
by the violence of the winds; the place has a Greek
name meaning 'canalized,' and is 600 yards long. On
the peninsula is the town of Leucas, formerly called
Neritus. Then come the Acarnanian cities of Alyzia,

Alyzia, Stratos, Argos Amphilochicum cognomina
tum, amnis Achelous e Pindo fluens atque Acarnaniam
ab Aetolia dirimens et Artemitam insulam adsiduo
terrae invectu continenti adnectens.

6 II. Aetolorum populi Athamanes, Tymphaei,
Ephyri, Aenienses, Perrhaebi, Dolopes, Maraces,
Atraces, a quibus Atrax amnis Ionio mari infunditur.
Aetoliae oppidum Calydon VII D passuum a mari
iuxta Evenum amnem, dein Macynia, Molycria,
cuius a tergo Chalcis mons et Taphiassus. at in
ora promunturium Antirrium, ubi ostium Corinthiaci sinus minus M p. latitudine influentis Aetolos-
que dirimentis a Peloponneso. promunturium quod
contra procedit appellatur Rhion. sed in Corinthio
sinu oppida Aetoliae Naupactus, Eupalimna, et in
mediterraneo Pleuron, Halicarna. montes clari in
Dodone Tomarus, in Ambracia Crania, in Acarnania
Aracynthus, in Aetolia Achaton, Panaetolium,
Macynium.

7 III. Proxumi Aetolis Locri cognominantur Ozolae,
immunes. oppidum Oeanthe, portus Apollinis Pha-
estii, sinus Crisaeus; intus oppida Argyna, Eupalia,
Phaestum, Calamisus. ultra Cirrhaei Phocidis campi, oppidum Cirrha, portus Chalaeon, a quo VII p.
introrsus liberum oppidum Delphi sub monte Parnaso
8 clarissimi in terris oraculi Apollinis. fons Castalius,
amnis Cephisus praefluens Delphos, ortus in Lilaea

---

^a ' Strong-smelling '—so called either from their wearing
undressed hides or from the asphodel growing in their country
or from its vaporous springs.

122

Stratos, and Argos surnamed Amphilochian, and the river Achelous flowing from Mount Pindus and separating Acarnania from Aetolia; the continual deposits of earth that it brings down are linking the island of Artemita to the main land.

II. The Aetolian peoples are the Athamanes, Tymphaei, Ephyri, Aenienses, Perrhaebi, Dolopes, Maraces and Atraces in whose district is the source of the river Atrax that flows into the Ionian Sea. The towns of Aetolia are Calydon on the river Evenus seven miles and a half from the sea, and then Macynia and Molycria, behind which are Mount Chalcis and Taphiassus. On the coast is the Promontory of Antirrhium, at which is the mouth of the Gulf of Corinth, less than a mile broad, whose channel separates the Aetolians from the Morea. The promontory that juts out opposite is called Rhium. Aetolian towns on the Gulf of Corinth are Lepanto, Eupalimna, and inland Pleuron and Halicarna. Notable mountains are Tomarus in the district of Dodona, Crania in Ambracia, Aracynthus in Acarnania, and Achaton, Panaetolium and Macynium in Aetolia. *North side of Gulf of Corinth.*

III. Next to the Aetolians are the Locrians, surnamed Ozolae,[a] who are exempt from tribute. Here are the town of Oeanthe, the harbour of Apollo Phaestius and the gulf of Salona; and inland the towns of Argyna, Eupalia, Phaestum and Calamisus. Beyond are the Cirrhaean Plains of Phocis, the town of Cirrha and the port of Chalaeon, seven miles inland from which is Delphi, a free town at the foot of Mount Parnassus and the seat of the oracle of Apollo, the most famous in the world. Here are the Castalian Spring and the river Cephisus flowing past Delphi;

urbe. quondam praeterea oppidum Crisa et cum
Bulensibus Anticyra, Naulochum, Pyrrha, Amphisa
immunis, Tithrone, Tithorea, Ambrysus, Mirana,
quae regio Daulis appellatur. deinde in intumo
sinu angulus Boeotiae adluitur cum oppidis Siphis,
Thebis quae Corsiae cognominatae sunt iuxta montem
Heliconem. tertium ab hoc mari Boeotiae oppidum
Pagae, unde Peloponnesi prosilit cervix.

9   IV. Peloponnesus, Apia antea appellata et Pelasgia, paeninsula haut ulli terrae nobilitate postferenda,
inter duo maria Aegaeum et Ionium, platani folio
similis, propter angulosos recessus circuitu D̄L̄X̄Ī̄Ī̄Ī̄ p.
colligit auctore Isidoro; eadem per sinus paene
tantundem adicit. angustiae unde procedit Isthmos
appellantur. in eo loco inrumpentia e diverso
quae dicta sunt maria a septentrione et exortu eius
omnem ibi latitudinem vorant, donec contrario
incursu tantorum aequorum in quinque milium
passuum intervallum exesis utrimque lateribus
angusta cervice Peloponnesum contineat Hellas.

10 Corinthiacus hinc, illinc Saronicus appellatur sinus;
Lecheae hinc, Cenchreae illinc angustiarum termini,
longo et ancipiti navium ambitu quas magnitudo
plaustris transvehi prohibet, quam ob causam per-

---

[a] The modern name Morea means ' like a mulberry leaf.'
[b] This common noun, meaning a neck of land, came to be
attached as a proper name to the neck joining the Morea to
Central Greece.
[c] The harbour of Corinth.
[d] The harbour on the Gulf of Egina.

it rises at the city of Lilaea. There was also formerly the town of Crisa, and together with the people of Bulis there are Anticyra, Naulochus, Pyrrha, the tax-free town of Salona, Tithrone, Tithorea, Ambrysus and Mirana, the district also called Daulis. Then right up the bay is the sea-board corner of Boeotia with the towns of Siphae and Thebes surnamed the Corsian, near Mount Helicon. The third town of Boeotia up from this sea is Pagae, from which projects the neck of the Morea.

IV. The Peloponnese, which was previously called *Isthmus of Corinth.* Apia and Pelasgia, is a peninsula inferior in celebrity to no region of the earth. It lies between two seas, the Aegean and the Ionian, and resembles in shape the leaf of a plane-tree *a* ; on account of the angular indentations the circuit of its coast-line, according to Isidore, amounts to 563 miles, and nearly as much again in addition, measuring the shores of the bays. The narrow neck of land from which it projects is called the Isthmus.*b* At this place the two seas that have been mentioned encroach on opposite sides from the north and east and swallow up all the breadth of the peninsula at this point, until in consequence of the inroad of such large bodies of water in opposite directions the coasts on either side have been eaten away so as to leave a space between them of only five miles, with the result that the Morea is only attached to Greece by a narrow neck of land. The inlets on either side are called the Gulf of Lepanto and the Gulf of Egina, the former ending in Lecheae *c* and the latter in Cenchreae.*d* The circuit of the Morea is a long and dangerous voyage for vessels prohibited by their size from being carried across the

fodere navigabili alveo angustias eas temptavere
Demetrius rex, dictator Caesar, Gaius princeps,
Domitius Nero, nefasto, ut omnium exitu patuit,
11 incepto. in medio hoc intervallo quod Isthmon
appellavimus adplicata colli habitatur colonia Corinthus antea Ephyra dicta sexagenis ab utroque litore
stadiis, e summa sua arce quae vocatur Acrocorinthos,
in qua fons Pirene, diversa duo maria prospectans.
L̄X̄X̄X̄V̄Ī̄Ī̄ p. ad Corinthiacum sinum traiectus est
Patras a Leucade. Patrae, colonia in longissimo
promunturio Peloponnesi condita ex adverso Aetoliae
et fluminis Eveni, minus м p., ut dictum est, intervallo
in ipsis faucibus sinum Corinthiacum L̄X̄X̄X̄V̄ in
longitudinem usque ad Isthmon transmittunt.

12 V. Achaiae nomen provinciae ab Isthmo incipit.
antea Aegialos vocabatur propter urbes in litore per
ordinem dispositas. primae ibi quas diximus Lecheae
Corinthiorum portus, mox Olyros Pellenaeorum
castellum, oppida Helice, Bura, in quae refugere
haustis prioribus, Sicyon, Aegira, Aegium, Erineos.
13 intus Cleonae, Hysiae. Panhormus portus demonstra-
tumque iam Rhium, a quo promunturio v̄ absunt
Patrae quas supra memoravimus, locus Pherae.

---

^a The project was renewed in 1889 and completed in 1893,
without disastrous results except to the finances of the
original promoters. The canal is about four miles long.
^b Originally the district of Phthia in the south of Thessaly
had this name.
^c The Sea-coast.
^d Headquarters of the old Achaean League.
^e Owing to an earthquake in 373 B.C.

isthmus on trolleys, and consequently successive
attempts were made by King Demetrius, Caesar the
dictator and the emperors Caligula and Nero, to dig
a ship-canal through the narrow part—an undertaking *Canal.*
which the end that befell them all proves to have
been an act of sacrilege.^a   In the middle of this neck
of land which we have called the Isthmus is the
colony of Corinth, the former name of which was
Ephyra; its habitations cling to the side of a hill,
7½ miles from the coast on either side, and the top of
its citadel, called the Corinthian Heights, on which is
the spring of Pirene, commands views of the two seas
in opposite directions.   The distance across the
Isthmus from Leucas to Patras on the Gulf of Corinth
is 88 miles.   The colony of Patras is situated on the
longest projection of the Peloponnese opposite to
Aetolia and the river Evenus, separated from them
at the actual mouth of the gulf by a gap of less than
a mile, as has been said; but in length the Gulf of § 6.
Corinth extends 85 miles from Patras to the Isthmus.

V. At the Isthmus begins the province named *Morea.*
Achaia.^b   It was previously called Aegialos^c on account
of the cities situated in a row on its coast.   The first
place there is Lecheae the port of Corinth, already
mentioned, and then come Olyrus the fortress of the
people of Trikala, and the towns of Helice^d and Bura,
and those in which their inhabitants took refuge
when the former towns were swallowed up by
the sea,^e namely Basilica, Palaeokastro, Vostitza
and Artotina.   Inland are Klenes and Hysiae.   Then
come the port of Tekieh and Rhium already described,
the distance between which promontory and Patras
which we have mentioned above is five miles; and then
the place called Pherae.   Of the nine mountains in

in Achaia novem montium Scioessa notissimus, fons
Cymothoe. ultra Patras oppidum Olenum, colonia
Dyme, loca Buprasium, Hyrmine, promunturium
Araxus, Cyllenius sinus, promunturium Chelonates
unde Cyllenen v̄ p., castellum Phlium, quae regio ab
Homero Araethyrea dicta est, postea Asopis.

14   Inde Eliorum ager, qui antea Epioe vocabantur.
ipsa Elis in mediterraneo, et a Pylo xiii intus delubrum Olympii Iovis, ludorum claritate fastos Graeciae
complexum, Pisaeorum quondam oppidum, praefluente Alpheo amne. at in ora promunturium
Ichthys, amnis Alpheus—navigatur v̄ī—oppida
Aulon, Leprium, promunturium Platanodes, omnia
15 haec ad occasum versa.   ad meridiem autem Cyparis-
sius sinus cum urbe Cyparisso lxxv̄ circuitu, oppida
Pylos, Methone, locus Helos, promunturium Acritas,
sinus Asinaeus ab oppido Asine, Coronaeus a Corone;
finiuntur Taenaro promunturio. ibi regio Messenia
duodeviginti montium, amnis Pamisus, intus autem
ipsa Messene, Ithome, Oechalia, Arene, Pteleon,
Thryon, Dorion, Zancle, variis quaeque clara temporibus. huius sinus circuitus lxxx̄, traiectus vero
xxx̄.

16   Dehinc a Taenaro ager Laconicus liberae gentis
et sinus circuitu cv̄ī, traiectu xxxviii. oppida

---

  a *Iliad*, II. 57.
  b Destroyed by the Eleans in 572 B.C.

Achaia the best known is Scioessa; and there is also the spring of Cymothoe. Beyond Patras is the town of Kato-Achaia, the colony of Dyme, the places called Buprasium and Hyrmine, the promontory of Capo Papa, the Bay of Cyllene, the promontory of Cape Tornese 5 miles from Cyllene, the fortress of Phlius, the district round which was called Araethyrea by Homer[a] and afterwards Asopis.

Then begins the territory of the Eleans, who were formerly called the Epioi. Elis itself is in the interior, and 13 miles inland from Pilo is the shrine of Zeus of Olympus, which owing to the celebrity of its Games has taken possession of the calendar of Greece; here once was the town of Pisa,[b] on the banks of the river Rufia. On the coast are the promontory of Katakolo, the river Rufia, navigable for 6 miles, the towns of Aulon and Leprium, and the promontory of Platanodes, all these places lying westward. Southward are the Gulf of Cyparissus with the city of Cyparissus on its shore, which is 75 miles round, the towns of Pilo and Modon, the place called Helos, the promontory of Capo Gallo, the Asinaean Gulf named from the town of Asine, and the Coronaean named from Corone; the list ends with the promontory of Cape Matapan. Here is the territory of Messenia with its 18 mountains, and the river Pyrnatza; and inland, the city of Messene, Ithome, Oechalia, Sareni, Pteleon, Thryon, Dorion and Zancle, all of them celebrated at different periods. The gulf measures 80 miles round and 30 miles across.

At Cape Matapan begins the territory of the free *Sparta.* nation of Laconia, and the Laconian Gulf, which measures 106 miles round and 38 miles across. The

Taenarum, Amyclae, Pherae, Leuctra, et intus
Sparta, Therapne, atque ubi fuere Cardamyle,
Pitane, Anthea, locus Thyrea, Gerania, mons
Taygetus, amnis Eurotas, sinus Aegilodes, oppidum
Psamathus, sinus Gytheates ab oppido ex quo
Cretam insulam certissimus cursus. omnes autem
Maleo promunturio includuntur.

17 Qui sequitur sinus ad Scyllaeum Argolicus
appellatur, traiectu L̄, idem ambitu C̄L̄X̄ĪĪ. oppida
Boea, Epidaurus Limera cognomine, Zarax, Cyphans
portus. amnes Inachus, Erasinus, inter quos Argos
Hippium cognominatum supra locum Lernen a
mari MM, novemque additis milibus Mycenae et ubi
fuisse Tiryntha tradunt et locus Mantinea. montes
Artemisius, Apesantus, Asterion, Parparus aliique
XI numero; fontes Niobe, Amymone, Psamathe.

18 A Scyllaeo ad Isthmum L̄X̄X̄X̄ p. oppida Hermione,
Troezen, Coryphasium, appellatumque alias Inachium
alias Dipsium Argos; portus Schoenitas, sinus
Saronicus olim querno nemore redimitus, unde nomen
ita Graecia antiqua appellante quercum. in eo Epidaurum oppidum Aesculapi delubro celebre, Spiraeum
promunturium, portus Anthedus et Bucephalus et
quas supra dixeramus Cenchreae, Isthmi pars altera
cum delubro Neptuni quinquennalibus incluto ludis.

---

^a This recurring use of *locus* may imply that the town of
the name had disappeared, though this is more explicitly
stated in other cases.

^b From its breed of horses.   ^c Now the Gulf of Egina.

^d Σαρωνίδες, αἱ διὰ παλαιότητα κεχηνυῖαι δρύες, Hesychius;
σαρωνίδας, δρῦς, διὰ τὸ σεσηρότα καὶ συνεστραμμένον τὸν φλοιὸν
ἔχειν, Schol. ad. Callimachum *Jov.* 22 ἦ πολλὰς ἐφύπερθε
σαρωνίδας.

^e A mistake: the Isthmian, like the Nemean, Games were
every two years: *cf.* ταυροφόνῳ τριετηρίδι, Pindar, *Nem.* VI. 40.

towns are Kimaros, Amyclae, Chitries, Levtros, and inland Sparta, Therapne, the sites of the former Cardamyle, Pitane and Anthea, the place called *a* Thyrea, Gerania, the mountain range of Pente Dactyli, the river Niris, the Gulf of Scutari, the town of Psamathus, the Gulf of Gytheum called from the town of that name, from which is the safest crossing to the island of Crete. All these places are bounded by the promontory of Capo Sant' Angelo.

The bay that comes next, extending to Capo Skyli, *Gulf of* is called the Gulf of Nauplia; it is 50 miles across *Argos.* and 162 miles round. The towns on it are Boea, Epidaurus surnamed Limera, Zarax, and the port of Cyphanta. The rivers are the Banitza and the Kephalari, between which lies Argos surnamed Hippium,*b* above the place called Lerne, two miles from the sea, and nine miles further on Mycenae and the traditional site of Tiryns and the place called Mantinea. The mountains are Malvouni, Fuka, Asterion, Parparus and others numbering eleven; the springs, Niobe, Amymone and Psamathe.

From Capo Skyli to the Isthmus of Corinth is 80 *Saronic* miles. The towns are Hermione, Troezen, Cory- *Gulf.* phasium and Argos, sometimes called Inachian Argos and sometimes Dipsian; then comes the harbour of Schoenitas, and the Saronic Gulf,*c* formerly encircled with oak woods from which it takes its name, this being the old Greek word for an oak.*d* On it is the town of Epidaurus famous for its shrine of Aescula- pius; the promontory of Capo Franco; the ports of Anthedus and Bucephalus, and that of Cenchreae mentioned above, on the south side of the Isthmus, with the temple of Poseidon, famous for the Isthmian Games celebrated there every four *e* years.

19   Tot sinus Peloponnesi oram lancinant, tot maria
adlatrant, siquidem a septentrione Ionium inrumpit,
ab occidente Siculo pulsatur, a meridie Cretico
urguetur, ab oriente brumali Aegaeo, ab oriente
solstitiali Myrtoo quod a Megarico incipiens sinu
totam Atticen adluit.

20   VI. Mediterranea eius Arcadia maxime tenet
undique a mari remota, initio Drymodes,[a] mox
Pelasgis appellata. oppida eius Psophis, Mantinea,[b]
Stymphalum, Tegea, Antigonea, Orchomenum, Phe-
neum, Pallantium unde Palatium Romae, Megale
Polis, Gortyna, Bucolium, Carnion, Parrhasie, Thel-
pusa, Melaenae, Heraea, Pylae, Pallene, Agrae,
Epium, Cynaethae, Lepreon Arcadiae, Parthenium,
Alea, Methydrium, Enispe, Macistum, Lampia,
Clitorium, Cleonae.[c] inter quae duo oppida regio
21 Nemea est Bembinadia[d] vocitata. montes in Arcadia
Pholoe cum oppido, item Cyllene, Lycaeus in quo
Lycaei Iovis delubrum, Maenalus, Artemisius, Par-
thenius, Lampeus, Nonacris, praeterque ignobiles
VIII. amnes Ladon e paludibus Phenei, Erymanthus
e monte eiusdem nominis in Alpheum defluens.
22 reliquae civitates in Achaia dicendae Alipheraei,
Abeatae, Pyrgenses, Paroreatae, Paragenitae, Tor-
tuni, Typanei, Thriusi, Tritienses. universae Achaiae

---

[a] Δρυμώδης, 'wooded.'
[b] I.e. Mantinea, which was taken and partly destroyed by
Aratus, and renamed after Antigonus Doson, who had
assisted him and who restored it.
[c] There was another place of the same name in Elis.
[d] From the village of Bembina there.

So many are the bays that pierce the coast of the
Peloponnese, and so many seas howl round it, inasmuch as it is invaded on the north by the Ionian Sea,
lashed on the west by the Sicilian, and beset by the
Cretan on the south, by the Aegean on the south-east
and on the north-east by the Myrtoan which starting at
the Gulf of Megara washes the whole coast of Attica.

VI. Most of the interior of the Peloponnese is *Interior of
Morea.*
occupied by Arcadia, which on every side is remote
from the sea; it was originally called Drymodes,*a*
and later Pelasgis. Its towns are Psophis, Mantinea,
Stymphalus, Tegea, Antigonea,*b* Orchomenus,
Pheneus, Pallantium (from which the Palatium at
Rome gets its name), Megalopolis, Gortyna, Bucolium, Carnion, Parrhasia, Thelpusa, Melaenae,
Heraea, Pylae, Pallene, Agrae, Epium, Cynaethae,
Lepreon in Arcadia,*c* Parthenium, Alea, Methydrium, Enispe, Macistum, Lampia, Clitorium and
Cleonae. Between the last two towns is the district
of Nemea commonly called Bembinadia.*d* The
mountains in Arcadia are Pholoe,*e* with a town of
the same name, Cyllene also with a town, Lycaeus
on which is the shrine of Zeus Lycaeus, Maenalus,
Artemisius, Parthenius, Lampeus, Nonacris, and
also eight others of no note. The rivers are the
Landona flowing from the marshes of Fonia and the
Dogana flowing down from the mountain of the same
name into the Alpheus. The remaining states in
Achaia deserving of mention are those of the Alipheraei, Abeatae, Pyrgenses, Paroreatae, Paragenitae, Tortuni, Typanei, Thriusi and Tritinenses.
Freedom was given to the whole of Achaia by

e This and the six following are now named Olono, Zyria,
Nomiai, Roinon, Turniki, Partheni, Zembi.

libertatem Domitius Nero dedit. Peloponnesus
in latitudinem a promunturio Maleae ad oppidum
Aegium Corinthiaci sinus $\overline{\text{cxc}}$ patet, at in transversum ab Elide Epidaurum $\overline{\text{cxxv}}$, ab Olympia Argos
per Arcadiam $\overline{\text{lxviii}}$; ab eodem loco ad Pylum iam
dicta mensura est.[1] universa autem, velut pensante
aequorum incursus natura, in montes VI atque LXX
attollitur.

23   VII. Ab Isthmi angustiis Hellas incipit, a nostris
Graecia appellata. in ea prima Attice, antiquitus
Acte vocata. attingit Isthmum parte sui quae
appellatur Megaris ab colonia Megara, e regione
Pagarum. duo haec oppida excurrente Peloponneso
sita sunt, utraque ex parte velut in umeris Helladis,
Pagaei et amplius Aegosthenenses contributi Mega-
rensibus. in ora autem portus Schoenos, oppida
Sidous, Cremmyon, Scironia saxa $\overline{\text{vi}}$ longitudine,
24 Gerania, Megara, Eleusin; fuere et Oenoe et
Probalinthos. nunc sunt ab Isthmo $\overline{\text{lv}}$ Piraeeus et
Phalera portus muro $\overline{\text{v}}$ [2] recedentibus Athenis iuncti.
libera haec civitas, nec indiga ullius praeconii
amplius, tanta claritas superfluit. in Attica fontes
Cephisia, Larine, Callirroe Enneacrunos, montes
Brilessus, Aegialeus, Icarius, Hymettus, Lycabettus,

---

[1] [ab eodem loco . . . mensura est]? *Rackham.*
[2] *Rackham :* $\overline{\text{v}}$ muro.

---

[a] Nero gave up his family name of Domitius when adopted
by Claudius to succeed him as Emperor.

[b] Viz. in § 14; but this irrelevant insertion looks like an
interpolation. The measurements of the Peloponnese are
given from south to north and then from west to east, first
at the widest point and afterwards farther south at the level
of the Gulf of Nauplia.

Domitius Nero.[a] The Peloponnese measures 190 miles across from Cape Malea to the town of Vostitza on the Gulf of Corinth, and in the other direction 125 miles from Elis to Epidauros and 68 miles from Olympia through Arcadia to Argos. (The distance between Olympia and Pylos has been given already.[b]) Nature has compensated for the inroads of the sea by the mountainous character of the entire region, there being 76 peaks in all.

VII. At the narrow part of the Isthmus begins *Attica.* Hellas, called in our language Greece. In this the first region is Attica, named in antiquity Acte. It touches the Isthmus with the part of it named Megaris, from Megara, the colony on the opposite side of the Isthmus from Pagae. These two towns are situated where the Peloponnese projects, and stand on either side of the Isthmus, as it were on the shoulders of Hellas, Pagae and also Aegosthena[c] being assigned to the jurisdiction of Megara. On the coast are the harbour of Porto Cocosi, the towns Leandra and Cremmyon, the Scironian Rocks[d] six miles in length, Gerania, Megara and Levsina; formerly there were also Oenoe and Probalinthos. There now are the harbours of Piraeus and Phaleron, 55 miles from the Isthmus, and joined by wall to Athens 5 miles away. Athens is a free city, and requires no further advertisement here as her celebrity is more than ample. In Attica are the springs of Cephisia, Larine, and the Nine Wells of Callirrhoe, and the mountains of Brilessus,[e] Aegialeus, Icarius, Hymettus

[c] Just north of Pagae at the east end of the Gulf of Corinth.
[d] Now Kaki Scala.
[e] Believed to be another name for Pentelicus, now Mendeli, famous for its marble quarries.

135

locus Ilisos, a Piraeeo x̄l̄v̄ Sunium promunturium,
Thoricos promunturium, Potamos, Steria, Brauron,
quondam oppida, Rhamnus pagus, locus Marathon,
campus Thriasius, oppidum Melita et Oropus in
confinio Boeotiae.

25   Cuius Anthedon, Onchestos, Thespiae liberum
oppidum, Lebadea, nec cedentes Athenis claritate
quae cognominantur Boeotiae Thebae, duorum
numinum Liberi atque Herculis, ut volunt, patria.
et Musis natale in nemore Heliconis adsignant.
datur et his Thebis saltus Cithaeron, amnis Ismenus.
praeterea fontes in Boeotia Oedipodia, Psamathe,
Dirce, Epicrane, Arethusa, Hippocrene, Aganippe,
Gargaphie; montes extra praedictos Mycalesus,
26 Hadylius, Acontius. reliqua oppida inter Megari-
cam et Thebas Eleutherae, Haliartus, Plataeae,
Pherae, Aspledon, Hyle, Thisbe, Erythrae, Glissa,
Copae, iuxta Cephisum amnem Lamiae et Anichiae,
Medeon, Phlygone, Acraephia, Coronea, Chaeronea.
in ora autem infra Thebas Ocalee, Heleon, Scolos,
Schoenos, Peteon, Hyrie, Mycalesos, Ireseum,
Pteleon, Olyarum, Tanagra liber populus, et in ipsis
faucibus Euripi quem facit obiecta insula Euboea
Aulis capaci nobilis portu. Boeotos Hyantas anti-
27 quitus dixere. Locri deinde Epicnemidii cognomi-
nantur olim Leleges appellati, per quos amnis
Cephisus defertur in mare; oppida Opus, unde et
sinus Opuntius, Cynus. Phocidis in litore unum

ᵃ In distinction from places of the same name in Egypt,
Phthiotis and Lucania.
ᵇ *I.e.* on the promontory of Cnemides below Mount
Cnemis.
ᶜ Golfo di Talanti.

and Lycabettus; the place called Ilissus; the promontories of Capo Colonna, 45 miles from Piraeus, and Thoricos; the former towns of Potamos, Steria and Brauron, the village of Rhamnus, the place called Marathon, the Thriasian Plain, the town of Melita, and Ropo on the border of Boeotia.

To Boeotia belong Anthedon, Onchestus, the free town of Thespiae, Livadhia, and Thebes, surnamed Boeotian,[a] which does not yield even to Athens in celebrity, and which is reputed to be the native place of two deities, Liber and Hercules. The Muses also are assigned a birth-place in the grove of Helicon. To this city of Thebes also are attributed the forest of Cithaeron and the river Ismenus. Besides these Boeotia contains the Springs of Oedipus and those of Psamathe, Dirce, Epicrane, Arethusa, Hippocrene, Aganippe and Gargaphie; and in addition to the mountains previously mentioned, Mycalesus, Hadylius and Acontius. The remaining towns between the Megarid and Thebes are Eleutherae, Haliartus, Plataea, Pherae, Aspledon, Hyle, Thisbe, Erythrae, Glissa, Copae, Lamiae and Anichiae on the river Cephisus, Medeon, Phlygone, Acraephia, Coronea and Chaeronea. On the coast below Thebes are Ocalee, Heleon, Scolos, Schoenos, Peteon, Hyrie, Mycalesos, Ireseum, Pteleon, Olyarum, Tanagra Free State, and right in the channel of the Euripus, formed by the island of Euboea lying opposite, Aulis famous for its spacious harbour. The Boeotians had the name of Hyantes in earlier days. Then come the Locri surnamed Epicnemidii,[b] and formerly called Leleges, through whose territory the river Cephisus flows down to the sea; and the towns of Opus, which gives its name to the Opuntian Bay,[c] and Cynus.

North-east coast of Greece.

137

Daphnus, introrsus autem Larisa Elatea et in ripa
Cephisi, ut diximus, Lilaea, Delphosque versae
Cnemis et Hyampolis. rursus Locrorum ora, in
qua Larumna, Thronium, iuxta quod Boagrius amnis
defertur in mare, oppida Narycum, Alope, Scarphia.
postea Maliacus sinus ab incolis dictus, in quo
oppida Halcyone, Aeconia, Phalara.

28   Doris deinde, in qua Sperchios, Erineon, Boion,
Pindus, Cytinum.   Doridis a tergo mons Oeta est.

Sequitur mutatis saepe nominibus Haemonia,
eadem Pelasgis et Pelasgicon Argos, Hellas, eadem
Thessalia et Dryopis, semper a regibus cognominata:
ibi genitus rex nomine Graecus a quo Graecia, ibi
Hellen a quo Hellenes. hos eosdem Homerus
tribus nominibus appellavit Myrmidonas et Hellenas
et Achaeos. ex his Phthiotae nominantur Dorida
accolentes; eorum oppida Echinus, in faucibus
Sperchii fluminis Thermopylarum angustiae, quo
argumento IV inde Heraclea Trechin dicta est.
mons ibi Callidromus, oppida celebrata Hellas, Halos,
Lamia, Phthia, Arne.

29   VIII. In Thessalia autem Orchomenus Minyius
antea dictus et oppidum Alimon, ab aliis Holmon,
Atrax, Palamna, fons Hyperia, oppida Pherae,
quarum a tergo Pieria ad Macedoniam protenditur,

---

^a Now the Gulf of Zeitoun.
^b From τραχύς, ' rugged.'

The only town of Phocis on the coast is Daphnus, but inland are Larisa, Elatea, and on the banks of the Cephisus, as we have said, Lilaea, and, facing Delphi, Cnemis and Hyampolis. Then there is the Locrian coast, on which are Larumna and Thronium, near which the river Boagrius flows into the sea, and the towns of Narycum, Alope and Scarphia. Afterwards comes the Malian Gulf *a* named from its inhabitants and on it are the towns of Halcyone, Aeconia and Phalara.

Then comes Doris, in which are Sperchios, Erineon, Boion, Pindus and Cytinum. In the rear of Doris is Mount Oeta.

There follows Haemonia, which has often changed its name, having been successively called Pelasgis or Pelasgic Argos, and Hellas, Thessaly and Dryopis, always taking its surname from its kings: it was the birthplace of the king named Graecus from whom Greece is named, and of king Hellen from whom the Hellenes get their name. These same people are called by three different names in Homer, Myrmidons, Hellenes and Achaeans. The section of the Hellenes adjacent to Doris are named Phthiotae; their towns are Akhino and Heraclea, which takes the name of Trechin *b* from the Pass of Thermopylae four miles away in the gorge of the river Ellada. Here is Mount Callidromus, and the notable towns are Hellas, Halos, Lamia, Phthia and Arne.

VIII. The places in Thessaly are Orchomenus, *Thessaly.* formerly called the Minyan, and the town of Alimon, otherwise Holmon, Atrax, Palamna, the Hyperian Spring, the towns of Pherae (behind which lies Pieria spreading in the direction of Macedonia),

Larisa, Gomphi, Thebae Thessalae, nemus Pteleon,
sinus Pagasicus, oppidum Pagasa, idem postea
Demetrias dictum, Tricca, Pharsali campi cum civitate libera, Crannon, Iletia. montes Phthiotidis
Nymphaeus quondam topiario naturae opere spec-
tabilis, Buzygaeus, Donacoessa, Bromiaeus, Daphusa,
30 Chimarone, Athamas, Stephane. in Thessalia quattuor atque triginta, quorum nobilissimi Cercetii,
Olympus Pierius, Ossa, cuius ex adverso Pindus et
Othrys Lapitharum sedes, hi ad occasum vergentes,
ad ortus Pelius, omnes theatrali modo inflexi, caveatis
ante eos LXXV urbibus. flumina Thessaliae Apidanus, Phoenix, Enipeus, Onochonus, Pamisus, fons
Messeis, lacus Boebeis, et ante cunctos claritate
Penius ortus iuxta Gomphos interque Ossam et
Olympum nemorosa convalle defluens D stadiis,
31 dimidio eius spati navigabilis. in eo cursu Tempe
vocant v̄ passuum longitudine et ferme sesquiiugeri
latitudine ultra visum hominis attollentibus se dextra
laevaque leniter convexis iugis intus valle luco[1] viri-
dante. hac[2] labitur Penius, vitreus calculo, amoenus circa ripas gramine, canorus avium concentu.
accipit amnem Orcon, nec recipit, sed olei modo
supernatantem, ut dictum est Homero, brevi spatio

---

[1] Detlefsen: sua luce (silva late Mayhoff).
[2] ac Mayhoff.

---

[a] The iugerum was about two-thirds of an acre, but was
measured in an oblong 240 ft. long by 120 ft. broad, so that
here presumably its breadth is meant, making the gorge 180 ft.
across.
[b] Il. II. 751 ff.

οἵ τ' ἀμφ' ἱμερτὸν Τιταρήσιον ἔργα νέμοντο,
ὅς ῥ' ἐς Πηνειὸν προΐει καλλίρροον ὕδωρ,

Larisa, Gomphi, Thessalian Thebes, Elm Wood, the
Gulf of Volo, the town of Pagasa subsequently
called Demetrias, Tricca, the Pharsalian Plains with
their free city, Crannon, Iletia. The mountains of
Phthiotis are Nymphaeus, once so beautiful for its
natural landscape gardening, Buzygaeus, Donacoessa,
Bromiaeus, Daphusa, Chimarone, Athamas, Stephane. In Thessaly there are 34, of which the most
famous are Cercetii, Pierian Olympus and Ossa, facing
which are Pindus and Othrys the abode of the Lapi-
thae—these looking to the west; and looking east is
Pelion; all form a curve like a theatre, and in the
hollow in front of them lie 75 cities. Thessaly
contains the rivers Apidanus, Phoenix, Enipeus,
Onochonus and Pamisus; the spring Messeis; Lake
Boebeis; and before all alike in celebrity the river
Peneus, rising close to Gomphi and flowing down a
wooded glen between Ossa and Olympus for 62½
miles, for half of which distance it is navigable. Part
of this course is called the Vale of Tempe, 5 miles
long and nearly an acre and a half *a* in breadth, with
gently sloping hills rising beyond human sight on
either hand, while the valley between is verdant with
a grove of trees. Along it glides the Peneus, glittering
with pebbles and adorned with grassy banks, melodi-
ous with the choral song of birds. Into it flows the
river Orcus, to which it gives no intimate welcome,
but merely carries it for a brief space floating on its
surface like a skin of oil, in Homer's phrase,*b* and then

οὐδ' ὅ γε Πηνειῷ συμμίσγεται ἀργυροδίνῃ
ἀλλά τέ μιν καθύπερθεν ἐπιρρέει ἠΰτ' ἔλαιον·
ὅρκον γὰρ δεινοῦ Στυγὸς ὕδατός ἐστιν ἀπορρώξ.

Homer's ὅρκον, 'a thing to swear by,' is read by Pliny as a
proper name.

141

portatum abdicat poenales aquas Dirisque genitas argenteis suis misceri recusans.

32 IX. Thessaliae adnexa Magnesia est, cuius fons Libethra, oppida Iolcus, Ormenium, Pyrrha, Methone, Olizon, promunturium Sepias, oppida Castana, Spalathra, promunturium Aeantium, oppida Meliboea, Rhizus, Erymnae, ostium Penii, oppida Homolium, Orthe, Iresiae, Pelinna, Thaumacie, Gyrton, Crannon, Acharne, Dotion, Melite, Phylace, Potniae.

Epiri, Achaiae, Atticae, Thessaliae in porrectum longitudo $\overline{\text{ccccxc}}$ traditur, latitudo $\overline{\text{cciiic}}$.

33 X. Macedonia postea CL populorum, duobus incluta regibus quondamque terrarum imperio, Emathia antea dicta. haec ad Epiroticas gentes in solis occasum recedens post terga Magnesiae atque Thessaliae infestatur a Dardanis: partem eius septentrionalem Paeonia ac Pelagonia protegunt a Triballis. oppida Aegiae, in quo sepeliri mos reges, Beroea, et in regione quae Pieria appellatur a 34 nemore Aeginium. in ora Heraclea, flumen Apilas, oppida Pydna, Oloros, amnis Haliacmon. intus Aloritae, Vallaei, Phylacaei, Cyrrestae, Tyrissaei, Pella colonia, oppidum Stobi civium Romanorum. mox Antigonea, Europus ad Axium amnem, eodemque nomine per quod Rhoedias fluit, Scydra, Eordaea, 35 Mieza, Gordyniae. mox in ora Ichnae, fluvius

---

ᵃ Philip and Alexander.

rejects it, refusing to allow the punitive waters engendered for the service of the Furies to mingle with its own silver flood.

IX. Adjoining Thessaly is Magnesia, to which belong the spring Libethra, the towns of Iolcus, Ormenium, Pyrrha, Methone and Olizon, Cape Sepias, the towns of Castana and Spalathra, Cape Aeantium, the towns Meliboea, Rhizus and Erymnae, the mouth of the Peneus, the towns Homolium, Orthe, Iresiae, Pelinna, Thaumacie, Gyrton, Crannon, Acharne, Dotion, Melite, Phylace and Potniae. *Coast N.E. of Thessaly.*

The total length of Epirus, Achaia, Attica and Thessaly is said to be 490 miles and the total breadth 297 miles. *Dimensions of Greece.*

X. Next comes Macedonia, with 150 nations, and famous for two kings [a] and for its former world-wide empire; it was previously called Emathia. It stretches westward to the races of Epirus, on the back of Magnesia and Thessaly, and on this side is exposed to the inroads of the Dardani, but its northern part is protected from the Triballi by Paeonia and Pelagonia. Its towns are Aegiae, the customary burial place of its kings, Beroea, and in the district called Pieria from the forest of that name, Aeginium. On the coast are Heraclea, the river Platamona, the towns of Pydna and Olorus, and the river Vistritza. Inland are the Aloritae, Vallaei, Phylacaei, Cyrrestae and Tyrissaei, the colony of Pella, and the town of Stobi, which has the Roman citizenship. Then come Antigonea, Europus on the river Axius, and the town of the same name through which flows the Rhoedias, Scydra, Eordaea, Mieza and Gordyniae. Then on the coast Ichnae and the river Axius. The neighbours of Macedonia on this *North coast of Aegean Sea: Macedonia.*

PLINY: NATURAL HISTORY

Axius; ad hunc finem Dardani, Treres, Pieres
Macedoniam accolunt, ab hoc amne Paeoniae gentes
Paroraei, Eordenses, Almopi, Pelagones, Mygdones,
montes Rhodope, Scopius, Orbelus; dein praeia-
cente gremio terrarum Arethusii, Antiochienses,
Idomenenses, Doberi, Aestrienses, Allantenses,
Audaristenses, Morylli, Garresci, Lyncestae, Othryo-
nei et liberi Amantini atque Orestae, coloniae
Bullidenses et Dienses, Xylopolitae, Scotussaei
36 liberi, Heraclea Sintica, Tymphaei, Toronaei. in
ora sinus Macedonica oppidum Chalastra et intus
Pyloros, Lete, medioque litoris flexu Thessalonice
liberae condicionis (ad hanc a Dyrrhachio $\overline{\text{CCXLV}}$),
Therme, in Thermaico sinu oppida Dicaea, Palinan-
drea, Scione, promunturium Canastraeum, oppida
Pallene, Phlegra. qua in regione montes Hypsizonus,
Epitus, Algion, Elaeuomne, oppida Nyssos, Phryxelon,
Mendae, et in Pallenensi isthmo quondam Potidaea,
nunc Cassandrea colonia, Anthemus, Olophyxus,
37 sinus Mecyberna, oppida Miscella, Ampelos, Torone,
Singos, Telos, fretum quo montem Atho Xerxes
Persarum rex continenti abscidit in longitudine
passuum MD. mons ipse a planitie excurrit in mare
ad $\overline{\text{XXV}}$ [1] passuum, ambitus radicis $\overline{\text{CL}}$ colligit. oppidum in cacumine fuit Acrathoon, nunc sunt Urano-
polis, Palaehorium, Thyssus, Cleonae, Apollonia
38 cuius incolae Macrobi cognominantur. oppidum
Cassera, faucesque alterae isthmi, Acanthus, Stagira,

---

[1] *Detlefsen* : in maria $\overline{\text{LXXV}}$.

---

[a] Now Monte Santo.
[b] The MSS. give 75 miles; the actual length is 40.
[c] Long-lived.

144

frontier are the Dardani, Treres and Pieres, and
after the river Axius come the Paeonian races of the
Paroraei, Eordenses, Almopi, Pelagones and Mygdones,
and the mountains of Rhodope, Scopius and Orbelus;
then, in the fold of ground lying in front of them,
the Arethusii, Antiochienses, Idomenenses, Doberi,
Aestrienses, Allantenses, Audaristenses, Morylli,
Garresci, Lyncestae, Othryonei, and the free peoples
of the Amantini and Orestae; the colonies Bullidenses
and Dienses; the Xylopolitae, the free Scotussaei,
Heraclea Sintica, the Tymphaei, the Toronaei. On
the Macedonian coast of the gulf are the town of
Chalastra and, farther in, Pylorus, Lete, and at
the centre of the curve of the coast the free city of
Saloniki (from there to Durazzo is 245 miles), Therme,
and on the Gulf of Saloniki the towns of Dicaea,
Palinandrea and Scione, Cape Paliuri, and the towns
of Pallene and Phlegra. The mountains in this
district are Hypsizonus, Epitus, Algion and
Elaeuomne; the towns are Nyssus, Phryxelon,
Mendae, and on the Isthmus of Pallene what was
formerly Potidaea but is now the colony of Cassandrea,
Anthemus, Olophyxus, Mecyberna Bay, the towns
of Miscella, Ampelos, Torone, Singos, Telos, and the
canal, a mile and a half in length, by which the
Persian king Xerxes cut off Mount Athos [a] from the
mainland. The actual mountain projects from the
level plain into the sea for a distance of 25 miles,[b] and
its circumference at its base amounts to 150 miles.
There was once a town on its summit called Acrathoon; the present towns on it are Uranopolis,
Palaehorium, Thyssus, Cleonae, and Apollonia, the
inhabitants of which are called Macrobii.[c] Then the
town of Cassera, and the other side of the isthmus,

Sithone, Heraclea, et regio Mygdoniae subiacens, in qua recedentes a mari Apollonia, Arethusa. in ora rursus Posidium et sinus cum oppido Cermoro, Amphipolis liberum, gens Bisaltae. dein Macedoniae terminus amnis Strymo ortus in Haemo; memorandum in septem lacus eum fundi priusquam dirigat cursum.

39   Haec est Macedonia terrarum imperio potita quondam, haec Asiam, Armeniam, Hiberiam, Albaniam, Cappadociam, Syriam, Aegyptum, Taurum, Caucasum transgressa, haec in Bactris, Medis, Persis dominata toto oriente possesso, haec etiam Indiae victrix per vestigia Liberi Patris atque Herculis vagata, haec eadem est Macedonia cuius uno die Paulus Aemilius imperator noster LXXII urbes direptas vendidit. tantam differentiam sortis praestitere duo homines.

40   XI. Thracia sequitur, inter validissimas Europae gentes, in strategias L divisa. populorum eius quos nominare non pigeat amnem Strymonem accolunt dextro latere Denseletae et Medi ad Bisaltas usque supra dictos, laevo Digerri Bessorumque multa nomina ad Mestum amnem ima Pangaei montis ambientem inter Haletos, Diobessos, Carbilesos, inde Brysas, Sapaeos, Odomantos. Odrysarum gens fundit Hebrum accolentibus Cabyletis, Pyrogeris, Drugeris, Caenicis, Hypsaltis, Benis, Cor-
41 pillis, Bottiaeis, Edonis. eodem sunt in tractu

ᵃ Alexander the Great and L. Aemilius Paullus, who conquered the Macedonian monarch Perseus at Pydna, 181 B.C., and by the order of the Senate gave his soldiers 72 towns to pillage because they had sided with Perseus.

ᵇ The Roman *praefecturae*.

Acanthus, Stagira, Sithone, Heraclea, and the district of Mygdonia lying below, in which at some distance from the sea are Apollonia and Arethusa, and on the coast again Posidium and the bay with the town of Cermorus, the free city of Amphipolis, and the tribe of the Bisaltae. Then comes the river Struma which rises in Mount Haemus and forms the boundary of Macedonia; it is worth recording that it spreads out into seven lakes before it proceeds on its course.

Such is Macedonia, which once won a world-wide empire, marched across Asia, Armenia, Iberia, Albania, Cappadocia, Syria, Egypt, Mount Taurus and the Hindu Kush, was lord over the Bactrians, Medes and Persians, owned the entire East, and even roamed in the tracks of Father Liber and of Hercules and conquered India; and this also is the Macedonia 72 of whose cities our general Aemilius Paullus pillaged and sold in a single day. So great the difference in her lot bestowed upon her by two individuals![a]

XI. Next comes Thrace, one of the most powerful *Thrace.* nations of Europe, divided into fifty commands.[b] Of its peoples those whom we ought not to omit to name are the Denseletae and the Medi, who live on the right bank of the river Struma right up to the Bisaltae above mentioned, and the Digerri and the various sections of the Bessi on the left bank, as far as the river Mesto that winds round the foot of Mount Pilat Tepeh, passing through the Haleti, Diobessi and Carbilesi, and then the Brysae, Sapaei and Odomanti. The race of the Odrysae owns the source of the Maritza, on the banks of which live the Cabyleti, Pyrogeri, Drugeri, Caenici, Hypsalti, Beni, Corpilli, Bottiaei and Edoni. In the same district

147

Staletae, Priantae, Dolongae, Thyni, Celaletae
maiores Haemo, minores Rhodopae subditi. inter
quos Hebrus amnis, oppidum sub Rhodope Poneropolis antea, mox a conditore Philippopolis, nunc a
situ Trimontium dicta. Haemi excelsitas vī passuum
subitur. aversa eius et in Histrum devexa Moesi,
Getae, Aodi, Scaugdae Clariaeque, et sub iis Arraei
Sarmatae quos Areatas vocant Scythaeque et circa
Ponti litora Moriseni Sithonique Orphei vatis
genitores optinent.

42 Ita finit Hister a septentrione, ab ortu Pontus ac
Propontis, a meridie Aegaeum mare, cuius in ora
a Strymone Apollonia, Oesyma, Neapolis, Batos.
intus Philippi colonia (absunt a Dyrrhachio cccxxv)
Scotussa, Topiros civitas, Mesti amnis ostium, mons
Pangaeus, Heraclea, Olynthos, Abdera libera civitas,
stagnum Bistonum et gens. oppidum fuit Tirida
Diomedis equorum stabulis dirum; nunc sunt
Dicaea, Ismaron, locus Parthenion, Phalesina, Maro-
43 nea prius Orthagurea dicta, mons Serrium, Zone; tum
locus Doriscum x̄ hominum capax: ita Xerxes ibi
dinumeravit exercitum; os Hebri, portus Stentoris,
oppidum Aenos liberum cum Polydori tumulo, Cico-

---

^a Son of Priam and Hecuba, murdered for his treasure by
their son-in-law Polymnestor, king of Thrace, Virgil, *Aen.*
III. 45.

are the Staletae, Priantae, Dolongae, Thyni, and the Greater Celaletae at the foot of the Great Balkan and the Lesser at the foot of Mount Rhodope. Between these tribes runs the river Maritza, and below Rhodope is the town formerly called Poneropolis, then Philippopolis after its founder, and now Trimontium from its site. To the summit of the Great Balkan is a journey of six miles. Its opposite side sloping down towards the Danube is inhabited by the Moesi, Getae, Aodi, Scaugdae and Clariae, and below them the Sarmatian Arraei called Areatae, and the Scythians, and round the shores of the Black Sea the Moriseni and the Sithoni, the ancestry of the poet Orpheus.

Thus Thrace is bounded by the Danube on the north, the Black Sea and Sea of Marmara on the east, and the Aegean Sea on the south, on the coast of which after leaving the Struma we come to Apollonia, Osima, Kavallo and Batos. Inland is the colony of Filiba, at a distance of 325 miles from Durazzo, Scotussa, the state of Topiros, the mouth of the river Mestus, the mountain of Pilat Tepeh, Melenik, Agia Maria, the free city of Abdera, the Lagos Buru and the people of the Bistoni. Here once was the town of Tirida, formidable on account of the stables of the horses of Diomede; and there now are the towns of Dicaea and Ismaron, the place called Parthenion, Phalesina, Marogna formerly called Orthagurea, Mount Serrium, Zone; and then the place called Doriscus, a plain large enough to hold 10,000 men, as it was in detachments of that number that Xerxes there counted his army; the mouth of the Maritza, the harbour of Stentor, the free town of Enos with the Funeral Mound of Polydorus,[a] a district

num quondam regio. a Dorisco incurvatur ora ad
Macron Tichos $\overline{\text{CXII}}$ p., circa quem locum fluvius Melas
a quo sinus appellatur. oppida Cypsela, Bisanthe,
Macron Tichos dictum quia a Propontide ad Melana
sinum inter duo maria porrectus murus procurrentem
44 excludit Cherronesum. namque Thracia altero
latere a Pontico litore incipiens, ubi Hister amnis
inmergitur, vel pulcherrimas in ea parte urbes habet,
Histropolin Milesiorum, Tomos, Callatim quae antea
Cerbatis vocabatur. Heracleam habuit et Bizonen
terrae hiatu raptam, nunc habet Dionysopolim
Crunon antea dictam: adluit Zyras amnis. totum
eum tractum Scythae Aroteres cognominati tenuere.
eorum oppida Aphrodisias, Libistus, Zygere, Rhocobae, Eumenia, Parthenopolis, Gerania, ubi Pygmaeorum gens fuisse proditur: Catizos barbari vocabant,
45 creduntque a gruibus fugatos. in ora a Dionyso-
poli est Odessus Milesiorum, flumen Pannysis, oppidum Tetranaulochus. mons Haemus vasto iugo
procumbens in Pontum oppidum habuit in vertice
Aristaeum; nunc in ora Mesembria, Anchialum, ubi
Messa fuerat. Astice regio habuit oppidum Anthium, nunc est Apollonia. flumina Panisos, Iuras,
Tearus, Orosines, oppida Thynias, Halmydesos,
Develcon (cum stagno quod nunc Deultum vocatur)
veteranorum, Phinopolis, iuxta quam Bosporus.

---

[a] Now the Gulf of Enos.
[b] See § 92 n.

formerly belonging to the Cicones. From Doriscus
the coast makes a curve of 112 miles to Long Wall,
round which flows the Black River that gives its
name to the bay.[a] The towns are Ipsala, Rodosto,
Long Wall, so called because its fortifications extend
between the two seas, from the Sea of Marmara to the
Gulf of Enos, cutting off the projecting Gallipoli
Peninsula. For the other side of Thrace begins at *East coast*
the coast of the Black Sea where the Danube flows *of Thrace.*
into it; and this region comprises its finest cities,
Kostendsje, a colony from Miletus, Temesvar and
Collat, formerly called Cerbatis. It formerly had
Heraclea and Bizone, which was swallowed up by an
earthquake, and it still has the City of Dionysus,
previously called Crunos, which is washed by the
river Zyras. The whole of this region was occupied
by the Scythian tribe called the Ploughmen, their
towns being Aphrodisias, Libistus, Zygere, Rhocobae,
Eumenia, Parthenopolis and Gerania, stated to have
been the abode of the race of Pigmies: their name
in the local dialect used to be Catizi, and there is a
belief that they were driven away by cranes. On
the coast after the City of Dionysus come the Milesian
colony of Varna, the river Daphne-Soni and the town
of Four Roadsteads. The enormous ridge of the
Great Balkan projecting into the Black Sea formerly
had on its summit the town of Aristaeum, and on the
coast now are Missiori and Akiali on the former site
of Messa. The region of Astice had a town of
Anthium, which is now Apollonia.[b] The rivers are
the Panisos, Iuras, Tearus, Orosines; the towns
Tiniada, Midjeh, Zagora (with its marsh now called
Deultum), a colony of veterans, and Phinopolis, near
which are the Straits of Constantinople. From the

ab Histri ostio ad os Ponti passuum $\overline{\text{DLII}}$ fecere,
Agrippa $\overline{\text{LX}}$ adiecit; inde ad murum supra dictum
$\overline{\text{CL}}$, ab eo Cherronesus $\overline{\text{CXXVI}}$.

46   Sed a Bosporo sinus Casthenes, portus Senum et
alter qui Mulierum cognominatur, promunturium
Chryseon Ceras in quo oppidum Byzantium liberae
condicionis antea Lygos dictum; abest a Dyrrhachio
$\overline{\text{DCCXI}}$ p.: tantum patet longitudo terrarum inter
47 Hadriaticum mare et Propontidem. amnes Bathy-
nias, Pidaras sive Athidas, oppida Selymbria, Perinthus latitudine cc pedum continenti adnexa. intus
Bizye arx regum Thraciae a Terei nefasto invisa
hirundinibus, regio Caenica, colonia Flaviopolis ubi
antea Caela oppidum vocabatur, et a Bizye $\overline{\text{L}}$ p.
Apros colonia, quae a Philippis abest $\overline{\text{CLXXXIX}}$. at
in ora amnis Erginus, oppidum fuit Ganos; deseritur
48 et Lysimachea iam in Cherroneso. alius namque
ibi Isthmos angustias similes eodem nomine et pari
latitudine inlustrat; duae urbes utrimque litora haut
dissimili modo tenuere, Pactye a Propontide, Cardia
a Melane sinu, haec ex facie loci nomine accepto,
utraeque conprehensae postea Lysimachea $\overline{\text{V}}$ p. a
Longis Muris. Cherronesos a Propontide habuit

---

    [a] Constantinople, Stamboul.

    [b] The legendary king of Thrace, who violated Philomela the
sister of his wife Procne. Philomela became a nightingale
and Procne a swallow; or according to another account Philomela a swallow and Procne a nightingale.

    [c] Hexamila now occupies the site.

    [d] The word is regarded as a proper name, properly belonging
to the Isthmus of Corinth.

    [e] Like Corinth and Lechaeum on their Isthmus.

    [f] See § 43.

    [g] The Greek for 'heart,' καρδία.   [h] See § 43.

mouth of the Danube to the outlet of the Black Sea
was reckoned as 552 miles, but Agrippa made it 60
miles more; and from that point to the wall above
mentioned is 150 miles, and from there to the end
of the Gallipoli Peninsula 126 miles.

On leaving the Dardanelles we come to the Bay of *Stamboul.*
Casthenes, the Old Men's Harbour and the other
called the Women's Harbour, and the promontory of
the Golden Horn, on which is the town of Byzantium,[a]
a free state, formerly called Lygos; it is 711 miles
from Durazzo, so great being the space of land
between the Adriatic and the Sea of Marmara.
There are the rivers Bathynias and Pidaras or
Athidas, and the towns of Selymbria and Perinthus
which are connected with the mainland by an isthmus
200 ft. wide.   Inland are Vizia, a citadel of the
kings of Thrace that is hated by swallows because
of the outrage committed by Tereus,[b] the district of
Caenica, the colony of Flaviopolis on the site of
the former town called Caela, and 50 miles from Vizia
the colony of Apros, which is 189 miles distant from
Philippi.   On the coast is the river Erkene, and once
stood the town of Ganos; Lysimachea [c] on the
Gallipoli Peninsula is also now becoming deserted.
But at this point there is another [d] Isthmus which *Gallipoli.*
marks similar narrows with the same name and is of
about equal width; and in a not dissimilar manner [e]
two cities occupied the shores on either side, Pactye
on the side of the Sea of Marmara and Cardia on
that of the Gulf of Enos,[f] the latter city taking its
name [g] from the conformation of the place; both were
subsequently united with the city of Lysimachea,
five miles from Long Wall.[h]   On the Marmara
side of Gallipoli Peninsula were Tiristasis, Crithotes

Tiristasin, Crithoten, Cissam flumini Aegos adpositam;
nunc habet a colonia Apro $\overline{\text{XXII}}$ p. Resisthon ex ad-
49 verso coloniae Parianae. et Hellespontus VII ut
diximus [1] stadiis Europam ab Asia dividens IV inter
se contrarias urbes habet, in Europa Callipolim et
Seston et in Asia Lampsacon et Abydon. dein
promunturium Cherronesi Mastusia adversum Sigeo,
cuius in fronte obliqua Cynossema (ita appellatur
Hecubae tumulus), statio Achaeorum, et turris,
delubrum Protesilai et in extrema Cherronesi
fronte, quae vocatur Aeolium, oppidum Elaeus.
dein petenti Melana sinum portus Coelos et Panhormus et supra dicta Cardia.
50 Tertius Europae sinus ad hunc modum clauditur.
montes extra praedictos Thraciae Edonus, Gygemeros, Meritus, Melamphyllos, flumina in Hebrum
cadentia Bargus, Syrmus. Macedoniae, Thraciae,
Hellesponti longitudo est supra dicta (quidam
$\overline{\text{DCCXX}}$ faciunt), latitudo $\overline{\text{CCCLXXXIV}}$ est.
51 Aegaeo mari nomen dedit scopulus inter Tenum
et Chium verius quam insula, Aex nomine a specie
caprae (quae ita Graecis appellatur), repente e
medio mari exiliens. cernunt eum ab dextera parte
Antandrum [2] navigantes ab Achaia, dirum ac pesti-
ferum. Aegaei pars Myrtoo datur; appellatur ab
insula parva quae cernitur Macedoniam a Geraesto

---

[1] [ut diximus]? *edd.*   [2] *Detlefsen*: Andrum.

---

[a] This has not in fact been said before.
[b] Kilidbhas, a little south of Anzac.

and Cissa lying on the Goat's River; and there is now Resisthos, 22 miles from the colony of Apros, opposite to the colony of Parium. Also the Dardanelles, which as we have said *a* divide Europe from Asia by a space not quite a mile across, have four cities facing one another on the opposite sides, Gallipoli and Ialova in Europe and Lamsaki and Avido in Asia. Then on Gallipoli there is the promontory of Capo Helles opposite to Jeni-Hisari, on the slanting side of which is the Bitch's Tomb (the name given to the funeral mound of Hecuba), the naval station of the Greeks in the Trojan war, and a tower, the shrine of Protesilaus, and at the point of the peninsula, which is called Aeolium, the town of Elaeus. Then as you make for the Gulf of Enos you have the harbours of Coelos *b* and Panormus and Cardia above mentioned.

This rounds off the third Gulf of Europe. The mountains of Thrace, beside those already mentioned, are Edonus, Gygemeros, Meritus and Melamphyllus; the rivers are the Bargus and the Syrmus, which fall into the Maritza. The length of Macedonia, Thrace and the Hellespont has been mentioned previously §46. (some make it 720 miles); the breadth is 384 miles.

The Aegean Sea takes its name from an island, or *Aegean Sea.* more truly a rock suddenly springing out of the middle of the sea, between Tenos and Chios, named Aex from its resemblance to a she-goat—αἴξ being the Greek word for the animal. In sailing from Achaia to Antandro, this rock is sighted on the starboard side, and it is a sinister threat of disaster. One section of the Aegean is distinguished as the Myrtoan Sea; it takes its name from the small island of Myrtos sighted as you sail from Geraestus in the direction of

petentibus haut procul Euboeae Carysto. Romani
omnia haec maria duobus nominibus appellant,
Macedonicum quacumque Macedoniam aut Thraciam
attingit, Graeciense qua Graeciam adluit; nam
Graeci et Ionium dividunt in Siculum ac Creticum
ab insulis, item Icarium quod est inter Samum et
Myconum, cetera nomina sinus dedere quos diximus.

52   XII. Et maria quidem gentesque in tertio Europae
sinu ad hunc modum se habent, insulae autem:
ex adverso Thesprotiae a Buthroto $\overline{\text{XII}}$ p., eadem ab
Acrocerauniis $\overline{\text{L}}$, cum urbe eiusdem nominis Corcyra
liberae civitatis et oppido Cassiope temploque Cassi
Iovis, $\overline{\text{XCVII}}$ in longitudinem patens, Homero dicta
Scheria et Phaeacia, Callimacho etiam Drepane.
circa eam aliquot, sed ad Italiam vergens Othronos,
ad Leucadiam Paxoe duae, $\overline{\text{V}}$ discretae a Corcyra,
53 nec procul ab iis ante Corcyram Ericusa, Marathe,
Elaphusa, Malthace, Trachie, Pythionia, Ptychia,
Tarachie, et a Phalario Corcyrae promunturio
scopulus in quem mutatam Ulixis navem a simili
specie fabula est. ante Leucadiam autem et
Aetoliam [1] permultae, quarum Teleboides, eaedem-
que Taphiae ab incolis appellantur, Taphias, Carnos,
Oxia, Prinoessa, ante Aetoliam Echinades, Aegialia,
Cotonis, Thyatira, Geoaris, Dionysia, Cyrnus, Chalcis,
54 Pinara, Nystrus. ante eas in alto Cephallania,
Zacynthus, utraque libera, Ithaca, Dulichium, Same,

---

[1] *Mayhoff*: Achaiam.

[a] Now Magnisi, Kalamota and Kastos.

Macedonia, not far from Carystus in Euboea. The
Romans call all these seas by two names, the Macedonian Sea wherever it touches Macedonia or
Thrace and the Grecian Sea where it washes the
coast of Greece; while the Greeks divide the Ionian
Sea too into the Sicilian and the Cretan, named from
the islands, and also give the name of Icarian to the
part between Samos and Myconos, and the other
Greek names are taken from the gulfs that we
have mentioned.

XII. So much for the arrangement of the seas and   *Islands down
the nations in the third Gulf of Europe. The islands   *west coast
are as follows: opposite to Thesprotia, 12 miles from   *of Greece.*
Buthrotus and also 50 from Acroceraunia, lies Corfu,
with a city of the same name, a free state, and the
town of Cassopo, and the temple of Jupiter Cassius;
the island is 97 miles long. In Homer it has the names
of Scheria and Phaeacia, and in Callimachus also that
of Drepane. Several islands lie round it, especially
Fano on the side towards Italy and Paxo and Antipaxo
towards Leucadia, both 5 miles away from Corfu.
Not far from these, lying off Corfu, are Ericusa,
Marathe, Elaphusa, Malthace, Trachie, Pythionia,
Ptychia and Tarachie, and off the promontory of
Corfu called Capo Drasti the rock into which
(according to the story, which is due to the similarity
of shape) the ship of Ulysses was changed. Off
Leucadia and Aetolia are a very large number,
among which those called the Teleboides, and also
by their inhabitants the Taphiae, are Taphias,
Carnos, Oxia, and Prinoessa; *a* off Aetolia are the
Echinades, Aegialia, Cotonis, Thyatira, Geoaris,
Dionysia, Cyrnus, Chalcis, Pinara, Nystrus. Off
these out at sea lie Cephallenia and Zante, both free,

PLINY: NATURAL HISTORY

Crocyle. a Paxo Cephallania quondam Melaena dicta x̄ p. abest, circuitu patet x̄c̄ı̄ı̄ı̄; Same diruta a Romanis adhuc tamen oppida tria habet. inter hanc et Achaiam cum oppido magnifica et fertilitate praecipua Zacynthus, aliquando appellata Hyrie, Cephallaniae meridiana parte x̄x̄v̄ abest; mons Elatus ibi nobilis. ipsa circuitu colligit x̄x̄x̄v̄ı̄.

55 ab ea Ithaca x̄v̄ distat, in qua mons Neritus; tota vero circuitu patet x̄x̄v̄. ab ea Araxum Peloponnesi promunturium x̄v̄. ante hanc in alto Asteris, Prote, ante Zacynthum x̄x̄x̄v̄ in eurum ventum Strophades duae, ab aliis Plotae dictae. ante Cephallaniam Letoia, ante Pylum ııı Sphageae, totidem ante Messenen Oenussae.

56 In Asinaeo sinu tres Thyrides, in Laconico Teganissa, Cothon, Cythera cum oppido, antea Porphyris appellata—haec sita est a Maleae promunturio v̄ passuum ancipiti propter angustias ibi navium ambitu; in Argolico Pityusa, Arine, Ephyre; contra Hermionium agrum Tricarenus, Aperopia, Colonis, Aristera;

57 contra Troezenium Calauria ᴅ distans, Plateis, Belbina, Lasia, Baucidias; contra Epidaurum Cecryphalos, Pityonesos v̄ı̄ a continente, ab hac Aegina liberae condicionis x̄v̄, cuius x̄v̄ı̄ı̄ı̄ praenavigatio

---

a So called from its fir-trees; now Scopo.
b At the south of the Argolid.

158

Ithaca, Dulichium, Same, and Crocyle. Cephallenia, formerly called in Greek the Black Island, is 10 miles from Paxo, and measures 93 miles in circumference; Same has been demolished by the Romans, but still possesses three towns. Between Same and the coast of Achaia lies Zante, distinguished by its fine town and remarkable for the fertility of its soil; it was at one time called Hyrie. It is 25 miles from the southern part of Cephallenia, and on it is the celebrated mountain of Elatus.[a] It measures 36 miles in circumference. At a distance of 15 miles from Zante is Ithaca, on which is Monte Stefano; its whole circumference measures 25 miles. The distance from it to the Peloponnesian promontory of Araxus is 15 miles. Off Ithaca in the open sea are Asteris and Prote, and off Zante at a distance of 35 miles to the south-east are the two Strophades, called by other people the Plotae. Off Cephallenia is Letoia, off Pylos the three Sphageae and off Messene the three Oenussae.

In the Messenian Gulf are the three Thyrides, and in the Gulf of Laconia Teganissa, Cothon and Cerigo with the town of that name—the former name of this island was Porphyris; it lies 5 miles from Cape Malea, which is dangerous to circumnavigate because of the narrowness of the strait. In the Gulf of Nauplia are Pityusa, Arine and Ephyre; opposite the territory of Hermione [b] Tricarenus, Aperopia, Colonis and Aristera; opposite that of Troezen, Calauria half a mile away, Plateis, Belbina, Lasia and Baucidias; opposite Epidaurus, Cecryphalos and Pityonesus 6 miles from the mainland. Fifteen miles from Pityonesus is Aegina, a free state, which is 18 miles long as you sail past it, and 20 miles

Islands south of Greece.

PLINY: NATURAL HISTORY

est, eadem autem a Piraeeo Atheniensium portu $\overline{xx}$
abest, ante Oenone vocitata. Spiraeo promunturio
obiacent Eleusa, Adendros, Craugiae duae, Caeciae
duae, Selacosa; et a Cenchreis[1] Aspis $\overline{vii}$ et in
Megarico sinu Methurides $\overline{iv}$, Aegila autem $\overline{xv}$ a
Cythera, eademque a Cretae Phalasarna oppido $\overline{xxv}$.

58   Ipsa Creta altero latere ad austrum altero ad
septentrionem versa inter ortum occasumque porrigitur, centum urbium clara fama. Dosiades eam a
Crete nympha, Hesperidis filia, Anaximander a
rege Curetum, Philistides Mallotes et Crates primum Aeriam dictam, deinde postea Curetim, et
Macaron nonnulli a temperie caeli appellatam
existimavere. latitudine nusquam $\overline{L}$ excedens et
circa mediam sui partem maxime patens longitudine
implet $\overline{CCLXX}$, circuitu $\overline{DLXXXIX}$, flectensque se in
Creticum pelagus ab ea dictum qua longissima est ad
orientem promunturium Samonium adversum Rhodo,
ad occidentem Criumetopon Cyrenas versus expellit.

59   Oppida eius insignia Phalasarna, Elaea, Cisamon,
Pergamum, Cydonea, Minoium, Apteron, Pantoma-
trium, Amphomala, Rhithymna, Panhormum, Cytae-
um, Apollonia, Matium, Heraclea, Miletos, Ampelos,
Hierapytna, Lebena, Hierapolis, et in mediterraneo
Gortyna, Phaestum, Gnosus, Polyrrhenum, Myrina,
Lycastos, Rhamnus, Lyctus, Dium, Asium, Pyloros,
Rhytion, Elatos, Pherae, Holopyxos, Lasos, Eleu-
thernae, Therapnae, Marathusa, Gytisos, et aliorum

---

[1] *Mayhoff*: Selacosa, Dacenchrus.

[a] Probably Cape San Sidero, not Cape Salomon, in spite of
the name.
[b] The Greek name survives in the modern Capo Crio.
[c] The modern Canea.
[d] The site is now occupied by Candia.

distant from Piraeus, the port of Athens; its name used to be Oenone. Off the promontory of Spiraeum lie Eleusa, Adendros, the two Craugiae, the two Caeciae and Selacosa; and Aspis 7 miles from Cenchreae and Methurides in the Bay of Megara 4 miles; while Aegila is 15 miles from Cythera and 25 from the Cretan town of Phalasarna.

Crete itself stretches east and west with one side *Crete.* facing south and the other north; it is celebrated for the renown of its 100 cities. Dosiades held the view that it took its name from the nymph Crete, daughter of Hesperis, Anaximander that it was named from the king of the Curetes, Philistides of Mallos and Crates that it was first called Aeria and then subsequently Curetis; its Greek appellation, ' the Island of the Blest,' is thought by some to be due to the mildness of its climate. Its breadth nowhere exceeds 50 miles, its widest part being about the middle; its length is fully 270 miles and its circumference 589 miles; its longest side forms a curve towards the Cretan Sea which takes its name from it, its easternmost projection, Cape Samonium,[a] point ing towards Rhodes and its westernmost, the Ram's Forehead,[b] towards Cyrene.

The important cities of Crete are Phalasarna, Elaea, Cisamon, Pergamum, Cydonia,[c] Minoium, Apteron, Pantomatrium, Amphomala, Rhithymna, Panhormum, Cytaeum, Apollonia, Matium,[d] Heraclea, Miletos, Ampelos, Hierapytna, Lebena and Hierapolis; and in the interior Gortyna, Phaestus, Cnossus, Polyrrhenum, Myrina, Lycastos, Rhamnus, Lyctus, Dium, Asium, Pyloros, Rhytion, Elatos, Pherae, Holopyxos, Lasos, Eleuthernae, Therapnae, Marathusa, Gytisos, and about 60 other towns of which

circiter LX oppidorum memoria extat. montes
60 Cadistus, Idaeus, Dictynnaeus, Corycus. ipsa abest
promunturio suo quod vocatur Criumetopon, ut
prodit Agrippa, a Cyrenarum promunturio Phycunte
$\overline{\text{cxxv}}$, item Cadisto a Malea Peloponnesi $\overline{\text{lxxx}}$, a
Carpatho insula promunturio Samonio $\overline{\text{lx}}$ in favonium
ventum; haec inter eam et Rhodum interiacet.

61 Reliquae circa eam ante Peloponnesum duae
Corycoe, totidem Mylae, et latere septentrionali
dextra Cretam habenti contra Cydoneam Leuce
et duae Budroe, contra Matium Dia, contra Itanum
promunturium Onysia, Leuce, contra Hierapytnam
Chrysa, Gaudos. eodem tractu Ophiussa, Butoa,
Ramnus, circumvectisque Criumetopon tres Acusa-
gorus appellatae. ante Samonium promunturium
Phocoe, Platiae, Stirnides, Naulochos, Harmedon,
Zephyre.

62 At in Hellade, etiamnum in Aegaeo, Lichades,
Scarphia, Corese, Phocasia conpluresque aliae ex
adverso Atticae sine oppidis et ideo ignobiles; sed
contra Eleusina clara Salamis. ante eam Psyttalia,
a Sunio vero Helene $\overline{\text{v}}$ distans. dein Ceos ab ea
totidem, quam nostri quidam dixere Ceam, Graeci
et Hydrusam, avolsam Euboeae; quingentos longa
stadios fuit quondam, mox quattuor fere partibus
quae ad Boeotiam vergebant eodem mari devoratis

---

^a Now Ras el-Sem.

162

only the memory exists. The mountains are
Cadistus, Ida, Dictynna and Corycus. The distance
of the island at its promontory called the Ram's
Forehead from the promontory of Cyrene named
Phycus [a] is stated by Agrippa to be 125 miles, and
at Cadistus from Malea in the Morea 80; at the
promontory of Samonium it is 60 miles west of the
island of Skarpanto, which lies between it and
Rhodes.

The remaining islands lying round Crete are, *Islands of*
towards the Morea, the two called Corycos and the *Crete.*
two called Myla; on the north side having Crete
on the right and opposite to Cydonea are Leuce and
the two called Budroe, opposite to Matium is Dia,
opposite to the promontory of Itanum are Onysia
and Leuce, and opposite to Hierapytna Chrysa and
Gaudos. In the same region are Ophiussa, Butoa and
Rhamnus, and after rounding the Ram's Forehead
the three called Acusagorus. Off the promontory of
Samonium are the Phocoi, Platiae and Stirnides, and
Naulochos, Harmedon and Zephyre.

Forming part of Hellas but still in the Aegean Sea *Islands up*
are the Lichades, Scarphia, Corese, Phocasia, and a *the east coast*
number of others facing Attica that have no towns on *of Greece.*
them and are consequently unimportant. Opposite
Eleusis is the famous island of Salamis. In front of
it is Psyttalea, and, at a distance of 5 miles from
Sunium, Helene. Then at the same distance from
Helene is Ceos, called by some Romans Cea and by
the Greeks also Hydrusa. This is an island that has
been torn away from Euboea; it was formerly
62½ miles long, but more recently about four-fifths
of it lying in the direction of Boeotia has also been
swallowed up by the sea, leaving the towns of Iulis

oppida habet reliqua Iulida, Carthaeam; intercidere
Coresus, Poeeessa. ex hac profectam delicatiorem
feminis vestem auctor est Varro.

63　　Euboea et ipsa avolsa Boeotiae tam modico interfluente Euripo ut ponte iungatur, ad meridiem
promunturiis duobus, Geraesto ad Atticam vergente
et ad Hellespontum Caphereo, insignis, a septentrione
Cenaeo, nusquam latitudinem ultra $\overline{\text{XL}}$ extendit,
nusquam infra MM contrahit, sed in longitudinem
universae Boeotiae ab Attica ad Thessaliam usque
64 praetenta in $\overline{\text{CL}}$, circuitu vero $\overline{\text{CCCLXV}}$. abest ab Hellesponto parte Caipherei $\overline{\text{CCXXV}}$, urbibus quondam Pyrrha,
Porthmo, Neso, Cerintho, Oreo, Dio, Aedepso, Ocha,
Oechalia, nunc Chalcide cuius ex adverso in continenti Aulis est, Geraesto, Eretria, Carysto, Oritano,
Artemisio, fonte Arethusa, flumine Lelanto aquisque
calidis quae Hellopiae vocantur nobilis, notior tamen
marmore Carystio. antea vocitata est Chalcodontis
aut Macris, ut Dionysius et Ephorus tradunt, ut
Aristides Macra, ut Callidemus Chalcis aere ibi
primum reperto, ut Menaechmus Abantias, ut
poetae vulgo Asopis.

65　　Extra eam in Myrtoo multae, sed maxime inlustres
Glauconnesos et Aegila et a promunturio Geraesto
circa Delum in orbem sitae, unde et nomen traxere

and Carthaea, while Coresus and Grassy Island have
disappeared. Varro states that this island used to
export an exceptionally fine kind of cloth used for
ladies' dresses.

Euboea itself also is sundered from Boeotia by so
moderate a channel, the Euripus, that it is joined
to the mainland by a bridge. At the south end it
has two marked promontories, Capo Mandili pointing towards Attica and Kavo Doro towards the
Dardanelles; at the north it has Cape Lithadha.
Its breadth nowhere exceeds 40 miles and nowhere
contracts below two miles; its length stretches along
the whole of Boeotia from Attica to Thessaly and
measures 150 miles, while its circumference is 365
miles. At its south-easternmost point its distance
from the Dardanelles is 225 miles. Its notable
cities were formerly Pyrrha, Porthmos, Nesos, Cerin-
thos, Oreus, Dium, Aedepsos, Ocha and Oechalia;
those now noteworthy are Chalcis (opposite which on
the mainland is Aulis), Geraestus, Eretria, Carystus,
Oritanum and Artemisium, as well as the Spring of
Arethusa, the river Lelantus and the warm springs
known as the Hellopiae. Euboea is, however, still
better known for the marble of Carystus. It used
formerly to be called Chalcodontis or according to
Dionysius and Ephorus Macris, but Macra according
to Aristides, and according to Callidemus Chalcis,
because copper was first discovered there; according
to Menaechmus its name was Abantias, while in
poetry it is commonly called Asopis.

In the Myrtoan Sea besides Euboea are many *Islands of*
islands, the best known being Glauconnesus and the *Archipelago; western*
Aegila islands, and off Capo Mandili the Cyclades, *group.*
lying round Delos in a circle which has given them

165

Cyclades. prima earum Andrus cum oppido abest
a Geraesto x̄, a Ceo x̄x̄x̄v̄ī́īī. ipsam Myrsilus Cauron,
deinde Antandron cognominatam tradit, Callimachus
Lasiam, alii Nonagriam, Hydrusam, Epagrim. patet
circuitu x̄c̄īīī. ab eadem Andro passus mille et
a Delo x̄v̄ Tenos cum oppido in x̄v̄ porrecta, quam
propter aquarum abundantiam Aristoteles Hydrusam
66 appellatam ait, aliqui Ophiusam. ceterae Myconus
cum monte Dimasto a Delo x̄v̄, Siphnus ante Meropia
et Acis appellata circuitu x̄x̄v̄īīī, Seriphus x̄v̄, Prepesinthus, Cythnos, ipsaque longe clarissima et Cycladum media ac templo Apollinis et mercatu celebrata
Delos, quae diu fluctuata, ut proditur, sola motum
terrae non sensit ad M. Varronis aetatem: Mucianus
prodidit bis concussam. hanc Aristoteles ita appellatam tradidit quoniam repente apparuerit enata,
Aglaosthenes Cynthiam, alii Ortygiam, Asteriam,
Lagiam, Chlamydiam, Cynethum, Pyrpilen igne ibi
primum reperto. cingitur v̄ passuum, adsurgit
Cynthio monte.

67 Proxima ei Rhene quam Anticlides Celadusam
vocat, item Artemiten, Celadinen; Syros quam
circuitu patere x̄x̄ prodiderunt veteres, Mucianus

----

a Δῆλος, 'manifest.'

their name. The first of these is Andro with a town
of the same name, 10 miles from Mandili and 38 from
Ceos. Myrsilus tells us that Ceos was once called
Cauros, and later Antandros; Callimachus says it
had the name of Lasia, others Nonagria or Hydrusa or
Epagris. Its circuit measures 93 miles. At a distance
of a mile from Andros and 15 miles from Delos is
Tino, with a city of the same name; this island is 15
miles in length. Aristotle says that owing to its
abundance of springs it once was called Hydrusa;
others give its old name as Ophiusa. The other
islands are: Mykono, with Mount Two Breasts, 15
miles from Delos; Siphnus, previously called
Meropia and Acis, 28 miles round; Serpho 15 miles
round; Prepesinthus; Cythnos; and by far the
most famous of the Cyclades and lying in the middle
of them, Delos, celebrated for its temple of Apollo
and for its commerce. According to the story, Delos
for a long time floated adrift; also it was the only
island that down to the time of Marcus Varro had
never felt an earthquake shock; Mucianus however
states that it has suffered twice from earthquake.
Aristotle has recorded that it owes its name [a] to
its having suddenly appeared emerging from the
water; Aglaosthenes, however, calls it the Isle of
Cynthus, and others Quail Island, Star Island, Hare
Island, Cloak Island, Dog Island, and Fiery Island
because fire was first discovered there. It measures
five miles in circumference. Its only eminence is
Mount Cynthius.

Next to Delos is Rhene, which Anticlides calls
Celadusa, and also Artemites and Celadine; Syros,
stated by old writers to measure 20 miles in circuit,
but by Mucianus 160 miles; Olearos; Paros, with

$\overline{\text{CLX}}$; Olearus; Parus cum oppido, ab Delo $\overline{\text{xxxviii}}$ marmore nobilis, quam primo Platean, postea Minoida vocarunt. ab ea $\overline{\text{vii}}$ D Naxus, a Delo $\overline{\text{xviii}}$, cum oppido, quam Strongylen, deinde Diam, mox Dionysiada a vinearum fertilitate, alii Siciliam Minorem aut Callipolim appellarunt. patet circuitu $\overline{\text{lxxv}}$ p., dimidioque maior est quam Parus.

68   Et hactenus quidem Cycladas servant, ceteras quae secuntur Sporadas. sunt autem Helene, Phacusa, Nicasia, Schinusa, Pholegandros, et a Naxo $\overline{\text{xxxviii}}$ p. Icaros, quae nomen mari dedit, tantundem ipsa in longitudinem patens, cum oppidis duobus, tertio amisso, antea vocitata Doliche et Macris et Ichthyoessa. sita est ab exortu solstitiali Deli $\overline{\text{L}}$, eademque a Samo $\overline{\text{xxxv}}$, inter Euboeam et Andrum $\overline{\text{x}}$ passuum freto, ab ea Geraestum $\overline{\text{cxii}}$ D passuum.

69   Nec deinde servari potest ordo; acervatim ergo ponentur reliquae: Scyros; Ios a Naxo $\overline{\text{xviii}}$, Homeri sepulchro veneranda, longitudine $\overline{\text{xxii}}$, antea Phoenice appellata; Odia; Oletandros; Gyara cum oppido, circuitu $\overline{\text{xv}}$, abest ab Andro $\overline{\text{lxii}}$; ab ea Syrnos $\overline{\text{lxxx}}$; Cynethus; Telos unguento nobilis, a Callimacho Agathusa appellata; Donusa; Patmus circuitu $\overline{\text{xxx}}$; Corassiae, Lebinthus, Gyrus, Cinara, Sicinus quae antea Oenoe; Heraclia quae Onus; Casos quae Astrabe; Cimolos quae Echinusa; Melos cum oppido quam Aristides Mimblida appellat,

^a The Scattered Islands.
^b Now Pira, Tecussa, Racchia, Schinusa and Polecandro.
^c This is an overstatement.
^d Named from the son of Daedalus, who fell into the sea here; now Nikaria.

the town of that name, 38 miles from Delos, famous
for its marble, and originally called Platea and afterwards Minois. Seven and a half miles from Paros
and 18 from Delos is Naxos with its town, which was
called Strongyle and then Dia and afterwards the
Island of Dionysus because of the fertility of its
vineyards, and by others Little Sicily or Callipolis.
Its circuit measures 75 miles and it is half as large
again as Paros.

So far the islands are regarded as belonging to the *Islands of*
Cyclades, but the remainder that follow are called *the central*
the Sporades.[a] They are Helene, Phacusa, Nicasia, *Aegean.*
Schinusa, Pholegandros,[b] and 38 miles from Naxos
and the same number of miles in length,[c] Icaros,[d]
which has given its name to the surrounding sea;
it has two towns, a third having disappeared; it was
formerly called Doliche or Long Island, also Fish
Island. It lies 50 miles north-east of Delos and 35
miles from Samos; between Euboea and Andros
there is a channel 10 miles wide, and the distance
from Icaros to Geraestus is 112½ miles.

After these no regular order can be kept, so the *Other islands*
remaining islands shall be given in a group: Scyro; *in Southern*
Nio, 18 miles from Naxos, venerable as the burial- *Aegean.*
place of Homer, 22 miles long, previously called
Phoenice; Odia; Oletandros; Gioura, with a town
of the same name, 15 miles in circumference, 62 miles
distant from Andros; 80 miles from Gioura, Syrnos;
Cynethus; Telos, noted for its unguent, and called by
Callimachus Agathusa; Donusa; Patmos, 30 miles
in circumference; the Corassiae, Lebitha, Lero,
Zinari; Sikino, previously Oenoe; Heraclia or Onus;
Casos or Astrabe; Kimoli or Echinusa; Milo, with
the town of that name, called by Aristides Mimblis,

Aristoteles Zephyriam, Callimachus Mimallida, Heraclides Siphin et Acytan: haec insularum rotundis-
sima est; Buporthmos; Machia; Hypere, quondam
Patage, ut alii, Platage, nunc Amorgos; Polyaegas;
Sapyle; Thera, cum primum emersit Calliste dicta:
ex ea avolsa postea Therasia, atque inter duas enata
mox Automate, eadem Hiera, et in nostro aevo
Thia iuxta easdem enata. distat Ios a Thera
$\overline{\text{XXV}}$ p.

71 Secuntur Lea, Ascania, Anaphe, Hippuris. Asty-
palaea liberae civitatis, circuitus $\overline{\text{LXXXVIII}}$, abest a
Cadisto Cretae $\overline{\text{CXXV}}$, ab ea Platea $\overline{\text{LX}}$, unde Caminia
$\overline{\text{XXXVIII}}$; Azibintha, Lamse, Atragia, Pharmacusa,
Thetaedia, Chalcia, Calymna in qua oppidum, Coos,
Eulimna, a qua Carpathum quae nomen Carpathio
mari dedit $\overline{\text{XXV}}$. inde Rhodum Africo vento $\overline{\text{L}}$; a
Carpatho Casum $\overline{\text{VII}}$, a Caso Samonium Cretae pro-
munturium $\overline{\text{XXX}}$. in Euripo autem Euboico, primo
fere introitu, Petaliae IV insulae, et in exitu Atalante.
Cyclades et Sporades ab oriente litoribus Icariis
Asiae, ab occidente Myrtois Atticae, a septentrione
Aegaeo mari, a meridie Cretico et Carpathio inclusae
per $\overline{\text{DCC}}$ in longitudinem et per $\overline{\text{CC}}$ in latitudinem
iacent.

72 Pagasicus sinus ante se habet Euthiam, Cicyne-
thum, Scyrum supra dictam sed Cycladum et Spora-

---

a Between Crete and Rhodes.
b See § 29.

by Aristotle Zephyria, by Callimachus Mimallis and by Heraclides Siphis and Acytas—the most circular in shape of all the islands; Buporthmos; Machia; Hypere, formerly called Patage, or by others Platage, now Amorgo; Polyaegas; Sapyle; Santorin, called Fair Island when it first emerged from the water; Therasia subsequently detached from it, and Automate or Holy Island, which soon afterwards arose between the two, and Thia, which emerged near the same islands in our own day. The distance between Santorin and Nio is 25 miles.

There follow Lea, Ascania, Namphi, and Hippuris. Stampalia, a free state, measuring 88 miles in circumference, is 125 miles from Cadistus in Crete; Platea 60 miles from Stampalia, and Caminia 38 miles from Platea; Azibintha, Lamse, Atragia, Pharmacusa, Thetaedia, Karki, Kalymni with its town, Coos, Eulimna, and at a distance of 25 miles from it Skarpanto, which has given its name to the Carpathian Sea.[a] From there to Rhodes, a south-west course, is 50 miles; from Skarpanto to Casus is 7 miles, from Casus to Cape Samonium in Crete 30. In the Euripus between Euboea and the mainland, almost at the first entrance, are the four Petaliae Islands, and at its outlet Talanti. The Cyclades and the Sporades are bounded on the east by the Asiatic coasts of the Icarian Sea, on the west by the Attic coasts of the Myrtoan Sea, on the north by the Aegean Sea and on the south by the Cretan and Carpathian coasts; these islands occupy an area 700 miles long and 200 miles broad.

Across the mouth of the Gulf of Volo [b] lie Euthia, *Islands of* Trikeri, Skyro, previously mentioned, and in fact the *Northern Aegean.* outermost of the Cyclades and Sporades, Gerontia

171

dum extimam, Gerontiam, Scandiram; Thermaeus
Iresiam, Solymniam, Eudemiam, Neam quae Minervae
sacra est; Athos ante se IV, Peparethum cum oppido,
quondam Evoenum dictam novem milia, Sciathum
x̄v̄, Imbrum cum oppido ᴸxxxvī̄ī̄; eadem abest a
Mastusia Cherronesi x̄x̄ī̄ī̄ p., ipsa circuitus ᴸx̄ī̄ī̄ D
73 perfunditur amne Ilisso. ab ea Lemnos x̄x̄ī̄ī̄, quae
ab Atho ᴸxxxvī̄ī̄; circuitu patet c̄x̄v̄ D p., oppida
habet Hephaestiam et Myrinam in cuius forum
solstitio Athos eiaculatur umbram. ab ea Thasos
libera v̄ī̄, olim Aeria vel Aethria dicta; inde Abdera
continentis x̄x̄ī̄ī̄, Athos ᴸx̄ī̄ī̄ D, tantundem insula
Samothrace libera ante Hebrum, ab Imbro x̄x̄x̄ī̄ī̄,
a Lemno x̄x̄ī̄ī̄ D p., a Thraciae ora x̄x̄x̄vī̄ī̄ī̄, circuitus
x̄x̄x̄v̄; attollitur monte Saoce x̄ p. altitudinis, vel
inportuosissima omnium. Callimachus eam antiquo
nomine Dardaniam vocat.

74 Inter Cherronesum et Samothracen, utrimque fere
x̄v̄ Halonesos, ultra Gethone, Lamponia, Alopeconnesus haut procul a Coelo Cherronesi portu, et
quaedam ignobiles. desertis quoque reddantur in
hoc sinu quarum modo inveniri potuere nomina:
Avesticos, Sarnos, Cissyros, Charbrusa, Calathusa,
Scyllia, Dialeon, Dictaea, Melanthia, Dracanon,

---

^a This is nearly double the actual distance.

^b Cf. Sophocles (Schol. ad Theocr. *Id.* 6. 72) ῍Αθως σκιάζει
νῶτα Λημνίας ἁλός. Myrina at the S.W. corner of Lemnos lies
at a distance of about 50 miles due S.E. of Mount Athos,
which is 6350 ft. high.

^c The text clamours for emendation—Warmington sug-
gests M p.—unless indeed the figure really gives not the height
of the peak but the length of the path up it. Baedeker,
Mediterranean, p. 533, gives the highest point on Samothrace
as 5250 ft., a little under a mile, and the altitude of Mont
Blanc is just under 3 miles English: the Roman mile was
142 yards shorter than the English.

and Scandira; across the Gulf of Saloniki Iresia
Solymnia, Eudemia and Nea, the last an island
sacred to Minerva; across the Gulf of Athos lie four
islands, Piperi with the town of that name and formerly
called Evoenus, 9 miles off, Sciathos 15 miles, and
Embro with its town 88 miles; the distance between
Embro and Mastusia on the Gallipoli Peninsula is
22 miles. Embro is 62½ miles in circuit; it is watered
by the river Ilissus. Twenty-two miles from Embro
is Stalimene, which lies 87 [a] miles from Mount Athos;
its circuit measures 115½ miles, and on it are the towns
of Hephaestia and Myrina—the market place of the
latter is reached by the shadow of Mount Athos [b]
at mid-summer. Six miles from Stalimene is Thasos,
a free state, formerly called Aeria or Aethria; Abdera
on the mainland is 22 miles from Thasos, and
Athos 62½ miles, and the island of Samothrace, a
free state, off the river Maritza, is the same distance
from Thasos, 32 miles from Embro, 22½ from Stalimene, and 38 from the coast of Thrace; its circuit
measures 35 miles, and on it rises Monte Nettuno,
which is 10 miles high.[c] Embro gives the worst
anchorage for vessels of all the islands. It is mentioned by Callimachus under its ancient name of
Dardania.

Between the Gallipoli peninsula and Samothrace, *Islands of*
about 15 miles from each, is the island of Skopelo, *N.E.Aegean.*
and beyond it are Gethone, Lamponia, Alopeconnesus,
which is not far from Coelos the port of Gallipoli,
and some others of no importance. We may also
specify the names of uninhabited islands in the Gulf
so far as we have been able to ascertain them:
Avesticos, Sarnos, Cissyros, Charbrusa, Calathusa,
Scyllia, Dialeon, Dictaea, Melanthia, Dracanon,

Arconesus, Diethusa, Ascapos, Capheris, Mesate,
Aeantion, Pateronnesos, Pateria, Calathe, Neriphus,
Pelendos.

75 Quartus e magnis Europae sinus ab Hellesponto
incipiens Maeotis ostio finitur. sed totius Ponti
forma breviter conplectenda est, ut facilius partes
noscantur. vastum mare praeiacens Asiae et ab
Europa porrecto Cherronesi litore expulsum angusto meatu inrumpit in terras, VII stadiorum, ut
dictum est, intervallo Europam auferens Asiae.
primas angustias Hellespontum vocant; hac Xerxes
Persarum rex constrato in navibus ponte duxit exercitum. porrigitur deinde tenuis euripus L̄XXXV̄Ī
spatio ad Priapum urbem Asiae, qua Magnus
76 Alexander transcendit. inde exspatiatur aequor
rursusque in artum coit. laxitas Propontis appellatur,
angustiae Thracius Bosporus, latitudine quingen-
torum passuum qua Darius pater Xerxis copias ponte
transvexit; tota ab Hellesponto longitudo C̄C̄XXXIX̄.

Dein vastum mare Pontus Euxinus, qui quondam
Axenus, longe refugientes occupat terras magnoque
litorum flexu retro curvatus in cornua ab his utrimque porrigitur, ut sit plane arcus Scythici forma.
medio flexu iungitur ostio Maeotii lacus; Cimmerius
Bosporus id os vocatur, II quingentos passus latitu-
77 dine. at inter duos Bosporos Thracium et Cim-

ᵃ The Inhospitable Sea (cf. VI. 1), so described as being
stormy, cold and without the shelter of islands on which Greek
navigators were accustomed to rely; but the ominous name
was euphemistically altered into Euxine, ' Hospitable.'

ᵇ Shaped in two curves meeting in an angle at the middle.
This describes the north coast of the Black Sea, the central
projection being the Thracian Chersonese, the Crimea. The
more or less straight south coast is the bowstring.

Arconesus, Diethusa, Ascapos, Capheris, Mesate, Aeantion, Pateronnesus, Pateria, Calathe, Neriphus, Pelendos.

The fourth of the great Gulfs of Europe begins at *Black Sea.* the Dardanelles and ends at the entrance of the Sea of Azov. But in order more easily to indicate the divisions of the Black Sea we must give a brief description of its shape as a whole. It is a vast body of water lying in front of Asia and shut out from Europe by the promontory of Gallipoli; but it forces an entrance into the interior by a narrow winding channel, and separates Europe from Asia, as has been said, by a strait that is less than a mile wide. The :49. first part of the narrows is called the Dardanelles; here the Persian king Xerxes made the bridge of boats across which he led his army. From there a narrow channel 86 miles long extends to the Asiatic city of Priapus; it was here that Alexander the Great crossed. From this point the water begins to widen out, and afterwards narrows again. The wide part is called the Sea of Marmara and the narrows the Straits of Constantinople; at the point where Xerxes' father Darius conveyed his forces across by means of a bridge it is 500 yards wide, and its entire length from the Dardanelles is 239 miles.

Then comes the vast extent of the Black Sea, formerly the Axenus,[a] which encroaches on a large area of the continent, and with a great bend of its coasts curves back into horns and from them stretches out on either side, producing exactly the shape of a Scythian bow.[b] In the middle of the curve it is joined by the mouth of the Sea of Azov; this aperture is called the Straits of Kertsch, and measures two and a half miles across. The distance in a straight line

merium directo cursu, ut auctor est Polybius, $\overline{\mathrm{D}}$ intersunt. circuitu vero totius Ponti viciens semel L, ut auctor est Varro et fere veteres; Nepos Cornelius $\overline{\mathrm{CCCL}}$ adicit, Artemidorus vicies semel et decem novem milia facit, Agrippa $\lceil\overline{\mathrm{XXV}}\rceil$ $\overline{\mathrm{XL}}$, Mucianus $\lceil\overline{\mathrm{XXIV}}\rceil$ $\overline{\mathrm{XXV}}$. simili modo de Europae latere mensuram alii

78 $\lceil\overline{\mathrm{XIV}}\rceil$ $\overline{\mathrm{LXXIX}}$ determinavere, alii $\lceil\overline{\mathrm{XI}}\rceil$. M. Varro ad hunc modum metitur: ab ostio Ponti Apolloniam $\overline{\mathrm{CLXXXVII}}$ D p., Callatim tantundem, ad ostium Histri $\overline{\mathrm{CXXV}}$, ad Borysthenem $\overline{\mathrm{CCL}}$, Cherronesum Heracleotarum oppidum $\overline{\mathrm{CCCLXXV}}$ p., ad Panticapaeum quod aliqui Bosporum vocant, extremum in Europae ora, $\overline{\mathrm{CCXII}}$ D, quae summa efficit $\lceil\overline{\mathrm{XIII}}\rceil$ $\overline{\mathrm{XXXVII}}$ D. Agrippa a Byzantio ad flumen Histrum $\overline{\mathrm{DXL}}$, inde Panticapaeum $\overline{\mathrm{DCXXXV}}$.

Lacus ipse Maeotis Tanain amnem ex Ripaeis montibus defluentem accipiens, novissimum inter Europam Asiamque finem, $\lceil\overline{\mathrm{XIV}}\rceil$ $\overline{\mathrm{VI}}$ circuitu patere traditur, ab aliis $\lceil\overline{\mathrm{XI}}\rceil$ $\overline{\mathrm{XXV}}$. ab ostio eius ad Tanais ostium directo cursu $\overline{\mathrm{CCCLXXV}}$ esse constat. accolae sinus eius in mentione Thraciae dicti sunt Histropolin usque.

79 Inde ostia Histri. ortus hic in Germania iugis montis Abnouae ex adverso Raurici Galliae oppidi, multis ultra Alpes milibus ac per innumeras lapsus

---

[a] This name is applied vaguely to all the ranges of Northern Europe and Asia. As a matter of fact the Don rises in the centre of European Russia.

[b] At Donaueschingen.

[c] The Black Forest.

[d] Named after the Raurici of Gallia Belgica; probably Augst near Basel.

between the two straits, the Dardanelles and Kaffa, measures according to Polybius 500 miles. The whole circumference of the Black Sea according to Varro and the old authorities generally is 2150 miles, but Cornelius Nepos adds 350 miles, while Artemidorus makes it 2119 miles, Agrippa 2540, and Mucianus 2425. There is a similar difference of opinion as to the measurement of the European shore, some fixing it at 1479 miles and others at 1100. Marcus Varro gives the measurement as follows: from the mouth of the Black Sea to Apollonia 187½ miles; from there to Collat the same; to the mouth of the Danube 125; to the Dnieper 250; to the town of Cherronesus of the Heracleotae 375 miles; to Kertsch, by some called Bosporus, the last point on the coast of Europe, 212½ miles—the total making 1337½ miles. Agrippa makes it 540 miles from Istamboul to the river Danube and 635 miles from the Danube to Kertsch.

The actual Sea of Azov, which receives the Don *Sea of Azov.* flowing down from the Ripaean Mountains,[a] the river being the extreme boundary between Europe and Asia, is said to measure 1406, or according to other authorities 1125, miles in circumference. The distance in a straight line between the entrance of the Sea of Azov and the mouth of the Don is agreed to be 375 miles. The inhabitants of the coasts of *§ 44 f.* this great Gulf as far as Istere have been mentioned in our account of Thrace.

We then come to the mouths of the Danube. *Geography of* It rises [b] in Germany in the range of Mount Abnoua,[c] *the Danube.* opposite to the Gallic town of Rauricum,[d] and flows for a course of many miles beyond the Alps, and through innumerable tribes, under the name of Danube; then its volume of water increases enor-

gentes Danuvi nomine, immenso aquarum auctu et
unde primum Illyricum alluit Hister appellatus, LX
amnibus receptis, medio ferme eorum numero
navigabili, in Pontum vastis sex fluminibus evolvitur.
primum ostium Peuces, mox ipsa Peuce insula, in
qua proximus alveus Sacer [1] appellatus $\overline{XIX}$ p. magna
palude sorbetur. ex eodem alveo et super Histro-
polin lacus gignitur $\overline{LXIII}$ passuum ambitu: Halmyrin
vocant. secundum ostium Naracustoma appellatur,
tertium Calon Stoma iuxta insulam Sarmaticam,
quartum Pseudostomon, dein insula Conopon Dia-
basis, postea Borion Stoma et Psilon Stoma. singula
autem ora tanta sunt ut prodatur in $\overline{XL}$ passuum
longitudinis vinci mare dulcemque intellegi haustum.

80   Ab eo in plenum quidem omnes Scytharum sunt
gentes, variae tamen litori apposita tenuere, alias
Getae, Daci Romanis dicti, alias Sarmatae, Graecis
Sauromatae, eorumque Hamaxobii aut Aorsi, alias
Scythae degeneres et a servis orti aut Trogodytae,
mox Alani et Rhoxolani. superiora autem inter
Danuvium et Hercynium saltum usque ad Pannonica
hiberna Carnunti Germanorumque ibi confinium
campos et plana Iazyges Sarmatae, montes vero et
81 saltus pulsi ab his Daci ad Pathissum amnem. a
Maro, sive Duria est a Suebis regnoque Vanniano

---

[1] Sacer *add. Urlichs.*

---

[a] The mountains stretching round Bohemia and through
Moravia into Hungary.

mously and from the point where it first enters
Illyria it is called the Hister; after receiving 60
tributary rivers, nearly half of which are navigable,
it is discharged into the Black Sea by six vast channels.
The first of these is the mouth of Piczina, close to the
island of that name, at which the nearest channel,
called the Holy River, is swallowed up in a marsh
19 miles in extent. Opening from the same channel
and above Istere spreads a lake measuring 63
miles round, named the Saltings. The second is
called the Narakian Mouth; the third, next the
island of Sarmatica, Fair Mouth; the fourth,
False Mouth; then comes the island of Mosquito
Crossing, afterwards the North Mouth and the Barren
Mouth. These mouths are each of them so large
that for a distance of forty miles, so it is said, the
sea is overpowered and the water tastes fresh.

From this point all the races in general are *Populations*
Scythian, though various sections have occupied *north of the*
the lands adjacent to the coast, in one place the *Danube.*
Getae, called by the Romans Dacians, at another the
Sarmatae, called by the Greeks Sauromatae, and the
section of them called Waggon-dwellers or Aorsi,
at another the base-born Scythians, descended from
slaves, or else the Cave-dwellers, and then the
Alani and Rhoxolani. The higher parts between
the Danube and the Hercynian Forest [a] as far as
the winter quarters of Pannonia at Carnuntum and
the plains and level country of the German frontiers
there are occupied by the Sarmatian Iazyges, while
the Dacians whom they have driven out hold the
mountains and forests as far as the river Theiss.
From the river Maros, or else the Dora if it is that
which separates them from the Suebi and the

179

PLINY: NATURAL HISTORY

dirimens eos, aversa Basternae tenent aliique inde
Germani. Agrippa totum eum tractum ab Histro
ad oceanum bis ad decies centenum [1] milium passuum in longitudinem, quattuor milibus minus
$\overline{cccc}$ [2] in latitudinem, ad flumen Vistlam a desertis
Sarmatiae prodidit. Scytharum nomen usquequa-
que transiit [3] in Sarmatas atque Germanos; nec
aliis prisca illa duravit appellatio quam qui extremi
gentium harum ignoti prope ceteris mortalibus
degunt.

82   Verum ab Histro oppida Cremniscoe, Aepolium,
montes Macrocremni, clarus amnis Tyra, oppido
nomen inponens ubi antea Ophiusa dicebatur. in
eodem insulam spatiosam incolunt Tyragetae; abest
a Pseudostomo Histri ostio $\overline{cxxx}$. mox Axiacae
cognomines flumini, ultra quos Crobyzi, flumen
Rhode, sinus Sangarius, portus Ordesos. et a Tyra
$\overline{cxx}$ flumen Borysthenes lacusque et gens eodem
nomine et oppidum ab mari recedens $\overline{xv}$ passuum,
83 Olbiopolis et Miletopolis antiquis nominibus. rursus
litore portus Achaeorum, insula Achillis tumulo
eius viri clara, et ab ea $\overline{cxxv}$ passuum paeninsula ad
formam gladii in transversum porrecta, exercitatione
eiusdem cognominata Dromos Achilleos, cuius longitudinem $\overline{lxxx}$ tradidit Agrippa. totum eum tractum tenent Sardi Scythae et Siraci. inde silvestris
regio Hylaeum mare quo adluitur cognominavit;

---

[1] *Jan*: centum.
[2] *Mayhoff*: *varia codd.*
[3] *Niebuhr*: transit.

---

[a] A chief of the Vadi, made king of the Swabians by
Germanicus, A.D. 19.
[b] Now the Teligul.

180

Kingdom of Vannius,[a] the opposite side of the country is occupied by the Basternae and then other German tribes. Agrippa describes the whole of this area from the Danube to the sea as being 1200 miles in length by 396 in breadth, as far as the river Vistula in the direction of the Sarmatian desert. The name of Scythians has spread in every direction, as far as the Sarmatae and the Germans, but this old designation has not continued for any except the most outlying sections of these races, living almost unknown to the rest of mankind.

After the Danube come the towns of Cremniscoi and Aepolium, the Macrocremni Mountains, and the famous river Dniester, which gives its name to the town on the site which previously was called Ophiusa. A large island in the Dniester, inhabited by the Tyragetae, is 130 miles from the False Mouth of the Danube. Then come the Axiacae named from the river Axiaces,[b] and beyond them the Crobyzi, the river Rhode, the Sangarian Gulf, the port of Ordesus, and 120 miles from the Dniester the river Dnieper and the lake and tribe of the same name, and the town 15 miles inland from the sea, the old names of which were Olbiopolis and Miletopolis. Returning to the coast, we come to the Port of the Achaeans and the Isle of Achilles, famous for the tomb of that hero, and 125 miles from it a peninsula stretching out at a slant in the shape of a sword, and called the Race-course of Achilles from having been his exercising ground; its length is given by Agrippa as 80 miles. The whole of this stretch is occupied by the Scythian Sardi and Siraci. Then there is a wooded region that has given its name to the Forest Sea that washes its coast; the

North coast of Black Sea.

Enoecadioe vocantur incolae. ultra Panticapes
amnis qui Nomadas et Georgos disterminat, mox
Acesinus. quidam Panticapen confluere infra Ol-
biam cum Borysthene tradunt, diligentiores Hypanim, tanto errore eorum qui illum in Asiae parte
prodidere.

84 Mare subit magno recessu, donec v̄ passuum intervallo absit a Maeotide, vasta ambiens spatia mul-
tasque gentes; sinus Carcinites appellatur. flumen
Pacyris, oppida Navarum, Carcine, a tergo lacus
Buces fossa emissus in mare. ipse Buces a Coreto
Maeotis lacus sinu petroso discluditur dorso. recipit
amnes Bucem, Gerrhum, Hypanim, ex diverso
venientes tractu: nam Gerrhus Basilidas et Nomadas
separat, Hypanis per Nomadas et Hylaeos fluit
manu facto alveo in Bucen, naturali in Coretum:
regio Scythia Sindica nominatur.

85 Sed a Carcinite Taurica incipit, quondam mari
circumfusa et ipsa qua nunc campi iacent; dein
vastis attollitur iugis. triginta sunt eorum populi,
ex iis mediterranei XXIII, VI oppida Orgocyni, Characeni, Assyrani, Stactari, Acisalitae, Caliordi, iugum
ipsum Scythotauri tenent. cluduntur ab occidente

ᵃ On the west of the Tauric Chersonese, the modern Crimea.
ᵇ The 7 tribes named with the 23 above make up the 30.

inhabitants are called the tribe of the Indigenae. Beyond is the river Somara, which forms the boundary between the Nomad and Agricultural tribes, and then the Acesinus. Some authorities say that below Olbia the Somara flows into the Dnieper, but the more accurate make the Bug a tributary of the Dnieper—so erroneous it is to put the latter in a region of Asia.

Here the sea runs in, forming a large gulf, until *Gulf of* there is only a space of five miles separating it from *Negropoli.* the Sea of Azov, and it forms the coastline of vast tracts of land and numerous races; this is called the Gulf of Negropoli.[a] Here is the river Pacyris, the towns of Navarum and Carcine, and behind them Lake Buces, which discharges into the sea by an artificial channel. Lake Buces itself is shut off by a rocky ridge from the Bay of Coretus in the Sea of Azov. Into it run the rivers Buces, Gerrhus and Bug, coming from different directions: for the Gerrhus separates the Nomads and the Basilides, while the Bug flows through the Nomads and Foresters and discharges by an artificially made channel into the Buces and by a natural channel into the Coretus: this region has the name of Scythia Sindica.

At the river Carcinites begins the Crimea, itself *Crimea.* also formerly surrounded by the sea where there are now low-lying stretches of land, though afterwards it rises in huge mountain ridges. The population includes 30 tribes; of these 23 live in the interior, 6 towns are occupied by the Orgocyni, Characeni, Assyrani, Stactari, Acisalitae and Caliordi, and the Scythotauri[b] occupy the actual ridge. On the west side they are adjoined by the New Peninsula and on

183

Cherroneso Nea, ab ortu Scythis Sataucis. in ora
a Carcine oppida Taphrae in ipsis angustiis peninsulae,
mox Heraclea Cherronesus libertate a Romanis
donatum; Megarice vocabatur antea, praecipui
nitoris in toto eo tractu custoditis Graeciae moribus,
86 v̄ passuum ambiente muro. inde Parthenium
promunturium, Taurorum civitas Placia, Symbolum
portus, promunturium Criumetopon adversum Caram-
bicon Asiae promunturium per medium Euxinum
procurrens c̄l̄x̄x̄ intervallo, quae maxime ratio Scythici
arcus formam efficit. ab eo Taurorum portus multi et
lacus. oppidum Theodosia a Criumetopo c̄x̄x̄v̄ p., a
Cherroneso vero c̄l̄x̄v̄. ultra fuere oppida Cytae,
87 Zephyrium, Acrae, Nymphaeum, Dia; restat longe
validissimum in ipso Bospori introitu Panticapaeum
Milesiorum, a Theodosia l̄x̄x̄x̄v̄īī D p., a Cimmerio
vero oppido trans fretum sito MM D, ut diximus,
passus: haec ibi latitudo Asiam ab Europa separat,
eaque ipsa pedibus plerumque pervia glaciato freto.
Bospori Cimmerii longitudo [1] x̄īī D passuum oppida
habet Hermisium, Myrmecium et intus insulam
Alopecen. per Maeotim autem ab extremo isthmo,
qui locus Taphrae vocatur, ad os Bospori c̄c̄l̄x̄ longitudo colligitur.
88 A Taphris per continentem introrsus tenent
Auchetae apud quos Hypanis oritur, Neuroe apud

[1] *Pintianus*: latitudo.

---

[a] Aia-burun, the southern point of the Crimea.
[b] Cf. § 76.

the east by the Satauci Scythians. The towns on the coast after Carcine are Taphrae at the actual neck of the peninsula, and then the Heraclean Peninsula, a place on which Rome has recently bestowed freedom; it was formerly called Megarice, and is the most highly cultured community in all this region owing to its having preserved the manners of Greece; it is encircled by a wall measuring five miles. Then come the Virgin's Cape, Placia a city of the Tauri, the port of Balaklava, Ram's Head Cape,[a] jutting out into the middle of the Black Sea opposite to Cape Kerempi in Asia with a space between them of 170 miles, which is chiefly the reason that produces the shape of a Scythian bow.[b] After this come a number of harbours and lakes belonging to the Tauri. The town of Theodosia is 125 miles from Ram's Head and 165 from the Peninsula. Beyond it there were in former times the towns of Cytae, Zephyrium, Acrae, Nymphaeum and Dia; while by far the strongest of them all, the Milesian city of Kertsch, at the actual mouth of the Straits, still stands; it is 87½ miles from Theodosia and 2½ miles, as we have said, from the town of Cimmerium situated across the Straits—this is the width that here separates Asia from Europe, and even this can usually be crossed on foot when the Gulf is frozen over. On the Straits of Kertsch, the length of which is 12½ miles, are the towns of Hermisium and Myrmecium, and inside the Straits is the island of Alopece. The coast of the Sea of Azov, from the place called Taphrae at the end of the isthmus to the mouth of the Straits of Kertsch measures altogether 260 miles.

After Taphrae, the interior of the mainland is occupied by the Auchetai and the Neuroi, in whose

quos Borysthenes, Geloni, Thyssagetae, Budini,
Basilidae et caeruleo capillo Agathyrsi; super eos
Nomades, deinde Anthropophagi, a Buce vero super
Maeotim Sauromatae et Essedones. at per oram
ad Tanain usque Maeotae, a quibus lacus nomen
accepti, ultimique a tergo eorum Arimaspi. mox
Ripaei montes et adsiduo nivis casu pinnarum
similitudine Pterophoros appellata regio, pars mundi
damnata a rerum natura et densa mersa caligine,
neque in alio quam rigoris opere [1] gelidisque Aqui-
89 lonis conceptaculis. pone eos montes ultraque
Aquilonem gens felix (si credimus), quos Hyperboreos appellavere, annoso degit aevo, fabulosis
celebrata miraculis. ibi creduntur esse cardines
mundi extremique siderum ambitus semenstri luce
et una die [2] solis aversi,[3] non, ut imperiti dixere, ab
aequinoctio verno in autumnum: semel in anno
solstitio oriuntur iis soles, brumaque semel occidunt.
regio aprica felici temperie, omni adflatu noxio
carens. domus iis nemora lucique, et deorum
cultus viritim gregatimque, discordia ignota et
aegritudo omnis. mors non nisi satietate vitae,
epulatis delibutoque senio luxu, e quadam rupe in
mare salientibus [4]: hoc genus sepulturae beatissi-

---

[1] *Menda latet.*
[2] [et una die] *Solmsen.*
[3] *V. l.* adversi.
[4] *Caesarius*: salientium.

---

[a] See § 78, note.
[b] The Latin text is corrupt.

territories respectively are the sources of the Bug
and the Dnieper, the Geloni, Thyssagetae, Budini,
Basilidae and Agathyrsi, the last a dark-haired
people; above them are the Nomads and then the
Cannibals, and after Lake Buces above the Sea of
Azov the Sauromatae and Essedones. Along the
coast, as far as the river Don, are the Maeotae from
whom the sea receives its name, and last of all in the
rear of the Maeotae are the Arimaspi. Then come
the Ripaean Mountains [a] and the region called
Pterophorus, because of the feather-like snow con-
tinually falling there; it is a part of the world that
lies under the condemnation of nature and is plunged
in dense darkness, and occupied only by the work of
frost and the chilly lurking-places of the north wind.[b]
Behind these mountains and beyond the north wind *The Hyper-*
there dwells (if we can believe it) a happy race of *boreans.*
people called the Hyperboreans, who live to extreme
old age and are famous for legendary marvels. Here
are believed to be the hinges on which the firmament
turns and the extreme limits of the revolutions of
the stars, with six months' daylight and a single day
of the sun in retirement, not as the ignorant have
said, from the spring equinox till autumn: for these
people the sun rises once in the year, at midsummer,
and sets once, at midwinter. It is a genial region,
with a delightful climate and exempt from every
harmful blast. The homes of the natives are the
woods and groves; they worship the gods severally
and in congregations; all discord and all sorrow is
unknown. Death comes to them only when, owing
to satiety of life, after holding a banquet and anoint-
ing their old age with luxury, they leap from a certain
rock into the sea: this mode of burial is the most

90 mum. quidam eos in prima parte Asiae litorum
posuere, non in Europa, quia sunt ibi simili consuetudine et situ Attacorum nomine; alii medios fecere
eos inter utrumque solem, antipodum occasus
exorientemque nostrum, quod fieri nullo modo potest
tam vasto mari interveniente. qui non alibi quam
in semenstri luce constituere eos, serere matutinis,
meridie metere, occidente fetus arborum decerpere,
91 noctibus in specus condi tradiderunt. nec licet
dubitare de gente ea: tot auctores produnt frugum
primitias solitos Delum mittere Apollini, quem
praecipue colunt. virgines ferebant eas hospitiis
gentium per annos aliquot venerabiles, donec violata
fide in proximis accolarum finibus deponere sacra ea
instituere, hique ad conterminos deferre, atque ita
Delum usque. mox et hoc ipsum exolevit.

Sarmatiae, Scythiae, Tauricae, omnisque a Borys-
thene amne tractus longitudo $\overline{\text{DCCCCLXXX}}$, latitudo
$\overline{\text{DCCXVI}}$ a M. Agrippa tradita est; ego incertam in
hac terrarum parte mensuram arbitror.

Verum instituto ordine reliqua huius sinus dicantur; et maria quidem eius nuncupavimus.

---

^a *E.g.* Herodotus IV. 32 ff.

blissful. Some authorities have placed these people not in Europe but on the nearest part of the coasts of Asia, because there is a race there with similar customs and a similar location, named the Attaci; others have put them midway between the two suns, the sunsets of the antipodes and our sunrise, but this is quite impossible because of the enormous expanse of sea that comes between. Those who locate them merely in a region having six months of daylight have recorded that they sow in the morning periods, reap at midday, pluck the fruit from the trees at sunset, and retire into caves for the night. Nor is it possible to doubt about this race, as so many authorities [a] state that they regularly send the first fruits of their harvests to Delos as offerings to Apollo, whom they specially worship. These offerings used to be brought by virgins, who for many years were held in veneration and hospitably entertained by the nations on the route, until because of a violation of good faith they instituted the custom of depositing their offerings at the nearest frontiers of the neighbouring people, and these of passing them on to their neighbours, and so till they finally reached Delos. Later this practice itself also passed out of use.

The territories of Sarmatia, Scythia and Taurica, and the whole region from the river Dnieper are stated by Marcus Agrippa to measure 980 miles in length and 716 in breadth; but for my own part I consider that in this part of the world estimates of measurement are uncertain. *Measurements of S. Russia.*

But in conformity with the plan set out the remaining features of this gulf must be stated. Its seas we have specified. *§ 75 f.*

92 XIII. Hellespontus insulas non habet in Europa dicendas. in Ponto duae, M D ab Europa, $\overline{xiv}$ ab ostio, Cyaneae, ab aliis Symplegades appellatae, traditaeque fabulis inter se concucurrisse, quoniam parvo discretae intervallo ex adverso intrantibus geminae cernebantur paulumque deflexa acie coeuntium speciem praebebant. citra Histrum Apolloniarum [1] una $\overline{lxxx}$ a Bosporo Thracio, ex qua M. Lucullus Capitolinum Apollinem advexit. inter ostia Histri
93 quae essent diximus. ante Borysthenen Achillea est supra dicta, eadem Leuce et Macaron appellata. hanc temporum horum demonstratio a Borysthene $\overline{cxl}$ ponit, a Tyra $\overline{cxx}$, a Peuce insula $\overline{l}$. cingitur circiter $\overline{x}$ p. reliquae in Carcinite sinu Cephalonnesos, Spodusa, Macra. non est omittenda multorum opinio, priusquam digredimur a Ponto, qui maria omnia interiora illo capite nasci, non Gaditano freto, existimavere haut inprobabili argumento, quoniam aestus semper e Ponto profluens numquam reciprocet.
94 Exeundum deinde est ut extera Europae dicantur,

---

[1] *Rackham:* Apollonitarum *aut* Apolloniatarum.

---

[a] Later Sozopolis, now Sizeboli, see § 45; and for the other Apollonia see VI. 32.

[b] A colossal work about 50 ft. high, brought to Rome by M. Licinius Lucullus when he retired from his province of Macedonia in 71 B.C. After being carried in his triumph it was set up in the Capitol.

XIII. In the Dardanelles there are no islands *Islands of*
that deserve mention belonging to Europe. There *the Black*
are two in the Black Sea, 1½ miles from the European *Sea.*
coast and 14 miles from the mouth of the straits, the
Fanari, called by others the Symplegades, these
being the islands about which there is the tradition
that they once clashed together: the story is due
to the fact that they are separated by so small a
gap that by persons entering the Black Sea
directly facing them they were seen as two, and
then when the line of sight became slightly oblique
they gave the appearance of coming together. On
this side of the Danube there is one of the islands *a*
called Apollonia, 80 miles from the Thracian
Bosphorus; from this island Marcus Lucullus
brought the statue *b* of Apollo of the Capitol. We
have stated the places in the Delta of the Danube. § 79.
Off the mouth of the Dnieper is the Island of
Achilles mentioned above, which also has the Greek § 83.
names of the White Island and Island of the Blest.
Modern investigation shows the position of this
island to be 140 miles from the Dnieper, 120 from
the Dniester, and 50 from the island of Peuce. It is
about 10 miles in circuit. The remaining islands in
the Gulf of Carcinites are Cephalonnesus, Spodusa
and Macra. Before we leave the Black Sea, we must
not omit the opinion held by many persons that all
the waters of the Mediterranean are derived from this
source, and not from the Straits of Gibraltar; the
reason that they give for this view is not an improbable
one—viz. that the tide is always flowing out of the
Black Sea and never ebbing in the other direction.

Next we must leave the Black Sea to describe the *Islands of*
outer regions of Europe, and crossing the Ripaean *the Northern*
Ocean.

transgressisque Ripaeos montes litus oceani septentrionalis in laeva, donec perveniatur Gadis, legendum.
insulae complures sine nominibus eo situ traduntur,
ex quibus ante Scythiam quae appellatur Baunonia
unam abesse diei cursu, in quam veris tempore
fluctibus electrum eiciatur, Timaeus prodidit. reliqua litora incerta signata fama. septentrionalis[1]
oceanus: Amalchium eum Hecataeus appellat a
Parapaniso amne, qua Scythiam adluit, quod nomen
95 eius gentis lingua significat congelatum; Philemon
Morimarusam a Cimbris vocari, hoc est mortuum
mare, inde usque ad promunturium Rusbeas, ultra
deinde Cronium. Xenophon Lampsacenus a litore
Scytharum tridui navigatione insulam esse inmensae
magnitudinis Balciam tradit, eandem Pytheas
Basiliam nominat. feruntur et Oeonae in quis ovis
avium et avenis incolae vivant, aliae in quibus equinis
pedibus homines nascantur Hippopodes appellati,
Panotiorum[2] aliae in quibus nuda alioqui corpora
praegrandes ipsorum aures tota contegant.
96   Incipit deinde clarior aperiri fama ab gente In-
guaeonum quae est prima in Germania. mons
Saevo ibi inmensus nec Ripaeis iugis minor inmanem
ad Cimbrorum usque promunturium efficit sinum,
qui Codanus vocatur refertus insulis quarum clarissima est Scatinavia, inconpertae magnitudinis, por-

---

[1] *Vel* incerta. signata fama septentrionalis . . . *sed cf.*
§ 96 *init.*
[2] *Sillig ex Isidoro* (Phanesiorum *alii e Solino*): fanesiorum.

---

[a] See p. 176, note *a*.
[b] Presumably the islands of the Baltic.
[c] Heligoland, or perhaps Bornholm.

Mountains ^a must coast to the left along the shore of the northern ocean until we reach Cadiz. In this direction a number of islands ^b are reported to exist that have no names, but according to the account of Timaeus there is one named Baunonia,^c lying off Scythia, at a distance of a day's voyage from the coast, on the beach of which in spring time amber is cast up by the waves. The rest of these coasts are only known in detail by reports of doubtful authority. To the north is the ocean; beyond the river Parapanisus where it washes the coast of Scythia Hecataeus calls it the Amalchian Sea, a name that in the language of the natives means 'frozen'; Philemon says that the Cimbrian name for it is Morimarusa (that is, 'Dead Sea') from the Parapanisus to Cape Rusbeae, and from that point onward the Cronian Sea. Xenophon of Lampsacus reports that three days' sail from the Scythian coast there is an island of enormous size called Balcia; Pytheas gives its name as Basilia. Also some islands called the Oeonae are reported of which the inhabitants live on birds' eggs and oats, and others on which people are born with horses' feet, which gives them their Greek name; there are others called the All-ears Islands in which the natives have very large ears covering the whole of their bodies, which are otherwise left naked.

From this point more definite information begins to open up, beginning with the race of the Inguaeones, the first that we come to in Germany. Here there is an enormous mountain, the Saevo, as big as those of the Ripaean range, which forms an enormous bay reaching to the Cimbrian promontory; it is named the Codanian Gulf, and is studded with islands. The most famous of these is Scandinavia; its size

tionem tantum eius, quod notum sit, Hillevionum
gente quingentis incolente pagis, quae alterum
orbem terrarum eam appellat. nec minor est
97 opinione Aeningia. quidam haec habitari ad Vistlam usque fluvium a Sarmatis, Venedis, Sciris, Hirris
tradunt, sinum Cylipenum vocari, et in ostio insulam
Latrim, mox alterum sinum Lagnum conterminum
Cimbris. promunturium Cimbrorum excurrens in
maria longe paeninsulam efficit quae Tastris appellatur. XXIII inde insulae Romanis armis cognitae;
earum nobilissimae Burcana, Fabaria nostris dicta a
frugis multitudine [1] sponte provenientis, item
Glaesaria a sucino militiae appellata, a barbaris
Austeravia, praeterque Actania.

98   Toto autem mari ad Scaldim usque fluvium Germaniae accolunt gentes haud explicabili mensura:
tam immodica prodentium discordia est. Graeci
et quidam nostri $\overline{|XXV|}$ oram Germaniae tradiderunt,
Agrippa cum Raetia et Norico longitudinem $\overline{DCLXXXVI}$,
latitudinem $\overline{CCXLVIII}$, (XIV.) Raetiae prope unius
maiore latitudine, sane circa excessum eius subactae,
nam Germania multis postea annis nec tota percognita
99 est. si coniectare permittitur, haut multum ora
deerit Graecorum opinioni et longitudini ab Agrippa
proditae.

Germanorum genera quinque: Vandili quorum

---

[1] similitudine *vulg.*

---

[a] The cape of Skagen on the north of Jutland.
[b] Borkhum, at the mouth of the Ems.

has not been ascertained, and so far as is known, only part of it is inhabited, its natives being the Hilleviones, who dwell in 500 villages, and call their island a second world. Aeningia is thought to be equally big. Some authorities report that these regions as far as the river Vistula are inhabited by the Sarmati, Venedi, Sciri and Hirri, and that there is a gulf named Cylipenus, with the island of Latris at its mouth, and then another gulf, that of Lagnus, at which is the frontier of the Cimbri. The Cimbrian promontory projects a long way into the sea, forming a peninsula called Tastris.[a] Then there are twenty-three islands known to the armed forces of Rome; the most noteworthy of these are Burcana,[b] called by our people Bean Island from the quantity of wild beans growing there, and the island which by the soldiery is called Glass Island from its amber, but by the barbarians Austeravia, and also Actania.

The whole of the sea-coast as far as the German river *Population* Scheldt is inhabited by races the extent of whose terri- *of Northern* tories it is impossible to state, so unlimited is the dis- *Europe.* agreement among the writers who report about them. The Greek writers and some of our own have given the coast of Germany as measuring 2500 miles, while Agrippa makes the length of Germany includ- ing Raetia and Noricum 686 miles and the breadth 248 miles, (XIV.) whereas the breadth of Raetia alone almost exceeds that figure; though to be sure it was only conquered about the time of Agrippa's death— for Germany was explored many years after, and that not fully. If one may be allowed to conjecture, the coast will be found to be not much shorter than the Greek idea of it and the length given by Agrippa.

There are five German races: the Vandals, who *Germany.*

pars Burgodiones, Varinnae, Charini, Gutones;
alterum genus Inguaeones, quorum pars Cimbri,
100 Teutoni ac Chaucorum gentes; proximi autem
Rheno Istiaeones, quorum pars Sicambri; mediterranei Hermiones, quorum Suebi, Hermunduri, Chatti,
Cherusci; quinta pars Peucini, Basternae supra
dictis contermini Dacis. amnes clari oceanum
defluunt Guthalus, Visculus sive Vistla, Albis, Visur-
gis, Amisis, Rhenus, Mosa. introrsus vero nullo
inferius nobilitate Hercynium iugum praetenditur.

101   XV. In Rheno autem ipso, prope c̄ in longitudinem, nobilissima Batavorum insula et Cannene-
fatium, et aliae Frisiorum, Chaucorum, Frisiavonum,
Sturiorum, Marsaciorum quae sternuntur inter
Helinium ac Flevum. ita appellantur ostia in quae
effusus Rhenus a septentrione in lacus, ab occidente
in amnem Mosam se spargit, medio inter haec ore
modicum nomini suo custodiens alveum.

102   XVI. Ex adverso huius situs Britannia insula clara
Graecis nostrisque monimentis inter septentrionem
et occidentem iacet, Germaniae, Galliae, Hispaniae,
multo maximis Europae partibus magno intervallo
adversa. Albion ipsi nomen fuit, cum Britanniae
vocarentur omnes de quibus mox paulo dicemus.
haec abest a Gesoriaco Morinorum gentis litore
proximo traiectu l̄. circuitu patere |xxxxviii| lxxv
Pytheas et Isidorus tradunt, xxx prope iam annis

---

^a Perhaps the Oder.
^b Used as a general name for all the mountains of Southern
and Central Germany.
^c Dionysius *Periegesis*, Τάων τοι μέγεθος περιώσιον, οὐδέ τις
ἄλλη Νήσοις ἐν πάσαισι Βρετάννεσιν ἰσοφαρίζει.
^d Boulogne.
^e This is an overstatement even if measured to the Roman
fort of Rutupiae, Richborough.

include the Burgodiones, Varinnae, Charini and
Gutones; the second race the Inguaeones, including
Cimbri, Teutoni and the tribes of the Chauci; nearest
to the Rhine the Istiaeones, including the Sicambri;
inland the Hermiones, including the Suebi, Hermunduri, Chatti and Cherusci; and the fifth section
the Peucini, and the Basternae who march with the
Dacians above mentioned. Notable rivers that flow
into the Ocean are the Guthalus,[a] the Visculus or
Vistula, the Elbe, the Weser, the Ems, the Rhine and
the Meuse. In the interior stretches the Hercinian
range[b] of mountains, which is inferior to none in
grandeur.

XV. In the Rhine itself, the most notable island is *The Rhine.*
that of the Batavi and Cannenefates, which is almost
a hundred miles in length, and others are those
of the Frisii, Chauci, Frisiavones, Sturii and Marsacii,
which lie between Briel and Vlieland. The latter
give their names to the mouths into which the Rhine
divides, discharging itself on the north into the lakes
there and on the west into the river Meuse, while
at the middle mouth between these two it keeps a
small channel for its own name.

XVI. Opposite to this region lies the island of *Britain.*
Britain, famous in the Greek records[c] and in our
own; it lies to the north-west, facing, across a
wide channel, Germany, Gaul and Spain, countries
which constitute by far the greater part of Europe.
It was itself named Albion, while all the islands about
which we shall soon briefly speak were called the
Britains. Its distance from Gesoriacum[d] on the coast
of the Morini tribe by the shortest passage is 50
miles.[e] Its circumference is reported by Pytheas and
Isidorus to measure 4875 miles; nearly thirty years

notitiam eius Romanis armis non ultra vicinitatem
silvae Calidoniae propagantibus. Agrippa longitu-
dinem $\overline{\text{DCCC}}$ esse, latitudinem $\overline{\text{CCC}}$ credit, eandem
103 Hiberniae, sed longitudinem $\overline{\text{CC}}$ minorem. super
eam haec sita abest brevissimo transitu a Silurum
gente $\overline{\text{XXX}}$. reliquarum nulla cxxv amplior circuitu
proditur. sunt autem xl Orcades modicis inter se
discretae spatiis, vii Acmodae, xxx Hebudes, et inter
Hiberniam ac Britanniam Mona, Monapia, Riginia,
Vectis, Silumnus, Andros, infra vero Sambis et
Axanthos, et ab adversa in Germanicum mare sparsae
Glaesariae[1] quas Electridas Graeci recentiores
104 appellavere, quod ibi electrum nasceretur. ultima
omnium quae memorantur Tyle, in qua solstitio
nullas esse noctes indicavimus, cancri signum sole
transeunte, nullosque contra per brumam dies;
hoc quidam senis mensibus continuis fieri arbitrantur.
Timaeus historicus a Britannia introrsum sex dierum
navigatione abesse dicit insulam Mictim in qua
candidum plumbum proveniat; ad eam Britannos
vitilibus navigiis corio circumsutis navigare. sunt
qui et alias prodant, Scandias, Dumnam, Bergos,
maximamque omnium Berricen, ex qua in Tylen
navigetur. a Tyle unius diei navigatione mare
concretum a nonnullis Cronium appellatur.

---

[1] *Edd.*, cf. § 97 : Glaeriae.

---

[a] Probably the Grampian Hills.
[b] South Wales.
[c] See 97 *fin.*
[d] Possibly N.W. Norway.
[e] Probably St. Michael's Mount off Cornwall, in spite of the distance stated.
[f] Possibly Barra.
[g] Possibly Lewis.

ago, its exploration was carried by the armed forces
of Rome to a point not beyond the neighbourhood
of the Caledonian Forest.[a] Agrippa believes the
length of the island to be 800 miles and its breadth
300, and the breadth of Ireland the same but its
length 200 miles less. Ireland lies beyond Britain, *Ireland.*
the shortest crossing being from the district [b] of the
Silures, a distance of 30 miles. Of the remaining
islands it is said that none has a circumference of
more than 125 miles. There are the 40 Orkneys
separated by narrow channels from each other, the
7 Shetlands, the 30 Hebrides, and between Ireland
and Britain the Islands of Anglesea, Man, Racklin,
White-horn, Dalkey and Bardsey; south of Britain
are Sian and Ushant, and opposite, scattered about
in the direction of the German Sea, are the Glass
Islands,[c] which the Greeks in more modern times have
called the Electrides, from the Greek word for amber,
which is produced there. The most remote of all
those recorded is Thule,[d] in which as we have *Thule.*
pointed out there are no nights at midsummer when II. 187.
the sun is passing through the sign of the Crab, and
on the other hand no days at midwinter; indeed
some writers think this is the case for periods of six
months at a time without a break. The historian
Timaeus says there is an island named Mictis [e]
lying inward six days' sail from Britain where tin
is found, and to which the Britons cross in boats
of osier covered with stitched hides. Some writers
speak of other islands as well, the Scandiae, Dumna,
Bergos,[f] and Berrice,[g] the largest of all, from which
the crossing to Thule starts. One day's sail from
Thule is the frozen ocean, called by some the Cronian
Sea.

105 XVII. Gallia omnis Comata uno nomine appellata in tria populorum genera dividitur, amnibus maxime distincta: a Scalde ad Sequanam Belgica, ab eo ad Garunnam Celtica eademque Lugdunensis, inde ad Pyrenaei montis excursum Aquitanica, Aremorica antea dicta. universam oram |x̄v̄īī|L̄ Agrippa, Galliarum inter Rhenum et Pyrenaeum atque oceanum ac montes Cebennam et Iures, quibus Narbonensem Galliam excludit, longitudinem c̄c̄c̄c̄xx, latitudinem c̄c̄c̄xv̄ī̄īī computavit.

106 A Scaldi incolunt extera Texuandri pluribus nominibus, dein Menapi, Morini, Oromarsaci iuncti pago qui Chersiacus vocatur, Britanni, Ambiani, Bellovaci, Bassi; introrsus Catoslugi, Atrebates, Nervi liberi, Veromandui, Suaeuconi, Suessiones liberi, Ulmanectes liberi, Tungri, Sunuci, Frisiavones, Baetasi, Leuci liberi, Treveri liberi antea, et Lingones foederati, Remi foederati, Mediomatrici, Sequani, Raurici, Helveti; coloniae Equestris et Raurica. Rhenum autem accolentes Germaniae gentium in eadem provincia Nemetes, Triboci, Vangiones, in Ubiis colonia Agrippinensis, Guberni, Batavi et quos in insulis diximus Rheni.

107 XVIII. Lugdunensis Gallia habet Lexovios, Veliocasses, Galetos, Venetos, Abrincatuos, Ossismos, flumen clarum Ligerem, sed paeninsulam spectatiorem excurrentem in oceanum a fine Ossismorum

---

a Cologne, named after Agrippina (the wife of Claudius), who was born there.

b Brittany, ending in Cape Finistère.

200

XVII. The whole of Gaul included under the Gaul.
general name of Long-haired divides into three races
of people, which are chiefly separated by the rivers:
from the Scheldt to the Seine is Belgic Gaul, from
the Seine to the Garonne Celtic Gaul, also called
Lyonese, and from the Garonne to the projection
of the Pyrenees Aquitanian Gaul, previously called
Armorica. Agrippa reckoned the entire length of
the coast at 1750 miles, and the dimensions of the
Gauls between the Rhine and the Pyrenees and the
ocean and the mountains of the Cevennes and Jura,
which exclude the Narbonne division of Gaul, as—
length 420 miles, breadth 318 miles.

The part beginning at the Scheldt is inhabited by *Belgium and North-eastern France.*
the Texuandri, who have several names, and then the
Menapi, the Morini, the Oromarsaci adjacent to the
canton called Chersiacus, the Bretons, the Ambiani,
the Bellovaci and the Bassi; and more in the interior
the Catoslugi, Atrebates, Nervi (a free people),
Veromandui, Suaeuconi, Suessiones (free), Ulmanectes
(free), Tungri, Sunici, Frisiavones, Baetasi, Leuci
(free), Treveri (formerly free), Lingones (federated),
Remi (federated), Mediomatrici, Sequani, Raurici,
Helveti; and the Equestrian and Rauric colonies.
The races of Germany living on the banks of the
Rhine in the same province are the Nemetes,
Triboci and Vangiones, and among the Ubii the
Colony of Agrippina,[a] the Guberni, the Batavi and
the people whom we have already mentioned as § 101.
dwelling on the islands of the Rhine.

XVIII. To Lyonese Gaul belong the Lexovii, *Central and Western France.*
Veliocasses, Galeti, Veneti, Abrincatui, Ossismi, the
famous river Loire, and also the still more remarkable
peninsula[b] that runs out into the ocean from the

circuitu $\overline{\text{DCXXV}}$, cervice in latitudinem $\overline{\text{CXXV}}$. ultra
eum Namnetes, intus autem Aedui foederati,
Carnuteni foederati, Boi, Senones, Aulerci qui
cognominantur Eburovices et qui Cenomani, Neldi
liberi, Parisi, Tricasses, Andicavi, Viducasses, Bodiocasses, Venelli, Coriosvelites, Diablinti, Rhedones,
Turones, Atesui, Secusiani liberi, in quorum agro
colonia Lugdunum.

108 XIX. Aquitanicae sunt Ambilatri, Anagnutes,
Pictones, Santoni liberi, Bituriges liberi cognomine
Vivisci, Aquitani unde nomen provinciae, Sediboviates; mox in oppidum contributi Convenae,
Begerri, Tarbelli Quattuorsignani, Cocosates Sexsignani, Venami, Onobrisates, Belendi; saltus Pyrenaeus,
infraque Monesi, Oscidates Montani, Sybillates,
Camponi, Bercorcates, Pinpedunni, Lassunni, Vellates, Toruates, Consoranni, Ausci, Elusates, Sottiates, Oscidates Campestres, Successes, Latusates,
Basaboiates, Vassei, Sennates, Cambolectri Ages-
109 sinates. Pictonibus iuncti autem Bituriges liberi
qui Cubi appellantur, dein Lemovices, Arverni liberi,
Gabales. rursus Narbonensi provinciae contermini
Ruteni, Cadurci, Nitiobroges, Tarneque amne dis-
creti a Tolosanis Petrocori.

Maria circa oram ad Rhenum septentrionalis
oceanus, inter Rhenum et Sequanam Britannicus,
inter eum et Pyrenaeum Gallicus. insulae conplures
Venetorum, et quae Veneticae appellantur et in
Aquitanico sinu Uliaros.

---

[a] Belle Isle, Morbihan and others.

boundary of the Ossismi and measures 625 miles round and 125 miles across at its neck. Beyond that neck are the Namnetes, and in the interior the Aedui (federated), Carnuteni (federated), Boii, Senones, Aulerci (both those named Eburovices and those named Cenomani), Neldi (free), Parisii, Tricasses, Andicavi, Viducasses, Bodiocasses, Venelli, Coriosvelites, Diablinti, Rhedones, Turones, Atesui, and Secusiani (free), in whose territory is the colony of Lyons.

XIX. To Aquitanian Gaul belong the Ambilatri, *South-western France.* Anagnutes, Pictones, Santoni (free), Bituriges, also named Vivisci (free), Aquitani (who give their name to the province), Sediboviates; then the Convenae together forming one town, the Begerri, the Tarbelli Quattuorsignani, Cocosates Sexsignani, Venami, Onobrisates, Belendi; the Pyrenean pass; and below the Monesi, Mountain Oscidates, Sybillates, Camponi, Bercorcates, Pinpedunni, Lassunni, Vellates, Toruates, Consoranni, Ausci, Elusates, Sottiates, Oscidates of the Plain, Successes, Latusates, Basaboiates, Vassei, Sennates and the Cambolectri Agessinates. Joining on to the Pictones are the Bituriges called Cubi (free), then the Lemovices, Arverni (free), Gabales, and again, marching with the province of Gallia Narbonensis, the Ruteni, Cadurci, Nitiobroges, and separated by the river Tarn from the people of Toulouse, the Petrocori.

The seas round the coast are: as far as the Rhine the Northern ocean, between the Rhine and the Seine the British Sea, and between the Seine and the Pyrenees the Gallic Sea. There are a number of islands *a* of the Veneti, both those called the Veneticae and Oleron in the Gulf of Aquitania.

PLINY: NATURAL HISTORY

110   XX. A Pyrenaei promunturio Hispania incipit,[1]
angustior non Gallia modo verum etiam semetipsa,
ut diximus, inmensum quantum hinc oceano illinc
Hiberico mari comprimentibus. ipsa Pyrenaei iuga
ab exortu aequinoctiali fusa [2] in occasum brumalem [3]
breviores latere septentrionali [4] quam meridiano [5]
Hispanias faciunt. proxima ora Citerioris est eiusdemque Tarraconensis situs; a Pyrenaeo per oceanum Vasconum saltus, Olarso, Vardulorum oppida,
Morogi, Menosca, Vesperies, Amanum portus ubi
111   nunc Flaviobrica colonia; civitatium novem regio
Cantabrorum, flumen Sauga, portus Victoriae Iulio-
bricensium (ab eo loco fontes Hiberi x̄l̄ p.), portus
Blendium, Orgenomesci e Cantabris, portus eorum
Vereasueca, regio Asturum, Noega oppidum, in
paeninsula Pesici; et deinde conventus Lucensis, a
flumine Navialbione Cibarci, Egivarri cognomine
Namarini, Iadovi, Arroni, Arrotrebae; promunturium Celticum, amnes Florius, Nelo, Celtici
cognomine Neri et super Tamarci quorum in paeninsula tres arae Sestianae Augusto dicatae, Copori,

---

[1] incipit ⟨ibi⟩ ? *Detlefsen.*   [2] fusa *v.l. om.*
[3] brumali *Detlefsen.*   [4] septentrionali *v.l. om.*
[5] brumalem breviores quam latere meridiano *Mayhoff.*

---

[a] *I.e.* the eastern extremity of the Pyrenees, Cape Creux.
[b] *I.e.* than the size into which it widens out south and west
of where the Pyrenees cut it off from France. *Oceanus* means
the Bay of Biscay as part of the Atlantic; *Hibericum Mare*
is the Gulf of Lyons, *Sinus Gallicus,* which is more usually
described as part of *Mare Balearicum,* the name *Mare Hibericum* being kept for the part of the Mediterranean between
the Balearic Islands and the Straits of Gibraltar.
[c] Both text and meaning are extremely doubtful. Possibly
what is meant is that, whereas the south of Spain is all sea-

204

XX. At the promontory [a] of the Pyrenees begins Spain. Spain, which is narrower not only than Gaul but even than itself,[b] as we have said, seeing how enormously it is pressed together on one side by the ocean and on the other by the Iberian Sea. The actual chain of the Pyrenees, spreading from due east to south-west, makes the Spanish provinces shorter on the northern side than on the southern.[c] On the nearest coast is situated Hither or Tarragonian Spain; along the sea-coast [d] from the Pyrenees are the forest of the Vascones, Olarso, the towns of the Varduli, Morogi, Menosca, Vesperies and the port of Amanum, the present site of the colony of Flaviobrica; then the district of the nine states of the Cantabri, the river Sauga, the port of Victory of the Juliobricenses [e] (from this place the sources of the Ebro are 40 miles distant), the port of Blendium, the Orgenomesci (a branch of the Cantabrians), their port Vereasueca, the district of the Astures, the town of Noega,[f] the Pesici on a peninsula; and then, belonging to the jurisdiction of Lugo, starting from the river Navialbio, the Cibarci, the Egivarri surnamed Namarini, Iadovi, Arroni, Arrotrebae; the Celtic Promontory,[g] the rivers Florius and Nelo, the Celts surnamed Neri, and above them the Tamarci, on whose peninsula are the three Altars of Sestius dedicated to Augustus,

coast, part of the northern boundary is formed by the Pyrenees. That range, however, runs almost due east and west, though mountainous country does stretch from it S.W. across the peninsula.

[d] *I.e.* along the Spanish coast of the Bay of Biscay going westward.

[e] Now Santander.

[f] Now Navia.

[g] Finisterre.

oppidum Noeta, Celtici cognomine Praestamarci,
Cileni. ex insulis nominandae Corticata et Aunios.
112 a Cilenis conventus Bracarum Helleni, Grovi,
castellum Tyde, Graecorum sobolis omnia; insulae
Siccae, oppidum Abobrica, Minius amnis IV ore
spatiosus, Leuni, Seurbi, Bracarum oppidum Augusta,
quos super Gallaecia; flumen Limia; Durius amnis
ex maximis Hispaniae, ortus in Pelendonibus et
iuxta Numantiam lapsus, dein per Arevacos Vaccae-
osque disterminatis ab Asturia Vettonibus, a Lusitania Gallaecis, ibi quoque Turdulos a Bracaris
arcens. omnisque dicta regio a Pyrenaeo metallis
referta auri, argenti, ferri, plumbi nigri albique.

113 XXI. A Durio Lusitania incipit: Turduli veteres,
Paesuri, flumen Vagia, oppidum Talabrica, oppidum
et flumen Aeminium, oppida Coniumbrica, Collippo,
Eburobrittium. excurrit deinde in altum vasto
cornu promunturium, quod aliqui Artabrum appellavere, alii Magnum, multi Olisipponense ab oppido,
terras, maria, caelum discriminans. illo finitur
Hispaniae latus et a circuitu eius incipit frons.

114 XXII. Septentrio hinc oceanusque Gallicus, occasus
illinc et oceanus Atlanticus. promunturi excursum
LX prodidere, alii XC, ad Pyrenaeum inde non pauci
|XII|L, et ibi gentem Artabrum, quae numquam fuit,

---

  a See p. 6, note b.
  b A tribe descended from them were in Farther Spain, III 8.
  c Capo de la Roca.
  d I.e. the coast from Cape Roca at the mouth of the Tagus to
the Straits of Gibraltar. Pliny thinks that the coast from Cape
Roca to Finisterre faces north.

the Copori, the town of Noeta, the Celts surnamed
Praestamarci, the Cileni. Of the islands must be
specified Corticata and Aunios. After the Cileni,
in the jurisdiction of the Bracae are the Helleni, the
Grovi and Tyde Castle, all people of Greek stock;
the Dry Islands, the town of Abobrica, the river
Minho four miles wide at its mouth, the Leuni, the
Seurbi, Augusta, a town belonging to the Bracae,
above whom is Gallaecia; the Limia stream and the
river Douro, one of the largest in Spain, which
rises in the district of the Pelendones and passing
by Numantia then flows through the Arevaci and
Vaccaei, separating the Vettones from Asturia and
the Gallaeci from Lusitania, and at this point also
separating the Turduli from the Bracari. The whole
of the district mentioned, from the Pyrenees onward,
is full of mines of gold, silver, iron, lead and tin.

XXI. From the Douro begins Lusitania:[a] the _Portugal._
old Turduli,[b] the Paesuri, the river Vouga, the town
of Talabrica, the town and river Agueda, the towns
of Coimbra, Leiria and Eboro di Alcobaza. Then
there runs out into the sea a promontory[c] shaped
like a vast horn, called by some people Artabrum, by
others the Great Cape, and by many Cape Lisbon
after the town; this headland sharply divides the
land and sea and climate. This cape ends the side
of Spain, and after rounding it the front[d] of Spain
begins. XXII. On one side of it is the north
and the Gallic Ocean, and on the other the west
and the Atlantic. The distance to which this promontory projects has been given as 60 miles, and
by others as 90 miles; the distance from here to
the Pyrenees many give as 1250 miles, and place
here a race of Artabres, which never existed,

manifesto errore: Arrotrebas enim, quos ante
Celticum diximus promunturium, hoc in loco posuere
litteris permutatis.

115 Erratum et in amnibus inclutis. ab Minio, quem
supra diximus, cc (ut auctor est Varro) abest Ae-
minius, quem alibi quidam intellegunt et Limaeam
vocant, Oblivionis antiquis dictus multumque fabu-
losus. ab Durio Tagus $\overline{\text{cc}}$ interveniente Munda;
Tagus auriferis harenis celebratur. ab eo $\overline{\text{clx}}$
promunturium Sacrum e media prope Hispaniae
fronte prosilit. $\overline{|\text{xiv}|}$ inde ad Pyrenaeum medium
colligi Varro tradit, ad Anam vero, quo Lusitaniam
a Baetica discrevimus, $\overline{\text{cxxvi}}$, a Gadibus $\overline{\text{cii}}$ additis.

116 Gentes Celtici, Turduli et circa Tagum Vettones;
ab Ana ad Sacrum Lusitani. oppida a Tago memorabilia in ora Olisippo equarum e favonio vento conceptu nobile, Salacia cognominata Urbs Imperatoria,
Merobrica, promunturium Sacrum et alterum Cuneus,
oppida Ossonoba, Balsa, Myrtilis.

117 Universa provincia dividitur in conventus tres,
Emeritensem, Pacensem, Scallabitanum, tota populorum xlv, in quibus coloniae sunt quinque, munici-

---

^a Probably Punta de Sagres.

the error being obvious; they have put here, with
an alteration in the spelling of the name, the Arrotrebae, whom we spoke of before we came to the
Celtic Promontory.   § 111.

Mistakes have also been made in regard to the
important rivers. From the Minho, which we spoke
of above, the distance to the Agueda according to § 112.
Varro is 200 miles, though others place the latter
elsewhere and call it the Limaea; in early times it
was called the River of Forgetfulness, and a great
many stories were told about it. Two hundred miles
from the Douro is the Tagus, the Mondego coming
between them; the Tagus is famous for its auriferous
sands. At a distance of nearly 160 miles from the
Tagus is Cape St. Vincent, projecting from nearly
the middle of the front of Spain. The distance from
Cape St. Vincent to the middle of the Pyrenees is
stated by Varro to amount to 1400 miles; from St.
Vincent to the Guadiana, which we indicated as the
boundary between Lusitania and Baetica, he puts
at 126 miles, the distance from the Guadiana to
Cadiz adding another 102 miles.

The peoples are the Celtici, the Turduli, and on the
Tagus the Vettones; and between the Guadiana and
Cape St. Vincent the Lusitanians. The notable
towns on the coast, beginning at the Tagus, are:
Lisbon, famous for its mares which conceive from VIII. 166
the west wind; Alcazar do Sal, called the Imperial
City; Santiago de Cacem; Cape St. Vincent, and the
other promontory called the Wedge; [a] and the towns
of Estombar, Tavira and Mertola.

The whole province is divided into three associa- *Organization*
tions, centred at Merida, Beja and Santarem. It *of Province*
consists of 45 peoples in all, among whom there are *of Spain.*

pium civium Romanorum, Lati antiqui III, stipendiaria XXXVI. coloniae Augusta Emerita Anae fluvio
adposita, Metellinensis, Pacensis, Norbensis Caesarina cognomine (contributa sunt in eam Castra
Servilia, Castra Caecilia); quinta est Scallabis quae
Praesidium Iulium vocatur. municipium civium
Romanorum Olisippo Felicitas Iulia cognominatum.
oppida veteris Lati Ebora, quod idem Liberalitas
118 Iulia, et Myrtilis ac Salacia, quae diximus. stipen-
diariorum quos nominare non pigeat, praeter iam
dictos in Baeticae cognominibus, Augustobricenses,
Aeminienses, Aranditani, Axabricenses, Balsenses,
Caesarobricenses, Caperenses, Caurienses, Colarni,
Cibilitani, Concordienses, Elbocori, Interamnienses,
Lancienses, Mirobricenses qui Celtici cognominantur,
Medubricenses qui Plumbari, Ocelenses, Turduli qui
Bardili et Tapori.

Lusitaniam cum Asturia et Gallaecia patere
longitudine $\overline{\text{DXL}}$, latitudine $\overline{\text{DXXXVI}}$, Agrippa prodidit.
omnes autem Hispaniae a duobus Pyrenaei promun-
turiis per maria, totius orae circuitu $|\overline{\text{XXIX}}|$ $\overline{\text{XXIV}}$
colligere existimantur, ab aliis $\overline{|\text{XXVI}|}$.

119 Ex adverso Celtiberiae conplures sunt insulae Cas-
siterides dictae Graecis a fertilitate plumbi albi,[1] et
e regione Arrotrebarum promunturi Deorum VI, quas
aliqui Fortunatas appellavere. in ipso vero capite
mox Baeticae ab ostio freti p. $\overline{\text{XXV}}$ Gadis, longa, ut

---

[1] albi *add. Warmington.*

five colonies, one municipality of Roman citizens, three with the old Latin rights and 36 that pay tribute. The colonies are Merida on the river Guadiana, Medellin, Beja, and Alcantara surnamed Caesarina (to this Trucillo and Caceres are assigned); and the fifth is that of Santarem, which is called the Garrison of Julius. The municipality of Roman citizens is Lisbon, surnamed the Success of Julius. The towns with the old Latin rights are Evora, which is also called the Generosity of Julius, and Mertola and Alcazar do Sal which we have mentioned. Of §116. the tributary towns that deserve mention, besides those already specified in the list of names of those III 13. belonging to Baetica, are Augustobriga, Aemia, Arandita, Axabrica, Balsa, Caesarobrica, Capera, Coria, Colarna, Cibilita, Concordia, Elbocorium, Interamnium, Lancia, Malabriga surnamed Celtic, Medubriga surnamed Plumbaria, Ocelum, the Turduli also called Bardili, and the Tapori.

The dimensions of Lusitania combined with Asturia and Gallaecia are given by Agrippa as: length 540 miles, breadth 536 miles. The provinces of Spain taken all together, measured from the two promontories of the Pyrenees along the sea line, are estimated to cover by the circumference of the whole coast 2924 miles, or by others 2600 miles.

Opposite to Celtiberia are a number of islands *Islands off* called by the Greeks the Tin Islands in consequence *Spain.* of their abundance of that metal; and facing Cape Finisterre are the six Islands of the Gods, which some people have designated the Isles of Bliss. But immediately at the beginning of Baetica comes Cadiz, 25 miles from the mouth of the Strait, an island

---

a Probably the Scilly Islands.

Polybius scribit, $\overline{\text{XII}}$, lata $\overline{\text{III}}$. abest a continente
proxima parte minus pedes DCC, reliqua plus $\overline{\text{VII}}$;
ipsius spatium $\overline{\text{XV}}$ est. habet oppidum civium
Romanorum qui appellantur Augustani urbe Iulia
120 Gaditana. ab eo latere quo Hispaniam spectat
passibus fere C altera insula est M longa passus, M
lata, in qua prius oppidum Gadium fuit; vocatur
ab Ephoro et Philistide Erythea, a Timaeo et Sileno
Aphrodisias, ab indigenis Iunonis. maiorem Timaeus Potimusam a puteis vocitatam ait, nostri
Tarteson appellant, Poeni Gadir ita Punica lingua
saepem significante; Erythea dicta est, quoniam
Tyri aborigines eorum orti ab Erythro mari ferebantur. in hac Geryones habitasse a quibusdam
existimantur quorum [1] armenta Hercules abduxerit;
sunt qui aliam esse eam et contra Lusitaniam
arbitrentur, eodemque nomine quondam [2] ibi
appellatam. [3]

121 XXIII. Peracto ambitu Europae reddenda con-
summatio est, ne quid non in expedito sit noscere
volentibus. longitudinem eius Artemidorus atque
Isidorus a Tanai Gades $|\overline{\text{LXXVII}}|$ $\overline{\text{XIV}}$ prodiderunt.
Polybius latitudinem Europae ab Italia ad oceanum
scripsit $|\overline{\text{XI}}|\overline{\text{L}}$ esse, etiam tum inconperta magnitudine.
122 est autem ipsius Italiae, ut diximus, $|\overline{\text{X}}|$ $\overline{\text{XX}}$ ad Alpes,

---

[1] *V.l.* existimatur cuius.
[2] *Edd.* quandam.
[3] *Caesarius*: appellant.

according to Polybius's account measuring 12 miles
in length and 3 miles in breadth. Its distance from
the mainland at the nearest point is less than 233
yards, but at other places it is more than 7 miles;
the circuit of the island is 15 miles. It has a town
whose population have the Roman citizenship and
are called Augustans, the title of their city being
Julia Gaditana. On the side facing Spain at a
distance of about 100 yards is another island one
mile long and one mile broad, on which the town of
Cadiz was previously situated; Ephorus and Philistus
call this island Erythea, and Timaeus and Silenus
call it Aphrodisias, but its native name is the Isle
of Juno. The larger island according to Timaeus is
known as Potimusa from its wells, but our people call
it Tartesos and the Punic name is Gadir, which is
Carthaginian for a fence; it was called Erythea,
because the original ancestors of the Carthaginians,
the Tyrians, were said to have come from the Red
Sea. This island is believed by some people to have
been the home of the Geryones whose cattle were
carried off by Hercules; but others hold that that
was another island, lying off Lusitania, and that an
island there was once called by the same name.

XXIII. Having completed the circuit of Europe *Dimensions*
we must now give its complete dimensions, in order *of Europe.*
that those who desire this information may not be
left at a loss. Its length from the Don to Cadiz is
given by Artemidorus and Isidorus as 7714 miles.
Polybius stated the breadth of Europe from Italy
to the ocean as 1150 miles, but its exact magnitude
had not been ascertained even in his day. The length
of Italy itself up to the Alps is 1020 miles, as we
stated; and from the Alps through Lyons to the III 43.

unde per Lugdunum ad portum Morinorum Britannicum, qua videtur mensuram agere Polybius, |XI| LXIX; sed certior mensura ac longior ad occasum solis aestivi ostiumque Rheni per castra legionum Germaniae ab iisdem Alpibus dirigitur, |XII| XLIII.

Hinc deinde Africa atque Asia dicentur.

harbour[a] of the Morini, the port on the British channel, the line of measurement that Polybius appears to take, is 1169 miles, but a better ascertained measurement and a longer one is that starting also from the Alps but going north-west through the Camp of the Legions in Germany to the mouth of the Rhine—1243 miles.

Next after this we shall speak of Africa and Asia.

[a] Gesoriacum, now Boulogne.

BOOK V

LIBER V

1   I. Africam Graeci Libyam appellavere et mare
ante eam Libycum. Aegypto finitur; nec alia
pars terrarum pauciores recipit sinus longe ab
occidente [1] litorum obliquo spatio. populorum eius
oppidorumque nomina vel maxime sunt ineffabilia
praeterquam ipsorum linguis; et alias castella
ferme inhabitant.

2   Principio terrarum Mauretaniae appellantur,
usque ad C. Caesarem Germanici filium regna,
saevitia eius in duas divisae provincias. promunturium Oceani extremum Ampelusia nominatur a
Graecis.   oppida fuere Lissa et Cotte ultra columnas
Herculis, nunc est Tingi quondam ab Antaeo
conditum, postea a Claudio Caesare, cum coloniam
faceret, appellatum Traducta Iulia; abest a Baelone
oppido Baeticae proximo traiectu $\overline{xxx}$.   ab eo $\overline{xxv}$ in
ora Oceani colonia Augusti Iulia Constantia Zulil,
regum dicioni exempta et iura in Baeticam petere
iussa.   ab ea $\overline{xxxv}$ colonia a Claudio Caesare facta

---

[1] [longe ab occidente] *Dalecamp.*

---

  [a] Cape Spartel.
  [b] Presumably in memory of a previous colony 'transferred' from Tangier to Spain in the time of Julius Caesar.
  [c] Arzilla, in the territory of Fez.

218

BOOK V

I. THE Greeks give to Africa the name of Libya, and they call the sea lying in front of it the Libyan Sea. It is bounded by Egypt. No other part of the earth has fewer bays or inlets in its coast, which stretches in a long slanting line from the west. The names of its peoples and towns are absolutely unpronounceable except by the natives; and for the rest, they mostly reside in fortresses.

The list of its countries begins with the two called Mauretania, which down to the time of the emperor Caligula were kingdoms, but by his cruelty were divided into two provinces. The outermost promontory projecting into the ocean is named by the Greeks Ampelusia.ª Beyond the Straits of Gibraltar there were once the towns of Lissa and Cotte; but at the present day there is only Tangier, which was originally founded by Antaeus and subsequently entitled Traducta Julia *b* by the emperor Claudius when he established a colony there. It is 30 miles distant from the town of Baelon in Baetica, where the passage across is shortest. On the Atlantic coast 25 miles from Tangier is Julia Constantia Zulil,*c* a colony of Augustus, which is exempt from the government of the native kings and included under the jurisdiction of Baetica. Thirty-five miles from Zulil is Lixus, made a colony by the emperor

219

3 Lixos, vel fabulosissime antiquis narrata: ibi regia
Antaei certamenque cum Hercule, et Hesperidum
horti. adfunditur autem aestuarium e mari flexuoso
meatu, in quo draconis[1] custodiae instar fuisse nunc
interpretantur; amplectitur intra se insulam, quam
solam e vicino tractu aliquanto excelsiore non
tamen aestus maris inundant. exstat in ea et ara
Herculis nec praeter oleastros aliud ex narrato illo
4 aurifero nemore. minus profecto mirentur por-
tentosa Graeciae mendacia de his et amne Lixo
prodita qui cogitent nostros nuperque paulo minus
monstrifica quaedam de iisdem tradidisse, prae-
validam hanc urbem maioremque Magna Carthagine,
praeterea ex adverso eius sitam et prope inmenso
tractu ab Tingi, quaeque alia Cornelius Nepos
avidissime credidit.

5   Ab Lixo x̅l̅ in mediterraneo altera Augusti colonia
est Babba, Iulia Campestris appellata, et tertia
Banasa l̅x̅x̅v̅ p., Valentia cognominata. ab ea x̅x̅x̅v̅
Volubile oppidum, tantundem a mari utroque distans.
at in ora a Lixo l̅ amnis Sububus praeter Banasam
coloniam defluens, magnificus et navigabilis. ab eo

[1] V.l. dracones.

---

[a] Their golden apples were guarded by a serpent.
[b] Cf. the name ' Serpentine ' in London.
[c] The Wadi Draa.
[d] The original city, so called in distinction from its colony
in Spain, Carthago Nova, now Cartagena.
[e] I.e. on the same meridian; this is of course a mistake.

Claudius, about which the most marvellous legends are told by the old writers: this was the site of the palace of Antaeus and the scene of his combat with Hercules, and here were the gardens of the Ladies of the West.[a]   As a matter of fact an arm of the sea stretches inland here with a winding channel which, as people nowadays explain the story, had some resemblance to a guardian serpent;[b] it embraces within it an island which, although the neighbouring district is considerably elevated, is nevertheless the only portion not flooded by the tides.   On the island there also rises an altar of Hercules, but of the famous grove in the story that bore the golden fruit nothing else except some wild olive trees.   No doubt less wonder may be felt at the portentous falsehoods of Greece put about concerning these serpents and the river Lixus[c] by people who reflect that our own countrymen, and these quite recently, have reported little less miraculous stories about the same matters, stating that this city is exceedingly powerful and greater than Great Carthage[d] ever was, and moreover that it is situated in a line with[e] Carthage and at an almost immeasurable distance from Tangier, and all the other details swallowed so greedily by Cornelius Nepos.

In the interior, 40 miles from Lixus, is another colony of Augustus, Babba, called Julia.   On The Plains, and 75 miles further, a third, Banasa, which has the surname of Valentia.   Thirty-five miles from Banasa is the town of Volubile, which is at the same distance from the coasts of the Atlantic and the Mediterranean.   On the shore, 50 miles from Lixus, is the river Sebou, flowing by the colony of Banasa, a fine river available for navigation.   The same

totidem milibus oppidum Sala eiusdem nominis fluvio
inpositum, iam solitudinibus vicinum elephantorumque gregibus infestum, multo tamen magis
Autololum gente, per quam iter est ad montem
6 Africae vel fabulosissimum Atlantem. e mediis
hunc harenis in caelum attolli prodidere, asperum,
squalentem qua vergat ad litora oceani cui cognomen
imposuit, eundem opacum nemorosumque et scatebris
fontium riguum qua spectet Africam, fructibus
omnium generum sponte ita subnascentibus ut
7 numquam satias voluptatibus desit. incolarum neminem interdiu cerni, silere omnia haut alio quam
solitudinum horrore, subire tacitam religionem animos
propius accedentium praeterque horrorem elati
super nubila atque in vicina lunaris circuli; eundem
noctibus micare crebris ignibus, Aegipanum Satyrorumque lascivia inpleri, tibiarum ac fistulae cantu
tympanorumque et cymbalorum sonitu strepere.
haec celebrati auctores prodidere praeter Herculi
et Perseo laborata ibi. spatium ad eum inmensum
incertumque.
8   Fuere et Hannonis Carthaginiensium ducis com-
mentarii Punicis rebus florentissimis explorare
ambitum Africae iussi, quem secuti plerique a

---

^a Written in Punic and still extant in a Greek translation,
see Vol. I, Index, *Hanno*, and Book I, § 169.

number of miles from the Sebou is the town of Sallee, situated on the river of the same name; this town is on the very edge of the desert, and is beset by herds of elephants, but much more seriously harried by the Autololes tribe, through whose terri- *Mount Atlas.* tory lies the road to Mount Atlas, which is the subject of much the most marvellous stories of all the mountains in Africa. It is reported to rise into the sky out of the middle of the sands, a rugged eminence covered with crags on the side facing towards the coast of the Ocean to which it has given its name, but shaded by dense woods and watered by gushing springs on the side facing Africa, where fruits of all kinds spring up of their own accord with such luxuriance that pleasure never lacks satisfaction. It is said that in the day-time none of its inhabitants are seen, and that all is silent with a terrifying silence like that of the desert, so that a speechless awe creeps into the hearts of those who approach it, and also a dread of the peak that soars above the clouds and reaches the neighbourhood of the moon's orb; also that at night this peak flashes with frequent fires and swarms with the wanton gambols of Goat-Pans and Satyrs, and echoes with the music of flutes and pipes and the sound of drums and cymbals. These stories have been published by celebrated authors, in addition to the labours performed in this region by Hercules and Perseus. It is an immense distance away, across unexplored country.

There were also once extant some notes[a] of the *Exploration of West Coast* Carthaginian commander Hanno, who at the most *of Africa.* flourishing period of the Punic state was ordered to explore the circuit of Africa. It is Hanno whom

Graecis nostrisque et alia quidem fabulosa et urbes multas ab eo conditas ibi prodidere, quarum nec memoria ulla nec vestigium exstat.

9 Scipione Aemiliano res in Africa gerente Polybius annalium conditor ab eo accepta classe scrutandi illius orbis gratia circumvectus prodidit a monte eo ad occasum versus saltus plenos feris quas generat Africa; ad flumen Anatim $\overline{\text{ccccxcvi}}$, ab eo Lixum $\overline{\text{ccv}}$ Agrippa, Lixum a Gaditano freto $\overline{\text{cxii}}$ abesse; inde sinum qui vocetur Sagigi, oppidum in promunturio Mulelacha, flumina Sububum et Salat, portum Rutubis a Lixo $\overline{\text{ccxxiv}}$, inde promunturium Solis, portum Rhysaddir, Gaetulos Autoteles, flumen Quosenum, gentes Velatitos et Masatos, flumen Masathat, flumen Darat, in quo crocodilos gigni.

10 dein sinum dcxvi includi montis Bracae promunturio excurrente in occasum, quod appelletur Surrentium. postea flumen Salsum, ultra quod Aethiopas Perorsos, quorum a tergo Pharusios. his iungi in mediterraneo Gaetulos Daras, at in ora Aethiopas Daratitas, flumen Bambotum crocodilis et hippopotamis refertum. ab eo montes perpetuos usque ad eum quem Theon Ochema dicemus. inde ad promunturium Hesperium navigatione dierum ac

---

^a In the Third Punic War, when Carthage was destroyed, 146 B.C.
^b Perhaps the Om-Rabya.   ^c Mount Kakulima.

the majority of the Greek and Roman writers have followed in the accounts that they have published of a number of cities founded by him there of which no memory or trace exists, not to speak of other fabulous stories.

Scipio Aemilianus, during his command in Africa,[a] placed a fleet of vessels at the service of the historian Polybius for the purpose of making a voyage of discovery in that part of the world. After sailing round the coast, Polybius reported that beyond Mount Atlas in a westerly direction there are forests teeming with the wild animals that Africa engenders. Agrippa says that to the river Anatis[b] is a distance of 496 miles, and from the Anatis to Lixus 205 miles; that Lixus is 112 miles from the Straits of Gibraltar and that then come the gulf called Sagigi Bay, the town on Cape Mulelacha, the rivers Sebou and Sallee, the port of Mazagan 224 miles from Lixus, then Capo Blanco, the port of Safi, the Gaetulian Free State, the river Tensift, the Velatiti and Masati tribes, the river Mogador, and the river Sous, in which crocodiles are found. Then, he states, a gulf 616 miles across is enclosed by the promontory of the Atlas chain projecting westward, called Cape Ger. After this the river Assa, beyond which is the Aethiopian tribe of the Perorsi, and in their rear the Pharusii. Adjoining these in the interior are the Gaetulian Darae, and on the coast the Aethiopian Daratitae and the river Non, which is full of crocodiles and hippopotamuses. From the Non runs a line of mountains extending right to the peak[c] of which the Greek name is, as we shall state, the VI. 197. Chariot of the Gods. The distance from this peak to Cape Roxo he gives as a voyage of ten days and

noctium decem. in medio eo spatio Atlantem locavit a ceteris omnibus in extremis Mauretaniae proditum.

11 Romana arma primum Claudio principe in Mauretania bellavere Ptolemaeum regem a Gaio Caesare interemptum ulciscente liberto Aedemone, refugientibusque barbaris ventum constat ad montem Atlantem. nec solum consulatu perfunctis atque e senatu ducibus qui tum res gessere sed equitibus quoque Romanis qui ex eo praefuere ibi Atlantem

12 penetrasse in gloria fuit. quinque sunt (ut diximus) Romanae coloniae in ea provincia, perviumque fama[1] videri potest; sed id plerumque fallacissimum experimento deprehenditur, quia dignitates, cum indagare vera pigeat, ignorantiae pudore mentiri non piget, haut alio fidei proniore lapsu quam ubi falsae rei gravis auctor existit. equidem minus miror inconperta quaedam esse equestris ordinis viris, iam vero et senatum inde intrantibus, quam luxuriae, cuius efficacissima vis sentitur atque maxima, cum ebori, citro silvae exquirantur, omnes

13 scopuli Gaetuli muricibus, purpuris. indigenae ta-

---

[1] *V.l.* famae.

nights; and in the middle of this space he places Mount Atlas, which all other authorities give as situated at the farthest point of Mauretania.

The first occasion on which the armed forces of Rome fought in Mauretania was in the principate of Claudius, when King Ptolemy had been put to death by Caligula and his freedman Aedemon were seeking to avenge him; and it is an accepted fact that our troops went as far as Mount Atlas in pursuit of the routed natives. And not only were the ex-consuls and generals drawn from the senate who commanded in that campaign able to boast of having penetrated the Atlas range, but this distinction was also shared by the Knights of Rome who subsequently governed the country. The province contains, as we have said, five Roman colonies, and, to judge by common report, the place might well be thought to be easily accessible; but upon trial this criterion is discovered to be for the most part exceedingly fallacious, because persons of high position, although not inclined to search for the truth, are ashamed of ignorance and consequently are not reluctant to tell falsehoods, as credulity is never more easily let down than when a false statement is attested by an authority of weight. For my own part I am less surprised that some things are outside the knowledge of gentlemen of the equestrian order, some of whom indeed nowadays actually get into the senate, than that anything should be unknown to luxury, which acts as an extremely great and powerful stimulus, inasmuch as forests are ransacked for ivory and citrus-wood and all the rocks of Gaetulia explored for the murex and for purple. The natives, however, inform us that on the coast

Roman penetration into N.W. Africa.

§§ 2 ff.

227

PLINY: NATURAL HISTORY

men tradunt in ora ab Salat $\overline{CL}$ flumen Asanam marino haustu sed portu spectabile, mox amnem quem vocant Fut, ab eo ad Dirim—hoc enim Atlanti nomen esse eorum lingua convenit—$\overline{CC}$, interveniente flumine cui nomen est Ivor; ibi pauca [1] extare circa vestigia habitati quondam soli, vinearum palmetorumque reliquias.

14 Suetonius Paulinus, quem consulem vidimus, primus Romanorum ducum transgressus quoque Atlantem aliquot milium spatio prodidit de excelsitate quidem eius quae ceteri, imas radices densis altisque repletas silvis incognito genere arborum, proceritatem spectabilem esse enodi nitore, frondes cupressi similes praeterquam gravitate odoris, tenui eas obduci lanugine, quibus addita arte posse quales e bombyce vestes confici. verticem altis etiam

15 aestate operiri nivibus. decumis se eo pervenisse castris et ultra ad fluvium qui Ger vocatur per solitudines nigri pulveris, eminentibus interdum velut exustis cautibus, loca inhabitabilia fervore quamquam hiberno tempore experto. qui proximos inhabitent saltus refertos elephantorum ferarumque et serpentium omni genere Canarios appellari, quippe

---

[1] *Mayhoff*: ibi favo, ibi fama *et alia*.

---

[a] The modern Daran.
[b] Consul 66 A.D., propraetor in Mauretania 42 A.D.; the father of the biographer of the Caesars.

150 miles from the Sallee is the River Asana, which is a tidal river but which is notable for its harbour; and then the river which they call the Fut, and 200 miles from it, after crossing a river named Ivor, the Diris *a* range—that is agreed to be the native name for the Atlas; and that in the neighbourhood are traces of the land having formerly been inhabited—remains of vineyards and palm-groves.

Suetonius Paulinus, who was consul in our own times,*b* was the first Roman commander who actually crossed the Atlas range and advanced a distance of many miles beyond it. His report as to its remarkable altitude agrees with that of all the other authorities, but he also states that the regions at the base of the range are filled with dense and lofty forests of trees of an unknown kind, with very tall trunks remarkable for their glossy timber free from knots, and foliage like that of the cypress except for its oppressive scent, the leaves being covered with a thin downy floss, so that with the aid of art a dress-material like that obtained from the silk-worm can be made from them. The summit (the report continued) is covered with deep snow-drifts even in summer. Ten days' march brought him to this point and beyond it to the river called the Ger, across deserts covered with black dust occasionally broken by projections of rock that looked as if they had been burnt, a region rendered uninhabitable by its heat, although it was winter time when he explored it. He states that the neighbouring forests swarm with every kind of elephant and snake, and are inhabited by a tribe called the Canarii, owing to the fact that they have their

victum eius animalis promiscuum his esse et dividua ferarum viscera.

16 Iunctam Aethiopum gentem quos Perorsos vocant satis constat. Iuba Ptolemaei pater, qui primus utrique Mauretaniae imperitavit, studiorum claritate memorabilior etiam quam regno, similia prodidit de Atlante, praeterque gigni herbam ibi euphorbeam nomine ab inventore medico suo appellatam, cuius lacteum sucum miris laudibus celebrat in claritate visus contraque serpentes et venena omnia privatim dicato volumine.—Et satis superque de Atlante.

17 Tingitanae provinciae longitudo $\overline{\text{CLXX}}$ est. gentes in ea: quondam praecipua Maurorum (unde nomen) quos plerique Maurusios dixerunt, attenuata bellis ad paucas recidit familias. proxima illi Masaesylorum fuerat; simili modo extincta est. Gaetulae nunc tenent gentes, Baniurae multoque validissimi Autoteles et horum pars quondam Nesimi, qui avolsi his 18 propriam fecere gentem versi ad Aethiopas. ipsa provincia ab oriente montuosa fert elephantos, in Abyla quoque monte et quos Septem Fratres a

---

ᵃ Spurge.　ᵇ Or possibly 'dedicated to him personally.'
ᶜ Now Djebel Mousa.

diet in common with the canine race and share with it the flesh of wild animals.

It is well ascertained that the next people are the Aethiopian tribe called the Perorsi. Juba, the father of Ptolemy, who was the first ruler to hold sway over both the Mauretanias, and who is even more distinguished for his renown as a student than for his royal sovereignty, has published similar facts about Mount Atlas, and has stated in addition that a plant grows there called the euphorbia,[a] named after his doctor who discovered it; in a volume devoted solely to the subject of this plant[b] he sings the praises of its milky juice in very remarkable terms, stating it to be an aid to clear sight and an antidote against snake-bite and poisons of all kinds.—This is enough, or more than enough, about Mount Atlas.

The province of Tangier is 170 miles in length. It contains the following tribes: the Moors (from whom it takes its name of Mauretania), by many writers called the Maurusii, were formerly the leading race, but they have been thinned by wars and are now reduced to a few families. The next race to this was previously that of the Masaesyli, but this has been wiped out in a similar manner. The country is now occupied by the Gaetulian tribes, the Baniurae and the Free State, by far the most powerful of them all, and the Nesimi, who were formerly a section of the Autoteles, but have split off from them and formed a separate tribe of their own in the direction of the Aethiopians. The province itself produces elephants in its mountainous district on the eastern side and also on Mount Ceuta and the range of peaks called the Seven Brothers[c] from

North coast of Africa: Tangier, Algeria.

simili altitudine appellant; freto imminent ii iuncti
Abylae. ab his ora interni maris, flumen Tamuda
navigabile, quondam et oppidum; flumen Laud et
ipsum navigiorum capax, Rhysaddir oppidum et
19 portus, Malvane fluvius navigabilis. Siga oppidum
ex adverso Malacae in Hispania situm, Syphacis
regia, alterius iam Mauretaniae; namque diu regum
nomina optinuere, ut Bogutiana appellaretur extuma,
itemque Bocchi quae nunc Caesariensis. ab ea
Portus Magnus a spatio appellatus, civium Romanorum oppidum[1]; amnis Mulucha, Bocchi Masae-
sylorumque finis; Quiza Xenitana (Peregrinorum
20 Oppidum); Arsennaria Latinorum, III a mari;
Cartenna colonia Augusti legione[2] secunda, item
colonia eiusdem deducta cohorte praetoria Gunugu;
promunturium Apollinis oppidumque ibi celeberrimum Caesarea, antea vocitatum Iol, Iubae regia a
divo Claudio coloniae iure donata; eiusdem iussu
deductis veteranis Oppidum Novum et Latio dato
Tipasa, itemque a Vespasiano imperatore eodem
munere donatum Icosium; colonia Augusti Rusguniae, Rusucurium civitate honoratum a Claudio,
Rusazus colonia Augusti, Saldae colonia eiusdem,
item Igilgili; oppidum Tucca inpositum mari et
21 flumini Ampsagae. intus colonia Augusta quae

---

[1] *V.l.* oppido.
[2] *I. Mueller*: legio.

---

[a] Mauretania Caesariensis, now Algeria.
[b] A Latinised adjective from ξένος.
[c] Perhaps Algiers.
[d] Now the Wadi-el-Kebir.

their similarity of height; these mountains join on
to Mount Ceuta and overlook the Straits of Gibraltar.
At the Seven Brothers begins the coast of the
Mediterranean, and next come the navigable river
Bedia and the site of a former town of the same
name, the river Gomera, also navigable for vessels,
the town and harbour of Safi, and the navigable
river Maluia. Opposite to Malaga in Spain is
situated the town of Aresgol, the capital of King
Syphax, where we reach the second Mauretania [a]—
for these regions for a long time took the names
of their kings, Further Mauretania being called the
Land of Bogut and similarly the present Caesariensis
the Land of Bocchus. After Aresgol come the port
called from its size Great Harbour, a town with
Roman citizenship; the river Mulucha, the frontier
between the Land of Bocchus and the Masaesyli;
Quiza Xenitana [b] ('Alienville'); Arzen, a town
with Latin rights, three miles from the sea; Tenez,
a colony of Augustus, where the Second Legion was
settled, and Gunugu, likewise a colony of the same
emperor and the settlement of a praetorian cohort;
Cape Mestagan, and on it the famous town of
Caesarea,[c] previously called Iol, the capital of King
Juba, to which colonial rights were granted by his
late Majesty Claudius; New Town, founded as a
settlement of veteran troops, and Tipasa, granted
Latin rights by the same emperor's orders, and also
Icosium given the same privilege by the emperor
Vespasian; Rusguniae, a colony of Augustus, Rusucurium, given the honour of citizenship by Claudius,
Rusazus, a colony of Augustus, Saldae, a colony of the
same, Igilgili likewise; the town of Zucca, situated
on the sea and the river Ampsaga.[d] In the interior

item Succhabar, item Tubusuptu, civitates Timici, Tigavae, flumina Sardaval, Aves, Nabar, gens Macurebi, flumen Usar, gens Nababes. flumen Ampsaga abest a Caesarea $\overline{\text{CCCXXII}}$.[1] utriusque Mauretaniae longitudo $\overline{|\text{X}|}$ $\overline{\text{XXXVIII}}$, latitudo $\overline{\text{CCCCLXVII}}$.

22 II. Ab Ampsaga Numidia est Masinissae clara nomine, Metagonitis terra a Graecis appellata, Numidae vero Nomades a permutandis pabulis, mapalia sua, hoc est domos, plaustris circumferentes. oppida Cullu, Rusiccade, et ab eo ad $\overline{\text{XLVIII}}$ in mediterraneo colonia Cirta Sitianorum cognomine, et alia intus Sicca, liberumque oppidum Bulla Regia. at in ora Tacatua, Hippo Regius, flumen Armua, oppidum Tabraca civium Romanorum. Tusca fluvius Numidiae finis. nec praeter marmoris Numidici ferarumque proventum aliud insigne ei.

23 III. A Tusca Zeugitana regio et quae proprie vocetur Africa est. tria promunturia, Candidum, mox Apollinis adversum Sardiniae, Mercuri adversum Siciliae, in altum procurrentia duo efficiunt sinus, Hipponiensem proximum ab oppido quod Hipponem Dirutum vocant, Diarrhytum Graecis dictum propter aquarum inrigua, cui finitimum Theudalis immune

24 oppidum, longius a litore; dein promunturium Apollinis, et in altero sinu Utica civium Romanorum,

---

[1] $\overline{\text{CCXII}}$ *Brotier.*

---

[a] The modern Constantine. Sitius served under Caesar, and received a grant of the place after the defeat of Juba.

[b] A residence or foundation of the Kings of Numidia; there was also a small place named Bulla Mensa south of Carthage.

[c] 'Irrigated,' 'canalised.'

is the colony of Augusta, also called Succhabar, and
likewise Tubusuptu, the independent cities of
Timici and Tigavae, the rivers Sardaval, Aves and
Nabar, the Macurebi tribe, the river Usar, and the
Nababes tribe. From the river Ampsaga to Caesarea
is 322 miles. The length of the two Mauretanias is
1038 miles and the breadth 467 miles.

II. At the river Ampsaga begins Numidia, a *Numidia.*
country rendered famous by the name of Masinissa.
The Greeks called it Metagonitis, and they named
its people the Nomads, from their custom of frequently changing their pasturage, carrying their
mapalia, that is their homes, about the country on
waggons. The towns are Chollum and Sgigada,
and in the interior about 48 miles from the latter
the colony of Cirta, called Cirta of the Sitiani,[a] and
another colony further inland, Sicca, and the free
town of King's Bulla.[b] On the coast are Tagodet,
King's Hippo, the river Mafragg, and the town of
Tabraca, which has Roman citizenship. The boundary of Numidia is the river Zaina. The country
produces nothing remarkable beside the Numidian
marble and wild beasts.

III. Beyond the Zaina is the district of Zeugitana *Africa proper (Tunisia and Tripoli).*
and the region properly to be called Africa. Three
promontories run out into the sea, White Cape and
then Cape Farina facing Sardinia and Cape Bon
facing Sicily; these form two bays—the Bay of
Hippo next the town called Hippo Dirutus, in Greek
Diarrhytus,[c] which name is due to its irrigation
channels, and adjacent to this, further from the
coast, Theudalis, a town exempt from tribute; and
then Cape Farina, and on the second bay Utica,
which has the rights of Roman citizenship; it is

Catonis morte nobilis, flumen Bagrada, locus Castra
Cornelia, colonia Carthago Magnae in vestigiis
Carthaginis, colonia Maxula, oppida Carpi, Misua
et liberum Clypea in promunturio Mercuri, item
libera Curubis, Neapolis.

Mox Africae ipsius alia distinctio. Libyphoenices
vocantur qui Byzacium incolunt: ita appellatur
regio $\overline{\text{CCL}}$ p. circuitu, fertilitatis eximiae, cum cente-
25 sima fruge agricolis fenus reddente terra. hic
oppida libera Leptis, Hadrumetum, Ruspina, Thapsus.
inde Thenae, Aves, Macomades, Tacape, Sabrata
contingens Syrtim Minorem, ad quam Numidiae et
Africae ab Ampsaga longitudo $\overline{\text{DLXXX}}$, latitudo qua
cognitum est $\overline{\text{CC}}$. ea pars quam Africam appellavimus dividitur in duas provincias, Veterem et
Novam, discretas fossa inter Africanum sequentem et
reges Thenas usque perducta, quod oppidum a
Carthagine abest $\overline{\text{CCXVI}}$.

26 IV. Tertius sinus dividitur in geminos, duarum
Syrtium vadoso ac reciproco mari diros. ad
proximam, quae minor est, a Carthagine $\overline{\text{CCC}}$ Polybius
tradit, ipsam centum milium passuum aditu, tre-
centorum ambitu. et terra autem siderum observatione ad eam per deserta harenis perque serpentes
iter est. excipiunt saltus repleti ferarum multitudine,

---

[a] Scipio Africanus the elder camped here on landing in
Africa 204 B.C.
[b] See § 4 note.
[c] Scipio Aemilianus, son of Aemilius Paulus.
[d] Micipsa and two other sons of Masinissa.

famous as the scene of the death of Cato. Then there is the river Merjerdah, the place called the Camp of Cornelius,[a] the colony of Carthage on the *Carthage.* site of Great Carthage,[b] the colony of Maxula, the towns of Carpi, Misua and Clypea, the last a free town on Cape Mercury, where are also the free towns Kurbah and Nabal.

Then comes another section of Africa proper. The inhabitants of Byzacium are called Libyphoenicians, Byzacium being the name given to a region measuring 250 miles round, a district of exceptional fertility, the soil paying the farmers interest at the rate of a hundredfold. Here are the free towns of Lempta, Sousa, Monastir, Demas, and then Taineh, Aves, Mahometa, Cabès and Sabart on the edge of the Lesser Syrtis; from the Ampsaga to this point the length of Numidia and Africa is 580 miles and the breadth so far as ascertained 200 miles. The part that we have called Africa is divided into two provinces, the Old and the New; the division between these, as agreed between the younger Scipio [c] and the Kings,[d] is a dyke running right through to the town of Taineh, which is 216 miles from Carthage.

IV. The third gulf is divided into two bays, which *The Gulf of Cabès and the Gulf of Sydra.* are rendered formidable by the shallow tidal waters of the two Syrtes. The distance between the nearest Syrtis, which is the smaller of the two, and Carthage is said by Polybius to be 300 miles; and he gives its width across as 100 miles and its circuit as 300 miles. There is however also a way to it by land, that can be found by observation of the stars, across a desert abandoned to the sand and swarming with serpents. Next come forests filled with a

et introrsus elephantorum solitudines, mox deserta
vasta ultraque Garamantes ab Augilis dierum XII
27 itinere distantes.   super illos fuere gens Psylli, super
quos lacus Lycomedis desertis circumdatus.   Augilae
ipsi medio fere spatio locantur, ab Aethiopia quae
ad occidentem vergit et a regione quae duas Syrtis
interiacet pari utrimque intervallo.   sed litore inter
duas Syrtis c̄c̄l̄; ibi civitas Oeensis, Cinyps fluvius ac
regio, oppida Neapolis, Taphra, Habrotonum, Leptis
altera quae cognominatur Magna.   inde Syrtis Maior
circuitu d̄c̄xxv̄, aditu autem c̄c̄c̄xī̄ī; accolit[1] gens
28 Cisippadum.   in intimo sinu fuit Ora Lotophagon
quos quidam Machroas[2] dixere, ad Philaenorum Aras:
ex harena sunt hae.   ab his non procul a continente
palus vasta amnem Tritonem nomenque ab eo
accipit, Pallantias appellata Callimacho et citra
Minorem Syrtim esse dicta, multis vero inter duas
Syrtis.   promunturium quod Maiorem includit
Borion appellatur; ultra Cyrenaica provincia.
29   Ad hunc finem Africa a fluvio Ampsaga populos
DXVI habet qui Romano pareant imperio; in his
colonias sex, praeter iam dictas Uthinam, Thuburbi;
oppida civium Romanorum xv, ex quibus in mediterraneo dicenda Absuritanum, Abutucense, Abo-

---

[1] *Mayhoff*: inde accolit.
[2] *V.l.* Alachroas.

---

[a] Here denoting the denizens of Phazania, Fezzan, the
largest oasis in the Sahara.
[b] One legend gave it as her birthplace.

multitude of wild beasts, and further inland desolate
haunts of elephants, and then a vast desert, and
beyond it the Garamantes [a] tribe, at a distance of
twelve days' journey from Aujelah. Beyond these
was formerly the Psylli tribe, and beyond them
Lake Lynxama, surrounded by desert. Aujelah
itself is situated almost in the middle, at an equal
distance on either side from the Ethiopia that
stretches westward and from the region lying between
the two Syrtes. But by the coast between the two
Syrtes it is 250 miles; here are the independent
city of Oea, the river Cinyps and the district of that
name, the towns of Neapolis, Taphra, Habrotonum
and the second Leptis, called Great Leptis. Then
comes the Greater Syrtis, measuring 625 miles
round and 312 wide at the entrance, near which
dwells the race of the Cisippades. At the end of
this Gulf was once the Coast of the Lotus-eaters,
the people called by some the Machroae, extending
to the Altars of the Philaeni—these are formed of
heaps of sand. After these, not far from the shore
of the mainland, there is a vast swamp into which
flows the river Tritonis, the name of which it bears;
Callimachus calls it the Lake of Pallas.[b] He places
it on the nearer side of the Lesser Syrtis, but many
writers put it between the two Syrtes. The promontory shutting in the Greater Syrtis is called Cape
Trajuni; beyond it is the province of Cyrene.

Between the river Ampsaga and this boundary
Africa contains 516 peoples that accept allegiance
to Rome. These include six colonies, Uthina and
Thuburbi, in addition to those already mentioned; §§ 22, 24.
15 towns with Roman citizenship, among which in
the interior must be mentioned those of Absurae,

riense, Canopicum, Chimavense, Simittuense, Thunusidense, Thuburnicense, Thinidrumense, Tibigense, Ucitana duo, Maius et Minus, Vagense; oppidum Latinum unum Uzalitanum; oppidum stipendiarium
30 unum Castris Corneliis; oppida libera xxx, ex quibus dicenda intus Achollitanum, Accaritanum, Avinense, Abziritanum, Canopitanum, Melizitanum, Materense, Salaphitanum, Tusdritanum, Tiphicense, Tunisense, Theudense, Tagesense, Tigense, Ulusubritanum, Vagense aliud, Vigense, Zamense. ex reliquo numero non civitates tantum sed pleraeque etiam nationes iure dici possunt, ut Natabudes, Capsitani, Musulami, Sabarbares, Massyli, Nicives, Vamacures, Cinithi, Musuni, Marchubi, et tota Gaetulia ad flumen Nigrim, qui Africam ab Aethiopia dirimit.

31 V. Cyrenaica (eadem Pentapolitana regio) inlustratur Hammonis oraculo quod a Cyrenis abest $\overline{\text{cccc}}$ p., fonte Solis, urbibus maxime quinque, Berenice, Arsinoe, Ptolemaide, Apollonia ipsaque Cyrene. Berenice in Syrtis extimo cornu est, quondam vocata Hesperidum supra dictarum, vagantibus Graeciae fabulis; nec procul ante oppidum fluvius Leton, lucus sacer, ubi Hesperidum horti memorantur.
32 abest ab Lepti $\overline{\text{ccclxxv}}$; ab ea Arsinoe Teuchira vocitata $\overline{\text{xliii}}$, et deinde Ptolemais antiquo nomine Barce $\overline{\text{xxii}}$; mox $\overline{\text{xl}}$ promunturium Phycuus per

---

a From which Tunis takes its name.
b The birthplace of St. Augustine.

240

Abutucum, Aborium, Canopicum, Chimavis, Simit-tuum, Thunusidum, Thuburnicum, Thinidrumum, Tibiga, the two towns called Ucita, the Greater and the Lesser, and Vaga; one town with Latin rights, Uzalita; one tributary town at the Camp of Cornelius; 30 free towns, of which must be mentioned in the interior the towns of Achollita, Accarita, Avina, Abzirita, Canopita, Melizita, Matera, Salaphita, Tusdrita, Tiphica, Tunisa,[a] Theuda, Tagesa, Tiga, Ulusubrita, a second Vaga, Viga and Zama.[b] Of the remaining number most can rightly be entitled not merely cities but also tribes, for instance the Natabudes, Capsitani, Musulami, Sabarbares, Massyli, Nicives, Vamacures, Cinithi, Musuni, Marchubi, and the whole of Gaetulia as far as the river Quorra, which separates Africa from Ethiopia.

V. Notable places in the district of Cyrenaica *Cyrenaica* (the Greek name of which is the Land of the Five *(Barca).* Cities) are the Oracle of Ammon, which is 400 miles from the city of Cyrene, the Fountain of the Sun, and especially five cities, Benghazi, Arsinoe, Tolmeita, Marsa Sousah and Cyrene itself. Benghazi is situated at the tip of the horn of the Syrtis; it was formerly called the City of the Ladies of the West, mentioned above, as the myths of Greece § 3. often change their locality; and in front of the town not far away is the river Leton, with a sacred grove, reputed to be the site of the gardens of the Ladies of the West. Benghazi is 375 miles from Leptis; and Arsinoe is 43 miles from Benghazi, commonly called Teuchira, and then 22 miles further Ptolemais, the old name of which was Barce; then 40 miles on the cape of Ras Sem projects into the Cretan

Creticum mare excurrit, distans $\overline{\text{CCCL}}$ p. a Taenaro
Laconicae promunturio, a Creta vero ipsa $\overline{\text{CCXXV}}$.
post id Cyrene, a mari XI passuum, ab Phycunte
Apolloniam $\overline{\text{XXIV}}$, ad Cherronesum $\overline{\text{LXXXVIII}}$, unde
Catabathmum $\overline{\text{CCXVI}}$. accolunt Marmaridae, a Parae-
toni ferme regione ad Syrtim Maiorem usque por-
33 recti; post eos Acrauceles ac iam in ora Syrtis Nasamones, quos antea Mesammones Grai appellavere
ab argumento loci, medios inter harenas sitos.
Cyrenaicus ager $\overline{\text{XV}}$ p. latitudine a litore et arboribus
fertilis habetur, intus eodem spatio frugibus tantum,
mox $\overline{\text{XXX}}$ latitudine et $\overline{\text{CCL}}$ longitudine lasari modo.
34   Post Nasamonas Asbytae et Macae vivont; ultra
eos Amantes XII dierum itinere a Syrtibus Maioribus,
ad occidentem et ipsi versus harenis circumdati,
puteos tamen haut difficile binum ferme cubitorum
altitudine inveniunt ibi restagnantibus Mauretaniae
aquis. domus sale montibus suis exciso ceu lapide
construunt. ab his ad Trogodytas hiberni occasus
plaga dierum septem iter, cum quibus commercium
gemmae tantum quam carbunculum vocamus ex
35 Aethiopia invectae. intervenit ad solitudines Africae
supra Minorem Syrtim dictas versa Phazania, ubi

---

^a The distance is said to be really 264 miles.

Sea, 350 miles *a* distant from Cape Matapan in Laconia and 225 miles from Crete itself. After the cape of Ras Sem is Cyrene, 11 miles from the sea, from Ras Sem to the harbour of Cyrene being 24 miles and to Ras El Tin 88 miles, from which it is 216 miles to the Canyon. The inhabitants of this coast are the Marmaridae, reaching almost all the way from the region of El Bareton to the Greater Syrtis; after these are the Acrauceles and then on the edge of the Syrtis the Nasamones, formerly called by the Greeks Mesammones by reason of their locality, the word meaning ' in the middle of the sands '. The territory of Cyrene for a breadth of 15 miles from the coast is thought to be good even for growing trees, but for the same space further inland to grow only corn, and afterwards over a strip 30 miles wide and 250 miles long nothing but silphium.

After the Nasamones, we come to the dwellings of the Asbytae and Macae; and beyond them, twelve days' journey from the Greater Syrtis, the Amantes. These also are surrounded by sands in the western direction, but nevertheless they find water without difficulty at a depth of about three feet, as the district receives the overflow of the waters of Mauretania. They build their houses of blocks of salt quarried out of their mountains like stone. From these it is a journey of 7 days in a south-westerly quarter to the Cave-dwellers, with whom our only intercourse is the trade in the precious stone imported from Ethiopia which we call the carbuncle. Before reaching them, in the direction § 26. of the African desert stated already to be beyond the Lesser Syrtis, is Fezzan, where we have subju-

gentem Phazaniorum urbesque Alelen et Cillibam
subegimus, item Cydamum e regione Sabratae. ab
his mons longo spatio in occasum ab ortu tendit Ater
nostris dictus a natura, adusto similis aut solis
36 repercussu accenso. ultra eum deserta, mox Thelgae
oppidum Garamantum, itemque Debris adfuso fonte
a medio die ad mediam noctem aquis ferventibus
totidemque horis ad medium diem rigentibus,
clarissimumque Garama caput Garamantum : omnia
armis Romanis superata et a Cornelio Balbo triumph-
ata, uni huic[1] omnium externo curru[2] et Quiritium
iure donato : quippe Gadibus genito civitas Romana
cum Balbo maiore patruo data est. et hoc mirum,
supra dicta oppida ab eo capta auctores nostros
prodidisse, ipsum in triumpho praeter Cydamum et
Garamam omnium aliarum gentium urbiumque
nomina ac simulacra duxisse, quae iere hoc ordine :
37 Tabudium oppidum, Niteris natio, Milgis Gemella
oppidum, Bubeium natio vel oppidum, Enipi natio,
Thuben oppidum, mons nomine Niger, Nitibrum,
Rapsa oppida, Viscera natio, Decri oppidum, flumen
Nathabur, Thapsagum oppidum, Tamiagi natio,
Boin oppidum, Pege oppidum, flumen Dasibari ;
mox oppida continua Baracum, Buluba, Alasit, Galsa,

---

[1] *Hardouin* : unius.
[2] *V.l.* curru externo (*fortasse* curru uni huic omnium externo
Rackham).

gated the Fezzan tribe and the cities of Mellulen
and Zala, as well as Gadamez in the direction of
Sabrata. After these a long range stretches from
east to west which our people from its nature call
the Black Mountain, as it has the appearance of
having suffered from fire, or else of being scorched
by the reflection of the sun. Beyond this mountain
range is the desert, and then a town of the Garamantes called Thelgae, and also Bedir (near which
there is a spring of which the water is boiling hot
from midday to midnight and then freezing cold for
the same number of hours until midday) and Garama,
the celebrated capital of the Garamantes: all of
which places have been subdued by the arms of
Rome, being conquered by Cornelius Balbus, who
was given a triumph—the only foreigner ever so
honoured—and citizen rights, since, although a
native of Cadiz, he together with his great-uncle,
Balbus, was presented with our citizenship. There
is also this remarkable circumstance, that our writers
have handed down the names of the towns mentioned
above as having been taken by him, and have stated
that in his own triumphal procession beside Cydamum
and Garama were carried the names and images of
all the other races and cities, which went in this
order: the town of Tibesti, the Niteris tribe, the
town of Milgis Gemella, the tribe or town of Febabo,
the tribe of the Enipi, the town of Thuben, the
mountain known as the Black Mountain, the towns
called Nitibrum and Rapsa, the Im-Zera tribe, the
town of Om-El-Abid, the river Tessava, the town of
Sava, the Tamiagi tribe, the town of Boin, the town
of Winega, the river Dasibari; then a series of
towns, Baracum, Buluba, Alasit, Galsa, Balla, Misso-

Balla, Maxalla, Cizania; mons Gyri in quo gemmas
nasci titulus praecessit.

38   Ad Garamantas iter inexplicabile adhuc fuit
latronibus gentis eius puteos—qui sunt non alte fodi-
endi si locorum notitia adsit—harenis operientibus.
proxumo bello, quod cum Oeensibus gessere initiis
Vespasiani imperatoris, conpendium viae quadridui
deprehensum est; hoc iter vocatur Praeter Caput
Saxi. finis Cyrenaicus Catabathmos appellatur,
oppidum et vallis repente convexa. ad eum ter-
minum Cyrenaica Africa a Syrti Minore |x̄| l̄x in
longitudinem patet, in latitudinem qua cognitum est
d̄ccccx.

39   VI. Quae sequitur regio Mareotis Libya appellatur
Aegypto contermina. tenent Marmarides, Adyrmachidae, dein Mareotae. mensura a Catabathmo
Paraetonium l̄xxxvi. in eo tractu intus Apis interest,
nobilis religione Aegypti locus. ab eo Paraetonium
l̄xii d, inde Alexandriam c̄c. latitudo c̄lxix est.
Eratosthenes a Cyrenis Alexandriam terrestri itinere

40   d̄xxv prodit. Agrippa totius Africae a mari Atlantico
cum Inferiore Aegypto |xxx| longitudinem, Polybius
et Eratosthenes diligentissimi existimati ab oceano
ad Carthaginem Magnam |x̄ī|, ab ea Canopum, Nili

lat, Cizania; and Mount Goriano, its effigy preceded by an inscription that it was a place where precious stones were produced.

Hitherto it has been impossible to open up the road to the Garamantes country, because brigands of that race fill up the wells with sand—these do not need to be dug very deep if you are aided by a knowledge of the localities. In the last war waged with the people of Oea, at the beginning of the principate of Vespasian, a short route of only four days was discovered, which is known as By the Head of the Rock. The last place in Cyrenaica is called the Canyon, a town and a suddenly descending valley. The length of Cyrenaic Africa from the Lesser Syrtis to this boundary is 1060 miles, and the breadth, so far as ascertained, 810 miles.

VI. The district that follows is called Libya *Libya.* Mareotis; it borders upon Egypt. It is occupied by the Marmarides, the Adyrmachidae, and then the Mareotae. The distance between the Canyon and Paraetonium is 86 miles. Between them in the interior of this district is Apis, a place famous in the Egyptian religion. The distance from Apis to Paraetonium is $62\frac{1}{2}$ miles, and from Paraetonium to Alexandria 200 miles. The district is 169 miles in breadth. Eratosthenes gives the distance by land from Cyrenae to Alexandria as 525 miles. Agrippa made the length of the whole of Africa from the Atlantic, including Lower Egypt, 300 miles; Polybius and Eratosthenes, who are deemed extremely careful writers, made the distance from the Ocean to Great Carthage 1100 miles, and from Great Carthage to the nearest mouth of the Nile,

proximum ostium, $\overline{|\mathrm{xvi}|}$ $\overline{\mathrm{xxviii}}$ fecerunt, Isidorus a Tingi Canopum $\overline{|\mathrm{xxxv}|}$ $\overline{\mathrm{xcix}}$, Artemidorus xl m minus quam Isidorus.

41 VII. Insulas non ita multas complectuntur haec maria. clarissima est Meninx, longitudine $\overline{\mathrm{xxv}}$, latitudine $\overline{\mathrm{xxii}}$, ab Eratosthene Lotophagitis appellata. oppida habet duo, Meningen ab Africae latere et ab[1] altero Thoar, ipsa a dextro Syrtis Minoris promunturio passibus md sita. ab ea $\overline{\mathrm{c}}$ p. contra laevum Cercina cum urbe eiusdem nominis libera, longa $\overline{\mathrm{xxv}}$, lata dimidium eius ubi plurimum, at in extremo non plus $\overline{\mathrm{v}}$—huic perparva Carthaginem versus Cercinitis 42 ponte iungitur. ab his $\overline{\mathrm{L}}$ fere passuum Lopadusa, longa $\overline{\mathrm{vi}}$; mox Gaulos et Galata, cuius terra scorpiones, dirum animal Africae, necat. dicuntur et in Clupea emori, cuius ex adverso Cossyra cum oppido. at contra Carthaginis sinum duae Aegimoeroe; Arae autem, scopuli verius quam insulae, inter Siciliam maxime et Sardiniam; auctores sunt et has quondam habitatas subsedisse.

43 VIII. Interiore autem ambitu Africae ad meridiem versus superque Gaetulos, intervenientibus desertis, primi omnium Libyes Aegyptii, deinde Leucoe Aethiopes habitant. super eos Aethiopum gentes

[1] ab *add. Rackham.*

248

Canopus, 1628 miles; Isidorus makes the distance from Tangier to Canopus 3599 miles, but Artemidorus makes it 40 miles less than Isidorus.

VII. These seas do not contain very many islands. *Islands off N. Africa.* The most famous is Zerba, 25 miles long and 22 miles broad, called by Eratosthenes Lotus Eaters' Island. It has two towns, Meninx on the side of Africa and Thoar on the other side, the island itself lying off the promontory on the right-hand side of the Lesser Syrtis, at a distance of a mile and a half away. A hundred miles from Zerba and lying off the left-hand promontory is the island of Cercina, with the free city of the same name; it is 25 miles long and measures half that distance across where it is widest, but not more than 5 miles across at its end; and joined to it by a bridge is the extremely small island of Cercinitis, which looks towards Carthage. About 50 miles from these is Lopadusa, 6 miles long; then come Gaulos and Galata, the soil of the latter having the property of killing scorpions, that pest of Africa. It is also said that scorpions cannot live at Clupea, opposite to which lies Pantellaria with its town. Opposite the Gulf of Carthage lie the two Aegimoeroi; but the Altars, which are more truly rocks than islands, are chiefly between Sicily and Sardinia. Some authorities state that even the Altars were formerly inhabited but that their level has sunk.

VIII. In the interior circuit of Africa towards the *Peoples of the interior.* south and beyond the Gaetulians, after an intermediate strip of desert, the first inhabitants of all are the Egyptian Libyans, and then the people called in Greek the White Ethiopians. Beyond these are the Ethiopian clans of the Nigritae,

Nigritae a quo dictum est flumine, Gymnetes Pharusii, iam oceanum attingentes quos in Mauretaniae fine diximus Perorsi. ab his omnibus vastae solitudines orientem versus usque ad Garamantas Augilasque et Trogodytas, verissima opinione eorum qui desertis Africae duas Aethiopias superponunt, et ante omnis Homeri qui bipertitos tradit Aethiopas, ad orientem occasumque versos.

44　Nigri fluvio eadem natura quae Nilo; calamum ac papyrum et easdem gignit animantes iisdemque temporibus augescit. oritur inter Tarraelios Aethiopas et Oechalicas; horum oppidum Magium. quidam solitudinibus interposuerunt Atlantas eosque iuxta Aegipanas semiferos et Blemmyas et Gamphasantas et Satyros et Himantopodas.

45　Atlantes degeneres sunt humani ritus, si credimus; nam neque nominum ullorum inter ipsos appellatio est, et solem orientem occidentemque dira inprecatione contuentur ut exitialem ipsis agrisque, neque in somno visunt qualia reliqui mortales. Trogodytae specus excavant; hae illis domus, victus serpentium carnes, stridorque, non vox: adeo sermonis commercio carent. Garamantes matrimoniorum exortes passim cum feminis degunt. Augilae inferos tantum

---

　　a *Od.* I. 23 f.
　　b It is not certain that this is the river now known by this name.
　　c Herod. IV. 183 τετρίγασι κατά περ αἱ νυκτερίδες.

named after the river which has been mentioned, § 30.
the Pharusian Gymnetes, and then bordering on the
Ocean the Perorsi whom we have spoken of at the § 10.
frontier of Mauretania. Eastward of all of these there
are vast uninhabited regions spreading as far as the
Garamantes and Augilae and the Cave-dwellers—
the most reliable opinion being that of those who
place two Ethiopias beyond the African desert, and
especially Homer,[a] who tells us that the Ethiopians
are divided into two sections, the eastward and the
westward.

The river Niger[b] has the same nature as the Nile:
it produces reeds and papyrus, and the same animals,
and it rises at the same seasons of the year. Its
source is between the Ethiopic tribes of the Tarraelii
and the Oechalicae; the town of the latter is
Magium. In the middle of the desert some place
the Atlas tribe, and next to them the half-animal
Goat-Pans and the Blemmyae and Gamphasantes
and Satyrs and Strapfoots.

The Atlas tribe have fallen below the level of
human civilization, if we can believe what is said;
for they do not address one another by any names,
and when they behold the rising and setting sun,
they utter awful curses against it as the cause of
disaster to themselves and their fields, and when
they are asleep they do not have dreams like the
rest of mankind. The Cave-dwellers hollow out
caverns, which are their dwellings; they live on the
flesh of snakes, and they have no voice, but only
make squeaking noises,[c] being entirely devoid of intercourse by speech. The Garamantes do not practise
marriage but live with their women promiscuously.
The Augilae only worship the powers of the lower

colunt. Gamphasantes nudi proeliorumque expertes
46 nulli externo congregantur. Blemmyis traduntur
capita abesse ore et oculis pectori adfixis. Satyris
praeter figuram nihil moris humani. Aegipanum
qualis vulgo pingitur forma. Himantopodes lori-
pedes quidam quibus serpendo ingredi natura sit.
Pharusi, quondam Persae, comites fuisse dicuntur
Herculis ad Hesperidas tendentis.

Nec de Africa plura quae memorentur occurrunt.

47 IX. Adhaeret Asia, quam patere a Canopico ostio
ad Ponti ostium Timosthenes $\overline{|xxvi|}$ $\overline{xxxviii}$ p. tradidit,
ab ore autem Ponti ad os Maeotis Eratosthenes $\overline{|xv|}$
$\overline{xlv}$, universam vero cum Aegypto ad Tanain Arte-
midorus et Isidorus $\overline{|L|}$ $\overline{xiii}$ dccl.[1] maria eius conplura
ab accolis traxere nomina, quare simul indicabuntur.

48 Proxima Africae incolitur Aegyptus, introrsus ad
meridiem recedens donec a tergo praetendantur
Aethiopes. inferiorem eius partem Nilus dextera
laevaque divisus amplexu suo determinat, Canopico
ostio ab Africa, ab Asia Pelusiaco, $\overline{clxx}$ passuum
intervallo. quam ob causam inter insulas quidam
Aegyptum retulere, ita se findente Nilo ut triquetram

---

[1] *Varia edd.*

---

[a] These figures are uncertain in the Latin text.

world. The Gamphasantes go naked, do not engage in battle, and hold no intercourse with any foreigner. The Blemmyae are reported to have no heads, their mouth and eyes being attached to their chests. The Satyrs have nothing of ordinary humanity about them except human shape. The form of the Goat-Pans is that which is commonly shown in pictures of them. The Strapfoots are people with feet like leather thongs, whose nature it is to crawl instead of walking. The Pharusi, originally a Persian people, are said to have accompanied Hercules on his journey to the Ladies of the West. Nothing more occurs to us to record about Africa.

IX. Joining on to Africa is Asia, the extent of which from the Canopic mouth of the Nile to the mouth of the Black Sea is given by Timosthenes as 2638 miles; Eratosthenes gives the distance from the mouth of the Black Sea to the mouth of the Sea of Azov as 1545 miles; and Artemidorus and Isidorus give the whole extent of Asia including Egypt as far as the river Don as $5013\frac{3}{4}$ miles.[a] It possesses several seas, named after the tribes on their shores, for which reason they will be mentioned together.

The inhabited country next to Africa is Egypt, *Egypt.* which stretches southward into the interior to where the Ethiopians border it in the rear. The boundaries of its lower part are formed by the two branches of the Nile embracing it on the right and on the left, the Canopic mouth separating it from Africa and the Pelusiac from Asia, with a space of 170 miles between the two mouths. This has caused some authorities to class Egypt as an island, because the Nile divides in such a manner as to produce a

terrae figuram efficiat; ideoque multi Graecae
litterae vocabulo Delta appellavere Aegyptum.
mensura ab unitate alvei, unde se primum findit in
latera, ad Canopicum ostium $\overline{\text{CXLVI}}$, ad Pelusiacum
$\overline{\text{CLVI}}$ est.

49 Summa pars contermina Aethiopiae Thebais vocatur. dividitur in praefecturas oppidorum quas
nomos vocant—Ombiten, Apollonopoliten, Hermon-
thiten, Thiniten, Phaturiten, Coptiten, Tentyriten,
Diospoliten, Antaeopoliten, Aphroditopoliten, Lyco-
politen. quae iuxta Pelusium est regio nomos
habet Pharbaethiten, Bubastiten, Sethroiten, Tani-
ten. reliqua autem Arabicum, Hammoniacum ten-
dentem ad Hammonis Iovis oraculum, Oxyrynchiten,
Leontopoliten, Athribiten, Cynopoliten, Hermo-
politen, Xoiten, Mendesium, Sebennyten, Cabasiten,
Latopoliten, Heliopoliten, Prosopiten, Panopoliten,
Busiriten, Onuphiten, Saiten, Ptenethum, Ptem-
phum, Naucratiten, Metelliten, Gynaecopoliten,
Menelaiten, Alexandriae regionem; item Libyae
50 Mareotis. Heracleopolites est in insula Nili longa
p. $\overline{\text{L}}$, in qua et oppidum Herculis appellatum.
Arsinoitae duo sunt; hi et Memphites usque ad
summum Delta perveniunt, cui sunt contermini ex
Africa duo Oasitae. quidam ex his aliqua nomina
permutant et substituunt alios nomos, ut Hero-
opoliten et Crocodilopoliten. inter Arsinoiten autem
ac Memphiten lacus fuit circuitu $\overline{\text{CCL}}$ aut, ut Mucianus

254

piece of land shaped like a triangle; and consequently many have called Egypt by the name of
the Greek letter Delta. The distance from the
point where the single channel first splits into
branches to the Canopic mouth is 146 miles and to
the Pelusiac mouth 156 miles.

The uppermost part of Egypt, marching with
Ethiopia, is called the Thebaid. It is divided into
prefectures of towns, called ' nomes '—the Ombite,
Apollonopolite, Hermonthite, Thinite, Phaturite,
Coptite, Tentyrite, Diospolite, Antaeopolite, Aphro-
ditopolite and Lycopolite nomes. The nomes be-
longing to the district in the neighbourhood of Pelu-
sium are the Pharbaethite, Bubastite, Sethroite and
Tanite. The remaining nomes are called the Arabic,
Hammoniac (on the way to the oracle of Jupiter
Ammon), Oxyrhynchite, Leontopolite, Athribite,
Cynopolite, Hermopolite, Xoite, Mendesian, Seben-
nyte, Cabasite, Latopolite, Heliopolite, Prosopite,
Panopolite, Busirite, Onuphite, Saite, Ptenethus,
Ptemphus, Naucratite, Metellite, Gynaecopolite,
Menelaite—these forming the region of Alexandria;
and likewise Mareotis belonging to Libya. The
Heracleopolite nome is on an island of the Nile
measuring 50 miles long, on which is also the town
called the City of Hercules. There are two nomes
called the Arsinoite; these and the Memphite extend to the apex of the Delta, adjacent to which
on the side of Africa are the two Oasite nomes.
Certain authorities alter some out of these names
and substitute other nomes, for instance the Hero-
polite and Crocodilopolite. Between the Arsinoite
and Memphite nomes there was once a lake
measuring 250, or according to Mucianus's account

tradit, $\overline{\text{CCCCL}}$ et altitudinis quinquaginta passuum,
manu factus, a rege qui fecerat Moeridis appellatus.
inde $\overline{\text{LXII}}$ p. abest Memphis, quondam arx Aegypti
regum, unde ad Hammonis oraculum XII dierum iter
est, ad scissuram autem Nili, quod appellavimus
Delta, xv.

51   X. Nilus incertis ortus fontibus, ut per deserta et
ardentia et inmenso longitudinis spatio ambulans
famaque tantum inermi quaesitus sine bellis quae
ceteras omnis terras invenere, originem, ut Iuba rex
potuit exquirere, in monte inferioris Mauretaniae
non procul oceano habet lacu protinus stagnante,
quem vocant Niliden. ibi pisces reperiuntur ala-
betae, coracini, siluri; crocodilus quoque inde ob
argumentum hoc Caesareae in Iseo dicatus ab eo
spectatur hodie. praeterea observatum est, prout
in Mauretania nives imbresve satiaverint, ita Nilum
52 increscere. ex hoc lacu profusus indignatur fluere
per harenosa et squalentia, conditque se aliquot
dierum itinere, mox alio lacu maiore in Caesariensis
Mauretaniae gente Masaesylum erumpit et hominum coetus veluti circumspicit, iisdem animalium
argumentis. iterum harenis receptus conditur rursus
xx dierum desertis ad proximos Aethiopas, atque ubi

450, miles round, and 250 feet deep, an artificial sheet of water, called the Lake of Moeris after the king who made it. Its site is 62 miles from Memphis, the former citadel of the kings of Egypt, and from Memphis it is 12 days' journey to the Oracle of Ammon and 15 days' journey to the place where the Nile divides and forms what we have called the Delta.

X. The sources from which the Nile rises have *The Nile.* not been ascertained, proceeding as it does through scorching deserts for an enormously long distance and only having been explored by unarmed investigators, without the wars that have discovered all other countries; but so far as King Juba was able to ascertain, it has its origin in a mountain of lower Mauretania not far from the Ocean, and immediately forms a stagnant lake called Nilides. Fish found in this lake are the alabeta, coracinus and silurus; also a crocodile was brought from it by Juba to prove his theory, and placed as a votive offering in the temple of Isis at Caesarea, where it is on view to-day. Moreover it has been observed that the Nile rises in proportion to excessive falls of snow or rain in Mauretania. Issuing from this lake the river disdains to flow through arid deserts of sand, and for a distance of several days' journey it hides underground, but afterwards it bursts out in another larger lake in the territory of the Masaesyles clan of Mauretania Caesariensis, and so to speak makes a survey of the communities of mankind, proving its identity by having the same fauna. Sinking again into the sand of the desert it hides for another space of 20 days' journey till it reaches the nearest Ethiopians, and when it has once more

iterum sensit hominem, prosilit fonte, ut verisimile
53 est, illo quem Nigrum vocavere. inde Africam ab
Aethiopia dispescens, etiamsi non protinus populis,
feris tamen et beluis frequens silvarumque opifex,
medios Aethiopas secat cognominatus Astapus, quod
illarum gentium lingua significat aquam e tenebris
profluentem. insulas ita innumeras spargit, quasdamque tam vastae magnitudinis, quamquam rapida
celeritate, ut tamen dierum v cursu, non breviore,
travolet, circa clarissimam earum Meroen Astobores
laevo alveo dictus, hoc est ramus aquae venientis e
tenebris, dextra vero Astusapes, quod lateris signi-
54 ficationem adicit, nec ante Nilus quam se totum aquis
rursus concordibus iunxit, sic quoque etiamnum Giris
ante nominatus per aliquot milia, et in totum Homero
Aegyptus aliisque Triton. subinde insulis impactus,
totidem incitatus inritamentis, postremo inclusus
montibus, nec aliunde torrentior, vectus aquis pro-
perantibus ad locum Aethiopicum [1] qui Catadupi
vocatur,[2] novissimo catarracte inter occursantis
scopulos non fluere inmenso fragore creditur sed
ruere. postea lenis et confractis [3] aquis domitaque
violentia, aliquid et spatio fessus, multis quamvis

---

[1] *Rackham* : Aethiopum.
[2] *V.l.* vocantur.
[3] *V.l.* levis et confractus.

---

[a] *Od.* iv. 477.
[b] The northernmost, now the First Cataract.

become aware of man's proximity it leaps out in a
fountain, probably the one called the Black Spring.
From this point it forms the boundary line between
Africa and Ethiopia, and though the river-side is not
immediately inhabited, it teems with wild beasts
and animal life and produces forests; and where
the river cuts through the middle of Ethiopia it
has the name of Astapus, which in the native
language means 'water issuing from the shades
below.' It strews about such a countless number of
islands, and some of them of such vast size, that in
spite of its very rapid flow it nevertheless only flies
past them in a course of five days, and not shorter;
while making the circuit of the most famous of these
islands, Meroe, the left-hand channel is called
Astobores, that is 'branch of water coming out of
the shades,' and the right-hand channel Astusapes,
which means 'side branch.' It is not called Nile
until its waters are again reconciled and have united
in a single stream, and even then for some miles
it still has the name of Giris which it had previously. Its name in Homer [a] is Aegyptus over its
whole course, and with other writers it is the Triton.
Every now and then it impinges on islands, which
are so many incitements spurring it forward on its
way, till finally it is shut in by mountains, its flow
being nowhere more rapid; and it is borne on with
hurrying waters to the place in Ethiopia called in
Greek the Downcrash, where at its last cataract [b]
owing to the enormous noise it seems not to run
but to riot between the rocks that bar its way.
Afterwards it is gentle, the violence of its waters
having been broken and subdued, and also it is
somewhat fatigued by the distance it has raced,

faucibus in Aegyptium mare se evomat, certis tamen diebus auctu magno per totam spatiatus Aegyptum fecundus innatat terrae.

55 Causas huius incrementi varias prodidere, sed maxime probabiles etesiarum eo tempore ex adverso flantium repercussum, ultra in ora acto mari, aut imbres Aethiopiae aestivos iisdem etesiis nubila illo ferentibus e reliquo orbe. Timaeus mathematicus occultam protulit rationem: Phialam appellari fontem eius, mergique in cuniculos ipsum amnem vapore anhelantem fumidis cautibus ubi conditur; verum sole per eos dies comminus facto extrahi ardoris vi et suspensum abundare ac ne devoretur

56 abscondi; id evenire a canis ortu per introitum solis in leonem, contra perpendiculum fontis sidere stante, cum eo tractu absumantur umbrae—plerisque e diverso opinatis largiorem fluere ad septentriones sole discedente, quod in cancro et leone evenit, ideoque tunc minus siccari, rursus in capricornum et austrinum

---

^a The south-eastern Mediterranean along the coast of Egypt.
^b These blow for forty days at midsummer.

and it belches out, by many mouths it is true, into
the Egyptian Sea.[a] For a certain part of the year
however its volume greatly increases and it roams
abroad over the whole of Egypt and inundates the
land with a fertilising flood.

Various explanations of this rising of the river have
been given; but the most probable are either the
backwash caused by what are called in Greek the
Annual Winds,[b] which blow in the opposite direction to the current at that period of the year, the
sea outside being driven into the mouths of the
river, or the summer rains of Ethiopia which are
due to the same Annual Winds bringing clouds
from the rest of the world to Egypt. The mathe-
matician Timaeus produced a very recondite theory
—that the source of the Nile is a spring called
Phiala, and that the river buries itself in burrows
underground and breathes forth vapour owing to the
steaming hot rocks among which it hides itself; but
that as the sun at the period in question comes
nearer the river water is drawn out by the force
of the heat and rises up and overflows, and with-
draws itself to avoid being swallowed up. This,
he says, begins to occur at the rising of the Dogstar,
when the sun is entering the sign of the Lion, the
sun standing in a vertical line above the spring, at
which season in that region shadows entirely dis-
appear—though the general opinion on the contrary
is that the flow of the Nile is more copious when
the sun is departing towards the north, which
happens when it is in the Crab and the Lion, and
that consequently the river is dried up less then;
and again when the sun returns to Capricorn and
towards the south pole its waters are absorbed and

polum reverso sorberi et ob id parcius fluere. sed
Timaeo si quis extrahi posse credat, umbrarum
defectus his diebus et locis sine fine adest.

57   Incipit crescere luna nova quaecumque post
solstitium est, sensim modiceque cancrum sole
transeunte, abundantissime autem leonem, et residit
in virgine iisdem quibus adcrevit modis. in totum
autem revocatur intra ripas in libra, ut tradit Herodotus, centesimo die. cum crescit, reges aut prae-
fectos navigare eo nefas iudicatum est. auctus per
58   puteos mensurae notis deprehenduntur. iustum
incrementum est cubitorum XVI. minores aquae
non omnia rigant, ampliores detinent tardius re-
cedendo; hae serendi tempora absumunt solo
madente, illae non dant sitiente. utrumque reputat
provincia; in XII cubitis famem sentit, in XIII etiamnum esurit, XIV cubita hilaritatem adferunt, XV
securitatem, XVI delicias. maximum incrementum
ad hoc aevi fuit cubitorum XVIII Claudio principe,
minimum V Pharsalico bello, veluti necem Magni
prodigio quodam flumine aversante. cum stetere
aquae, apertis molibus admittuntur; ut quaeque

----

[a] Even when the sun is in the south, so that if Timaeus's
explanation were right, the Nile would be high all the year
round.
[b] II. 19.
262

its volume consequently reduced. But if anybody is inclined to accept the possibility of Timaeus's explanation that the waters of the river are drawn out of the earth, there is the fact that in these regions absence of shadows goes on continuously at this season.[a]

The Nile begins to rise at the next new moon after midsummer, the rise being gradual and moderate while the sun is passing through the Crab and at its greatest height when it is in the Lion; and when in Virgo it begins to fall by the same degrees as it rose. It subsides entirely within its banks, according to the account given by Herodotus,[b] on the hundredth day, when the sun is in the Scales. The view has been held that it is unlawful for kings or rulers to sail on the Nile when it is rising. Its degrees of increase are detected by means of wells marked with a scale. An average rise is one of 24 feet. A smaller volume of water does not irrigate all localities, and a larger one by retiring too slowly retards agriculture; and the latter uses up the time for sowing because of the moisture of the soil, while the former gives no time for sowing because the soil is parched. The province takes careful note of both extremes: in a rise of 18 feet it senses famine, and even at one of 19½ feet it begins to feel hungry, but 21 feet brings cheerfulness, 22½ feet complete confidence and 24 feet delight. The largest rise up to date was one of 27 feet in the principate of Claudius, and the smallest 41–54 A.D. 7½ feet in the year of the war of Pharsalus, as if the 48 B.C. river were attempting to avert the murder of Pompey by a sort of portent. When the rise comes to a standstill, the floodgates are opened and irrigation

liberata est terra, seritur. idem amnis unus
omnium nullas exspirat auras.

59 Dicionis Aegyptiae esse incipit a fine Aethiopiae
Syene: ita vocatur paeninsula mille passuum ambitu
in qua Castra sunt latere Arabiae et ex adverso
insulae IV Philae, DC p. a Nili fissura, unde appellari
diximus Delta. hoc spatium edidit Artemidorus, et
in eo CCL oppida fuisse, Iuba CCCC, Aristocreon ab
Elephantide ad mare DCCL. Elephantis insula intra
novissimum catarracten IV p. et supra Syenen XVI
habitatur, navigationis Aegyptiae finis, ab Alexandria
DLXXXV p.—in tantum erravere supra scripti. ibi
Aethiopicae conveniunt naves; namque eas plicatiles
umeris transferunt quotiens ad catarractas ventum
est.

60 XI. Aegyptus super ceteram antiquitatis gloriam
XX urbium sibi Amase regnante [habitata][1] praefert,
nunc quoque multis etiamsi ignobilibus frequens.
celebratur tamen Apollinis, mox Leucotheae, Diospolis Magna, eadem Thebe, portarum centum nobilis
fama, Coptos Indicarum Arabicarumque mercium
Nilo proximum emporium, mox Veneris oppidum et
iterum Iovis ac Tentyris, infra quod Abydus Mem-

---

[1] *Om. cum uno codice Rackham.*

begins; and each strip of land is sown as the flood relinquishes it. It may be added that the Nile is the only river that emits no exhalations.

It first comes within the territory of Egypt at the Ethiopian frontier, at Assuan—that is the name of the peninsula a mile in circuit in which, on the Arabian side, the Camp is situated and off which lie the four islands of Philae, 600 miles from the place where the Nile splits into two channels—the point at which, as we have said, the island called the Delta begins. This is the distance given by Artemidorus, who also states that the island formerly contained 250 towns; Juba, however, gives the distance as 400 miles. Aristocreon says that the distance from Elephantis to the sea is 750 miles—Elephantis is an inhabited island 4 miles below the last cataract and 16 above Assuan; it is the extreme limit of navigation in Egypt, being 585 miles from Alexandria—so far out in their calculations have the above-named authors been. Elephantis is the point of rendezvous for Ethiopian vessels, which are made collapsible for the purpose of portage on reaching the cataracts.

XI. In addition to boasting its other glories of the past Egypt can claim the distinction of having had in the reign [a] of King Amasis 20,000 cities; and even now it contains a very large number, although of no importance. However, the City of Apollo is notable, as is also the City of Leucothea and the Great City of Zeus, also called Thebes, renowned for the fame of its hundred gates, Coptos the market near the Nile for Indian and Arabian merchandise, and also the Town of Venus and the Town of Jove and Tentyris, below which is Abydos, famous for

Cities of Egypt.

nonis regia et Osiris templo inclutum, VII D p. in
61 Libyam remotum a flumine. dein Ptolemais et
Panopolis ac Veneris iterum, et in Libyco Lycon, ubi
montes finiunt Thebaidem. ab iis oppida Mercuri,
Alabastron, Canum et supra dictum Herculis.
deinde Arsinoes ac iam dicta Memphis, inter quam
et Arsinoiten nomon in Libyco turres quae pyramides
vocantur, labyrinthus in Moeridis lacu nullo addito
ligno exaedificatus et oppidum Crialon.[1] unum
praeterea intus et Arabiae conterminum claritatis
magnae, Solis oppidum.

62 Sed iure laudetur in litore Aegyptii maris Alexandria a Magno Alexandro condita in Africae parte
ab ostio Canopico XII p. iuxta Mareotim lacum, qui
locus antea Rhacotes nominabatur. metatus est
eam Dinochares architectus pluribus modis memorabili ingenio, V p. laxitate insessa ad effigiem Mace-
donicae chlamydis orbe gyrato laciniosam, dextra
laevaque anguloso procursu, iam tum tamen quinta
63 situs parte regiae dicata. Mareotis lacus a meridiana
urbis parte euripo e Canopico ostio mittit ex mediterraneo commercia, insulas quoque plures amplexus,
XXX traiectu, CCL ambitu, ut tradit Claudius Caesar.
alii schoenos in longitudinem patere XL faciunt,

---

[1] Crocodilon *Hardouin ex Hdt.* II. 147.

---

[a] At XII. 53 Pliny gives the *schoenus* (a Persian measure)
as either 40 or 32 stades (see p. 98, n. *a*), *viz.* nearly 5 or
nearly 4 miles.

the palace of Memnon and the temple of Osiris, in the interior of Libya $7\frac{1}{2}$ miles from the river. Then Ptolemais and Panopolis and another Town of Venus, and on the Libyan side Lycon, where the Province of Thebes is bounded by a mountain range. Beyond this are the Towns of Mercury, and of the Alabastri, the Town of Dogs, and the Town of Hercules mentioned above. Then Arsinoe's Town and Memphis already mentioned, between which and the Arsinoite district on the Libyan side are the towers called pyramids, and on Lake Moeris the Labyrinth, in the construction of which no timber was used with the masonry, and the town of the Criali. There is one place besides in the interior and bordering on the Arabian frontier which is of great renown, Heliopolis.

But justice requires that praise shall be bestowed *Alexandria.* on Alexandria, built by Alexander the Great on the coast of the Egyptian Sea on the side of Africa, 12 miles from the Canopic mouth and adjoining Lake Mariout; the site was previously named Rhacotes. It was laid out by the architect Dinochares, who is famous for his talent in a variety of ways; it covered an area spreading 15 miles in the shape of a Macedonian soldier's cape, with indentations in its circumference and projecting corners on the right and left side; while at the same time a fifth of the site was devoted to the King's palace. Lake Mariout, which lies on the south side of the city, carries traffic from the interior by means of a canal from the Canopic mouth of the Nile; also it includes a considerable number of islands, being 30 miles across and 250 miles in circumference, according to Claudius Caesar. Others make it 40 *schoeni* [a] long and reckon

schoenumque stadia xxx, ita fieri longitudinis cl p., tantundem et latitudinis.

64   Sunt in honore et intra decursus Nili multa oppida, praecipue quae nomina ostiis dedere, non omnibus—xii enim reperiuntur, superque quattuor quae ipsi falsa ora appellant—sed celeberrimis vii, proximo Alexandriae Canopico, dein Bolbitino, Sebennytico, Phatnitico, Mendesico, Tanitico, ultimoque Pelusiaco. praeterea Butos, Pharbaethos, Lentopolis, Athribis, Isidis Oppidum, Busiris, Cynopolis, Aphrodites, Sais, Naucratis, unde ostium quidam Naucratiticum nominant quod alii Heracleoticum, Canopico cui proximum est praeferentes.

65   XII. Ultra Pelusiacum Arabia est, ad Rubrum Mare pertinens et odoriferam illam ac divitem et beatae cognomine inclutam. haec Cattabanum et Esbonitarum et Scenitarum Arabum vocatur, sterilis praeterquam ubi Syriae confinia attingit, nec nisi Casio monte nobilis. his Arabes iunguntur, ab oriente Canchlei, a meridie Cedrei, qui deinde ambo Nabataeis. Heroopoliticus vocatur alterque Aelaniticus [1] sinus Rubri maris in Aegyptum vergentis, $\overline{\text{CL}}$ intervallo inter duo oppida, Aelana et in nostro mari

---

[1] *V.ll.* Laelaniticus *et alia*: Laeaniticus *vel* Aelaniticus *Mayhoff coll.* VI. 156, 165.

---

[a] *I.e.* Arabia Petraea, adjoining Egypt.
[b] Arabia Felix.
[c] 'Tent-dwellers' (*cf.* VI. 143), the modern Bedouins.

the *schoenus* as 30 furlongs, which makes the length 150 miles, and they give the same figure for the breadth.

There are also many considerable towns in the region of the lower parts of the Nile, especially those that have given their names to the mouths of the river, though not all of these are named after towns—for we find that there are twelve of them, besides four more that the natives call 'false mouths'—but the seven best known are the Canopic mouth nearest to Alexandria and then the Bolbitine, Sebennytic, Phatnitic, Mendesic, Tanitic, and last the Pelusiac. Besides the towns that give their names to the mouths there are Butos, Pharbaethos, Leontopolis, Athribis, the Town of Isis, Busiris, Cynopolis, Aphrodite's Town, Sais, and Naucratis, after which some people give the name of Naucratitic to the mouth called by others the Heracleotic, and mention it instead of the Canopic mouth which is next to it.

XII. Beyond the Pelusiac mouth of the Nile is Arabia,[a] extending to the Red Sea and to the Arabia known by the surname of Happy[b] and famous for its perfumes and its wealth. This bears the names of the Cattabanes, Esbonitae and Scenitae[c] tribes of Arabs; its soil is barren except where it adjoins the frontier of Syria, and its only remarkable feature is the El Kas mountain. The Arabian tribe of the Canchlei adjoin those mentioned on the east and that of the Cedrei on the south, and both of these in their turn adjoin the Nabataei. The two gulfs of the Red Sea where it converges on Egypt are called the Gulf of Suez and the Gulf of Akaba; between the two towns of Akaba and Guzzah, which is on the Mediterranean, there is a

Towns of lower Nile.

Arabia. Petraea.

269

Gazain. Agrippa a Pelusio Arsinoen Rubri maris
oppidum per deserta cxxv p. tradit. tam parvo
distat ibi tanta rerum naturae diversitas!

66   XIII. Iuxta Syria litus occupat, quondam terrarum
maxuma et plurimis distincta nominibus: namque
Palaestine vocabatur qua contingit Arabas, et Iudaea,
et Coele, exin Phoenice, et qua recedit intus Damascena, ac magis etiamnum meridiana Babylonia, et
eadem Mesopotamia inter Euphraten et Tigrin,
quaque transit Taurum Sophene, citra vero eam
Commagene, et ultra Armeniam Adiabene Assyria
67 ante dicta, et ubi Ciliciam attingit Antiochia. longitudo eius inter Ciliciam et Arabiam $\overline{\text{CCCCLXX}}$ p. est,
latitudo a Seleucia Pieria ad oppidum in Euphrate
Zeugma $\overline{\text{CLXXV}}$. qui subtilius dividunt circumfundi
Syria Phoenicen volunt, et esse oram maritimam
Syriae, cuius pars sit Idumaea et Iudaea, dein
Phoenicen, dein Syriam. id quod praeiacet mare
totum Phoenicium appellatur. ipsa gens Phoenicum
in magna gloria litterarum inventionis et siderum
navaliumque ac bellicarum artium.

68   XIV. A Pelusio Chabriae castra, Casius mons,
delubrum Iovis Casii, tumulus Magni Pompei.
Ostracine Arabia finitur, a Pelusio $\overline{\text{LXV}}$ p. mox
Idumaea incipit et Palaestina ab emersu Sirbonis

space of 150 miles. Agrippa says that the distance from Pelusium across the desert to the town of Ardscherud on the Red Sea is 125 miles: so small a distance in that region separates two such different regions of the world!

XIII. The next country on the coast is Syria, *Syria.* formerly the greatest of lands. It had a great many divisions with different names, the part adjacent to Arabia being formerly called Palestine, and Judaea, and Hollow Syria, then Phoenicia and the more inland part Damascena, and that still further south Babylonia as well as Mesopotamia between the Euphrates and the Tigris, the district beyond Mount Taurus Sophene, that on this side of Sophene Commagene, that beyond Armenia Adiabene, which was previously called Assyria, and the part touching Cilicia Antiochia. Its length between Cilicia and Arabia is 470 miles and its breadth from Seleukeh Pieria to Bridgetown on the Euphrates 175 miles. Those who divide the country into smaller parts hold the view that Phoenicia is surrounded by Syria, and that the order is—the seacoast of Syria of which Idumaea and Judaea are a part, then Phoenicia, then Syria. The whole of the sea lying off the coast is called the Phoenician Sea. The Phoenician race itself has the great distinction of having invented the alphabet and the sciences of astronomy, navigation and strategy.

XIV. After Pelusium come the Camp of Chabrias, *Idumaea,* Mount El Kas the temple of Jupiter Casius, and the *Palestine,* *Samaria.* tomb of Pompey the Great. At Ras Straki, 65 miles from Pelusium, is the frontier of Arabia. Then begins Idumaea, and Palestine at the point where the Serbonian Lake comes into view. This

lacus, quem quidam C̄L̄ circuitu tradidere: Herodotus
Casio monti adplicuit; nunc est palus modica.
oppida Rhinocolura et intus Rhaphea, Gaza et intus
Anthedon, mons Argaris. regio per oram Samaria,
oppidum Ascalo liberum, Azotos, Iamneae duae,
69 altera intus; Iope Phoenicum, antiquior terrarum
inundatione, ut ferunt, insidet collem praeiacente
saxo in quo vinculorum Andromedae vestigia
ostendunt; colitur illic fabulosa Ceto. inde Apollonia, Stratonis turris, eadem Caesarea, ab Herode
rege condita, nunc colonia Prima Flavia a Vespasiano
imperatore deducta, finis Palaestines C̄L̄X̄X̄X̄I̅X̅ p. a
confinio Arabiae. dein Phoenice, intus autem
Samaria; oppida Neapolis, quod antea Mamortha
dicebatur, Sebaste in monte, et altiore Gamala.
70 XV. Supra Idumaeam et Samariam Iudaea longe
lateque funditur. pars eius Syriae iuncta Galilaea
vocatur, Arabiae vero et Aegypto proxima Peraea,
asperis dispersa montibus et a ceteris Iudaeis Iordane
amne discreta. reliqua Iudaea dividitur in toparchias
decem quo dicemus ordine: Hiericuntem palmetis
consitam, fontibus riguam, Emmaum, Lyddam,
Iopicam, Acrebitenam, Gophaniticam, Thamniticam,
Bethleptephenen, Orinen, in qua fuere Hierosolyma

---

^a Deucalion's, not Noah's, is meant.
^b To be eaten by the sea-monster, κῆτος, from which she
was rescued by Perseus. The monster seems to have been
commemorated in the local cult.

lake is recorded by some writers as having measured 150 miles round—Herodotus gave it as reaching the foot of Mount El Kas; but it is now an inconsiderable fen. There are the towns of El-Arish and inland Refah, Gaza and inland Anthedon, and Mount Argaris. Further along the coast is the region of Samaria, the free town Ascalon, Ashdod, the two towns named Iamnea, one of them inland; and the Phoenician city of Joppa. This is said to have existed before the flood;[a] it is situated on a hill, and in front of it is a rock on which they point out marks made by the chains with which Andromeda was fettered;[b] here there is a cult of the legendary goddess Ceto. Next Apollonia, and the Tower of Strato, otherwise Caesarea, founded by King Herod, but now the colony called Prima Flavia established by the Emperor Vespasian; this is the frontier of Palestine, 189 miles from the confines of Arabia. After this comes Phoenicia, and inland Samaria; the towns are Naplous, formerly called Mamortha, Sebustieh on a mountain, and on a loftier mountain Gamala.

XV. Beyond Idumaea and Samaria stretches the *Judaea.* wide expanse of Judaea. The part of Judaea adjoining Syria is called Galilee, and that next to Arabia and Egypt Peraea. Peraea is covered with rugged mountains, and is separated from the other parts of Judaea by the river Jordan. The rest of Judaea is divided into ten Local Government Areas in the following order: the district of Jericho, which has numerous palm-groves and springs of water, and those of Emmaus, Lydda, Joppa, Accrabim, Jufna, Timnath-Serah, Beth-lebaoth, the Hills, the district that formerly contained Jerusalem, by far the most

longe clarissima urbium orientis, non Iudaeae modo, Herodium cum oppido inlustri eiusdem nominis.

71 Iordanes amnis oritur e fonte Paniade, qui cognomen dedit Caesareae de qua dicemus. amnis amoenus et quatenus locorum situs patitur ambitiosus accolisque se praebens velut invitus Asphaltiten lacum dirum natura petit, a quo postremo ebibitur aquasque laudatas perdit pestilentibus mixtas. ergo ubi prima convallium fuit occasio, in lacum se fundit quem plures Genesaram vocant, $\overline{\text{xvi}}$ p. longitudinis, $\overline{\text{vi}}$ latitudinis, amoenis circumsaeptum oppidis, ab oriente Iuliade et Hippo, a meridie Tarichea, quo nomine aliqui et lacum appellant, ab occidente 72 Tiberiade aquis calidis salubri. Asphaltites nihil praeter bitumen gignit, unde et nomen. nullum corpus animalium recipit, tauri camelique fluitant; inde fama nihil in eo mergi. longitudine excedit $\overline{\text{c}}$ p., latitudine maxima $\overline{\text{lxxv}}$ implet, minima $\overline{\text{vi}}$. prospicit eum ab oriente Arabia Nomadum, a meridie Machaerus, secunda quondam arx Iudaeae ab Hierosolymis. eodem latere est calidus fons medicae salubritatis Callirroe aquarum gloriam ipso nomine praeferens.

---

^a The valley of the Jordan runs in a straight line almost to the Dead Sea, but the stream itself winds in numerous curves.

famous city of the East and not of Judaea only, and Herodium with the celebrated town of the same name.

The source of the river Jordan is the spring of Panias from which Caesarea described later takes its second name. It is a delightful stream, winding about *a* so far as the conformation of the locality allows, and putting itself at the service of the people who dwell on its banks, as though moving with reluctance towards that gloomy lake, the Dead Sea, which ultimately swallows it up, its much-praised waters mingling with the pestilential waters of the lake and being lost. For this reason at the first opportunity afforded by the formation of the valleys it widens out into a lake usually called the Sea of Gennesareth. This is 16 miles long and 6 broad, and is skirted by the pleasant towns of Bethsaida and Hippo on the east, El Kereh on the south (the name of which place some people also give to the lake), and Tabariah with its salubrious hot springs on the west. The only product of the Dead Sea is bitumen, the Greek word for which gives it its Greek name, Asphaltites. The bodies of animals do not sink in its waters, even bulls and camels floating; this has given rise to the report that nothing at all can sink in it. It is more than 100 miles long, and fully 75 miles broad at the broadest part but only 6 miles at the narrowest. On the east it is faced by Arabia of the Nomads, and on the south by Machaerus, at one time next to Jerusalem the most important fortress in Judaea. On the same side there is a hot spring possessing medicinal value, the name of which, Callirrhoë, itself proclaims the celebrity of its waters.

The Jordan and the Dead Sea.

§ 74.

275

73   Ab occidente litora Esseni fugiunt usque qua
nocent, gens sola et in toto orbe praeter ceteras
mira, sine ulla femina, omni venere abdicata, sine
pecunia, socia palmarum. in diem ex aequo con-
venarum turba renascitur large frequentantibus quos
vita fessos ad mores eorum fortuna [1] fluctibus agitat.
ita per seculorum milia (incredibile dictu) gens
aeterna est in qua nemo nascitur: tam fecunda illis
aliorum vitae paenitentia est!

Infra hos Engada oppidum fuit, secundum ab
Hierosolymis fertilitate palmetorumque nemoribus,
nunc alterum bustum. inde Masada castellum in
rupe et ipsum haut procul Asphaltite. et hactenus
Iudaea est.

74   XVI. Iungitur ei latere Syriae Decapolitana regio
a numero oppidorum, in quo non omnes eadem
observant, plurimi tamen Damascum epoto riguis
amne Chrysorroa fertilem, Philadelphiam, Rhap-
hanam (omnia in Arabiam recedentia), Scythopolim
(antea Nysam, a Libero Patre sepulta nutrice ibi)
Scythis deductis, Gadara Hieromice praefluente, et
iam dictum Hippon, Dion, Pellam aquis divitem,
Galasam, Canatham. intercurrunt cinguntque has
urbes tetrarchiae, regnorum instar singulae, et in [2]
regna contribuuntur, Trachonitis, Panias (in qua

---

[1] *Mayhoff*: fortunae.   [2] in *v.l. om*

On the west side of the Dead Sea, but out of range of the noxious exhalations of the coast, is the solitary tribe of the Essenes, which is remarkable beyond all the other tribes in the whole world, as it has no women and has renounced all sexual desire, has no money, and has only palm-trees for company. Day by day the throng of refugees is recruited to an equal number by numerous accessions of persons tired of life and driven thither by the waves of fortune to adopt their manners. Thus through thousands of ages (incredible to relate) a race in which no one is born lives on for ever: so prolific for their advantage is other men's weariness of life!

Lying below the Essenes was formerly the town of Engedi, second only to Jerusalem in the fertility of its land and in its groves of palm-trees, but now like Jerusalem a heap of ashes. Next comes Masada, a fortress on a rock, itself also not far from the Dead Sea. This is the limit of Judaea.

XVI. Adjoining Judaea on the side of Syria is the region of Decapolis, so called from the number *The Decapolis.* of its towns, though not all writers keep to the same towns in the list; most however include Damascus, with its fertile water-meadows that drain the river Chrysorrhoë, Philadelphia, Raphana (all these three withdrawn towards Arabia), Scythopolis (formerly Nysa, after Father Liber's nurse, whom he buried there) where a colony of Scythians are settled; Gadara, past which flows the river Yarmak; Hippo mentioned already, Dion, Pella rich with its § 71. waters, Galasa, Canatha. Between and around these cities run tetrarchies, each of them equal to a kingdom, and they are incorporated into kingdoms—Trachonitis, Panias (in which is Caesarea § 71.

Caesarea cum supra dicto fonte), Abila, Arca, Ampeloessa, Gabe.

75 XVII. Hinc redeundum est ad oram atque Phoenicen. fuit oppidum Crocodilon, est flumen; memoria urbium Dorum, Sycaminum. promunturium Carmelum et in monte oppidum eodem nomine, quondam Acbatana dictum. iuxta Getta, Geba, rivus Pacida sive Belus, vitri fertiles harenas parvo litori miscens; ipse e palude Cendebia a radicibus Carmeli profluit. iuxta colonia Claudi Caesaris Ptolemais, quae quondam Acce, oppidum

76 Ecdippa, promunturium Album. Tyros, quondam insula praealto mari DCC passibus divisa, nunc vero Alexandri oppugnantis operibus continens, olim partu clara urbibus genitis Lepti, Utica, et illa Romani imperii aemula terrarumque orbis avida Carthagine, etiam Gadibus extra orbem conditis: nunc omnis eius nobilitas conchylio atque purpura constat. circuitus $\overline{XIX}$ est, in ora [1] Palaetyro inclusa; oppidum ipsum XXII stadia optinet. inde Sarepta et Ornithon oppida et Sidon artifex vitri Thebarumque Boeotiarum parens.

77 A tergo eius Libanus mons orsus MD stadiis Zimyram usque porrigitur Coeles Syriae quae [2] cognominatur. huic par interveniente valle mons

---

[1] in ora? *Mayhoff*: intra.
[2] *Rackham*: quae Coeles Syriae *aut* quae Coele Syria.

---

[a] Τὰ Δῶρα and Συκαμίνων πόλις.
[b] Believed to have been named after Ptolemy I, who enlarged it.
[c] Now Acre.
[d] *I.e.* Ras el Abiad, its modern name.
[e] Founded by Cadmus, son of Agenor King of Sidon.

with the spring mentioned above), Abila, Arca, Ampeloessa and Gabe.

XVII. From this point we must go back to the *Phoenicia.* coast and to Phoenicia. There was formerly a town called Crocodilon, and there is still a river of that name; and the cities of Dora and Sycamini,[a] of which only the memory exists. Then comes Cape Carmel, and on a mountain the town of the same name, formerly called Acbatana. Next are Getta, Geba, and the river Pacida or Belus, which covers its narrow bank with sand of a kind used for making glass; the river itself flows out of the marsh of Cendebia at the foot of Mount Carmel. Close to this river is Ptolemais,[b] a colony of the Emperor Claudius, formerly called Acce;[c] and then the town of Ach-Zib, and the White Cape.[d] Next Tyre, *Tyre and* once an island separated from the mainland by *Sidon.* a very deep sea-channel 700 yards wide, but now joined to it by the works constructed by Alexander when besieging the place, and formerly famous as the mother-city from which sprang the cities of Leptis, Utica and the great rival of Rome's empire in coveting world-sovereignty, Carthage, and also Cadiz, which she founded outside the confines of the world; but the entire renown of Tyre now consists in a shell-fish and a purple dye! The circumference of the city, including Old Tyre on the coast, measures 19 miles, the actual town covering $2\frac{3}{4}$ miles. Next are Zarephath and Bird-town, and the mother-city of Thebes[e] in Boeotia, Sidon, where glass is made.

Behind Sidon begins Mount Lebanon, a chain ex- *Mount* tending as far as Zimyra in the district called Hollow *Lebanon.* Syria, a distance of nearly 190 miles. Facing Lebanon, with a valley between, stretches the

adversus Antilibanus obtenditur quondam muro
coniunctus. post eum introrsus Decapolitana regio
praedictaeque cum ea Tetrarchiae et Palaestines tota
78 laxitas; in ora autem subiecta Libano fluvius
Magoras, Berytus colonia quae Felix Iulia appellatur,
Leontos Oppidum, flumen Lycos, Palaebyblos,
flumen Adonis, oppida Byblos, Botrys, Gigarta,
Trieris, Calamos, Tripolis quam Tyrii et Sidonii et
Aradii optinent, Orthosia, Eleutheros flumen, oppida
Zimyra, Marathos, contraque Arados septem stadiorum oppidum et insula ducentis passibus a continente
distans; regio in qua supradicti desinunt montes;
et interiacentibus campis Bargylus mons.
79   XVIII. Incipit hinc rursus Syria, desinente
Phoenice. oppida Carne, Balanea, Paltos, Gabala,
promunturium in quo Laodicea libera, Dipolis,
Heraclea, Charadrus, Posidium. dein promunturium
Syriae Antiochiae; intus ipsa Antiochia libera,
Epi Daphnes cognominata, Oronte amne dividitur; in
promunturio autem Seleucia libera Pieria appellata.
80 super eam mons eodem quo alius nomine, Casius,
cuius excelsa altitudo quarta vigilia orientem per
tenebras solem aspicit, brevi circumactu corporis
diem noctemque pariter ostendens. ambitus ad
cacumen $\overline{\text{XIX}}$ p. est, altitudo per directum $\overline{\text{IV}}$. at

---

ᵃ A celebrated grove dedicated to Apollo.

equally long range of Counter-Lebanon, which was
formerly connected with Lebanon by a wall. Behind
Counter-Lebanon inland is the region of the Ten
Cities, and with it the tetrarchies already men- §74.
tioned, and the whole of the wide expanse of Palestine; while on the coast, below Mount Lebanon,
are the river Magoras, the colony of Beyrout called
Julia Felix, Lion's Town, the river Lycus, Palaebyblos, the river Adonis, the towns of Jebeil, Batrun,
Gazis, Trieris, Calamos; Tarablis, inhabited by people
from Tyre, Sidon and Ruad; Ortosa, the river Eleutheros, the towns of Zimyra and Marathos; and facing
them the seven-furlong town and island of Ruad,
330 yards from the mainland; the region in which
the mountain ranges above mentioned terminate;
and beyond some intervening plains Mount Bargylus.

XVIII. At this point Phoenicia ends and Syria *Syria*
begins again. There are the towns of Tartus, *Antiochia.*
Banias, Bolde and Djebeleh; the cape on which
the free town of Latakia is situated; and Dipolis,
Heraclea, Charadrus and Posidium. Then the cape
of Antiochian Syria, and inland the city of Antioch
itself, which is a free town and is called ' Antioch
Near Daphne,' [a] and which is separated from Daphne
by the river Orontes; while on the cape is the free
town of Seleukeh, called Pieria. Above Seleukeh is a
mountain having the same name as the other one, §68.
Casius, which is so extremely lofty that in the
fourth quarter of the night it commands a view of
the sun rising through the darkness, so presenting
to the observer if he merely turns round a view of
day and night simultaneously. The winding route
to the summit measures 19 miles, the perpendicular
height of the mountain being 4 miles. On the coast

in ora amnis Orontes natus inter Libanum et Antilibanum iuxta Heliopolim. oppida Rhosos—et a tergo Portae quae Syriae appellantur, intervallo Rhosiorum montium et Tauri,—in ora oppidum Myriandros, mons Amanus in quo oppidum Bomitae. ipse ab Syris Ciliciam separat.

81 XIX. Nunc interiora dicantur. Coele habet Apameam Marsya amne divisam a Nazerinorum tetrarchia, Bambycen quae alio nomine Hierapolis vocatur, Syris vero Mabog—ibi prodigiosa Atargatis, Graecis autem Derceto dicta, colitur—, Chalcidem cognominatam Ad Belum, unde regio Chalcidena fertilissima Syriae, et inde Cyrresticae Cyrrum, Gazetas, Gindarenos, Gabenos, tetrarchias duas quae Granucomatitae vocantur, Hemesenos, Hylatas, Ituraeorum gentem et qui ex his Baethaemi vocantur,
82 Mariamnitanos, tetrarchiam quae Mammisea apellatur, Paradisum, Pagras, Penelenitas, Seleucias praeter iam dictam duas, quae ad Euphraten et quae ad Belum vocantur, Tardytenses. reliqua autem Syria habet (exceptis quae cum Euphrate dicentur) Arbethusios, Beroeenses, Epiphanenses ad Orontem, Laodicenos qui ad Libanum cognominantur, Leucadios, Larisaeos, praeter tetrarchias in regna discriptas barbaris nominibus XVII.

ᵃ Astarte, half woman, half fish.

is the river Orontes, which rises between Lebanon and Counter-Lebanon, near Baalbec. The towns are Rhosos,—and behind it the pass called the Gates of Syria, in between the Rhosos Mountains and Mount Taurus,—and on the coast the town of Myriandros, and Mount Alma-Dagh, on which is the town of Bomitae. This mountain separates Cilicia from Syria.

XIX. Now let us speak of the places inland. *Inland Syria.* Hollow Syria contains the town of Kulat el Mudik, separated by the river Marsyas from the tetrarchy of the Nosairis; Bambyx, which is also named the Holy City, but which the Syrians call Mabog—here the monstrous goddess Atargatis,[a] the Greek name for whom is Derceto, is worshipped; the place called Chalcis on Belus,[b] which gives its name to the region of Chalcidene, a most fertile part of Syria; and then, belonging to Cyrrestica, Cyrrus and the Gazetae, Gindareni and Gabeni; the two tetrarchies called Granucomatitae; the Hemeseni, the Hylatae, the Ituraei tribe and a branch of them called the Baethaemi; the Mariamnitani; the tetrarchy called Mammisea; Paradise, Pagrae, Penelenitae; two places called Seleucia in addition to the place of that name already mentioned, Seleucia on the Euphrates §79. and Seleucia on Belus; and the Tardytenses. The remainder of Syria (excepting the parts that will be spoken of with the Euphrates) contains the Arbethusii, the Beroeenses, the Epiphanenses on the Orontes, the Laodiceans on Lebanon, the Leucadii and the Larisaei, besides seventeen tetrarchies divided into kingdoms and bearing barbarian names.

[b] Perhaps the mountain Djebel el Semmaq.

83   XX. Et de Euphrate hoc in loco dixisse aptissimum fuerit. oritur in praefectura Armeniae Maioris Caranitide, ut prodidere ex iis qui proxime viderant Domitius Corbulo in monte Aga, Licinius Mucianus sub radicibus montis quem Capoten appellat, supra Zimaram $\overline{\text{XII}}$ p., initio Pyxurates nominatus. fluit Derzenen primum, mox Anaeticam, Armeniae
84 regiones a Cappadocia excludens. Dascusa abest a Zimara $\overline{\text{LXXV}}$ p. inde navigatur Sartonam $\overline{\text{L}}$, Melitenen Cappadociae $\overline{\text{XXIV}}$, Elegeam Armeniae $\overline{\text{x}}$ acceptis fluminibus Lyco, Arsania, Arsano. apud Elegeam occurrit ei Taurus mons, nec resistit quamquam $\overline{\text{XII}}$ p. latitudine praevalens.[1] Ommam vocant inrumpentem, mox ubi perfregit, Euphraten,
85 ultra quoque saxosum et violentum. Arabiam inde laeva, Orroeon dictam regionem, trischoena mensura dextraque Commagenen disterminat, pontis tamen etiam ubi Taurum expugnat patiens. apud Claudiopolim Cappadociae cursum ad occasum solis agit; primo hunc illic in pugna Taurus aufert, victusque et abscisus sibimet alio modo vincit ac fractum expellit in meridiem. ita naturae dimicatio illa aequatur

[1] *V.l.* praevalenti.

XX. A description of the Euphrates also will come *The river* *Euphrates.*
most suitably at this place. It rises in Caranitis, a
prefecture of Greater Armenia, as has been stated
by two of the persons who have seen it nearest to
its source—Domitius Corbulo putting its source in
Mount Aga and Licinius Mucianus at the roots of
a mountain the name of which he gives as Capotes,
twelve miles above Zimara. Near its source the
river is called Pyxurates. Its course divides first the
Derzene region of Armenia and then the Anaetic
from Cappadocia. Dascusa is 75 miles from Zimara;
and from Dascusa the river is navigable to Sartona,
a distance of 50 miles, to Melitene in Cappadocia
24 miles, and to Elegea in Armenia 10 miles, receiving
the tributary streams Lycus, Arsania and Arsanus.
At Elegea it encounters Mount Taurus, which however does not bar its passage although forming an
extremely powerful barrier 12 miles broad. The
river is called the Omma where it forces its way
into the range, and later, where it emerges, the
Euphrates; beyond the range also it is full of rocks
and has a violent current. From this point it forms
the frontier between the district of Arabia called
the country of the Orroei on the left and Commagene
on the right, its breadth being three cables' length,
although even where it forces its passage through
the Taurus range it permits of a bridge. At Claudio-
polis in Cappadocia it directs its course towards the
west; and there for the first time in this combat
Mount Taurus carries the stream out of its course,
and though conquered and cleft in twain gains the
victory in another manner by breaking its career
and forcing it to take a southerly direction. Thus
this duel of nature becomes a drawn battle, the

hoc eunte quo vult, illo prohibente ire qua velit. a
catarractis iterum navigatur. $\overline{XL}$ p. inde Com-
magenes caput Samosata.

86   XXI. Arabia supra dicta habet oppida Edessam
quae quondam Antiochia dicebatur, Callirrhoen a
fonte nominatam, Carrhas Crassi clade nobiles.
iungitur praefectura Mesopotamiae ab Assyriis
originem trahens, in qua Anthemusia et Nicephorium
oppida. mox Arabes qui Praetavi vocantur; horum
caput Singara. a Samosatis autem, latere Syriae,
Marsyas amnis influit. Cingilla Commagenen finit,
Imeneorum civitas incipit. oppida adluuntur Epiphania et Antiochia quae ad Euphraten vocatur,[1]
item Zeugma $\overline{LXXII}$ p. a Samosatis, transitu Euphratis
nobile: ex adverso Apameam Seleucus, idem utri-
87 usque conditor, ponte iunxerat. qui cohaerent
Mesopotamiae Rhoali vocantur. at in Syria oppida
Europum, Thapsacum quondam, nunc Amphipolis,
Arabes Scenitae. ita fertur usque Suram locum, in
quo conversus ad orientem relinquit Syriae Palmyrenas solitudines quae usque ad Petram urbem et
regionem Arabiae Felicis appellatae pertinent.

88   Palmyra urbs nobilis situ, divitiis soli et aquis
amoenis, vasto undique ambitu harenis includit

[1] *Rackham* : vocantur.

    • See § 65 n.

river reaching the goal of its choice but the mountain preventing it from reaching it by the course of its choice. After passing the Cataracts the stream is again navigable; and 40 miles from this point is Samosata the capital of Commagene.

XXI. Arabia above mentioned contains the towns *Mesopo-* Edessa, which was formerly called Antiochia, *tamia; Syria on the* Callirrhoe, named from its spring, and Carrhae, *Euphrates.* famous for the defeat of Crassus there. Adjoining it is the prefecture of Mesopotamia, which derives its origin from the Assyrians and in which are the towns of Anthemusia and Nicephorium. Then comes the Arab tribe called the Praetavi, whose capital is Singara. Below Samosata, on the Syrian side, the river Marsyas flows into the Euphrates. At Cingilla the territory of Commagene ends and the state of the Imenei begins. The towns washed by the river are Epiphania and Antioch (called Antioch on the Euphrates), and also Bridgetown, 72 miles from Samosata, famous as a place where the Euphrates can be crossed, Apamea on the opposite bank being joined to it by a bridge constructed by Seleucus, the founder of both towns. The people contiguous to Mesopotamia are called the Rhoali. In Syria are the town of Europus and the town formerly called Thapsacus and now Amphipolis, and an Arab tribe of Scenitae.[a] So the river flows on to the place named Sura, where it takes a turn to the east and leaves the Syrian desert of Palmyra which stretches right on to the city of Petra and the region called Arabia Felix.

Palmyra is a city famous for its situation, for the rich- *Palmyra.* ness of its soil and for its agreeable springs; its fields are surrounded on every side by a vast circuit of sand,

287

agros, ac velut terris exempta a rerum natura, privata
sorte inter duo imperia summa Romanorum Parthorumque, et [1] prima in discordia semper utrimque
cura. abest ab Seleucia Parthorum quae vocatur ad
Tigrim $\overline{\text{cccxxxvii}}$ p., a proximo vero Syriae litore
$\overline{\text{cciii}}$ et a Damasco xxvii propius.

89   Infra Palmyrae solitudines Stelendena regio est
dictaeque iam Hierapolis ac Beroea et Chalcis. ultra
Palmyram quoque ex solitudinibus his aliquid obtinet
Hemesa, item Elatium, dimidio propior Petrae quam
Damascus. a Sura autem proxime est Philiscum
oppidum Parthorum ad Euphraten; ab eo Seleuciam
dierum decem navigatio, totidemque fere Babylonem.

90   scinditur Euphrates a Zeugmate $\overline{\text{dlxxxxi}}$ p. circa
vicum Massicen, et parte laeva in Mesopotamiam
vadit per ipsam Seleuciam, circa eam praefluenti
infusus Tigri; dexteriore autem alveo Babylonem
quondam Chaldaeae caput petit, mediamque permeans, item quam Mothrim vocant, distrahitur in
paludes. increscit autem et ipse Nili modo statis
diebus paulum differens ac Mesopotamiam inundat
sole optinente xx partem cancri; minui incipit in
virginem e leone transgresso, in totum vero remeat in
xxix parte virginis.

91   XXII. Sed redeamus ad oram Syriae, cui proxima
est Cilicia. flumen Diaphanes, mons Crocodilus.

----

[1] est Mayhoff.

and it is as it were isolated by Nature from the world, having a destiny of its own between the two mighty empires of Rome and Parthia, and at the first moment of a quarrel between them always attracting the attention of both sides. It is 337 miles distant from Parthian Seleucia, generally known as Seleucia on the Tigris, 203 miles from the nearest part of the Syrian coast, and 27 miles less from Damascus.

Below the Desert of Palmyra is the district of Stelendena, and Holy City, Beroea and Chalcis already mentioned. Beyond Palmyra also a part of §§ 81, 82. this desert is claimed by Hemesa, and a part by Elatium, which is half as far as Damascus is from Petrae. Quite near to Sura is the Parthian town of Philiscum on the Euphrates; from Philiscum to Seleucia is a voyage of ten days, and about the same to Babylon. At a point 594 miles from Bridgetown, the Euphrates divides round the village of Massice, the left branch passing through Seleucia itself into Mesopotamia and falling into the Tigris as it flows round that city, while the right-hand channel makes for Babylon, the former capital of Chaldea, and passing through the middle of it, and also through the city called Mothris, spreads out into marshes. Like the Nile, the Euphrates also increases in volume at fixed periods with little variation, and floods Mesopotamia when the sun has reached the 20th degree of the Crab; but when the sun has passed through the Lion and entered Virgo it begins to sink, and when the sun is in the 29th degree of Virgo it returns to its channel entirely.

XXII. But let us return to the coast of Syria, *Asia Minor:* adjoining which is Cilicia. Here are the river *Cilicia and* Diaphanes, Mount Crocodile, the Gates of Mount *adjoining nations.*

portae Amani montis, flumina Androcus, Pinarus,
Lycus, sinus Issicus, oppidum Issos, item Alexandria,
flumen Chlorus, oppidum Aegaeae liberum, amnis
Pyramus, portae Ciliciae, oppida Mallos, Magirsos
et intus Tarsos, campi Alei, oppida Casyponis, Mopsos
liberum Pyramo inpositum, Tyros, Zephyrium,

92 Anchiale; amnes Saros, Cydnos Tarsum liberam
urbem procul a mari secans; regio Celenderitis cum
oppido, locus Nymphaeum, Soloe Cilicii nunc Pompeiopolis, Adana, Cibyra, Pinare, Pedalie, Ale,
Selinus, Arsinoe, Iotape, Dorion, iuxtaque mare
Corycos, eodem nomine oppidum et portus et specus.
mox flumen Calycadnus, promunturium Sarpedon,
oppida Holmoe, Myle, promunturium et oppidum

93 Veneris a quo proxime Cyprus insula. sed in continente oppida Mysanda, Anemurium, Coracesium,
finisque antiquus Ciliciae Melas amnis. intus autem
dicendi Anazarbeni qui nunc Caesarea, Augusta,
Castabala, Epiphania quae antea Oeniandos, Eleusa,
Iconium, Seleucia supra amnem Calycadnum Tracheotis cognomine, ab mari relata ubi vocabatur
Hermia. praeterea intus flumina Liparis, Bombos,
Paradisus, mons Imbarus.

94 XXIII. Ciliciae Pamphyliam omnes iunxere
neglecta gente Isaurica. oppida eius intus Isaura,
Clibanus, Lalasis; decurrit autem ad mare Anemuri
e regione supra dicti. simili modo omnibus qui

---

a Founded by Alexander the Great to commemorate his
victory over Darius; the name survives as Scanderoon.

Alma-Dagh, the rivers Androcus, Pinarus and Lycus, the Gulf of Issos, the town of Issos, likewise Alexandria,[a] the river Chlorus, the free town of Aegaeae, the river Pyramus, the Gates of Cilicia, the towns of Mallos and Magirsos and in the interior Tarsus, the Aleian Plains, the towns of Casyponis, Mopsos (a free town on the river Pyramus), Tyros, Zephyrium and Anchiale; and the rivers Saros and Cydnos, the latter cutting through the free city of Tarsus at a great distance from the sea; the district of Celenderitis with its town, the place Nymphaeum, Soloi of Cilicia now Pompeiopolis, Adana, Cibyra, Pinare, Pedalie, Ale, Selinus, Arsinoe, Iotape, Dorion, and on the coast Corycos, there being a town and harbour and cave of the same name. Then the river Calycadnus, Cape Sarpedon, the towns of Holmoe and Myle, and the promontory and town of Venus, a short distance from which lies the island of Cyprus. On the mainland are the towns of Mysanda, Anemurium and Coracesium and the river Melas, the former boundary of Cilicia. Places worthy of mention in the interior are Anazarbeni (the present Caesarea), Augusta, Castabala, Epiphania (previously called Oeniandos), Eleusa, Iconium, and beyond the river Calycadnus Seleucia, called Seleucia Tracheotis, a city moved from the seashore, where it used to be called Hermia. Besides these there are in the interior the rivers Liparis, Bombos and Paradisus, and Mount Imbarus.

XXIII. All the authorities have made Pamphylia *Isauria.* join on to Cilicia, overlooking the people of Isauria. The inland towns of Isauria are Isaura, Clibanus and Lalasis; it runs down to the sea over against Anemurium above mentioned. Similarly all who § 93.

eadem composuere ignorata est contermina illi gens Omanadum quorum intus oppidum Omana. cetera castella XLIV inter asperas convalles latent.

XXIV. Insident verticem Pisidae quondam appellati Solymi, quorum colonia Caesarea, eadem Antiochia, oppida Oroanda, Sagalessos.

95 XXV. Hos includit Lycaonia in Asiaticam iurisdictionem versa, cum qua conveniunt Philomelienses, Tymbriani, Leucolithi, Pelteni, Tyrienses. datur et tetrarchia ex Lycaonia qua parte Galatiae contermina est, civitatium XIV, urbe celeberrima Iconio. ipsius Lycaoniae celebrantur Thebasa in Tauro, Ide in confinio Galatiae atque Cappadociae. a latere autem eius super Pamphyliam veniunt Thracum suboles Milyae, quorum Arycanda oppidum.

96 XXVI. Pamphylia antea Mopsopia appellata est. mare Pamphylium Cilicio iungitur. oppida Side et in monte Aspendum, Plantanistum, Perga; promunturium Leucolla; mons Sardemisus; amnes Eurymedon iuxta Aspendum fluens, Catarractes, iuxta quem Lyrnessus et Olbia ultimaque eius orae Phaselis.

97 XXVII. Iunctum mare Lycium est gensque Lycia, unde vastos[1] sinus Taurus mons ab Eois veniens litoribus Chelidonio promunturio disterminat, in-

---

[1] *Sillig*: vastus.

have written on the same subject have ignored the tribe of the Omanades bordering on Isauria, whose town of Omana is in the interior. There are 44 other fortresses lying hidden among rugged valleys.

XXIV. The crest of the mountains is occupied by *Pisidia.* the Pisidians, formerly called the Solymi, to whom belong the colony of Caesarea also named Antioch and the towns of Oroanda and Sagalessos.

XXV. The Pisidians are bordered by Lycaonia, *Lycaonia.* included in the jurisdiction of the province of Asia, which is also the centre for the peoples of Philomelium, Tymbrium, Leucolithium, Pelta and Tyriaeum. To that jurisdiction is also assigned a tetrarchy that forms part of Lycaonia in the division adjoining Galatia, consisting of 14 states, the most famous city being Iconium. Notable places belonging to Lycaonia itself are Thebasa on Mount Taurus and Ida on the frontier between Galatia and Cappadocia. At the side of Lycaonia, beyond Pamphylia, come the Milyae, a tribe of Thracian descent; their town is Arycanda.

XXVI. Pamphylia was previously called Mopsopia. *Pamphylia.* The Pamphylian Sea joins on to the Sea of Cilicia. Pamphylia includes the towns of Side and, on the mountain, Aspendus, Plantanistus and Perga, Cape Leucolla and Mount Sardemisus; its rivers are the Eurymedon flowing past Aspendus and the Catarrhactes on which are Lyrnessus and Olbia and Phaselis, the last place on the coast.

XXVII. Adjoining Pamphylia are the Sea of Lycia *Mount* and the Lycian tribe, at the point where Mount *Taurus.* Taurus coming from the Eastern shores forms the Chelidonian Promontory as a boundary between vast bays. It is itself an immense range, and holds

mensus ipse et innumerarum gentium arbiter, dextro
latere septentrionalis, ubi primum ab Indico mari
exsurgit, laevo meridianus, et ad occasum tendens
mediamque distrahens Asiam, nisi opprimenti terras
occurrerent maria. resilit ergo ad septentriones,
flexusque inmensum iter quaerit, velut de industria
rerum natura subinde aequora opponente, hinc
Phoenicium, hinc Ponticum, illinc Caspium et
98 Hyrcanium contraque Maeotium lacum. torquetur
itaque collisus inter haec claustra, et tamen victor
flexuosus evadit usque ad cognata Ripaeorum
montium iuga, numerosis nominibus et novis quacumque incedit insignis, Imaus prima parte dictus,
mox Emodus, Paropanisus, Circius, Cambades,
Pariades, Choatras, Oreges, Oroandes, Niphates,
Taurus, atque ubi se quoque exuperat Caucasus, ubi
brachia emittit subinde temptanti maria similis
Sarpedon, Coracesius, Cragus, iterumque Taurus;
99 etiam ubi dehiscit seque populis aperit portarum
tamen nomine unitatem sibi vindicans quae aliubi
Armeniae aliubi Caspiae aliubi Ciliciae vocantur.
quin etiam confractus, effugiens quoque maria,
plurimis se gentium nominibus hinc et illinc implet, a
dextra Hyrcanius, Caspius, a laeva Parihedrus,

---

a 'Himaeus' and 'Emodus' both mean 'Himalaya,' and
Paropanisus is Hindu Kush.

the balance between a countless number of tribes; its right-hand side, where it first rises out of the Indian Ocean, faces north, and its left-hand side faces south; it also stretches westward, and would divide Asia in two at the middle, were it not that in dominating the land it encounters the opposition of seas. It therefore recoils in a northerly direction, and forming a curve starts on an immense route, Nature as it were designedly throwing seas in its way at intervals, here the Phoenician Sea, here the Black Sea, there the Caspian and the Hyrcanian, and opposite to them the Sea of Azov. Consequently owing to their impact the mountain twists about between these obstacles, and nevertheless sinuously emerging victorious reaches the kindred ranges of the Ripaean Mountains. The range is designated by a number of names, receiving new ones at each point in its advance: its first portion is called Imaus, then Emodus,[a] Paropanisus, Circius, Cambades, Pariades, Choatras, Oreges, Oroandes, Niphates, Taurus, and where it overtops even itself, Caucasus, while where it occasionally throws out arms as if trying to invade the sea, it becomes Sarpedon, Coracesius, Cragus, and once again Taurus; and even where it gapes open and makes a passage for mankind, nevertheless claiming for itself an unbroken continuity by giving to these passes the name of Gates: in one place they are called the Armenian Gates, in another the Caspian, and in another the Cilician. Moreover when it has been cut short in its career, retiring also from the sea, it fills itself on either side with the names of numerous races, on the right-hand side being called the Hyrcanian Mountain and the Caspian, and on

Moschicus, Amazonicus, Coraxicus, Scythicus appellatus, in universum vero Graece Ceraunius.

100 XXVIII. In Lycia igitur a promunturio eius oppidum Simena, mons Chimaera noctibus flagrans, Hephaestium civitas et ipsa saepe flagrantibus iugis. oppidum Olympus ibi fuit, nunc sunt montana Gagae, Corydalla, Rhodiopolis, iuxta mare Limyra cum amne in quem Arycandus influit, et mons Masicitus, Andria civitas, Myra, oppida Aperiae et Antiphellos quae quondam Habesos, atque in recessu Phellos. dein Pyrrha itemque Xanthus a mari $\overline{xv}$, flumenque eodem nomine; deinde Patara, quae prius Pataros, et in monte Sidyma, promun-
101 turium Cragus. ultra par sinus priori; ibi Pinara et quae Lyciam finit Telmessus. Lycia LXX quondam oppida habuit, nunc XXXVI habet; ex his celeberrima praeter supra dicta Canas, Candyba ubi laudatur Eunias nemus, Podalia, Choma praefluente Aedesa, Cyaneae, Ascandiandalis, Amelas, Noscopium, Tlos, Telandrus. conprehendit in mediterraneis et Cabaliam, cuius tres urbes Oenianda, Balbura, Bubon.
102 a Telmesso Asiaticum mare sive Carpathium et quae proprie vocatur Asia. in duas eam partes Agrippa divisit. unam inclusit ab oriente Phrygia et Lycaonia, ab occidente Aegaeo mari, a meridie Aegyptio,

the left the Parihedrian, Moschian, Amazonian, Coraxian, Scythian; whereas in Greek it is called throughout the whole of its course the Ceraunian Mountain.

XXVIII. In Lycia therefore after leaving the *Lycia.* promontory of Mount Taurus we have the town of Simena, Mount Chimaera, which sends forth flames at night, and the city-state of Hephaestium, which also has a mountain range that is often on fire. The town of Olympus stood here, and there are now the mountain villages of Gagae, Corydalla and Rhodio-polis, and near the sea Limyra with the river of which the Arycandus is a tributary, and Mount Masicitus, the city-state of Andria, Myra, the towns of Aperiae and Antiphellos formerly called Habesos, and in a corner Phellos. Then comes Pyrrha, and also Xanthus 15 miles from the sea, and the river of the same name; and then Patara, previously Pataros, and Sidyma on its mountain, and Cape Cragus. Beyond Cape Cragus is a bay as large as the one before; here are Pinara and Telmessus, the frontier town of Lycia. Lycia formerly contained 70 towns, but now it has 36; of these the most famous besides those mentioned above are Canas, Candyba the site of the famous grove of Eunia, Podalia, Choma past which flows the Aedesa, Cyaneae, Ascandiandalis, Amelas, Noscopium, Tlos, Telandrus. It includes also in its interior Cabalia, with its three cities, Oenianda, Balbura and Bubon. After Telmessus begins the Asiatic or Carpathian Sea, and Asia properly so called. Agrippa divided this country into two parts. One of these he en-closed on the east by Phrygia and Lycaonia, on the west by the Aegean Sea, on the south by the

a septentrione Paphlagonia; huius longitudinem
$\overline{\text{CCCCLXX}}$, latitudinem $\overline{\text{CCCXX}}$ fecit. alteram deter-
minavit ab oriente Armenia minore, ab occidente
Phrygia, Lycaonia, Pamphylia, a septentrione provincia Pontica, a meridie mari Pamphylio, longam
$\overline{\text{DLXXV}}$, latam $\overline{\text{CCCXXV}}$.

103　XXIX. In proxima ora Caria est, mox Ionia, ultra
eam Aeolis. Caria mediae Doridi circumfunditur,
ad mare utroque latere ambiens. in ea promunturium
Pedalium, amnis Glaucus deferens Telmedium, oppida
Daedala, Crya fugitivorum, flumen Axon, oppidum
Calynda. amnis Indus in Cibyratarum iugis ortus
recipit LX perennes fluvios, torrentes vero amplius
104 centum. oppidum Caunos liberum, dein Pyrnos,
portus Cressa, a quo Rhodus insula passuum $\overline{\text{XX}}$,
locus Loryma, oppida Tisanusa, Paridon, Larymna,
sinus Thymnias, promunturium Aphrodisias, oppidum Hydas, sinus Schoenus, regio Bubassus;
oppidum fuit Acanthus, alio nomine Dulopolis. est
in promunturio Cnidos libera, Triopia, dein Pegusa
105 et Stadia appellata. ab ea Doris incipit.

　　Sed prius terga et mediterraneas iurisdictiones
indicasse conveniat. una appellatur Cibyratica;
ipsum oppidum Phrygiae est; conveniunt eo xxv
civitates celeberrima urbe Laodicea. inposita est
Lyco flumini, latera adluentibus Asopo et Capro,

Egyptian Sea, and on the north by Paphlagonia; the length of this part he made 470 miles and the breadth 320 miles. The other half he bounded on the east by Lesser Armenia, on the west by Phrygia, Lycaonia and Pamphylia, on the north by the Province of Pontus and on the south by the Pamphylian Sea, making it 575 miles long and 325 miles broad.

XXIX. On the adjoining coast is Caria and then *Caria.* Ionia and beyond it Aeolis. Caria entirely surrounds Doris, encircling it right down to the sea on both sides. In Caria are Cape Pedalium and the river Glaucus, with its tributary the Telmedius, the towns of Daedala and Crya, the latter a settlement of refugees, the river Axon, and the town of Calynda. The river Indus, rising in the mountains of the Cibyratae, receives as tributaries 60 streams that are constantly flowing and more than 100 mountain torrents. There is the free town of Caunos, and then Pyrnos, Port Cressa, from which the island of Rhodes is 20 miles distant, the place Loryma, the towns of Tisanusa, Paridon and Larymna, Thymnias Bay, Cape Aphrodisias, the town of Hydas, Schoenus Bay, and the district of Bubassus; there was formerly a town Acanthus, otherwise named Dulopolis. On a promontory stand the free city of Cnidus, Triopia, and then Pegusa, also called Stadia. After Pegusa begins Doris.

But before we go on it may be as well to describe the back parts of Caria and the jurisdictions of the interior. One of these is called Cibyratica; the actual town of Cibyra belongs to Phrygia, and is the centre for 25 city-states, the most famous being the city of Laodicea. Laodicea is on the river Lycus, its sides being washed by the Asopus and the Caprus;

appellata primo Diospolis, dein Rhoas. reliqui in eo
conventu quos nominare non pigeat Hydrelitae,
Themisones, Hierapolitae. alter conventus a Syn-
nade accepit nomen; conveniunt Lycaones, Appiani,
Corpeni, Dorylaei, Midaei, Iulienses, et reliqui
106 ignobiles populi xv. tertius Apameam vadit ante
appellatam Celaenas, dein Ciboton; sita est in radice
montis Signiae, circumfusa Marsya, Obrima, Orba
fluminibus in Maeandrum cadentibus; Marsyas ibi
redditur ortus ac paulo mox conditur.[1] ubi certavit
tibiarum cantu cum Apolline, Aulocrene est: ita
vocatur convallis x̄ p. ab Apamea, Phrygiam petentibus. ex hoc conventu deceat nominare Metro-
politas, Dionysopolitas, Euphorbenos, Acmonenses,
Peltenos, Silbianos; reliqui ignobiles ix.

107 Doridis in sinu Leucopolis, Hamaxitos, Eleus,
Etene; dein Cariae oppida Pitaium, Eutane, Hali-
carnassus. sex oppida contributa ei sunt a Magno
Alexandro, Theangela, Side, Medmassa, Uranium,
Pedasum, Telmisum; habitatur inter duos sinus,
Ceramicum et Iasium. inde Myndus et ubi fuit
Palaemyndus, Nariandos, Neapolis, Caryanda, Ter-
mera libera, Bargylia et (a quo sinus Iasius) oppidum
108 Iasus. Caria interiorum nominum fama praenitet:
quippe ibi sunt oppida Mylasa libera, Antiochia ubi

---

[1] *Rackham*: conditus.

its original name was the City of Zeus, and it was afterwards called Rhoas. The rest of the peoples belonging to the same jurisdiction whom it may not be amiss to mention are the Hydrelitae, Themisones and Hierapolitae. Another centre has received its name from Synnas; it is the centre for the Lycaones, Appiani, Corpeni, Dorylaei, Midaei, Julienses and 15 other peoples of no note. A third jurisdiction centres at Apamea, previously called Celaenae, and then Cybotos; Apamea is situated at the foot of Mount Signia, with the rivers Marsyas, Obrima and Orba, tributaries of the Maeander, flowing round it; the Marsyas here emerges from underground, and buries itself again a little later. Aulocrene is the place where Marsyas had a contest in flute-playing with Apollo: it is the name given to a gorge 10 miles from Apamea, on the way to Phrygia. Out of this jurisdiction it would be proper to name the Metropolitae, Dionysopolitae, Euphorbeni, Acmonenses, Pelteni and Silbiani; and there are nine remaining tribes of no note.

On the Gulf of Doris are Leucopolis, Hamaxitos, Eleus, Etene; then there are the Carian towns of Pitaium, Eutane and Halicarnassus. To the jurisdiction of Halicarnassus six towns were assigned by Alexander the Great, Theangela, Side, Medmassa, Uranium, Pedasum and Telmisum; the last is situated between two bays, those of Ceramus and Iasus. Next we come to Myndus and the former site of Old Myndus, Nariandos, Neapolis, Caryanda, the free town Termera, Bargylia and Iasus, the town that gives its name to the bay. Caria is especially distinguished for the famous list of places in its interior, for here are Mylasa, a free town, and

301

fuere Symmaethos et Cranaos oppida; nunc eam
circumfluunt Maeander et Orsinus. fuit in eo tractu
et Maeandropolis; est Eumenia Cludro flumini adposita, Glaucus amnis, Lysias oppidum et Orthosia,
Berecynthius tractus, Nysa, Trallis, eadem Euanthia
et Seleucia et Antiochia dicta. adluitur Eudone
109 amne, perfunditur Thebaide; quidam ibi Pygmaeos
habitasse tradunt. praeterea sunt Thydonos,
Pyrrha, Eurome, Heraclea, Amyzon, Alabanda
libera quae conventum eum cognominavit, Stratonicea libera, Hynidos, Ceramus, Troezene, Phorontis.
longinquiores eodem foro disceptant Orthronienses,
Alidienses, Euhippini, Xystiani, Hydissenses, Apolloniatae, Trapezopolitae, Aphrodisienses liberi. praeter
haec sunt Coscinus, Harpasa adposita fluvio Harpaso,
quo et Trallicon cum fuit adluebatur.

110   XXX. Lydia autem perfusa flexuosis Maeandri
amnis recursibus super Ioniam procedit, Phrygiae ab
exortu solis vicina, ad septentrionem Mysiae, meridiana parte Cariam amplectens, Maeonia antea
appellata. celebratur maxime Sardibus in latere
Tmoli montis, qui antea Timolus appellabatur, vitibus
consito conditis [1]; ex quo profluente Pactolo eodemque Chrysorroa ac fonte Tarni, a Maeonis civitas
111 ipsa Hyde vocitata est, clara stagno Gygaeo. Sardi-

---

[1] vitibus consito conditis *Rackham*: conditus *aut* conditis
aut vitibus consitus.

Antiochia which occupies the sites of the former towns of Symmaethus and Cranaos; it is now surrounded by the rivers Maeander and Orsinus. This region formerly also contained Maeandropolis; in it are Eumenia on the river Cludrus, the river Glaucus, the town of Lysias, and Orthosia, the district of Berecynthus, Nysa, and Trallis also called Euanthia and Seleucia and Antiochia. It is washed by the river Eudon and the Thebais flows through it; some record that a race of Pygmies formerly lived in it. There are also Thydonos, Pyrrha, Eurome, Heraclea, Amyzon, the free town of Alabanda which has given its name to this jurisdiction, the free town of Stratonicea, Hynidos, Ceramus, Troezene and Phorontis. At a greater distance but resorting to the same centre for jurisdiction are the Orthronienses, Alidienses, Euhippini, Xystiani, Hydissenses, Apolloniatae, Trapezopolitae and Aphrodisienses, a free people. Besides these places there are Coscinus and Harpasa, the latter on the river Harpasus, which also passes the site of the former town of Trallicon.

XXX. Lydia, bathed by the ever-returning *Lydia.* sinuosities of the river Maeander, extends above Ionia; it is bordered by Phrygia to the east and Mysia to the north, and with its southern portion it embraces Caria. It was previously called Maeonia. It is specially famous for the city of Sardis, situated on the vine-clad side of Mount Tmolus, the former name of which was Timolus. From Tmolus flows the Pactolus, also called the Chrysorrhoas, and the source of the Tarnus; and the city-state of Sardis itself, which is famous for the Gygaean Lake, used to be called Hyde by the people of Maeonia. This

ana nunc appellatur ea iurisdictio, conveniuntque in eam extra praedictos Macedones Cadieni, Philadelphini, et ipsi in radice Tmoli Cogamo flumini adpositi Maeonii, Tripolitani, iidem et Antoniopolitae—Maeandro adluuntur—, Apollonihieritae, Mysotimolitae et alii ignobiles.

112   XXXI. Ionia ab Iasio sinu incipiens numerosiore ambitu litorum flectitur.   in ea primus sinus Basilicus, Posideum promunturium et oppidum oraculum Branchidarum appellatum, nunc Didymaei Apollinis, a litore stadiis xx, et inde cLxxx Miletus Ioniae caput, Lelegeis antea et Pityusa et Anactoria nominata, super xc urbium per cuncta maria genetrix, nec fraudanda cive Cadmo qui primus prorsam orationem

113 condere instituit. amnis Maeander ortus e lacu in monte Aulocrene plurimisque adfusus oppidis et repletus fluminibus crebris, ita sinuosus flexibus ut saepe credatur reverti, Apamenam primum pervagatur regionem, mox Eumeneticam, ac dein Hyrgaleticos campos, postremo Cariam, placidus omnisque eos agros fertilissimo rigans limo, ad decumum a Mileto stadium lenis inlabitur mari. inde mons Latmus, oppida Heraclea montis eius cognominis Carice, Myuus quod primo condidisse Iones narrantur Athenis profecti, Naulochum,

jurisdiction is now called the district of Sardis, and
besides the people before-named it is the centre for
the Macedonian Cadieni, the Philadelphini, and the
Maeonii themselves who are situated on the river
Cogamus at the foot of Mount Tmolus, the Tripolitani,
also called Antoniopolitae—their territory is washed
by the river Maeander—, the Apollonihieritae, the
Mysotimolitae and other people of no note.

XXXI. At the Gulf of Iasus Ionia begins. It has a *Ionia.*
winding coast, with a rather large number of bays.
The first is the Royal Bay, then the cape and
town of Posideum, and the shrine once called the
oracle of the Branchidae, now that of Didymaean
Apollo, 2½ miles from the coast; and 22½ miles from
it Miletus, the capital of Ionia, which formerly bore
the names of Lelegeis and Pityusa and Anactoria,
the mother of over 90 cities scattered over all the
seas; nor must she be robbed of her claim to Cadmus
as her citizen, the author who originated composition
in prose. From the mountain lake of Aulocrene
rises the river Maeander, which washes a large
number of cities and is replenished by frequent
tributaries; its windings are so tortuous that it is
often believed to turn and flow backwards. It first
wanders through the region of Apamea, afterwards
that of Eumenia, and then the plains of Hyrgale,
and finally the country of Caria, its tranquil waters
irrigating all these regions with mud of a most
fertilising quality; and it glides gently into the sea
a mile and a quarter from Miletus. Next comes
Mount Latmus, the towns of Heraclea belonging to
the mountain so designated in the Carian dialect,
Myus which is recorded to have been first founded
by Ionian emigrants from Athens, Naulochum, and

Priene. in ora quae Troglea appellatur Gessus amnis. regio omnibus Ionibus sacra et ideo Panionia 114 appellata. iuxta a fugitivis conditum (uti nomen indicio est) Phygela fuit et Marathesium oppidum. supra haec Magnesia Maeandri cognomine insignis, a Thessalica Magnesia orta; abest ab Epheso xv p., Trallibus eo amplius MMM. antea Thessaloche et Androlitia nominata; et litori adposita Derasidas insulas secum abstulit mari. intus et Thyatira 115 adluitur Lyco, Pelopia aliquando et Euhippia cognominata.

In ora autem Matium, Ephesus Amazonum opus, multis antea expetita nominibus: Alopes cum pugnatum apud Troiam est, mox Ortygiae, Amorges; vocata est et Smyrna cognomine Trachia et Haemonion et Ptelea. attollitur monte Pione, adluitur Caystro in Cilbianis iugis orto multosque amnes deferente et stagnum Pegaseum, quod Phyrites amnis expellit. ab his multitudo limi est quae terras propagat mediisque iam campis Syrien insulam adiecit. fons in urbe Callippia et templum Dianae conplexi e diversis regionibus duo Selinuntes.

116 Ab Epheso Matium aliud Colophoniorum et intus ipsa Colophon, Haleso adfluente. inde Apollinis Clarii fanum, Lebedos—fuit et Notium oppidum—,

---

a I.e. the channel between the islands and the shore has dried up, and they are now part of Magnesia.

b, c Sillig reads *Mantium* ($\mu\alpha\nu\tau\epsilon\hat{\iota}o\nu$, oracular shrine).

Priene. At the part of the coast called Troglea is
the river Gessus. The district is sacred with all
Ionians, and is consequently called Panionia. Next
there was formerly a town founded by refugees—
as its name Phygela indicates—and another called
Marathesium. Above these places is Magnesia,
distinguished by the name of Magnesia on Maeander,
an offshoot from Magnesia in Thessaly; it is 15
miles from Ephesus, and 3 miles more from Tralles.
It previously had the names of Thessaloche and
Androlitia. Being situated on the coast it has appro-
priated the Derasides islands from the sea.[a] Inland
also is Thyatira, washed by the Lycus; once it was
called Pelopian or Euhippian Thyatira.

On the coast again is Matium,[b] and Ephesus built
by the Amazons, previously designated by many
names—that of Alope at the time of the Trojan
War, later Ortygia and Amorge; it was also called
Smyrna Trachia and Haemonion and Ptelea. It is
built on the slope of Mount Pion, and is watered by
the Cayster, which rises in the Cilbian range and
brings down the waters of many streams, and also
drains the Pegasaean Marsh, an overflow of the river
Phyrites. From these comes a quantity of mud
which advances the coastline and has now joined
the island of Syrie on to the mainland by the flats
interposed. In the city of Ephesus is the spring
called Callippia, and a temple of Diana surrounded
by two streams, both called Selinus, coming from
different directions.

After leaving Ephesus there is another Matium,[c]
which belongs to Colophon, and Colophon itself
lying more inland, on the river Halesus. Then the
temple of Clarian Apollo, Lebedos—formerly there

promunturium Cyrenaeum, mons Mimas CL p.
excurrens atque in continentibus campis residens.
quo in loco Magnus Alexander intercidi planitiem
eam iusserat VII M D p. longitudine, ut duos sinus
iungeret Erythrasque cum Mimante circumfunderet.
117 iuxta eas fuerunt oppida Pteleon, Helos, Dorion,
nunc est Aleon fluvius, Corynaeum Mimantis promunturium, Clazomenae, Parthenie et Hippi, Chytrophoria appellatae cum insulae essent; Alexander
idem per duo stadia continenti adnecti iussit. interiere
intus Daphnus et Hermesta et Sipylum quod ante
Tantalis vocabatur, caput Maeoniae, ubi nunc est
stagnum Sale; obiit et Archaeopolis substituta
Sipylo et inde illi Colpe et huic Libade.

118   Regredientibus inde abest $\overline{\text{XII}}$ p. ab Amazone condita, restituta ab Alexandro, in ora Smyrna, amne
Melete gaudens non procul orto. montes Asiae
nobilissimi in hoc tractu fere explicant se: Mastusia
a tergo Smyrnae et Termetis Olympi radicibus iunctis
in Dracone desinit, Draco in Tmolo, Tmolus in
119 Cadmo, ille in Tauro. a Smyrna Hermus amnis
campos facit[1] et nomini suo adoptat. oritur iuxta
Dorylaum Phrygiae civitatem, multosque colligit
fluvios, inter quos Phrygem qui nomine genti dato a

[1] secat *Mayhoff*.

---

[a] An unknown town: or perhaps 'Termetis,' another
mountain.
[b] Perhaps the text should be altered to give 'cuts through
the plains and gives them its name.'

308

was also the town of Notium—, Cape Cyrenaeum,
and Mount Mimas which projects 150 miles into the
sea and slopes down into the plains adjoining. It
was here that Alexander the Great had given orders
for a canal 7½ miles long to be cut across the level
ground in question so as to join the two bays and to
make an island of Erythrae with Mimas. Near
Erythrae were formerly the towns of Pteleon, Helos
and Dorion, and there is now the river Aleon,
Corynaeum the promontory of Mimas, Clazomenae,
and Parthenie and Hippi, which were called the
Chytrophoria when they were islands; these
Alexander also ordered to be joined to the mainland
by a causeway a quarter of a mile in length. Places
in the interior that exist no longer were Daphnus
and Hermesta and Sipylum previously called Tantalis,
the capital of Maeonia, situated where there is now
the marsh named Sale; Archaeopolis which replaced
Sipylus has also perished, and later Colpe which
replaced Archaeopolis and Libade which replaced
Colpe.

On returning thence to the coast, at a distance of
12 miles we come to Smyrna, founded by an Amazon
and restored by Alexander; it is refreshed by the
river Meles which rises not far off. The most famous
mountains of Asia mostly lie in this district: Mastusia
behind Smyrna and Termes,[a] joining on to the
roots of Olympus, ends, and is followed by Mount
Draco, Draco by Tmolus, Tmolus by Cadmus, and
that range by Taurus. After Smyrna the river
Hermus forms level plains [b] to which it gives its name.
It rises at the Phrygian city-state of Dorylaus, and
has many tributary rivers, among them the Phryx
which forms the frontier between the race to which

Caria eam determinat, Hyllum et Cryon, et ipsos Phrygiae, Mysiae, Lydiae amnibus repletos. fuit in ore eius oppidum Temnos, nunc in extremo sinu Myrmeces scopuli, oppidum Leucae in promunturio quod insula fuit finisque Ioniae Phocaea.

120 Smyrnaeum conventum magna pars et Aeoliae quae mox dicetur frequentat, praeterque Macedones Hyrcani cognominati et Magnetes a Sipylo. verum Ephesum alterum lumen Asiae remotiores conveniunt Caesarienses, Metropolitae, Cilbiani inferiores et superiores, Mysomacedones, Mastaurenses, Briullitae, Hypaepeni, Dioshieritae.

121 XXXII. Aeolis proxima est, quondam Mysia appellata, et quae Hellesponto adiacet Troas. ibi a Phocaea Ascanius portus; dein fuerat Larisa, sunt Cyme, Myrina quae Sebastopolim se vocat, et intus Aegaeae, Itale, Posidea, Neon Tichos, Temnos. in ora autem Titanus amnis et civitas ab eo cognominata; fuit et Grynia, nunc tantum portus, olim insula adprehensa; oppidum Elaea et ex Mysia veniens Caicus amnis; oppidum Pitane; Canaitis

122 amnis. intercidere Canae, Lysimachea, Atarnea, Carene, Cisthene, Cilla, Cocylium, Thebe, Astyre, Chrysa, Palaescepsis, Gergitha, Neandros: nunc est Perperene civitas, Heracleotes tractus, Coryphas oppidum, amnes Grylios, Ollius, regio Aphrodisias quae antea Politice Orgas, regio Scepsis, flumen

it gives its name and Caria, and the Hyllus and the
Cryos, themselves also augmented by the rivers of
Phrygia, Mysia and Lydia. At the mouth of the
Hermus there was once the town of Temnos, and
now at the end of the bay are the rocks called the
Ants, the town of Leucae on a headland that was
formerly an island, and Phocaea, the frontier town
of Ionia. The jurisdiction of Smyrna is also the centre
resorted to by a large part of Aeolia which will
now be described, and also by the Macedonians
called Hyrcani and the Magnesians from Sipylus.
But Ephesus, the other great luminary of Asia, is
the centre for the Caesarienses, Metropolitae, Upper
and Lower Cilbiani, Mysomacedones, Mastaurenses,
Briullitae, Hypaepeni and Dioshieritae.

XXXII. Next is Aeolis, once called Mysia, and *Aeolis.*
Troas lying on the coast of the Dardanelles. Here
after passing Phocaea we come to Port Ascanius,
and then to the place where once stood Larisa and
where now are Cyme, Myrina which styles itself
Sebastopolis, and inland Aegaeae, Itale, Posidea, New
Wall, Temnos. On the coast are the river Titanus
and the city-state named after it, and also once there
was Grynia, now only a harbour, formerly an island
that had been joined to the mainland; the town of
Elaea and the river Caicus coming from Mysia; the
town of Pitane; the river Canaitis. Canae has disappeared, as have Lysimachea, Atarnea, Carene,
Cisthene, Cilla, Cocylium, Thebe, Astyre, Chrysa,
Palaescepsis, Gergitha Neandros; but there still
exist the city-state of Perperene, the district of Heracleotes, the town of Coryphas, the rivers Grylios
and Ollius, the district of Aphrodisias which was
formerly Politice Orgas, the district of Scepsis, and

Evenum, cuius in ripis intercidere Lyrnesos et
Miletos. in hoc tractu Ide mons, et in ora quae
sinum cognominavit et conventum Adramytteos
olim Pedasus dicta, flumina Astron, Cormalos,
Crianos, Alabastros, Hieros ex Ida; intus mons
123 Gargara eodemque nomine oppidum. rursus in
litore Antandros Edonis prius vocata, dein Cimmeris,
Assos, eadem Apollonia; fuit et Palamedium oppi-
dum. promunturium Lectum disterminans Aeolida
et Troada. fuit et Polymedia civitas, Chrysa et
Larisa alia: Zminthium templum durat. intus
Colone intercidit. deportant Adramytteum negotia
Apolloniatae a Rhyndaco amne, Eresi, Miletopolitae,
Poemaneni, Macedones Asculacae,[1] Polichnaei, Pio-
nitae, Cilices Mandacandeni, Mysi[2] Abretteni et
Hellespontii appellati et alii ignobiles.

124 XXXIII. Troadis primus locus Hamaxitus, dein
Cebrenia ipsaque Troas Antigonia dicta, nunc
Alexandria, colonia Romana; oppidum Nee; Scamander amnis navigabilis et in promunturio quondam
Sigeum oppidum. dein portus Achaeorum, in
quem influit Xanthus Simoenti iunctus stagnumque
prius faciens Palaescamander. ceteri Homero celebrati, Rhesus, Heptaporus, Caresus, Rhodius, vestigia
non habent; Granicus diverso tractu in Propontida

---

[1] a Scylace *Detlefsen.*
[2] *Mayhoff*: Mysia (in Mysia *Hermolaus*).

the river Evenus, on the banks of which stood
Lyrnesus and Miletos, both now in ruins. In this
region is Mount Ida, and on the coast Adramytteos,
formerly called Pedasus, which has given its name to
the bay and to the jurisdiction, and the rivers
Astron, Cormalos, Crianos, Alabastros, and Holy
River coming from Mount Ida; inland are Mount
Gargara and the town of the same name. On the
coast again are Antandros previously called Edonis,
then Cimmeris, and Assos, which is the same as
Apollonia; and formerly there was also the town
of Palamedium. Then Cape Lectum which marks
the frontier between the Aeolid and the Troad; also
there was once the city-state of Polymedia, and
Chrysa and another Larisa: the temple of Zmintheus
still stands. Colone inland has disappeared.
Adramytteos is resorted to for legal business by
the people of Apollonia on the river Rhyndacus,
the Eresi, Miletopolitae, Poemaneni, Macedonian
Asculacae, Polichnaei, Pionitae, the Cilician Mandacandeni, the Mysian peoples known as the Abretteni and the Hellespontii, and others of no note.

XXXIII. The first place in the Troad is Hamaxitus, *The Troad,*
then come Cebrenia, and then Troas itself, formerly *and the adjoining*
called Antigonia and now Alexandria, a Roman *regions.*
colony; the town of Nee; the navigable river
Scamander; and on a promontory was formerly the
town of Sigeum. Then the Harbour of the Achaeans,
into which flows the Xanthus united with the Simois,
and the Palaescamander, which previously forms a
marsh. Of the rest of the places celebrated in Homer,
Rhesus, Heptaporus, Caresus, Rhodius, no traces
remain; and the Granicus flows by a different route
into the Sea of Marmara. However there is even

fluit. est tamen et nunc Scamandria civitas parva,
ac MM D p. remotum a portu Ilium immune, unde
125 omnis rerum claritas. extra sinum sunt Rhoetea
litora Rhoeteo et Dardanio et Arisbe oppidis habitata.
fuit et Achilleon oppidum iuxta tumulum Achillis
conditum a Mytilenaeis et mox Atheniensibus ubi
classis eius steterat in Sigeo; fuit et Aeantion a
Rhodiis conditum in altero cornu, Aiace ibi sepulto,
XXX stadiorum intervallo a Sigeo et ipsa statione
classis suae. supra Aeolida et partem Troadis in
mediterraneo est quae vocatur Teuthrania, quam
Mysi antiquitus tenuere: ibi Caicus amnis iam dictus
oritur; gens ampla per se, etiam cum totum Mysia
126 appellaretur. in ea Pioniae, Andera, Idale, Stabulum, Conisium, Teium, Balce, Tiare, Teuthranie,
Sarnaca, Haliserne, Lycide, Parthenium, Cambre,
Oxyopum, Lygdamum, Apollonia, longeque clarissimum Asiae Pergamum, quod intermeat Selinus,
praefluit Cetius profusus Pindaso monte. abest
haut procul Elaea, quam in litore diximus. Perga-
mena vocatur eius tractus iurisdictio; ad eam conveniunt Thyatireni, Mossyni, Mygdones, Bregmeni,
Hierocometae, Perpereni, Tiareni, Hierolophienses,
Hermocapelitae, Attalenses, Panteenses, Apollo-
127 nidienses aliaeque inhonorae civitates. a Rhoeteo
Dardanium oppidum parvum abest stadia LXX.

now the small city-state of Scamander, and 2½ miles from its harbour Ilium, a town exempt from tribute, the scene of all the famous story. Outside the bay are the Rhoetean coasts, occupied by the towns of Rhoeteum, Dardanium and Arisbe. Formerly there was also the town of Achilleon, founded near to the tomb of Achilles by the people of Mitylene and afterwards rebuilt by the Athenians, where the fleet of Achilles was stationed at Sigeum; and also there once was Aeantion, founded by the Rhodians on the other horn of the bay, which is the place where Ajax was buried, at a distance of 3¾ miles from Sigeum, and from the actual place where his fleet was stationed. Inland behind Aeolis and a part of the Troad is the district called Teuthrania, inhabited in ancient times by the Mysians—this is where the river Caicus already mentioned rises; Teuthrania was § 121. a considerable independent clan, even when the whole district bore the name of Mysia. Places in Teuthrania are Pioniae, Andera, Idale, Stabulum, Conisium, Teium, Balce, Tiare, Teuthranie, Sarnaca, Haliserne, Lycide, Parthenium, Cambre, Oxyopum, Lygdamum, Apollonia, and by far the most famous place in Asia, Pergamum, which is traversed by the river Selinus and bordered by the river Cetius, flowing down from Mount Pindasus. Not far away is Elaea, which we mentioned, on the coast. The § 121. jurisdiction of this district is called the Pergamene, and it is the centre for the Thyatireni, Mossyni, Mygdones, Bregmeni, Hierocometae, Perpereni, Tiareni, Hierolophienses, Hermocapelitae, Attalenses, Panteenses, Apollonidienses and other city-states of no note. At a distance of 8¾ miles from Rhoeteum is the small town of Dardanium.

inde $\overline{\text{XVIII}}$ promunturium Trapeza, unde primum concitat se Hellespontus. ex Asia interisse gentes tradit Eratosthenes Solymorum, Lelegum, Bebrycum, Colycantiorum, Tripsedorum; Isidorus Arieneos et Capreatas ubi sit Apamea condita a Seleuco rege, inter Ciliciam, Cappadociam, Cataoniam, Armeniam et, quoniam ferocissimas gentes domuisset, initio Damea vocata.[1]

128 XXXIV. Insularum ante Asiam prima est in Canopico ostio Nili, a Canopo Menelai gubernatore, ut ferunt, dicta. altera iuncta ponte Alexandriae, colonia Caesaris dictatoris, Pharos, quondam diei navigatione distans ab Aegypto, nunc a turri nocturnis ignibus cursum navium regens; namque fallacibus vadis Alexandria tribus omnino aditur alveis maris, Stegano, Posideo, Tauro. in Phoenicio deinde mari est ante Iopen Paria, tota oppidum, in qua obiectam beluae Andromedam ferunt, et iam dicta Arados, inter quam et continentem L cubita alto mari, ut auctor est Mucianus, e fonte dulcis aqua tubo coriis facta usque a vado trahitur.

129 XXXV. Pamphylium mare ignobilis insulas habet, Cilicium ex quinque maximis Cyprum ad ortum occasumque Ciliciae ac Syriae obiectam, quondam novem regnorum sedem. huius circuitum Timosthenes $\overline{\text{CCCCXXVII}}$ D p. prodidit, Isidorus $\overline{\text{CCCLXXV}}$.

---

[1] *Rackham*: Dameam vocatam.

[a] From the Greek δαμάζω.

Eighteen miles from it is Cape Trapeza, from which point the Dardanelles start. A list of Asiatic races now extinct given by Eratosthenes includes the Solymi, Leleges, Bebryces, Colycantii and Tripsedi; Isidore gives the Arienei and the Capreatae at the place where Apamea stands, founded by King Seleucus, between Cilicia, Cappadocia, Cataonia and Armenia. Apamea was originally called Damea [a] because it had subdued some extremely fierce tribes.

XXXIV. Of the islands off the coast of Asia the first is at the Canopic mouth of the Nile, and takes its name, it is said, from Menelaus's helmsman Canopus. The second, called Pharos, joined by a bridge to Alexandria, was settled by the Dictator Caesar; it was formerly a day's sail from Egypt, but now it carries a lighthouse to direct the course of vessels at night; for owing to the treacherous shoals Alexandria can be reached by only three channels of the sea, those of Steganus, Posideum and Taurus. Then in the Phoenician Sea off Joppa lies Paria, the whole of which is a town—it is said to have been the place where Andromeda was exposed to the monster,—and Arados, mentioned already; between which and the mainland, according to Mucianus, fresh water is brought up from a spring at the bottom of the sea, which is 75 feet deep, by means of a leather pipe.

XXXV. The Pamphylian Sea contains some islands of no note. The Cilician Sea has five of considerable size, among them Cyprus, which lies east and west off the coasts of Cilicia and Syria; it was formerly the seat of nine kingdoms. Its circumference is given by Timosthenes as measuring $427\frac{1}{2}$ miles and by Isidore as 375 miles. Its length between the two

Islands off Asiatic Coast.

§ 78.

Cyprus.

317

longitudinem inter duo promunturia, Clidas et Aca-
manta, quod est ab occasu, Artemidorus $\overline{\text{CLXII}}$ D,
Timosthenes $\overline{\text{CC}}$. vocatam antea Acamantida Philonides, Cerastim Xenagoras et Aspeliam et Ama-
thusiam et Macariam, Astynomus Crypton et
130 Colinian. oppida in ea xv, Neapaphos, Palaepaphos,
Curias, Citium, Corinaeum, Salamis, Amathus, Lapethos, Soloe, Tamasos, Epidaurum, Chytri, Arsinoe,
Carpasium, Golgoe; fuere et [1] Cinyria, Mareum,
Idalium. abest ab Anemurio Ciliciae $\overline{\text{L}}$; mare quod
praetenditur vocant Aulona Cilicium. in eodem situ
Eleusa insula est, et quattuor ante promunturium
ex adverso Syriae Clides, rursusque ab altero capite
Stiria, contra Neam Paphum Hiera et Cepia, contra
131 Salamina Salaminiae. in Lycio autem mari Illyris,
Telendos, Attelebussa, Cypriae tres steriles et Dionysia prius Charaeta dicta; dein contra Tauri
promunturium pestiferae navigantibus Chelidoniae
totidem. ab his cum oppido Leucolla Pactyae, Lasia,
Nymphais, Macris, Megista cuius civitas interiit;
multae deinde ignobiles. sed contra Chimaeram Dolichiste, Choerogylion, Crambusa, Rhoge, Xenagora [2]
viii, Daedaleon duae, Cryeon tres, Strongyle, et
contra Sidyma Antiochi Glaucumque versus amnem
Lagussa, Macris, Didymae, Helbo, Scope, Aspis, et
(in qua oppidum interiit) Telandria proximaque
Cauno Rhodussa.

---

[1] *Mayhoff*: et ibi *aut* et in.
[2] *V.ll.* Genagora, Enagora.

capes of Clidae and Acamas, the latter at its west end, is given by Artemidorus as 162½ and by Timosthenes as 200 miles. According to Philonides it was previously called Acamantis, according to Xenagoras Cerastis and Aspelia and Amathusia and Macaria, and according to Astynomus Cryptos and Colinias. It contains 15 towns, New and Old Paphos, Curias, Citium, Corinaeum, Salamis, Amathus, Lapethos, Soloe, Tamasos, Epidaurus, Chytri, Arsinoe, Carpasium and Golgoe; and formerly there were also Cinyria, Mareum and Idalium. It is 50 miles from Anemurius in Cilicia; the sea lying between is called the Cilician Aulon. In the same neighbourhood is the island of Eleusa, and the four Clides off the cape facing Syria, and again off a second headland Stiria, and towards New Paphos Hiera and Cepia, and towards Salamis the Salaminiae. In the Lycian Sea are Illyris, Telendos, Attelebussa, the three barren Cyprian islands and Dionysia, formerly called Charaeta; then opposite to Cape Taurus, the Chelidonian islands, the same in number, fraught with disaster for passing vessels. Next to these the Pactyae with the town of Leucolla, Lasia, Nymphais, Macris and Megista, the city-state on which has ceased to exist; and then a number of islands of no note. But opposite to Chimaera are Dolichiste, Choerogylion, Crambusa, Rhoge, the eight called the Xenagora islands, the two called Daedaleon, and the three called Cryeon; Strongyle, and opposite Sidyma Antiochi and towards the river Glaucus Lagussa, Macris, Didymae, Helbo, Scope, Aspis and Telandria (the town on which has ceased to exist) and nearest to Mount Caunus Rhodussa.

132 XXXVI. Sed pulcherrima est libera Rhodos.
circuitu c̄x̄x̄v̄ aut, si potius Isidoro credimus, c̄ĪĪĪ.
habitata urbibus Lindo, Camiro, Ialyso, nunc Rhodo,
distat ab Alexandria Aegypti d̄l̄x̄x̄x̄ĪĪĪ, ut Isidorus
tradit, ut Eratosthenes c̄c̄c̄c̄l̄x̄v̄ĪĪĪ, ut Mucianus d̄, a
Cypro c̄l̄x̄x̄v̄ī. vocitata est antea Ophiussa, Asteria,
Aethria, Trinacrie, Corymbia, Poeeessa, Atabyria ab
133 rege, dein Macaria et Oloessa. Rhodiorum insulae
Carpathus quae mari nomen dedit, Casos Achne
olim, Nisyros distans a Cnido x̄v̄ D, Porphyris antea
dicta, et eodem tractu media inter Rhodum Cni-
dumque Syme. cingitur x̄x̄x̄v̄ĪĪ D; portus benigne
praebet VIII. praeter has circa Rhodum Cyclopis,
Teganon, Cordylusa, Diabatae IV, Hymos, Chalce
cum oppido, Teutlusa, Narthecusa, Dimastos,
Progne, et a Cnido Cisserusa, Therionarcia, Calydne
cum tribus oppidis Notio, Nisyro, Mendetero, et
in Arconneso oppidum Ceramus. in Cariae ora quae
vocantur Argiae numero XX, et Hyetusa, Lepsia,
134 Leros. nobilissima autem in eo sinu Coos ab Halicarnaso x̄v̄ distans, circuitu c̄, ut plures existimant
Merope vocata, Cea ut Staphylus, Meropis ut
Dionysius, dein Nymphaea. mons ibi Prion; et
Nisyron abruptam illi putant, quae Porphyris antea

---

a Built about 408 B.C. by the three old towns conjointly,
to serve as the capital of the island.

XXXVI. But the most beautiful is the free island *Rhodes.*
of Rhodes, which measures 125, or, if we prefer to
believe Isidore, 103 miles round, and which contains
the cities of Lindus, Camirus and Ialysus, and now that
of Rhodes.[a] Its distance from Alexandria in Egypt
is 583 miles according to Isidore, 468 according to
Eratosthenes, 500 according to Mucianus; and it is
176 miles from Cyprus. It was previously called
Ophiussa, Asteria, Aethria, Trinacrie, Corymbia,
Poeeessa, Atabyria after its king, and subsequently
Macaria and Oloessa. Islands belonging to the
Rhodians are Carpathus which has given its name
to the Carpathian Sea, Casos, formerly Achne,
Nisyros, previously called Porphyris, 15½ miles distant from Cnidus, and in the same neighbourhood
lying between Rhodes and Cnidus, Syme. Syme
measures 37½ miles in circumference; it provides
the welcome of eight harbours. Other islands
in the neighbourhood of Rhodes besides those
mentioned are Cyclopis, Teganon, Cordylusa, the
four Diabatae, Hymos, Chalce with its town,
Teutlusa, Narthecusa, Dimastos, Progne, and in
the direction of Cnidus Cisserusa, Therionarcia,
Calydne with the three towns of Notium, Nisyrus and
Mendeterus, and the town of Ceramus on Arconnesus.
Off the coast of Caria are the Argiae, a group of
twenty islands, and Hyetusa, Lepsia and Leros. But
the most famous island in this gulf is that of Cos, which
is 15 miles distant from Halicarnassus and 100 miles
in circumference; it is generally believed to have
been called Merope, but according to Staphylus its
former name was Cea and according to Dionysius
Meropis and later Nymphaea. On Cos is Mount
Prion; and the island of Nisyros, formerly called

dicta est. hinc Caryanda cum oppido; nec procul ab Halicarnaso Pidossus. in Ceramico autem sinu Priaponesos, Hipponesos, Pserema, Lampsa, Aemyndus, Passala, Crusa, Pyrrhaeciusa, Sepiusa, Melano, paulumque a continente distans quae vocata est Cinaedopolis probrosis ibi relictis a rege Alexandro.

135   XXXVII. Ioniae ora Aegeas et Corseas habet et Icaron, de qua dictum est, Laden quae prius Late vocabatur, atque inter ignobiles aliquot duas Camelitas Mileto vicinas, Mycalae Trogilias tres, Philion, Argennon, Sandalion, Samon liberam circuitu $\overline{\text{LXXXVII}}$ D aut, ut Isidorus, $\overline{\text{c}}$. Partheniam primum appellatam Aristoteles tradit, postea Dryusam, deinde Anthemusam; Aristocritus adicit Melamphyllum, dein Cyparissiam, alii Parthenoarrhusam, Stephanen. amnes in ea Imbrasus, Chesius, Hibiethes, fontes Gigartho, Leucothea, mons Cercetius. adiacent insulae Rhypara, Nymphaea, Achillea.

136   XXXVIII. Par claritate ab ea distat $\overline{\text{XCIV}}$ cum oppido Chios libera, quam Aethaliam Ephorus prisco nomine appellat, Metrodorus et Cleobulus Chiam a Chione nympha, aliqui a nive, et Macrin et Pityusam. montem habet Pelinnaeum, marmor Chium.[1] circuitu $\overline{\text{CXXV}}$ colligit, ut veteres tradidere, Isidorus $\overline{\text{IX}}$ adicit.

---

[1] [marmor Chium]? *Rackham.*

Porphyris, is believed to have been severed from Cos. Next to Cos we come to Caryanda with its town; and not far from Halicarnassus, Pidossus. In the Ceramic Bay are Priaponesus, Hipponesus, Pserema, Lampsa, Aemyndus, Passala, Crusa, Pyrrhaeciusa, Sepiusa, Melano, and at only a small distance from the mainland the island named Cinaedopolis, because certain persons of disgraceful character were deposited there by Alexander the Great.

XXXVII. Off the coast of Ionia are Aegeae and Corseae, and Icarus previously mentioned, Lade, formerly called Late, and among some islands of no importance the two Camelitae near Miletus, the three Trogiliae near Mycala, Philios, Argennos, Sandalios, and the free island of Samos, which measures 87½, or according to Isidore, 100 miles in circumference. Aristotle records that it was first called Parthenia, afterwards Dryusa, and then Anthemusa; Aristocritus adds the names Melamphyllus, and later Cyparissia, others Parthenoarrhusa and Stephane. Samos contains the rivers Imbrasus, Chesius and Hibiethes, the springs Gigartho and Leucothea, and Mount Cercetius. Adjacent islands are Rhypara, Nymphaea and Achillea.

Islands off Ionian coasts: Samos. IV. 68.

XXXVIII. Ninety-four miles from Samos is the equally famous free island of Chios with its town. This island Ephorus designates by its ancient name of Aethalia, while Metrodorus and Cleobulus call it Chia after the nymph Chione, though some say that name is derived from the Greek word for snow. Other names for it are Macris and Pityusa. It contains Mount Pelinnaeus, in which Chian marble is quarried. Its circumference amounts to 125 miles, according to old accounts, but Isidore adds 9 miles to that

Chios.

posita est inter Samum et Lesbum, ex adverso maxime
137 Erythrarum. finitimae sunt Tellusa quam alii
Daphnusam scribunt, Oenusa, Elaphitis, Euryanassa,
Arginusa cum oppido. iam hae circa Ephesum et
quae Pisistrati vocantur Anthinae, Myonnesos, Diar-
rheusa (in utraque oppida intercidere), Pordoselene
cum oppido, Cerciae, Halone, Commone, Illetia,
Lepria, Aethre, Sphaeria, Procusae, Bolbulae, Pheate,
Priapos, Syce, Melane, Aenare, Sidusa, Pele,
Drymusa, Anhydros, Scopelos, Sycussa, Marathusa,
138 Psile, Perirrheusa, multaeque ignobiles. clara vero
in alto Teos cum oppido, a Chio $\overline{\text{LXXI}}$ D, tantundem ab
Erythris. iuxta Zmyrnam sunt Peristerides, Carteria,
Alopece, Elaeusa, Bacchina, Pystira, Crommyonnesos,
Megale. ante Troada Ascaniae, Plateae tres, dein
Lamiae, Plitaniae duae, Plate, Scopelos, Getone,
Arthedon, Coele, Lagusae, Didymae.

139   XXXIX. Clarissima autem Lesbos, a Chio $\overline{\text{LXV}}$,
Himerte et Lasia, Pelasgia, Aegira, Aethiope, Ma-
caria appellata. fuit IX oppidis incluta: ex his
Pyrrha hausta est mari, Arisbe terrarum motu
subversa, Antissam Methymna traxit in se, ipsa IX
urbibus Asiae in $\overline{\text{XXXVII}}$ p. vicina. et Agamede obiit
et Hiera; restant Eresos, Pyrrha et libera Mytilene
annis MD potens. tota insula circuitur, ut Isidorus,
140 $\overline{\text{CLXVIII}}$, ut veteres $\overline{\text{CXCV}}$. montes habet Lepetym-

---

[a] This was the harbour-suburb of the town of the same
name stated just above to have been submerged: Strabo
XIV. 618.

figure. It is situated between Samos and Lesbos and directly opposite to Erythrae. Neighbouring islands are Tellusa, by other writers called Daphnusa, Oenusa, Elaphitis, Euryanassa and Arginusa with its town. These islands bring us to the neighbourhood of Ephesus, where are also those called the Islands of Pisistratus, Anthinae, Myonnesus, Diarrheusa (the towns on both these islands have disappeared), Pordoselene with its town, Cerciae, Halone, Commone, Illetia, Lepria, Aethre, Sphaeria, Procusae, Bolbulae, Pheate, Priapos, Syce, Melane, Aenare, Sidusa, Pele, Drymusa, Anhydros, Scopelos, Sycussa, Marathusa, Psile, Perirrheusa, and many others of no note. Out at sea is the famous island of Teos with its town, 71½ miles from Chios and the same distance from Erythrae. Near Smyrna are the Peristerides, Carteria, Alopece, Elaeusa, Bacchina, Pystira, Crommyonnesos, Megale. Off the Troad are Ascaniae, the three Plateae, then Lamiae, the two Plitaniae, Plate, Scopelos, Getone, Arthedon, Coele, Lagusae, Didymae.

XXXIX. The most famous island is Lesbos, 65 *Lesbos.* miles from Chios; it was formerly called Himerte and Lasia, Pelasgia, Aegira, Aethiope and Macaria. It had nine noteworthy towns: of these Pyrrha has been swallowed up by the sea, Arisbe destroyed by earthquake and Antissa absorbed by Methymna, which itself lies near nine cities of Asia, along a coastline of 37 miles. Agamede and Hiera have also ceased to exist; but there remain Eresos, Pyrrha*a* and the free city of Mytilene, which has been powerful for 1500 years. The circuit of the whole island measures 168 miles according to Isidore and 195 miles according to old authorities. The mountains

num, Ordymnum, Macistum, Creonem, Olympum.
a proxima continente abest VII D p. insulae adpositae
Sandalium, Leucae v, ex iis Cydonea cum fonte
calido; Arginussae ab Aege IV p. distant, dein
Phellusa, Pedna. extra Hellespontum adversa Sigeo
litori iacet Tenedus, Leucophrys dicta et Phoenice et
Lyrnesos; abest a Lesbo LVI, a Sigeo XII D.

141 XL. Impetum deinde sumit Hellespontus, et
mari[1] incumbit, vorticibus limitem fodiens donec
Asiam abrumpat Europae. promunturium id appellavimus Trapezam. ab eo X p. Abydum oppidum,
ubi angustiae VII stadiorum; deinde Percote oppidum et Lampsacum antea Pityusa dictum, Parium
colonia quam Homerus Adrastiam appellavit, oppidum Priapos, amnis Aesepus, Zelia, Propontis (ita
appellatur ubi se dilatat mare), flumen Granicum,
142 Artace portus ubi oppidum fuit. ultra insula quam
continenti iunxit Alexander, in qua oppidum Milesiorum Cyzicum ante vocitatum Arctonnesos et
Dolionis et Didymis, cuius a vertice mons Didymus.
mox oppida Placia, Ariace, Scylace, quorum a tergo
mons Olympus Mysius dictus, civitas Olympena.
amnes Horisius et Rhyndacus ante Lycus vocatus;
oritur in stagno Artynia iuxta Miletopolim, recipit
Maceston et plerosque alios, Asiam Bithyniamque

---

[1] *Urlichs*: mare.

[a] One of the Leucae, 'White Islands'; should its name be
Aegle, 'Radiance'?
[b] *Il*. II. 828.

on Lesbos are Lepetymnus, Ordymnus, Macistus, Creone and Olympus. It is 7½ miles distant from the nearest point of the mainland. Adjacent islands are Sandalium and the five Leucae, which include Cydonea with its hot spring; four miles from Aege [a] are the Arginussae and then Phellusa and Pedna. Outside the Dardanelles and opposite the coast of Sigeum lies Tenedos, also called Leucophrys and Phoenice and Lyrnesos; it is 56 miles from Lesbos and 12½ from Sigeum.

XL. Here the current of the Dardanelles becomes *The Hellespont and Mysia.* stronger, and comes into collision with the sea, undermining the bar with its eddies until it separates Asia from Europe. We have already given the name of § 127. the promontory here as Trapeza. Ten miles from it is the town of Abydus, where the strait is only 7 furlongs wide; then the town of Percote, and Lampsacus formerly called Pityusa, the colony of Parium, called by Homer [b] Adrastia, the town of Priapos, the river Aesepus, Zelia, and the Sea of Marmara (the name given to the Straits where the sea widens out), the river Granicus and the harbour of Artace, where there once was a town. Beyond is the island which Alexander joined to the mainland and on which is the Milesian town of Cyzicus, formerly called Arctonnesus and Dolionis and Didymis; above it is Mount Didymus. Then the towns of Placia, Ariace and Scylace, and in their rear the mountain called the Mysian Olympus and the city-state of Olympena. The rivers are the Horisius and the Rhyndacus, formerly called the Lycus: this rises in the marsh of Artynia near Miletopolis, and into it flow the Macestos and several other rivers; it forms the boundary between Asia

327

143 disterminans. ea appellata est Cronia, dein Thessalis
dein Malianda et Strymonis; hos Homerus Hali-
zonas dixit, quando praecingitur gens mari. urbs
fuit inmensa Atussa nomine, nunc sunt xii civitates,
inter quas Gordiu Come quae Iuliopolis vocatur, et in
ora Dascylos. dein flumen Gelbes, et intus Helgas
oppidum quae Germanicopolis, alio nomine Boos Coete,
sicut Apamea quae nunc Myrlea Colophoniorum,
flumen Echeleos anticus Troadis finis et Mysiae
144 initium. postea sinus in quo flumen Ascanium,
oppidum Bryalion, amnes Hylas et Cios cum oppido
eiusdem nominis, quod fuit emporium non procul
accolentis Phrygiae, a Milesiis quidem conditum, in
loco tamen qui Ascania Phrygiae vocabatur; quapropter non aliubi aptius de ea dicatur.

145   XLI. Phrygia Troadi superiecta populisque a
promunturio Lecto ad flumen Echeleum praedictis
septentrionali sui parte Galatiae contermina, meridiana Lycaoniae, Pisidiae Mygdoniaeque, ab oriente
Cappadociam attingit. oppida ibi celeberrima praeter iam dicta Ancyra, Andria, Celaenae, Colossae,
Carina, Cotyaion, Ceraine, Conium, Midaium. sunt
auctores transisse ex Europa Moesos et Brygos et
Thynos, a quibus appellentur Mysi, Phryges, Bithyni.

146   XLII. Simul dicendum videtur et de Galatia, quae
superposita agros maiore ex parte Phrygiae tenet

---

^a *Il.* II. 856.

and Bithynia. This district was formerly named Cronia, then Thessalis, and then Malianda and Strymonis; its inhabitants were called by Homer[a] the Halizones, as the tribe is ' girdled by the sea.' It once had a vast city named Atussa, and it now includes twelve city-states, among them Gordiu Come otherwise called Juliopolis, and on the coast Dascylos. Then there is the river Gelbes, and inland the town of Helgas, also called Germanicopolis, another name for it being Boos Coete; as also Apamea now known as Myrlea of the Colophonii; and the river Echeleos which in early times was the frontier of the Troad, and at which Mysia began. Afterwards the bay in which are the river Ascanius, the town of Bryalion, the rivers Hylas and Cios, with the town also named Cios, formerly a trading station for the neighbouring district of Phrygia, founded by the people of Miletus but on a site formerly known as Ascania of Phrygia: consequently this is as suitable a place as any other to speak about Phrygia.

XLI. Phrygia lies behind Troas and the peoples *Phrygia.* already mentioned between Cape Lectum and the river Echeleus. On its northern side it marches with Galatia, on its southern side with Lycaonia, Pisidia and Mygdonia, and on the east it extends to Cappadocia. Its most famous towns beside the ones already mentioned are Ancyra, Andria, Celaenae, *§ 105 f.* Colossae, Carina, Cotyaion, Ceraine, Conium and Midaium. Some authorities say that the Mysians, Phrygians and Bithynians take their names from three parties of immigrants who crossed over from Europe, the Moesi, Brygi and Thyni.

XLII. At the same time it seems proper to speak *Galatia and* also about Galatia, which lies above Phrygia and holds *adjoining regions.*

329

caputque quondam eius Gordium. qui partem eam
insedere Gallorum Tolistobogii et Voturi et Ambitouti
vocantur, qui Maeoniae et Paphlagoniae regionem
Trogmi. praetenditur Cappadocia a septentrione et
solis ortu, cuius uberrimam partem occupavere
Tectosages ac Toutobodiaci. et gentes[1] quidem hae;
populi vero ac tetrarchiae omnes numero cxcv.
oppida Tectosagum Ancyra, Trogmorum Tavium,
147 Tolistobogiorum Pisinuus. praeter hos celebres Actalenses, Alassenses, Comenses, Didienses, Hierorenses,
Lystreni, Neapolitani, Oeandenses, Seleucenses,
Sebasteni, Timoniacenses, Thebaseni. attingit Galatia et Pamphyliae Cabaliam et Milyas qui circa
Barim sunt et Cyllanicum et Oroandicum Pisidiae
tractum, item Lycaoniae partem Obizenen. flumina
sunt in ea praeter iam dicta Sangarium et Gallus, a
quo nomen traxere Matris Deum sacerdotes.

148   XLIII. Nunc reliqua in ora. a Cio intus in
Bithynia Prusa ab Hannibale sub Olympo condita—
inde Nicaeam xxv p. interveniente Ascanio lacu—,
dein Nicaea in ultimo Ascanio sinu, quae prius Olbia,
et Prusias, item altera sub Hypio monte. fuere
Pythopolis, Parthenopolis, Coryphanta. sunt in ora

---

[1] Tectosages. ac toto tractu gentes *Mayhoff (scilicet nomina
in hoc loco incertissime traduntur)*.

lands that for the most part were taken from
that country, as was Gordium, its former capital.
This district is occupied by Gallic settlers called
the Tolistobogii, Voturi and Ambitouti, and those
occupying the Maeonian and Paphlagonian region
are the Trogmi. Along the north and east of Galatia
stretches Cappadocia, the most fertile part of which
has been occupied by the Tectosages and Toutobodiaci. These are the races that inhabit the
country; the peoples and tetrarchies into which
they are divided number 195 in all. The towns are
Ancyra belonging to the Tectosages, Tavium to the
Trogmi and Pisinûs to the Tolistobogii. Noteworthy people besides these are the Actalenses,
Alassenses, Comenses, Didienses, Hierorenses,
Lystreni, Neapolitani, Oeandenses, Seleucenses,
Sebasteni, Timoniacenses and Thebaseni. Galatia
also touches on Cabalia in Pamphylia and the Milyae
about Baris; also on Cyllanicum and the district of
Oroanda in Pisidia, and Obizene which is part of
Lycaonia. The rivers in it beside those already
mentioned are the Sakarya and the Gallus; from
the latter the priests of the Mother of the Gods take
their name.

XLIII. Now we give the remainder of the places *Bithynia.*
on this coast. Inland from Cios, in Bithynia, is Prusa,
at the foot of Olympus, founded by Hannibal
—from there to Nicaea is 25 miles, Lake Ascanius
coming in between—; then, on the innermost bay of
the lake, Nicaea, which was formerly called Olbia,
and Prusias; then a second place also named
Prusias at the foot of Mount Hypius. Places that
exist no longer are Pythopolis, Parthenopolis and
Coryphanta. On the coast are the rivers Aesius,

amnes Aesius, Bryazon, Plataneus, Areus, Aesyros,
Geodos qui et Chrysorroas, promunturium in quo
Megarice oppidum fuit: unde[1] Craspedites sinus
vocabatur, quoniam id oppidum velut in lacinia erat.
fuit et Astacum, unde et ex eo Astacenus idem sinus.
fuit et Libyssa oppidum ubi nunc Hannibalis tantum
tumulus; est et in intimo sinu Nicomedia Bithyniae
149 praeclara. Leucatas promunturium quo includitur
Astacenus sinus a Nicomedia X̄X̄X̄V̄ĪĪ D p. rursusque
coeuntibus terris angustiae pertinentes usque ad
Bosporum Thracium. in his Calchadon libera, a Nicomedia L̄X̄ĪĪ D p., Procerastis ante dicta, dein Colpusa,
postea Caecorum Oppidum, quod locum eligere
nescissent, VII stadiis distante Byzantio tanto feli-
ciore omnibus modis sede. ceterum intus in Bithynia
colonia Apamena, Agrippenses, Iuliopolitae, Bithynion. flumina Syrium, Laphias, Pharnacias,
Alces, Serinis, Lilaeus, Scopius, Hieros qui Bithyniam
150 et Galatiam determinat. ultra Calchadona Chrysopolis fuit. dein Nicopolis, a qua nomen etiamnum
sinus retinet in quo portus Amyci; dein Naulochum
promunturium, Hestiae,[2] templum Neptuni. Bosporos
D p. intervallo Asiam Europae iterum auferens abest a
Calchadone X̄ĪĪ D p., inde fauces primae VIII DCCL p.,
ubi Spiropolis oppidum fuit. tenent oram omnem

---

[1] *V.l.* inde.
[2] *Rackham* ('Εστία et *Mueller*): Estiae.

---

[a] 'On the fringe,' used of the last person in a Greek chorus.
[b] This form is well attested, though Chalcedon is more usual.

Bryazon, Plataneus, Areus, Aesyrus and Geodos,
another name for which is Chrysorrhoas, and the headland on which formerly the town of Megarice stood:
owing to which the gulf used to have the name of
Craspedites,[a] because that town was a sort of tassel
on its fringe. There was also formerly the town of
Astacus, owing to which the gulf in question was
also called Astacus Bay. Also there was a town
called Libyssa at the place where there is now only
the tomb of Hannibal; and also at the far extremity
of the bay stands the famous city of Bithynian
Nicomedia. Cape Leucatas which shuts in Astacus
Bay is 37½ miles from Nicomedia; and then the
coastlines come together again, forming narrows
that extend as far as the Straits of Constantinople.
On these narrows are the free city of Calchadon,[b]
previously called Procerastis, 62½ miles from Nico-
demia, then Colpusa, afterwards Blind Men's Town
—a name implying that its founders did not know
how to choose a site, Byzantium a site so much more
attractive in every respect being less than a mile
away! Inland in Bithynia are the colony of Apamea,
Agrippenses, Juliopolitae and Bithynion. The rivers
are the Syrium, Laphias, Pharnacias, Alces, Serinis,
Lilaeus, Scopius and Hieros, which forms the frontier
between Bithynia and Galatia. Beyond Calchadon
formerly stood Chrysopolis. Then Nicopolis, from
which comes the name still given to the bay containing Port of Amycus; then Cape Naulochum, Hestiae
and Neptune's Temple. Then come the Straits of
Constantinople, the channel half a mile wide which
again separates Asia from Europe, 12½ miles from
Calchadon. Then the mouth of the Straits, 8¾ miles
wide, where once stood the town of Spiropolis. The

Thyni, interiora Bithyni. is finis Asiae est populorumque CCLXXXII qui ad cum locum a fine Lyciae numerantur. spatium Hellesponti et Propontidis ad Bosporum Thracium esse $\overline{\text{CCXXXIX}}$ p. diximus; a Calchadone Sigeum Isidorus $\overline{\text{CCCXXII}}$ D p. tradit.

151 XLIV. Insulae in Propontide ante Cyzicum Elaphonnesus, unde Cyzicenum marmor, eadem Neuris et Proconnesus dicta; secuntur Ophiussa, Acanthus, Phoebe, Scopelos, Porphyrione, Halone cum oppido, Delphacie, Polydora, Artacaeon cum oppido. est et contra Nicomediam Demonnesos, item ultra Heracleam adversa Bithyniae Thynias quam barbari Bithyniam vocant. est et Antiochia et contra fauces Rhyndaci Besbicos $\overline{\text{XVIII}}$ p. circuitu; est Elaea et duae Rhodusae, Erebinthote, Megale, Chalcitis, Pityodes.

whole of the coast is inhabited by the Thynians and the interior by the Bithynians. This is the end of Asia and of the 282 peoples who can be counted between the frontier of Lycia and this point. The length of the Dardanelles and the Sea of Marmara to the Straits of Constantinople we stated above as 239 miles, and the distance from Calchadon to Sigeum is given by Isidore as 322½ miles. IV. 76.

XLIV. The islands in the Marmara are, Elaphon- *Islands in* nesus off Cyzicus, from which is obtained the Cyzicus *the* *Propontis.* marble—it is also called Neuris and Proconnesus—, and then Ophiussa, Acanthus, Phoebe, Scopelos, Porphyrione, Halone with its town, Delphacie, Polydora and Artacaeon with its town. Also off Nicomedia is Demonnesus, and also beyond Heraclea and off Bithynia Thynias, the native name of which is Bithynia. There is also Antiochia, and off the mouth of the Rhyndacus Besbicos, an island 18 miles in circumference; and also Elaea and the two Rhodusae, Erebinthote, Megale, Chalcitis and Pityodes.

BOOK VI

LIBER VI

1   I. Pontus Euxinus, antea ab inhospitali feritate
Axinus appellatus, peculiari invidia naturae sine
ullo fine indulgentis aviditati maris et ipse in[1]
Europam Asiamque funditur. non fuerat satis
oceano ambisse terras et partem earum aucta
inmanitate abstulisse, non inrupisse fractis montibus Calpeque Africae avolsa tanto maiora absorbuisse
quam reliquerit spatia, non per Hellespontum Propontida infudisse iterum terris devoratis : a Bosporo
quoque in aliam vastitatem panditur nulla satietate,
donec exspatianti lacus Maeotii rapinam suam iun-
2 gant. invitis hoc accidisse terris indicio sunt tot
angustiae atque tam parva naturae repugnantis intervalla, ad Hellespontum DCCCLXXV p., ad Bosporos duos
vel bubus meabili transitu—unde nomen ambobus,—
etiam quaedam in dissociatione germanitas concors :
alitum quippe cantus canumque latratus invicem
audiuntur, vocis etiam humanae commercia, inter
duos orbes manente conloquio, nisi cum id ipsum
auferunt venti.

[1] *V.l.* inter

---

   [a] See IV. 76 *note.* Some of the ancients thought that the
name was due to the inhospitable savagery of the natives.
   [b] *I.e.* double paces, say 5 feet.
   [c] The Thracian and the Cimmerian Bosporus ; the name ' Ox-
ford,' supposed to be due to Io, who as a cow traversed the
former strait, was also given to others.

BOOK VI

I. The Euxine or Black Sea, formerly because of its *The Black* inhospitable roughness called the Axine,[a] owing to a *Sea.* peculiar jealousy on the part of Nature, which here indulges the sea's greed without any limit, actually spreads into Europe and Asia. The Ocean was not content to have encircled the earth, and with still further cruelty to have reft away a portion of her surface, nor to have forced an entrance through a breach in the mountains and rent Gibraltar away from Africa, so devouring a larger area than it left remaining, nor to have swallowed up a further space of land and flooded the Sea of Marmara through the Dardanelles; even beyond the Straits of Constantinople also it widens out into another desolate expanse, with an appetite unsatisfied until the Sea of Azov links on its own trespass to its encroachments. That this event occurred against the will of the earth is proved by the number of narrows, and by the smallness of the gaps left by Nature's resistance, measuring at the Dardanelles 875 paces,[b] at the Straits of Constantinople and Kertsch the passage being actually fordable by oxen—which fact gives both of them their name[c];—and also by a certain harmonious affinity contained in their disseverance, as the singing of birds and barking of dogs on one side can be heard on the other, and even the interchange of human speech, conversation going on between the two worlds, save when the actual sound is carried away by the wind.

3 Mensuram Ponti a Bosporo ad Maeotium lacum
quidam fecere ⌈xiv⌉ xxxviii d, Eratosthenes c̄ minorem
Agrippa a Calchadone ad Phasim ⌈x⌉, inde Bosporum
Cimmerium c̄c̄clx. nos intervalla generatim ponemus [1] conperta in aevo nostro, quando etiam in ipso
ore Cimmerio pugnatum est.

4 Ergo a faucibus Bospori est amnis Rebas, quem
aliqui Rhesum dixerunt; dein Syris, portus Calpas,
Sangarius fluvius ex inclutis; oritur in Phrygia, accipit
vastos amnes, inter quos Tembrogium et Gallum,
idem Sagiarius plerisque dictus; Coralius, a quo
incipiunt Mariandyni, sinus oppidumque Heraclea
Lyco flumini adpositum—abest a Ponti ore c̄c̄,—portus Aconae veneno aconito dirus, specus Acherusia,
flumina Paedopides, Callichorum, Sonautes, oppidum
5 Tium ab Heraclea xxxviii p., fluvius Billis. II. ultra
quem gens Paphlagonia, quam Pylaemeniam aliqui
dixerunt, inclusam a tergo Galatia, oppidum Mastya
Milesiorum, dein Cromna, quo loco Enetos adicit
Nepos Cornelius, a quibus in Italia ortos cognomines
eorum Venetos credi debere [2] putat, Sesamon
oppidum, quod nunc Amastris, mons Cytorus a Tio
lxiii p., oppida Cimolis, Stephane, amnis Parthenius.
6 promunturium Cerambis vasto excursu abest a
Ponti ostio c̄c̄cxxv, ut aliis placuit, c̄c̄cl, tantundem a

---

[1] *Gelenius*: ponimus.
[2] *Mayhoff*: credere (ea de re *Detlefsen*).

The dimension of the Black Sea from the Dardanelles to the Sea of Azov is given by some authorities as 1438½ miles, but Eratosthenes makes it 100 miles less. Agrippa gives the distance from Calchadon to the river Rion as 1000 miles and from that river to the Straits of Kertsch as 360 miles. We shall state the distances in sections as ascertained in our own time, inasmuch as there has been dispute even about the mouth of the Straits of Kertsch.

Well then, after the mouth of the Dardanelles is the river Rebas, called by some the Rhesus; then Syris, and Port Calpas, and the Sakarya, a famous river which rises in Phrygia and into which flow some very large tributaries, among them the Tembrogius and the Gallus; its name is commonly given as Sagiarius; the Coralius where the Mariandyni territory begins; the bay of Heraclea, and the town of that name on the river Lycus—it is 200 miles from the mouth of the Black Sea,—the port of Aconae, of evil repute for the poison called aconite, the Acherusian Cavern, the rivers Paedopides, Callichorus and Sonautes, the town of Tium 38 miles from Heraclea, and the river Billis. II. Beyond *Paphlagonia.* this river is the Paphlagonian race, called by some the Pylaemenian, enclosed to the rear by Galatia, the Milesian town of Mastya, then Cromna, a place with which Cornelius Nepos connects the Eneti, from whom he thinks the Veneti in Italy bearing a similar name must be believed to be descended; the town of Sesamon, now called Amastris; Mount Cytorus, 63 miles from Tium; the towns of Cimolis and Stephane and the river Parthenius. The great projection of Cape Cerambis is 325 miles, or according to others 350 miles, distant from the mouth of the

Cimmerio aut, ut aliqui maluere, $\overline{\text{CCCXII}}$ D. fuit et
oppidum eodem nomine et aliud inde Armine; nunc
est colonia Sinope a Cytoro $\overline{\text{CLXIV}}$; flumen Evarchum,[1]
gens Cappadocum, oppidum Caturia Zaceplum, amnis
Halys a radicibus Tauri per Cataoniam Cappado-
7 ciamque decurrens; oppida Gamge, Carusa, Amisum
liberum a Sinope $\overline{\text{CXXX}}$, eiusdemque nominis sinus
tanti recessus ut Asiam paene insulam faciat, $\overline{\text{CC}}$ haut
amplius per continentem ad Issicum Ciliciae sinum.
quo in omni tractu proditur tres tantum gentes
Graecas iure dici, Doricam Ionicam Aeolicam,
ceteras barbarorum esse. Amiso iunctum fuit
oppidum Eupatoria a Mithridate conditum; victo
eo utrumque Pompeiopolis appellatum est.

8 III. Cappadocia intus habet coloniam Claudi
Caesaris Archelaidem quam praeterfluit Halys,
oppida Comana quod Salius, Neocaesaream quod
Lycus, Amasiam quod Iris in regione Gazacena, in
Colopene vero Sebastiam et Sebastopolim (haec
parva sed paria supra dictis), reliqua sui parte
Melitam a Samiramide conditam haud procul
Euphrate, Diocaesaream, Tyana, Castabala, Magno-
polim, Zelam et sub monte Argaeo Mazacum quae
9 nunc Caesarea nominatur. Cappadociae pars
praetenta Armeniae Maiori Melitene vocatur,

---

[1] *Hardouin*: Varecum.

---

[a] The Kizil Irmak or Red River.
[b] This strange belief goes back to Herodotus. The distance
across to the Gulf of Issus, Scanderoon, is at least 300 miles.
[c] King of Pontus, finally defeated in 63 B.C., by Pompey.

Black Sea, and the same distance, or, by an estimate which some prefer, 312½ miles from the Straits of Kertsch. There was formerly also a town of the same name, and then another called Armine; and at the present day there is the colony of Sinâb, 164 miles from Mount Cytorus; the river Evarchus, a tribe of Cappadocians, the town of Caturia Zaceplum, and the river Halys[a] that flows down from the base of Mount Taurus through Cataonia and Cappadocia; the towns of Gamge and Carusa, the free town of Amisus 130 miles from Sinâb, and the bay of the same name which runs so far inland as to give to Asia the shape of a peninsula,[b] the isthmus measuring not more than 200 miles across to the Gulf of Issus in Cilicia. It is reported that in all this region there are only three races that can rightly be designated Greek, the Dorian, the Ionian and the Aeolian, all the rest being tribes of barbarians. To Amisus was attached the town of Eupatoria, founded by Mithridates;[c] after he had been conquered, the two places were united under the name of Pompeiopolis.

III. Cappadocia contains in its interior a colony *Cappadocia.* of Claudius Caesar named Archelais, past which flows the river Halys, and the towns of Comana on the Salius, Neocaesarea on the Lycus, and Amasia on the Iris in the region of Gazacena; while in the Colopene region are Sebastia and Sebastopol, which are small towns but equal in importance to those mentioned above; and in the remaining part of Cappadocia are Melita, founded by Samiramis, not far from the Euphrates, Diocaesarea, Tyana, Castabala, Magnopolis, Zela, and under Mount Argaeus Mazacus, now named Caesarea. The part of Cappadocia adjacent to Greater Armenia is called

Commagenis Cataonia, Phrygiae Garsauritis, Sargaurasana Cammaneni, Galatiae Morimene, ubi
disterminat eas Cappadox amnis, a quo nomen
traxere antea Leucosyri dicti. a Neocaesarea supra
dicta Minorem Armeniam Lycus amnis disterminat.
est et Coeranus intus clarus, in ora autem ab Amiso
oppidum et flumen Chadisia, Lycastum, a quo
10 Themiscyrena regio. Iris flumen deferens Lycum.
civitas Ziela intus, nobilis clade Triarii et victoria
C. Caesaris. in ora amnis Thermodon ortus ad
castellum quod vocant Phanorian praeterque radices
Amazoni montis lapsus; fuit oppidum eodem nomine
et alia quinque, Amazonium, Themiscyra, Sotira,
11 Amasia, Comana, nunc Matium[1]; (IV) gentes Cae-
narum, Chalybum, oppidum Cotyorum, gentes
Tibareni, Massyni notis signantes corpora, gens
Macrocephali, oppidum Cerasus, portus Cordule,
gentes Bechires, Buxeri, flumen Melas, gens Machorones, Sideni flumenque Sidenum quo alluitur
oppidum Polemonium ab Amiso $\overline{cxx}$. inde flumina
Iasonium, Melanthium, et ab Amiso $\overline{lxxx}$ Pharnacea
oppidum, Tripolis castellum et fluvius, item Philocalia
et sine fluvio item Liviopolis, et a Pharnacea $\overline{c}$

---

[1] Mantium *Hermolaus* (cf. V. 115, 116).

[a] In the war against Mithradates, 67 B.C.

[b] Over Pharnaces, son of Mithradates—the victory (in
47 B.C.) reported by Julius Caesar to the senate in the words
Veni, vidi, vici.

[c] Or perhaps 'Comana, which is now an Oracular Shrine.'

Melitene, the part bordering on Commagene Cataonia, that on Phrygia Garsauritis, that on Cammanene Sargaurasana, that on Galatia Morimene, where the boundary between the two countries is formed by the river Cappadox, from which the Cappadocians take their name—they were formerly called the White Syrians. The boundary between Neocaesarea above mentioned and Lesser Armenia is the river Lycus. In the interior there is also the notable river Coeranus, and on the coast after Amisus the town of Chadisia with the river of the same name, and the town of Lycastus, after which the district of Themiscyra begins. The river here is the Iris, *Themiscyra.* with a tributary the Lycus. Inland is Ziela, the city-state famous for the defeat [a] of Triarius and the victory of Gaius Caesar.[b] On the coast is the river Thermodon, which rises at the fortress called Phanorias and flows past the foot of the mountain Mason Dagh; there was formerly a town of the same name as the river, and five others, Amazonium, Themiscyra, Sotira, Amasia and Comana, and now there is Matium;[c] (IV) the Caenares and Chalybes tribes, the town of the Cotyi, the tribes of the Tibareni and the Massyni—the latter practise tattooing,—the Longhead tribe, the town of Cerasus, the harbour of Cordule, the Bechires and Buxeri tribes, the Black River, the Machorones tribe, the Sideni, and the river Sidenus which washes the town of Polemonium 120 miles from Amisus. Then come the rivers Iasonius and Melanthius, and 80 miles from Amisus the town of Pharnacea, the fortress and river Tripolis, the fortress and river Philocalia and the fortress of Liviopolis, which is not on a river, and 100 miles from Pharnacea the free town of Trebizond, shut in

345

12 Trapezus liberum monte vasto clausum. ultra quod
gens Armenochalybes, et Maior Armenia $\overline{\text{xxx}}$ p.
distans. in ora ante Trapezunta flumen est Pyxites,
ultra vero gens Sannorum Heniochorum, flumen
Absarrum cum castello cognomini [1] in faucibus, a
Trapezunte $\overline{\text{cxl}}$. eius loci a tergo montium Hiberia
est, in ora vero Heniochi, Ampreutae, Lazi, flumina
Acampseon, Isis, Mogrus, Bathys, gentes Col-
chorum, oppidum Matium, flumen Heracleum et
promunturium eodem nomine, clarissimusque Ponti
13 Phasis. oritur in Moschis, navigatur quamlibet
magnis navigiis $\overline{\text{xxxviii}}$ D p., inde minoribus longo
spatio, pontibus $\overline{\text{cxx}}$ pervius. oppida in ripis habuit
conplura, celeberrima Tyndarida, Circaeum, Cygnum
et in faucibus Phasim; maxime autem inclaruit Aea,
$\overline{\text{xv}}$ p. a mari, ubi Hippos et Cyaneos vasti amnes e
diverso in eum confluunt. nunc habet Surium
tantum, et ipsum ab amne influente ibi cognominatum usque quo magnarum navium capacem esse
diximus. et alios accipit fluvios magnitudine numero-
que mirabiles, inter quos Glaucum; in ore eius
14 insula est [2] sine nomine, ab Absarro $\overline{\text{lxx}}$. inde aliud
flumen Charien, gens Saltiae antiquis Phthirophagi
dicti et alia Sanni, flumen Chobum e Caucaso per
Suanos fluens, dein Rhoan, regio Cegritice, amnes
Sigania, Thersos, Astelphus, Chrysorroas, gens

---

[1] cognomini? *Mayhoff*: cognomine.
[2] *Mayhoff*: insulae.

by a vast mountain range. Beyond Trebizond begins the Armenochalybes tribe, and 30 miles further Greater Armenia. On the coast before reaching Trebizond is the river Pyxites, and beyond Trebizond the Charioteer Sanni, and the river Absarrus with the fortress of the same name in its gorge, 140 miles from Trapezus. Behind the mountains of this district is Hiberia, and on the coast the Charioteers, the Ampreutae and the Lazi, the rivers Acampseon, Isis, Mogrus and Bathys, the Colchian tribes, the town of Matium, the River of Heracles and the cape of the same name, and the Rion, the most celebrated river of the Black Sea region. The Rion rises among the Moschi and is navigable for ships of any size for 38½ miles, and a long way further for smaller vessels; it is crossed by 120 bridges. It had a considerable number of towns on its banks, the most notable being Tyndaris, Circaeus, Cygnus, and at its mouth Phasis; but the most famous was Aea, 15 miles from the sea, where two very large tributaries join the Rion from opposite directions, the Hippos and the Cyaneos. At the present day the only town on the Rion is Surium, which itself also takes its name from a river that enters the Rion at the point up to which we said that it is navigable for large vessels. It also receives other tributaries remarkable for their size and number, among them the Glaucus; at its mouth is an island with no name, 70 miles from the mouth of the Absarrus. Then there is another river, the Charieis, the Saltiae tribe called of old the Pine-seed-eaters, and another tribe, the Sanni; the river Chobus flowing from the Caucasus through the Suani territory; then Rhoan, the Cegritic district, the rivers Sigania, Thersos, Astelphus and

The river Rion.

347

Absilae, castellum Sebastopolis a Phaside c̄, gens
Sanicarum, oppidum Cygnus, flumen et oppidum
Penius; deinde multis nominibus Heniochorum
gentes.

15   V. Subicitur Ponti regio Colica, in qua iuga
Caucasi ad Ripaeos montes torquentur, ut dictum est,
altero latere in Euxinum et Maeotium devexa, altero
in Caspium et Hyrcanium mare. reliqua litora fere
nationes tenent Melanchlaeni, Coraxi urbe Col-
chorum Dioscuriade iuxta fluvium Anthemunta nunc
deserta, quondam adeo clara ut Timosthenes in eam
CCC nationes dissimilibus linguis descendere prodiderit; et postea a nostris CXXX interpretibus negotia
16   gesta ibi. sunt qui conditam eam ab Amphito et
Thelchio Castoris ac Pollucis aurigis putent, a quibus
ortam Heniochorum gentem fere constat. c̄ a[1] Dioscuriade oppidum Heracleum distat, a Sebastopoli
L̄X̄X̄. Achaei, Mardi, Cercetae, post eos Serri,
Cephalotomi. in intimo eo tractu Pityus oppidum
opulentissimum ab Heniochis direptum est. a tergo
eius Epagerritae, Sarmatarum populus, in Caucasi
17   iugis, post quem Sauromatae. ad hos profugerat
Mithridates Claudio principe, narravitque Thalos iis
esse confinis qui ab oriente Caspii maris fauces

---

[1] *Mayhoff*: ca *aut* a.

---

[a] Established as king of Bosporus by Claudius in A.D. 41,
but later replaced by his brother Cotys.
[b] See p. 364, note *b*.

Chrysorrhoas, the Absilae tribe, the fortress of Sebastopol 100 miles from Phasis, the Sanicae tribe, the town of Cygnus, the river and town of Penius; and then tribes of the Charioteers with a variety of names.

V. Below this lies the Black Sea district named *Colica.* Colica, in which the Caucasus range curves round to the Ripaean Mountains, as we have previously v. 98. stated, one side sloping down towards the Black Sea and the Sea of Azov, and the other towards the Caspian and Hyrcanian Sea. The tribes occupying almost all the rest of the coasts are the Blackcloaks and the Coraxi, with the Colchian city of Dioscurias on the river Anthemus, now deserted, but once so famous that according to Timosthenes 300 tribes speaking different languages used to resort to it; and subsequently business was carried on there by Roman traders with the help of a staff of 130 interpreters. Some people think that Dioscurias was founded by the charioteers of Castor and Pollux, Amphitus and Thelchius, from whom it is virtually certain that the Charioteer tribe are descended. The town of Heracleum is 100 miles from Dioscurias and 70 miles from Sebastopol. The tribes here are the Achaei, Mardi and Cercetae, and after these the Serri and Cephalotomi. In the interior of this region was the extremely wealthy town of Pityus, which was sacked by the Charioteers. Behind Pityus are the Epagerritae, a Sarmatian people on the Caucasus range, and after them come the Sauromatians. It was with this tribe that Mithridates [a] took refuge in the principate of Claudius, and from him we learn that there is a neighbouring tribe, the Thali, who on the eastern side extend to the mouth [b] of the Caspian

349

attingerent; siccari eas aestu recedente. in ora
autem iuxta Cercetas flumen Icarus, Achaei[1] cum
oppido Hiero et flumine, ab Heracleo C͞X͞X͞X͞V͞I. inde
promunturium Crunoe, a quo supercilium arduum
tenent Toretae, civitas Sindica ab Hiero L͞X͞V͞I͞I D,
flumen Secheries.

18   VI. Inde ad Bospori Cimmerii introitum L͞X͞X͞X͞V͞I͞I͞I D.
Sed ipsius paeninsulae inter Pontum et Maeotium lacum excurrentis non amplior L͞X͞V͞I͞I D p. longitudo est,
latitudo nusquam infra duo iugera; Eonem vocant.
ora ipsa Bospori utrimque ex Asia atque Europa
curvatur in Maeotim. oppida in aditu [Bospori
primo][2] Hermonasa, dein Cepoe Milesiorum, mox
Stratoclia et Phanagoria ac paene desertum Apaturos
ultimoque in ostio Cimmerium, quod antea Cerberion
vocabatur. VII. Inde Maeotis lacus in Europa
dictus.

19   A Cimmerio accolunt Maeotici, Hali, Sernes, Serrei,
Scizi, Gnissi. dein Tanain amnem gemino ore
influentem incolunt Sarmatae, Medorum (ut ferunt)
suboles, et ipsi in multa genera divisi. primi Sauromatae Gynaecocratumenoe, Amazonum conubia;
dein Naevazae, Coitae, Cizici, Messeniani, Cotobacchi, Cetae, Zigae, Tindari, Thussegetae, Tyrcae
usque ad solitudines saltuosis convallibus asperas,
ultra quas Arimphaei qui ad Ripaeos pertinent
20 montes. Tanaim ipsum Scythae Sinum vocant,

---

[1] *Hermolaus* : acaesum *et alia codd.*
[2] *Mayhoff.*

Sea, where, he tells us, the channel dries up at low tide. On the coast of the Black Sea near the Cercetae is the river Icarus, and the Achaei, with their Holy Town and River, 136 miles from Heracleum. Then comes Cape Cruni, after which a steep cliff is occupied by the Toretae, and then the city-state of Sindica, 67½ miles from Holy Town, and the river Secheries.

VI. The distance from the Secheries to the entrance *Straits of* to the Straits of Kertsch is 88½ miles. But the *Kertsch.* actual peninsula projecting between the Black Sea and the Sea of Azov is not more than 67½ miles long, its breadth being nowhere below 80 yards; it is called Eone. The actual coast of the Straits on both the Asiatic and the European sides curves into the Sea of Azov. The towns at its entrance are Hermonasa and next the Milesian town of Cepi, then Stratoclia and Phanagoria and the almost deserted town of Apaturos, and at the extreme end of the mouth Cimmerium, the former name of which was Cerberion. VII. Then comes the Sea of Azov, which is held to be in Europe.

After passing Cimmerium, the tribes inhabit- *The Don* ing the coast are the Macotici, Hali, Sernes, Serrei, *coast* Scizi and Gnissi. Next come the two mouths *beyond.* of the river Don, where the inhabitants are the Sarmatae, said to be descended from the Medes, and themselves divided into a number of sections. The first of these are the Matriarchal Sauromatae, the husbands of the Amazons; then the Naevazae, Coitae, Cizici, Messeniani, Cotobacchi, Cetae, Zigae, Tindari, Thussegetae and Tyrcae, which brings us to uninhabited deserts intersected by wooded glens, beyond which are the Arimphaei, who reach to the Ripaean Mountains. The Don itself is called by the

Maeotim Temarundam, quo significant matrem maris.
oppidum in Tanais quoque ostio. tenuere finitima
primo Cares, dein Clazomeni; et Maeones, postea
Panticapaeenses. sunt qui circa Maeotim ad Ceraunios montes has tradant gentes: a litore Napras,
21 supraque Essedonas Colchis iunctos montium cacu-
minibus. dein Camacas, Oranos, Autacas, Mazama-
cas, Cantiocaptas, Agamathas, Picos, Rymosolos,
Acascomarcos, et ad iuga Caucasi Icatalas, Imado-
chos, Ramos, Andacas, Tydios, Carastaseos, Authian-
das; Lagoum amnem ex montibus Catheis in quem
defluat Opharus, ibi gentes Cauthadas, Opharitas;
amnes Menotharum, Imityen ex montibus Cissiis;
infra [1] Agdeos, Carnas, Oscardeos, Accisos, Gabros,
Gegaros, circaque fontem Imityis Imityos et Apar-
22 taeos. alii influxisse eo Scythas Auchetas, Ather-
neos, Asampatas, ab his Tanaitas et Inapaeos viritim
deletos. aliqui flumen Ocharium labi per Canticos
et Sapeos, Tanain vero transisse Satharcheos Herti-
cheos, Spondolicos, Synhietas, Anasos, Issos, Cataee-
tas, Tagoras, Caronos, Neripos, Agandeos, Meanda-
raeos, Satharcheos Spalaeos.
23   VIII. Peracta est interior ora a Cio amne omnesque
accolae, nunc reddatur ingens in mediterraneo situs,[2]

----
[1] *Mayhoff*: inter.   [2] *Mayhoff*: sinus.

natives the Sinus, and the Sea of Azov the Temarunda, which means in their language 'the mother of the sea.' There is also a town at the mouth of the Don. The neighbouring districts were first occupied by the Carians, then by the Clazomenii and Maeones, and afterwards by the Panticapaeans. Some give the following list of tribes round the Sea of Azov near the Ceraunian Mountains: starting from the coast the Naprae, and higher up the Essedones, joining on to the Colchians on the tops of the mountains. Then the Camacae, Orani, Autacae, Mazamacae, Cantiocaptae, Agamathae, Pici, Rymosoli and Acascomarci, and near the Caucasus range the Icatalae, Imadochi, Rami, Andacae, Tydii, Carastasei and Authiandes; the river Lagous flowing down from the Cathean Mountains, with its tributary the Opharus, where are the Cauthadae and Opharitae tribes; the rivers Menotharus and Imityes flowing from the Cissian Mountains; below these the Agdaei, Carnae, Oscardei, Accisi, Gabri and Gegari, and round the source of the Imityes the Imityi and Apartaei. Other writers say that the Scythian tribes of the Auchetae, Athernei and Asampatae have spread into this country, and have destroyed the Tanaitae and Inapaei to a man. Some state that the river Ocharius runs through the Cantici and Sapei, but that the Don has passed through the Hertichean tribe of Satharchei, the Spondolici, Synhietae, Anasi, Issi, Cataeetae, Tagorae, Caroni, Neripi, Agandei, Meandaraei and Spalaean Satharchei.

VIII. We have gone over the inner coast of Asia *The interior.* from the river Cius and all the tribes dwelling on it; let us now give an account of the vast region that lies

in quo multa aliter ac veteres proditurum me non eo
infitias, anxia perquisitis [1] cura rebus nuper in eo
situ gestis a Domitio Corbulone regibusque inde
missis supplicibus aut regum liberis obsidibus.
24 ordiemur autem a Cappadocum gente. longissime
haec Ponticarum omnium introrsus recedens Minorem
Armeniam Maioremque et Commagenen laevo suo
latere transit, dextro vero omnes in Asia dictas
gentes, plurimis superfusa populis magnoque impetu
scandens ad ortum solis et Tauri iuga transit Lycaoniam, Pisidiam, Ciliciam, vadit super Antiochiae
tractum, et usque ad Cyrresticam eius regionem
parte sua quae vocatur Cataonia contendit. itaque ibi
longitudo Asiae $\overline{|XII|}$ $\overline{L}$ efficit, latitudo $\overline{DCXL}$.

25 IX. Armenia autem Maior incipit a Parihedris
montibus, Euphrate amne, ut dictum est, aufertur
Cappadociae et, qua discedit Euphrates, Mesopotamiae haut minus claro amne Tigri. utrumque
fundit ipsa, et initium Mesopotamiae facit inter duos
amnes sitae; quod interest ibi tenent Arabes Orroei.
sic finem usque in Adiabenen perfert; ab ea trans-
versis iugis inclusa latitudinem in laeva pandit ad
Cyrum amnem transversa Araxen, longitudinem vero
ad Minorem usque Armeniam, Absarro amne in

[1] *Rackham* : perquisita.

---

[a] *I.e.* when it runs the farthest to the west.
[b] A translation of ' Mesopotamia '.

in the interior. I do not deny that my description of it will differ in many points from that of the old writers, as I have devoted much care and attention to ascertaining thoroughly the recent events in that region from Domitius Corbulo and the kings sent from there as suppliants or king's children sent as hostages. We will however begin with the Cappadocian tribe. This extends farthest into the interior of all the peoples of Pontus, passing on its left-hand side Lesser and Greater Armenia and Commagene and on its right all the tribes of Asia mentioned above; it spreads over a very large number of peoples, and rises rapidly in elevation towards the east in the direction of the Taurus range, passing Lycaonia, Pisidia and Cilicia, and then advances above the district of Antiochia, the part of it called Cataonia reaching as far as the department of Antiochia named Cyrrestica. Consequently the length of Asia at this point is 1250 miles and its breadth 640 miles.

IX. Greater Armenia begins at the Parihedri *Greater* Mountains, and is separated from Cappadocia, as we *Armenia.* have said, by the river Euphrates and, when the v. 83. Euphrates turns aside,[a] from Mesopotamia by the equally famous river Tigris. Both rivers rise in Armenia, and it forms the beginning of Mesopotamia, the tract of country lying between these two rivers;[b] the intervening space is occupied by the Orroean Arabs. It thus extends its frontier as far as Adiabene, where it is enclosed by ranges of mountains that stretch across it; here it spreads its width on the left, crossing the Aras, to the river Kur, while its length reaches right to Lesser Armenia, from which it is separated by the river Absarrus, which flows

Pontum defluente et Parihedris montibus qui
fundunt Absarrum discreta ab illa.

26 X. Cyrus oritur in Heniochis montibus quos alii
Coraxicos vocavere, Araxes eodem monte quo
Euphrates $\overline{\text{vi}}$ p. intervallo, auctusque amne Usi et
ipse, ut plures existimavere, a Cyro defertur in
Caspium mare.

Oppida celebrantur in Minore Caesarea, Aza,
Nicopolis, in Maiore Arsamosata Euphrati proximum,
Tigri Carcathiocerta, in excelso autem Tigranocerta,
27 at in campis iuxta Araxen Artaxata. universae
magnitudinem Aufidius quinquagiens centena milia
prodidit, Claudius Caesar longitudinem a Dascusa ad
confinium Caspii maris $\lceil$xiii$\rceil$ p., latitudinem dimidium eius a Tigranocerta ad Hiberiam. dividitur,
quod certum est, in praefecturas, quas strategias
vocant, quasdam ex his vel singula regna quondam,
barbaris nominibus cxx. claudunt eam montes ab
oriente, sed non statim, Cerauni, nec Adiabene regio.
28 quod interest spatii Cepheni tenent; ab his iuga ultra
Adiabeni tenent, per convalles autem proximi
Armeniae sunt Menobardi et Moscheni. Adiabenen
Tigris et montes invii cingunt. ab laeva eius regio
Medorum est ad prospectum Caspii maris; ex

ª The Aras formed a separate mouth of its own in 1897.

into the Black Sea, and by the Parihedri Mountains in which the Absarrus rises.

X. The source of the Kur is in the Heniochi Mountains, which are called by some persons the Coraxici; while the Aras rises in the same mountains as the Euphrates, at a distance of six miles from it, and after being augmented by the river Usis, itself also, in the opinion of the majority of writers, joins the Kur and is carried by it down into the Caspian Sea.[a] *The river Kur.*

The notable towns in Lesser Armenia are Caesarea, Ezaz and Nicopolis; those in Greater Armenia are Arsamosata, which is near the Euphrates, Kharput on the Tigris and Sert on the high ground, with Artaxata in the plains adjoining the Araxes. Aufidius gives the circumference of the whole of Armenia as 5000 miles, while Claudius Caesar makes its length from Dascusa to the edge of the Caspian Sea 1300 miles and its breadth from Sert to Hiberia half that amount. It is a well-known fact that it is divided into 120 administrative districts with native names, called in Greek military commands, some of which were formerly actual separate kingdoms. It is shut in on the east, but not immediately, by the Ceraunian Mountains and similarly by the Adiabene district. The intervening space is occupied by the Cepheni, and next to them the mountain district beyond is occupied by the Adiabeni, while along the valleys the peoples adjoining Armenia are the Menobardi and Moscheni. Adiabene is encircled by the Tigris and by impassable mountains. The district on the left of Adiabene belongs to the Medes, as far as the point where the Caspian Sea comes into view; this sea derives its water from the Ocean, as we shall say in *Lesser Armenia.*

357

oceano hoc, ut suo loco dicemus, infunditur, totumque
Caucasis montibus cingitur.

Incolae per confinium Armeniae nunc dicentur.

29 XI. Planitiem omnem a Cyro usque Albanorum
gens tenet, mox Hiberum discreta ab his amne
Alazone[1] in Cyrum Caucasis montibus defluente.
praevalent oppida Albaniae Cabalaca, Hiberiae
Hermastus iuxta flumen et[2] Neoris. regiones[3] Thasie
et Thriare usque ad Parihedros montes; ultra sunt
Colchicae solitudines, quarum a latere ad Ceraunios
verso Armenochalybes habitant et Moschorum
tractus ad Hiberum amnem in Cyrum defluentem et
infra eos Sacasani et deinde Macerones ad flumen
Absarrum. sic plana aut devexa optinentur; rursus
ab Albaniae confinio tota montium fronte gentes
Silvorum ferae et infra Lupeniorum, mox Diduri et
Sodi.

30 XII. Ab iis sunt Portae Caucasiae magno errore
multis Caspiae dictae, ingens naturae opus montibus
interruptis repente, ubi fores additae[4] ferratis
trabibus, subter medias amne diri odoris fluente
citraque in rupe castello quod vocatur Cumania com-
munito ad arcendas transitu gentes innumeras, ibi
loci terrarum orbe portis discluso, ex adverso maxime
Hermasti oppidi Hiberum. a portis Caucasis per

---

[1] *Hermolaus e Strab.* : Ocazane.   [2] *et add. Rackham.*
         [3] *Rackham* : regio.   [4] *V.l.* obditae.

---

[a] Probably the pass of Dariel, nearly in the centre of the
Caucasus range; also called Sarmaticae Pylae. Another
important pass is between the chief north-eastern spur of the
range and the Caspian Sea, near Derbend; it was called
Albaniae or Caspiae Pylae.

the proper place, and is entirely surrounded by the §36. Caucasus Mountains.

We shall now mention the peoples dwelling along the border of Armenia.

XI. All the plain from the Kur onward is oc- *The Armenian coasts.* cupied by the race of the Albani and then that of the Hiberes, separated from the Albani by the river Alazon, which flows down from Mount Caucasus into the Cyrus. Important towns are Kablas-Var in Albania and Hermastus on the river and Neoris in Hiberia. The districts of Thasie and Thriare reach to the Parihedri Mountains, and beyond them is the Colchian desert, on the side of which towards the Ceraunii dwell the Armenochalybes, and the country of the Moschi reaching to the river Hiberus, a tributary of the Kur, and below them the Sacasani and then the Macerones reaching to the river Absarrus. This gives the population of the plains or mountain slopes; then after the frontier of Albania the whole face of the mountains is occupied by the wild tribes of the Silvi and below them those of the Lupenii, and afterwards the Diduri and Sodi.

XII. On leaving these one comes to the Gates of the *A Caucasian pass.* Caucasus,[a] which many very erroneously call the Caspian Gates, an enormous work of Nature, who has here suddenly rent the mountains asunder. Here gates have been placed, with iron-covered beams, under the centre of which flows a river emitting a horrible odour; and on this side of it on a rock stands the fortress called Cumania, erected for the purpose of barring the passage of the innumerable tribes. At this spot therefore the world is divided by gates into two portions; it is just opposite the Hiberian town of Hermastus. Beyond the Gates of

montes Gurdinios Valli, Suani, indomitae gentes, auri
tamen metalla fodiunt. ab his ad Pontum usque
Heniochorum plurima genera, mox Achaeorum.
ita se habet terrarum situs [1] e clarissimis.

31 Aliqui inter Pontum et Caspium mare $\overline{\text{CCCLXXV}}$ p.
non amplius interesse tradiderunt, Cornelius Nepos
$\overline{\text{CCL}}$: tantis iterum angustiis infestatur Asia. Claudius
Caesar a Cimmerio Bosporo ad Caspium mare $\overline{\text{CL}}$ prodidit, eaque perfodere cogitasse Nicatorem Seleucum
quo tempore sit ab Ptolomaeo Cerauno interfectus.
a portis Caucasiis ad Pontum $\overline{\text{CC}}$ esse constat fere.

32 XIII. Insulae in Ponto Planctae sive Cyaneae sive
Symplegades, deinde Apollonia, Thynias dicta ut
distingueretur ab ea quae est in Europa—distat
continente p. M, cingitur $\overline{\text{III}}$—et contra Pharnaceam
Chalceritis, quam Graeci Ariam dixerunt Martique
sacram, et in ea volucres cum advenis pugnasse
pinnarum ictu.

33 XIV. Nunc omnibus quae sunt Asiae interiora
dictis Ripaeos montes transcendat animus dextraque
litore oceani incedat. tribus hic partibus caeli
adluens Asiam Scythicus a septentrione, ab oriente

---

[1] *Rackham* (cf. § 23): sinus.

---

[a] Cf. § 7.
[b] In reality the shortest distance across is nearly 600 miles.
[c] The Urek-Jaki.
[d] At the mouth of the Danube, IV. 45, 92.
[e] See § 11.

the Caucasus among the Gurdinian Mountains are the Valli and the Suani, races never yet quelled, who nevertheless work gold-mines. After these, right on to the Black Sea, are a large number of tribes of Charioteers and then of Achaei. Such is the present state of one of the most famous regions in the world.

Some authorities have reported the distance between the Black Sea and the Caspian as not more than 375 miles, while Cornelius Nepos makes it 250 miles: by such narrow straits is Asia for a second time [a] beset. Claudius Caesar gives the distance from the Straits of Kertsch to the Caspian Sea as 150 miles,[b] and states that Seleucus Nicator at the time when he was killed by Ptolemy Ceraunus was contemplating cutting a channel through this isthmus. It is practically certain that the distance from the Gates of the Caucasus to the Black Sea is 200 miles.

XIII. The islands in the Black Sea are the Planctae,[c] otherwise named the Cyaneae or Symplegades, and then Apollonia, called Thynias to distinguish it from the island [d] of the same name in Europe— it is a mile away from the mainland and three miles in circumference—and opposite to Pharnacea [e] Chalceritis, called by the Greeks the Isle of Ares and sacred to the god of war; they say that on it there were birds which used to attack strangers with blows of their wings. *Black Sea Islands.*

XIV. Having now completed our description of the interior of Asia let us in imagination cross the Ripaean Mountains and proceed to the right along the shores of the Ocean. This washes the coast of Asia towards three points of the compass, under the name of Scythian Ocean on the north, Eastern Ocean on the east *Races north of Black Sea.*

Eous, a meridie Indicus vocatur; varieque per sinus et accolas in conplura nomina dividitur. verum Asiae quoque magna portio apposita septentrioni
34 iniuria sideris rigens vastas solitudines habet. ab extremo aquilone ad initium orientis aestivi Scythae sunt; extra eos ultraque aquilonis initia Hyperboreos aliqui posuere, pluribus in Europa dictos. primum inde noscitur promunturium Celticae Lytharmis, fluvius Carambucis, ubi lassata cum siderum vi Ripaeorum montium deficiunt iuga, ibique Arimphaeos quosdam accepimus, haut dissimilem Hyper-
35 boreis gentem. sedes illis nemora, alimenta bacae, capillus iuxta feminis virisque in probro existimatur, ritus clementes. itaque sacros haberi narrant inviolatosque esse etiam feris accolarum populis, nec ipsos modo sed illos quoque qui ad eos profugerint. ultra eos plane iam Scythae, Cimmerii, Cissi, Anthi, Georgi et Amazonum gens, haec usque ad Caspium et Hyrcanium mare.
36 XV. Nam et inrumpit e Scythico oceano in aversa Asiae, pluribus nominibus accolarum appellatum, celeberrimum[1] duobus Caspium et Hyrcanium. non minus hoc esse quam Pontum Euxinum Clitarchus putat, Eratosthenes ponit et mensuram ab exortu

---

[1] *Rackham*: celeberrimis *aut* Celtiberium et.

---

[a] *I.e.* North-east.

and Indian Ocean on the south; and it is subdivided
into a variety of designations according to the bays
that it forms and the people dwelling on its coasts. A
great portion of Asia however also, adjoining the north,
owing to the severity of its frosty climate contains
vast deserts. From the extreme north-north-east to
the northernmost point at which the sun rises in
summer [a] there are the Scythians, and outside of them
and beyond the point where north-north-east begins
some have placed the Hyperboreans, who are said
by a majority of authorities to be in Europe. After
that point the first place known is Lytharmis, a
promontory of Celtica, and the river Carambucis,
where the range of the Ripaean Mountains terminates and with it the rigour of the climate relaxes;
here we have reports of a people called the Arimphaei, a race not unlike the Hyperboreans. They
dwell in forests and live on berries; long hair is
deemed to be disgraceful in the case of women and
men alike; and their manners are mild. Consequently they are reported to be deemed a sacred race
and to be left unmolested even by the savage tribes
among their neighbours, this immunity not being con-
fined to themselves but extended also to people who
have fled to them for refuge. Beyond them we come
directly to the Scythians, Cimmerians, Cissi, Anthi,
Georgi, and a race of Amazons, the last reaching to
the Caspian and Hyrcanian Sea.

XV. For the sea actually forces a passage from *The Caspian*
the Scythian Ocean to the back of Asia, where the *Sea and the*
inhabitants call it by a variety of names, but it is best *Ocean.*
known by two of them, as the Caspian Sea and the
Hyrcanian. Clitarchus is of opinion that the Caspian
is as large as the Black Sea; Eratosthenes also gives

et meridie per Cadusiae et Albaniae oram v̄cccc
stadia, inde per Atiacos, Amarbos, Hyrcanos ad
ostium Zoni fluminis ꟾꟾꟾꟾdccc, ab eo ad ostium
Iaxartis mmcccc, quae summa efficit |xv| lxxv p.

37 Artemidorus hinc detrahit xxv p. Agrippa Caspium
mare gentesque quae circa sunt et cum iis Armeniam,
determinatas ab oriente oceano Serico, ab occidente
Caucasi iugis, a meridie Tauri, a septentrione oceano
Scythico, patere qua cognitum est ccccLxxx in longitudinem, in latitudinem ccxc prodidit. non desunt
vero qui eius maris universum circuitum a freto
|xxv| tradunt.

38 Inrumpit autem artis faucibus et in longitudinem
spatiosis, atque ubi coepit in latitudinem pandi
lunatis obliquatur cornibus, velut ad Maeotium lacum
ab ore descendens, sicilis, ut auctor est M. Varro,
similitudine. primus sinus appellatur Scythicus.
utrimque enim accolunt Scythae et per angustias
inter se commeant hinc Nomades et Sauromatae
multis nominibus, illinc Abzoae non paucioribus. ab
introitu dextra mucronem ipsum faucium tenent
Udini Scytharum populus; dein per oram Albani, ut
ferunt, ab Iasone orti, unde[1] quod mare ibi est[2]

39 Albanum nominatur. haec gens superfusa montibus
Caucasis ad Cyrum amnem, Armeniae confinium

---

[1] *Mayhoff*: ante.   [2] ibi est *Mayhoff*: est *aut* abest.

[a] This really discharges into the Aral Sea, not into the
Caspian.
[b] *I.e.* the imaginary passage by which it was supposed to
communicate with the Scythian Ocean.

its dimensions on the south-east side along the coast
of Cadusia and Albania as 725 miles, from there
through the territories of the Atiaci, Amarbi and
Hyrcani to the mouth of the river Zonus 600 miles,
and from there to the mouth of the Syr Daria *a*
300 miles, making a total of 1575 miles. Artemidorus subtracts 25 miles from this total. Agrippa
states that the Caspian Sea and the races surrounding
it, including Armenia, bounded on the east by the
Chinese Ocean, on the west by the ranges of the
Caucasus, on the south by those of the Taurus and on
the north by the Scythian Ocean, so far as is known
extend 480 miles in length and 290 miles in breadth.
But there are some authors who give the entire circuit of the sea in question from the straits *b* as 2500
miles.

Its waters make their way into this sea by a narrow
mouth of considerable length; and where it begins
to widen out it curves obliquely with crescent-
shaped horns, as though descending from the mouth
to the Sea of Azov, in the likeness of a sickle, as
Marcus Varro states. The first part of it is called
the Scythian Gulf, because the inhabitants on both
sides are Scythians, who hold communication across
the narrows, on one side being the Nomads and the
Sauromatae, who have a variety of names, and on
the other the Abzoae, with just as many. Starting
at the entrance, on the right-hand side the actual
point of the mouth is occupied by the Scythian tribe
of the Udini; then along the coast are the Albani,
said to be descended from Jason, after whom the sea
at that point is called the Alban Sea. This race
overflows the Caucasus Mountains and, as previously § 29.
stated, comes down as far as the river Kur, which

365

atque Hiberiae, descendit, ut dictum est. supra
maritima eius Udinorumque gentem Sarmatae,
Utidorsi, Aroteres praetenduntur, quorum a tergo
indicatae iam Amazones et Sauromatides. flumina
per Albaniam decurrunt in mare Casus et Albanus,
dein Cambyses in Caucasis ortus montibus, mox
Cyrus in Coraxicis, ut diximus. oram omnem a Caso
praealtis rupibus accessum negare[1] per $\overline{\text{ccccxxv}}$ p.
auctor est Agrippa. a Cyro Caspium mare vocari
incipit; accolunt Caspi.

40 Corrigendus est in hoc loco error multorum, etiam
qui in Armenia res proxime cum Corbulone gessere.
namque hi Caspias appellavere portas Hiberiae quas
Caucasias diximus vocari, situsque depicti et inde
missi hoc nomen inscriptum habent. et Neronis
principis comminatio ad Caspias portas tendere
dicebatur, cum peteret illas quae per Hiberiam in
Sarmatas tendunt, vix ullo propter oppositos montes
aditu ad Caspium mare. sunt autem aliae Caspiis
gentibus iunctae, quod dinosci non potest nisi comitatu rerum Alexandri Magni.

41 XVI. Namque Persarum regna, quae nunc Parthorum intellegimus, inter duo maria Persicum et

[1] *Mayhoff* (accessu carere *coll.* XII. 33 *Jan*): *corrupta.*

forms the boundary between Armenia and Hiberia.
Above the coastward parts of Albania and the Udini
tribe stretch the Sarmatae, Utidorsi and Aroteres, in
the rear of whom we have already indicated the § 35.
Amazons and Sauromatides. The rivers running
down to the sea through Albania are the Casus and
the Albanus, then the Cambyses, which rises in the
Caucasus Mountains, and then the Kur, rising in the
Coraxaci, as we have said. The whole of the coast § 26.
from the Casus is stated by Agrippa to be formed of
very lofty cliffs which prohibit landing for 425 miles.
The sea begins to have the name of Caspian from
the mouth of the Kur, the coast being inhabited by
the Caspii.

In this place we must correct a mistake made by *Northern*
many people, even those who recently served with *passes.*
Corbulo in the war in Armenia. These have given
the name of Caspian Gates to the pass in Hiberia,
which, as we have stated, is called the Gates of the § 30.
Caucasus, and maps of the region sent home from
the front have this name written on them. Also the
expedition threatened by the Emperor Nero was
spoken of as intended to penetrate to the Caspian
Gates, whereas it was really aimed at the pass that
gives a road through Hiberia to Sarmatia, the
mountain barrier affording scarcely any access to the
Caspian Sea. There are however other Caspian
Gates adjoining the Caspian tribes; the distinction
between the two passes can only be established by
means of the report of those who accompanied the
expedition of Alexander the Great.

XVI. The kingdom of the Persians, which we *Countries*
now know as Parthia, lies between the two seas, the *bordering*
on Greater
Persian and the Caspian, on the heights of the *Armenia.*

367

Hyrcanium Caucasi iugis attolluntur. utrimque per
devexa laterum Armeniae Maiori a frontis parte
quae vergit in Commagenen Cephenia, ut diximus,
copulatur, eique Adiabene Assyriorum initium, cuius
pars est Arbilitis, ubi Darium Alexander debellavit,
42 proxima[1] Syriae. totam eam Macedones Mygdo-
niam cognominaverunt a similitudine. oppida Alexandria, item Antiochia quam Nesebin vocant; abest
ab Artaxatis $\overline{\text{DCCL}}$ p. fuit et Ninos inposita Tigri
ad solis occasum spectans, quondam clarissima.
reliqua vero fronte, qua tendit ad Caspium mare,
Atrapatene ab Armeniae Otene regione discreta
Araxe; oppidum eius Gazae, ab Artaxatis $\overline{\text{CCCCL}}$ p.,
totidem ab Ecbatanis Medorum, quorum pars sunt
Atrapateni.

43 XVII. Ecbatana caput Mediae Seleucus rex
condidit, a Seleucia Magna $\overline{\text{DCCL}}$ p. a Portis vero
Caspiis $\overline{\text{XX}}$; reliqua Medorum oppida Phazaca,
Aganzaga[2], Apamea Rhagiane cognominata. causa
Portarum nominis eadem quae supra, interruptis
angusto transitu iugis ita ut vix singula meent
plaustra, longitudine $\overline{\text{VIII}}$ p. toto opere manu facto.
dextra laevaque ambustis similes inpendent scopuli,
sitiente tractu per $\overline{\text{XXVIII}}$ p.; angustias impedit
corrivatus salis e cautibus liquor atque eadem

---

[1] *V.l.* proxime.
[2] Phazaca, Aganzaga *Hardouin coll. Ptol.* VI. 2: Phizgan-
zaga.

Caucasus range. Greater Armenia, which occupies
the front of the mountain sloping towards Commagene, is adjoined, as we have said, by Cephenia, §28.
which lies on the descent on both sides of it, and this
by Adiabene, where the land of the Assyrians begins;
the part of Adiabene nearest to Syria is Arbilitis,
where Alexander conquered Darius. The Macedonians have given to the whole of Adiabene the
name of Mygdonia, from its likeness to Mygdonia in
Macedon. Its towns are Alexandria and Antiochia,
the native name for which is Nesebis; it is 750 miles
from Artaxata. There was also once the town of
Nineveh, which was on the Tigris facing west, and was
formerly very famous. Adjoining the other front of
Greater Armenia, which stretches to the Caspian
Sea, is Atrapatene, separated from the district of
Otene in Armenia by the Aras; its chief town is
Gazae, 450 miles from Artaxata and the same
distance from Hamadan, the city of the Medes, to
which race the Atrapateni belong.

XVII. Hamadan, the capital of Media, which was *Media.*
founded by King Seleucus, is 750 miles from Great
Seleucia and 20 miles from the Caspian Gates. The
other towns of Media are Phazaca, Aganzaga and
Apamea, called Rhei. The reason for the name
'Gates' is the same as that stated above: the §30.
range is here pierced by a narrow pass 8 miles long,
scarcely broad enough for a single line of waggon
traffic, the whole of it a work of engineering. It is
overhung on either side by crags that look as if they
had been exposed to the action of fire, the country
over a range of 28 miles being entirely waterless;
the narrow passage is impeded by a stream of salt
water that collects from the rocks and finds an exit

emissus. praeterea serpentium multitudo nisi hieme transitum non sinit.

44 Adiabenis conectuntur Carduchi quondam dicti, nunc Cordueni, praefluente Tigri, his Pratitae παρ' ὁδὸν appellati, qui tenent Caspias Portas. his ab latere altero occurrunt deserta Parthiae et Citheni iuga; mox eiusdem Parthiae amoenissimus situs qui vocatur Choara. duae urbes ibi Parthorum oppositae quondam Medis, Calliope et alia¹ in rupe Issatis; ipsum vero Parthiae caput Hecatompylos abest a Portis c̄xxxiii p.—ita Parthorum quoque 45 regna foribus discluduntur. egressos Portis excipit protinus gens Caspia ad litora usque, quae nomen portis et mari dedit; laeva montuosa. ab ea gente retrorsus ad Cyrum amnem produntur c̄cxxv p., ab eodem amne si subeatur ad Portas D̄CC; hunc enim cardinem Alexandri Magni itinerum fecere ab his Portis ad Indiae principium stadia x̄vDCLxxxx prodendo, inde² ad Bactra oppidum, quod appellant Zariasta, MMMDCC, inde ad Iaxartem amnem v̄.

46 XVIII. A Caspiis ad orientem versus regio est Apavortene dicta, et in ea fertilitatis inclutae locus Dareium. mox gentes Tapyri, Anariaci, Staures, Hyrcani, a quorum litoribus idem mare Hyrcanium vocari incipit a flumine Sideri; citra id amnes Mazi-

---

¹ alta? *Rackham.*   ² inde *add. Rackham.*

ᵃ Or 'which has the name of Zariasta': see § 48 note.

by the same way. Moreover the number of snakes renders the route impracticable except in winter.

Joining on to the Adiabeni are the people formerly called the Carduchi and now the Cordueni, past whom flows the river Tigris, and adjoining these are the 'Roadside' Pratitae, as they are called, who hold the Caspian Gates. Running up to these on the other side are the Parthian deserts and the Citheni range; and then comes the very agreeable locality, also belonging to Parthia, called Choara. Here are the two Parthian towns formerly serving for protection against the Medes, Calliope and, on another rock, Issatis; but the actual capital of Parthia, Hecatompylos, is 133 miles from the Gates—so effectively is the Parthian kingdom also shut off by passes. Going out of the Gates one comes at once to the Caspian nation, which extends down to the coast: it is from this people that the pass and the sea obtain their name. On the left there is a mountainous district. Turning back from this people to the river Kur the distance is said to be 225 miles, and going up from the river Kur to the Gates 700 miles; for in the Itineraries of Alexander the Great this pass is made the turning-point of his expeditions, the distance from these Gates to the frontier of India being given as 1961 miles, from the frontier to the town of Balkh, which is the name given to Zariasta,[a] 462 miles, and from Zariasta to the river Syr Darya 620 miles.

XVIII. Lying to the east of the Caspians is the region called Apavortene, in which is Dareium, a place noted for its fertility. Then there are the tribes of the Tapyri, Anariaci, Staures and Hyrcani, from whose shores the Caspian beyond the river Sideris begins to be called the Hyrcanian Sea;

ris, Straor, omnia ex Caucaso. sequitur regio
Margiane apricitatis inclutae, sola in eo tractu viti-
fera, undique inclusa montibus amoenis ambitu
stadiorum MD, difficilis aditu propter harenosas
solitudines per c̄x̄x̄ p., et ipsa contra Parthiae tractum
47 sita. in qua Alexander Alexandriam condiderat;
qua diruta a barbaris Antiochus Seleuci filius eodem
loco restituit Syrianam interfluente Margo qui corri-
vatur in Zotha lacu¹; maluerat illam Antiochiam
appellari. urbis amplitudo circumitur stadiis LXX.
in hanc Orodes Romanos Crassana clade captos
deduxit. ab huius excelsis per iuga Caucasi protenditur ad Bactros usque gens Mardorum fera, sui
iuris. sub eo tractu gentes Orciani, Commori,
Berdrigae, Harmatotropi, Citomarae, Comani, Mur-
48 rasiarae, Mandruani; flumina Mandrum, Chindrum,
ultraque Chorasmi, Gandari, Paricani, Zarangae,
Arasmi, Marotiani, Arsi, Gaeli quos Graeci Cadusios
appellavere, Matiani; oppidum Heraclea ab Alexandro conditum, quod deinde subversum ac restitu-
tum Antiochus Achaida appellavit; Drebices quorum
medios finis secat Oxus amnis ortus in lacu Oaxo;
Syrmatae, Oxyttagae, Moci, Bateni, Saraparae;
Bactri quorum oppidum Zariasta, quod postea

¹ *V.l.* Zothale; is.

ᵃ Now Merv.   ᵇ See V. 86.

while on this side of the Sideris are the rivers Maziris
and Straor, all three streams rising in the Caucasus.
Next comes the Margiane country, famous for its
sunny climate—it is the only district in that region
where the vine is grown; it is shut in all round by a
beautiful ring of mountains, 187 miles in circuit, and
is difficult of access on account of sandy deserts
stretching for a distance of 120 miles; and it is
itself situated opposite to the region of Parthia.
In Margiane Alexander had founded a city [a] bearing
his name, which was destroyed by the barbarians, but Antiochus son of Seleucus re-estab-
lished a Syrian city on the same site, intersected
by the river Murghab, which is canalized into
Lake Zotha; he had preferred that the city should
be named after himself. Its circuit measures $8\frac{3}{4}$
miles. This is the place to which the Roman
prisoners taken in the disaster [b] of Crassus were
brought by Orodes. From the heights of Merv
across the ridges of the Caucasus right on to the
Bactrians extend the fierce tribe of the Mardi, an
independent state. Below this region are the
tribes of the Orciani, Commori, Berdrigae, Harmatotropi, Citomarae, Comani, Murrasiarae and Mandruani; the rivers Mandrum and Chindrum, and
beyond them the Chorasmi, Gandari, Paricani,
Zarangae, Arasmi, Marotiani, Arsi, Gaeli (called
by the Greeks the Cadusii), and Matiani; the town
of Heraclea, founded by Alexander and subsequently
overthrown, but restored by Antiochus, who gave it
the name of Achais; the Drebices, whose territory is
intersected by the river Amu Darya rising in Lake
Oaxus; the Syrmatae, Oxyttagae, Moci, Bateni,
Saraparae; and the Bactri, whose town was called

Bactra,[1] a flumine appellatum est. gens haec
optinet aversa montis Paropanisi exadversus fontes
49 Indi; includitur flumine Ocho. ultra Sogdiani, oppidum Panda et in ultimis eorum finibus Alexandria ab
Alexandro Magno conditum. arae ibi sunt ab
Hercule ac Libero Patre constitutae, item Cyro et
Samiramide atque Alexandro: finis omnium eorum
ductus ab illa parte terrarum, includente flumine
Iaxarte, quod Scythae Silim vocant, Alexander
militesque eius Tanain putavere esse. transcendit
eum amnem Demodamas, Seleuci et Antiochi regum
dux, quem maxime sequimur in his, arasque Apollini
Didymaeo statuit.

50   XIX. Ultra sunt Scytharum populi. Persae illos
Sacas in universum [2] appellavere a proxima gente,
antiqui Aramios. Scythae ipsi Persas Chorsaros et
Caucasum montem Croucasim, hoc est nive candidum.
multitudo populorum innumera et quae cum Parthis
ex aequo degat; celeberrimi eorum Sacae, Massagetae, Dahae, Essedones, Astacae, Rumnici, Pestici,
Homodoti, Histi, Edones, Camae, Camacae, Euchatae,
Cotieri, Authusiani, Psacae, Arimaspi, Antacati,
Chroasai, Oetaei; ibi Napaei interisse dicuntur a
51 Palaeis. nobilia apud eos flumina Mandragaeum et

---

[1] *Rackham, cf.* § 45: Zariastes . . . Bactrum.
[2] *Gelen.*: inversos, inversum, universos.

---

[a] Or 'whose town is Zariasta, which was afterwards called
Bactra, from the river.' Authorities differ as to which was
the name of the river. Cf. § 45.

Zariasta from the river, but its name was afterwards changed to Balkh.[a] This race occupies the opposite side of the Hindu Kush over against the sources of the Indus, and is enclosed by the river Ochus. Beyond are the Sogdiani and the town of Panda, and on the farthest confines of their territory Alexandria, founded by Alexander the Great. At this place there are altars set up by Hercules and Father Liber, and also by Cyrus and Samiramis and by Alexander, all of whom found their limit in this region of the world, where they were shut in by the river Syr Darya, which the Scythians call the Silis and which Alexander and his soldiers supposed to be the Don. But this river was crossed by Demodamas, the general of King Seleucus and King Antiochus, whom we are chiefly following in this part of our narrative; and he set up altars to Apollo Didymaeus.

XIX. Beyond are some tribes of Scythians. To these the Persians have given the general name of Sacae, from the tribe nearest to Persia, but old writers call them the Aramii, and the Scythians themselves give the name of Chorsari to the Persians and call Mount Caucasus Croucasis, which means 'white with snow.' There is an uncountable number of tribes, numerous enough to live on equal terms with the Parthians; most notable among them are the Sacae, Massagetae, Dahae, Essedones, Astacae, Rumnici, Pestici, Homodoti, Histi, Edones, Camae, Camacae, Euchatae, Cotieri, Authusiani, Psacae, Arimaspi, Antacati, Chroasai and Oetaei; among them the Napaei are said to have been destroyed by the Palaei. Notable rivers in their country are the Mandragaeus and the Caspasus.

Scythian tribes.

375

Caspasum. nec in alia parte maior auctorum inconstantia, credo propter innumeras vagasque gentes.
haustum ipsius maris dulcem esse et Alexander
Magnus prodidit et M. Varro talem perlatum
Pompeio iuxta res gerenti Mithridatico bello, magnitudine haut dubie influentium amnium victo sale.
52 adicit idem Pompei ductu exploratum, in Bactros
septem diebus ex India perveniri ad Bactrum flumen
quod in Oxum influat, et ex eo per Caspium in Cyrum
subvectas [1] et v non amplius dierum terreno itinere
ad Phasim in Pontum Indicas posse devehi merces.

Insulae toto in eo mari multae, volgata una maxime
Zazata.

53 XX. A Caspio mari Scythicoque oceano in Eoum
cursus inflectitur ad orientem conversa litorum fronte.
inhabitabilis eius prima pars a Scythico promunturio
ob nives, proxima inculta saevitia gentium. Anthropophagi Scythae insident humanis corporibus vescentes; ideo iuxta vastae solitudines ferarumque
multitudo haut dissimilem hominum inmanitatem
obsidens. iterum deinde Scythae iterumque deserta
cum beluis, usque ad iugum incubans mari quod

[1] *Gelen.* : subvectos.

---

[a] The second was against Mithridates, 74-65 B.C.

And in regard to no other region is there more discrepancy among the authorities, this being due as I believe to the countless numbers and the nomadic habits of the tribes. The water of the Caspian Sea itself was said by Alexander the Great to be sweet to drink, and also Marcus Varro states that good drinking water was conveyed from it for Pompey when he was operating in the neighbourhood of the river during the Mithridatic War;[a] doubtless the size of the rivers flowing into it overcomes the salt. Varro further adds that exploration under the leadership of Pompey ascertained that a seven days' journey from India into the Bactrian country reaches the river Bactrus, a tributary of the Amu Darya, and that Indian merchandize can be conveyed from the Bactrus across the Caspian to the Kur and thence with not more than five days' portage by land can reach Phasis in Pontus.

There are many islands in all parts of the Caspian Sea, but only one of them, Zazata, is particularly notable.

XX. After leaving the Caspian Sea and the *The Farther* Scythian Ocean our course takes a bend towards *East.* the Eastern Sea as the coast turns to face eastward. The first part of the coast after the Scythian promontory is uninhabitable on account of snow, and the neighbouring region is uncultivated because of the savagery of the tribes that inhabit it. This is the country of the Cannibal Scythians who eat human bodies; consequently the adjacent districts are waste deserts thronging with wild beasts lying in wait for human beings as savage as themselves. Then we come to more Scythians and to more deserts inhabited by wild beasts, until we reach

vocant Tabim; nec ante dimidiam ferme longitudinem eius orae quae spectat aestivom orientem
54 inhabitatur illa regio. primi sunt hominum qui
vocantur[1] Seres, lanicio silvarum nobiles, perfusam
aqua depectentes frondium canitiem, unde geminus
feminis nostris labos redordiendi fila rursusque texendi: tam multiplici opere, tam longinquo orbe petitur ut in publico matrona traluceat. Seres mites
quidem, sed et ipsi feris similes coetum reliquorum
55 mortalium fugiunt, commercia exspectant. primum
eorum noscitur flumen Psitharas, proximum Cambari,
tertium Lanos, a quo promunturium Chryse, sinus
Cirnaba, flumen Atianos, sinus et gens hominum Attacorarum,[2] apricis ab omni noxio adflatu seclusa
collibus, eadem qua Hyperborei degunt temperie;
de iis privatim condidit volumen Amometus, sicut
Hecataeus de Hyperboreis. ab Attacoris gentis
Thuni et Focari, et, iam Indorum, Casiri introrsus ad
Scythas versi—humanis corporibus vescuntur; Nomades quoque Indiae vagantur huc. aliqui[3] ab
aquilone contingi ab ipsis et Ciconas dixere et
Brisaros.
56　XXI. Sed unde plane constent gentes, Hemodi

---

[1] *V.l.* noscantur.
[2] Attacorarum? *Brotier*: Attacorum.
[3] huc. aliqui? *Mayhoff*: huic cui (sunt qui *edd.*).

---

[a] The substance referred to, though confused with silk, is
probably cotton made into calico or muslin. For silk see
XI. 76.

a mountain range called Tabis which forms a cliff over the sea; and not until we have covered nearly half of the length of the coast that faces north-east is that region inhabited. The first human occupants *China.* are the people called the Chinese, who are famous for the woollen substance [a] obtained from their forests; after a soaking in water they comb off the white down of the leaves, and so supply our women with the double task of unravelling the threads and weaving them together again; so manifold is the labour employed, and so distant is the region of the globe drawn upon, to enable the Roman matron to flaunt transparent raiment in public. The Chinese, though mild in character, yet resemble wild animals, in that they also shun the company of the remainder of mankind, and wait for trade to come to them. The first river found in their territory is the Psitharas, next the Cambari, and third the Lanos, after which come the Malay Peninsula, the Bay of Cirnaba, the river Atianos and the tribe of the Attacorae on the bay of the same name, sheltered by sunbathed hills from every harmful blast, with the same temperate climate as that in which dwell the Hyperborei. The Attacorae are the subject of a monograph by Amometus, while the Hyperborei have been dealt with in a volume by Hecataeus. After the Attacorae there are the Thuni and Focari tribes, and (coming now to natives of India) the Casiri, situated in the interior in the direction of the Scythians—the Casiri are cannibals; also the Nomad tribes of India reach this point in their wanderings. Some writers state that these tribes are actually in contact with the Cicones and IV. 43. also the Brisari on the north.

XXI. We now come to a point after which there *India.*

montes adsurgunt, Indorumque gens incipit, non
Eoo tantum mari adiacens verum et meridiano quod
Indicum appellavimus. quae pars orienti est adversa,
recto praetenditur spatio ad flexum et initio Indici
maris |XVIII| LXXV colligit, deinde quae se flexit[1] in
meridiem, |XXIV| LXXV, ut Eratosthenes tradit, usque
ad Indum amnem qui est ab occidente finis Indiae.
57 conplures autem totam eius longitudinem XL dierum
noctiumque velifico navium cursu determinavere, et
a septentrione ad meridiem |XXVIII| L. Agrippa longi-
tudinis |XXXIII|, latitudinis |XXIII| prodidit. Posi-
donius ab aestivo solis ortu ad hibernum exortum
metatus est eam, adversam Galliae statuens, quam
ab occidente aestivo ad occidentem hibernum meta-
batur, totam a favonio; itaque adverso[2] eius venti
adflatu iuvari Indiam salubremque fieri haut dubia
58 ratione docuit. alia illi caeli facies, alii siderum ortus,
binae aestates in anno, binae messes media inter
illas hieme etesiarum flatu, nostra vero bruma lenes
ibi aurae, mare navigabile. gentes ei urbesque
innumerae, si quis omnes persequi velit. etenim
patefacta est non modo Alexandri Magni armis
regumque qui successere ei, circumvectis etiam in
Hyrcanium mare et Caspium Seleuco et Antiocho
praefectoque classis eorum Patrocle, verum et aliis

---

[1] *Mayhoff*: deinde qua (*aut* se) flexit.
[2] *V.l.* adversum (-sam *Hardouin*).

is complete agreement as to the races—the range of
mountains called the Himalayas. Here begins the
Indian race, bordering not only on the Eastern Sea
but on the southern also, which we have designated
the Indian Ocean. The part facing east stretches §33.
in a straight line until it comes to a bend, and at the
point where the Indian Ocean begins its total length
is 1875 miles; while from that point onward the
southerly bend of the coast according to Eratosthenes
covers 2475 miles, finally reaching the river Indus,
which is the western boundary of India. A great
many authors however give the entire length of
the coast as being forty days' and nights' sail and
the measurement of the country from north to south
as 2850 miles. Agrippa says that it is 3300 miles
long and 2300 miles broad. Posidonius gives its
measurement from north-east to south-east, making
the whole of it face the west side of Gaul, of
which he gives the measurement from north-west
to south-west; and accordingly he shows by an
unquestionable line of argument that India has the
advantage of being exposed to the current of the
west wind, which makes it healthy. In that country the aspect of the heavens and the rising of the
stars are different, and there are two summers and
two harvests yearly, separated by a winter accompanied by etesian winds, while at our midwinter it
enjoys soft breezes and the sea is navigable. Its
races and cities are beyond counting, if one wished
to enumerate all of them. For it has been brought to
knowledge not only by the armed forces of Alexander
the Great and the kings who succeeded him, Seleucus
and Antiochus, and their admiral of the fleet Pat-
rocles having sailed round even into the Hyrcanian

auctoribus Graecis, qui cum regibus Indicis morati,
sicut Megasthenes et Dionysius a Philadelpho missus
59 ex ea causa, vires quoque gentium prodidere.   non
tamen est diligentiae locus, adeo diversa et incredibilia traduntur.   Alexandri Magni comites in eo
tractu Indiae quem is subegerit scripserunt v̄ oppidorum fuisse, nullum MM minus,[1] gentium IX,[2]
Indiamque tertiam partem esse terrarum omnium,
multitudinem populorum innumeram, probabili sane
ratione: Indi enim gentium prope soli numquam
migravere finibus suis.   colliguntur a Libero Patre
ad Alexandrum Magnum reges eorum CLIII annis
60 V̄I.CCCCLI—adiciunt et menses III.   amnium mira
vastitas: proditur Alexandrum nullo die minus
stadia DC navigasse Indo nec potuisse ante menses v
enavigare adiectis paucis diebus, et tamen minorem
Gange esse constat.   Seneca etiam apud nos temp-
tata Indiae commentatione LX amnes eius prodidit
gentes duodeviginti centumque.   par labos sit
montes enumerare; iunguntur inter se Imavus,
Hemodus, Paropanisus, Caucasus, a quibus tota
decurrit in planitiem inmensam et Aegypto similem.
61 Verum ut terrena demonstratio intellegatur,

---

[1] *Detlefsen*: cogiminus (Coo minus *Jan*).
[2] ĪX, *Detlefsen*; MM? *Mayhoff*.

---

[a] Or perhaps 'none with a population of less than 2000';
but the text is doubtful, as is that of the following numeral.
[b] Imavus and Hemodus constitute the Himalayas and
Paropanisus is the Hindu Kush.

and Caspian Sea, but also by other Greek authors
who have stayed as guests with the Indian kings,
for instance Megasthenes, and Dionysius sent by
Philadelphus for that purpose, and have also reported
as to the strength of these nations. Nevertheless
there is no possibility of being exact as to this matter,
so discrepant and so difficult to believe are the accounts
given. Those who accompanied Alexander the
Great have written that the region of India subdued
by him contained 5000 towns, none less than two
miles in circuit,[a] and nine nations, and that India
forms a third of the entire surface of the earth, and
that its populations are innumerable—which is
certainly a very probable theory, inasmuch as the
Indians are almost the only race that has never
migrated from its own territory. From the time
of Father Liber to Alexander the Great 153 kings
of India are counted in a period of 6451 years and
three months. The rivers are of enormous size:
it is stated that Alexander sailing on the Indus did
never less thar 75 miles a day and yet could not
reach the mouth of the river in less time than five
months and a few days over, and nevertheless it is
certain that the Indus is smaller than the Ganges.
Seneca also, who among our own writers essayed
an account of India, gives its rivers as 60 in number
and its races as 118. It would be an equally laborious
task to enumerate its mountains; there is a continuous chain formed by Imavus, Hemodus, Paropanisus [b] and Caucasus, from which the whole country
slopes down into an immense plain resembling that
of Egypt.

However, in order to give an idea of the geo- *Northern*
graphical description of India we will follow in the *India.*

Alexandri Magni vestigiis insistemus.[1]   Diognetus et
Baeton itinerum eius mensores scripsere a portis
Caspiis Hecatompylon Parthorum quot diximus milia
esse, inde Alexandriam Arion, quam urbem is rex
condidit, $\overline{\text{DLXXV}}$, Prophthasiam Drangarum $\overline{\text{CXCIX}}$,
Arachosiorum oppidum $\overline{\text{DLXV}}$, Hortospanum $\overline{\text{CLXXV}}$,
62 inde ad Alexandri Oppidum L. (in quibusdam
exemplaribus diversi numeri reperiuntur)—hanc
urbem sub ipso Caucaso esse positam; ab ea ad
flumen Copheta et oppidum Indorum Peucolatim
$\overline{\text{CCXXXVII}}$, unde ad flumen Indum et oppidum Taxilla
$\overline{\text{LX}}$, ad Hydaspen fluvium clarum $\overline{\text{CXX}}$, ad Hypasim non
ignobiliorem $\overline{\text{CCCXC}}$ [2] qui fuit Alexandri itinerum
terminus exuperato tamen amne arisque in adversa
ripa dicatis. epistulae quoque regis ipsius con-
63 sentiunt his.   reliqua inde Seleuco Nicatori peragrata
sunt: ad Sydrum $\overline{\text{CLXIX}}$, Iomanem amnem tantundem (aliqua exemplaria adiciunt $\overline{\text{V}}$ passuum), inde
ad Gangen $\overline{\text{CXIID}}$, ad Rhodaphan $\overline{\text{DLXIX}}$ (alii $\overline{\text{CCCXXV}}$ in
hoc spatio produnt), ad Callinipaza oppidum $\overline{\text{CLXVII}}$
D (alii $\overline{\text{CLXV}}$),[3] inde ad confluentem Iomanis amnis et
Gangis $\overline{\text{DCXXV}}$ (plerique adiciunt $\overline{\text{XIIID}}$), ad oppidum
Palibothra $\overline{\text{CCCCXXV}}$, ad ostium Gangis $\overline{\text{DCXXXVID}}$.
64 gentes quas memorare non pigeat a montibus
Hemodis (quorum promunturium Imaus vocatur
incolarum lingua nivosum sic [4] significante) Isari, Cosiri, Izi et per iuga Chirotosagi multarumque gentium

---

[1] *Rackham*: insistimus *aut* insistamus.
[2] *Mayhoff*: |$\overline{\text{XXV}}$|$\overline{\text{rVCCCXC}}$ *codd.*
[3] *Warmington*: CCLXV *codd.*
[4] sic *add. Mueller.*

---

^a § 44.   ^b Now Herat.   Now Kandahar.

footsteps of Alexander the Great. Diognetus and
Baeton, the surveyors of his expeditions, write that the
distance from the Caspian Gates to the Parthian City
of Hecatompylos is the number of miles that we stated
above; [a] from thence to the city of Alexandria [b] of
the Arii, which Alexander founded, 575 miles, to
the city of the Drangae, Prophthasia, 199 miles, to
the town [c] of the Arachosii 565 miles, to Kabul
175 miles, and thence to Alexander's Town 50 miles
(in some copies of this record we find different
numbers): this city is stated to be situated immediately below the Caucasus; from it to the river
Kabul and the Indian town of Peucolatis 237
miles, and thence to the river Indus and the town
of Taxilla 60 miles, to the famous river Jhelum
120 miles, to the not less notable river Beas 390 miles
—this was the terminus of Alexander's journeys,
although he crossed the river and dedicated altars
upon the opposite bank. The king's actual dis-
patches also agree with these figures. The remaining distances after the Beas were ascertained by the exploration of Seleucus Nicator;
to the Sutlej 169 miles, to the river Jumna the same
(some copies add 5 miles), thence to the Ganges
112½, to Rhodapha 569 (others give 325 miles in this
space), to the town of Callinipaza 167½ (others 165),
thence to the confluence of the river Jumna and
the Ganges 625 (a great many add 13½), to the town
of Patna 425, to the mouth of the Ganges 637½.
The races worth mentioning after leaving the
Hemodi Mountains (a projection of which is called
the Imaus, which in the vernacular means 'snowy')
are the Isari, Cosiri, Izi, and spread over the range
the Chirotosagi and a number of tribes with the

cognomen Bragmanae, quorum Mactocalingae; flumina Prinas et Cainnas, quod in Gangen influit, ambo navigabilia; gentes Calingae mari proximi et supra Mandaei, Malli quorum mons Mallus, finisque tractus eius Ganges.

65 XXII. Hunc alii incertis fontibus ut Nilum rigantemque vicina eodem modo, alii in Scythicis montibus nasci dixerunt, influere in eum XIX amnes, ex his navigabiles praeter iam dictos Crenaccam, Rhamnumbovam, Casuagum, Sonum. alii cum magno fragore ipsius statim fontis erumpere, deiectumque per scopulosa et abrupta, ubi primum molles planities contingat, in quodam lacu hospitari, inde lenem fluere, ubi minimum, VIII p. latitudine, ubi modicum, stadiorum c, altitudine nusquam minore passuum xx, novissima gente Gangaridum Calingarum: regia

66 Pertalis vocatur. regi LX peditum, equites M, elephanti DCC in procinctu bellorum excubant. namque vita mitioribus populis Indorum multipertita degitur: tellurem exercent, militiam alii capessunt, merces alii suas evehunt externasque invehunt, res publicas optumi ditissimique temperant, iudicia reddunt, regibus adsident. quintum genus celebratae illis[1] et prope in religionem versae sa-

---

[1] illis? *Mayhoff*: illi *aut* illic.

name of Bragmanae, among them the Mactocalingae; the rivers are the Prinas and Cainnas, the latter a tributary of the Ganges, both of them navigable; then the tribes of the Calingae nearest the sea, and further inland the Mandaei, the Malli occupying Mount Mallus, and the river Ganges, which is the boundary of this region.

XXII. The Ganges is said by some people to rise *The Ganges* from unknown sources like the Nile and to irrigate *and adja-* the neighbouring country in the same manner, but *cent regions.* others say that its source is in the mountains of Scythia, and that it has nineteen tributaries, among which the navigable ones besides those already mentioned are the Crenacca, Rhamnumbova, Casuagus and Sonus. Others state that it bursts forth with a loud roar at its very source, and after falling over crags and cliffs, as soon as it reaches fairly level country finds hospitality in a certain lake, and flows out of it in a gentle stream with a breadth of 8 miles where narrowest, and $12\frac{1}{2}$ miles as its average width, and nowhere less than 100 feet deep, the last race situated on its banks being that of the Gangarid Calingae: the city where their king lives is called Pertalis. This monarch has 60,000 infantry, 1000 cavalry and 700 elephants always equipped ready for active service. For the peoples of the more civilised Indian races are divided into many classes in their mode of life: they cultivate the land, others engage in military service, others export native merchandise and import goods from abroad, while the best and wealthiest administer the government and serve as judges and as counsellors of the kings. There is a fifth class of persons devoted to wisdom, which is held in high honour with these

pientiae deditum voluntaria semper morte vitam
accenso prius rogo finit. unum super haec est semi-
ferum ac plenum laboris inmensi—a quo [1] supra dicta
continentur—venandi elephantos domandique; his
arant, his invehuntur, haec maxime novere pecuaria,
his militant dimicantque pro finibus: dilectum in
67 bella vires et aetas atque magnitudo faciunt. insula
in Gange est magnae amplitudinis gentem continens
unam nomine Modogalingam. ultra siti sunt Modubae, Molindae, Uberae cum oppido eiusdem nominis
magnifico, Modressae, Praeti, Aclissae, Sasuri,
Fassulae, Colebae, Orumcolae, Abali, Thalutae:
rex horum peditum $\bar{\text{L}}$, equitum $\overline{\text{IV}}$, elephantorum $\overline{\text{IV}}$
in armis habet. validior deinde gens Andarae,
plurimis vicis, xxx oppidis quae muris turribusque
muniuntur, regi praebet peditum $\bar{\text{c}}$, equitum $\bar{\text{II}}$,
elephantos M. fertilissimi sunt auri Dardae, Setae
68 vero et argenti. sed omnia in India prope, non
modo in hoc tractu, potentia claritateque antecedunt
Prasi amplissima urbe ditissimaque Palibothra, unde
quidam ipsam gentem Palibothros vocant, immo vero
tractum universum a Gange. regi eorum peditum
$\overline{\text{DC}}$, equitum $\overline{\text{xxx}}$, elephantorum $\overline{\text{IX}}$ per omnes dies

---

[1] *V.l.* e quo.

[a] The text is uncertain; perhaps the sense is 'by which ...
are supported.'   [b] The ancient Andhras.

people and almost elevated into a religion; those of this class always end their life by a voluntary death upon a pyre to which they have previously themselves set light. There is one class besides these, half-wild people devoted to the laborious task—from which the classes above mentioned are kept away [a]—of hunting and taming elephants; these they use for ploughing and for transport, these are their commonest kind of cattle, and these they employ when fighting in battle and defending their country: elephants to use in war are chosen for their strength and age and size. There is a very spacious island in the Ganges containing a single race named the Modogalinga race. Beyond it are situated the Modubae, the Molindae, the Uberae with a magnificent town of the same name, the Modressae, Praeti, Aclissae, Sasuri, Fassulae, Colebae, Orumcolae, Abali and Thalutae: the king of the latter tribe has an army of 50,000 infantry, 4000 cavalry and 4000 elephants. Next come the Andarae,[b] a more powerful tribe, with a great many villages and thirty towns fortified with walls and towers; they furnish their king with 100,000 infantry, 2000 cavalry and 1000 elephants. The country of the Dardae produces gold in great quantity, and that of the Setae silver also. But almost the whole of the peoples of India and not only those in this district are surpassed in power and glory by the Prasi, with their very large and wealthy city of Patna, from which some people give the name of Palibothri to the race itself, and indeed to the whole tract of country from the Ganges. Their king maintains and pays a standing army of 60,000 foot, 30,000 horse and 9000 elephants, from which

stipendiantur, unde coniectatio ingens opum est.
69 ab his in interiore situ Monaedes et Suari, quorum
mons Maleus in quo umbrae ad septentrionem cadunt
hieme, aestate in austrum, per senos menses. septentriones eo tractu semel anno adparere, nec nisi
quindecim diebus, Baeton auctor est, hoc idem
pluribus locis Indiae fieri Megasthenes. austrinum
polum Indi Diamasa vocant. amnis Iomanes in
Gangen per Palibothros decurrit inter oppida Methora
70 et Chrysobora. a Gange versa ad meridiem plaga
tinguntur sole populi, iam quidem infecti, nondum
tamen Aethiopum modo exusti; quantum ad Indum
accedunt tantum colorem [1] praeferunt. Indus statim
a Prasiorum gente, quorum in montanis Pygmaei
traduntur. Artemidorus inter duos amnes |XXI|
interesse tradit.
71 XXIII. Indus incolis Sindus appellatus in iugo
Caucasi montis quod vocatur Paropanisus adversus
solis ortum effusus et ipse undeviginti recipit amnes,
sed clarissimos Hydaspen quattuor alios adferentem,
Cantabam tris, per se vero navigabiles Acesinum et
Hypasim, quadam tamen aquarum modestia nusquam latior L stadiis aut altior xv passibus, amplissi-
mam insulam efficiens quae Prasiane nominatur et
72 aliam minorem quae Patale. ipse per |XII|XL

---

[1] V.l. colore (colore prae ⟨se⟩ ferunt Detlefsen).

[a] The Indus Delta.

the vastness of his wealth may be conjectured. Further up country from these are the Monaedes and the Suari, in whose domain is Mount Maleus upon which shadows fall towards the north in winter and towards the south in summer, for periods of six months alternately. According to Baeton the constellation of the Great Bear is only visible in this region one time in the year, and only for a period of a fortnight; and Megasthenes says that the same thing occurs in many other places in India. The Indian name for their southern region is Diamasa. The river Jumna runs through the Palibothri country into the Ganges between the towns of Muttra and Chrysobora. In the region to the south of the Ganges the tribes are browned by the heat of the sun to the extent of being coloured, though not as yet burnt black like the Ethiopians; the nearer they get to the Indus the more colour they display. We come to the Indus immediately after leaving the Prasii, a tribe in whose mountain regions there is said to be a race of Pygmies. Artemidorus gives the distance from the Ganges to the Indus as 2100 miles.

XXIII. The Indus, the native name for which is *The Indus.* Sindus, rises on the east side of a ridge of Mount Caucasus called Hindu Kush; in its course it receives nineteen tributaries, the best known being the Jhelum which brings with it four other streams, the Cantaba which brings three, and the Chenab and the Beas, themselves navigable rivers. Owing however to a certain limitation in its supply of water the Indus is nowhere more than $6\frac{1}{4}$ miles wide or 75 feet deep; and it forms an island of considerable size named Prasiane and another smaller one named Patale.[a] The main river is navigable for a distance

passuum parcissimis auctoribus navigatur et quodam
solis comitatu in occasum versus oceano infunditur.
mensuram orae ad eum ponam, ut invenio, generatim, quamquam inter se nullae congruunt: ab ostio
Gangis ad promunturium Calingon et oppidum
Dandaguda $\overline{\text{DCXXV}}$, ad Tropina $\lceil\text{XII}\rceil$ $\overline{\text{XXV}}$, ad Perimulae
promunturium, ubi est celeberrimum Indiae em-
porium, $\overline{\text{DCCL}}$, ad oppidum in insula quam supra
diximus Patalam $\overline{\text{DCXX}}$.

73 Gentes montanae inter eum et Iomanem Caesi,
Caetriboni silvestres, dein Megallae (quorum regi D
elephanti, peditum equitumque numerus incertus),
Chrysei, Parasangae, Asmagi, tigri fera scatentes;
armant peditum $\overline{\text{XXX}}$, elephantos CCC, equites DCCC.
hos Indus includit montium corona circumdatos et
solitudinibus. $\overline{\text{DCXXV}}$ infra solitudines Dari, Surae,
iterumque solitudines per $\overline{\text{CLXXXVII}}$, plerumque harenis
ambientibus haut alio modo quam insulas mari.

74 infra deserta haec Maltaecorae, Singae, Moroae,
Rarungae, Moruni. hi montium qui perpetuo
tractu oceani in[1] ora pertinent incolae liberi et regum
expertes multis urbibus montanos optinent colles.
Nareae deinde, quos claudit mons altissimus Indi-
corum Capitalia. huius incolae alio latere late auri

---

[1] in *add. Mayhoff.*

of 1240 miles according to the most moderate accounts, and it discharges into the ocean after following the sun's course in some measure westward. I will give the measurement of the coast-line to the mouth of the river by stages as I find it, although none of the various reports of it agree with one another; from the mouth of the Ganges to the Cape of the Calingae and the town of Dandaguda 625 miles, to Tropina 1225 miles, to the Cape of Perimula, where is the most celebrated trading-place of India, 750 miles, to the town of Patala on the island which we have mentioned above, 620 miles.

Between the Indus and the Jumna are the *Races beyond* mountain tribes of the Caesi, the forester Caetriboni, *the Indus.* and then the Megallae (whose king possesses 500 elephants and an uncertain number of infantry and cavalry), the Chrysei, the Parasangae and the Asmagi, whose district is infested by the wild tiger; they have an armed force of 30,000 foot, 300 elephants and 800 cavalry. They are bounded by the river Indus and surrounded by a ring of mountains and by deserts. Below the deserts at a distance of 625 miles are the Dari and Surae, and then desert again for a distance of 187 miles, these places for the most part being surrounded by sands exactly as islands are surrounded by the sea. Below these deserts are the Maltaecorae, Singae, Moroae, Rarungae and Moruni. These peoples are the inhabitants of the mountains that stretch in a continuous range on the coast of the ocean; they are free people having no kings, and they occupy the mountain slopes with a number of cities. Next come the Nareae, who are shut in by the Capitalia range, the highest of the mountains of India. The

75 et argenti metalla fodiunt. ab his Oratae, quorum
regi elephanti quidem x, sed amplae vires peditum,
Suarataratae—et hi sub rege elephantos non alunt
fiducia equitum peditumque—Odonbaeoraes, Arabastrae Thorace urbe pulchra fossis palustribus
munita per quas crocodili humani corporis avidissimi
aditum nisi ponte non dant. et aliud apud illos
laudatur oppidum Automula, inpositum litori quinque
amnium in unum confluente [1] concursu, emporio
nobili; regi eorum elephanti MDC, peditum $\overline{\text{CL}}$,
equitum $\bar{\text{v}}$. pauperior Charmarum rex elephantos
76 LX parvasque reliquas vires habet. ab his gens
Pandae, sola Indorum regnata feminis. unam
Herculi sexus eius genitam ferunt ob idque grati-
orem, praecipuo regno donatam. ab ea deducentes
originem imperitant CCC oppidis; peditum $\overline{\text{CL}}$,
elephantes D. post hanc trecentarum urbium seriem
Derangae, Posingae, Butae, Gogaraei, Umbrae,
Nereae, Brangosi, Nobundae, Cocondae, Nesei,
Palatitae, Salobriasae, Orostrae Patalam insulam
attingentes, a cuius extremo litore ad Caspias portas
$\overline{|\text{XIX}|\text{XXV}}$ produntur.

77 Hinc deinde accolunt Indum adverso eo scandente [2]
demonstratione Mathoae, Bolingae, Gallitalutae,

---

[1] *V.l.* confluentium.
[2] *Mayhoff*: adversus eos cadente (scandente *Urlichs*).

inhabitants of the other side of this mountain work a wide range of gold and silver mines. Next to these come the Oratae, whose king has only ten elephants but a large force of infantry, the Suarataratae—these also though ruled by a king do not keep elephants but rely on cavalry and infantry—the Odonbaeoraes and the Arabastrae, whose fine city Thorax is guarded by marshy canals which crocodiles, creatures with an insatiable appetite for human flesh, render impassable save by way of a bridge. Another town in their country is also highly spoken of, Automula, which is situated on the coast at the point of confluence of five rivers, and has a celebrated market; their king possesses 1600 elephants, 150,000 foot and 5000 horse. The king of the Charmae is not so wealthy, having 60 elephants and small forces of the other kinds. The race next to these is that of the Pandae, the only people in India ruled by queens. They say that only one child of the female sex was born to Hercules, and that she was in consequence his favourite and he bestowed on her a specially large kingdom. The queens deriving their descent from her rule over 300 towns, and have an army of 150,000 foot and 500 elephants. After this list of 300 cities we have the Derangae, Posingae, Butae, Gogaraei, Umbrae, Nereae, Brangosi, Nobundae, Cocondae, Nesei, Palatitae, Salobriasae and Orostrae, the last people being adjacent to the island of Patala, the distance from the extreme point of which to the Caspian Gates is given as 1925 miles.

From this point onward the tribes dwelling on the Indus—our enumeration proceeding up stream—are the Mathoae, Bolingae, Gallitalutae, Dimuri,

Dimuri, Megari, Ardabae, Mesae, Abi, Suri, Silae,
mox deserta in $\overline{\text{CCL}}$, quibus exuperatis Organagae,
Abortae, Bassuertae, et ab his solitudines prioribus
pares. dein Sorofages, Arbae, Marogomatrae, Umbritae Ceaeque quorum xii nationes singulisque
binae urbes, Asini trium urbium incolae : caput
eorum Bucephala Alexandri regis equo, cui fuerat
78 hoc nomen, ibi sepulto conditum. montani super
hos Caucaso subiecti Sosaeadae, Sondrae ; transgressisque Indum et cum eo decurrentibus Samarabiae, Sambraceni, Bisambritae, Orsi, Andiseni,
Taxilae cum urbe celebri. iam in plana demisso
tractu, cui universo nomen Amendae, populi quattuor, Peucolitae, Arsagalitae, Geretae, Assoi : etenim
plerique ab occidente non Indo amne determinant
sed adiciunt quattuor satrapias, Gedrosos, Arachotas,
Arios, Paropanisidas, ultimo fine Cophete fluvio,
79 quae omnia Ariorum esse aliis placet. nec non et
Nysam urbem plerique Indiae adscribunt montem-
que Merum Libero Patri sacrum (unde origo fabulae
Iovis femine editum), item Aspaganos gentem vitis
et lauri et buxi pomorumque omnium in Graecia
nascentium fertilem. quae memoranda ac prope
fabulosa de fertilitate terrae et genere [1] frugum
arborumque aut ferarum ac volucrum et aliorum
animalium traduntur suis quaeque locis in reliqua

---

[1] generibus *vel* generatione ? *Rackham.*

Megari, Ardabae, Mesae, Abi, Suri and Silae; then 250 miles of desert; and after traversing that, the Organagae, Abortae and Bassuertae; and next to these an uninhabited stretch equal in extent to the preceding one. Then the Sorofages, Arbae and Marogomatrae; the Umbritae and Ceae comprising twelve tribes and each race possessing two cities; the Asini inhabiting three cities, their chief place being Oxhead, founded to be the burial-place of King Alexander's charger bearing that name. Mountain tribes above these under the Hindu Kush range are the Sosaeadae and Sondrae; and crossing the Indus and following it down-stream we come to the Samarabiae, Sambraceni, Bisambritae, Orsi and Andiseni, and the Taxilae with their famous city. Then the region slopes down to level ground, the whole having the name of Amenda; and there are four tribes, the Peucolitae, Arsagalitae, Geretae and Assoi; indeed, most authorities do not put the western frontier at the river Indus but include four satrapies, the Gedrosi, Arachotae, Arii and Paropanisidae, with the river Kabul as the final boundary—the whole of which region others consider to belong to the Arii. Moreover most people also assign to India the city of Nisa and Mount Merus which is sacred to Father Liber (this being the place from which originated the myth of the birth of Liber from the thigh of Jove), and the same as to the Aspagani tribe, a district producing the vine, the bay and the box and all the kinds of fruit indigenous to Greece. Remarkable and almost fabulous reports as to fertility of soil and variety of crops and trees or wild animals and birds and other living creatures will be recorded in their

397

parte operis commemorabuntur, quattuor satrapiae
mox paulo, ad Taprobanen insulam festinante animo.

80   Sed ante sunt aliae: Patale quam significavimus
in ipsis faucibus Indi, triquetra figura, $\overline{\text{CCXX}}$ p.
latitudine; extra ostium Indi Chryse et Argyre,
fertilis metalli, ut credo: nam quod aliqui tradidere
aureum argenteumque his solum esse haut facile
crediderim. ab his $\overline{\text{XX}}$ p. Crocala et ab ea $\overline{\text{XII}}$ Bibaga
ostreis ac conchyliis referta, dein Coralliba $\overline{\text{VIII}}$ a
supra dicta, multaeque ignobiles.

81   XXIV. Taprobanen alterum orbem terrarum esse
diu existimatum est Antichthonum appellatione:
ut insulam esse liqueret Alexandri Magni aetas
resque praestitere. Onesicritus classis eius praefectus elephantos ibi maiores bellicosioresque quam
in India gigni scripsit; Megasthenes flumine dividi,
incolasque Palaeogonos appellari, auri margaritarum-
que grandium fertiliores quam Indos. Eratosthenes
et mensuram prodidit, longitudinis $\overline{\text{VII}}$ stadium,
82 latitudinis $\overline{\text{V}}$, nec urbes esse sed vicos DCC.[1] incipit
ab Eoo mari inter ortum occasumque solis Indiae
praetenta et quondam credita xx dierum navigatione
a Prasiana gente distare, mox, quia papyraceis

---

[1] DCC ⟨L⟩ *Siegelin ex Aeliano.*

---

   [a] Suggesting the inhabitants of another land-mass balanc-
ing our own in the southern hemisphere—but not on the
opposite side of the earth : there is of course no suggestion
of the Antipodes.
   [b] Ceylon is really 271½ miles long and 137½ broad.
   [c] An Indian race on the Ganges.

several places in the remainder of the work, and the four satrapies will be described a little below, as at present our mind hastens on to the island of Ceylon.

But before Ceylon come some other islands: Patale, which we have indicated as situated at the very mouth of the Indus, an island of triangular shape, 220 miles in breadth; and outside the mouth of the Indus Chryse and Argyre, both of which I believe to be rich in minerals—for I find it hard to believe the statement of some writers that they only have gold and silver mines. Twenty miles beyond these is Crocala, and 12 miles further Bibaga, which is full of oysters and other shell-fish, and then Coralliba 8 miles beyond the above-mentioned island, and many of no note. *Indian Islands. § 71.*

XXIV. Ceylon, under the name of the Land of the Counterlanders,[a] was long considered to be another world; but the epoch and the achievements of Alexander the Great supplied clear proof of its being an island. Onesicritus, a commander of Alexander's navy, writes that elephants are bred there of larger size and more warlike spirit than in India; and Megasthenes says that it is cut in two by a river, that the inhabitants have the name of Aborigines, and that they produce more gold and large pearls than the Indians. Eratosthenes further gives the dimensions [b] of the island as 875 miles in length and 625 miles in breadth, and says that it contains no cities, but 700 villages. Beginning at the eastern sea it stretches along the side of India from east to west; and it was formerly believed to be a distance of 20 days' sail from the nation of the Prasii,[c] but at later times, inasmuch as the voyage to it used to be made with vessels constructed of *Ceylon.*

navibus armamentisque Nili peteretur, ad nostrarum
navium cursus VII dierum intervallo taxata. mare
interest vadosum, senis non amplius altitudinis
passibus, sed certis canalibus ita profundum ut nullae
anchorae sidant: ob id navibus utrimque prorae, ne
per angustias alvei circumagi sit necesse; magnitudo
83 ad terna milia amphorum. siderum in navigando
nulla observatio—septentrio non cernitur; volucres
secum vehunt emittentes saepius, meatumque
earum terram petentium comitantur. nec plus
quaternis mensibus anno navigant: cavent a solstitio
maxime centum dies, tunc illo mari hiberno.

84 Hactenus a priscis memorata. nobis diligentior
notitia Claudi principatu contigit legatis etiam ex ea
insula advectis. id accidit hoc modo: Anni Plocami,
qui Maris Rubri vectigal a fisco redemerat, libertus
circa Arabiam navigans aquilonibus raptus praeter
Carmaniam, XV die Hippuros portum eius invectus,
hospitali regis clementia sex mensum tempore
inbutus adloquio percontanti postea narravit Ro-
85 manos et Caesarem. mirum in modum in auditis

ᵃ The big two-handled clay wine-jar served as a standard
measure of a ship's capacity, as with us the ton.

reeds and with the rigging used on the Nile, its
distance was fixed with reference to the speeds made
by our ships as seven days' sail. The sea between
the island and the mainland is shallow, not more
than 18 feet deep, but in certain channels so deep
that no anchors hold the bottom: for this reason
ships are used that have bows at each end, so as to
avoid the necessity of coming about while negotiating
the narrows of the channel; the tonnage of these
vessels is as much as three thousand barrels.[a] The
Cingalese take no observations of the stars in navigation—indeed, the Great Bear is not visible; but
they carry birds on board with them and at fairly
frequent intervals set them free, and follow the
course they take as they make for the land. They
only use four months in the year for voyages, and
they particularly avoid the hundred days following
midsummer, when those seas are stormy.

So far the facts stated have been recorded by *Geography*
the early writers. We however have obtained more *and
ethnology of*
accurate information during the principate of *Ceylon.*
Claudius, when an embassy actually came to Rome
from the island of Ceylon. The circumstances were
as follows: Annius Plocamus had obtained a contract
from the Treasury to collect the taxes from the Red
Sea; a freedman of his while sailing round Arabia
was carried by gales from the north beyond the
coast of Carmania, and after a fortnight made the
harbour of Hippuri in Ceylon, where he was entertained with kindly hospitality by the king, and
in a period of six months acquired a thorough
knowledge of the language; and afterwards in reply
to the king's enquiries he gave him an account of
the Romans and their emperor. The king among

iustitiam ille suspexit, quod paris[1] pondere denarii
essent in captiva pecunia, cum diversae imagines
indicarent a pluribus factos. et hoc maxime sol-
licitatus ad amicitiam legatos quattuor misit principe
eorum Rachia. ex his cognitum D esse oppida,
portum contra meridiem adpositum oppido Palaesi-
mundo omnium ibi clarissimo ac regio,[2] $\overline{cc}$ plebis.
86 stagnum intus Megisba $\overline{ccclxxv}$ p. ambitu, insulas
pabuli tantum fertiles complexu; ex eo duos
amnes erumpere, Palaesimundum iuxta oppidum
eiusdem nominis influentem in portum tribus alveis,
quinque stadiorum artissimo, xv amplissimo, alterum
ad septentriones Indiamque versum, Cydara nomine.
proximum esse Indiae promunturium quod vocetur
Coliacum, quadridui navigatione medio in cursu
87 Solis insula occurrente; mare ibi[3] colore perviridi,
praeterea fruticosum[4] arboribus, iubas earum guber-
naculis detergentibus. Septentriones Vergiliasque
apud nos veluti in novo caelo mirabantur, ne lunam
quidem apud ipsos nisi ab octava in xvi supra
terram aspici fatentes, Canopum lucere noctibus,

---

[1] *V.l.* pari.
[2] *V.l.* regia (-iae *aut* -iam *edd.*).
[3] ibi? *Mayhoff:* in *aut* id.
[4] *V.l.* fructuosum.

---

[a] Perhaps a title, Rajah.
[b] This seems to be a description of mangrove-swamps.

all that he heard was remarkably struck with admiration for Roman honesty, on the ground that among the money found on the captive the denarii were all equal in weight, although the various figures on them showed that they had been coined by several emperors. This strongly attracted his friendship, and he sent four envoys, the chief of whom was Rachias.[a] From them we learnt the following facts about Ceylon: it contains 500 towns, and a harbour facing south, adjacent to the town of Palaesimundus, which is the most famous of all the places in the island and a royal residence, with a population of 200,000. Inland (we were told) there is a marsh named Megisba measuring 375 miles round and containing islands that only produce pasturage; and out of this marsh flow two rivers, Palaesimundus running through three channels into the harbour near the town that bears the same name as the river, and measuring over half a mile in breadth at the narrowest point and nearly two miles at the widest, and the other, named Cydara, flowing north in the direction of India. The nearest cape in India (according to our informants) is the one called Cape Comorin, at a distance of four days' sail, passing in the middle of the voyage the Island of the Sun; and the sea there is of a deep green colour, and also has thickets of trees growing in it,[b] the tops of which are brushed by the rudders of passing vessels. The envoys marvelled at the new aspect of the heavens visible in our country, with the Great and Little Bear and the Pleiads, and they told us that in their own country even the moon only appears above the horizon from the 8th to the 16th day of the month, and that Canopus, a large and

sidus ingens et clarum. sed maxime mirum iis
erat umbras suas in nostrum caelum cadere, non in
suum, solemque ab laeva oriri et in dextram occidere
88 potius quam e diverso. iidem narravere latus
insulae quod praetenderetur Indiae $\bar{x}$ stadiorum
esse ab oriente hiberno; ultra montes Hemodos
Seras quoque ab ipsis aspici notos etiam commercio:
patrem Rachiae commeasse eo: advenis sibi Seras[1]
occursare. ipsos vero excedere hominum magnitudinem, rutilis comis, caeruleis oculis, oris sono
truci, nullo commercio linguae. cetera eadem quae
nostri negotiatores: fluminis ulteriore ripa merces
positas iuxta venalia tolli ab iis si placeat permutatio,
non aliter odio iustiore luxuriae quam si perducta
mens illuc usque cogitet quid et quo petatur et
quare.
89 Sed ne Taprobane quidem, quamvis extra orbem[a]
a natura relegata, nostris vitiis caret: aurum argen-
tumque et ibi in pretio, marmor testudinis simile,
margaritae gemmaeque in honore; multo praestantior
est[2] totus[3] luxuriae nostra[4] cumulus. ipsorum
opes maiores esse dicebant, sed apud nos opulentiae

---

[1] *Hardouin*: advenis ibi feras.
[2] *Mayhoff*: praestantiores et.
[3] *V.l.* totius.
[4] *Warmington*: nostrae.

---

[a] *I.e.*, towards the north, not the south.

brilliant star, lights them by night. But what surprised them most was that their shadows fell towards our sky and not towards theirs,[a] and that the sun rose on the left-hand side of the observer and set towards the right instead of *vice versa*. They also told us that the side of their island facing towards India is 1250 miles long and lies south-east of India; that beyond the Himalayas they also face towards the country of the Chinese, who are known to them by intercourse in trade as well, the father of Rachia having travelled there, and that when they arrived there the Chinese always hastened down to the beach to meet them. That people themselves (they told us) are of more than normal height, and have flaxen hair and blue eyes, and they speak in harsh tones and use no language in dealing with travellers. The remainder of the envoys' account agreed with the reports of our traders—that commodities were deposited on the opposite bank of a river by the side of the goods offered for sale by the natives, and they took them away if satisfied by the barter,—hatred of luxury being in no circumstances more justifiable than if the imagination travels to the Far East and reflects what is procured from there and what means of trade are employed and for what purpose.

But even Ceylon, although banished by Nature beyond the confines of the world, is not without the vices that belong to us: gold and silver are valued there also, and a kind of marble resembling tortoise-shell and pearls and precious stones are held in honour; in fact the whole mass of luxury is there carried to a far higher pitch than ours. They told us that there was greater wealth in their own

Cingalese manners and customs.

maiorem usum: servom nemini, non in diem aut
interdiu somnum, aedificia modice ab humo exstantia,
annonam numquam augeri, non fora litesve esse, coli
Herculem, eligi regem a populo senecta clementiaque
liberos non habentem, et si postea gignat, abdicari,

90 ne fiat hereditarium regnum. rectores ei a populo
xxx dari, nec nisi plurium sententia quemquam capitis
damnari; sic quoque appellationem esse ad populum
et septuaginta iudices dari; si liberent ii reum,
amplius xxx iis nullam esse dignationem, gravissimo
probro. regi cultum Liberi Patris, ceteris Arabum.

91 regem, si quid delinquat, morte multari, nullo
interimente, aversantibus cunctis et commercia etiam
sermonis negantibus. festa venatione absumi: gratis-
simam eam tigribus elephantisque constare. agros
diligenter coli, vitis usum non esse, pomis abundare.
esse et in piscatu voluptatem, testudinum maxime,
quarum superficie familias habitantium contegi:
tanta reperiri magnitudine. vitam hominum centum
annis modicam.

ᵃ A long robe with a train

country than in ours, but that we made more use of
our riches: with them nobody kept a slave, everybody got up at sunrise and nobody took a siesta
in the middle of the day; their buildings were of
only moderate height; the price of corn was never
inflated; there were no lawcourts and no litigation;
the deity worshipped was Hercules; the king was
elected by the people on the grounds of age and
gentleness of disposition, and as having no children,
and if he afterwards had a child, he was deposed,
to prevent the monarchy from becoming hereditary.
Thirty Governors, they told us, were assigned to the
king by the people, and capital punishment could
only be inflicted by a vote of a majority of these;
and even then there was a right of appeal to the
people, and a jury of seventy members was appointed
to try the case, and if these acquitted the accused
the thirty Governors were no more held in any
esteem, being utterly disgraced. The king's costume
was that _a_ of Father Liber, and the other people wore
Arabian dress. If the king committed a delinquency
he was punished by being condemned to death,
though nobody executed the sentence, but the whole
of the people turned their backs on him and refused
to have any communication with him or even to speak
to him. Holidays, they told us, were spent in hunting,
tiger hunts and elephant hunts being always the
most popular. Agriculture was industriously practised, but the vine was not grown, although orchard
fruit was abundant. They were also fond of fishing,
especially for turtle, the shells of which were used
as roofs for family dwellings—they were found
of so large a size. They looked upon a hundred
years as a moderate span of life.

Haec conperta de Taprobane.

92 XXV. Quattuor satrapiae quas in hunc locum distulimus ita se habent. a proximis Indo gentibus montana. Capisene habuit Capisam urbem quam diruit Cyrus; Arachosia cum flumine et oppido eiusdem nominis, quod quidam Cufim dixere, a Samiramide conditum; amnis Erymandus praefluens Parabesten Arachosiorum. proximos his a meridie ad partem Arachotarum faciunt Dexendrusos, a septentrione Paropanisidas, Cartana oppidum sub Caucaso, quod postea Tetragonis dictum. haec regio est ex adverso Bactriae; Arianorum[1] deinde cuius oppidum Alexandria a conditore dictum; Syndraci, Dangalae, Parapinae, Cataces, Mazi; ad Caucasum Cadrusi, oppidum ab Alexandro 93 conditum. infra haec omnia planiora.[2] ab Indo Ariana regio ambusta fervoribus desertisque circumdata, multa tamen interfusa opacitate cultores congregat circa duos maxime fluvios, Tonberon et Arosapen. oppidum Artacoana, Arius amnis qui praefluit Alexandriam ab Alexandro conditam: patet oppidum stadia xxx; multoque pulchrius sicut antiquius Artacabene, iterum ab Antiocho munitum,

[1] *Mayhoff*: adverso Bactrianorum.
[2] *Mayhoff, cf.* § 92: omnia ora.

---

[a] Now Kandahar. [b] Now Herat.

This is the information that was given to us about Ceylon.

XXV. The following is the arrangement of the four satrapies which we deferred to this place in our account. After leaving the races nearest to India, you come to the mountain districts. That of Capisene formerly had a city named Capisa, which was destroyed by Cyrus; next Arachosia, with a river and town *a* of the same name—the town, which was founded by Samiramis, being called by some writers Cufis; then the river Erymandus, flowing past the Arachosian town of Parabeste. Next to the Arachosii writers place the Dexendrusi on the south side, adjoining a section of the Arachotae, and the Paropanisadae on the north; and beneath the Hindu Kush the town of Cartana, later called Tetragonis. This region is opposite to Bactria, and then comes the region of the Ariani, whose town is called Alexandria *b* after its founder; the Syndraci, Dangalae, Parapinae, Cataces and Mazi; near the Hindu Kush the Cadrusi, whose town was founded by Alexander. Below these places the whole country is more level. In the direction of the Indus is the Arian region, which is scorched by glowing heat and encircled by deserts, yet extending in the district between them with plenty of shade, it is occupied by numerous farmers, settled especially on the banks of two rivers, the Tonberos and the Arosapes. There is a town, Artacoana, and a river, Arius, which flows past Alexandria, a town founded by Alexander which covers an area of nearly four miles; and the much more beautiful as well as older town of Artacabene, the fortifications of which were renewed by Antiochus, covers an area of $6\frac{1}{4}$

409

94 stadia quinquaginta. Dorisdorsigi gens; amnes
Pharnacotis, Ophradus; Prophthasia; oppidum Zaraspadum, Drangac, Euergetae,[1] Zarangae, Gedrusi;
oppida Peucolis, Lyphorta, Methorcum; deserta;
amnis Manain, Acutri gens, flumen Eorum, gens
Orbi, flumen navigabile Pomanus Pandarum finibus,
item Cabirus Suarorum, ostio portuosum, oppidum
Condigramma, flumen Cophes. influunt in eum
95 navigabilia Saddaros, Parospus, Sodamus. Arianae
partem esse Daritim aliqui volunt, mensuramque
produnt utriusque longitudinem $\overline{|XIX|}$ $\bar{L}$, latitudinem
dimidio minorem quam Indiae. alii Gedrusos et
Sires posuere per $\overline{CXXXVIII}$ p., mox Ichthyophagos
Oritas propria, non Indorum lingua loquentes per
$\overline{CC}$ p. (Ichthyophagos omnes Alexander vetuit piscibus
vivere.) deinde posuere Arbiorum gentem per $\overline{CC}$ p.
ultra deserta, dein Carmania ac Persis atque Arabia.
96 XXVI. Sed priusquam generatim haec perse-
quamur indicari convenit quae prodidit Onesicritus
classe Alexandri circumvectus in mediterranea
Persidis ex India, enarrata proxime a Iuba, deinde
eam navigationem quae his annis comperta servatur
hodie.

Onesicriti et Nearchi navigatio nec nomina
habet mansionum nec spatia; primumque Xylinepolis

---

[1] *Hardouin e Strabone*: Arietae.

miles. Then the Dorisdorsigi tribe; the rivers Pharnacotis and Ophradus; Prophthasia; the town of Zaraspadum, the Drangae, Euergetae, Zarangae and Gedrusi; the towns of Peucolis, Lyphorta and Methorcum; a space of desert; the river Manain, the Acutri tribe, the river Eorus, the Orbi tribe, the navigable river Pomanus at the frontier of the Pandae and the Cabirus at that of the Suari, forming a good harbour at its mouth; the town of Condigramma and the river Kabul. Navigable tributaries of the Kabul are the Saddaros, Parospus and Sodamus. Some hold that Daritis is part of Ariana, and they give the dimensions of both as—length 1950 miles, breadth one half that of India. Others place the Gedrusi and Sires as covering an area of 138 miles, and then the Fish-eating Oritae, who do not speak the Indian language but have one of their own, covering a space of 200 miles. (Alexander made an order forbidding a fish diet to all the Fish-eaters.) Next they put the race of the Arbii, covering 200 miles. Beyond them there is a region of desert, and then come Carmania, Farsistan and Arabia.

XXVI. But before we go on to a detailed account of these countries, it is suitable to indicate the facts reported by Onesicritus after sailing with the fleet of Alexander round from India to the interior of Farsistan, and quite recently related in detail by Juba, and then to state the sea-route that has been ascertained in recent times and is followed at the present day.

Voyage of Nearchus and Onesicritus.

The record of the voyage of Onesicritus and Nearchus does not include the names of the official stopping places nor the distances travelled; and

ab Alexandro condita, unde ceperunt exordium,
iuxta quod flumen aut ubi fuerit non satis explanatur.
97 haec tamen digna memoratu produntur: Arbis [1]
oppidum a Nearcho conditum in navigatione et
flumen Arbium [2] navium capax, contra insula distans
LXX stadia; Alexandria condita a Leonnato iussu
Alexandri in finibus gentis; Argenus portu salubri;
flumen Tonberum navigabile, circa quod Parirae;
deinde Ichthyophagi tam longo tractu ut xxx dierum
spatio praenavigaverint; insula quae Solis appellatur
et eadem Nympharum Cubile, rubens, in qua nullum
98 non animal absumitur incertis causis; Ori gens;
flumen Carmaniae Hyctanis portuosum et auro
fertile. ab eo primum Septentriones apparuisse
adnotavere, Arcturum neque omnibus cerni noctibus
nec totis umquam; Achaemenidas usque illo tenuisse;
aeris et ferri metalla et arrenici ac mini exerceri.
inde promunturium Carmaniae est, ex quo in adversam
oram ad gentem Arabiae Macas traiectus distat
$\bar{v}$ p.; insulae tres, quarum Oracta tantum habitatur
99 aquosa a continente $\overline{xxv}$ p., insulae quattuor iam in
sinu ante Persida—circa has hydri marini vicenum
cubitorum adnatantes terruere classem—, insula

---

[1] *Hardouin*: ab iis *aut* ab his *aut* abies.
[2] *Mayhoff*: Nabrum.

to begin with, no sufficiently clear account is given of the position of the city of Timbertown, founded by Alexander, which was their starting point, nor is the river on which it stood indicated. Nevertheless they give the following places worth mentioning: the town of Arbis, founded by Nearchus during his voyage, and the river Arbium, navigable by ships, and an island opposite to Arbis, 8¾ miles distant; Alexandria, founded in the territory of this race by Leonnatus at the order of Alexander; Argenus, with a serviceable harbour; the navigable river Tonberum, in the neighbourhood of which are the Parirae; then the Fish-eaters, covering so wide a space of coast that it took 30 days to sail past them; the island *a* called the Isle of the Sun and also the Couch of the Nymphs, the soil of which is red in colour, and on which all animals without exception die, from causes not ascertained; the Ori tribe; the Carmanian river Hyctanis, affording harbourage and producing gold. The travellers noted that it was here that the Great and Little Bear first became visible, and that Arcturus is not visible at all on some nights and never all night long; that the rule of the Persian kings extended to this point; and that copper, iron, arsenic and red-lead are mined here. Next there is the Cape of Carmania, from which it is a passage of five miles to cross to the Arabian tribe of the Macae on the opposite coast; three islands, of which only Oracta, 25 miles from the mainland, has a supply of fresh water and is inhabited; four islands quite in the gulf, off the coast of Farsistan—in the neighbourhood of these the fleet was terrified by sea-serpents 30 ft. long that swam alongside—;

---

a Now Ashtola.

Aradus, item Gauratae, in quibus Gyani gens; flumen
Hyperis in medio sinu Persico, onerariarum navium
capax; flumen Sitioganus, quo Pasargadas septimo
die navigatur; flumen navigabile Phrystimus; insula
sine nomine. flumen Granis modicarum navium[1]
per Susianen fluit, dextra eius accolunt Deximontani
qui bitumen perficiunt; flumen Zarotis ostio difficili
nisi peritis; insulae duae parvae. inde vadosa
navigatio palustri similis per euripos tamen quosdam
peragitur; ostium Euphratis; lacus quem faciunt
Eulaeus et Tigris iuxta Characen, inde Tigri Susa.
100 festos dies ibi agentem Alexandrum invenerunt
septimo mense postquam digressus ab iis fuerat
Patalis, tertio navigationis. sic Alexandri classis
navigavit; postea ab Syagro Arabiae promunturio
Patalen favonio, quem Hippalum ibi vocant, peti
certissimum videbatur, $\overline{|XIII|}$ $\overline{XXXII}$ p. aestimatione.
101 secuta aetas propiorem cursum tutioremque iudicavit
si ab eodem promunturio Sigerum portum Indiae
peteret, diuque ita navigatum est, donec conpendia
invenit mercator, lucroque India admota est; quippe
omnibus annis navigatur sagittariorum cohortibus
inpositis; etenim piratae maxime infestabant.

[1] navium ⟨capax⟩ edd. vet.

* The name of the explorer who discovered the proper use
of monsoons between Arabia and India.

the island of Aradus and that of Gauratae, both inhabited by the Gyani tribe; at the middle of the Persian Gulf the river Hyperis, navigable for merchant vessels; the river Sitioganus, up which it is seven days' voyage to Pasargadae; the navigable river Phrystimus; and an island that has no name. The river Granis, carrying vessels of moderate size, flows through Susiane, and on its right bank dwell the Deximontani, who manufacture asphalt; the river Zarotis, the mouth of which is difficult to navigate except for those familiar with it; and two small islands. Then comes a shallow stretch of water like a marsh which nevertheless is navigable by way of certain channels; the mouth of the Euphrates; a lake formed in the neighbourhood of Charax by the Eulaeus and the Tigris; then by the Tigris they reached Susa. There after three months' voyaging they found Alexander celebrating a festival; it was seven months since he had left them at Patala. Such was the route followed by the fleet of Alexander; but subsequently it was thought that the safest line is to start from Ras Fartak in Arabia with a west wind (the native name for which in those parts is Hippalus [a]) and make for Patale, the distance being reckoned as 1332 miles. The following period considered it a shorter and safer route to start from the same cape and steer for the Indian harbour of Sigerus,[b] and for a long time this was the course followed, until a merchant discovered a shorter route, and the desire for gain brought India nearer; indeed, the voyage is made every year, with companies of archers on board, because these seas used to be very greatly infested by pirates.

Sea-route from Arabia to India.

[b] Probably Jaigarh.

Nec pigebit totum cursum ab Aegypto exponere nunc primum certa notitia patescente. digna res, nullo anno minus HS⌐D⌐ [1] imperii nostri exhauriente India et merces remittente quae apud nos centiplicato 102 veneant. MM p. ab Alexandria abest oppidum Iuliopolis. inde navigant Nilo Coptum $\overline{\text{CCCIX}}$ p. qui cursus etesiis flantibus peragitur XII diebus. a Copto camelis itur, aquationum ratione mansionibus dispositis: prima appellatur Hydreuma $\overline{\text{XXII}}$; secunda in monte diei itinere; tertia in altero Hydreumate a Copto $\overline{\text{LXXXV}}$; deinde in monte; mox ad Hydreuma Apollinis a Copto $\overline{\text{CLXXXIV}}$; rursus in monte; 103 mox ad Novum Hydreuma a Copto $\overline{\text{CCXXX}}$. est et aliud Hydreuma vetus—Trogodyticum nominatur— ubi praesidium excubat deverticulo duum milium; distat a Novo Hydreumate $\overline{\text{VII}}$. inde Berenice oppidum, ubi portus Rubri maris, a Copto $\overline{\text{CCLVII}}$ p. sed quia maior pars itineris conficitur noctibus propter aestus et stativis dies absumuntur, totum a Copto Berenicen iter duodecimo die peragitur. 104 navigare incipiunt aestate media ante canis ortum aut ab exortu protinus, veniuntque tricesimo circiter die Ocelim Arabiae aut Canen turiferae regionis.

[1] *V.l.* ⌐DL⌐.

---

[a] Say £425,000, taking *mille sestertium* as £8 10s. gold.
[b] *I.e.* 'Watering Place.'
[c] Near Ras Benas.
[d] Hisn Ghorab.

And it will not be amiss to set out the whole of *Sea-route from Egypt to India* the voyage from Egypt, now that reliable knowledge of it is for the first time accessible. It is an important subject, in view of the fact that in no year does India absorb less than fifty million sesterces *a* of our empire's wealth, sending back merchandise to be sold with us at a hundred times its prime cost. Two miles from Alexandria is the town of Juliopolis. The voyage up the Nile from there to Keft is 309 miles, and takes 12 days when the midsummer trade-winds are blowing. From Keft the journey is made with camels, stations being placed at intervals for the purpose of watering; the first, a stage of 22 miles, is called Hydreuma *b*; the second is in the mountains, a day's journey on; the third at a second place named Hydreuma, 85 miles from Keft; the next is in the mountains; next we come to Apollo's Hydreuma, 184 miles from Keft; again a station in the mountains; then we get to New Hydreuma, 230 miles from Keft. There is also another old Hydreuma known by the name of Trogodyticum, where a guard is stationed on outpost duty at a caravanserai accommodating two thousand travellers; it is seven miles from New Hydreuma. Then comes the town of Berenice,*c* where there is a harbour on the Red Sea, 257 miles from Keft. But as the greater part of the journey is done by night because of the heat and the days are spent at stations, the whole journey from Keft to Berenice takes twelve days. Travelling by sea begins at midsummer before the dogstar rises or immediately after its rising, and it takes about thirty days to reach the Arabian port of Cella or Cane *d* in the frankincense-producing district. There is also a

417

est et tertius portus qui vocatur Muza, quem Indica
navigatio non petit, nec nisi turis odorumque Ara-
bicorum mercatores. intus oppidum, regia eius,
appellatur Sapphar, aliudque Save. Indos autem
petentibus utilissimum est ab Oceli egredi; inde
vento Hippalo navigant diebus XL ad primum emporium Indiae Muzirim, non expetendum propter vicinos
piratas qui optinent locum nomine Nitrias, neque est
abundans mercibus; praeterea longe a terra abest
navium statio, lintribusque adferuntur onera et
egeruntur. regnabat ibi, cum proderem haec,
105 Caelobothras. alius utilior portus gentis Neacyndon,
qui vocatur Becare; ibi regnabat Pandion, longe ab
emporio in[1] mediterraneo distante oppido quod
vocatur Modura; regio autem ex qua piper monoxylis
lintribus Becaren convehunt vocatur Cottonara.
quae omnia gentium portuumve aut oppidorum
nomina apud neminem priorum reperiuntur, quo
106 apparet mutari locorum status. ex India renavigant
mense Aegyptio Tybi incipiente, nostro Decembri,
aut utique Mechiris Aegyptii intra diem sextum,
quod fit intra idus Ianuarias nostras; ita evenit ut
eodem anno remeent. navigant autem ex India
vento Volturno et, cum intravere Rubrum Mare,
Africo vel Austro.

[1] *V.l. om.* in.

---

[a] See above, § 100.
[b] Probably Pigeon Island.
[c] In fact, it was with the N.E. monsoon.

third port named Mokha, which is not called at on the voyage to India, and is only used by merchants trading in frankincense and Arabian perfumes. Inland there is a town, the residence of the king of the district, called Sapphar, and another called Save. But the most advantageous way of sailing to India is to set out from Cella; from that port it is a 40 days' voyage, if the Hippalus [a] is blowing, to the first trading-station in India, Cranganore—not a desirable port of call, on account of the neighbouring pirates, who occupy a place called Nitriae,[b] nor is it specially rich in articles of merchandise; and furthermore the roadstead for shipping is a long way from the land, and cargoes have to be brought in and carried out in boats. The king of Muziris, at the date of publication, was Caelobothras. There is another more serviceable port, belonging to the Neacyndi tribe, called Porakad; this is where king Pandion reigned, his capital being a town in the interior a long way from the port, called Madura; while the district from which pepper is conveyed to Becare in canoes made of hollowed tree-trunks is called Cottonara. But all these names of tribes and ports or towns are to be found in none of the previous writers, which seems to show that the local conditions of the places are changing. Travellers set sail from India on the return voyage at the beginning of the Egyptian month Tybis, which is our December, or at all events before the sixth day of the Egyptian Mechir, which works out at before January 13 in our calendar—so making it possible to return home in the same year. They set sail from India with a southeast wind,[c] and after entering the Red Sea, continue the voyage with a south-west or south wind.

Nunc revertemur ad propositum.

107 XXVII. Carmaniae oram patere duodeciens quinquaginta milia passuum Nearchus scripsit, ab initio
eius ad flumen Sabim c̄ p.; inde vineas coli et arva
ad flumen Ananim xxv milium spatio. regio vocatur
Armysia; oppida Carmaniae Zetis et Alexandria.

XXVIII. Inrumpit deinde et in hac parte geminum
mare in [1] terras, quod Rubrum dixere nostri, Graeci
Erythrum a rege Erythra, aut, ut alii, solis repercussu
talem reddi existimantes colorem, alii ab harena
108 terraque, alii tali aquae ipsius natura. sed in duos
dividitur sinus. is qui ab oriente est Persicus
appellatur, $\overline{|xxv|}$ circuitu, ut Eratosthenes tradit.
ex adverso est Arabia, cuius $\overline{|xv|}$ longitudo; rursus
altero ambitur sinu Arabico nominato, oceanum qui
influit Azanium appellant. Persicum introitu v̄
latitudinis alii,[2] alii īv fecerunt; ab eo ad intimum
sinum recto cursu $\overline{|xi|}$ $\overline{|xxv|}$ propemodum constat esse,
109 et situm eius humani capitis effigie. Onesicritus et
Nearchus ab Indo amne in sinum Persicum atque
illinc Babylonem Euphratis paludibus scripserunt
$\overline{|\text{λvii}|}$ esse.

In Carmaniae angulo Chelonophagi, testudinum

---

[1] *V.l. om.* in.   [2] alii *add. Rackham.*

---

[a] *I.e.*, forms two bays in succession, the Red Sea and
the Persian Gulf, both included here under the name of *Rubrum
Mare.*

We will now return to our main subject.

XXVII. Nearchus writes that the length of the coast of Carmania is 1250 miles, and the distance from its beginning to the river Sabis 100 miles; and that from that river to the river Ananis, a space of 25 miles, there are vineyards and arable land. The district is called Armysia; and towns of Carmania are Zetis and Alexandria.

Carmania.

XXVIII. Moreover in this region the sea then makes a double inroad [a] into the land; the name given to it by our countrymen is the Red Sea, while the Greeks call it Erythrum, from King Erythras, or, according to others, in the belief that the water is given a red colour by the reflexion of the sun, while others say that the name comes from the sand and the soil, and others that it is due to the actual water being naturally of such a character. However, this sea is divided into two bays. The one to the east is called the Persian Gulf, and according to the report of Eratosthenes measures 2500 miles round. Opposite is Arabia, with a coastline 1500 miles in length, and on its other side Arabia is encompassed by the second bay, named the Arabian Gulf; the ocean flowing into this is called the Azanian Sea. The width of the Persian Gulf at its entrance some make five and others four miles; the distance in a straight line from the entrance to the innermost part of the Gulf has been ascertained to be nearly 1125 miles, and its outline has been found to be in the likeness of a human head. Onesicritus and Nearchus write that from the river Indus to the Persian Gulf and from there to Babylon by the marshes of the Euphrates is a voyage of 1700 miles.

The Red Sea and Persian Gulf.

In an angle of Carmania are the Turtle-eaters,

superficie casas tegentes, carne vescentes; a flumine
Arabi promunturium ipsum inhabitant, praeter
capita toto corpore hirti coriisque piscium vestiti.
110 ab horum tractu Indiam versus Cascandrus deserta
insula in oceano L̄ p. traditur, iuxtaque eam freto
interfluente Stoidis quaestuosa margaritis. a promunturio Carmanis iunguntur Harmozaei; quidam
interponunt Arbios, C̄C̄C̄C̄X̄X̄Ī p. toto litore. ibi
Portus Macedonum et Arae Alexandri in promun-
111 turio, amnes Siccanas, dein Dratinus et Salsum. ab
eo promunturium Themisteas; insula Aphrodisias
habitatur. inde Persidis initium ad flumen Oratim
quo dividitur ab Elymaide. contra Persidem insulae Psilos, Cassandra, Aracha cum monte praealto
Neptuno sacra. ipsa Persis adversus occasum sita
optinet litore D̄L̄ p., etiam in luxum dives, in Parthorum iam pridem translata nomen.

Horum de imperio nunc in paucis.

112 XXIX. Regna Parthorum duodeviginti sunt omnia;
ita enim dividunt provincias circa duo, ut diximus,
maria, Rubrum a meridie, Hyrcanium a septentrione.
ex his XI quae superiora dicuntur incipiunt a confinio

who roof their houses with the shells and live on the flesh of turtles. These people inhabit the promontory that is reached next after leaving the river Arabis. They are covered all over, except their heads, with shaggy hair, and they wear clothes made of the skins of fishes. After the district belonging to these people, in the direction of India there is said to be an uninhabited island, Cascandrus, 50 miles out at sea, and next to it, with a strait flowing between, Stoidis, with a valuable pearl-fishery. After the promontory the Carmanians are adjoined by the Harmozaei, though some authorities place the Arbii between them, stretching all along the coast for 421 miles. Here are the Port of the Macedonians and the Altars of Alexander situated on a promontory; the rivers are Siccanas and then the Dratinus and the Salsum. After the Salsum is Cape Themisteas, and the inhabited island of Aphrodisias. Here is the beginning of Farsistan, at the river Tab, which separates Farsistan from Elymais. Off the coast of Farsistan lie the islands of Psilos, Cassandra and Aracha, the last with an extremely lofty mountain, and consecrated to Neptune. Farsistan itself occupies 550 miles of coast, facing west. It is wealthy even to the point of luxury. It has long ago changed its name to Parthia.

We will now give a brief account of the Parthian empire.

XXIX. The Parthi possess in all eighteen king- *Parthia.* doms, such being the divisions of their provinces on the coasts of two seas, as we have stated, the Red §41. Sea on the south and the Caspian Sea on the north. Of these provinces the eleven designated the Upper Kingdoms begin at the frontiers of Armenia and the

Armeniae Caspiisque litoribus pertinent ad Scythas,
cum quibus ex aequo degunt. reliqua VII regna
inferiora appellantur. quod ad Parthos attinet,
semper fuit Parthyaea in radicibus montium saepius
113 dictorum qui omnes eas gentes praetexunt. habet
ab ortu Arios, a meridie Carmaniam et Arianos, ab
occasu Pratitas Medos, a septentrione Hyrcanos, undique desertis cincta. ulteriores Parthi Nomades
appellantur. citra deserta ab occasu urbes eorum
quas diximus, Issatis et Calliope, ab oriente aestivo
Pyropum, ab hiberno Maria, in medio Hecatompylos,
Arsace, regio Nisiaea Parthyenes nobilis, ubi
Alexandropolis a conditore.

114   Necessarium est hoc in loco signare et Medorum
situm terrarumque faciem circumagere ad Persicum
mare, quo facilius dein reliqua noscantur. namque
Media ab occasu transversa oblique Parthiae occurrens utraque regna praecludit. habet ergo ipsa ab
ortu Caspios et Parthos, a meridie Sittacenen et
Susianen et Persida, ab occasu Adiabenen, a septen-
115 trione Armeniam. Persae Rubrum mare semper
accoluere, propter quod is sinus Persicus vocatur.
regio ibi maritima Cyropolis,[1] qua vero ipsa subit ad
Medos Climax Megale appellatur, locus arduo montis

---

[1] *Hermolaus e Ptolemaeo*: Cyribo *aut* Ceribobus *et alia.*

shores of the Caspian, and extend to the Scythians, with whom the Parthians live on terms of equality. The remaining seven kingdoms are called the Lower Kingdoms. So far as the Parthi are concerned, there has always been a country named Parthyaea at the foot of the mountain range, already mentioned more than once, which forms the boundary § 41. of all these races. To the east of Parthyaea are the Arii, to the south Carmania and the Ariani, to the west the Pratitae, a Median race, and to the north the Hyrcani; and it is surrounded on all sides by desert. The more remote Parthians are called the Nomads. Short of the desert on the west side are the Parthian cities mentioned above, Issatis and Calliope; north- § 44. east is Pyropum, south-east Maria, and in the middle Hecatompylos, Arsace, and the fine district of Parthyene, Nisiaea, containing the city named Alexandropolis after its founder.

At this point it is necessary also to indicate the *Geography* geographical position of the Medes, and to trace *of Media* the formation of the country round to the Persian *and Parthia.* Sea, in order that the rest of the account that follows may be more easily understood. Media lies crosswise on the west side, meeting Parthia at an angle, and so shutting off both groups of Parthian kingdoms. Consequently it has the Caspian and Parthian people on its east side, Sittacene, Susiane and Farsistan on the south, Adiabene on the west, and Armenia on the north. The Persians have always lived on the shore of the Red Sea, which is the reason why it is called the Persian Gulf. The coastal region there is called Cyropolis, but the Greek name of the place where it runs up towards the Medes is the Great Staircase, from a steep gorge ascending the

ascensu per gradus, introitu angusto, ad Persepolim caput regni dirutam ab Alexandro. praeterea habet in extremis finibus Laodiceam ab Antiocho conditam.

116 inde ad orientem Magi optinent Phrasargida castellum, in quo Cyri sepulchrum; est et horum Ecbatana oppidum translatum ab Dario rege ad montes. inter Parthos et Arianos excurrunt Paraetaceni. his a gentibus et Euphrate inferiora regna includuntur; reliqua dicemus a Mesopotamia excepto mucrone eius Arabumque populis in priore dictis volumine.

117 XXX. Mesopotamia tota Assyriorum fuit, vicatim dispersa praeter Babylona et Ninum. Macedones eam in urbes congregavere propter ubertatem soli. oppida praeter iam dicta habet Seleuciam, Laodiceam, Artemitam; item in Arabum gente qui Orroei vocantur et Mandani Antiochiam quae a praefecto Mesopotamiae Nicanore condita Arabs[1] vocatur.

118 iunguntur his Arabes introrsus Eldamari, supra quos ad Pallacontam flumen Bura oppidum, Salmani et Masei Arabes; Gurdiaeis vero iuncti Azoni, per quos Zerbis fluvius in Tigrim cadit, Azonis Silices montani et Orontes, quorum ad occidentem oppidum Gauga-

---

[1] *Rackham*: Arabis *aut* Arabes.

---

[a] To distinguish it from several other cities of the same name; its site is not known.

mountain by stages, with a narrow entrance, leading to the former capital of the kingdom, Persepolis, which was destroyed by Alexander. Right on the frontier the region also possesses the city of Laodicea, founded by Antiochus. To the east of Laodicea is the fortress of Phrasargis, occupied by the Magi, which contains the tomb of Cyrus; and another place belonging to the Magi is the town of Ecbatana which King Darius transferred to the mountains. Between the Parthi and the Ariani projects the territory of the Paraetaceni. The Lower Kingdoms are enclosed by these races and by the Euphrates; of the remaining kingdoms we shall speak after describing Mesopotamia, with the exception of the point of that country and the Arabian peoples mentioned in the preceding volume. V. 86 ff.

XXX. The whole of Mesopotamia once belonged *Mesopo-*
to the Assyrians, and the population was scattered *tamia.*
in villages, with the exception of Babylon and Nineveh. The Macedonians collected its population into cities, because of the fertility of the soil. Besides the cities already mentioned it has the towns of Seleucia, Laodicea and Artemita; and also, in the territory of the Arabian tribe called the Orroei and Mandani, Antioch, which was founded by Nicanor when Governor of Mesopotamia, and which is called Arabian Antioch.[a] Adjoining these, in the interior, are the Arabian tribe of the Eldamari, above whom on the river Pallaconta is the town of Bura, and the Arabian Salmani and Masei; but adjoining the Gurdiaei are the Azoni, through whose country flows the Zerbis, a tributary of the Tigris, and adjoining the Azoni the mountain tribe of the Silices and the Orontes; west of whom is the town

mela, item Suae in rupibus. supra Silicas Sitrae,
per quos Lycus ex Armenia fertur, ab Sitris ad
hibernum exortum Azochis oppidum, mox in cam-
pestribus oppida Dios Pege, Polytelia, Stratonicea,
119 Anthemus. in vicinia Euphratis Nicephorion, quod
diximus; Alexander iussit condi propter loci oppor-
tunitatem. dicta est et in Zeugmate Apamea;
ex qua orientem petentes excipit oppidum Caphrena
munitum, quondam stadiorum LXX amplitudine et
Satraparum Regia appellatum quo tributa con-
120 ferebantur, nunc in arcem redactum. durant ut
fuere Thebata et ductu Pompei Magni terminus
Romani imperi Oruros, a Zeugmate $\overline{\text{CCL}}$.[1] sunt
qui tradunt Euphraten Gobaris praefecti opere
diductum esse ubi [2] diximus findi, ne praecipiti cursu
Babyloniam infestaret, ab Assyriis vero universis
appellatum Narmalchan, quod significat regium
flumen. qua dirivatur oppidum fuit Agranis e
maximis quod diruere Persae.

121 Babylon Chaldaicarum gentium caput diu summam
claritatem inter urbes obtinuit in toto orbe, propter
quam reliqua pars Mesopotamiae Assyriaeque
Babylonia appellata est, $\overline{\text{LX}}$ p. amplexa II[3] muris

---

[1] $\overline{\text{L}}$.cc *Mueller.* [2] *Mueller :* diductum ubi esse.
[3] II *add. Mayhoff.*

of Gaugamela, and also Suae on a cliff. Above the Silices are the Sitrae, through whom flows the Lycus from its source in Armenia, and south-east of the Sitrae the town of Azochis, and then in level country the towns of Zeus's Spring, Polytelia, Stratonicea and Anthemus. In the neighbourhood of the Euphrates is Nicephorion, mentioned above; it was founded ^{V. 86.} by order of Alexander because of the convenience of the site. We have also mentioned Apamea opposite ^{V. 86.} Bridgetown; travelling eastward from which one comes to the fortified town of Caphrena, which formerly measured $8\frac{3}{4}$ miles in extent and was called the Court of the Satraps, being a centre for the collection of tribute, but which has now been reduced to a fortress. Thebata remains in the same condition as it was formerly, and so does the place which marked the limit of the Roman Empire under the leadership of Pompey, Oruros, 250 miles from Bridgetown. Some writers record that the Euphrates was diverted into an artificial channel by the governor Gobares at the place where we have stated that it divides, in ^{V. 89.} order to prevent the violence of its current from threatening damage to the district of Babylonia; and that its name among the whole of the Assyrians is Narmalchas, which means the Royal River. At the point where the channel divides there was once a very large town named Agranis, which was destroyed by the Persians.

Babylon, which is the capital of the Chaldaean *Babylon.* races, long held an outstanding celebrity among the cities in the whole of the world, and in consequence of this the remaining part of Mesopotamia and Assyria has received the name of Babylonia. It has two walls with a circuit of 60 miles, each wall being

ducenos pedes altis, quinquagenos latis, in singulos pedes ternis digitis mensura ampliore quam nostra, interfluo Euphrate, mirabili opere utrobique. durat adhuc ibi Iovis Beli templum—inventor hic fuit

122 sideralis scientiae: cetero ad solitudinem rediit exhausta vicinitate Seleuciae ob id conditae a Nicatore intra xc lapidem in confluente Euphratis fossa perducti atque Tigris, quae tamen Babylonia cognominatur, libera hodie ac sui iuris Macedonumque moris. ferunt ei plebis urbanae $\overline{\text{DC}}$ esse, situm vero moenium aquilae pandentis alas, agrum totius orientis fertilissimum. invicem ad hanc exhauriendam Ctesiphontem iuxta tertium ab ea lapidem in Chalonitide condidere Parthi, quod nunc caput est regnorum. et postquam nihil proficiebatur, nuper Vologesus rex aliud oppidum Vologesocertam in

123 vicino condidit. sunt etiamnum in Mesopotamia oppida: Hippareni,[1] Chaldaeorum doctrina [2] et hoc sicut Babylon, iuxta fluvium qui cadit in Narragam unde civitati nomen (muros Hipparenorum Persae diruere); Orcheni quoque, tertia Chaldaeorum doctrina, in eodem situ locantur ad meridiem versi; ab his Notitae et Orothophanitae et Gnesiochartae.

[1] *Rackham*: Hipparenum.
[2] doctrina clarum *edd. vet.*

[a] The name *Baal* or *Bel* is interpreted by Eusebius as meaning 'heaven'.
[b] With this use of *doctrina* cf. *studium generale,* 'university'.

200 ft. high and 50 ft. wide (the Assyrian foot measures 3 inches more than ours). The Euphrates flows through the city, with marvellous embankments on either side. The temple of Jupiter Belus [a] in Babylon is still standing—Belus was the discoverer of the science of astronomy; but in all other respects the place has gone back to a desert, having been drained of its population by the proximity of Seleucia, founded for that purpose by Nicator not quite 90 miles away, at the point where the canalised Euphrates joins the Tigris. However, Seleucia is still described as being in the territory of Babylon, although at the present day it is a free and independent city and retains the Macedonian manners. It is said that the population of the city numbers 600,000; that the plan of the walls resembles the shape of an eagle spreading its wings; and that its territory is the most fertile in the whole of the east. For the purpose of drawing away the population of Seleucia in its turn, the Parthians founded Ctesiphon, which is about three miles from Seleucia in the Chalonitis district, and is now the capital of the kingdoms of Parthia. And after it was found that the intended purpose was not being achieved, another town was recently founded in the neighbourhood by King Vologesus, named Vologesocerta. There are in addition the following towns in Mesopotamia: Hippareni—this also a school [b] of Chaldaean learning like Babylon—situated on a tributary of the river Narraga, from which the city-state takes its name (the walls of Hippareni were demolished by the Persians); also Orcheni, a third seat [b] of Chaldaean learning, is situated in the same neighbourhood towards the south; and next Notitae and Orothophanitae and Gnesiochartae.

124 Euphrate navigari Babylonem e Persico mari
CCCCXII p. tradunt Nearchus et Onesicritus, qui vero
postea scripsere ad Seleuciam CCCCXL, Iuba a Baby-
lone Characen CLXXV D. fluere aliqui ultra Babylona
continuo alveo, priusquam distrahatur ad rigua,
LXXXVII, universo autem cursu |XII| p. inconstantiam
mensurae diversitas auctorum facit, cum Persae
quoque schoenos et parasangas alii alia mensura
125 determinent. ubi desiit alveo munire, ad confinium
Characis accedente tractu, statim infestant Attali
latrones, Arabum gens, ultra quos Scenitae. ambitu
vero Euphratis Nomades Arabiae usque ad deserta
Syriae, unde in meridiem flecti eum diximus, soli-
126 tudines Palmyrenas relinquentem. Seleucia abest
a capite Mesopotamiae Euphrate [1] navigantibus
|XI| XXV p., a Mari Rubro, si Tigri navigetur, CCCXX,
a Zeugmate DCCXXIV. Zeugma abest Seleucia Syriae
ad nostrum litus CLXXV. haec est ibi latitudo terrarum inter duo maria, Parthici vero regni DCCCCXVIII.

XXXI. Est etiamnum oppidum Mesopotamiae in
ripa Tigris circa confluentes, quod vocant Digbam.

---

[1] *Mayhoff*: Euphraten.

---

[a] See p. 266, n. *a*. The *parasang* was 30 stades, say 3¾
miles.
[b] Including the Persian Gulf, p. 420, n. *a*.

Nearchus and Onesicritus report that the Euphrates *The*
is navigable from the Persian Sea to Babylon, a *Euphrates.*
distance of 412 miles; but subsequent writers say
it is navigable up to Seleucia, 440 miles, and Juba
from Babylon as far as Charax, 175½ miles. Some
report that it continues to flow in a single channel
for a distance of 87 miles beyond Babylon before it is
diverted into irrigation-channels, and that its entire
course is 1200 miles long. This discrepancy of
measurement is due to the variety of authors that
have dealt with the matter, as even among the
Persians different writers give different measurements
for the length of the *schoenus* ᵃ and the *parasang*.
Where it ceases to afford protection by its channel,
as it does when its course approaches the boundary
of Charax, it immediately begins to be infested by
the Attali, an Arabian tribe of brigands, beyond
whom are the Scenitae. But the winding course
of the Euphrates is occupied by the Nomads of
Arabia right on to the desert of Syria, where, as we
have stated, the river makes a bend to the south, v. 87.
quitting the uninhabited districts of Palmyra. The
distance of Seleucia from the beginning of Mesopotamia is a voyage by the Euphrates of 1125 miles; its
distance from the Red Sea, if the voyage by made by
the Tigris, is 320 miles, and from Bridgetown 724
miles. Bridgetown is 175 miles from Seleucia on
the Mediterranean coast of Syria. This gives the
breadth of the country lying between the Mediterranean and the Red Sea.ᵇ The extent of the kingdom
of Parthia is 918 miles.

XXXI. Moreover there is a town belonging to *The Tigris.*
Mesopotamia on the bank of the Tigris near its
confluence with the Euphrates, the name of which

433

127 sed et de Tigri ipso dixisse conveniat. oritur in
regione Armeniae Maioris fonte conspicuo in planitie;
loco nomen Elegosini [1] est, ipsi qua tardior fluit
Diglito, unde concitatur, a celeritate Tigris incipit
vocari—ita appellant Medi sagittam. influit in
lacum Aretissam, omnia inlata pondera sustinentem
et nitrum nebulis exhalantem. unum genus ei
piscium est, idque transcurrentis non miscetur alveo
sicut neque e Tigri pisces in lacum transnatant;
128 fertur autem et cursu et colore dissimilis, trans-
vectusque occurrente Tauro monte in specum mergitur subterque lapsus a latere altero eius erumpit.
locus vocatur Zoaranda; eundem esse manifestum
est quod demersa perfert. alterum deinde transit
lacum qui Thespites appellatur rursusque in cuniculos
mergitur et post XXII p. circa Nymphaeum redditur.
tam vicinum Arsaniae fluere eum in regione Archene
Claudius Caesar auctor est, ut cum intumuere
confluant nec tamen misceantur, leviorque Arsanias
innatet MMMM ferme spatio, mox divisus in Euphraten

¹ *Rackham*: Elegosine.

is Digba. But some statement about the Tigris itself may also be suitable here. The source of the Tigris is in a region of Greater Armenia, and is clearly visible, being on level ground; the name of the place is Elegosine, and the stream itself in its comparatively sluggish part is named Diglitus, but where its flow accelerates, it begins to be called the Tigris, owing to its swiftness—*tigris* is the Persian word for an arrow. It flows into Lake Aretissa, heavy objects thrown into which always float on the surface, and which gives off nitrous vapours. The lake contains a single species of fish, which never enters the current of the Tigris flowing through the lake, as likewise the fish of the river do not swim out of its stream into the water of the lake; but the river travels on in a distinct course and with a different colour, and when after traversing the lake it comes against Mount Taurus, it plunges into a cave, glides underground, and bursts out again on the other side of the mountain. The name of the place where it emerges is Zoaranda; and the identity of the stream is proved by the fact that objects thrown into it are carried through the tunnel. Then it crosses a second lake called Thespites, and again burrows into underground passages, re-emerging 22 miles further on in the neighbourhood of Nymphaeum. According to Claudius Caesar, the course of the Tigris in the Archene district is so close to that of the Arsanias that when they are in flood they flow together, although without intermingling their waters; that of the Arsanias being of less specific gravity floats on the surface for a distance of nearly four miles, after which the two rivers separate, and the Arsanias discharges into the

129 mergatur. Tigris autem ex Armenia acceptis
fluminibus claris Parthenia ac Nicephorione Arabas
Orroeos Adiabenosque disterminans et quam diximus Mesopotamiam faciens, lustratis montibus
Gurdiaeorum circa Apameam Mesenes oppidum,
citra Seleuciam Babyloniam $\overline{\text{cxxv}}$ p. divisus in alveos
duos, altero meridiem ac Seleuciam petit Mesenen
perfundens, altero ad septentrionem flexus eiusdem
gentis tergo campos Cauchas secat, ubi remeavere
130 aquae, Pasitigris appellatus. postea recipit ex
Media Choaspen, atque, ut diximus, inter Seleuciam
et Ctesiphontem vectus in Lacus Chaldaicos se fundit
eosque $\overline{\text{LXII}}$ p. amplitudine implet. mox vasto alveo
profusus dextra Characis oppidi infertur mari Persico
$\overline{\text{x}}$ p. ore. inter duorum amnium ostia $\overline{\text{xxv}}$ p. fuere,
ut alii tradunt, $\overline{\text{vii}}$,[1] utroque navigabili; sed longo
tempore Euphraten praeclusere Orcheni et [2] accolae
agros rigantes, nec nisi per Tigrim defertur in mare.
131 Proxima Tigri regio Parapotamia appellatur. in
ea dictum est de Mesene—oppidum eius Dabitha;
iungitur Chalonitis cum Ctesiphonte, non palmetis
modo verum et olea pomisque arbusta[3]. ad eam
pervenit Zagrus mons ex Armenia inter Medos

[1] xvii ? *Rackham.*
[2] ut *aut del.* et *edd.,* et ⟨alii⟩ ? *Rackham.*
[3] *Detlefsen :* arbustis.

---

[a] It seems more probable that the alternative figure was 17.

Euphrates. The Tigris however after receiving as
tributaries from Armenia those notable rivers the
Parthenias and Nicephorion, makes a frontier between
the Arab tribes of the Orroei and Adiabeni and forms
the region of Mesopotamia mentioned above; it §25.
then traverses the mountains of the Gurdiaei, flowing
round Apamea, a town belonging to Mesene, and
125 miles short of Babylonian Seleucia splits into
two channels, one of which flows south and reaches
Seleucia, watering Mesene on the way, while the
other bends northward and passing behind the same
people cuts through the plains of Cauchae; when
the two streams have reunited, the river is called
Pasitigris. Afterwards it is joined by the Kerkhah
from Media, and, as we have said, after flowing §122.
between Seleucia and Ctesiphon empties itself into
the Chaldaean Lakes, and broadens them out to a
width of 62 miles. Then it flows out of the Lakes
in a vast channel and passing on the right-hand side
of the town of Charax discharges into the Persian
Sea, the mouth of the river being 10 miles wide.
The mouths of the two rivers used to be 25 miles
apart, or as others record 7[a] miles, and both were
navigable; but a long time ago the Euphrates was
dammed by the Orcheni and other neighbouring
tribes in order to irrigate their lands, and its water
is only discharged into the sea by way of the Tigris.

The country adjacent to the Tigris is called Para- *The Tigris*
potamia. It contains the district of Mesene, men- *region.*
tioned above; a town in this is Dabitha, and adjoining §129.
it is Chalonitis, with the town of Ctesiphon, a wooded
district containing not only palm groves but also
olives and orchards. Mount Zagrus extends as far
as Chalonitis from Armenia, coming between the

Adiabenosque veniens supra Paraetacenen et Persida.
Chalonitis abest a Perside $\overline{\text{CCCLXXX}}$ p.; tantum a
Caspio mari et a Syria abesse conpendio itineris
132 aliqui tradunt. inter has gentes atque Mesenen
Sittacene est, eadem Arbelitis et Palaestine dicta.
oppidum eius Sittace Graecorum, ab ortu et Sabdata,
ab occasu autem Antiochia inter duo flumina Tigrim
et Tornadotum, item Apamea, cui nomen Antiochus
matris suae inposuit; Tigri[1] circumfunditur haec,
133 dividitur Archoo. infra est Susiane, in qua vetus
regia Persarum Susa a Dario Hystaspis filio condita.
abest ab Seleucia Babylonia $\overline{\text{CCCCL}}$ p., tantundem ab
Ecbatanis Medorum per montem Carbantum. in
septentrionali Tigris alveo oppidum est Barbitace;
abest a Susis $\overline{\text{CXXXV}}$ p. ibi mortalium solis[2] aurum
in odio; contrahunt id defodiuntque, ne cui sit in
usu. Susianis ad orientem versus iunguntur Oxii
latrones et Mizaeorum XL populi liberae feritatis.
134 supra eos parent Parthis Mardi et Saitae ii qui
praetenduntur supra Elymaida, quam Persidi in ora
iunximus. Susa a Persico mari absunt $\overline{\text{CCL}}$ p. qua
subiit ad eam classis Alexandri Pasitigri, vicus ad
lacum Chaldaicum vocatur Aple, unde Susa navi-
gatione $\overline{\text{LXII}}$ D p. absunt. Susianis ab oriente proximi sunt Cossiaei, supra Cossiaeos ad septentionem

---

[1] *Gronovius*: Tigris.
[2] *Pintianus*: soli (soli auri miro odio contrahunt *Mayhoff*).

Medes and the Adiabeni above Paraetacene and
Farsistan. The distance of Chalonitis from Farsistan
is 380 miles, and some persons say that by the shortest
route it is the same distance from the Caspian Sea
and from Syria. Between these races and Mesene
is Sittacene, which is also called Arbelitis and
Palaestine. Its town of Sittace is of Greek origin,
and also to the east of this is Sabdata and to the
west Antiochia, which lies between the two rivers,
Tigris and Tornadotus, and also Apamea, which
Antiochus named after his mother; this town is
surrounded by the Tigris, and the Archous intersects
it. Below is Susiane, in which is situated Susa, the
ancient capital of the Persian monarchy, founded by
Darius son of Hystaspes. Babylonia is 450 miles
from Seleucia, and the same distance from Ecbatana
of the Medes, by way of Mount Carbantus. On the
northern channel of the Tigris is the town of Barbitace,
which is 135 miles from Susa. Here are the only
people among mankind who have a hatred for gold,
which they collect together and bury, to prevent anyone from using it. Adjoining the Susiani on the east
are the brigand Oxii and the forty independent and
savage tribes of the Mizaei. Above these and subject
to the Parthians are the Mardi and Saitae stretching
above Elymais, which we described as adjacent to §111.
Farsistan on the coast. The distance of Susa from
the Persian Gulf is 250 miles. Near where the fleet
of Alexander came up the Pasitigris to the city of
Susa is a village on the Chaldaic lake called Aple,
the distance of which from Susa is a voyage of 62½
miles. The nearest people to the Susiani on the
east side are the Cossiaei, and beyond the Cossiaei
to the north is Massabatene, lying below Mount

Massabatene sub monte Cambalido, qui est Caucasi
ramus, inde mollissimo transitu in Bactros.

135 Susianen ab Elymaide disterminat amnis Eulaeus
ortus in Medis modicoque spatio cuniculo conditus
ac rursus exortus et per Massabatenen lapsus. cir-
cumit arcem Susorum ac Dianae templum augustissi-
mum illis gentibus, et ipse in magna caerimonia,
siquidem reges non ex alio bibunt et ob id in longinqua
portant. recipit amnes Hedyphon praeter Asylum
Persarum venientem, Adunam ex Susianis. oppi-
dum iuxta eum Magoa, a Charace $\overline{xv}$ p.; quidam hoc
in extrema Susiane ponunt solitudinibus proximum.

136 infra Eulaeum Elymais est in ora iuncta Persidi, a
flumine Orati ad Characem $\overline{ccxl}$ p.; oppida eius
Seleucia et Sostrate adposita monti Chasiro. oram
quae praeiacet Minorum Syrtium vice diximus
inaccessam coeno, plurimum limi deferentibus Brixa
et Ortacia amnibus, madente et ipsa Elymaide in
tantum ut nullus sit nisi circuitu eius ad Persidem
aditus. infestatur et serpentibus quos flumina
deportant. pars eius maxume invia Characene
vocatur ab oppido Arabiae claudente regna ea;

Cambalidus, which is a spur of the Caucasus range; from this point is the easiest route across to the country of the Bactri.

The territory of Susa is separated from Elymais *Susa.* by the river Karún, which rises in the country of the Medes, and after running for a moderate distance underground, comes to the surface again and flows through Massabatene. It passes round the citadel of Susa and the temple of Diana, which is regarded with the greatest reverence by the races in those parts; and the river itself is held in great veneration, inasmuch as the kings drink water drawn from it only, and consequently have it conveyed to places a long distance away. Tributaries of the Karún are the Hedyphos, which flows past the Persian town of Asylum, and the Aduna coming from the territory of the Susiani. On the Karún lies the town of Magoa, 15 miles from Charax—though some people locate Magoa at the extreme edge of the territory of Susa, close to the desert. Below the Karún on the coast is Elymais, which marches with Farsistan and extends from the river Oratis to the Charax, a distance of 240 miles; its towns are Seleucia and Sostrate, situated on the flank of Mount Chasirus. The coast lying in front, as we have stated above, is rendered inaccessible § 99. by mud, like the Lesser Syrtes, as the rivers Brixa and Ortacia bring down a quantity of sediment, and the Elymais district is itself so marshy that it is only possible to reach Farsistan by making a long détour round it. It is also infested with snakes carried down by the streams. A particularly inaccessible part of it is called Characene, from Charax, a town of Arabia that marks the frontier of these kingdoms; about

de quo dicemus exposita prius M. Agrippae sententia.
137 namque is Mediam et Parthiam et Persidem ab
oriente Indo, ab occidente Tigri, a septentrione
Tauro, Caucaso, a meridie Rubro mari terminatas
patere in longitudinem $\overline{|XIII|}$ $\overline{XX}$ p., in latitudinem
$\overline{DCCCXL}$ prodidit, praeterea per se Mesopotamiam
ab oriente Tigri, ab occasu Euphrate, a septentrione
Tauro, a meridie mari Persico inclusam, longitudine
$\overline{DCCC}$ p., latitudine $\overline{CCCLX}$.

138 Charax oppidum Persici sinus intimum, a quo
Arabia Eudaemon cognominata excurrit, habitatur
in colle manu facto inter confluentes dextra Tigrim,
laeva Eulaeum, $\overline{II}$ [1] p. laxitate. conditum est primum
ab Alexandro Magno colonis ex urbe regia Durine
quae tum interiit deductis militumque [2] inutilibus
ibi relictis; Alexandriam appellari iusserat, pagum-
que Pellaeum a patria sua quem proprie Macedo-
139 num fecerat. flumina id oppidum expugnavere.
postea restituit Antiochus quintus regum et suo
nomine appellavit; iterum quoque infestatum Spaosines Sagdodonaci filius, rex finitimorum Arabum,
quem Iuba satrapen Antiochi fuisse falso tradit,
oppositis molibus restituit nomenque suum dedit

---

[1] $\overline{III}$ *aut* $\overline{VI}$ *edd.*   [2] *V.l. om.* que.

---

[a] The figure should perhaps be emended to 3 or even 6.
[b] Or perhaps 'these settlers being invalided soldiers who
had been left at Durine'.
[c] *I.e.* Charax Spaosinou.

this town we will now speak, after first stating the opinion of Marcus Agrippa. According to his account the countries of Media, Parthia and Farsistan are bounded on the east by the Indus, on the west by the Tigris, on the north by the Taurus and Caucasus mountains, and on the south by the Red Sea, and cover an area 1320 miles in length and 840 miles in breadth; he adds that the area of Mesopotamia by itself, bounded by the Tigris on the east, the Euphrates on the west, Mount Taurus on the north and the Persian Sea on the south, is 800 miles in length by 360 miles in breadth.

The town of Charax is situated in the innermost *Charax* recess of the Persian Gulf, from which projects the country called Arabia Felix. It stands on an artificial elevation between the Tigris on the right and the Karún on the left, at the point where these two rivers unite, and the site measures two [a] miles in breadth. The original town was founded by Alexander the Great with settlers brought from the royal city of Durine, which was then destroyed, and with [b] the invalided soldiers from his army who were left there. He had given orders that it was to be called Alexandria, and a borough which he had assigned specially to the Macedonians was to be named Pellaeum, after the place where he was born. The original town was destroyed by the rivers, but it was afterwards restored by Antiochus, the fifth king of Syria, who gave it his own name; and when it had been again damaged it was restored and named after himself [c] by Spaosines son of Sagdodonacus, king of the neighbouring Arabs, who is wrongly stated by Juba to have been a satrap of Antiochus; he constructed embankments for the protection of

443

emunito situ iuxta in longitudinem $\overline{\text{vi}}$ p., in latitudinem paulo minus. primo afuit a litore stadios x et maritimum etiam ipsa portum habuit, Iuba
140 vero prodente $\overline{\text{l}}$ p.; nunc abesse a litore $\overline{\text{cxx}}$ legati Arabum nostrique negotiatores qui inde venere adfirmant. nec ulla in parte plus aut celerius profecere terrae fluminibus invectae; magis illud [1] mirum est, aestu longe ultra id accedente non repercussas.

141 Hoc in loco genitum esse Dionysium terrarum orbis situs recentissimum auctorem, quem ad commentanda omnia in orientem praemiserit divus Augustus ituro in Armeniam ad Parthicas Arabicasque res maiore filio, non me praeteriit, nec sum oblitus sui quemque situs diligentissimum auctorem visum nobis introitu operis; in hac tamen parte arma Romana sequi placet nobis Iubamque regem ad eundem Gaium Caesarem scriptis voluminibus de eadem expeditione Arabica.

142 XXXII. Arabia, gentium nulli postferenda amplitudine, longissime a monte Amano e regione Ciliciae Commagenesque descendit, ut diximus, multis gentibus eorum deductis illo a Tigrane Magno, sponte vero ad mare nostrum litusque Aegyptium,

---

[1] illud *Rackham*: id.

---

[a] The emperor's adopted son, his grandson Gaius.

the town, and raised the level of the adjacent ground over a space of six miles in length and a little less in breadth. It was originally at a distance of 1¼ miles from the coast, and had a harbour of its own, but when Juba published his work it was 50 miles inland; its present distance from the coast is stated by Arab envoys and our own traders who have come from the place to be 120 miles. There is no part of the world where earth carried down by rivers has encroached on the sea further or more rapidly; and what is more surprising is that the deposits have not been driven back by the tide, as it approaches far beyond this point.

It has not escaped my notice that Charax was the birthplace of Dionysius, the most recent writer dealing with the geography of the world, who was sent in advance to the East by his late majesty Augustus to write a full account of it when the emperor's elder son [a] was about to proceed to Armenia to take command against the Parthians and Arabians; nor have I forgotten the view stated at the III. 2. beginning of my work that each author appears to be most accurate in describing his own country; in this section however my intention is to be guided by the Roman armies and by King Juba, in his volumes dedicated to the above-mentioned Gaius Caesar describing the same expedition to Arabia.

XXXII. In regard to the extent of its terri- *Arabia.* tory Arabia is inferior to no race in the world; its longest dimension is, as we have said, the slope V. 85. down from Mount Amanus in the direction of Cilicia and Commagene, many of the Arabian races having been brought to that country by Tigranes the Great, while others have migrated of their own accord to the Mediterranean and the Egyptian coast,

ut docuimus, nec non in media Syriae ad Libanum
montem penetrantibus Nubeis, quibus iunguntur
143 Ramisi, dein Teranei, dein Patami. ipsa vero
paeninsula Arabia inter duo maria Rubrum Persi-
cumque procurrens, quodam naturae artificio ad
similitudinem atque magnitudinem Italiae mari
circumfusa, in eandem etiam caeli partem nulla
differentia spectat, haec quoque in illo situ felix.
populos eius a nostro mari usque ad Palmyrenas[1]
solitudines diximus, reliqua nunc inde peragemus.

Nomadas infestatoresque Chaldaeorum Scenitae,
ut diximus, cludunt, et ipsi vagi, sed a tabernaculis
144 cognominati quae ciliciis metantur ubi libuit. deinde
Nabataei oppidum incolunt Petram nomine in con-
valle, paulo minus $\overline{\text{II}}$ p. amplitudinis, circumdatum
montibus inaccessis, amne interfluente. abest ab
Gaza oppido litoris nostri $\overline{\text{DC}}$, a sinu Persico $\overline{\text{DCXXXV}}$.[2]
huc convenit utrumque bivium, eorum qui ex Syria
Palmyram petiere et eorum qui a Gaza venerunt.
145 a Petra incoluere Omani ad Characen usque oppidis
quondam claris ab Samiramide conditis Abaesamide
et Soractia; nunc sunt solitudines. deinde est
oppidum quod Characenorum regi paret in Pasitigris
ripa, Forat nomine, in quod a Petra conveniunt,
Characenque inde $\overline{\text{XII}}$ p. secundo aestu navigant.

[1] *Edd*. Palmyrenae, -rene (*an* Palmyrenes ? *Mayhoff*).
[2] DCXXXV (*vel* DCCXXXV) *Warmington*: CXXXV.

[a] Perhaps we should read 735; the MSS. give 135.

as we have explained, and also the Nubei penetrating v. 65.
to the middle of Syria as far as Mount Lebanon
adjoining whom are the Ramisi and then the Teranei
and then the Patami. Arabia itself however is a
peninsula projecting between two seas, the Red
Sea and the Persian Gulf, some device of nature
having surrounded it by sea with a conformation
and an area resembling Italy, and also with exactly
the same orientation, so that it also has the advantage
of that geographical position. We have stated the
peoples that inhabit it from the Mediterranean to
the deserts of Palmyra, and we will now recount
the remainder of them from that point onward.

Bordering on the Nomads and the tribes that
harry the territories of the Chaldaeans are, as we
have said, the Scenitae, themselves also a wandering v. 65, 86.
people, but taking their name from their tents made VI. 125.
of goat's-hair cloth, which they pitch wherever they
fancy. Next are the Nabataeans inhabiting a town
named Petra; it lies in a deep valley a little less
than two miles wide, and is surrounded by inaccessible mountains with a river flowing between
them. Its distance from the town of Gaza on the
Mediterranean coast is 600 miles, and from the
Persian Gulf 635 miles.ᵃ At Petra two roads meet,
one leading from Syria to Palmyra, and the other
coming from Gaza. After Petra the country as far
as Charax was inhabited by the Omani, with the once
famous towns of Abaesamis and Soractia, founded
by Samiramis; but now it is a desert. Then there
is a town on the bank of the Pasitigris named Forat,
subject to the king of the Characeni; this is resorted
to by people from Petra, who make the journey
from there to Charax, a distance of 12 miles by

e Parthico autem regno navigantibus vicus Teredon infra confluentem Euphratis et Tigris; laeva fluminis
146 Chaldaei optinent, dextra nomades Scenitae. quidam et alia duo oppida longis intervallis Tigri praenavigari tradunt, Barbatiam, mox Dumatham, quod abesse a Petra dierum x navigatione. nostri negotiatores dicunt Characenorum regi parere et Apameam, sitam ubi restagnatio Euphratis cum Tigri confluat, itaque molientes incursionem Parthos operibus obiectis inundatione arceri.

147 Nunc a Charace dicemus oram Epiphani primum exquisitam. locus ubi Euphratis ostium fuit, flumen salsum, promunturium Caldone, voragini similius quam mari aestuarium[1] per L̄ orae,[2] flumen Achenum, deserta c̄ p. usque ad insulam Icarum,[3] sinus Capeus quem accolunt Gaulopes et Gattaei, sinus Gerraicus, oppidum Gerra v̄ p. amplitudine; turres habet ex
148 salis quadratis molibus. a litore L̄ regio Attene; ex adverso Tyros insula totidem milibus a litore, plurimis margaritis celeberrima cum oppido eiusdem nominis, iuxtaque altera minor a promunturio eius XĪI D p. ultra magnas aspici insulas tradunt ad quas

---

[1] aestuarium *add. Mayhoff*.　　　[2] *V.l.* ore.
[3] *Hermolaus*: Barum.

• Bahrein.

water, using the tide. But those travelling by water
from the kingdom of Parthia come to the village
of Teredon below the confluence of the Euphrates
and the Tigris; the left bank of the river is occupied
by the Chaldaeans and the right bank by the Scenitae
tribe of nomads. Some report that two other towns
at long distances apart are also passed on the voyage
down the Tigris, Barbatia and then Dumatha, the
latter said to be ten days' voyage from Petra. Our
merchants say that the king of the Characeni also
rules over Apamea, a town situated at the confluence of the overflow of the Euphrates with the
Tigris; and that consequently when the Parthians
threaten an invasion they are prevented by the
construction of dams across the river, which cause
the country to be flooded.

We will now describe the coast from Charax *The Persian*
onward, which was first explored for King Epiphanes. *Gulf—*
There is the place where the mouth of the Euphrates *Arabian side.*
formerly was, a salt-water stream; Cape Caldone;
an estuary more resembling a whirlpool than open
sea, stretching 50 miles along the coast; the river
Achenum; 100 miles of desert, extending as far as
Icarus Island; Capeus Bay, on which dwell the
Gaulopes and the Gattaei; the Bay of Gerra and the
town of that name, which measures five miles round
and has towers made of squared blocks of salt.
Fifty miles inland is the Attene district; and opposite
to it and the same number of miles distant from the
coast is the island of Tyros,[a] extremely famous for
its numerous pearls, with a town of the same name,
and next another smaller island 12½ miles away
from the cape of Tyros. It is reported that beyond
Tyros some large islands are in view which have

non sit perventum, huius ambitum $\overline{\text{CXII}}$ D p., a Perside
longius abesse, adiri uno alveo angusto. insula
Ascliae, gentes Nochaeti, Zurazi, Borgodi, Catharrei
149 nomades, flumen Cynos. ultra navigationem incom-
pertam ab eo latere propter scopulos tradit Iuba
praetermissa mentione oppidi Omanorum Batrasa-
vaves et Omanae, quod priores celebrem portum
Carmaniae fecere, item Homnae et Attanae, quae
nunc oppida maxime celebrari a Persico mari nostri
negotiatores dicunt. a flumine Canis, ut Iuba, mons
adusto similis, gentes Epimaranitae, mox Ichthyophagi, insula deserta, gentes Bathymi, Eblythaci
montes, insula Omoemus, portus Mochorbae, insulae
150 Etaxalos, Inchobrichae, gens Cadaei; insulae sine
nominibus multae, celebres vero Isura, Rhinnea et
proxima in qua scriptae sunt stelae lapideae litteris
incognitis; Coboea portus, Bragae insulae desertae,
gens Taludaei, Dabanegoris regio, mons Orsa cum
portu, sinus Duatas, insulae multae, mons Tricory-
phos, regio Chardaleon, insulae Solanades, Cachinna,
item Ichthyophagorum. dein Clari, litus Mamaeum
ubi auri metalla, regio Canauna, gentes Apitami,
Casani, insula Devade, fons Coralis, Carphati, insulae
151 Alaea, Amnamethus, gens Darae; insulae Chelonitis,

---

[a] I.e., on the Arabian side of the Persian Gulf.
[b] I.e., the Cynos, § 148 fin. taken to mean κυνός.

never been visited; that the circumference of Tyros measures 112½ miles; that its distance from Farsistan is more than that; and that it is accessible only by one narrow channel. Then the island of Ascliae, tribes named Nochaeti, Zurazi, Borgodi and the nomad Catharrei, and the river Cynos. According to Juba the voyage beyond on that side [a] has not been explored, because of the rocks—Juba omits to mention Batrasavave, the town of the Omani, and the town of Omana which previous writers have made out to be a famous port of Carmania, and also Homna and Attana, towns said by our traders to be now the most frequented ports in the Persian Gulf. After the Dog's River,[b] according to Juba, there is a mountain looking as if it had been burnt; the Epimaranitae tribes, then the Fish-eaters, an uninhabited island, the Bathymi tribes, the Eblythaean Mountains, the island of Omoemus, Port Mochorbae, the islands of Etaxalos and Inchobrichae, the Cadaei tribe; a number of islands without names, and the well-known islands of Isura and Rhinnea, and the adjacent island on which there are some stone pillars bearing inscriptions written in an unknown alphabet; Port Coboea, the unhabited Bragae islands, the Taludaei tribe, the Dabanegoris district, Mount Orsa with its harbour, Duatas Bay, a number of islands, Mount Three Peaks, the Chardaleon district, the Solonades and Cachinna, also islands belonging to the Fish-eaters. Then Clari, the Mamaean coast with its gold-mines, the Canauna district, the Apitami and Casani tribes, Devade Island, the spring Coralis, the Carphati, the islands of Alaea and Amnamethus, the Darae tribe; Chelonitis Island and a number of

451

Ichthyophagon multae, Odanda deserta, Basa, multae Sabaeorum. flumina Thanar, Amnum, insulae Doricae, fontes Daulotos, Dora, insulae Pteros, Labatanis, Coboris, Sambrachate et oppidum eodem nomine in continente. a meridie insulae multae, maxima Camari, flumen Musecros, portus Laupas; Scenitae Sabaei, insulae multae, emporium eorum
152 Acila, ex quo in Indiam navigatur; regio Amithoscatta, Damnia, Mizi Maiores et Minores, Drymatina, Macae; horum[1] promunturium contra Carmaniam distat $\overline{\text{L}}$ p. mira res ibi traditur, Numenium ab Antiocho rege Mesenae praepositum ibi vicisse eodem die classe aestuque reverso iterum equitatu contra Persas dimicantem et gemina tropaea eodem in loco Iovi ac Neptuno statuisse.

153 Insula in alto obiacet Ogyris, clara Erythra rege ibi sepulto; distat a continente $\overline{\text{CXXV}}$ p., circumitur $\overline{\text{CXII}}$ D. nec minus altera clara in Azanio mari Dioscuridu, distans a Syagro extumo promunturio $\overline{\text{CCLXXX}}$.

Reliqui in continente a noto etiamnum Autaridae, in montes VII dierum transitus, gens Larendani et Catapani, Gebbanitae pluribus oppidis sed maximis Nagia et Thomna templorum LXV: haec est amplitudinis significatio. promunturium, a quo ad con-
154

---

[1] *Gutschmidt*: drimati naumachaeorum *aut alia.*

---

[a] See V. 65, n.   [b] Ras Musandam.
[c] Ras Fartak in Arabia.

islands of the Fish-eaters, the uninhabited Odanda, Basa, a number of islands belonging to the Sabaei. The rivers Thanar and Amnum, the Doric Islands, the Daulotos and Dora springs, the islands of Pteros, Labatanis, Coboris and Sambrachate with the town of the same name on the mainland. Many islands to the southward, the largest of which is Camari, the river Musecros, Port Laupas; the Sabaei, a tribe of Scenitae,[a] owning many islands and a trading-station at Kalhat which is a port of embarkation for India; the district of Amithoscatta, Damnia, the Greater and Lesser Mizi, Drymatina, the Macae; a cape[b] in their territory points towards Carmania, 50 miles away. A remarkable event is said to have occurred there: the governor of Mesene appointed by King Antiochus, Numenius, here won a battle against the Persians with his fleet and after the tide had gone out a second battle with his cavalry, and set up a couple of trophies, to Jupiter and to Neptune, on the same spot.

Out at sea off this coast lies the island of Ogyris, famous as the burial-place of King Erythras; its distance from the mainland is 125 miles and it measures $112\frac{1}{2}$ miles round. Equally famous is a second island in the Azanian Sea, the island of Socotra, lying 280 miles away from the extreme point of Cape Syagrus.[c]

The remaining tribes on the mainland situated *The rest of* further south are the Autaridae, seven days' journey *Arabia.* into the mountains, the Larendani and Catapani tribe, the Gebbanitae with several towns, of which the largest are Nagia and Thomna, the latter with sixty-five temples, a fact that indicates its size. Then a cape the distance between which and the

tinentem Trogodytarum L̄; Thoani, Actaei, Chatramotitae, Tonabaei, Antiadalei et Lexianae, Agraei,
Cerbani, Sabaei Arabum propter tura clarissimi ad
utraque maria porrectis gentibus. oppida eorum in
Rubro litore Merme, Marma, Corolia, Sabbatha,
intus oppida Nascus, Cardava, Carnus et quo merces
155 odorum deferunt Thomala. pars eorum Atramitae,
quorum caput Sabota LX templa muris includens;
regia tamen[1] omnium Mareliabata sinum obtinet[2]
xcvi, refertum insulis odoriferis. Atramitis in mediterraneo iunguntur Minaei; mare accolunt et
Aelamitae oppido eiusdem nominis, iis iuncti Chaculatae oppido[3] Sibi quod Graeci Apaten vocant, Arsi,
Codani, Vadaei oppido magno Barasasa, et Lechieni;
Sygaros insula quam canes non intrant expositique
156 circa litora errando moriuntur. sinus intimus in
quo Laeanitae, qui nomen ei dedere. regia eorum
Agra et in sinu Laeana vel, ut alii, Aelana; nam et
ipsum sinum nostri Laeaniticum[4] scripsere, alii
Aelaniticum, Artemidorus Alaeniticum, Iuba Leani-
ticum.[5] circuitus Arabiae a Charace Laeana colligere

---

[1] *V.l.* tamen est.
[2] *V.l.* obtinent.
[3] oppido? *Mayhoff*: oppidum.
[4] *Mayhoff, cf.* 165, V. 65: Aelaniticum.
[5] *Mayhoff, cf. Ptol.* VI. 6.18: Laeniticum.

---

a, d Both names seem to survive in the name Hadramaut

mainland in the Cave-dwellers' territory is 50 miles;
then the Thoani, the Actaei, the Chatramotitae,[a]
the Tonabaei, the Antiadalei and Lexianae, the
Agraei, the Cerbani and the Sabaei,[b] the best
known of all the Arabian tribes because of their
frankincense—these tribes extend from sea to sea.[c]
Their towns on the coast of the Red Sea are Merme,
Marma, Corolia, Sabbatha, and the inland towns are
Nascus, Cardava, Carnus, and Thomala to which
they bring down their perfumes for export. One
division of them are the Atramitae,[d] whose chief
place is Sabota, a walled town containing sixty
temples; the royal capital of all these tribes however
is Mareliabata, which lies on a bay measuring 94
miles round, studded with islands that produce
perfumes. Adjoining the Atramitae in the interior
are the Minaei; and dwelling on the coast are also
the Aelamitae with a town of the same name, and
adjoining them the Chaculatae with the town of
Sibis, the Greek name of which is Apate, the Arsi,
the Codani, the Vadaei with the large town of
Barasasa, and the Lechieni; and the island of
Sygaros, into which dogs are not admitted, and so
being exposed on the seashore they wander about
till they die. Then a bay running far inland on which
live the Laeanitae, who have given it their name.
Their capital is Agra, and on the bay[e] is Laeana, or
as others call it Aelana; for the name of the bay
itself has been written by our people 'Laeanitic',
and by others 'Aelanitic', while Artemidorus gives
it as 'Alaenitic' and Juba as 'Leanitic'. The
circumference of Arabia from Charax to Laeana is

[b] Of Yemen. [c] *I.e.* from the Red Sea to the Arabian.
[e] The Gulf of Akaba.

455

proditur $\overline{\lvert \text{XLVI} \rvert}$ $\overline{\text{LXV}}$ p., Iuba paulo minus $\overline{\lvert \text{XL} \rvert}$ putat;
latissima est a septentrione inter oppida Heroeum
et Characen.

157 Iam[1] et reliqua mediterranea eius dicantur.
Nabataeis Timaneos iunxerunt veteres; nunc sunt
Taveni, Suelleni, Araceni, Arreni oppido in quod[2]
negotiatio omnis convenit, Hemnatae, Avalitae
(oppida Domata, Haegra), Tamudaei (oppidum
Baclanaza), Cariati, Acitoali (oppidum Phoda), ac
Minaei a rege Cretae Minoe, ut existimant, originem
trahentes, quorum Carmei. oppidum $\overline{\text{XIV}}$ p. Maribba,
Paramalacum, et ipsum non spernendum, item
158 Canon. Rhadamaei (et horum origo Rhadamanthus
putatur, frater Minois), Homeritae Mesala oppido,
Hamiroei, Gedranitae, Phryaei, Lysanitae, Bachylitae, Samnaei, Amaitaei oppidis Messa et Chenne-
seri, Zamareni oppidis Sagiatta, Canthace, Bacaschami Riphearina oppido, quo vocabulo hordeum
appellant, Autaei, Ethravi, Cyrei Elmataeis oppido,
Chodae Aiathuri in montibus oppido $\overline{\text{XXV}}$ p. (in quo
fons Aenuscabales, quod significat camelorum),
159 oppidum Ampelome, colonia Milesiorum, Athrida
oppidum, Calingi, quorum Mariba oppidum significat
dominos omnium, oppida Pallon, Murannimal iuxta
flumen per quod Euphraten emergere putant, gentes
Agraei et Ammoni, oppidum Athenae, Caunaravi

---

[1] *Detlefsen*: nam.
[2] *Mayhoff*: oppidum in quo.

said to amount to 4665 miles, though Juba thinks it is a little less than 4000 miles; it is widest at the north, between the towns of Heroeum and Charax.

The rest of its inland places also must now be stated. Adjoining the Nabataei the old authorities put the Timanei, but now there are the Taveni, Suelleni, Araceni, Arreni (with a town which is a centre for all mercantile business), Hemnatae, Avalitae (with the towns of Domata and Haegra), Tamudaei (town Baclanaza), Cariati, Acitoali (town Phoda), and the Minaei, who derive their origin, as they believe, from King Minos of Crete; part of them are the Carmei. Fourteen miles further is the town of Maribba, then Paramalacum, also a considerable place, and Canon, to which the same applies. Then the Rhadamaei (these also are believed to descend from Rhadamanthus the brother of Minos), the Homeritae with the town of Mesala, the Hamiroei, Gedranitae, Phryaei, Lysanitae, Bachylitae, Samnaei, the Amaitaei with the towns of Messa and Chenneseris, the Zamareni with the towns of Sagiatta and Canthace, the Bacaschami with the town of Riphearina (a name which is the native word for barley), the Autaei, Ethravi, Cyrei with the town of Elmataei, Chodae with the town of Aiathuris 25 miles up in the mountains (in which is the spring called Aenuscabales, which means 'the fountain of the camels'), the town of Ampelome, a colony from Miletus, the town of Athrida, the Calingi, whose town is named Mariba, meaning 'lords of all men', the towns of Pallon and Murannimal, on a river through which the Euphrates is believed to discharge itself, the Agraei and Ammoni tribes, a town named Athenae, the Caunaravi (which means

(quod significat ditissimos armento), Chorranitae,
Cesani, Choani. fuerunt et Graeca oppida Arethusa,
Larisa, Chalcis, deleta variis bellis.

160 Romana arma solus in eam terram adhuc intulit
Aelius Gallus ex equestri ordine; nam C. Caesar
Augusti filius prospexit tantum Arabiam. Gallus
oppida diruit non nominata auctoribus qui ante
scripserunt: Negranam, Nestum, Nescam, Magusum,
Caminacum, Labaetiam, et supra dictam Maribam
circuitu $\overline{\text{VI}}$, item Caripetam, quo longissime processit.

161 cetera explorata retulit: Nomadas lacte et ferina
carne vesci; reliquos vinum ut Indos palmis ex-
primere, oleum sesamae; numerosissimos esse
Homeritas; Minaeis fertiles agros palmetis arbusto-
que, in pecore divitias; Cerbanos et Agraeos armis
praestare, maxime Chatramotitas; Carreis latissimos
et fertilissimos agros; Sabaeos ditissimos silvarum
fertilitate odorifera, auri metallis, agrorum riguis,
mellis ceraeque proventu: de odoribus suo dicemus

162 volumine. Arabes mitrati degunt aut intonso crine,
barba abraditur praeterquam in superiore labro;
aliis et haec intonsa. mirumque dictu ex innumeris
populis pars aequa in commerciis aut latrociniis

458

'very rich in herds'), the Chorranitae, the Cesani and the Choani. Here were also the Greek towns of Arethusa, Larisa and Chalcis, but they have been destroyed in various wars.

Aelius Gallus, a member of the Order of Knights, *Expedition of Aelius Gallus.* is the only person who has hitherto carried the arms of Rome into this country; for Gaius Caesar son of Augustus only had a glimpse of Arabia. Gallus destroyed the following towns not named by the authors who have written previously—Negrana, Nestus, Nesca, Magusus, Caminacus, Labaetia; as well as Mariba above mentioned, which measures §159. 6 miles round, and also Caripeta, which was the farthest point he reached. The other discoveries that he reported on his return are: that the Nomads live on milk and the flesh of wild animals; that the rest of the tribes extract wine out of palm trees, as the natives do in India, and get oil from sesame; that the Homeritae are the most numerous tribe; that the Minaei have land that is fertile in palm groves and timber, and wealth in flocks; that the Cerbani and Agraei, and especially the Chatramotitae, excel as warriors; that the Carrei have the most extensive and most fertile agricultural land; that the Sabaei are the most wealthy, owing to the fertility of their forests in producing scents, their gold mines, their irrigated agricultural land and their production of honey and wax: of their scents we shall speak in Book XII. the volume dealing with that subject. The Arabs wear turbans or else go with their hair unshorn; they shave their beards but wear a moustache— others however leave the beard also unshaven. And strange to say, of these innumerable tribes an equal part are engaged in trade or live by brigandage;

degit; in universum gentes ditissimae, ut apud quas maximae opes Romanorum Parthorumque subsidant, vendentibus quae e mari aut silvis capiunt, nihil invicem redimentibus.

163 XXXIII. Nunc reliquam oram Arabiae contrariam persequemur. Timosthenes totum sinum quadridui navigatione in longitudinem taxavit, bidui in latitudinem, angustias $\overline{\text{VII}}$ D [1] p., Eratosthenes ab ostio |XII| in quamque partem; Artemidorus Arabiae latere

164 |XVII| L, Trogodytico vero |XI| LXXXIV D p. Ptolomaida usque; Agrippa |XVII| XXXII sine differentia laterum. plerique latitudinem CCCCLXXV prodiderunt, faucisque hiberno orienti obversas alii IV, alii VII, alii XII patere.

165 Situs autem ita se habet: a sinu Laeanitico alter sinus quem Arabes Aean vocant, in quo Heroon oppidum est. fuit et Cambysu inter Nelos et Marchadas deductis eo aegris exercitus. gens Tyro, Daneon Portus, ex quo navigabilem alveum perducere in Nilum qua parte ad Delta dictum decurrit, LXII D intervallo, quod inter flumen et Rubrum Mare interest, primus omnium Sesostris Aegypti rex cogitavit, mox Darius Persarum, deinde Ptolemaeus

---

[1] *Numeros in §§ 163 sq. varie tradunt codd. et edd.*

[a] Presumably a MS. error for 'forty'.

taken as a whole, they are the richest races in the world, because vast wealth from Rome and Parthia accumulates in their hands, as they sell the produce they obtain from the sea or their forests and buy nothing in return.

XXXIII. We will now follow along the rest of the coast lying opposite to Arabia. Timosthenes esti- *The coasts of the Red Sea.* mated the length of the whole gulf at four ^a days' sail, the breadth at two, and the width of the Straits of Bab-el-Mandeb as $7\frac{1}{2}$ miles; Eratosthenes makes the length of the coast on either side from the mouth of the gulf 1200 miles; Artemidorus gives the length of the coast on the Arabian side as 1750 miles and on the side of the Cave-dweller country as far as Ptolemais $1184\frac{1}{2}$ miles; Agrippa says that there is no difference between the two sides, and gives the length of each as 1732 miles. Most authorities give the breadth as 475 miles, and the mouth of the gulf facing south-west some make 4 miles wide, others 7 and others 12.

The lie of the land is as follows: on leaving the Laeanitic Gulf there is another gulf the Arabic name of which is Aeas, on which is the town of Heroön. Formerly there was also the City of Cambyses, between the Neli and the Marchades; this was the place where the invalids from the army of Cambyses were settled. Then come the Tyro tribe and the Harbour of the Daneoi, from which there was a project to carry a ship-canal through to the Nile at the *Canal from* place where it flows into what is called the Delta, *Nile to Red* over a space of $62\frac{1}{2}$ miles, which is the distance *Sea.* between the river and the Red Sea; this project was originally conceived by Sesostris King of Egypt, and later by the Persian King Darius and then again

PLINY: NATURAL HISTORY

Sequens, qui et duxit [1] fossam latitudine pedum c,
altitudine xxx, in longitudinem $\overline{\text{xxxiv}}$ D p. usque ad
166 Fontes Amaros. ultra deterruit inundationis metus,
excelsiore tribus cubitis Rubro Mari conperto quam
terra Aegypti. aliqui non eam adferunt causam,
sed ne inmisso mari corrumperetur aqua Nili, quae
sola potus praebet. nihilominus iter totum terreno
frequentatur, a mari Aegyptio, quod est triplex:
unum a Pelusio per harenas, in quo nisi calami
defixi regant via non reperitur subinde aura vestigia
167 operiente; alterum $\overline{\text{ii}}$ ultra Casium Montem, quod
a $\overline{\text{lx}}$ p. redit in Pelusiacam viam—accolunt Arabes
Autaei; tertium a Gerro, quod Agipsum [2] vocant,
per eosdem Arabas [3] $\overline{\text{lx}}$ propius, sed asperum montibus et inops aquarum. eae omnes viae Arsinoen
ducunt conditam sororis nomine in sinu Carandra a
Ptolomaeo Philadelpho, qui primus Trogodyticen
excussit, amnem qui Arsinoen praefluit Ptolomaeum
168 appellavit. mox oppidum parvum est Aenum—alii
pro hoc Philoterias scribunt—, deinde sunt Asarri,
ex Trogodytarum conubiis Arabes feri, insulae
Sapirine, Scytala, mox deserta ad Myoshormon,

[1] *V.l.* qui eduxit.   [2] *V.l.* Adipsum.
[3] *Brotier:* Arabes.

---

[a] A variant gives 'the Not Thirsty route'.
[b] Ardscherûd near Suez.

462

by Ptolemy the Second, who did actually carry a trench 100 ft. broad and 30 ft. deep for a distance of 34½ miles, as far as the Bitter Springs. He was deterred from carrying it further by fear of causing a flood, as it was ascertained that the level of the Red Sea is 4½ ft. above that of the land of Egypt. Some persons do not adduce this reason for the abandonment of the project, but say that it was due to fear lest making an inlet from the sea would pollute the water of the Nile, which affords to Egypt its only supply of drinking-water. Nevertheless the whole journey from the Egyptian Sea is constantly performed by land, there being three routes: one from Pelusium across the sands, a route on which the only mode of finding the way is to follow a line of reeds fixed in the sand, as the wind causes footprints to be covered up immediately; another route beginning two miles beyond Mount Casius and after 60 miles rejoining the road from Pelusium—along this route dwell the Arab tribe of the Autaei; and a third starting from Gerrum, called the Agipsum *a* route, passing through the same Arab tribe, which is 60 miles shorter but rough and mountainous, as well as devoid of watering-places. All these routes lead to Arsinoë,*b* the city on Caran- *African coast* dra Bay founded and named after his sister by *of Red Sea.* Ptolemy Philadelphus, who first thoroughly explored the Cave-dweller country and gave his own name to the river on which Arsinoë stands. Soon after comes the small town of Aenum—other writers give the name as Philoteriae instead,—and then there are the Asarri, a wild Arab tribe sprung from inter-marriage with the Cave-dwellers, the islands of Sapirine and Scytala, and then desert stretching

ubi fons est Ainos, mons Eos, insula Iambe, portus
multi, Berenice oppidum matris Philadelphi nomine,
ad quod iter a Copto diximus, Arabes Autaei et
169 Gebadaei. XXXIV. Trogodytice, quam prisci
Midoen, alii Midioen dixere, mons Pentedactylos,
insulae Stenae Dirae aliquot, Halonesi non pauciores,
Cardamine, Topazos, quae gemmae nomen dedit.
sinus insulis refertus, ex his quae Matreu vocantur
aquosae, quae Eratonos sitientes; regum his praefecti fuere. introrsus Candaei, quos Ophiophagos
vocant, serpentibus vesci adsueti; neque alia regio
170 fertilior est earum. Iuba, qui videtur diligentissime
persecutus haec, omisit in hoc tractu (nisi exem-
plarium vitium est) Berenicen alteram quae Pan-
chrysos cognominata est et tertiam quae Epi Dires,
insignem loco: est enim sita in cervice longe pro-
currente, ubi fauces Rubri Maris VII D [1] p. ab Arabia
distant. insula ibi Cytis, topazum ferens et ipsa.
171 ultra silvae sunt,[2] ubi Ptolomais a Philadelpho condita
ad venatus elephantorum, ob id Epi Theras cognominata, iuxta lacum Monoleum. haec est regio
secundo volumine a nobis significata, in qua XLV

---

[1] *V.l.* IV D, *cf.* § 163.   [2] *Mayhoff*: ultra silvas.

---

[a] Abu Schaar.
[b] See § 103.
[c] Zebirget Island. The stone is really chrysolite, not topaz.
[d] So called from the neighbouring mines of Jebel Allaki
from which the Egyptians obtained their chief supply of gold.

as far as Myoshormos,[a] where is the spring of Ainos, Mount Eos, Iambe Island, a number of harbours, the town of Berenice[b] named from the mother of Philadelphus, the road to which from Coptus we have §103. described, and the Arab tribes of the Autaei and Gebadaei. XXXIV. Cave-dwellers' country, called *Trogodytice.* in former times Midoë and by other people Midioë, Mount Five-fingers, some islands called the Narrow Necks, the Halonesi about the same in number, Cardamine, and Topazos,[c] which has given its name to the precious stone. A bay crowded with islands, of which the ones called the Islands of Matreos have springs on them and those called Erato's Islands are dry; these islands formerly had governors appointed by the kings. Inland are the Candaei, who are called the Ophiophagi because it is their habit to eat snakes, of which the district is exceptionally productive. Juba, who appears to have investigated these matters extremely carefully, has omitted to mention in this district (unless there is an error in the copies of his work) a second town called Berenice which has the additional name of All-golden,[d] and a third called Berenice on the Neck, which is remarkable for its situation, being placed on a neck of land projecting a long way out, where the straits at the mouth of the Red Sea separate Africa from Arabia by a space of only 7½ miles. Here is the island of Cytis, which itself also produces the chrysolite. Beyond there are forests, in which is Ptolemais, built by Ptolemy Philadelphus for the purpose of elephant-hunting and consequently called Ptolemy's Hunting Lodge; it is close to Lake Monoleus. This is the district referred to by us in Book II, in which during the 45 days before II. 83.

465

diebus ante solstitium totidemque postea hora
sexta consumuntur umbrae, et in meridiem reliquis
horis cadunt, ceteris diebus in septentrionem, cum
in Berenice quam primam posuimus ipso die solstitii
sexta hora umbrae in totum absumantur nihilque
adnotetur aliud novi, $\overline{\text{DCII}}$ D[1] p. intervallo a Ptolemaide: res ingentis exempli locusque subtilitatis
inmensae, mundo ibi deprehenso, cum indubitata
ratione umbrarum Eratosthenes mensuram terrae
prodere inde conceperit. [2]

172 Hinc Azanium mare, promunturium quod aliqui
Hippalum scripsere, lacus Mandalum, insula Colocasitis, et in alto multae in quibus testudo pluruma.
oppidum Sacae, insula Daphnidis, oppidum Aduliton
—Aegyptiorum hoc servi profugi a dominis condidere.

173 maximum hic emporium Trogodytarum, etiam
Aethiopum—abest a Ptolemaide II[3] dierum navigatione; deferunt plurimum ebur, rhinocerotum
cornua, hippopotamiorum coria, chelium[4] testudinum, sphingia, mancipia. supra Aethiopas Aroteras
insulae quae Aliaeu vocantur, item Bacchias et
Antibacchias et Stratioton. hinc in ora Aethiopiae
sinus incognitus, quod miremur, cum ulteriora
mercatores scrutentur; promunturium in quo fons
174 Cucios, expetitus navigantibus; ultra Isidis portus,

---

[1] D add.? Mayhoff, cf. II. 183.   [2] V.l. ceperit.
[3] V.l. v.   [4] chelium (χέλειον) Mueller: celtium.

---

[a] In § 168; two others in § 170.
[b] Or perhaps ' the place was the scene of infinitely profound
research '.
[c] Ἄδουλις or Ἄδουλι, now Zula. The vernacular name
seems to have suggested ' unenslaved,' and the spurious
genitive Ἀδουλιτῶν is Latinized below, § 174, as ' Adulitarum.'

midsummer and the same number of days after
midsummer shadows contract to nothing an hour
before noon, and during the rest of the day fall to the
south, while all the other days of the year they fall
to the north; on the other hand at the first Berenice
mentioned above,[a] on the actual day of the summer
solstice the shadow disappears altogether an hour
before noon, but nothing else unusual is observed—
this place is 602½ miles from Ptolemais. The phen-
omenon is extremely remarkable, and the topic is
one involving infinitely profound research,[b] it being
here that the structure of the world was discovered,
because Eratosthenes derived from it the idea of
working out the earth's dimensions by the certain
method of noting the shadows.

Next come the Azanian Sea, the cape whose name *N.E. Africa.*
some writers give as Hippalus, Lake Mandalum,
Colocasitis Island, and out at sea a number of islands
containing a large quantity of turtle. The town of
Sacae, the island of Daphnis, Freemen's Town,[c]
founded by slaves from Egypt who had run away
from their masters. Here is very large trading
centre of the Cave-dwellers and also the Ethiopians
—it is two days' sail from Ptolemais; they bring
into it a large quantity of ivory, rhinoceros horns,
hippopotamus hides, tortoise shell, apes and slaves.
Beyond the Ploughmen Ethiopians are the islands
called the Isles of Aliaeos, and also Bacchias and
Antibacchias, and Soldiers' Island. Next there is a
bay in the coast of Ethiopia that has not been
explored, which is surprising, in view of the fact
that traders ransack more remote districts; and a
cape on which is a spring named Cucios, resorted
to by seafarers; and further on, Port of Isis, ten

467

decem dierum remigio ab oppido Adulitarum
distans; in eum Trogodytis[1] myrra confertur. insulae
ante portum duae Pseudopylae vocantur, interiores
totidem Pylae, in altera stelae lapideae litteris
ignotis. ultra sinus Abalitu, dein insula Diodori et
aliae desertae, per continentem quoque deserta,
oppidum Gaza; promunturium et portus Mossylites,
quo cinnamum devehitur: hucusque Sesostris exer-
175 citum duxit. aliqui unum Aethiopiae oppidum
ultra ponunt in litore Baragaza.

A Mossylite promunturio Atlanticum mare incipere vult Iuba, praeter Mauretanias suas Gadis
usque navigandum coro; cuius tota sententia hoc in
loco subtrahenda non est. a promunturio Indorum
quod vocetur Lepte Acra, ab aliis Depranum, proponit
recto cursu praeter Exustam ad[2] Malichu insulas
$\overline{XV}$ p. esse, inde ad locum quem vocant Scaeneos
$\overline{CCXXV}$ p., inde ad insulam Sadanum $\overline{CL}$; sic fieri ad
176 apertum mare $\overline{XVIII}$ $\overline{LXXV}$ p. reliqui omnes propter
ardorem solis navigari posse non putaverunt; quin
et commercia ipsa infestant ex insulis Arabes
Ascitae appellati, quoniam bubulos utres binos
insternentes ponte piraticam exercent sagittis vene-

---

[1] Trogodytica? cf. XII. 69, *Rackham.*
[2] ad *Sol.*: et.

---

[a] See § 172 n.
[b] See XII 69.
[c] Perim Island.
[d] Rameses II, King of Egypt 1333 B.C., subdued Ethiopia,
a great part of Asia, Thrace and Scythia: Herodotus II. 102 ff.
[e] On his Ethiopian expedition.
[f] Broach in N.W. India is meant.
[g] Really African: a common confusion in early sources
used by Pliny.

days' row distant from Freemen's Town,[a] and a centre to which Cave-dwellers' myrrh [b] is brought. There are two islands off the harbour called the False Gates, and two inside it called the Gates, on one of which are some stone monuments with inscriptions in an unknown alphabet. Further on is the Bay of Abalitos, and then Diodorus's Island [c] and other uninhabited islands, and also along the mainland a stretch of desert; the town of Gaza; Mossylites Cape and Harbour, the latter the port of export for cinnamon. This was the farthest point to which Sesostris [d] led his army.[e] Some writers place one Ethiopian town on the coast beyond this point, Baragaza.[f]

Juba holds that at Cape Mossylites begins the Atlantic Ocean, navigable with a north-west wind along the coast of his kingdom of the Mauretanias as far as Cadiz; and his whole opinion must not be omitted at this point in the narrative. He puts forward the view that the distance from the cape in the Indian[g] territory called in Greek the Narrow Head, and by others the Sickle, in a straight course past Burnt Island to Malichas's Islands is 1500 miles, from there to the place called Scaenei 225 miles, and on from there to Sadanus Island 150 miles— making 1875 miles to the open sea. All the rest of the authorities have held the view that the heat of the sun makes the voyage impossible; moreover actual goods conveyed for trade are exposed to the depredations of an Arabian tribe living on the islands: who are called the Ascitae [h] because they make rafts of timber placed on a pair of inflated oxhides and practise piracy, using poisoned arrows.

[h] From ἀσκός, a wine-skin.

natis. gentes Trogodytarum idem Iuba tradit Therothoas a venatu dictos, mirae velocitatis, sicut Ichthyophagos, natantes ceu maris animalia, Bangenos, Zangenas, Thalibas, Saxinas, Sirecas, Daremas,

177 Domazenes. quin et accolas Nili a Syene non Aethiopum populos sed Arabum esse dicit usque Meroen, Solis quoque oppidum, quod non procul Memphi in Aegypti situ diximus, Arabas conditores habere. sunt qui et ulteriorem ripam Aethiopiae auferant adnectantque Africae. (ripas autem incoluere propter aquam.)[1] nos relicto cuique intellegendi arbitrio oppida quo traduntur ordine utrimque ponemus a Syene.

178 XXXV. Et prius Arabiae latere gens Catadupi, deinde Syenitae, oppida Tacompson (quam quidam appellarunt Thaticen), Aramum, Sesamos, Andura, Nasarduma, Aindoma Come cum Arabeta et Boggiana, Leuphitorga, Tautarene, Meae, Chindita, Noa, Goploa, Gistate, Megada, Lea, Remni, Nups, Direa, Patigga, Bagada, Dumana, Radata (in quo felis aurea pro deo colebatur), Boron, in mediterraneo

179 Mallo proximum Meroe. sic prodidit Bion. Iuba aliter: oppidum munitum[2] Mega Tichos inter Aegyptum et Aethiopiam, quod Arabes Mirsion vocaverunt, dein Tacompson, Aramum, Sesamum, Pide, Mamuda, Corambim iuxta bituminis fontem, Amodata, Prosda, Parenta, Mania, Tessata, Galles,

---

[1] ripas . . . aquam *secl. Mayhoff, alii post* Meroen *vel* habere *tr.*
[2] *Mayhoff*: Munto *et alia.*

---

[a] This sentence is probably misplaced or interpolated.

Juba also speaks of some tribes of Cave-dwellers called the Jackal-hunters, because of their skill in hunting, who are remarkable for their swiftness, and also of the Fish-eaters, who can swim like creatures of the sea; also the Bangeni, Zangenae, Thalibae, Saxinae, Sirecae, Daremae and Domazenes. Juba states moreover that the people inhabiting the banks of the Nile from Syene as far as Meroë are not Ethiopian but Arabian tribes and also that the City of the Sun, which in our description of Egypt we spoke of as not far from Memphis, had v. 61. Arab founders. The further bank also is by some authorities taken away from Ethiopia and attached to Africa. (But they lived on the banks for the sake of the water.[a]) We however shall leave this point to the reader to form his own opinion on it, and shall enumerate the towns on either bank in the order in which they are reported, starting from Syene.

XXXV. And taking the Arabian side of the Nile *Ethiopia;* first, we have the Catadupi tribe, and then the Syeni- *the Nile* tae, and the towns of Tacompson (which some have *valley;* called Thatice), Aramum, Sesamos, Andura, Nasar- *Meroë.* duma, Aindoma Village with Arabeta and Bongiana, Leuphitorga, Tautarene, Meae, Chindita, Noa, Goploa, Gistate, Megada, Lea, Remni, Nups, Direa, Patinga, Bagada, Dumana, Radata (where a golden cat used to be worshipped as a god), Boron, and inland Meroë, near Mallos. This is the account given by Bion. Juba's is different: he says that there is a fortified town called the Great Wall between Egypt and Ethiopia, the Arabic name for which is Mirsios, and then Tacompson, Aramum, Sesamos, Pide, Mamuda, Corambis near a spring of mineral pitch, Amodota, Prosda, Parenta, Mania, Tessata, Galles, Zoton,

471

Zoton, Graucomen, Emeum, Pidibotas, Endonda-
cometas, Nomadas in tabernaculis viventes, Cystaepen,
Magadalen Parvam, Prumin, Nups, Dicelin, Patin-
gan, Breves, Magus Neos, Egasmala, Cramda,
Denna, Cadeum, Mathena, Batta, Alanam, Macua,
Scammos, Goram, in insula ab iis Abale, Androcalim,
Serem, Mallos, Agocem.

180 Ex Africae latere tradita sunt eodem nomine
Tacompsos altera sive pars prioris, Mogore, Saea,
Aedosa, Pelenariae, Pindis, Magassa, Buma, Lin-
tuma, Spintum, Sidopt, Gensoe, Pindicitor, Agugo,
Orsum, Suara, Maumarum, Urbim, Mulon (quod
oppidum Graeci Hypaton vocarunt), Pagoartas,
Zamnes (unde elephanti incipiant), Mambli, Berressa,
Coetum. fuit quondam et Epis oppidum contra
Meroen, antequam Bion scriberet deletum.

181 Haec sunt prodita usque Meroen, ex quibus hoc
tempore nullum prope utroque latere exstat; certe
solitudines nuper renuntiavere principi Neroni
missi ab eo milites praetoriani cum tribuno ad
explorandum, inter reliqua bella et Aethiopicum
cogitanti. intravere autem et eo arma Romana divi
Augusti temporibus duce P. Petronio et ipso equestris
ordinis praefecto Aegypti. is oppida eorum ex-
pugnavit quae sola invenimus quo dicemus ordine:
Pselcin, Primi, Bocchin, Forum Cambusis, Atteniam,

Graucome, Emeus, Pidibotae, Endondacometae, Nomad tribes living in tents, Cystaepe, Little Magadale, Prumis, Nups, Dicelis, Patingas, Breves, New Magus, Egasmala, Cramda, Denna, Cadeus, Mathena, Batta, Alana, Macua, Scammos, Gora, and on an island off these places Abale, Androcalis, Seres, Mallos and Agoces.

The places on the African side are given as Tacompsus (either a second town of the same name or a suburb of the one previously mentioned), Mogore, Saea, Aedosa, Pelenariae, Pindis, Magassa, Buma, Lintuma, Spintum, Sidopt, Gensoe, Pindicitor, Agugo, Orsum, Suara, Maumarum, Urbim, Mulon (the town called by the Greeks Hypaton), Pagoartas, Zamnes (after which elephants begin to be found), Mambli, Berressa, Coetum. There was also formerly a town called Epis, opposite to Meroë, which had been destroyed before Bion wrote.

These are the places that were reported as far as Meroë, though at the present day hardly any of them still exist on either side of the river; at all events an exploring party of praetorian troops under the command of a tribune lately sent by the emperor Nero, when among the rest of his wars he was actually contemplating an attack on Ethiopia, reported that there was nothing but desert. Nevertheless in the time of his late Majesty Augustus the arms of Rome had penetrated even into those regions, under the leadership of Publius Petronius, himself also a member of the Order of Knighthood, when he was Governor of Egypt. Petronius captured the Arabian towns of which we will give a list, the only ones we have found there: Pselcis, Primi, Bocchis, Cambyses' Market, Attenia and Stadissis,

Stadissim, ubi Nilus praecipitans se fragore auditum
182 accolis aufert; diripuit et Napata. longissime autem
a Syene progressus est $\overline{\text{DCCCLXX}}$ p. nec tamen arma
Romana ibi solitudinem fecerunt: Aegyptiorum
bellis attrita est Aethiopia vicissim imperitando
serviendoque, clara et potens etiam usque ad Troiana
bella Memnone regnante; et Syriae imperitasse
eam nostroque litori aetate regis Cephei patet
Andromedae fabulis.

183 Simili modo et de mensura eius varia prodidere,
primus Dalion ultra Meroen longe subvectus, mox
Aristocreon et Bion et Basilis, Simonides minor
etiam quinquennio in Meroe moratus cum de Aethiopia scriberet. nam Timosthenes classium Philadelphi
praefectus sine mensura dierum LX a Syene Meroen
iter prodidit, Eratosthenes $\overline{\text{DCXXV}}$, Artemidorus $\overline{\text{DC}}$,
Sebosus ab Aegypti extremis $\overline{|\text{XVI}|}$ LXXII, unde proxime
184 dicti $\overline{|\text{XII}|}$ $\bar{\text{L}}$.[1] verum omnis haec finita nuper disputatio
est, quoniam a Syene $\overline{\text{DCCCXLV}}$ [1] Neronis exploratores
renuntiavere his modis: a Syene Hieran Sycaminon
$\overline{\text{LIV}}$, inde Tama $\overline{\text{LXXII}}$ [1] regione Evonymiton Aethiopum, Primi $\overline{\text{CXX}}$, Acinam $\overline{\text{LXIV}}$,[1] Pitaram $\overline{\text{XXII}}$,[1] Ter-

---

[1] *Numeros varie tradunt codd.*

---

[a] The numerals throughout this passage vary considerably
in the MSS.

where there is a cataract of the Nile the noise of
which affects people dwelling near it with deafness;
he also sacked the town of Napata. The farthest
point he reached was 870 miles from Syene; but
nevertheless it was not the arms of Rome that made
the country a desert: Ethiopia was worn out by
alternate periods of dominance and subjection in a
series of wars with Egypt, having been a famous
and powerful country even down to the Trojan
wars, when Memnon was king; and the stories about
Andromeda show that it dominated Syria and the
coasts of the Mediterranean in the time of King
Cepheus.

Similarly there have also been various reports as
to the dimensions of the country, which were first
given by Dalion, who sailed up a long way beyond
Meroë, and then by Aristocreon and Bion and
Basilis, and also by the younger Simonides, who
stayed at Meroë for five years while writing his
account of Ethiopia. Further, Timosthenes, who commanded the navies of Philadelphus, has stated the
distance from Syene to Meroë as sixty days' journey,
without specifying the mileage *per diem*, while
Eratosthenes gives it as 625 miles and Artemidorus
as 600 miles; and Sebosus says that from the extreme
point of Egypt to Meroë is 1672 miles, whereas the
authors last mentioned give it as 1250 [a] miles. But all
this discrepancy has recently been ended, inasmuch
as the expedition sent by Nero to explore the
country have reported that the distance from Syene
to Meroë is 945 miles, made up as follows: from
Syene to Holy Mulberry 54 miles, from there to
Tama 72 miles through the district of the Ethiopian
Euonymites, to Primi 120 miles, Acina 64 miles, Pitara

gedum CIII.[1] insulam Gagauden esse in medio eo
tractu; inde primum visas aves psittacos et ab altera,
quae vocetur Articula, animal sphingion, a Tergedo
cynocephalos. inde Nabata LXXX, oppidum id parvum
inter praedicta solum, ab eo ad insulam Meroen

185 CCCLX. herbas circa Meroen demum viridiores,
silvarumque aliquid apparuisse[2] et rhinocerotum
elephantorumque vestigia. ipsum oppidum Meroen
ab introitu insulae abesse LXX p., iuxtaque aliam
insulam Tadu dextro subeuntibus alveo, quae portum

186 faceret; aedificia oppidi pauca. regnare feminam
Candacen, quod nomen multis iam annis ad reginas
transisset;[3] delubrum Hammonis et ibi religiosum
et toto tractu sacella. cetero cum potirentur rerum
Aethiopes, insula ea magnae claritatis fuit. tradunt
armatorum CCL dare solitam, artificum[4] III. alii[5]

187 reges Aethiopum XLV esse[6] hodie traduntur. universa vero gens Aetheria appellata est, deinde
Atlantia, mox a Vulcani filio Aethiope.[7] animalium
hominumque monstrificas effigies circa extremitates
eius gigni minime mirum, artifici ad formanda
corpora effigiesque caelandas mobilitate ignea.

---

[1] *Numeros varie tradunt codd.*
[2] *V.l.* viridiores silvarum apparuisse.
[3] *Rackham* : transit *aut* transiit.
[4] elephantum *Detlefsen.*
[5] *Mayhoff* : alare *aut* alere.
[6] esse (ēē) *Mayhoff* : et.
[7] *V.l.* Aethiope Aethiopia.

---

[a] Perhaps the text should be altered to ' elephants '.

22 miles, Tergedus 103 miles. The report stated that the island of Gagaudes is half-way between Syene and Meroë, and that it was after passing this island that the birds called parrots were first seen, and after another, named Articula, the *sphingion* ape, and after Tergedus dog-faced baboons. The distance from Tergedus to Nabata is 80 miles, that little town being the only one among those mentioned that survives; and from Nabata to the island of Meroë is 360 miles. Round Meroë, they reported, greener herbage begins, and a certain amount of forest came into view, and the tracks of rhinoceroses and elephants were seen. The actual town of Meroë they said is at a distance of 70 miles from the first approach to the island, and beside it in the channel on the right hand as one goes up stream lies another island, the Isle of Tados, this forming a harbour; the town possesses few buildings. They said that it is ruled by a woman, Candace, a name that has passed on through a succession of queens for many years; and that religious ceremonies take place in a temple of Hammon in the town and also in shrines of Hammon all over the district. Moreover at the time of the Ethiopic dominion this island was extremely celebrated. It is reported that it used to furnish 250,000 armed men and 3000 artisans.[a] At the present day there are reported to be forty-five other kings of Ethiopia. But the whole race was called Aetheria, and then Atlantia, and finally it took its name from Aethiops the son of Vulcan. It is by no means surprising that the outermost districts of this region produce animal and human monstrosities, considering the capacity of the mobile element of fire to mould their bodies and carve their outlines.

477

ferunt certe ab orientis parte intima gentes esse
sine naribus, aequali totius oris planitie, alias supe-
188 riore labro orbas, alias sine linguis. pars etiam ore
concreto et naribus carens uno tantum foramine
spirat potumque calamis avenae trahit et grana
eiusdem avenae sponte provenientis ad vescendum.
quibusdam pro sermone nutus motusque membrorum est; quibusdam ante Ptolomaeum Lathyrum
regem Aegypti ignotus fuit usus ignium. quidam
et Pygmaeorum gentem prodiderunt inter paludis
ex quibus Nilus oriretur. in ora autem ubi dicemus [1] continui montes ardentibus similes rubent.

189   Trogodytis et Rubro Mari a Meroe tractus omnis
superponitur, a Napata tridui itinere ad Rubrum
litus, aqua pluvia ad usum conpluribus locis servata,
fertilissima regione quae interest auri. ulteriora
Atabuli Aethiopum gens tenent; dein contra
Meroen Megabarri, quos aliqui Adiabaros nomina-
vere, oppidum habent Apollinis; pars eorum
190 Nomades, quae elephantis vescitur. ex adverso in
Africae parte Macrobii, rursus a Megabarris Memnones et Dabelli dierumque xx intervallo Critensi.
ultra eos Dochi, dein Gymnetes semper nudi, mox
Anderae, Mattitae, Mesagches: hi pudore [2] atri

---

[1] *Mayhoff coll.* § 197 : desiimus (*cf.* § 173 *fin.*).
[2] *Mayhoff* : hipdores (Hypsodores *Detlefsen*).

It is certainly reported that in the interior on the east side there are tribes of people without noses, their whole face being perfectly flat, and other tribes that have no upper lip and others no tongues. Also one section has the mouth closed up and has no nostrils, but only a single orifice through which it breathes and sucks in drink by means of oat straws, as well as grains of oat, which grows wild there, for food. Some of the tribes communicate by means of nods and gestures instead of speech; and some were unacquainted with the use of fire before the reign of King Ptolemy Lathyrus in Egypt. Some writers have actually reported a race of Pygmies living among the marshes in which the Nile rises. On the coast, in a region which we shall describe later, there is a § 197. range of mountains of a glowing red colour, which have the appearance of being on fire.

After Meroë all the region is bounded by the Cave-dwellers and the Red Sea, the distance from Napata to the coast of the Red Sea being three days' journey; in several places rainwater is stored for the use of travellers, and the district in between produces a large amount of gold. The parts beyond are occupied by the Atabuli, an Ethiopian tribe; and then, over against Meroë, are the Megabarri, to whom some give the name of Adiabari; they have a town named the Town of Apollo, but one division of them are Nomads, and live on the flesh of elephants. Opposite to them, on the African side, are the Macrobii, and again after the Megabarri come the Memnones and Dabelli, and 20 days' journey further on the Critensi. Beyond these are the Dochi, next the Gymnetes, who never wear any clothes, then the Anderae, Mattitae and Mesanches: the last are

479

coloris tota corpora rubrica inlinunt. at ex Africae
parte Medimni, dein Nomades cynocephalorum
lacte viventes, Alabi, Syrbotae qui octonum cubito-
191 rum esse dicuntur. Aristocreon Libyae latere a
Meroe oppidum Tollen dierum v itinere tradit.
inde dierum XII Aesar oppidum Aegyptiorum qui
Psammetichum fugerint (in eo produntur annis [1] $\overline{\text{CCC}}$
habitasse), contra in Arabico latere Diaron oppidum
esse eorum. Bion autem Sapen vocat quod ille
Aesar, et ipso nomine advenas ait significari; caput
eorum in insula Sembobitin, et tertium in Arabia
Sinat. inter montes autem et Nilum Simbarri sunt,
Palugges, in ipsis vero montibus Asachae multis
nationibus; abesse a mari dicuntur dierum v itinere;
vivunt elephantorum venatu. insula in Nilo Sem-
192 britarum reginae paret. ab ea Nubaei Aethiopes
dierum VIII itinere (oppidum eorum Nilo inpositum
Tenupsis), Sesambri, apud quos quadrupedes omnes
sine auribus, etiam elephanti. at ex Africae parte
Ptonebari, Ptoemphani qui canem pro rege habent,
motu eius imperia augurantes, Harusbi oppido longe
ab Nilo sito, postea Archisarmi, Phalliges, Marigarri,
193 Chasamari. Bion et alia oppida in insulis tradit:
a Sembobiti Meroen versus dierum toto itinere XX,

[1] *Edd. vet.*: prodente se.

ashamed of their black colour and smear themselves all over with red clay. On the African side are the Medimni, and then a Nomad tribe that lives on the milk of the dog-faced baboon, the Alabi, and the Syrbotae who are said to be 12 ft. high. Aristocreon reports that on the Lybian side five days' journey from Meroë is the town of Tolles, and twelve days beyond it another town, Aesar, belonging to Egyptians who fled to escape from Psammetichus (they are said to have been living there for 300 years), and that the town of Diaron on the Arabian side opposite belongs to them. To the town which Aristocrates calls Aesar Bion gives the name of Sapes, which he says means that the inhabitants are strangers; their chief city is Sembobitis, situated on an island, and they have a third town named Sinat, in Arabia. Between the mountains and the Nile are the Simbarri, the Palunges and, on the actual mountains, the numerous tribes of Asachae, who are said to be five days' journey from the sea; they live by hunting elephants. An island in the Nile, belonging to the Sembritae, is governed by a queen. Eight days' journey from this island are the Nubian Ethiopians, whose town Tenupsis is situated on the Nile, and the Sesambri, in whose country all the four-footed animals, even the elephants, have no ears. On the African side are the Ptonebari; the Ptoemphani, who have a dog for a king and divine his commands from his movements; the Harusbi, whose town is situated a long distance away from the Nile; and afterwards the Archisarmi, Phalliges, Marigarri and Chasamari. Bion also reports other towns situated on islands: after Sembobitis, in the direction of Meroë, the whole distance being twenty days' journey, on the first

481

proximae insulae oppidum Semberritarum sub regina
et aliud Asara; alterius oppidum Darden; tertiam
Medoen vocant, in qua oppidum Asel; quartam
eodem quo oppidum nomine Garroen. inde per
ripas oppida Nautis, Madum, Demadatin,[1] Secande,
Navectabe cum agro Psegipta, Candragori, Arabam,
194 Summaram. regio supra Sirbitum, ubi desinunt
montes, traditur a quibusdam habere maritimos
Aethiopas, Nisicathas, Nisitas, quod significat ternum
et quaternum oculorum viros, non quia sic sint, sed
quia sagittis praecipua contemplatione utantur. ab
ea vero parte Nili quae supra Syrtes Maiores oceanum-
que meridianum protendatur Dalion Vacathos esse
dicit pluvia tantum aqua utentis, Cisoros, Logon-
poros ab Oecalicibus dierum v itinere, Usibalchos,
Isbelos, Perusios, Ballios, Cispios; reliqua deserta.
195 dein fabulosa: ad occidentem versus Nigroe, quorum
rex unum oculum in fronte habeat, Agriophagi
pantherarum leonumque maxime carnibus viventes,
Pamphagi omnia mandentes, Anthropophagi humana carne vescentes, Cynamolgi caninis capitibus,
Artabatitae quadrupedes, ferarum modo vagi, deinde
Hesperioe, Perorsi et quos in Mauretaniae confinio
diximus. pars quaedam Aethiopum locustis tantum
vivit fumo et sale duratis in annua alimenta; hi
quadragesimum vitae annum non excedunt.

[1] *Post* Demadatin *codd.* secundum collocat, *nempe gloss.*
(Secundum, Collocat *edd.*).

---

[a] Two words follow in the MSS. which appear to be a
topographical note, but which editors print as names of towns,
as they do the words that follow Navectabe, which are here
rendered ' with ' and ' territory '.

[b] Perhaps the real name was Tettarabatitae.

island reached, a town of the Semberritae, governed by a queen, and another town named Asara; on the second island, the town of Darde; the third island is called Medoë, and the town on it is Asel; the fourth is Garroë, with a town of the same name. Then along the banks are the towns of Nautis, Madum, Demadatis,[a] Secande, Navectabe with the territory of Psegipta, Candragori, Araba, Summara. Above is the region of Sirbitum, where the mountain range ends, and which is stated by some writers to be occupied by Ethiopian coast-tribes, the Nisicathae and Nisitae, names that mean 'men with three' or 'with four eyes'—not because they really are like that but because they have a particularly keen sight in using arrows. On the side of the Nile that stretches inland from the Greater Syrtes and the southern ocean Dalion says there are the Vacathi, who use only rain-water, the Cisori, the Logonpori five days' journey from the Oecalices, the Usibalchi, Isbeli, Perusii, Ballii and Cispii; and that all the rest of the country is uninhabited. Then come regions that are purely imaginary: towards the west are the Nigroi, whose king is said to have only one eye, in his forehead; the Wild-beast-eaters, who live chiefly on the flesh of panthers and lions; the Eatalls, who devour everything; the Man-eaters, whose diet is human flesh; the Dog-milkers, who have dogs' heads; the Artabatitae,[b] who have four legs and rove about like wild animals; and then the Hesperioi, the Perorsi and the people we have mentioned as in-habiting the border of Mauretania. One section of the Ethiopians live only on locusts, dried in smoke and salted to keep for a year's supply of food; these people do not live beyond the age of forty.

v. 10.

483

196   Aethiopum terram universam cum mari Rubro
patere in longitudinem |xxi| l̄x̄x̄ p., in latitudinem
cum superiore Aegypto |xii| x̄c̄v̄ı̄ Agrippa existima-
vit. quidam longitudinem ita diviserunt: a Meroe
Sirbitum xii dierum navigationem, ab eo[1] xii ad
Dabellos, ab his ad oceanum Aethiopicum vi dierum
iter. in totum autem ab oceano ad Meroen d̄c̄x̄x̄v̄
p. esse inter auctores fere convenit, inde Syenen
197   quantum diximus. sita est Aethiopia ab oriente
hiberno ad occidentem hibernum meridiano cardine.
silvae, hebeno[2] maxime, virent. a media eius parte
imminens mari mons excelsus aeternis ardet ignibus,
Theon Ochema dictus a Graecis; a quo navigatione[3]
quadridui[4] promunturium quod Hesperu Ceras
vocatur confine Africae iuxta Aethiopas Hesperios.
quidam et in eo tractu modicos colles amoena
opacitate vestitos Aegipanum Satyrorumque produnt.
198   XXXVI. Insulas toto Eoo mari et Ephorus con-
pluris esse tradidit et Eudoxus et Timosthenes, Clitarchus vero Alexandro regi renuntiatam unam[5] adeo
divitem ut equos incolae talentis auri permutarent,
alteram ubi sacer mons opacus silva repertus esset,
destillante arboribus odore mirae suavitatis. contra
sinum Persicum Cerne nominatur insula adversa

----

[1] *Rackham*: ea.
[2] hiberno *Detlefsen*.
[3] *Detlefsen*: navigatio.
[4] quadridui ad *edd. vet.*
[5] unam *add. Rackham*.

----

[a] The figures in this section are again uncertain, cf. § 183*n*.
[b] *I.e.*, it is an isosceles triangle with its (very obtuse) apex
pointing north. Previous edd. take *meridiano cardine* with
following words.
[c] Mount Kakulima.

The length of the whole of the territory of the
Ethiopians including the Red Sea was estimated by
Agrippa as 2170[a] miles and its breadth including
Upper Egypt 1296 miles. Some authors give the
following divisions of its length: from Meroë to
Sirbitus 12 days' sail, from Sirbitus to the Dabelli 12
days' sail, and from the Dabelli to the Ethiopic Ocean
6 days' journey by land. But authorities are virtually
agreed that the whole distance from the ocean to
Meroë is 625 miles and that the distance from
Meroë to Syene is what we have stated above. The § 184.
conformation of Ethiopia spreads from south-east to
south-west with its centre line running south.[b] It
has flourishing forests, mostly of ebony trees.
Rising from the sea at the middle of the coast is a
mountain[c] of great height which glows with eternal
fires—its Greek name is the Chariot of the Gods;
and four days' voyage from it is the cape called the
Horn of the West, on the confines of Africa, adjacent
to the Western Ethiopians. Some authorities also
report hills of moderate height in this region, clad
with agreeable shady thickets and belonging to the
Goat-Pans and Satyrs.

XXXVI. It is stated by Ephorus, and also by *Islands off*
Eudoxus and Timosthenes, that there are a large *Africa.*
number of islands scattered over the whole of the
Eastern Sea; while Clitarchus says that King
Alexander received a report of one that was so
wealthy that its inhabitants gave a talent of gold for
a horse, and of another on which a holy mountain had
been found, covered with a dense forest of trees
from which fell drops of moisture having a marvel-
lously agreeable scent. An island opposite the
Persian Gulf and lying off Ethiopia is named Cerne;

Aethiopiae, cuius neque magnitudo neque intervallum a continente constat; Aethiopas tantum populos
199 habere proditur. Ephorus auctor est a Rubro Mari
navigantis in eam non posse propter ardores ultra
quasdam columnas (ita appellantur parvae insulae)
provehi. Polybius in extrema Mauretania contra
montem Atlantem a terra stadia VIII abesse prodit
Cernen, Nepos Cornelius ex adverso maxime
Carthaginis a continente p. $\bar{x}$, non ampliorem circuitu $\overline{\text{II}}$. traditur et alia insula contra montem
Altantem, et ipsa Atlantis appellata; ab ea II dierum
praenavigatione solitudines ad Aethiopas Hesperios
et promunturium quod vocavimus Hesperu Ceras,
inde primum circumagente se terrarum fronte in
200 occasum ac mare Atlanticum. contra hoc quoque
promunturium Gorgades insulae narrantur, Gorgonum
quondam domus, bidui navigatione distantes a
continente, ut tradit Xenophon Lampsacenus.
penetravit in eas Hanno Poenorum imperator
prodiditque hirta feminarum corpora, viros pernicitate evasisse; duarumque Gorgadum cutes argumenti et miraculi gratia in Iunonis templo posuit
201 spectatas usque ad Carthaginem captam. ultra has
etiamnum duae Hesperidum insulae narrantur;
adeoque omnia circa hoc incerta sunt ut Statius

---

a Hanno called these natives gorillas, but they were really
chimpanzees or baboons.

neither its size nor its distance from the mainland has been ascertained, but it is reported to be inhabited solely by Ethiopian tribes. Ephorus states that vessels approaching it from the Red Sea are unable because of the heat to advance beyond the Columns —that being the name of certain small islands. Polybius informs us that Cerne lies at the extremity of Mauretania, over against Mount Atlas, a mile from the coast; Cornelius Nepos gives it as being nearly in the same meridian as Carthage, and 10 miles from the mainland, and as measuring not more than 2 miles round. There is also reported to be another island off Mount Atlas, itself also called Atlantis, from which a two days' voyage along the coast reaches the desert district in the neighbourhood of the Western Ethiopians and the cape mentioned above named the Horn of the West, §197 the point at which the coastline begins to curve westward in the direction of the Atlantic. Opposite this cape also there are reported to be some islands, the Gorgades, which were formerly the habitation of the Gorgons, and which according to the account of Xenophon of Lampsacus are at a distance of two days' sail from the mainland. These islands were reached by the Carthaginian general Hanno,[a] who reported that the women had hair all over their bodies, but that the men were so swift of foot that they got away; and he deposited the skins of two of the female natives in the Temple of Juno as proof of the truth of his story and as curiosities, where they were on show until Carthage was taken by Rome. Outside the Gorgades there are also said to be two Islands of the Ladies of the West; and the whole of the geography of this neighbourhood is so uncertain that

Sebosus a Gorgonum insulis praenavigatione Atlantis dierum XL ad Hesperidum insulas cursum prodiderit, ab his ad Hesperu Ceras unius. nec Mauretaniae insularum certior fama est: paucas modo constat esse ex adverso Autololum a Iuba repertas, in quibus Gaetulicam purpuram tinguere instituerat.

202 XXXVII. Sunt qui ultra eas Fortunatas putent esse quasdamque alias quarum[1] numero idem Sebosus etiam spatia conplexus Iunoniam abesse a Gadibus $\overline{\text{DCCL}}$ p. tradit, ab ea tantundem ad occasum versus Pluvialiam Caprariamque; in Pluvialia non esse aquam nisi ex imbribus; ab iis $\overline{\text{CCL}}$ Fortunatas contra laevam Mauretaniae in VIII horam solis, vocari Invallem a convexitate et Planasiam a specie, Invallis circuitu $\overline{\text{CCC}}$ p.; arborum ibi proceritatem ad CXL 203 pedes adolescere. Iuba de Fortunatis ita inquisivit: sub meridiem positas esse prope occasum, a Purpurariis $\overline{\text{DCXXV}}$ p., sic ut CCL supra occasum navigetur, dein per $\overline{\text{CCCLXXV}}$ ortus petatur primam vocari Ombrion nullis aedificiorum vestigiis, habere, in montibus stagnum, arbores similes ferulae ex quibus aqua exprimatur, e nigris amara, ex candidioribus 204 potui iucunda; alteram insulam Iunoniam appellari,

1 *V.l.* quorum : *Mayhoff* quo in.

---

a The Canaries.   b Fuerteventura.
c Ferro.   d Gomera.
e The Island of Teneriffe.   f Great Canary Island.
g *I.e.*, its level surface.   h See § 201 *fin.*
i The Greek name of Pluvialia, § 202.

488

Statius Sebosus has given the voyage along the coast
from the Gorgons' Islands past Mount Atlas to the Isles
of the Ladies of the West as forty days' sail and from
those islands to the Horn of the West as one day's sail.
Nor is there less uncertainty with regard to the report
of the islands of Mauretania: it is only known for
certain that a few were discovered by Juba off the
coast of the Autololes, in which he had established a
dyeing industry that used Gaetulian purple.

XXXVII. Some people think that beyond the *The
Fortunate
Islands.*
islands of Mauretania lie the Isles of Bliss,[a] and
also some others of which Sebosus before mentioned
gives not only the number but also the distances,
reporting that Junonia[b] is 750 miles from Cadiz, and
that Pluvialia[c] and Capraria[d] are the same distance
west from Junonia; that in Pluvialia there is no
water except what is supplied by rain; that the
Isles of Bliss are 250 miles W.N.W. from these, to
the left hand of Mauretania, and that one is called
Invallis[e] from its undulating surface and the other
Planasia[f] from its conformation,[g] Invallis measuring
300 miles round; and that on it trees grow to a
height of 140 ft. About the Isles of Bliss Juba has
ascertained the following facts: they lie in a south-
westerly direction, at a distance of 625 miles' sail
from the Purple Islands,[h] provided that a course
be laid north of due west for 250 miles and then
east for 375 miles; that the first island reached is
called Ombrios,[i] and there are no traces of buildings
upon it, but it has a pool surrounded by mountains,
and trees resembling the giant fennel, from which
water is extracted, the black ones giving a bitter
fluid and those of brighter colour a juice that is
agreeable to drink; that the second island is called

in ea aediculam esse tantum uno[1] lapide exstructam;
ab ea in vicino eodem nomine minorem, deinde
Caprariam lacertis grandibus refertam; in con-
spectu earum esse Ninguariam, quae hoc nomen
205 acceperit a perpetua nive, nebulosam; proximam ei
Canariam vocari a multitudine canum ingentis
magnitudinis (ex quibus perducti sunt Iubae duo);
apparere[2] ibi vestigia aedificiorum; cum omnes
autem copia pomorum et avium omnis generis
abundent, hanc et palmetis caryotas ferentibus ac
nuce pinea abundare; esse copiam et mellis, papyrum
quoque et siluros in amnibus gigni; infestari eas
beluis, quae expellantur[3] adsidue, putrescentibus.

206   XXXVIII. Et abunde orbe terrae extra intra
indicato colligenda in artum mensura aequorum
videtur.

Polybius a Gaditano freto longitudinem directo
cursu ad os Maeotis $\overline{|XXXIV|}$ $\overline{XXXVII}$ D prodidit, ab
eodem initio ad orientem recto cursu Siciliam $\overline{|XII|}$
L, Cretam $\overline{CCCLXXV}$, Rhodum $\overline{CLXXXVII}$ D, Chelidonias
tantundem, Cyprum $\overline{CCXXV}$, inde Syriae Seleuciam
207 Pieriam $\overline{CXV}$, quae computatio efficit $\overline{|XXIII|}$ $\overline{XL}$.
Agrippa hoc idem intervallum a freto Gaditano ad
sinum Issicum per longitudinem directam $\overline{|XXXIV|}$ $\overline{XL}$
taxat, in quo haud scio an sit error numeri, quoniam

---

[1] uno add. *Sillig.*
[2] *Mayhoff*: apparent.
[3] expuantur ⟨aestu⟩ *Detlefsen.*

Junonia, and that there is a small temple on it built
of only a single stone; and that in its neighbourhood
there is a smaller island of the same name, and then
Capraria, which swarms with large lizards; and
that in view from these islands is Ninguaria, so
named from its perpetual snow, and wrapped in
cloud; and next to it one named Canaria, from its
multitude of dogs of a huge size (two of these were
brought back for Juba). He said that in this
island there are traces of buildings; that while they
all have an abundant supply of fruit and of birds of
every kind, Canaria also abounds in palm-groves
bearing dates, and in conifers; that in addition to
this there is a large supply of honey, and also papyrus
grows in the rivers, and sheat-fish; and that these
islands are plagued with the rotting carcases of
monstrous creatures that are constantly being cast
ashore by the sea.

XXXVIII. And now that we have fully described *Dimensions*
the outer and inner regions of the earth, it seems *of seas*
proper to give a succinct account of the dimensions *and straits.*
of its various bodies of water.

According to Polybius the distance in a straight
line from the Straits of Gibraltar to the outlet of the
Sea of Azov is 3437½ miles, and the distance from
the same starting point due eastward to Sicily 1250
miles, to Crete 375 miles, to Rhodes 187½ miles, to the
Swallow Islands the same, to Cyprus 225 miles, and
from Cyprus to Seleukeh Pieria in Syria 115 miles
—which figures added together make a total of
2340 miles. Agrippa calculates the same distance in
a straight line from the Straits of Gibraltar to the
Gulf of Scanderoon at 3440 miles, in which calculation I suspect there is a numerical error, as he has

idem a Siculo freto Alexandriam cursus |XIII| L
tradidit. universus autem circuitus per sinus dictos
ab eodem exordio colligit ad¹ Maeotim lacum |CLV|
IX; Artemidorus adicit DCCLVI, idem cum Maeotide
|CLXXIII| XC p. esse tradit.²

208 Haec est mensura inermium et pacata audacia
Fortunam provocantium hominum.

Nunc ipsarum partium magnitudo conparabitur,
utcumque difficultatem adferet auctorum diversitas;
aptissime tamen spectabitur ad longitudinem latitudine addita. est ergo ad hoc praescriptum Europae
magnitudo . . . longitudo³ |LXXXI| XLVIII.⁴ Africae
(ut media ex omni varietate prodentium sumatur
computatio) efficit longitudo |XXXVII| XCVIII, latitudo,
209 qua colitur nusquam DCCL⁵ excedit; sed quoniam in
Cyrenaica eius parte DCCCCX eam fecit Agrippa,
deserta eius ad Garamantas usque, qua noscebantur,
complectens, universa mensura quae veniet in
computationem⁶ |XLVII|VIII| efficit. Asiae longitudo
in confesso est |LX| III DCCL, latitudo sane computetur
ab Aethiopico mari Alexandriam iuxta Nilum sitam,
ut per Meroen et Syenen mensura currat, |XVIII|
210 LXXV. apparet ergo Europam paulo minus dimidia

---

¹ V.l. intra.   ² (?)Mayhoff: tradidit.
³ Lacunam statuit et longitudo add. Pintianus.
⁴ Numeri (ut alibi) incerti.
⁵ Rackham: CCL.
⁶ V.l. comparationem (cf. VII. 132).

ᵃ Scholars have taken the words to mean ' by adding the
breadth to the length ', and have charged Pliny with thinking
that this would give the area !
ᵇ The word ' length ' is a conjectural insertion, the figures for
the breadth preceding it having also apparently been omitted
by a copyist.

also given the length of the route from the Straits of Sicily to Alexandria as 1350 miles. The whole length of the coastline round the bays specified, starting at the same point and ending at the Sea of Azov, amounts to 15,509 miles—although Artemidorus puts it at 756 miles more, and also reports that the total coastline including the shores of Azov measures 17,390 miles.

This is the measurement made by persons throwing out a challenge to Fortune not by force of arms, but by the boldness they have displayed in time of peace.

We will now compare the dimensions of particular *Dimensions* parts of the earth, however great the difficulty *of continents.* that will arise from the discrepancy of the accounts given by authors; nevertheless the matter will be most suitably presented by giving the breadth in addition to the length.[a] The following, then, is the formula for the area of Europe . . . length [b] 8148 miles. As for Africa—to take the average of all the various accounts given of its dimensions—its length works out at 3798 miles, and the breadth of the inhabited portions nowhere exceeds 750 miles; but as Agrippa made it 910 miles at the Cyrenaic part of the country, by including the African desert as far as the country of the Garamantes, the extent then known, the entire length that will come into the calculation amounts to 4708 miles. The length of Asia is admittedly 6375 miles, and the breadth should properly be calculated from the Ethiopic Sea to Alexandria on the Nile, making the measurement run through Meroë and Syene, which gives 1875 miles. It is consequently clear that Europe is a little less than

493

Asiae parte maiorem esse quam Asiam, eandem altero
tanto et sexta parte Africae ampliorem quam Africam. quod si misceantur omnes summae, liquido
patebit Europam totius terrae tertiam esse partem et
octavam paulo amplius, Asiam vero quartam et
quartamdecimam, Africam autem quintam et insuper
sexagesimam.

211   XXXIX. His addemus etiamnum unam Graecae inventionis sententiam[1] vel exquisitissmae subtilitatis
ut nihil desit in spectando terrarum situ, indicatisque
regionibus noscatur et quae[2] cuique earum societas
sit sive cognatio dierum ac noctium, quibusque inter
se pares umbrae et aequa mundi convexitas. ergo
reddetur hoc etiam, terraque universa in membra
caeli digeretur.[3]

212   Plura sunt autem segmenta mundi quae nostri
circulos appellavere, Graeci parallelos. principium
habet Indiae pars versa ad austrum; patet usque
Arabiam et Rubri Maris accolas. continentur
Gedrosi, Carmani, Persae, Elymaei, Parthyene, Aria,
Susiane, Mesopotamia, Seleucia cognominata Babylonia, Arabia ad Petram[4] usque, Syria Coele, Pelusium, Aegypti inferiora quae Chora vocatur, Alexandria, Africae maritima, Cyrenaica oppida omnia, Thapsus, Hadrumetum, Clupea, Carthago, Utica, uterque
Hippo, Numidia, Mauretania utraque, Atlanticum
mare, Columnae Herculis. in hoc caeli circumplexu
aequinoctii die medio umbilicus quem gnomonem
vocant septem pedes longus umbram non amplius
quattuor pedes longam reddit, noctis vero dieique

---

[1] scientiam *codd. plurimi.*
[2] et cum qua *codd. plurimi* (et cum qua cuique siderum
Mayhoff).   [3] *V.l.* terraeque universae . . . digerentur.
[4] *Warmington*: Petras *codd.*

494

one and a half times the size of Asia, and two and one sixth times the width of Africa. Combining all these figures together, it will be clearly manifest that Europe is a little more than $\frac{1}{3} + \frac{1}{8}$th, Asia $\frac{1}{4} + \frac{1}{14}$th, and Africa $\frac{1}{5} + \frac{1}{60}$th, of the whole earth.

XXXIX. To these we shall further add one theory of Greek discovery showing the most recondite ingenuity, so that nothing may be wanting in our survey of the geography of the world, and so that now the various regions have been indicated, it may be also learnt what alliance or relationship of days and nights each of the regions has, and in which of them the shadows are of the same length and the world's convexity is equal. An account will therefore be given of this also, and the whole earth will be mapped out in accordance with the constituent parts of the heavens. *Division of the earth's surface into Parallels.*

The world has a number of segments to which our countrymen give the name of 'circles' and which the Greeks call 'parallels'. The first place belongs to the southward part of India, extending as far as Arabia and the people inhabiting the coast of the Red Sea. This segment includes the Gedrosians, Carmanians, Persians, and Elymaeans, Parthyene, Aria, Susiane, Mesopotamia, Babylonian Seleucia, Arabia as far as Petra, Hollow Syria, Pelusium, the lower parts of Egypt called Chora, Alexandria, the coastal parts of Africa, all the towns of Cyrenaica, Thapsus, Hadrumetum, Clupea, Carthage, Utica, the two Hippos, Numidia, the two Mauretanias, the Atlantic Ocean, the Straits of Gibraltar. In this latitude, at noon at the time of the equinox a sundial-pin or 'gnomon' 7 ft. long casts a shadow not more than 4 ft. long, while the longest night

longissima spatia xiv horas aequinoctiales habent,
brevissima ex contrario x.

213   Sequens circulus incipit ab India vergente ad
occasum, vadit per medios Parthos, Persepolim,
citima Persidis, Arabiam citeriorem, Iudaeam,
Libani montis accolas, amplectitur Babylonem,
Idumaeam, Samariam, Hierosolyma, Ascalonem,
Iopen, Caesaream, Phoenicen, Ptolemaidem, Sido-
nem, Tyrum, Berytum, Botryn, Tripolim, Byblum,
Antiochiam, Laodiceam, Seleuciam, Ciliciae maritima, Cypri austrina, Cretam, Lilybaeum in Sicilia,
septentrionalia Africae et Numidiae. umbilicus
xxxv pedum aequinoctio [1] umbram xxiv pedes longam
facit, dies autem noxque maxima xiv horarum
aequinoctialium est accedente bis quinta parte unius
horae.

214   Tertius circulus ab Indis Imavo proximis oritur;
tendit per Caspias Portas, Mediae proxuma, Cataoniam, Cappadociam, Taurum, Amanum, Issum, Cilicias
Portas, Solos, Tarsum, Cyprum, Pisidiam, Pamphyliam, Siden, Lycaoniam, Lyciam, Patara, Xan-
thum, Caunum, Rhodum, Coum, Halicarnassum,
Cnidum, Dorida, Chium, Delum, Cycladas medias,
Gythium, Malean, Argos, Laconicam, Elim, Olym-
piam, Messeniam Peloponnesi, Syracusas, Catinam,
Siliciam mediam, Sardiniae austrina, Carteiam, Gades.
gnomonis c unciae umbram lxxvii unciarum faciunt.
longissimus dies est aequinoctialium horarum xiv
atque dimidiae cum tricesima unius horae.

---

    [1] *Rackham*: umbilicus aequinoctio xxxv pedum.

and the longest day contain 14 equinoctial hours,[a] and the shortest on the contrary 10.

The next parallel begins with the western part of India, and runs through the middle of Parthia, Persepolis, the nearest parts of Farsistan, Hither Arabia, Judaea and the people living near Mount Lebanon, and embraces Babylon, Idumaea, Samaria, Jerusalem, Ascalon, Joppa, Caesarea, Phoenicia, Ptolemais, Sidon, Tyre, Berytus, Botrys, Tripolis, Byblus, Antioch, Laodicea, Seleucia, seaboard Cilicia, Southern Cyprus, Crete, Lilybaeum in Sicily, Northern Africa and Northern Numidia. At the equinox a 35 ft. gnomon throws a shadow 24 ft. long, while the longest day and the longest night measure $14\frac{2}{5}$ equinoctial hours.[b]

The third parallel begins at the part of India nearest to the Himalayas, and passes through the Caspian Gates, the nearest parts of Media, Cataonia, Cappadocia, Taurus, Amanus, Issus, the Cilician Gates, Soli, Tarsus, Cyprus, Pisidia, Pamphylia, Side, Lycaonia, Lycia, Patara, Xanthus, Caunus, Rhodes, Cos, Halicarnassus, Cnidus, Doris, Chios, Delos, the middle of the Cyclades, Gythium, Malea, Argos, Laconia, Elis, Olympia and Messenia in the Peloponnese, Syracuse, Catania, the middle of Sicily, the southern parts of Sardinia, Carteia, Cadiz. A gnomon 100 inches long throws a shadow 77 inches long. The longest day is $14\frac{8}{15}$ equinoctial hours.

[a] The Roman hour only corresponded in length to the modern hour ($\frac{1}{24}$th of day plus night) at the equinoxes, since they divided the periods from sunrise to sunset and from sunset to sunrise each into 12 hours all the year round.

[b] See preceding note.

PLINY: NATURAL HISTORY

215 Quarto subiacent circulo quae sunt ab altero latere
Imavi, Cappadociae austrina, Galatia, Mysia, Sardis,
Zmyrna, Sipylus mons [1], Tmolus mons, Lydia, Caria,
Ionia, Trallis, Colophon, Ephesus, Miletus, Chios,
Samos, Icarium mare, Cycladum septentrio, Athenae,
Megara, Corinthus, Sicyon, Achaia, Patrae, Isthmus,
Epirus, septentrionalia Siciliae, Narbonensis Galliae
exortiva, Hispaniae maritima a Carthagine Nova et
inde ad occasum. gnomoni xxi pedum respondent
umbrae xvi pedum. longissimus dies habet aequi-
noctiales horas xiv et tertias duas unius horae.

216 Quinto continentur segmento ab introitu Caspii
maris Bactria, Hiberia, Armenia, Mysia, Phrygia,
Hellespontus, Troas, Tenedus, Abydos, Scepsis,
Ilium, Ida mons, Cyzicum, Lampsacum, Sinope,
Amisum, Heraclea in Ponto, Paphlagonia, Lemnus,
Imbrus, Thasus, Cassandria, Thessalia, Macedonia,
Larisa, Amphipolis, Thessalonice, Pella, Edesus,
Beroea, Pharsalia, Carystum, Euboea Boeotum,
Chalcis, Delphi, Acarnania, Aetolia, Apollonia,
Brundisium, Tarentum, Thurii, Locri, Regium,
Lucani, Neapolis, Puteoli, Tuscum mare, Corsica
Baliares, Hispania media. gnomoni septem pedes,
umbris sex. magnitudo diei summa horarum aequi-
noctialium xv.

217 Sexta comprehensio, qua continetur urbs Roma,
amplectitur Caspias gentes, Caucasum, septentrionalia Armeniae, Apolloniam supra Rhyndacum,
Nicomediam, Nicaeam, Calchedonem, Byzantium,
Lysimacheam, Cherronesum, Melanem Sinum, Ab-
deram, Samothraciam, Maroneam, Aenum, Bessicam,
Thraciam, Maedicam, Paeoniam, Illyrios, Durra-
chium, Canusium, Apuliae extuma, Campaniam,

¹ mons add.—vel Tmolus [mons]—Rackham.

498

Under the fourth parallel lie the regions on the other side of the Imavus, the southern parts of Cappadocia, Galatia, Mysia, Sardis, Smyrna, Mount Sipylus, Mount Tmolus, Lydia, Caria, Ionia, Trallis, Colophon, Ephesus, Miletus, Chios, Samos, the Icarian Sea, the northern part of the Cyclades, Athens, Megara, Corinth, Sicyon, Achaia, Patras, the Isthmus, Epirus, the northern districts of Sicily, the eastern districts of Gallia Narbonensis, and the coast of Spain from New Carthage westward. A 21-ft. gnomon has 16-ft. shadows. The longest day has 14⅔ equinoctial hours.

The fifth division, beginning at the entrance of the Caspian Sea, contains Bactria, Hiberia, Armenia, Mysia, Phrygia, the Dardanelles, the Troad, Tenedos, Abydos, Scepsis, Ilium, Mount Ida, Cyzicus, Lampsacus, Sinope, Amisus, Heraclea in Pontus, Paphlagonia, Lemnos, Imbros, Thasos, Cassandria, Thessaly, Macedon, Larisa, Amphipolis, Thessalonica, Pella, Edesus, Beroea, Pharsalia, Carystum, Euboea belonging to Boeotia, Chalcis, Delphi, Acarnania, Aetolia, Apollonia, Brindisi, Taranto, Thurii, Locri, Reggio, the Lucanian territory, Naples, Pozzuoli, the Tuscan Sea, Corsica, the Balearic Islands and the middle of Spain. A 7-ft. gnomon throws a 6-ft. shadow. The longest day is 15 equinoctial hours.

The sixth group, the one containing the city of Rome, comprises the Caspian tribes, the Caucasus, the northern parts of Armenia, Apollonia on the Rhyndacus, Nicomedia, Nicaea, Chalcedon, Byzantium, Lysimachea, the Chersonese, the Gulf of Melas, Abdera, Samothrace, Maronea, Aenos, Bessica, Thrace, Maedica, Paeonia, Illyria, Durazzo, Canosa, the edge of Apulia, Campania,

Etruriam, Pisas, Lunam, Lucam, Genuam, Liguriam,
Antipolim, Massiliam, Narbonem, Tarraconem,
Hispaniam Tarraconensem mediam et inde per
Lusitaniam. gnomoni pedes ix umbrae viii. longis-
sima diei[1] spatia horarum aequinoctialium xv addita
ix parte unius horae aut, ut Nigidio placuit, quinta.

218 Septima divisio ab altera Caspii maris ora incipit,
vadit super Callatim, Bosporum, Borysthenen,
Tomos, Thraciae aversa, Triballos, Illyrici reliqua,
Hadriaticum mare, Aquileiam, Altinum, Venetiam,
Vicetiam, Patavium, Veronam, Cremonam, Ravennam, Anconam, Picenum, Marsos, Paelignos, Sabinos,
Umbriam, Ariminum, Bononiam, Placentiam, Mediolanum omniaque ab Apennino, transque Alpis
Galliam Aquitanicam, Viennam, Pyrenaeum, Celti-
beriam. umbilico xxxv pedum umbrae xxxvi, ut
tamen in parte Venetiae exaequetur umbra gnomoni.
amplissima diei spatia[2] horarum aequinoctialium
219 xv et quintarum partium horae trium.

Hactenus antiquorum exacta celebravimus. se-
quentium diligentissimi quod superest terrarum supra
tribus adsignavere segmentis: a Tanai per Maeotim
lacum et Sarmatas usque Borysthenen atque ita per
Dacos partemque Germaniae, Gallias oceani litora
amplexi, quod esset horarum xvi, alterum per Hyperboreos et Britanniam horarum ·xvii, postremum Scy-
thicum a Ripaeis iugis in Tylen, in quo dies continua-
220 rentur, ut diximus, noctesque per vices. iidem et ante

---

[1] diei *add. Beda.*
[2] *Mayhoff*: amplissima dies.

---

[a] Imaginary mountains in unknown north Europe and Asia.
[b] See IV. 104 *n.*

Etruria, Pisa, Luna, Lucca, Genoa, Liguria, Antibes, Marseilles, Narbonne, Tarragon, the middle of Tarragonian Spain; and then runs through Lusitania. A 9-ft. gnomon throws an 8-ft. shadow. The longest day-time is $15\frac{1}{9}$, or, according to Nigidius, $15\frac{1}{5}$ equinoctial hours.

The seventh division starts from the other side of the Caspian Sea and passes above Collat, the Straits of Kertsch, the Dnieper, Tomi, the back parts of Thrace, the Triballi, the remainder of Illyria, the Adriatic Sea, Aquileia, Altinum, Venice, Vicenza, Padua, Verona, Cremona, Ravenna, Ancona, Picenum, the Marsians, Paelignians and Sabines, Umbria, Rimini, Bologna, Piacenza, Milan and all the districts at the foot of the Apennines, and across the Alps Aquitanian Gaul, Vienne, the Pyrenees and Celtiberia. A 35-ft. gnomon throws 36-ft. shadows, except that in part of the Venetian district the shadow and the gnomon are equal. The longest day-time consists of $15\frac{3}{5}$ equinoctial hours.

Up to this point we have been setting forth the results worked out by the ancients. The rest of the earth's surface has been allotted by the most careful among subsequent students to three additional parallels: from the Don across the Sea of Azov and the country of the Sarmatae to the Dnieper and so across Dacia and part of Germany, and including the Gallic provinces forming the coasts of the Ocean, making a parallel with a sixteen-hour longest day; the next across the Hyperboreans and Britain, with a seventeen-hour day; the last the Scythian parallel from the Ripaean mountain-range [a] to Thule,[b] in which, as we said above, there are alternate periods of perpetual daylight and perpetual night.

principia quae fecimus posuere circulos duos: primum per insulam Meroen et Ptolemaidem in Rubro Mari ad elephantorum venatus conditam, ubi longissimus dies XII horarum esset dimidia hora amplior, secundum per Syenen Aegypti euntem, qui esset horarum XIII; iidemque singulis dimidia horarum spatia usque ad ultimum adiecere circulis.

Et hactenus de terris.

The same authorities also place two parallels before what we made the starting point, the first running through the island of Meroë and Ptolemy's Lodge built on the Red Sea for the sake of elephant-hunting, in which parallel the longest day will be 12½ hours, and the second passing through Syene in Egypt, with a 13-hour day; and they also add half an hour to each of the parallels up to the last.

So far as to the geography of the world.

BOOK VII

LIBER VII

Mundus et in eo terrae, gentes, maria, flumina[1]
insignia, insulae, urbes ad hunc modum se habent.

Animantium in eodem natura nullius prope partis
contemplatione minor est, etsi ne hic[2] quidem
omnia exsequi humanus animus queat.[3]

Principium iure tribuetur homini, cuius causa
videtur cuncta alia genuisse natura magna,[4] saeva
mercede contra tanta sua munera, ut non sit satis
aestimare, parens melior homini an tristior noverca
2 fuerit. ante omnia unum animantium cunctorum
alienis velat opibus, ceteris varie tegimenta tribuit,
testas, cortices, spinas, coria, villos, saetas, pilos,
plumam, pinnas, squamas, vellera; truncos etiam
arboresque cortice, interdum gemino, a frigoribus et
calore tutata est: hominem tantum nudum et in
nuda humo natali die abicit ad vagitus statim et
ploratum, nullumque tot animalium aliud pronius[5] ad
lacrimas, et has protinus vitae principio; at Hercule
risus praecox ille et celerrimus ante XL diem nulli
3 datur. ab hoc lucis rudimento quae ne feras quidem

---

[1] flumina *add. Mayhoff.*   [2] ne hic *add. Mayhoff.*
[3] *V.l.* nequeat.   [4] [magna]? *Rackham.*
[5] pronius *add. edd. vet.*

---

[a] ' Great ' is perhaps to be omitted, as an interpolated gloss
on *saeva.*

BOOK VII

The above is a description of the world, and of the lands, races, seas, important rivers, islands and cities that it contains.

The nature of the animals also contained in it is *Zoology.* not less important than the study of almost any other department, albeit here too the human mind is not capable of exploring the whole field.

The first place will rightly be assigned to man, for *Man the* whose sake great [a] Nature appears to have created *highest species, but* all other things—though she asks a cruel price for all *dependent on* her generous gifts, making it hardly possible to judge *the others.* whether she has been more a kind parent to man or more a harsh stepmother. First of all, man alone of all animals she drapes with borrowed resources. On all the rest in various wise she bestows coverings —shells, bark, spines, hides, fur, bristles, hair, down, feathers, scales, fleeces; even the trunks of trees she has protected against cold and heat by bark, sometimes in two layers: but man alone on the day of his birth she casts away naked on the naked ground, to burst at once into wailing and weeping, and none other among all the animals is more prone to tears, and that immediately at the very beginning of life; whereas, I vow, the much-talked-of smile of infancy even at the earliest is bestowed on no child less than six weeks old. This initiation into the

507

inter nos genitas vincula excipiunt et omnium
membrorum nexus; itaque feliciter natus iacet
manibus pedibusque devinctis flens, animal ceteris
imperaturum, et a suppliciis vitam auspicatur unam
tantum ob culpam, quia natum est. heu dementiam
ab his initiis existimantium ad superbiam se genitos!
4 Prima roboris spes primumque temporis munus
quadripedi similem facit. quando homini incessus!
quando vox! quando firmum cibis os! quam diu
palpitans vertex, summae inter cuncta animalia
inbecillitatis indicium! iam morbi, totque medicinae
contra mala excogitatae, et hae quoque subinde
novitatibus victae! et cetera sentire naturam suam,
alia pernicitatem usurpare, alia praepetes volatus,
alia nare: hominem nihil scire nisi doctrina, non
fari, non ingredi, non vesci, breviterque non aliud
naturae sponte quam flere! itaque multi extitere
qui non nasci optimum censerent aut[1] quam ocissime
5 aboleri. uni animantium luctus est datus, uni
luxuria et quidem innumerabilibus modis ac per
singula membra, uni ambitio, uni avaritia, uni
inmensa vivendi cupido, uni superstitio, uni sepulturae cura atque etiam post se de futuro. nulli
vita fragilior, nulli rerum omnium libido maior, nulli
pavor confusior, nulli rabies acrior. denique cetera

---

[1] aut ⟨natum⟩ ? *Rackham.*

---

[a] Cf. XII. 104.

light is followed by a period of bondage such as
befalls not even the animals bred in our midst,
fettering all his limbs; and thus when successfully
born he lies with hands and feet in shackles, weeping—the animal that is to lord it over all the rest,
and he initiates his life with punishment because of
one fault only, the offence of being born. Alas the
madness of those who think that from these beginnings they were bred to proud estate!

His earliest promise of strength and first grant of *Man's*
time makes him like a four-footed animal. When *limitations*
does man begin to walk? when to speak? when is his *divisions.*
mouth firm enough to take food? how long does his
skull throb,[a] a mark of his being the weakest among
all animals? Then his diseases, and all the cures
contrived against his ills—these cures also subsequently defeated by new disorders! And the fact
that all other creatures are aware of their own
nature, some using speed, others swift flight, others
swimming, whereas man alone knows nothing save
by education—neither how to speak nor how to walk
nor who to eat; in short the only thing he can do by
natural instinct is to weep! Consequently there have
been many who believed that it were best not to be
born, or to be put away as soon as possible. On
man alone of living creatures is bestowed grief, on
him alone luxury, and that in countless forms and
reaching every separate part of his frame; he alone
has ambition, avarice, immeasurable appetite for
life, superstition, anxiety about burial and even
about what will happen after he is no more. No
creature's life is more precarious, none has a greater
lust for all enjoyments, a more confused timidity, a
fiercer rage. In fine, all other living creatures pass

509

animantia in suo genere probe degunt: congregari videmus et stare contra dissimilia—leonum feritas inter se non dimicat, serpentium morsus non petit serpentis, ne maris quidem beluae ac pisces nisi in diversa genera saeviunt: at Hercule homini plurima ex homine sunt mala.

6   I. Et de universitate quidem generis humani magna ex parte in relatione gentium diximus.[a] neque enim ritus moresque nunc tractabimus innumeros ac totidem paene quot sunt coetus hominum; quaedam tamen haud omittenda duco, maximeque longius ab mari degentium, in quibus prodigiosa aliqua et incredibilia multis visum iri haud dubito. quis enim Aethiopas antequam cerneret credidit? aut quid non miraculo est cum primum in notitiam venit? quam multa fieri non posse priusquam sunt facta

7   iudicantur? naturae vero rerum vis atque maiestas in omnibus momentis fide caret si quis modo partes eius ac non totam conplectatur animo. ne pavones ac tigrium pantherarumque maculas et tot animalium picturas commemorem, parvum dictu sed inmensum aestimatione, tot gentium sermones, tot linguae, tanta loquendi varietas ut externus alieno paene non

8   sit hominis vice! iam in facie vultuque nostro cum sint decem aut paulo plura membra, nullas duas in tot milibus hominum indiscretas effigies existere,

---

[a] In the geographical books.

their time worthily among their own species: we
see them herd together and stand firm against other
kinds of animals—fierce lions do not fight among
themselves, the serpent's bite attacks not serpents,
even the monsters of the sea and the fishes are only
cruel against different species; whereas to man, I
vow, most of his evils come from his fellow-man.

I. And about the human race as a whole we have *Man's racial*
in large part spoken in our account of the various *and*
individual
nations.[a] Nor shall we now deal with manners *varieties.*
and customs, which are beyond counting and almost
as numerous as the groups of mankind; yet there
are some that I think ought not to be omitted, and
especially those of the people living more remote
from the sea; some things among which I doubt
not will appear portentous and incredible to many.
For who ever believed in the Ethiopians before
actually seeing them? or what is not deemed
miraculous when first it comes into knowledge?
how many things are judged impossible before they
actually occur? Indeed the power and majesty of the
nature of the universe at every turn lacks credence
if one's mind embraces parts of it only and not the
whole. Not to mention peacocks, or the spotted
skins of tigers and panthers and the colourings of so
many animals, a small matter to tell of but one of
measureless extent if pondered on is the number
of national languages and dialects and varieties of
speech, so numerous that a foreigner scarcely counts
as a human being for someone of another race!
Again though our physiognomy contains ten features
or only a few more, to think that among all the
thousands of human beings there exist no two
countenances that are not distinct—a thing that no

511

quod ars nulla in paucis numero praestet adfectando!
nec tamen ego in plerisque eorum obstringam fidem
meam, potiusque ad auctores relegabo qui dubiis
reddentur omnibus, modo ne sit fastidio Graecos
sequi tanto maiore eorum diligentia vel cura
vetustiore.

9   II. Esse Scytharum genera, et quidem plura, quae
corporibus humanis vescerentur indicavimus—id
ipsum incredibile fortasse ni cogitemus, in medio
orbe terrarum [ac Sicilia et Italia [1]] fuisse gentes
huius monstri, Cyclopas et Laestrygonas, et nuper-
rime trans Alpis hominem immolari gentium earum
10 more solitum, quod paulum a mandendo abest. sed
iuxta eos qui sunt ad septentrionem versi, haut
procul ab ipso aquilonis exortu specuque eius dicto,
quem locum Ges Clithron appellant, produntur
Arimaspi, quos diximus, uno oculo in fronte media
insignes. quibus adsidue bellum esse circa metalla
cum grypis, ferarum volucri genere, quale vulgo
traditur, eruente ex cuniculis aurum, mira cupiditate
et feris custodientibus et Arimaspis rapientibus,
multi sed maxime inlustres Herodotus et Aristeas
Proconnesius scribunt.

11   Super alios autem Anthropophagos Scythas in
quadam convalle magna Imavi montis regio est quae
vocatur Abarimon, in qua silvestres vivunt homines
aversis post crura plantis, eximiae velocitatis, passim

---

[1] *V.l.* ab Italia et Sicilia: *secl. Mayhoff.*

---

[a] The MSS. add 'and in Italy and Sicily,' or 'away from
Italy and Sicily.'

[b] *I.e.* the extreme limit of the world; the κλεῖθρον was a
wooden or iron bar with which a door was made fast.

[c] III. 116, IV. 13, 27.

art could supply by counterfeit in so small a number
of specimens! Nevertheless in most instances of
these I shall not myself pledge my own faith, and
shall preferably ascribe the facts to the authorities
who will be quoted for all doubtful points: only do
not let us be too proud to follow the Greeks, because
of their far greater industry or older devotion to study.

II. We have pointed out that some Scythian tribes, *Cannibals*
and in fact a good many, feed on human bodies—a *and savages*
statement that perhaps may seem incredible if we IV. 88,
do not reflect that races of this portentous character VI. 53.
have existed in the central region of the world,[a]
named Cyclopes and Laestrygones, and that quite
recently the tribes of the parts beyond the Alps
habitually practised human sacrifice, which is not
far removed from eating human flesh. But also a
tribe is reported next to these, towards the North,
not far from the actual quarter whence the North
Wind rises and the cave that bears its name, the
place called the Earth's Door-bolt[b]—the Arimaspi
whom we have spoken of already, people remarkable IV. 88,
for having one eye in the centre of the forehead. VI. 50.
Many authorities, the most distinguished being
Herodotus[c] and Aristeas of Proconnesus, write that
these people wage continual war around their mines
with the griffins, a kind of wild beast with wings, as
commonly reported, that digs gold out of mines,
which the creatures guard and the Arimaspi try to
take from them, both with remarkable covetousness.

But beyond the other Scythian cannibals, in a
certain large valley in the Himalayas, there is a
region called Abarimon where are some people dwelling in forests who have their feet turned backward
behind their legs, who run extremely fast and range

513

cum feris vagantes. hos in alio non spirare caelo ideoque ad finitimos reges non pertrahi neque ad Alexandrum Magnum pertractos Baeton itinerum

12 eius mensor prodidit. priores Anthropophagos, quos ad septentrionem esse diximus, decem dierum itinere supra Borysthenen amnem, ossibus humanorum capitum bibere cutibusque cum capillo pro mantelibus ante pectora uti Isigonus Nicaeensis. idem in Albania gigni quosdam glauca oculorum acie, pueritia statim canos, qui noctu plus quam interdiu cernant. idem itinere dierum tredecim supra Borysthenen Sauromatas tertio die cibum capere semper.

13 Crates Pergamenus in Hellesponto circa Parium genus hominum fuisse, quos Ophiogenes vocat, serpentium ictus contactu levare solitos et manu inposita venena extrahere corpori. Varro etiamnum esse paucos ibi quorum salivae contra ictus serpentium

14 medeantur. similis et in Africa Psyllorum gens fuit, ut Agatharchides scribit, a Psyllo rege dicta, cuius sepulchrum in parte Syrtium maiorum est. horum corpori ingenitum fuit virus exitiale serpentibus et cuius odore sopirent eas, mos vero liberos genitos protinus obiciendi saevissimis earum eoque genere pudicitiam coniugum experiendi, non profugientibus adulterino sanguine natos serpentibus. haec gens

514

abroad over the country with the wild animals. It is stated by Baeton, Alexander the Great's route-surveyor on his journeys, that these men are unable to breathe in another climate, and that consequently none of them could be brought to the neighbouring kings or had ever been brought to Alexander. According to Isogonus of Nicaea the former cannibal tribes whom we stated to exist to the north, ten days' journey beyond the river Dnieper, drink out of human skulls and use the scalps with the hair on as napkins hung round their necks. The same authority states that certain people in Albania are born with keen grey eyes and are bald from childhood, and that they see better by night than in the daytime. He also says that the Sauromatae, thirteen days' journey beyond the Dnieper, always take food once every two days.

Crates of Pergamum states that there was a race of men round Parium on the Dardanelles, whom he calls Ophiogenes, whose custom it was to cure snake-bites by touch and draw the poison out of the body by placing their hand on it. Varro says that there are still a few people there whose spittle is a remedy against snake-bites. According to the writings of Agatharchides there was also a similar tribe in Africa, the Psylli, named after King Psyllus, whose tomb is in the region of the greater Syrtes. In their bodies there was engendered a poison that was deadly to snakes, and the smell of which they employed for sending snakes to sleep, while they had a custom of exposing their children as soon as they were born to the most savage snakes and of using that species to test the fidelity of their wives, as snakes do not avoid persons born with adulterous blood in them. This tribe itself has been almost

Tribes immune from snake-bites,

515

ipsa quidem prope internicione sublata est a Nasa-
monibus qui nunc eas tenent sedes, genus tamen
hominum ex iis qui profugerant aut cum pugnatum
15 est afuerant hodie [1] remanet in paucis. simile et in
Italia Marsorum genus durat, quos a Circae filio
ortos ferunt et ideo inesse iis vim naturalem eam. et
tamen omnibus hominibus contra serpentes inest vene-
num : ferunt ictum salivae ut ferventis aquae contactum fugere ; quod si in fauces penetraverit, etiam
mori, idque maxime humani ieiuni oris.

Supra Nasamonas confinesque illis Machlyas
Androgynos esse utriusque naturae inter se vicibus
coeuntes Calliphanes tradit. Aristoteles adicit
dextram mammam is virilem, laevam muliebrem esse.
16 in eadem Africa familias quasdam effascinantium
Isigonus et Nymphodorus tradunt, quorum laudatione
intereant prata, arescant arbores, emoriantur infantes.
esse eiusdem generis in Triballis et Illyris adicit
Isigonus qui visu quoque effascinent interimantque
quos diutius intueantur, iratis praecipue oculis ;
quod eorum malum facilius sentire puberes ; nota-
bilius esse quod pupillas binas in singulis habeant
17 oculis. huius generis et feminas in Scythia, quae
Bitiae vocantur, prodit Apollonides, Phylarchus et
in Ponto Thibiorum genus multosque alios eiusdem
naturae, quorum notas tradit in altero oculo geminam
pupillam in altero equi effigiem, eosdem praeterea

---

[1] *Rackham* : hodieque.

---

[a] Agrius, whose father was Ulysses.

exterminated by the Nasamones who now occupy
that region, but a tribe of men descended from those
who had escaped or had been absent when the fighting
took place survives to-day in a few places. A
similar race lingers on in Italy also, the Marsi, said
to be descended from the son[a] of Circe and to possess
this natural property on that account. However,
all men contain a poison available as a protection
against snakes: people say that snakes flee from
contact with saliva as from the touch of boiling
water, and that if it gets inside their throats they
actually die; and that this is especially the case
with the saliva of a person fasting.

Beyond the Nasamones and adjacent to them *and with*
Calliphanes records the Machlyes, who are Androgyni *other strange*
and perform the function of either sex alternately. *qualities.*
Aristotle adds that their left breast is that of a man
and their right breast that of a woman. Isogonus and
Nymphodorus report that there are families in the
same part of Africa that practise sorcery, whose praises
cause meadows to dry up, trees to wither and infants
to perish. Isogonus adds that there are people of
the same kind among the Triballi and the Illyrians,
who also bewitch with a glance and who kill those
they stare at for a longer time, especially with a look
of anger, and that their evil eye is most felt by adults;
and that what is more remarkable is that they have
two pupils in each eye. Apollonides also reports
women of this kind in Scythia, who are called the
Bitiae, and Phylarchus also the Thibii tribe and many
others of the same nature in Pontus, whose distinguishing marks he records as being a double pupil
in one eye and the likeness of a horse in the other,
and he also says that they are incapable of drowning,

non posse mergi, ne veste quidem degravatos. haut dissimile his genus Pharmacum in Aethiopia Damon, quorum sudor tabem contactis corporibus efferat.

18 feminas quidem omnes ubique visu nocere quae duplices pupillas habeant Cicero quoque apud nos auctor est. adeo naturae, cum ferarum morem vescendi humanis visceribus in homine genuisset, gignere etiam in toto corpore et in quorundam oculis quoque venena placuit, ne quid usquam mali esset quod in homine non esset.

19 Haut procul urbe Roma in Faliscorum agro familiae sunt paucae quae vocantur Hirpi; hae sacrificio annuo quod fit ad montem Soractem Apollini super ambustam ligni struem ambulantes non aduruntur, et ob id perpetuo senatus consulto militiae omniumque aliorum munerum vacationem

20 habent. quorundam corpori partes nascuntur ad aliqua mirabiles, sicut Pyrro regi pollex in dextro pede, cuius tactu lienosis medebatur; hunc cremari cum reliquo corpore non potuisse tradunt, conditumque loculo in templo.

21 Praecipue India Aethiopumque tractus miraculis scatent. maxima in India gignuntur animalia: indicio sunt canes grandiores ceteris. arbores quidem tantae proceritatis traduntur ut sagittis superiaci nequeant et [facit ubertas soli, temperies caeli, aquarum abundantia],[1] si libeat credere, ut sub una fico turmae condantur equitum; harundines

<hr />

[1] *Secl. Detlefsen.*

<hr />

[a] This clause seems to be an interpolation.

even when weighed down with clothing. Damon
records a tribe not unlike these in Ethiopia, the
Pharmaces, whose sweat relieves of diseases bodies
touched by it. Also among ourselves Cicero states·
that the glance of all women who have double pupils
is injurious everywhere. In fact when nature
implanted in man the wild beasts' habit of devouring
human flesh, she also thought fit to implant poisons
in the whole of the body, and with some persons in
the eyes as well, so that there should be no evil any-
where that was not present in man.

There are a few families in the Faliscan territory,
not far from the city of Rome, named the Hirpi,
which at the yearly sacrifice to Apollo performed on
Mount Soracte walk over a charred pile of logs without being scorched, and who consequently enjoy
exemption under a perpetual decree of the senate
from military service and all other burdens. Some
people are born with parts of the body possessing
special remarkable properties, for instance King
Pyrrhus in the great toe of his right foot, to touch
which was a cure for inflammation of the spleen; it
is recorded that at his cremation it proved impossible
to burn the toe with the rest of the body, and it was
stored in a chest in a temple.

India and parts of Ethiopia especially teem with *Oriental*
marvels. The biggest animals grow in India: for *monstrosities*
instance Indian dogs are bigger than any others. *customs.*
Indeed the trees are said to be so lofty that it is not
possible to shoot an arrow over them, and [the richness of the soil, temperate climate and abundance
of springs bring it about ^a] that, if one is willing to
believe it, squadrons of cavalry are able to shelter
beneath a single fig-tree; while it is said that reeds

vero tantae proceritatis ut singula internodia alveo
22 navigabili ternos interdum homines ferant. multos
ibi quina cubita constat longitudine excedere, non
expuere, non capitis aut dentium aut oculorum ullo
dolore adfici, raro aliarum corporis partium : tam
moderato solis vapore durari ; philosophos eorum,
quos gymnosophistas vocant, ab exortu ad occasum
perstare contuentes solem inmobilibus oculis, ferventibus harenis toto die alternis pedibus insistere. in
monte cui nomen est Nulo homines esse aversis
23 plantis octonos digitos in singulis habentes auctor
est Megasthenes, in multis autem montibus genus
hominum capitibus caninis ferarum pellibus velari,
pro voce latratum edere, unguibus armatum venatu
et aucupio vesci ; horum supra $\overline{\text{cxx}}$ fuisse prodente
se. Ctesias scribit et in quadam gente Indiae feminas
semel in vita parere genitosque confestim canescere ;
idem hominum genus qui Monocoli vocentur [1]
singulis cruribus mirae pernicitatis ad saltum,
eosdem Sciapodas vocari, quod in maiori aestu humi
iacentes resupini umbra se pedum protegant ; non
longe eos a Trogodytis abesse, rursusque ab his
occidentem versus quosdam sine cervice oculos
24 in umeris habentes. sunt et satyri subsolanis

[1] *Sillig*: vocarentur.

———

[a] Μονόκωλοι.
[b] Doubtless a kind of monkey.

are of such height that sometimes a single section between two knots will make a canoe that will carry three people. It is known that many of the inhabitants are more than seven feet six inches high, never spit, do not suffer from headache or toothache or pain in the eyes, and very rarely have a pain in any other part of the body—so hardy are they made by the temperate heat of the sun; and that the sages of their race, whom they call Gymnosophists, stay standing from sunrise to sunset, gazing at the sun with eyes unmoving, and continue all day long standing first on one foot and then on the other in the glowing sand. Megasthenes states that on the mountain named Nulus there are people with their feet turned backwards and with eight toes on each foot, while on many of the mountains there is a tribe of human beings with dogs' heads, who wear a covering of wild beasts' skins, whose speech is a bark and who live on the produce of hunting and fowling, for which they use their nails as weapons; he says that they numbered more than 120,000 when he published his work. Ctesias writes that also among a certain race of India the women bear children only once in their life-time, and the children begin to turn grey directly after birth; he also describes a tribe of men called the Monocoli[a] who have only one leg, and who move in jumps with surprising speed; the same are called the Umbrella-foot tribe, because in the hotter weather they lie on their backs on the ground and protect themselves with the shadow of their feet; and that they are not far away from the Cave-dwellers; and again westward from these there are some people without necks, having their eyes in their shoulders. There are also satyrs[b] in the

Indorum montibus (Catarcludorum dicitur regio),
pernicissimum animal, iam quadripedes, iam recte
currentes humana effigie; propter velocitatem nisi
senes aut aegri non capiuntur. Choromandarum
gentem vocat Tauron silvestrem, sine voce, stridoris
horrendi, hirtis corporibus, oculis glaucis, dentibus
caninis. Eudoxus in meridianis Indiae viris plantas
esse cubitales, feminis adeo parvas ut Struthopodes
25 appellentur. Megasthenes gentem inter Nomadas
Indos narium loco foramina tantum habentem
anguium modo, loripedem, vocari Sciritas. ad ex-
tremos fines Indiae ab oriente circa fontem Gangis
Astomorum gentem sine ore, corpore toto hirtam,
vestiri frondium lanugine, halitu tantum viventem et
odore quem naribus trahant; nullum illis cibum
nullumque potum, radicum tantum florumque varios
odores et silvestrium malorum, quae secum portant
longiore itinere ne desit olfactus; graviore paulo
26 odore haut difficulter exanimari. Super hos extrema
in parte montium Trispithami [1] Pygmaeique narrantur, ternas spithamas longitudine, hoc est ternos
dodrantes, non excedentis, salubri caelo semperque
vernante montibus ab aquilone oppositis; quos a
gruibus infestari Homerus quoque prodidit. fama
est insidentes arietum caprarumque dorsis armatos
sagittis veris tempore universo agmine ad mare
descendere et ova pullosque earum alitum con-

---

[1] *Hardouin* (*i.e.* montium III spithami): montium spithami.

a Iliad, III. 6.

mountains in the east of India (it is called the district of the Catarcludi); this is an extremely swift animal, sometimes going on all fours and sometimes standing upright as they run, like human beings; because of their speed only the old ones or the sick are caught. Tauron gives the name of Choromandae to a forest tribe that has no speech but a horrible scream, hairy bodies, keen grey eyes and the teeth of a dog. Eudoxus says that in the south of India men have feet eighteen inches long and the women such small feet that they are called Sparrow-feet. Megasthenes tells of a race among the Nomads of India that has only holes in the place of nostrils, like snakes, and bandy-legged; they are called the Sciritae. At the extreme boundary of India to the East, near the source of the Ganges, he puts the Astomi tribe, that has no mouth and a body hairy all over; they dress in cottonwool and live only on the air they breathe and the scent they inhale through their nostrils; they have no food or drink except the different odours of the roots and flowers and wild apples, which they carry with them on their longer journeys so as not to lack a supply of scent; he says they can easily be killed by a rather stronger odour than usual. Beyond these in the most outlying mountain region we are told of the Three-span men and Pygmies, who do not exceed three spans, i.e. twenty-seven inches, in height; the climate is healthy and always spring-like, as it is protected on the north by a range of mountains; this tribe Homer [a] has also recorded as being beset by cranes. It is reported that in springtime their entire band, mounted on the backs of rams and she-goats and armed with arrows, goes in a body down to the sea and eats the cranes' eggs

523

sumere, ternis expeditionem eam mensibus confici,
aliter futuris gregibus non resisti; casas eorum luto
27 pinnisque et ovorum putaminibus construi. Aristoteles in cavernis vivere Pygmaeos tradit, cetera de
his ut reliqui. Cyrnos Indorum genus Isigonus
annis centenis quadragenis vivere tradit, item
Aethiopas Macrobios et Seras existimat et qui
Athon montem incolant, hos quidem quia viperinis
carnibus alantur, itaque nec capiti nec vestibus eorum
28 noxia corpori inesse animalia. Onesicritus quibus
locis Indiae umbrae non sint corpora hominum
cubitorum quinum et binorum palmorum existere, et
vivere annos cxxx, nec senescere sed in [1] medio
aevo mori. Crates Pergamenus Indos qui centenos
annos excedant Gymnetas appellat, non pauci
Macrobios. Ctesias gentem ex his quae appelletur
Pandae, in convallibus sitam annos ducenos vivere,
in iuventa candido capillo qui in senectute nigrescat;
29 contra alios quadragenos non excedere annos,
iunctos Macrobiis, quorum feminae semel pariant.
idque et Agatharchides tradit, praeterea locustis eos
ali et esse pernices. Mandorum nomen his dedit
Clitarchus, et Megasthenes trecentos quoque eorum
vicos adnumerat, feminas septimo aetatis anno
30 parere, senectam quadragesimo accidere. Artemidorus in Taprobane insula longissimam vitam sine
ullo corporis languore traduci. Duris Indorum

---

[1] *Mayhoff*: ut.

[a] About eight feet.

and chickens, and that this outing occupies three months; and that otherwise they could not protect themselves against the flocks of cranes that would grow up; and that their houses are made of mud and feathers and egg-shells. Aristotle says that the Pygmies live in caves, but in the rest of his statement about them he agrees with the other authorities. The Indian race of Cyrni according to Isigonus live to 140; and he holds that the same is true of the Long-lived Ethiopians, the Chinese and the inhabitants of Mount Athos—in the last case because of their diet of snakes' flesh, which causes their head and clothes to be free from creatures harmful to the body. Onesicritus says that in the parts of India where there are no shadows there are men five cubits and two spans *a* high, and people live a hundred and thirty years, and do not grow old but die middle-aged. Crates of Pergamum tells of Indians who exceed a hundred years, whom he calls Gymnetae, though many call them Long-livers. Ctesias says that a tribe among them called the Pandae, dwelling in the mountain valleys, live two hundred years, and have white hair in their youth that grows black in old age; whereas others do not exceed forty years, this tribe adjoining the Long-livers, whose women bear children only once. Agatharchides records this as well, and also that they live on locusts, and are very swift-footed. Clitarchus gave them the name of Mandi; and Megasthenes also assigns them three hundred villages, and says that the women bear children at the age of seven and old age comes at forty. Artemidorus says that on the Island of Ceylon the people live very long lives without any loss of bodily activity. Duris says that some

quosdam cum feris coire mixtosque et semiferos esse
partus, in Calingis eiusdem Indiae gente quinquennes
concipere feminas, octavum vitae annum non
excedere, et alibi cauda villosa homines nasci pernicitatis eximiae, alios auribus totos contegi.

Oritas ab Indis Arabis fluvius disterminat. hi
nullum alium cibum novere quam piscium, quo
unguibus dissectos sole torreant atque ita panem ex
31 iis faciunt,[1] ut refert Clitarchus. Trogodytas super
Aethiopiam velociores equis esse Pergamenus Crates,
item Aethiopas octona cubita longitudine excedere,
Syrbotas vocari gentem eam. Nomadum Aethiopum
secundum flumen Astragum ad septentrionem
vergentium gens Menisminorum appellata abest ab
oceano dierum itinere viginti; animalium quae
cynocephalos vocamus lacte vivit, quorum armenta
pascit maribus interemptis praeterquam subolis
32 causa. in Africae solitudinibus hominum species
obviae subinde fiunt momentoque evanescunt.

Haec atque talia ex hominum genere ludibria sibi,
nobis miracula, ingeniosa fecit natura. et singula [2]
quidem quae facit in dies ac prope horas quis enumerare valeat? ad detegendam eius potentiam
satis sit inter prodigia posuisse gentes. hinc ad
confessa in homine pauca.

33 III. Tergeminos nasci certum est Horatiorum
Curiatiorumque exemplo; super inter ostenta ducitur

---

[1] V.l. faciant.
[2] V.l. ex singulis.

Indians have union with wild animals and the off-spring is of mixed race and half animal; that among the Calingi, a tribe of the same part of India, women conceive at the age of five and do not live more than eight years, and that in another part men are born with a hairy tail and extremely swift, while others are entirely covered by their ears.

The river Arabis is the frontier between the Indians and the Oritae. These are acquainted with no other food but fish, which they cut to pieces with their nails and roast in the sun and thus make bread out of them, as is recorded by Clitarchus. Crates of Pergamum says that the Cavemen beyond Ethiopia are swifter than horses; also that there are Ethiopians more than twelve feet in height, and that this race is called the Syrbotae. The tribe of the Ethiopian nomads along the river Astragus towards the north called the Menismini is twenty days' journey from the Ocean; it lives on the milk of the animals that we call dog-headed apes, herds of which it keeps in pastures, killing the males except for the purpose of breeding. In the deserts of Africa ghosts of men suddenly meet the traveller and vanish in a moment.

These and similar varieties of the human race have been made by the ingenuity of Nature as toys for herself and marvels for us. And indeed who could possibly recount the various things she does every day and almost every hour? Let it suffice for the disclosure of her power to have included whole races of mankind among her marvels. From these we turn to a few admitted marvels in the case of the individual human being.

III. The birth of triplets is attested by the case *Exceptional* of the Horatii and Curiatii; above that number is *and monstrous births.*

praeterquam in Aegypto, ubi fetifer potu Nilus amnis. proxime supremis divi Augusti Fausta quaedam e plebe Ostiae duos mares totidemque feminas enixa famem quae consecuta est portendit haud dubie. reperitur et in Peloponneso quinos[1] quater enixa, maioremque partem ex omni eius vixisse partu. et in Aegypto septenos uno utero simul gigni auctor est Trogus.

34 Gignuntur et utriusque sexus quos Hermaphroditos vocamus, olim androgynos vocatos et in prodigiis habitos, nunc vero in deliciis. Pompeius Magnus in ornamentis theatri mirabiles fama posuit effigies ob id diligentius magnorum artificum ingeniis elaboratas, inter quas legitur Eutychis a viginti liberis rogo inlata Trallibus enixa xxx partus, Alcippe elephantum, quamquam id inter ostenta est, namque et serpentem peperit inter initia Marsici[a]

35 belli ancilla et multiformes pluribus modis inter monstra partus eduntur. Claudius Caesar scribit hippocentaurum in Thessalia natum eodem die interisse, et nos principatu eius allatum illi ex Aegypto in melle vidimus. est inter exempla in uterum protinus reversus infans Sagunti quo anno urbs[2] deleta ab Hannibale est.[b]

---

[1] quinos] *Sabellius coll. Arist. h. an.* 7, 5, 1 : binos.
[2] urbs *add. Rackham.*

---

[a] The Social War, 91–88 B.C.
[b] 218 B.C.

considered portentous, except in Egypt, where drinking the water of the Nile causes fecundity. Recently on the day of the obsequies of his late Majesty Augustus a certain woman of the lower orders named Fausta at Ostia was delivered of two male and two female infants, which unquestionably portended the food shortage that followed. We also find the case of a woman in the Peloponnese who four times produced quintuplets, the greater number of each birth surviving. In Egypt also Trogus alleges cases of seven infants born at a single birth.

Persons are also born of both sexes combined—what we call Hermaphrodites, formerly called *androgyni* and considered as portents, but now as entertainments. Pompey the Great among the decorations of his theatre placed images of celebrated marvels, made with special elaboration for the purpose by the talent of eminent artists; among them we read of Eutychis who at Tralles was carried to her funeral pyre by twenty children and who had given birth 30 times, and Alcippe who gave birth to an elephant—although it is true that the latter case ranks among portents, for one of the first occurrences of the Marsian War[a] was that a maidservant gave birth to a snake, and also monstrous births of various kinds are recorded among the ominous things that happened. Claudius Caesar writes that a hippocentaur was born in Thessaly and died the same day; and in his reign we actually saw one that was brought here for him from Egypt preserved in honey. One case is that of an infant at Saguntum which at once went back into the womb, in the year[b] in which that city was destroyed by Hannibal.

36   IV. Ex feminis mutari in mares non est fabulosum. invenimus in annalibus P. Licinio Crasso C. Cassio Longino coss. Casini puerum factum ex virgine sub parentibus, iussuque harispicum deportatum in insulam desertam. Licinius Mucianus prodidit visum a se Argis Arescontem, cui nomen Arescusae fuisset, nupsisse etiam, mox barbam et virilitatem provenisse uxoremque duxisse; eiusdem sortis et Zmyrnae puerum a se visum. ipse in Africa vidi mutatum in marem nuptiarum die L. Constitium civem Thysdri-

37 tanum. . . .[1] editis geminis raram esse aut puerperae aut puerperio praeterquam alteri vitam, si vero utriusque sexus editi sint gemini, rariorem utrique salutem; feminas celerius gigni quam mares, sicuti celerius senescere; saepius in utero moveri mares, et in dextera fere geri parte, in laeva feminas.

38   V. Ceteris animantibus statum et pariendi et partus gerendi tempus est: homo toto anno et incerto gignitur spatio, alius septimo mense, alius octavo et usque ad initium undecimi; ante septimum mensem haut umquam vitalis est. septimo non nisi pridie posterove pleniluni die aut interlunio concepti

<hr/>

[1] *Lacunam Urlichs.*

<hr/>

[a] 171 B.C.

[b] Some words seem to have been lost in the Latin here.

IV. Transformation of females into males is not an *Change of* idle story. We find in the Annals that in the *sex.* consulship[a] of Publius Licinius Crassus and Gaius Cassius Longinus a girl at Casinum was changed into a boy, under the observation of the parents, and at the order of the augurs was conveyed away to a desert island. Licinius Mucianus has recorded that he personally saw at Argos a man named Arescon who had been given the name of Arescusa and had actually married a husband, and then had grown a beard and developed masculine attributes and had taken a wife; and that he had also seen a boy with the same record at Smyrna. I myself saw in Africa a person who had turned into a male on the day of marriage to a husband; this was Lucius Constitius, a citizen of Thysdritum. . . .[b] (It is said that) at the birth of twins neither the mother nor more than one of the two children usually lives, but that if twins are born that are of different sex it is even more unusual for either to be saved; that females are born more quickly than males, just as they grow older more quickly; and that movement in the womb is more frequent in the case of males, and males are usually carried on the right side, females on the left.

V. All the other animals have a fixed season both *Human re-* for copulation and for bearing offspring, but human *production.* reproduction takes place all the year round and the period of gestation varies—in one case it may exceed six months, in another seven, and it may even exceed ten; a child born before the seventh month is usually still born. Only those conceived the day before or the day after full moon, or when there is no moon, are born in the seventh month. It is a common thing

39 nascuntur. tralaticium in Aegypto est et octavo
gigni, iam quidem et in Italia tales partus esse vitales
contra priscorum opiniones. variant haec pluribus
modis: Vistilia Gliti ac postea Pomponi atque
Orfiti clarissimorum civium coniunx ex his quattuor
partus enixa, septimo semper mense, genuit Suillium
Rufum undecimo, Corbulonem septumo, utrumque
consulem, postea Caesoniam Gai principis coniugem
40 octavo. in quo mensium numero genitis intra
quadragensimum diem maximus labor, gravidis
autem quarto et octavo mense, letalesque in his
abortus. Masurius auctor est L. Papirium praetorem
secundo herede lege agente bonorum possessionem
contra eum dedisse, cum mater partum se tredecim
mensibus diceret tulisse, quoniam nullum certum
tempus pariendi statutum videretur.

41 VI. A conceptu decimo die dolores capitis,
oculorum vertigines tenebraeque, fastidium in cibis,
redundatio stomachi indices sunt hominis inchoati.
melior color marem ferenti et facilior partus, motus
in utero quadragensimo die. contraria omnia in
altero sexu, ingestabile onus, crurum et inguinis levis
42 tumor, primus autem xc die motus. sed plurumum
languoris in utroque sexu capillum germinante partu

in Egypt for children to be born even in the eighth
month; and indeed in Italy also for such cases to
live, contrary to the belief of old times. These
matters vary in more ways also. Vistilia the wife
of Glitius and subsequently of Pomponius and of
Orfitius, citizens of the highest distinction, bore these
husbands four children, in each case after six months'
pregnancy, but subsequently gave birth to Suillius
Rufus after ten months and Corbulo after six—both
of these became consuls,—and subsequently bore
Caesonia, the consort of the Emperor Gaius, after
seven months. Infants born in this number of
months are weakest in health during the first six
weeks, the mothers in the fourth and eighth months
of pregnancy; and abortions in these cases are
fatal. Masurius states that Lucius Papirius as
praetor in a suit for an estate brought by an heir
presumptive gave judgement for the defendant;
the plaintiff's case was that the heir apparent's
mother said that he had been born after thirteen
months' pregnancy, and the ground for the judgement
was that there appeared to be no fixed period of
pregnancy.

VI. On the tenth day from conception pains in the *Pregnancy.*
head, giddiness and dim sight, distaste for food, and
vomiting are symptoms of the formation of the
embryo. If the child is a male, the mother has a
better colour and an easier delivery; there is movement in the womb on the fortieth day. In a case of
the other sex all the symptoms are the opposite:
the burden is hard to carry, there is a slight swelling
of the legs and groin, but the first movement is on
the ninetieth day. But in the case of both sexes
the greatest amount of faintness occurs when the

et in plenilunio, quod tempus editos quoque infantes
praecipue infestat. adeoque incessus atque omne
quicquid dici potest in gravida refert, ut salsioribus
cibis usae carentem unguiculis partum edant, et si
respiravere difficilius enitantur; oscitatio quidem in
enixu letalis est, sicut sternuisse a coitu abortivum.

43   VII. Miseret atque etiam pudet aestimantem quam
sit frivola animalium superbissimi origo, cum plerisque
abortus causa odor a lucernarum fiat extinctu. his
principiis nascuntur tyranni, his carnifex animus.
tu qui corporis viribus fidis, tu qui fortunae munera
amplexaris et te ne alumnum quidem eius existimas
44 sed partum, tu cuius imperatoria[1] est mens, tu qui
te deum credis aliquo successu tumens, tantine perire
potuisti ? atque etiam hodie minoris potes, quantulo
serpentis ictus dente, aut etiam ut Anacreon poeta
acino uvae passae, aut[2] ut Fabius Senator praetor
in lactis haustu uno pilo strangulatus. is demum
profecto vitam aequa lance pensitabit qui semper
fragilitatis humanae memor fuerit.

45   VIII. In pedes procidere nascentem contra naturam
est, quo argumento eos appellavere Agrippas ut
aegre partos; qualiter M. Agrippam ferunt genitum,
unico prope felicitatis exemplo in omnibus ad hunc
modum genitis—quamquam is quoque adversa
pedum valitudine misera iuventa, exercito aevo

---

[1] *Urlichs*: cuius semper tinctoria (*aut* in victoria).
[2] aut *add. Rackham.*

---

[a] *Aegre partus* is suggested as the etymology of *Agrippa*.

embryo begins to grow hair; and also at the full moon, which period is also specially inimical to infants after birth. The gait in walking and every thing that can be mentioned are so important during pregnancy that mothers eating food that is too salt bear children lacking nails, and that not holding the breath makes the delivery more difficult; indeed, to gape during delivery may cause death, just as a sneeze following copulation causes abortion.

VII. One feels pity and even shame in realizing *Abortion.* how trivial is the origin of the proudest of the animals, when the smell of lamps being put out usually causes abortion! These are the beginnings from which are born tyrants and the pride that deals slaughter. You who put confidence in your bodily strength, you who accept fortune's bounty and deem yourself not even her nurseling but her offspring, you whose thoughts are of empire, you who when swelling with some success believe yourself a god, could you have been made away with so cheaply? and even to-day you can be more cheaply, from being bitten by a snake's tiny tooth, or even choked by a raisin-stone like the poet Anacreon, or by a single hair in a draught of milk, like the praetor Fabius Senator. Assuredly only he who always remembers how frail a thing man is will weigh life in an impartial balance!

VIII. It is against nature to be born feet foremost; *Delivery.* this is the reason why the designation of 'Agrippa' has been applied to persons so born—meaning 'born with difficulty'[a]; Marcus Agrippa is said to have been born in this manner, almost the solitary instance of a successful career among all those so born— although he too is deemed to have paid the penalty which his irregular birth foretold, by a youth made

inter arma mortisque adeo obnoxio accessu, infelici
terris stirpe omni sed per utrasque Agrippinas
maxime, quae Gaium, quae Domitium Neronem
principes genuere totidem faces generis humani,
46 praeterea brevitate aevi quinquagesimo uno raptus
anno in [1] tormentis adulteriorum coniugis socerique
praegravi servitio, luisse augurium praeposteri
natalis existimatur. Neronem quoque paulo ante
principem et toto principatu suo hostem generis
humani pedibus genitum scribit parens eius Agrippina.
ritus [2] naturae capite hominem gigni, mos est pedibus
efferri.
47   IX. Auspicatius e necata [3] parente gignuntur, sicut
Scipio Africanus prior natus primusque Caesarum a
caeso matris utero dictus, qua de causa et Caesones
appellati. simili modo natus et Manilius qui Carthaginem cum exercitu intravit. X. Vopiscos appellabant
e geminis qui retenti utero nascerentur altero
interempto abortu—namque maxima etsi rara circa
hoc miracula existunt.
48   XI. Praeter mulierem pauca animalia coitum novere
gravida, unum quidem omnino aut alterum super-
fetat. extat in monimentis medicorum et eorum [4]
quibus talia consectari curae fuit uno abortu duodecim

[1] [in]? *Rackham.*   [2] *Hardouin*: ritu.
[3] *V.l.* enecta.   [4] eorum *add. Rackham.*

[a] The two Agrippinas.   [b] Julia.   [c] Julius.

unhappy by lameness, a lifetime passed amidst warfare and ever exposed to the approach of death, by the misfortune caused to the world by his whole progeny but especially due to his two daughters [a] who became the mothers of the emperors Gaius Caligula and Domitius Nero, the two firebrands of mankind; and also by the shortness of his life, as he was cut off at the age of fifty during the agony caused him by his wife's [b] adulteries and during his irksome subjection to his father-in-law Augustus. Nero also, who was emperor shortly before and whose entire rule showed him the enemy of mankind, is stated in his mother Agrippina's memoirs to have been born feet first. It is Nature's method for a human being to be born head first, and it is the custom for him to be carried to burial feet first.

IX. It is a better omen when the mother dies in giving birth to the child; instances are the birth of the elder Scipio Africanus and of the first [c] of the Caesars, who got that name from the surgical operation performed on his mother; the origin of the family name Caeso is also the same. Also Manilius who entered Carthage with his army was born in the same manner. X. The name Vopiscus used to be given to cases of a twin born after being retained in the womb when the other twin had been killed by premature delivery— for extremely remarkable though infrequent cases of this occur.

XI. Few animals except woman ever have sexual intercourse when pregnant—at all events superfetation only occurs with animals in very few cases. In the records of the medical profession and of writers who have been interested in collecting such occurrences, there is a case of miscarriage in which

537

puerperia egesta. sed ubi paululum temporis inter
49 duos conceptus intercessit, utrumque perfertur, ut
in Hercule et Iphicle fratre eius apparuit et in ea
quae gemino partu alterum marito similem alterum-
que adultero genuit, item in Proconnesia ancilla
quae eiusdem diei coitu alterum domino similem
alterum procuratori eius, et in alia quae unum iusto
partu, quinque mensium alterum edidit; rursus in alia
quae septem mensium edito puerperio insecutis
tribus [1] mensibus geminos enixa est.

50   Iam illa vulgata sunt [2]: varie ex integris truncos
gigni, ex truncis integros eademque parte truncos;
signa quaedam naevosque et cicatrices etiam regene-
rari, quarto partu aliquorum [3] originis nota in brachio
51 reddita [4] XII. (in Lepidorum gente tres, intermisso
ordine, obducto membrana oculo genitos accepimus);
similes quidem alios avo, et ex geminis quoque
alterum patri alterum matri, annoque post genitum
maiori similem fuisse ut geminum. quasdam sibi similes semper parere, quasdam viro, quasdam nulli,
quasdam feminam patri, marem sibi. indubitatum
exemplum est Nicaei nobilis pyctae Byzanti geniti

---

[1] *Detlefsen (viz. III):* in.
[2] *Mayhoff:* est *aut* et.
[3] *Barbarus:* Dacorum.
[4] *Mayhoff:* redditur.

twelve infants were still-born at once. When, however, a moderate interval of time separates two conceptions, both may be successful, as was seen in the instance of Hercules and his brother Iphicles and in the case of the woman who bore twins of whom one resembled her husband and the other an adulterer; and also in that of the maidservant of Marmara who, as a result of intercourse on the same day, bore one twin resembling her master and another resembling his steward, and that of another woman who bore one twin at the proper period and the other a five-months' child, and again of another who after bearing a seven months' child was delivered of twins three months later.

It is also well known that sound parents may have deformed children and deformed parents sound children or children with the same deformity, as the case may be; that some marks and moles and even scars reappear in the offspring, in some cases a birth-mark on the arm reappearing in the fourth generation XII. (we are told that in the Lepidus family three children were born, though not all in succession, with a membrane over the eyes); and indeed that other children have resembled their grandfather, and that also there has been a case of twins of which one resembled the father and the other the mother, and one of a child who resembled his brother like a twin although born a year later. Also that some women always bear children like themselves, some bear children like their husbands, some children with no family likeness, some a female child like its father and a male child like themselves. One unquestioned instance is that of the famous boxer Nicaeus, born at Istamboul, whose mother was the offspring of

Transmission of characteristics.

539

qui adulterio Aethiopis nata matre nihil a ceteris
colore differente ipse avum regeneravit Aethiopem.

52 Similitudinum quidem inmensa reputatio est et in
qua credantur multa fortuita pollere, visus, auditus
memoriae [1] haustaeque imagines sub ipso conceptu.
cogitatio etiam utriuslibet animum subito transvolans
effingere similitudinem aut miscere existimatur,
ideoque plures in homine quam in ceteris omnibus
animalibus differentiae quoniam velocitas cogita-
tionum animique celeritas et ingeni varietas multiformes notas inprimunt,[2] cum ceteris animantibus
inmobiles sint animi et similes omnibus singulisque
53 in suo cuique genere. Antiocho regi Syriae e plebe
nomine Artemo in tantum similis fuit ut Laodice
coniunx regia necato iam Antiocho mimum per eum
commendationis regnique successionis peregerit.
Magno Pompeio Vibius quidam e plebe et Publicius
etiam servitute liberatus indiscreta prope specie
fuere similes, illud os probum reddentes ipsumque
54 honorem eximiae frontis. qualis causa patri quoque
eius Menogenis coci sui cognomen inposuit (iam
Strabonis a specie oculorum habenti vitium imi-
tata et in servo), Scipioni Serapionis—is erat suarii

[1] *Rackham*: memoria.
[2] *Mayhoff*: imprimit *aut* imprimat.

---

[a] Or perhaps 'the rest of her family,' or 'other half-breeds.'
[b] Antiochus III, the Great, 223–187 B.C. Valerius Maximus,
IX. 14, says that the king's mimic was a member of the
royal family, and that he pretended to be the king lying ill
in bed and the public were admitted to see him; so Laodice
secured acceptance for her story that the king on his death-
bed had commended her and his children to the protection
of the people.
[c] 'Cross-eyed.'

adultery with an Ethiopian but had a complexion no different from that of other women,[a] whereas Nicaeus himself reproduced his Ethiopian grandfather.

Cases of likeness are indeed an extremely wide subject, and one which includes the belief that a great many accidental circumstances are influential—recollections of sights and sounds and actual sense-impressions received at the time of conception. Also a thought suddenly flitting across the mind of either parent is supposed to produce likeness or to cause a combination of features, and the reason why there are more differences in man than in all the other animals is that his swiftness of thought and quickness of mind and variety of mental character impress a great diversity of patterns, whereas the minds of the other animals are sluggish, and are alike for all and sundry, each in their own kind. A man of low station named Artemo so closely resembled Antiochus,[b] king of Syria, that the royal consort Laodice after she had murdered Antiochus successfully made use of him to stage a play of her being recommended for succession to the throne. Pompey the Great had two doubles almost indistinguishable from him in appearance, a plebeian named Vibius and one Publicius who was actually a liberated slave, both of whom reproduced that noble countenance and the actual dignity of his magnificent brow. A similar resemblance was the reason that saddled Pompey's father also with the surname Menogenes, that being the name of his cook, when he already had the surname Strabo[c] from the appearance of his eyes, which actually copied a defect in his slave; and a Scipio received the surname Serapio in a similar way,

Causes of transmission.

Cases of likeness of unrelated persons.

541

negotiatoris vile mancipium. eiusdem familiae Scipioni post eum nomen Salutio mimus dedit, sicut
Spinther secundarius tertiariusque,[1] Pamphilus col-
legio Lentuli et Metelli consulum, in quo perquam
inportune fortuitum hoc quoque fuit, duorum simul
55 consulum in scaena imagines cerni. e diverso L.
Plancus orator histrioni Rubrio cognomen inposuit,
rursus Curioni patri Burbuleius, itemque Messalae
censorio Menogenes, perinde histriones. Surae
quidem proconsulis etiam rictum in loquendo contrac-
tionemque linguae et sermonis tumultum, non
imaginem modo, piscator quidam in Sicilia reddidit.
Cassio Severo celebri oratori Armentarii murmillonis[2]
obiecta similitudo est. modo in Annaea[3] domo
Gallionem a Castellano liberto non discernebant,
nec a Sannio mimo Paride cognominato Agrippinum
56 senatorem. Toranius mango Antonio iam triumviro
duos[4] eximios forma pueros, alterum in Asia genitum
alterum trans Alpes, ut geminos vendidit: tanta
unitas erat. postquam deinde sermone puerorum
detecta fraude a furente increpitus Antonio est,
inter alia magnitudinem preti conquerente (nam
ducentis erat mercatus sestertiis), respondit versutus
ingenii mango id ipsum se tanti vendidisse, quoniam
non esset mira similitudo in ullis eodem utero editis,

---

[1] *Vulg.* secundarum tertiarumque.
[2] *Vel* armentarii Murmillonis.
[3] *Detlefsen:* in ea.
[4] duos *add. Rackham.*

---

[a] Or ' the cowherd Murmillo.'

Serapio being a low chattel belonging to a dealer in hogs. Another Scipio of a later generation received his name from an actor Salutio, just as Spinther and Pamphilus who played second and third roles respectively gave their names to the colleagues in the consulship Lentulus and Metellus, a situation which also (most inappropriately) resulted incidentally in the counterfeit presentations of two consuls being seen on the stage at once. *Vice versa*, Lucius Plancus an orator gave a surname to a player Rubrius, whereas Burbuleius gave his name to Curio senior and likewise Menogenes to the former censor Messala, both alike being actors. A fisherman in Sicily not only resembled the proconsul Sura in appearance but actually reproduced his gape while speaking and his tongue-tied stammering utterance. The famous orator Cassius Severus was taunted for his likeness to the gladiator Armentarius.[a] Recently in the household of Annaeus people used to mistake Gallio for the freedman Castellanus and the senator Agrippinus for the actor Sannius, surnamed Paris. The slave-dealer Toranius sold to Antony after he had become one of the triumvirate two exceptionally handsome boys, who were so identically alike that he passed them off as twins, although one was a native of Asia and the other of a district North of the Alps. Later the boys' speech disclosed the fraud, and a protest was made to the dealer by the wrathful Antony, who complained especially about the large amount of the price (he had bought them for 200,000 sesterces); but the crafty dealer replied that the thing protested about was precisely the cause of his having charged so much, because there was nothing remarkable in a likeness between any pair of twin

diversarum quidem gentium natales tam concordi
figura reperiri super omnem esse taxationem;
adeoque tempestivam admirationem intulit ut ille
proscriptor, minis [1] modo et contumelia furens, non
aliud in censu magis ex fortuna sua duceret.

57 XIII. Est quaedam privatim dissociatio corporum,
et inter se sterilis ubi cum aliis iunxere se, gignunt,
sicut Augustus et Livia; item alii. aliaeque feminas
tantum generant aut mares, plerumque et alternant,
sicut Gracchorum mater duodeciens, Agrippina
Germanici noviens; aliis sterilis est iuventa, aliis
semel in vita datur gignere; quaedam non perferunt
58 partus, quales, si quando medicina naturam [2] vicere,
feminam fere gignunt. divus Augustus in reliqua
exemplorum raritate neptis suae nepotem vidit
genitum quo excessit anno M. Silanum, qui cum
Asiam obtineret post consulatum Neronis principis
59 successione, veneno eius interemptus est. Q. Metellus Macedonicus, cum sex liberos relinqueret, XI
nepotes reliquit, nurus vero generosque et omnes
60 qui se patris appellatione salutarent XXVII. in actis
temporum divi Augusti invenitur duodecimo con-

---

[1] *Rhenanus*: animus.
[2] *Detlefsen*: medicina et cura.

---

[a] *I.e.* all but one of his grandchildren were married.
[b] 4 B.C.

brothers, whereas (he said) to find natives of different races so precisely alike in appearance was something above all appraisal; and this produced in Antony so convenient a feeling of admiration that the great inflictor of outlawry, who had just been in a fury of threats and abuse, considered that no other property that he possessed was more suited to his station!

XIII. Particular individuals may have a certain *Exceptional* physical incongruity between them, and persons whose *cases of fertility, etc.* union is infertile may have children when they form other connexions—for instance Augustus and Livia, and similarly others. Also some women have only female or only male children, though usually the sexes come alternately—for instance in the case of the mother of the Gracchi this occurred twelve times, and in that of Germanicus's wife Agrippina nine times; some women are childless in youth; on some parentage is bestowed once in a lifetime; certain women are always delivered prematurely, and those of this class, if ever they succeed in overcoming this tendency by the use of drugs, usually bear a female child. One of the many exceptional circumstances connected with his late Majesty Augustus is that he lived to see his daughter's grandson, Marcus Silanus, who was born in the year of his death; Silanus, after succeeding the emperor Nero as consul, held the province of Asia, and during his office Nero despatched him by poison. Quintus Metellus Macedonicus, leaving six children, left eleven grand-children, but including daughters-in-law and sons-in-law the total of those who greeted him by the title of father was twenty-seven.[a] In the annals of the period of his late Majesty Augustus is found a statement that in his twelfth consulship,[b] when

sulatu eius L. que Sulla collega a. d. III idus Aprilis C.
Crispinium Hilarum ex ingenua plebe Faesulana cum
liberis VIII, in quo numero filiae duae fuere, nepotibus
XXVII, pronepotibus XVIII, neptibus VIII, praelata
pompa cum omnibus his in Capitolio immolasse.

61 XIV. Mulier post quinquagensimum annum non
gignit, maiorque pars XL profluvium genitale sistit.
nam in viris Masinissam regem post LXXXVI annum
generasse filium quem Methimannum appellaverit
clarum est, Catonem censorium octogesimo exacto e
62 filia Saloni clientis sui: qua de causa aliorum eius
liberum propago Liciniani sunt cognominati, hi
Saloniani, ex quis Uticensis fuit. nuper etiam L.
Volusio Saturnino in urbis praefectura extincto notum
est e Cornelia Scipionum gentis Volusium Saturninum
qui fuit consul genitum post LXII annum. et usque
ad LXXV apud ignobiles vulgaris reperitur generatio.

63 XV. Solum autem animal menstruale mulier est;
inde unius utero quas appellaverunt molas. ea est
caro informis, inanima, ferri ictum et aciem respuens;
movetur sistitque menses, ut et partus, alias letalis
alias una senescens aliquando alvo citatiore excidens.
simile quiddam et viris in ventre gignitur, quod
vocant scirron, sicut Oppio Capitoni praetorio viro.

Lucius Sulla was his colleague, on the 9th April a freeman of humble station at Fiesole named Gaius Crispinius Hilarus went in procession preceded by eight children, including two daughters, twenty-seven grandchildren, eighteen great-grandchildren, and eight granddaughters by marriage, and with all of these in attendance offered sacrifice on the Capitol.

XIV. A woman does not bear children after the age of fifty, and with the majority menstruation ceases at 40. As for the case of men, it is well known that King Masinissa begot a son when over 86, whom he called Methimannus, and Cato the ex-censor had a son by the daughter of his client Salonius when he was 81: this is the reason why this branch of his family bears the surname of Salonianus, although that of the other branch is Licinianus; Cato of Utica belonged to the Salonian branch. Recently also Lucius Volusius Saturninus, who died while holding the office of City Praefect, is known to have had a son, by Cornelia of the Scipio family, born after he was 62, Volusius Saturninus, who was consul. Parentage even up to the age of 75 is commonly found in the lower classes. *Age of fertility.*

XV. Woman is, however, the only animal that has monthly periods; consequently she alone has what are called moles in her womb. This mole is a shapeless and inanimate mass of flesh that resists the point and the edge of a knife; it moves about, and it checks menstruation, as it also checks births: in some cases causing death, in others growing old with the patient, sometimes when the bowels are violently moved being ejected. A similar object is also formed in the stomach of males, called a tumour, as in the case of the praetorian Oppius *Menstruation.*

547

64 sed nihil facile reperiatur mulierum profluvio magis
monstrificum. acescunt superventu musta, sterile-
scunt contactae fruges, moriuntur insita, exuruntur
hortorum germina, fructus arborum [quibus insidere]¹
decidunt, speculorum fulgor adspectu ipso hebetatur,
acies ferri praestringitur, eboris nitor, alvi apium
moriuntur, aes etiam ac ferrum robigo protinus cor-
ripit odorque dirus aera, in rabiem aguntur gustato eo
65 canes atque insanabili veneno morsus inficitur. quin
et bituminum sequax alioquin ac lenta natura in
lacu Iudaeae qui vocatur Asphaltites certo tempore
anni supernatans non quit sibi avelli ad omnem
contactum adhaerens praeterquam filo quod tale
virus infecerit. etiam formicis, animali minimo,
inesse sensum eius ferunt, abicique gustatas fruges
66 nec postea repeti. et hoc tale tantumque omnibus
tricenis diebus malum in muliere exsistit et trimenstri
spatio largius, quibusdam vero saepius mense, sicut
aliquis numquam. sed tales non gignunt, quando
haec est generando homini materia, germine e
maribus coaguli modo hoc in sese glomerante, quod
deinde tempore ipso animatur corporaturque. ergo
cum gravidis fluxit, invalidi aut non vitales partus
67 eduntur aut saniosi, ut auctor est Nigidius. XVI.
(idem lac feminae non corrumpi alenti partum si ex

---

¹ *Seclusit Rackham.*

ᵃ The Dead Sea.

Capito. But nothing could easily be found that is more remarkable than the monthly flux of women. Contact with it turns new wine sour, crops touched by it become barren, grafts die, seeds in gardens are dried up, the fruit of trees falls off, the bright surface of mirrors in which it is merely reflected is dimmed, the edge of steel and the gleam of ivory are dulled, hives of bees die, even bronze and iron are at once seized by rust, and a horrible smell fills the air; to taste it drives dogs mad and infects their bites with an incurable poison. Moreover bitumen, a substance generally sticky and viscous, that at a certain season of the year floats on the surface of the lake of Judaea called the Asphalt Pool,[a] adheres to everything touching it, and cannot be drawn asunder except by a thread soaked in the poisonous fluid in question. Even that very tiny creature the ant is said to be sensitive to it, and throws away grains of corn that taste of it and does not touch them again. Not only does this pernicious mischief occur in a woman every month, but it comes in larger quantity every three months; and in some cases it comes more frequently than once a month, just as in certain women it never occurs at all. The latter, however, do not have children, since the substance in question is the material for human generation, as the semen from the males acting like rennet collects this substance within it, which thereupon immediately is inspired with life and endowed with body. Hence when this flux occurs with women heavy with child, the offspring is sickly or still-born or sanious, according to Nigidius. XVI. (The same writer holds that a woman's milk does not go bad while she is suckling

eodem viro rursus conceperit arbitratur). incipiente
autem hoc statu aut desinente conceptus facillimi
traduntur. fecunditatis in feminis praerogativam
accepimus inunctis medicamine oculis salivam infici.

68 Ceterum editis primores septimo mense gigni dentes, priusque in superna fere parte, haud dubium
est, septimo eosdem decidere anno aliosque suffici,
quosdam et cum dentibus nasci, sicut M'. Curium,
qui ob id Dentatus cognominatus est, et Cn. Papirium
Carbonem, praeclaros viros. in feminis ea res
inauspicati fuit exempli regum temporibus: cum ita
69 nata esset Valeria, exitio civitati in quam delata
esset futuram responso haruspicum vaticinante,
Suessam Pometiam illa tempestate florentissimam
deportata est, veridico exitu consecuto. (quasdam
concreto genitali gigni infausto omine Cornelia
Gracchorum mater indicio est.) aliqui vice dentium
continuo osse gignuntur, sicuti Prusiae regis Bithy-
niorum filius superna parte oris. dentes autem in [1]
70 tantum invicti sunt ignibus ut [2] nec crementur cum
reliquo corpore, iidemque flammis indomiti cavantur
tabe pituitae. candorem trahunt quodam medicamine. usu atteruntur, multoque prius [3] in aliquis
deficiunt. nec cibo tantum et alimentis necessarii,

[1] in *add. Mayhoff.*
[2] ut *add. Mayhoff.*
[3] *Sabellius:* primum.

---

[a] In Latium; conquered by the Romans under Tarquinius
Priscus. It revolted in 503 B.C. and was retaken by Sp. Cassius
in the following year and destroyed.

a baby if she has become pregnant again from the same male.) It is stated, however, that the easiest conceptions are when this condition is beginning or ceasing. We have it recorded as a sure sign of fertility in women if when the eyes have been anointed with a drug the saliva contains traces of it.

Moreover, it is known that children cut their first teeth when six months old, the upper ones mostly coming first, and that the first teeth fall out and are replaced by others when they are six years old; and that some children are born having teeth—two distinguished instances are Manius Curius, who received the surname Dentatus in consequence, and Gnaeus Papirius Carbo. In the regal period this occurrence was considered a sign of bad luck in females: Valeria was born with teeth, and the soothsayers in reply to inquiry prophesied that she would bring disaster to any community to which she was taken; she was deported to Suessa Pometia,[a] at that period a very flourishing place, the eventual result verifying the oracle. (Some females are born with the genitals closed; this is proved by the case of Cornelia the mother of the Gracchi to be a sign of bad luck.) Some infants are born with a ridge of bone instead of teeth; this was the case as regards the upper jaw with the son of Prusias, King of Bithynia. The teeth are so far indestructible by fire as not to burn when the rest of the body is cremated, but although they resist fire they are corroded by a morbid state of the saliva. A certain drug gives them whiteness. Use wears them down, and in some people they decay much before this. Nor are they only necessary for food and nourish-

Dentition of children.

551

quippe vocis sermonisque regimen primores tenent,
concentu quodam excipientes ictum linguae serieque
structurae atque magnitudine mutilantes molli-
entesve aut hebetantes verba et, cum defuere,
71 explanationem omnem adimentes. quin et augurium
in hac esse creditur parte. triceni bini viris adtri-
buuntur excepta Turdulorum gente; quibus plures
fuere longiora promitti vitae putant spatia. feminis
minor numerus, quibus in dextra parte gemini
superne a canibus cognominati fortunae blandimenta
pollicentur, sicut in Agrippina Domiti Neronis matre;
72 contra in laeva.—(Hominem prius quam genito dente
cremari mos gentium non est.[1])—sed mox plura de
hoc, cum membratim historia decurret.

Risisse eodem die quo genitus esset unum hominem accepimus Zoroastren, eidem cerebrum ita
palpitasse ut inpositam repelleret manum, futurae
praesagio scientiae.

73 In trimatu suae [2] cuique dimidiam esse mensuram
futurae staturae [3] certum est. in plenum autem
cuncto mortalium generi minorem in dies fieri pro-
pemodum observatur, rarosque patribus proceriores,
consumente ubertatem seminum exustione in cuius
vices nunc vergat aevom. in Creta terrae motu
rupto monte inventum est corpus stans XLVI cubitorum, quod alii Orionis alii Oti esse arbitrabantur.

---

[1] Hominem . . . est *post* pituitae § 70 *transferendum War-*
mington. [2] *Rackham :* suo.
[3] futurae staturae *Rackham :* futuras *aut* staturae.

---

[a] This sentence would come in better four lines from the
bottom of p. 551.

[b] Orion, a giant hunter, transported to heaven, gave his name
to the constellation; Otus was a gigantic son of Poseidon. Bones
of elephants, mastodons, whales, etc., discovered in alluvial
tracts have in the past been supposed to be the bones of giants.

ment, as the front teeth regulate the voice and speech, meeting the impact of the tongue with a kind of harmony, and according to their regularity of arrangement and size clipping or modulating or else dulling the words, and when they are lost preventing all clear articulation. Moreover this part of the body is believed to possess prophetic powers. Males (excepting the Turduli tribe) have 32 teeth; there have been cases of men with more—this is thought to foretell a longer term of life. Women have fewer; with them two dogteeth on the right side of the upper jaw are a promise of fortune's favours, as in the case of Domitius Nero's mother Agrippina; on the left side the opposite.—(It is the universal custom of mankind not to cremate a person who dies before cutting his teeth.[a])—But more of this later when our researches go through the parts of the body *seriatim*.

It is recorded of only one person, Zoroaster, that he laughed on the same day on which he was born, and also that his brain throbbed so violently as to dislodge a hand placed on his head—this foretelling his future knowledge. *Exceptional precocity.*

It is known that at the age of three a person's measurement is half his future stature. But it is almost a matter of observation that with the entire human race the stature on the whole is becoming smaller daily, and that few men are taller than their fathers, as the conflagration that is the crisis towards which the age is now verging is exhausting the fertility of the semen. When a mountain in Crete was cleft by an earthquake a body 69 feet in height was found, which some people thought must be that of Orion and others of Otus.[b] The records attest *Human stature diminishing.* *Giants and dwarfs.*

553

74 Orestis corpus oraculi iussu refossum septem cubitorum fuisse monimentis creditur. iam vero ante annos prope mille vates ille Homerus non cessavit minora corpora mortalium quam prisca conqueri. Naevii Pollionis amplitudinem annales non tradunt, sed quia populi concursu paene sit interemptus, vice prodigii habitam.[1] procerissimum hominem aetas nostra divo Claudio principe Gabbaram nomine ex Arabia advectum novem pedum et totidem unciarum

75 vidit. fuere sub divo Augusto duo [2] semipede addito, quorum corpora eius miraculi gratia in conditorio Sallustianorum adservabantur hortorum; Pusioni et Secundillae erant nomina. eodem praeside minimus homo duos pedes et palmum Conopas nomine in deliciis Iuliae neptis eius fuit, et minima [3] mulier Andromeda liberta Iuliae Augustae. Manium Maximum et M. Tullium equites Romanos binum cubitorum fuisse auctor est M. Varro, et ipsi vidimus in loculis adservatos. sesquipedales gigni, quosdam longiores, in trimatu inplentes vitae cursum, haud ignotum est.

76 Invenimus in monumentis Salamine Euthymenis filium in tria cubita triennio adcrevisse, incessu tardum, sensu hebetem, puberem etiam factum, voce robusta, absumptum contractione membrorum subita triennio circumacto. ipsi non pridem vidimus eadem ferme omnia praeter pubertatem in filio Corneli

---

[1] *Rackham*: habitum.
[2] duo *supplevit Rackham.*
[3] minima *supplevit Rackham.*

---

[a] By the Spartans, who then gained the victory in their long war with Tegea, 554 B.C. (Herodotus I. 65 ff.).

that the body of Orestes dug up *a* at the command of
an oracle measured 10 ft. 6 in.   Moreover, the famous
bard Homer nearly 1000 years ago never ceased to
lament that mortals were smaller of stature than in
the old days.   In the case of Naevius Pollio the
annals do not record his height, but they show that
it was deemed portentous, because he was almost
killed by the people flocking round him.   The tallest
person our age has seen was a man named Gabbara
brought from Arabia in the principate of his late
Majesty Claudius who was 9 ft. 9 in. in height.
Under his late Majesty Augustus there were two
persons 6 in. taller, whose bodies on account of this
remarkable height were preserved in the tomb in
Sallust's Gardens; their names were Pusio and
Secundilla.   When the same emperor was head of the
state the smallest person was a dwarf 2 ft. 5 in. high
named Conopas, the pet of his granddaughter Julia,
and the smallest female was Andromeda, a freed-
woman of Julia Augusta.   Marcus Varro states
that the Knights of Rome Manius Maximus and
Marcus Tullius were 3 ft. high, and we have ourselves
seen their bodies preserved in coffins.   It is a matter
of common knowledge that persons are born 18 in.
high and some taller, who complete their life's course
at the age of three.

   We find in the records that at Salamis the son of
Euthymenes grew to 4 ft. 6 in. in his third year;
he walked slowly, was dull of sense, became sexually
quite mature, had a bass voice, and was carried off
by a sudden attack of paralysis when he turned
three.   We ourselves recently saw almost all these
features except sexual maturity in a son of the Knight
of Rome Cornelius Tacitus, Deputy Finance Minister

Taciti equitis Romani Belgicae Galliae rationes
procurantis. ἐκτραπέλους Graeci vocant eos, in
Latio non habent nomen.

77 XVII. Quod sit homini spatium a vestigio ad
verticem id esse pansis manibus inter longissimos
digitos observatum est, sicuti vires[1] dextra parte
maiores, quibusdam aequas utraque, aliquis laeva
manu praecipuas, nec id umquam in feminis, mares
praestare pondere, et defuncta viventibus corpora
omnium animalium, et dormientia vigilantibus,
virorum cadavera supina fluitare, feminarum prona,
velut pudori defunctarum parcente natura.

78 XVIII. Concretis quosdam ossibus ac sine medullis
vivere accepimus; signum eorum esse nec sitim
sentire nec sudorem emittere, quamquam et voluntate
scimus sitim victam, equitemque Romanum Iulium
Viatorem e Vocontiorum gente foederata in pupillari-
bus annis aquae subter cutem fusae morbo prohibitum
umore a medicis naturam vicisse consuetudine atque
in senectam caruisse potu. nec non et alii multa
sibi imperavere.

79 XIX. Ferunt Crassum avum Crassi in Parthis
interempti numquam risisse, ob id Agelastum
vocatum, sicuti nec flesse multos, Socratem clarum
sapientia eodem semper visum vultu, nec aut hilaro
magis aut turbato. exit hic animi tenor aliquando in

---

[1] *V.l.* vires quibusdam.

---

[a] *I.e.* with the arms stretched out sideways.
[b] The 'triumvir,' who fell at Carrhae 63 B.C.

in Belgic Gaul. The Greeks call these cases ' perverts,' but in the Latin country there is no name for them.

XVII. It has been noticed that a man's height from head to foot is equal to his full span [a] measured from the tips of the middle fingers; likewise that the right-hand side of the frame is the stronger, though in some cases both sides are equally strong and there are people whose left side is the stronger, though this is never the case with women; and that males are the heavier; and that the bodies of all creatures are heavier when dead than when alive, and when asleep than when awake; and that men's corpses float on their backs, but women's on their faces, as if nature spared their modesty after death. *Human dimensions and weight.*

XVIII. Cases are recorded of persons living whose bones were solid and without marrow; and we are told that their distinguishing mark is insensibility to thirst and absence of perspiration, although we know that thirst can also be subdued by the will, and that a Knight of Rome of the allied tribe of the Vocontii named Julius Viator, suffering from dropsy when a minor, was forbidden liquid by the doctors and habituated himself to defeat nature, going without drink till old age. Moreover other persons also have exercised many kinds of self-control. *Varying need of liquid.*

XIX. It is stated that Crassus the grandfather of Crassus [b] who fell in Parthia never laughed, and was consequently called Agelastus, and that likewise there have been many cases of people who never wept, and that the famous philosopher Socrates always wore the same look on his countenance, never gayer and never more perturbed. This temperament sometimes develops into a kind of rigidity and a *Peculiar attributes.*

rigorem quendam torvitatemque naturae duram et
inflexibilem, affectusque humanos adimit, quales
80 ἀπαθεῖς Graeci vocant multos eius generis experti,
quodque mirum sit, auctores maxime sapientiae,
Diogenen   Cynicum,   Pyrrhonem,   Heraclitum,
Timonem, hunc quidem etiam in totius odium generis
humani evectum. sed haec parva naturae insignia
in multis varia cognoscuntur, ut in Antonia Drusi
numquam expuisse, in Pomponio consulari poeta
non ructasse. quibus natura concreta sunt ossa,
qui sunt rari admodum, cornei vocantur.

81   XX. Corpore vesco sed eximiis viribus Tritanum in
gladiatorio ludo Samnitium armatura celebrem,
filiumque eius militem Magni Pompei et rectos et
traversos cancellatim toto corpore habuisse nervos,
in brachiis etiam manibusque, auctor est Varro in
prodigiosarum virium relatione, atque etiam hostem
ab eo ex provocatione dimicantem inermi dextera
superatum et postremo correptum uno digito[1] in
82 castra tralatum. at Vinnius Valens meruit in praetorio divi Augusti centurio, vehicula cum culleis
onusta donec exinanirentur sustinere solitus, car-
penta adprehensa una manu retinere obnixus contra
nitentibus iumentis, et alia mirifica facere quae
insculpta monimento eius spectantur. idem M.
83 Varro: ' Rusticelius,' inquit, ' Hercules appellatus
mulum suum tollebat, Fufius Salvius duo centenaria

---

[1] uno digito *hic Mayhoff*:   *ante* superatum *codd.*

[a] Cf. § 78 above.

hard, unbending severity of nature, and takes away the emotions natural to humanity; persons of this sort are called 'apathetic' by the Greeks, who have known many men of the kind, and among them surprising to say, chiefly founders of schools of philosophy, Diogenes the Cynic, Pyrrho, Heraclitus, Timo—the last indeed going as far as to hate the whole human race. But these small peculiarities of nature are known to occur variously in many persons, for instance in the case of Drusus's daughter Antonia never spitting, in the poet and ex-consul Pomponius never belching. Persons whose bones are by nature solid,[a] a rather rare class, are called 'horny.'

XX. Varro in his account of cases of remarkable strength records that one Tritanus, famous in the gladiatorial exercise with the Samnite equipment, was slightly built but of exceptional strength, and that his son, a soldier of Pompey the Great, had a chequered criss-cross of sinews all over his body, even in his arms and hands; and moreover that once he challenged one of the enemy to single combat, defeated him without a weapon in his hand, and finally took hold of him with a single finger and carried him off to the camp. Vinnius Valens served as captain in the Imperial Guard of the late lamented Augustus; he was in the habit of holding carts laden with wine-sacks up in the air until they were emptied, and of catching hold of wagons with one hand and stopping them by throwing his weight against the efforts of the teams drawing them, and doing other marvellous exploits which can be seen carved on his monument. Marcus Varro likewise states: 'Rusticelius, who was nicknamed Hercules, used to lift his mule; Fufius Salvius used to walk up a ladder with two hundred-

pondera pedibus, totidem manibus, et ducenaria duo
umeris contra scalas ferebat.' nos quoque vidimus
Athanatum nomine, prodigiosae ostentationis, quin-
genario thorace plumbeo indutum cothurnisque
quingentum pondo calciatum per scaenam ingredi.
Milonem athletam cum constitisset nemo vestigio
educebat, malum tenenti nemo digitum corrigebat.

84 Cucurrisse MCXL stadia ab Athenis Lacedae-
monem biduo Phidippidem,[1] magnum erat, donec
Anystis cursor Lacedaemonius et Philonides Alexandri Magni a Sicyone Elim uno die MCCCV stadia
cucurrerunt. nunc quidem in circo quosdam $\overline{\text{CLX}}$
passuum tolerare non ignoramus, nuperque Fonteio
et Vipstano coss. annos VIII genitum a meridie ad
vesperam $\overline{\text{LXXV}}$ passuum cucurrisse. cuius rei
admiratio ita demum solida perveniet, si quis cogitet
nocte ac die longissimum iter vehiculis Tib. Neronem
emensum festinantem ad Drusum fratrem aegrotum
in Germaniam; ea fuerunt $\overline{\text{CC}}$ passuum.

85 XXI. Oculorum acies vel maxime fidem excedentia
invenit exempla. in nuce inclusam Iliadem Homeri
carmen in membrana scriptum tradit Cicero. idem
fuisse qui pervideret $\overline{\text{CXXXV}}$ passuum. huic et
nomen M. Varro reddit, Strabonem vocatum; soli-
tum autem Punico bello a Libybaeo Siciliae promunturio exeunte classe e Carthaginis portu etiam
numerum navium dicere. Callicrates ex ebore

---

[1] *Salmasius*: Philippidem.

---

[a] The courier sent to ask for aid against the Persian invaders,
490 B.C. (Herodotus VI. 105). The distances are given here
in rough figures, the stade being taken as 200 yards, and the
mille passus as 1600 yards. (Elsewhere, in topographical
passages, the usual renderings 'furlong' and 'mile' are
employed.) [b] 'Cross-eyed.'

pound weights fastened to his feet, the same weights
in his hands and two two-hundred-pound weights on
his shoulders.' We also saw a man named Athanatus,
who was capable of a miraculous display : he walked
across the stage wearing a leaden breast-plate
weighing 500 pounds and shod in boots of 500
pounds' weight. When the athlete Milo took a
firm stand, no one could make him shift his footing,
and when he was holding an apple no one could
make him straighten out a finger.

Phidippides's [a] running the 130 miles from Athens
to Sparta in two days was a mighty feat, until the
Spartan runner Anystis and Alexander the Great's
courier Philonides ran the 148 miles from Sicyon to
Elis in a day. At the present day indeed we are
aware that some men can last out 128 miles in the
circus, and that recently in the consulship of Fon-
teius and Vipstanus a boy of 8 ran 68 miles between
noon and evening. The marvellous nature of this
feat will only get across to us in full measure if we
reflect that Tiberius Nero completed by carriage
the longest twenty-four hours' journey on record
when hastening to Germany to his brother Drusus
who was ill : this measured 182 miles.

XXI. Keenness of sight has achieved instances *Exceptional*
transcending belief in the highest degree. Cicero *sight.*
records that a parchment copy of Homer's poem *The
Iliad* was enclosed in a nutshell. He also records a
case of a man who could see 123 miles. Marcus Varro
also gives this man's name, which was Strabo,[b] and
states that in the Punic wars he was in the habit
of telling from the promontory of Lilybaeum in Sicily
the actual number of ships in a fleet that was passing
out from the harbour of Carthage. Callicrates

formicas et alia tam parva fecit animalia ut partes
eorum a ceteris cerni non possent. Myrmecides
quidam in eodem genere inclaruit quadriga ex
eadem materia quam musca integeret alis fabricata
et nave quam apicula pinnis absconderet.

86   XXII. Auditus unum exemplum habet mirabile,
proelium quo Sybaris deleta est eo die quo gestum
erat auditum Olympiae. nam nuntii[1] Cimbrieae
victoriae Castoresque Romanis[2] qui Persicam
victoriam ipso die quo contigit nuntiavere visus et
numinum fuere praesagia.

87   XXIII. Patientia corporis, ut est crebra sors
calamitatum, innumera documenta peperit, clarissimum in feminis Leaenae meretricis, quae torta non
indicavit Harmodium et Aristogitonem tyrannicidas,
in viris Anaxarchi, qui simili de causa cum torqueretur
praerosam dentibus linguam unamque spem indici
in tyranni os expuit.

88   XXIV. Memoria necessarium maxime vitae bonum
cui praecipua fuerit haut facile dictu est tam multis
eius gloriam adeptis. Cyrus rex omnibus in exercitu
suo militibus nomina reddidit, L. Scipio populo Romano, Cineas Pyrrhi regis legatus senatui et equestri
ordini Romae postero die quam advenerat. Mithri-

---

[1] nuntii *add. Jan.*
[2] *Rackham* (Romam *Rhenanus*): Romani.

---

[a] Fought at the river Sagra in S. Italy, the Locrian settlers
defeating Crotona, 560 B.C.
[b] Won by Marius at Campus Raudius 101 B.C. For the
report conveyed by a miraculous noise of battle in the sky, see
II. 108.
[c] *I.e.* Castor and his brother Pollux.
[d] Won by Aemilius Paulus at Pydna, 168 B.C.
[e] At Athens, 514 B.C.

used to make such small ivory models of ants and
other creatures that to anybody else their parts were
invisible. A certain Myrmecides won fame in the
same department by making a four-horse chariot of
the same material that a fly's wings would cover,
and a ship that a tiny bee could conceal with its wings.

XXII. There is one marvellous instance of the *Exceptional transmission of a spoken message: the battle [a] that of sound.*
resulted in the destruction of Sybaris was heard of
at Olympia on the day on which it was fought. For
the messengers who brought news of the victory [b]
over the Cimbri and the brothers Castor [c] who
reported the victory [d] over Perseus to the Romans
on the very day on which it happened were visions
and warnings sent by the divine powers.

XXIII. Bodily endurance, so fertile of disasters is *Exceptional endurance.*
fate, has produced countless examples, the most
famous in the case of women being that of the harlot
Leaena who on the rack refused to betray the
tyrannicides Harmodius and Aristogiton,[e] and among
men that of Anaxarchus,[f] who when being tortured
for a similar reason bit off his tongue and spat the
only hope of betrayal in the tyrant's face.

XXIV. As to memory, the boon most necessary for *Exceptional memory.*
life, it is not easy to say who most excelled in it, so
many men having gained renown for it. King Cyrus
could give their names to all the soldiers in his
army, Lucius Scipio knew the names of the whole
Roman people, King Pyrrhus's envoy Cineas knew
those of the senate and knighthood at Rome the day
after his arrival.[g] Mithridates who was king of

---

[f] A philosopher in the court of Alexander, put to death by
Nicocreon King of Salamis for his freedom of speech.
[g] 280 B.C.

dates duarum et viginti gentium rex totidem linguis
iura dixit, pro contione singulas sine interprete
89 adfatus. Charmadas quidam in Graecia quae quis
exegerit volumina in bibliothecis legentis modo
repraesentavit. ars postremo eius rei facta et inventa est a Simonide melico, consummata a Metro-
doro Scepsio, ut nihil non iisdem verbis redderetur
90 auditum. nec aliud est aeque fragile in homine:
morborum et casus iniurias atque etiam metus sentit,
alias particulatim, alias universa. ictus lapide oblitus
est litteras tantum; ex praealto tecto lapsus matris
et adfinium propinquorumque cepit oblivionem, alius
aegrotus servorum etiam, sui vero nominis Messala
Corvinus orator. itaque saepe deficere temptat ac
meditatur vel quieto corpore et valido; somno
quoque serpente amputatur, ut inanis mens quaerat
ubi sit loci.
91   XXV. Animi vigore praestantissimum arbitror genitum[1] Caesarem dictatorem; nec virtutem constan-
tiamque nunc commemoro, nec sublimitatem omnium
capacem quae caelo continentur, sed proprium vigorem
celeritatemque quodam igne volucrem. scribere aut
legere, simul dictare aut audire solitum accepimus,
epistulas vero tantarum rerum quaternas pariter
92 dictare librariis aut, si nihil aliud ageret, septenas.[2]
idem signis conlatis quinquagiens dimicavit, solus
M. Marcellum transgressus, qui undequadragiens

---

[1] *V.ll.* gentium, Gaium.
[2] *V.l. om.* librariis—septenas.

---

[a] Some manuscripts omit the last clause

twenty-two races gave judgements in as many languages, in an assembly addressing each race in turn without an interpreter. A person in Greece named Charmadas recited the contents of any volumes in libraries that anyone asked him to quote, just as if he were reading them. Finally, a *memoria technica* was constructed, which was invented by the lyric poet Simonides and perfected by Metrodorus of Scepsis, enabling anything heard to be repeated in the identical words. Also no other human faculty is equally fragile: injuries from, and even apprehensions of, diseases and accident may affect in some cases a single field of memory and in others the whole. A man has been known when struck by a stone to forget how to read and write but nothing else. One who fell from a very high roof forgot his mother and his relatives and friends, another when ill forgot his servants also; the orator Messala Corvinus forgot his own name. Similarly tentative and hesitating lapses of memory often occur when the body even when uninjured is in repose; also the gradual approach of sleep curtails the memory and makes the unoccupied mind wonder where it is.

XXV. The most outstanding instance of innate mental vigour I take to be the dictator Caesar; and I am not now thinking of valour and resolution, nor of a loftiness embracing all the contents of the firmament of heaven, but of native vigour and quickness winged as it were with fire. We are told that he used to write or read and dictate or listen simultaneously, and to dictate to his secretaries four letters at once on his important affairs—or, if otherwise unoccupied, seven letters at once.[a] He also fought fifty pitched battles, and alone beat the record of Marcus Mar-

Exceptional intellect and character of Julius Caesar.

dimicavit—nam praeter civiles victorias undeciens
centena et nonaginta duo milia hominum occisa
proeliis ab eo non equidem in gloria posuerim, tantam
etiamsi [1] coactam humani generis iniuriam, quod ita
esse confessus est ipse bellorum civilium stragem non
prodendo.

93 Iustius Pompeio Magno tribuatur DCCCXLVI naves
piratis ademisse: Caesari proprium et peculiare
sit praeter supra dicta clementiae insigne qua
usque ad paenitentiam omnes superavit; idem
magnanimitatis praebuit exemplum cui comparari
94 non possit aliud. spectacula enim edita effusasque
opes aut operum magnificentiam in hac parte
numerare [2] luxuriae faventis est: illa fuit vera et
incomparabilis invicti animi sublimitas, captis apud
Pharsaliam Pompei Magni scriniis epistularum
iterumque apud Thapsum Scipionis concremasse ea
optima fide atque non legisse.

95 XXVI. Verum ad decus imperii Romani, non solum
ad viri unius pertinet, victoriarum Pompei Magni titulos
omnes triumphosque hoc in loco nuncupari, aequato
non modo Alexandri Magni rerum fulgore, sed etiam
96 Herculis prope ac Liberi patris. igitur Sicilia re-
cuperata, unde primum Sullanus in reip. causa
exoriens auspicatus est, Africa vero tota subacta et
in dicionem redacta, Magnique nomine in spolium

---

[1] *Detlefsen*: etiam (et incoactam? *Mayhoff*).
[2] *Mayhoff*: enumerare.

---

a The conqueror of Syracuse, 212 B.C.

cellus[a] who fought thirty-nine—for I would not myself count it to his glory that in addition to conquering his fellow-citizens he killed in his battles 1,192,000 human beings, a prodigious even if unavoidable wrong inflicted on the human race, as he himself confessed it to be by not publishing the casualties of the civil wars.

It would be more just to credit Pompey the Great with the 846 ships that he captured from the pirates; while to Caesar let us assign, in addition to the facts mentioned above, the peculiar distinction of the clemency in which (even to the point of subsequent regret) he surpassed all men; also he afforded an example of magnanimity that no other can parallel. For while to count under this head the shows that he gave and the wealth that he squandered, or the magnificence of his public works, would display indulgence to luxury, it showed the genuine and unrivalled sublimity of an unconquered spirit that, when Pompey the Great's despatch cases were captured at Pharsalia and again those of Scipio at Thapsus, he scrupulously burnt them and did not read them.

XXVI. But it concerns the glory of the Roman *Achievements and magnanimity of* Empire, and not that of one man, to mention in this *nanimity of* place all the records of the victories of Pompey the *Pompey.* Great and all his triumphs, which equal the brilliance of the exploits not only of Alexander the Great but even almost of Hercules and Father Liber. Well then, after the recovery of Sicily, which inaugurated his emergence as a champion of the commonwealth in the party of Sulla, and after the conquest of the whole of Africa and its reduction under our sway, and the acquirement as a trophy therefrom of

inde capto, Eques Romanus, id quod antea nemo,
curru triumphali revectus et statim ad solis occasum
trangressus, excitatis in Pyrenaeo tropaeis, oppida
DCCCLXXVI ab Alpibus ad finis Hispaniae ulterioris in dicionem redacta victoriae suae adscripsit et
maiore animo Sertorium tacuit, belloque civili quod
omnia externa conciebat extincto iterum triumphales
currus Eques Romam [1] induxit, totiens imperator
97 ante quam miles. postea ad tota maria et deinde
solis ortus missos infinitos retulit [2] patriae titulos
more sacris certaminibus vincentium—neque enim
ipsi coronantur, sed patrias suas coronant; hos ergo
honores urbi tribuit in delubro Minervae quod ex
manubiis dicabat:

Cn. Pompeius Magnus imperator bello XXX *annorum
confecto fusis fugatis occisis in deditionem acceptis hominum centiens viciens semel* $\overline{LXXXIII}$ *depressis aut captis
navibus* DCCCXLVI *oppidis castellis* MDXXXVIII *in fidem
receptis terris a Maeotis ad Rubrum mare subactis
votum merito Minervae.*

98 Hos est breviarium eius ab oriente. triumphi
vero quem duxit a. d. III kal. Oct. M. Pisone M.
Messala coss. praefatio haec fuit: *Cum oram maritimam praedonibus liberasset et imperium maris populo*

---

[1] *V.l.* Romanus.
[2] *Rackham:* missus hos rettulit *aut* missus infinitos.

---

[a] With Sertorius, ended 71 B.C.
[b] At Olympia etc.
[c] On the Sea of Azov. [d] 62 B.C.

the title of *The Great,* he rode back in a triumphal
chariot though only of equestrian rank, a thing which
had never occurred before ; and immediately afterwards he crossed over to the West, and after erecting
trophies in the Pyrenees he added to the record of
his victorious career the reduction under our sway of
876 towns from the Alps to the frontiers of Further
Spain, and with greater magnanimity refrained
from mentioning Sertorius, and after crushing the
civil war *a* which threatened to stir up all our foreign
relations, a second time led into Rome a procession
of triumphal chariots as a Knight, having twice
been commander-in-chief before having ever served
in the ranks. Subsequently he was despatched to
the whole of the seas and then to the far east, and
he brought back titles without limit for his country,
after the manner of those who conquer in the sacred
contests *b*—for these are not crowned with wreaths
themselves but crown their native land ; consequently he bestowed these honours on the city in
the shrine of Minerva that he was dedicating out of
the proceeds of the spoils of war :

*Gnaeus Pompeius Magnus, Commander in Chief,
having completed a thirty years' war, routed, scattered,
slain or received the surrender of 12,183,000 people,
sunk or taken 846 ships, received the capitulation of
1538 towns and forts, subdued the lands from the
Maeotians *c* to the Red Sea, duly dedicates his offering
vowed to Minerva.*

This is his summary of his exploits in the east. But
the announcement of the triumphal procession that
he led on September 28 in the consulship *d* of Marcus
Piso and Marcus Messala was as follows :

After having rescued the sea coast from pirates and

*Romano restituisset ex Asia Ponto Armenia Paphla-
gonia Cappadocia Cilicia Syria Scythis Iudaeis Albanis
Hiberia insula Creta Basternis et super haec de rege
Mithridate atque Tigrane triumphavit.*

99 Summa summarum in illa gloria fuit (ut ipse in
concione dixit cum de rebus suis dissereret) Asiam
ultimam provinciarum accepisse eandemque mediam
patriae reddidisse. si quis e contrario simili modo
velit percensere Caesaris res, qui maior illo apparuit,
totum profecto terrarum orbem enumeret, quod
infinitum esse conveniet.

100 XXVII. Ceteris virtutum generibus varie et multi
fuere praestantes. Cato primus Porciae gentis tres
summas in homine res praestitisse existimatur, ut esset
optimus orator, optimus imperator, optimus senator,
quae mihi omnia, etiamsi non prius, attamen clarius
fulsisse in Scipione Aemiliano videntur, dempto
praeterea plurimorum odio quo Cato laboravit.
itaque sit proprium Catonis quater et quadragiens
causam dixisse, nec quemquam saepius postulatum
et semper absolutum.

101 XXVIII. Fortitudo in quo maxime extiterit[1] inmensae quaestionis est, utique si poetica recipiatur fabu-
losita. Q. Ennius T. Caecilium Teucrum fratremque

[1] enituerit ? (*cf.* § 123) *Mayhoff.*

*restored to the Roman People the command of the sea,
he celebrated a triumph over Asia, Pontus, Armenia,
Paphlagonia, Cappadocia, Cicilia, Syria, the Scythians,
Jews and Albanians, Iberia, the Island of Crete, the
Basternae, and, in addition to these, over King Mithridates
and Tigranes.*

The crowning pinnacle of this glorious record was
(as he himself declared in assembly when discoursing
on his achievements) to have found Asia the remotest
of the provinces and then to have made her a central
dominion of his country. If anybody on the other
side desires to review in similar manner the achievements of Caesar, who showed himself greater than
Pompey, he must assuredly roll off the entire world,
and this it will be agreed is a task without limit.

XXVII. There have been various and numerous *Earlier cases*
cases of eminence in the other kinds of excellence. *of excep-*
Cato the first of that name in the Gens **Porcia** is *achievement.*
deemed to have exemplified the three supreme human
achievements, excelling alike as orator, as general
and as senator; all of which distinctions seem to
me to have been achieved though not previously
yet with greater brilliance in the case of Scipio
Aemilianus, and that moreover without the very
wide unpopularity that handicapped Cato. So it
may be counted an exceptional fact about Cato that
he took part in forty-four actions at law and was
sued more frequently than anybody else and always
acquitted.

XXVIII. What person has possessed the most outstanding courage is a subject of unending enquiry,
at all events if the legendary testimony of poetry be
accepted. Quintus Ennius had a particular admiration for Titus Caecilius Teucer and his brother,

eius praecipue miratus propter eos sextum decimum
adiecit annalem. L. Siccius Dentatus, qui tribunus
plebei fuit Sp. Tarpeio A. Aternio coss. haud multo
post exactos reges, vel numerosissima suffragia habet
centiens viciens proeliatus, octiens ex provocatione
victor, quadraginta quinque cicatricibus adverso
102 corpore insignis, nulla in tergo. idem spolia cepit
xxxiv, donatus hastis puris duodeviginti, phaleris
viginti quinque, torquibus tribus et octoginta,
armillis clx, coronis xxvi (in iis civicis xiv, aureis
octo, muralibus tribus, obsidionali una), fisco
aeris, x captivis et viginti simul bubus, imperatores
novem ipsius maxime opera triumphantes secutus,
praeterea (quod optumum in operibus eius reor)
103 uno ex ducibus T. Romilio ex consulatu ad populum
convicto male acti imperii. rei militaris [1] haut
minora forent Capitolini decora, ni perdidisset illa
exitu vitae. ante decem et septem annos bina
ceperat spolia; primus omnium eques muralem
acceperat coronam, sex civicas, xxxvii dona;
xxiii cicatrices adverso corpore exceperat; P.
Servilium magistrum equitum servaverat, ipse vul-
104 neratus umerum, femur; super omnia Capitolium
summamque rem in eo solus a Gallis servaverat, si
non regno suo servasset.

[1] *V.l.* male imperatae rei militaris.

---

[a] 454 B.C.
[b] A spear without a head was bestowed as a military
decoration, especially for saving the life of a fellow-citizen.
[c] M. Manlius; he was finally suspected of aspiring to restore
the monarchy, and was flung from the Tarpeian Rock, 384 B.C.

adding Book XVI to his *Annals* on their account. Lucius Siccius Dentatus, Tribune of the Plebs in the consulship[a] of Spurius Tarpeius and Aulus Aternius not long after the expulsion of the kings, scores an exceedingly large number of votes, as having fought in 120 battles, been challenged to and having won eight single combats, and having the distinction of 45 scars in front and none at all on his back. He also captured spoils 34 times, had bestowed upon him 18 spear-shafts,[b] 25 breast-badges, 83 necklets, 160 bracelets, 26 crowns (including 14 civic crowns, eight of gold, three mural crowns, one siege-rescue crown), a bag of money, ten prisoners of war and with them 20 cows; also he followed in the triumphs of nine generals whose victories were chiefly due to his aid, and in addition—and this in my opinion is his finest achievement—procured the conviction in the People's Court at the termination of his consulship of one of his leaders Titus Romilius on the charge of maladministration of his office. The military distinctions of Capitolinus[c] would be not inferior, if he had not cancelled them by the conclusion of his career. He had twice captured enemy's spoils before he was seventeen years old; he had been the first of any one to receive a mural crown as a Knight, as well as six civic crowns and 37 gifts; he had received 23 wounds on the front of his body; he had rescued Publius Servilius Master of the Horse, when himself wounded in the shoulder and thigh; above all he had alone saved the Capitol and the fortunes of the state therein from the Gauls[d]—if only he had not saved it to make himself king.

[d] 390 B.C.

Verum in his sunt quidem virtutis opera magna, sed
maiora fortunae: M. Sergio, ut equidem arbitror,
nemo quemquam hominum iure praetulerit, licet
pronepos Catilina gratiam nomini deroget. secundo
stipendio dextram manum perdidit, stipendiis duobus
ter et vicies vulneratus est, ob id neutra manu,
neutro pede satis utilis, animo tantum salvo,[1] plurimis postea stipendiis debilis miles. bis ab Hannibale
captus—neque enim cum quolibet hoste res fuit—,
bis vinculorum eius profugus, in viginti mensibus
nullo non die in catenis aut compedibus custoditus.
sinistra manu sola quater pugnavit, duobus equis
105 insidente eo suffossis. dextram sibi ferream fecit,
eaque religata proeliatus Cremonam obsidione
exemit, Placentiam tutatus est, duodena castra
hostium in Gallia cepit, quae omnia ex oratione eius
apparent habita cum in praetura sacris arceretur a
collegis ut debilis, quos hic coronarum acervos con-
106 structurus hoste mutato! etenim plurimum refert
in quae cuiusque virtus tempora inciderit. quas
Trebia Ticinusve aut Trasimenus civicas dedere?
quae Cannis corona merita, unde fugisse virtutis
summum opus fuit? ceteri profecto victores hominum
fuere, Sergius vicit etiam fortunam.

[1] *Detlefsen*: uno tantum servo (salvus *Mayhoff*).

---

[a] The four defeats of the Roman armies with which Hannibal's invasion began, 218–216 B.C. At the last of the four,
Cannae, one consul fell, and the other, Varro, escaped with
the remnant of his forces, and afterwards was thanked by
the Senate for not despairing of the State.

But, although these cases exhibit great achieve- *Exploits of*
ments of valour, yet they involve still greater *Sergius.*
achievements of fortune; whereas nobody, in my
judgement at all events, can rightly rank any
human being above Marcus Sergius, albeit his
greatgrandson Catiline diminishes the credit of his
name. Sergius in his second campaign lost his right
hand; in two campaigns he was wounded twenty-
three times, with the result that he was crippled
in both hands and both feet, only his spirit being
intact; yet although disabled, he served in numerous
subsequent campaigns. He was twice taken prisoner
by Hannibal (for it was with no ordinary foe that
he was engaged), and twice escaped from Hannibal's
fetters, although he was kept in chains or shackles
on every single day for twenty months. He fought
four times with only his left hand, having two horses
he was riding stabbed under him. He had a
right hand of iron made for him and going into
action with it tied to his arm, raised the siege of
Cremona, saved Piacenza, captured twelve enemy
camps in Gaul: all of which exploits are testified
by his speech delivered during his praetorship when
his colleagues wanted to debar him from the sacrifices as infirm—a man who with a different foe would
have accumulated what piles of wreaths! inasmuch
as it makes the greatest difference with what period
of history a particular man's valour happens to
coincide. What civic wreaths were bestowed by
Trebbia or Ticino or Trasimeno? what crown was
won at Cannae, where successful flight was valour's
highest exploit?[a] All other victors truly have
conquered men, but Sergius vanquished fortune
also.

575

107   XXIX. Ingeniorum gloriae quis possit agere de-
lectum per tot disciplinarum genera et tantam rerum
operumque varietatem? nisi forte Homero vate Graeco
nullum felicius extitisse convenit, sive operis forma [1]
sive materie aestimetur. itaque Alexander Magnus—
etenim insignibus iudiciis optume citraque invidiam
108 tam superba censura peragetur—inter spolia Darii
Persarum regis unguentorum scrinio capto quod
erat de [2] auro margaritis gemmisque pretiosum,
varios eius usus amicis demonstrantibus, quando
taedebat unguenti bellatorem et militia sordidum,
' Immo Hercule,' inquit, ' librorum Homeri custodiae
detur,' ut pretiosissimum humani animi opus quam
109 maxime diviti opere servaretur. idem Pindari vatis
familiae penatibusque iussit parci cum Thebas raperet, Aristotelis philosophi patriam suam credidit,[3]
tantaeque rerum claritati tam benignum testimonium miscuit. Archilochi poetae interfectores
Apollo arguit Delphis. Sophoclem tragici cothurni
principem defunctum sepelire Liber pater iussit,
obsidentibus moenia Lacedaemoniis, Lysandro eorum
rege in quiete saepius admonito ut pateretur humari
delicias suas. requisivit rex, qui supremum diem
Athenis obissent [4] nec difficulter ex his quem deus
significasset intellexit, pacemque funeri dedit.

    [1] *Strack*: fortuna.
    [2] *V.ll.* erat, erato : erat celato ? *Detlefsen.*
    [3] *V.l.* patriam condidit (Aristotelis Philippus patriam con-
didit *Longol.*).
    [4] *Urlichs*: obisset.

    [a] The restoration as well as the destruction of Aristotle's
birthplace, Stagira, is usually ascribed to Philip, but one
account says that he restored it at the request of his young
son Alexander.
    [b] In 406 B.C.

XXIX. Who could make an honours class-list of Cases of intellectual eminence: in poetry, geniuses, ranging through all the kinds of systems and all the varieties of subject and of treatment? unless perhaps it is agreed that no genius has ever existed who was more successful than Homer the bard of Greece, whether he be judged by the form or by the matter of his work. Consequently Alexander the Great—for so lordly an assessment will be effected best and least invidiously by the most supreme tribunals—when among the booty won from the Persian King Darius there was a case of unguents made of gold and enriched with pearls and precious stones, and when his friends pointed out the various uses to which it could be put, since a warrior soiled with warfare had no use for perfume, said, " No, by Hercules, rather let it be assigned to keeping the works of Homer "—so that the most precious achievement of the mind of man might be preserved in the richest possible product of the craftsman's art. Alexander also gave orders at the sack of Thebes for the household and home of the poet Pindar to be spared; and he felt the native place of the philosopher Aristotle to be his own, and blended that evidence of kindliness with all the glory of his exploits.[a] Apollo at Delphi exposed the murderers of the poet Archilochus. When Sophocles the prince of the tragic buskin died,[b] Father Liber gave orders for his burial though the Spartans were besieging the city walls, the Spartan king Lysander receiving frequent admonitions in dreams ' to permit the interment of the darling of the god.' The king enquired what persons had expired at Athens and had no difficulty in understanding which among them the god meant, and he granted an armistice for the funeral.

577

110   XXX. Platoni sapientiae antistiti Dionysius tyrannus alias saevitiae superbiaeque natus vittatam navem
misit obviam, ipse quadrigis albis egredientem in
litore excepit. viginti talentis unam orationem
Isocrates vendidit. Aeschines Atheniensis summus
orator, cum accusationem qua fuerat usus Rhodiis
legisset, legit et defensionem Demosthenis qua in
illud depulsus fuerat exilium, mirantibusque tum
magis fuisse miraturos dixit si ipsum orantem audi-
vissent, calamitate testis ingens factus inimici.

111 Thucydiden imperatorem Athenienses in exilium
egere, rerum conditorem revocavere, eloquentiam
mirati cuius virtutem damnaverant. magnum et
Menandro in comico socco testimonium regum
Aegypti et Macedoniae contigit classe et per legatos
petito, maius ex ipso regiae fortunae praelata litterarum conscientia.

112   Perhibuere et Romani proceres etiam exteris testi-
monia. Cn. Pompeius confecto Mithridatico bello
intraturus Posidonii sapientiae professione clari
domum forem percuti de more a lictore vetuit, et
fasces litterarum ianuae summisit is cui se oriens
occidensque summiserat. Cato censorius in illa

---

   [a] The younger Dionysius of Syracuse was visited by Plato
soon after his accession in 367 B.C. and again a few years
later.
   [b] *In Ctesiphontem.*
   [c] *De corona.*
   [d] In 424 B.C. Thucydides was in command of an Athenian
fleet that unavoidably arrived too late to save Amphipolis
from capture by the Spartan Brasidas. He avoided impeach-
ment by going into exile. He seems to have returned to

XXX. The tyrant Dionysius,[a] who was in other mat- *and in philo-*
ters by nature given to cruelty and pride, sent a ship *sophy, oratory and*
decked with garlands to meet Plato the high priest *drama.*
of wisdom, and as he disembarked received him at
the coast in person, in a chariot with four white
horses. Isocrates sold a single speech for 20 talents.
The eminent Athenian orator Aeschines, after reading to the citizens of Rhodes the speech[b] that he
had made in prosecuting, also read Demosthenes's
speech[c] in defence that had driven him into exile
at Rhodes, and on their expressing admiration said
that they would have admired it even more on
the actual occasion, if they had heard the orator
himself: thus his disaster constituted him a powerful
witness for his enemy's case. Thucydides as military commander was sentenced to exile by the
Athenians but as historian was recalled:[d] they
admired the eloquence of a man whose valour they
had condemned. High testimony was also born to
Menander's eminence in comedy by the kings of
Egypt and Macedon when they sent a fleet and an
embassy to fetch him, but higher testimony was
derived from himself by his preferment of the con-
sciousness of literary merit to royal fortune.

Roman leaders also have borne witness even to *Roman*
foreigners. At the conclusion of the war with *respect for*
Mithridates Gnaeus Pompey when going to enter *Greek*
the abode of the famous professor of philosophy *genius.*
Posidonius forbade his retainer to knock on the door
in the customary manner, and the subduer of the
East and of the West dipped his standard to the
portals of learning. Cato the censor, on the occa-

Athens in 403, when there was a general amnesty after the
restoration of the democracy.

nobili trium sapientiae procerum ab Athenis legatione
audito Carneade quamprimum legatos eos censuit
dimittendos, quoniam illo viro argumentante quid

113 veri esset haut facile discerni posset. quanta morum
commutatio! ille semper alioquin universos ex Italia
pellendos censuit Graecos, at pronepos eius Uticensis
Cato unum ex tribunatu militum philosophum,
alterum ex Cypria legatione deportavit; eandemque
linguam ex duobus Catonibus in illo abegisse, in hoc
importasse memorabile est.

114   Sed et nostrorum gloriam percenseamus. Prior
Africanus Q. Ennii statuam sepulchro suo inponi
iussit, clarumque illud nomen, immo vero spolium
ex tertia orbis parte raptum, in cinere supremo cum
poetae titulo legi. Divus Augustus carmina Vergilii
cremari contra testamenti eius verecundiam vetuit,
maiusque ita vati testimonium contigit quam si ipse

115 sua probavisset. M. Varronis in bibliotheca, quae
prima in orbe ab Asinio Pollione ex manubiis pub-
licata Romae est, unius viventis posita imago est,
haud minore, ut equidem reor, gloria principe oratore
et cive ex illa ingeniorum quae tunc fuit multitudine
uni hanc coronam dante quam cum eidem Magnus

116 Pompeius piratico ex bello navalem dedit. innu-

---

^a In 155 B.C., to deprecate the fine imposed on Athens for
the destruction of Oropus.

^b It is not known who this was. As to the second
philosopher at all events, it appears that it was his statue
that Cato brought to Rome; this was Zeno, the founder of
the Stoic school: see XXXIV. c. 19 *ad fin.*

sion when the famous embassy of the three leaders of philosophy was sent from Athens,[a] after hearing Carneades advised that these envoys should be sent away as soon as possible, because when Carneades was discoursing it was difficult to distinguish where the truth lay. What a complete change of fashion! The Cato in question always on other occasions recommended the total banishment of Greeks from Italy, whereas his great-grandson Cato of Utica brought home one philosopher[b] from his military tribunate and another from his mission to Cyprus; and of the two Catos the former has the distinction of having banished and the other of having introduced the same language.

But let us also pass in review the glory of our own countrymen. *Romans of intellectual eminence.* The elder Africanus gave orders for a statue of Quintus Ennius to be placed on his own tomb, and for that famous name, or rather trophy of war won from a third part of the world, to be read above his last ashes together with the memorial of a poet. His late Majesty Augustus overrode the modesty of Virgil's will and forbade the burning of his poems, and thus the bard achieved a stronger testimony than if he had commended his own works himself. In the library founded at Rome by Asinius Pollio, the earliest library in the world established out of the spoils of war, the only statue of a living person erected was that of Marcus Varro, the bestowal by a leading orator and citizen of this crowning honour on one only out of the multitude of men of genius then existing constituting no less a distinction, in my own opinion, than when Pompey the Great gave to that same Varro a naval crown for his conduct in the war with the pirates. There

merabilia deinde sunt exempla Romana, si persequi
libeat, cum plures una gens in quocumque genere
eximios tulerit quam ceterae terrae. sed quo te,
M. Tulli, piaculo taceam, quove maxime excellentem
insigni praedicem? quo potius quam universi populi
illius sciscentis [1] amplissimo testimonio, e tota vita
117 tua consulatus tantum operibus electis? te dicente
legem agrariam, hoc est alimenta sua, abdicarunt
tribus, te suadente Roscio theatralis auctori legis
ignoverunt notatasque se discrimine sedis aequo
animo tulerunt, te orante proscriptorum liberos
honores petere puduit, tuum Catilina fugit ingenium,
tu M. Antonium proscripsisti. salve primus omnium
parens patriae appellate, primus in toga triumphum
linguaeque lauream merite, et facundiae Latiarumque
litterarum parens atque, ut dictator Caesar hostis
quondam tuus de te scripsit, omnium triumphorum
laurea adepte [2] maiorem, quanto plus est ingenii
Romani terminos in tantum promovisse quam
imperii.
118 XXXI. Reliquis animi bonis praestitere ceteros
mortales: sapientia, ob id Cati, Corculi apud
119 Romanos cognominati, apud Graecos Socrates

---

[1] *Detlefsen*: genti, gentis (gentium *Welzhofer*).
[2] adepte *om. v.l.*

---

[a] 63 B.C.
[b] Of Rullus, for distribution of public lands.
[c] L. Roscius Otho: his law, in 67 B.C. reserved for the
Equites the 14 rows behind the patricians in the theatre. This
unpopular legislation four years later, when Cicero was consul,
led to rioting which it took all his eloquence to allay.
[d] *I.e.* ' brainy,' *cor* being the seat of the intellect. 'Catus
Aelius Sextus ' is quoted from Ennius by Cicero, *Tusc.* I, 18;

is a countless series of Roman examples, if one chose
to pursue them, since a single race has produced
more men of distinction in every branch whatever
than the whole of the other countries. But what
excuse could I have for omitting mention of you,
Marcus Tullius? or by what distinctive mark can I
advertise your superlative excellence? by what in
preference to the most honourable testimony of that
whole nation's decree, selecting out of your entire
life only the achievements of your consulship? [a]
Your oratory induced the tribes to discard the
agrarian law,[b] that is, their own livelihood; your
advice led them to forgive Roscius [c] the proposer of
the law as to the theatre, and to tolerate with
equanimity the mark put upon them by a distinction of seating; your entreaty made the children of
the men sentenced to proscription ashamed to stand
for office; your genius drove Catiline to flight; you
proscribed Mark Antony. Hail, first recipient of
the title of Father of the Country, first winner of a
civilian triumph and of a wreath of honour for
oratory, and parent of eloquence and of Latium's
letters; and (as your former foe, the dictator Caesar,
wrote of you) winner of a greater laurel wreath than
that of any triumph, inasmuch as it is a greater
thing to have advanced so far the frontiers of
the Roman genius than the frontiers of Rome's
empire.

XXXI. Persons who have surpassed the rest of *Eminent philosophers.*
mortal kind in the remaining gifts of the mind are: in
wisdom, the people who on this account won at Rome
the surnames of Wise and Sage,[d] and in Greece

Corculum (here pluralised in the masculine) was the surname
given to Scipio Nasica, consul 162 and 155 B.C.

oraculo Apollinis Pythii praelatus cunctis. XXXII.
Rursus mortales oraculorum societatem dedere Chiloni
Lacedaemonio tria praecepta eius Delphis consecrando
aureis litteris, quae sunt haec: nosse se quemque,
et nihil nimium cupere, comitemque aeris alieni
atque litis esse miseriam. quin et funus eius, cum
victore filio Olympiae expirasset gaudio, tota Graecia
prosecuta est.

XXXIII. Divinitas et quaedam caelitum societas
nobilissima ex feminis in Sibylla fuit, ex viris in
Melampode apud Graecos, apud Romanos in Marcio.

120 XXXIV. Vir optumus semel a condito aevo
iudicatus est Scipio Nasica a iurato senatu, idem in
toga candida bis repulsa notatus a populo. in summa
ei in patria mori non licuit, non Hercule magis quam
extra vincula illi sapientissimo ab Apolline iudicato
Socrati.

XXXV. Pudicissima femina semel matronarum
sententia iudicata est Sulpicia Paterculi filia, uxor
Fulvi Flacci, electa ex centum praeceptis quae
simulacrum Veneris ex Sibyllinis libris dedicaret,
iterum religionis experimento Claudia inducta
Romam deum matre.

---

[a] Sulpicia, daughter of Servius Sulpicius Paterculus and
wife of Quintus Fulvius Flaccus, was in 114 B.C. chosen as the
chastest woman in Rome to dedicate a statue of Venus Verti-
cordia, which was to be erected to raise the standard of
feminine morals (Valerius Maximus viii. 15. 12).

[b] Claudia Quinta, a Roman matron, accused of unchastity.
A statue of Cybele in 204 B.C. was being brought from Pessinus
to Rome, and the vessel conveying it grounded at the mouth
of the Tiber. The soothsayers announced that only a chaste

Socrates, whom Pythian Apollo's oracle placed before all other men. XXXII. Again, partnership with the oracles was bestowed by mortals on the Spartan Chilo, by canonizing in letters of gold at Delphi his three precepts, which are these : *Know thyself; Desire nothing too much ; The comrade of debt and litigation is misery.* Moreover when he expired from joy on his son's being victorious at Olympia, the whole of Greece followed in his funeral procession.

XXXIII. The most famous instances of the gift *and diviners.* of divination and so to speak communion with the heavenly beings are, among women, the Sibyl, and among men, Melampus in Greece and Marcius at Rome.

XXXIV. Scipio Nasica was judged by the verdict *The noblest* of the senate on oath to be once for all the noblest *Roman.* man since the foundation of time, although he was twice branded by the nation with defeat when a candidate for office. At the end he was not permitted to die in his native land, any more in truth than the great Socrates, whom Apollo judged to be the wisest of mankind, was allowed to die freed from fetters.

XXXV. The first case of a woman judged by the *The noblest* vote of the matrons to be the most modest was *Roman* *woman.* Sulpicia,[a] daughter of Paterculus and wife of Fulvius Flaccus, who was elected from a previously chosen list of 100 to dedicate the image of Venus in accordance with the Sibylline books ; and on a second occasion, by the test of religion, Claudia,[b] when the Mother of the Gods was brought to Rome.

woman could move it. Claudia coming forward took hold of the rope and at once pulled the vessel forward (Livy XXIX. 14, Ovid *Fasti* IV. 395).

585

121 XXXVI. Pietatis exempla infinita quidem toto orbe extitere, sed Romae unum cui comparari cuncta non possint. humilis in plebe et ideo ignobilis puerpera, supplicii causa carcere inclusa matre cum impetrasset aditum, a ianitore semper excussa ante[1] ne quid inferret cibi, deprehensa est uberibus suis alens eam. quo miraculo matris salus donata filiae pietati est ambaeque perpetuis alimentis, et locus ille eidem consecratus deae, C. Quinctio M'. Acilio coss. templo Pietatis extructo in illius carceris sede, ubi

122 nunc Marcelli theatrum est. Gracchorum pater anguibus prehensis in domo, cum responderetur ipsum victurum alterius sexus interempto: Immo vero, inquit, meum necate, Cornelia enim iuvenis est et parere adhuc potest. hoc erat uxori parcere et re publicae consulere; idque mox consecutum est. M. Lepidus Appuleiae uxoris caritate post repudium obiit. P. Rutilius morbo levi impeditus nunciata fratris repulsa in consulatus petitione ilico expiravit. P. Catienus Philotimus patronum adeo dilexit ut heres omnibus bonis institutus in rogum eius se iaceret.

---

[1] *Salmasius*: excussa *aut* excurrant *aut* excurante.

---

a 150 B.C.

XXXVI. Of filial affection there have it is true been unlimited instances all over the world, but one at Rome with which the whole of the rest could not compare. A plebeian woman of low position and therefore unknown, who had just given birth to a child, had permission to visit her mother who had been shut up in prison as a punishment, and was always searched in advance by the doorkeeper to prevent her carrying in any food; she was detected giving her mother sustenance from her own breasts. In consequence of this marvel the daughter's pious affection was rewarded by the mother's release and both were awarded maintenance for life; and the place where it occurred was consecrated to the Goddess concerned, a temple dedicated to Filial Affection being built on the site of the prison, where the Theatre of Marcellus now stands, in the consulship *a* of Gaius Quinctius and Manius Acilius. In the house of the father of the Gracchi two snakes were caught, and in reply to enquiry an oracle declared that he himself would live if the snake of the other sex were killed; " No," said he, " kill my snake: Cornelia is young and still able to bear children." This meant, to spare his wife and think of the public interest; and the result prophesied soon followed. Marcus Lepidus after divorcing his wife Appuleia died for love of her. Publius Rutilius when suffering from a slight illness received news of his brother's defeat in his candidature for the consulship, and at once expired. Publius Catienus Philotimus loved his patron so dearly that he threw himself upon his funeral pyre, although left heir to the whole of his property.

Eminence in filial affection.

587

123 XXXVII. Variarum artium scientia innumerabiles
enituere, quos tamen attingi par sit florem hominum
libantibus: astrologia Berosus, cui ob divinas praedic-
tiones Athenienses publice in gymnasio statuam
inaurata lingua statuere; grammatica Apollodorus,
cui Amphictyones Gracciae honorem habuere,
Hippocrates medicina, nam [1] venientem ab Illyriis
pestilentiam praedixit discipulosque ad auxiliandum
circa urbes dimisit, quod ob meritum honores illi quos
Herculi decrevit Graecia. eandem scientiam in
Cleombroto Ceo Ptolomaeus rex Megalensibus
124 sacris donavit centum talentis servato Antiocho rege.
magna et Critobulo fama est extracta Philippi regis
oculo sagitta et citra deformitatem oris curata orbitate
luminis, summa autem Asclepiadi Prusiensi condita
nova secta, spretis legatis et pollicitationibus Mithri-
datis regis, reperta ratione quá vinum aegris medetur,
relato e funere homine et conservato, sed maxime
sponsione facta cum fortuna ne medicus crederetur
si umquam invalidus ullo modo fuisset ipse: et vicit
suprema in senecta lapsu scalarum exanimatus.
125 Grande et Archimedi geometricae ac machinalis
scientiae testimonium M. Marcelli contigit interdicto
cum Syracusae caperentur ne violaretur unus, nisi

[1] *Detlefsen;* medicinam.

[a] Antiochus Soter, second of the Seleucid Kings of Syria
280–261 B.C.
[b] This accident happened to Philip of Macedon at the siege of
Methone, 354 B.C.

XXXVII. The people who have achieved distinc- *Eminent men*
tion in the knowledge of the various sciences are *of science,*
medicine
innumerable, but nevertheless they must be touched *and art.*
on when we are culling the flower of mankind: in
astronomy, Berosus, to whom on account of his
marvellous predictions Athens officially erected in
the exercising ground a statue with a gilt tongue;
in philology, Apollodorus, whom the Amphictyons
of Greece honoured; in medicine, Hippocrates, who
foretold a plague that was coming from Illyria and
despatched his pupils round the cities to render
assistance, in return for which service Greece voted
him the honours that it gave to Hercules. The same
knowledge in the case of Cleombrotus of Ceos was
rewarded by King Ptolemy at the Megalensian
Festival with 100 talents, after he had saved the life
of King Antiochus.[a] Critobulus also has a great
reputation for having extracted an arrow from
King Philip's eye,[b] and having treated his loss of
sight without causing disfigurement of his face; but
the highest reputation belongs to Asclepiades of
Prusa, for having founded a new school, despised the
envoys and overtures of King Mithridates, discovered
a method of preparing medicated wine for the sick,
brought back a man from burial and saved his life,
but most of all for having made a wager with
fortune that he should not be deemed a physician
if he were ever in any way ill himself: and he won
his bet, as he lost his life in extreme old age by
falling downstairs.

Archimedes also received striking testimony to
his knowledge of geometry and mechanics from
Marcus Marcellus, who at the capture of Syracuse
forbade violence to be done to him only—had not

fefellisset imperium militaris imprudentia. laudatus
est et Chersiphron Gnosius aede Ephesi Dianae
admirabili fabricata, Philon Athenis armamentario
CD [1] navium, Ctesibius pneumatica ratione et hydrau-
licis organis repertis, Dinochares metatus Alexandro
condenti [2] in Aegypto Alexandriam. idem hic imperator edixit ne quis ipsum alius quam Apelles
pingeret, quam Pyrgoteles scalperet, quam Lysippus
ex aere duceret, quae artes pluribus inclaruere ex-
126 emplis. XXXVIII. Aristidis Thebani pictoris unam
tabulam centum talentis rex Attalus licitus est,
octoginta emit duas Caesar dictator, Medeam et
Aiacem Timomachi, in templo Veneris Genetricis
dicaturus. Candaules rex Bularchi picturam Magne-
tum exiti, haud mediocris spati, pari rependit auro.
Rhodum non incendit rex Demetrius expugnator
cognominatus, ne tabulam Protogenis cremaret a
127 parte ea muri locatam. Praxiteles marmore nobilitatus est Gnidiaque Venere praecipue, vesano amore
cuiusdam iuvenis insigni, et Nicomedis aestimatione
regis grandi Gnidiorum aere alieno permutare eam
conati. Phidiae Iuppiter Olympius cotidie testimonium perhibet, Mentori Capitolinus et Diana
Ephesia, quibus fuere consecrata artis eius vasa.
128 XXXIX. Pretium hominis in servitio geniti maximum ad hunc diem, quod equidem conpererim, fuit

---

[1] *Mayhoff*: M.
[2] *Ritschl*: condente.

---

[a] Doubtless on a panel of wood. [b] Poliorcetes.

[c] There were three kings of this name, who came to the
throne of Bithynia in 278, 149 and 91 B.C. respectively. There
appears to be no evidence to show which of the three is here
alluded to.

the ignorance of a soldier foiled the command. Others who won praise were Chersiphron of Gnossus who constructed the wonderful temple of Diana at Ephesus, Philo who made a dockyard for 400 ships at Athens, Ctesibius who discovered the theory of the pneumatic pump and invented hydraulic engines, Dinochares who acted as surveyor for Alexander when founding Alexandria in Egypt. This ruler also issued a proclamation that only Apelles should paint his picture, only Pyrgoteles sculpture his statue, and only Lysippus cast him in bronze: there are many celebrated examples of these arts. XXXVIII. King Attalus bid 100 talents for one picture by the Theban painter Aristides; the dictator Caesar purchased two by Timomachus for 80, the Medea and the Ajax, to dedicate them in the temple of Venus Genetrix. King Candaules paid its weight in gold for a picture *a* of considerable size by Bularchus representing the downfall of the Magnesians. King Demetrius surnamed Besieger of Cities *b* refrained from setting fire to Rhodes for fear of burning a picture by Protogenes stored in that part of the fortification. Praxiteles is famous for his marbles, and especially for his Venus at Cnidos, which is celebrated because of the infatuation that it inspired in a certain young man, and because of the value set on it by King Nicomedes,*c* who attempted to obtain it in return for discharging a large debt owed by the Cnidians. Daily testimony is borne to Phidias by Olympian Jove, and to Mentor by Capitoline Jove and by Diana of Ephesus, works that have immortalized the tools of this craft.

XXXIX. The highest price hitherto paid, so far as I have ascertained, for a person born in slavery was *Exceptional prices for slaves.*

591

grammaticae artis Daphnin Attio Pisaurense vendente
et M. Scauro principe civitatis II$\overline{\text{i}}$. $\overline{\text{DCC}}$ licente. ex-
cessere hoc in nostro aevo, nec modice, histrionis
reditu[1] libertatem suam mercati, quippe cum iam
apud maiores Roscius histrio II$\overline{\text{i}}$. $\overline{\text{D}}$ annua meritasse
129 prodatur, nisi si quis in hoc loco disiderat Armeniaci
belli paulo ante propter Tiridaten gesti dispensa-
torem, quem Nero II$\overline{\text{i}}$. $|\overline{\text{cxxx}}|$ manumisit. sed
hoc pretium belli, non hominis, fuit, tam Hercule
quam libidinis, non formae, Paezontem e spadonibus
Seiani II$\overline{\text{i}}$. $|\overline{\text{D}}|$ mercante Clutorio Prisco. quam
quidem iniuriam lucri fecit ille mercatus in luctu
civitatis, quoniam arguere nulli vacabat.

130   XL. Gentium in toto orbe praestantissima una
omnium virtute haud dubie Romana extitit. felicitas
cui praecipua fuerit homini non est humani iudicii, cum
prosperitatem ipsam alius alio modo et suopte ingenio
quisque determinet. si verum facere iudicium volu-
mus ac repudiata omni fortunae ambitione decernere,
nemo mortalium est felix. abunde agitur[2] atque
indulgenter a fortuna deciditur[3] cum eo qui iure dici
non infelix potest. quippe ut alia non sint, certe ne
lassescat fortuna metus est, quo semel recepto solida
131 felicitas non est. quid quod nemo mortalium omnibus
horis sapit? utinamque falsum hoc et non ut a vate

---

[1] *Detlefsen* : reddi (sed hi *Mayhoff*).
[2] *Edd.* : igitur.
[3] indulgente fortuna deciditur ? *Brotier*.

when Attius of Pesaro was selling a skilled linguist named Daphnis and Marcus Scaurus, Head of the State, bid 700,000 sesterces. This has been exceeded, and considerably, in our own time by actors when buying their own freedom by means of their earnings, inasmuch as already in the time of our ancestors the actor Roscius is said to have earned 500,000 sesterces a year,—unless anybody expects a mention in this place of the commissary in the Armenian war carried on not long ago for Tiridates, whom Nero liberated for 13,000,000 sesterces. But this was the price paid for a war, not for an individual, just as in truth when Clutorius Priscus bought one of Sejanus's eunuchs Paezon for 50,000,000, this was the price of lust and not of beauty. But Clutorius got away with this outrageous affair during a period of national mourning, as nobody had time to show him up.

XL. The one race of outstanding eminence in virtue among all the races in the whole world is undoubtedly the Roman. What human being has had the greatest happiness is not a question for human judgement, since prosperity itself different people define in different ways and each according to his own temperament. If we wish to make a true judgement and discard all fortune's pomp in deciding the point, none among mortals is happy. Fortune deals lavishly and makes an indulgent bargain with the man whom it is possible justly to pronounce not unhappy. In fact, apart from other considerations, assuredly there is a fear that fortune may grow weary, and this fear once entertained, happiness has no firm foundation. What of the proverb that none among mortals is wise all the time? And would that as many men as possible may deem this proverb

Who is the happiest of mankind?

dictum quam plurimi iudicent! vana mortalitas et ad
circumscribendam se ipsam ingeniosa conputat more
Thraciae gentis, quae calculos colore distinctos pro
experimento cuiusque diei in urnam condit ac
supremo die separatos dinumerat atque ita de quoque
132 pronunciat. quid quod ipse[1] calculi candore illo
laudatus dies originem mali habuit? quam multos
accepta adflixere imperia! quam multos bona per-
didere et ultimis mersere suppliciis! ista nimirum
bona, si cui inter[2] illa hora in gaudio fuit! ita est profecto, alius de alio iudicat dies et tantum[3] supremus
de omnibus, ideoque nullis credendum est. quid quod
bona malis paria non sunt etiam pari numero, nec
laetitia ulla minimo maerore pensanda? heu vana
et imprudens diligentia! numerus dierum conputa-
tur,[4] ubi quaeritur pondus!

133　　XLI. Una feminarum in omni aevo Lampido Lace-
daemonia reperitur quae regis filia, regis uxor, regis
mater fuerit, una Berenice quae filia, soror, mater
Olympionicarum, una familia Curionum in qua tres
continua serie oratores exstiterint, una Fabiorum in
qua tres continui principes senatus, M. Fabius Ambustus, Fabius Rullianus filius, Q. Fabius Gurges nepos.

134 XLII. cetera exempla fortunae variantis innumera
sunt. etenim quae facit magna gaudia nisi ex malis,

[1] ipse? *Mayhoff*: iste.
[2] *V.l.* bona cum interim.
[3] *Mayhoff*: tamen.
[4] *Edd. vet.* (cf. VI. 209): comparatur.

---

[a] Really there were many, among them Olympias, mother
of Alexander the Great.

false, and not as the utterance of a prophet! Mortality, being so vain and so ingenious in self-deception, makes its calculation after the manner of the Thracian tribe that puts stone counters of different colours corresponding to each day's experience in an urn, and on the last day sorts them and counts them out and thus pronounces judgement about each individual. What of the fact that the very day commended by that stone of brilliant whiteness contained the source of misfortune? How many men have been overthrown by attaining power! How many have been ruined and plunged into the direst torments by wealth! Wealth forsooth it is called if a man has had an hour of joy while surrounded by it. So doubtless is it! Different days pass verdict on different men and only the last day a final verdict on all men; and consequently no day is to be trusted. What of the fact that goods are not equal to evils even if of equal number, and that no joy can counterbalance the smallest grief? Alas what vain and foolish application! we count the number of the days, when it is their weight that is in question!

XLI. Only one *a* woman can be found in the whole of history, the Spartan Lampido, who was daughter, *Fortune's mutability.* wife and mother of a king; only one, Berenice, who was daughter, sister and mother of Olympic winners; only one family, the Curios, that has produced three orators in unbroken series, only one, the Fabii, three successive Chiefs of the Senate, Marcus Fabius Ambustus, his son Fabius Rullianus and his grandson Quintus Fabius Gurges. XLII. All other cases are instances of changing Fortune, and are beyond counting. For what great joys does she produce except when

aut quae mala inmensa nisi ex ingentibus gaudiis?
XLIII. servavit proscriptum a Sulla M. Fidustium
senatorem annis XXXVI, sed iterum proscriptura: [1]
superstes Sullae vixit, sed usque ad Antonium,
constatque nulla alia de causa ab eo proscriptum
135 quam quia proscriptus fuisset. triumphare P. Ven-
tidium de Parthis voluit quidem solum, sed eundem
in triumpho Asculano Cn. Pompei duxit puerum,
quamquam Masurius auctor est bis in triumpho
ductum, Cicero mulionem castrensis furnariae fuisse,
plurimi iuventam inopem in caliga militari tolerasse.
136 fuit et Balbus Cornelius maior consul, sed accusatus
atque de iure virgarum in eum iudicum in consilium
missus, primus externorum atque etiam in oceano
genitorum usus illo honore quem maiores Latio
quoque negaverunt. est et L. Fulvius inter insignia
exempla, Tusculanorum rebellantium consul, eodemque honore, cum transisset, exornatus confestim
a p. R., qui solus eodem anno quo fuerat hostis
Romae triumphavit ex iis quorum consul fuerat.
137 unus hominum ad hoc aevi Felicis sibi cognomen
adseruit L. Sulla, civili nempe sanguine ac patriae
oppugnatione adoptatus.[2] et quibus felicitatis in-
ductus argumentis? quod proscribere tot milia
civium ac trucidare potuisset? o prava interpretatio

----

[1] *Sillig*: proscriptum.   [2] adoptatum *Hardouin*.

----

[a] The figure seems incorrect: Fidustius was proscribed in 81
B.C., and Antony's power only began after Caesar's assassina-
tion in 44 B.C.

[b] Balbus born in the island of Gades (Cadiz) served under
Pompey in Spain and was established by him at Rome.
Accused 56 B.C. of illegally assuming citizenship, he was de-
fended by Cicero and acquitted. Octavian made him consul
40 B.C.—Only aliens could be sentenced to flogging.

following on disasters, or what immeasurable disasters except when following on enormous joys? XLIII. She preserved the senator Marcus Fidustius for 36 [a] years after his proscription by Sulla, but only to proscribe him a second time: he survived Sulla, but he lived to see Antony, and it is known that Antony proscribed him for no other reason than that he had been proscribed before! It is true she willed that Publius Ventidius should alone win a triumph from the Parthians, but she also in his boyhood led him captive in Gnaeus Pompeius's triumph after Asculum —albeit Masurius states that he was led in triumph twice, and Cicero that he was a mule-driver for an army bakery, and many authorities say that in his youth he supported his poverty by foot-slogging in the ranks! Also the elder Cornelius Balbus was consul, but he was impeached and handed over to a court of justice to decide as to his legal liability to a flogging—he being the first foreigner and actual native of the Atlantic coast to have held an honour [b] refused by our ancestors even to Latium. Lucius Fulvius also is one of the notable examples, having been consul of the Tusculans at the time of their revolt and after coming over having been at once honoured with the same office by the Roman nation: he is the only man who ever in the same year in which he had been Rome's enemy won a triumph from the people whose consul he had been. Lucius Sulla is the sole human being hitherto who has assumed the surname Fortunate, in fact achieving the title by civil bloodshed and by making war upon his country. And what tokens of good fortune were his motive? His success in exiling and slaughtering so many thousands of his fellow-countrymen?

et futuro tempore infelix! non melioris sortis tunc
fuere pereuntes, quorum miseremur hodie cum
138 Sullam nemo non oderit? age, non exitus vitae eius
omnium proscriptorum ab illo calamitate crudelior
fuit erodente se ipso corpore et supplicia sibi gig-
nente? quod ut dissimulaverit et supremo somnio
eius, cui inmortuus quodammodo est, credamus ab
uno illo invidiam gloria victam, hoc tamen nempe [1]
felicitati suae defuisse confessus est quod Capitolium
non dedicavisset.

139 Q. Metellus in ea oratione quam habuit supremis
laudibus patris sui L. Metelli pontificis, bis consulis,
dictatoris, magistri equitum, xvviri agris dandis,
qui primus elephantos ex primo Punico bello duxit
in triumpho, scriptum reliquit decem maximas res
optumasque in quibus quaerendis sapientes aetatem
140 exigerent consummasse eum: voluisse enim pri-
marium bellatorem esse, optimum oratorem, fortissi-
mum imperatorem, auspicio suo maximas res geri,
maximo honore uti, summa sapientia esse, summum
senatorem haberi, pecuniam magnam bono modo
invenire, multos liberos relinquere et clarissimum in
civitate esse; haec contigisse ei nec ulli alii post
141 Romam conditam. Longum est refellere et super-

------

[1] [nempe]? *Mayhoff.*

------

[a] Plutarch, *Sulla* 37, gives a different account—that shortly
before his death he dreamt that his dead son came to him and
besought him to cease from anxiety and to go with him to join
his dead mother Metella and to live in happiness with her.

O what a false meaning to attach to the title! How doomed to misfortune in the future! Were not his victims more fortunate at the time when dying, whom we pity today when Sulla is universally hated? Come, was not the close of his life more cruel than the calamity of all the victims of his proscriptions, when his body ate itself away and bred its own torments? And although he dissembled the pangs, and although on the evidence of that last dream[a] of his, which may almost be said to have accompanied his death, we believed that he alone vanquished odium by glory, nevertheless he admitted forsooth that this one thing was wanting to his happiness—he had not dedicated the Capitol.

Quintus Metellus, in the panegyric that he delivered at the obsequies of his father Lucius Metellus the pontiff, who had been Consul twice, Dictator, Master of the Horse and Land-commissioner, and who was the first person who led a procession of elephants in a triumph, having captured them in the first Punic War, has left it in writing that his father had achieved the ten greatest and highest objects in the pursuit of which wise men pass their lives: for he had made it his aim to be a first-class warrior, a supreme orator and a very brave commander, to have the direction of operations of the highest importance, to enjoy the greatest honour, to be supremely wise, to be deemed the most eminent member of the senate, to obtain great wealth in an honourable way, to leave many children, and to achieve supreme distinction in the state; and that these things had fallen to his father's lot, and to that of no one else since Rome's foundation. It would be a lengthy matter to refute this, and it is superfluous to do so as it is

Even outstanding success interrupted by misfortune: the Metelli.

vacuum abunde uno casu refutante: siquidem is
Metellus orbam luminibus exegit senectam amissis
incendio cum Palladium raperet ex aede Vestae,
memorabili causa sed eventu misero. quo fit ut
infelix quidem dici non debeat, felix tamen non
possit. tribuit ei p. R. quod nulli alii ab condito
aevo, ut quotiens in senatum iret curru veheretur
ad curiam, magnum ei et sublime, sed pro oculis
datum.

142 XLIV. Huius quoque Q. Metelli qui illa de patre
dixit filius inter rara felicitatis humanae exempla
numeratur. nam praeter honores amplissimos cogno-
menque Macedonici a quattuor filiis inlatus rogo, uno
praetore, tribus consularibus (duobus triumphalibus),
uno censorio, quae singula quoque paucis contigere. in
143 ipso tamen flore dignationis suae a C. Atinio Labeone,
cui cognomen fuit Macerioni, tribuno plebis, quem e
senatu censor eiecerat, revertens e campo meridiano
tempore, vacuo foro et Capitolio, ad Tarpeium raptus
ut praecipitaretur, convolante quidem tam [1] numerosa
illa cohorte quae patrem eum appellabat, sed, ut
necesse erat in subito, tarde et tamquam in exse-
quias, cum resistendi sacroquesanctum repellendi ius
non esset, virtutis suae opera et censurae periturus,

[1] tum? *Mayhoff.*

abundantly rebutted by a single accidental misfortune: inasmuch as this Metellus passed an old age of blindness, having lost his sight in a fire when saving the statue of Pallas from the temple of Vesta, a memorable purpose but disastrous in its result. Consequently though he must not be pronounced unhappy, still he cannot be called happy. The nation bestowed on him a privilege given to no one else since the foundation of time, permission to ride to the senate-house in a chariot whenever he went to a meeting of the senate—a great and highly honourable privilege, but one that was bestowed on him as a substitute for sight.

XLIV. The son of this Metellus who made those remarks about his father is also counted among the exceptional instances of human happiness. Besides receiving an abundance of high honours and the surname of Macedonicus, he was borne to the tomb by four sons, one a praetor, three ex-consuls (two winners of triumphs), one an ex-censor—things that even separately have fallen to few men's lot. Nevertheless at the very height of his distinguished career, when coming back from the Field at midday, the market place and Capitol being empty, he was carried off to the Tarpeian Rock by Gaius Atinius Labeo, surnamed Macerio, tribune of the plebs, whom when censor he had ejected from the senate, with the intention of hurling him down the cliff; the numerous company of persons who called him their father did it is true hasten to his aid, but as was inevitable in this sudden emergency, too late and as if coming for his funeral, and as he had not the right to resist and to repel the hallowed person of a tribune his virtue and his strictness would have

aegre tribuno qui intercederet reperto a limine ipso
144 mortis revocatus, alieno beneficio postea vixit, bonis
inde etiam consecratis a damnato suo, tamquam
parum esset faucium reste[1] intortarum expressique
per aures sanguinis poena exacta.[2] equidem et
Africani sequentis inimicum fuisse inter calamitates
duxerim, ipso teste Macedonico, siquidem dixit:
ite filii, celebrate exequias; numquam civis maioris
funus videbitis. et hoc dicebat iam Baliaricis et
145 Dalmaticis,[3] iam Macedonicus ipse. verum ut illa
sola iniuria aestimetur, quis hunc iure felicem dixerit
periclitatum ad libidinem inimici, nec Africani saltem, perire? quos hostis vicisse tanti fuit? aut quos
non honores currusque illa sua violentia fortuna
retroegit, per mediam urbem censore tracto—
etenim sola haec morandi ratio fuerat,—tracto in
Capitolium idem[4] in quod triumphans ipse de eorum[5]
146 exuviis ne captivos quidem sic traxerat? maius
hoc scelus felicitate consecuta factum est, peri-
clitato Macedonico vel funus tantum ac tale perdere
in quo a triumphalibus liberis portaretur in rogum
velut exequiis quoque triumphans. nulla est pro-

---

[1] *Ruhnken*: certe.
[2] *V.l.* poenam exactam esse.
[3] *Beroaldus*: Diadematis.
[4] *Mayhoff*: ille.
[5] *Caesarius*: deorum (? dei ornatus *Mayhoff*).

---

[a] As praetor in 148 B.C. he carried on war in Macedonia
against the usurper Andriscus whom he defeated and took
prisoner. His eldest son, when consul 123 B.C., subdued the
Balearic Islands, and his nephew, consul 119 B.C., the Dalma-
tians.

[b] He had not been executed out of hand in order that this
further indignity might be inflicted on him.

resulted in his destruction, but with difficulty another tribune was found to intercede, and he was recalled from the very threshold of death; and subsequently he lived on the charity of another, as his own property had immediately been confiscated on the proposal of the very man whom he had himself caused to be condemned, just as though the penalty exacted from him of having his throat tied in a rope and the blood forced out through his ears were not sufficient! Although for my own part I should also reckon it as a disaster to have been at enmity with the second Africanus, on the evidence of Macedonicus himself, inasmuch as he said, " Go, my sons, celebrate his obsequies; you will never see the funeral of a greater citizen! " And he said this to sons who had already won the titles of Balearicus and Dalmaticus, while he himself was already Macedonicus.[a] But even if only that injury be taken into account, who could rightly pronounce happy this man who ran the risk of perishing at the will of an enemy, and him not even an Africanus? Victory over what enemies was worth so much? or what honours and triumphal cars did not fortune put into the shade by that violent stroke— a censor dragged through the middle of the city (for this had been the sole reason for delaying [b]), dragged to that same Capitol to which he himself had not thus dragged even prisoners when he was triumphing over the spoils taken from them? This was rendered a greater crime by the happiness that followed, as it placed Macedonicus in danger of losing even that great and glorious funeral in which he was carried to the pyre by his children who had themselves won triumphs, so that even his obsequies were a triumphal procession. Assuredly it is no firmly founded

fecto solida felicitas quam contumelia ulla vitae rupit,
nedum tanta. quod superest, nescio morum gloriae
an indignationis dolori accedat, inter tot Metellos tam
sceleratam C. Atini audaciam semper fuisse inultam.

147   XLV. In divo quoque Augusto, quem universa mortalitas in hac censura nuncupet, si diligenter aesti-
mentur cuncta, magna sortis humanae reperiantur
volumina: repulsa in magisterio equitum apud avun-
culum et contra petitionem eius praelatus Lepidus,
proscriptionis invidia, collegium in triumviratu pessi-
morum civium, nec aequa saltem portione, sed

148 praegravi Antonio, Philippensi proelio morbidi [1] fuga
et triduo in palude argroti et (ut fatentur Agrippa ac
Maecenas) aqua subter cutem fusa turgidi latebra,
naufragia Sicula et alia ibi quoque in spelunca occul-
tatio, iam in navali fuga urgente hostium manu
preces Proculeio mortis admotae, cura Perusinae
contentionis, sollicitudo Martis Actiaci, Pannonicis

149 bellis ruina e turri, tot seditiones militum, tot anci-
pites morbi corporis, suspecta Marcelli vota, pudenda
Agrippae ablegatio, totiens petita insidiis vita,
incusatae liberorum mortes; luctusque non tantum
orbitate tristis, adulterium filiae et consilia parricidae

[1] *Jan*: morbi.

---

[a] Julius Caesar, 46 B.C.
[b] His grandchildren, Lucius and Gaius, sons of Julia and
Agrippa, whom he adopted as his sons; their removal was
perhaps contrived by Livia, but Augustus was suspected of
complicity, to ensure the succession of Tiberius.
[c] Julia.

happiness that any outrage in a man's career has shattered, let alone so great an outrage as that. For the rest I know not whether it counts to the credit of our morals or increases the anguish of our indignation that among all the many Metelli that criminal audacity of Gaius Atinius for ever went unpunished.

XLV. Also in the case of his late Majesty Augustus, whom the whole of mankind enrols in the list of happy men, if all the facts were carefully weighed, great revolutions of man's lot could be discovered: his failure with his uncle *a* in regard to the office of Master of the Horse, when the candidate opposing him, Lepidus, was preferred; the hatred caused by the proscription; his association in the triumvirate with the wickedest citizens, and that not with an equal share of power but with Antony predominant; his flight in the battle of Philippi when he was suffering from disease, and his three days' hiding in a marsh, in spite of his illness and his swollen dropsical condition (as stated by Agrippa and Maecenas); his shipwreck off Sicily, and there also another period of hiding in a cave; his entreaties to Proculeius to kill him, in the naval rout when a detachment of the enemy was already pressing close at hand; the anxiety of the struggle at Perugia, the alarm of the Battle of Actium, his fall from a tower in the Pannonian Wars; and all the mutinies in his troops, all his critical illnesses, his suspicion of Marcellus's ambitions, the disgrace of Agrippa's banishment, the many plots against his life, the charge of causing the death of his children *b*; and his sorrows that were not due solely to bereavement, his daughter's *c* adultery and the disclosure of her plots

Chequered fortunes of Augustus.

605

palam facta, contumeliosus privigni Neronis secessus,
aliud in nepte adulterium, iuncta deinde tot mala,
inopia stipendi, rebellio Illyrici, servitiorum delectus,
iuventutis penuria, pestilentia urbis, fames Italiae,
destinatio expirandi et quadridui media maior pars
150 mortis in corpus recepta; iuxta haec Variana clades
et maiestatis eius foeda suggillatio, abdicatio Postumi
Agrippae post adoptionem, desiderium post relega-
tionem, inde suspicio in Fabium arcanorumque prodi-
tionem, hinc uxoris et Tiberi cogitationes, suprema
eius cura. in summa deus ille caelumque nescio
adeptus magis an meritus herede hostis sui filio
excessit.

151 XLVI. Subeunt in hac reputatione Delphica oracula
velut ad castigandam hominum vanitatem deo emissa.
duo sunt haec: Pedium felicissimum, qui pro patria
proxime occubuisset; iterum a Gyge rege tunc
amplissimo terrarum consultum,[1] Aglaum Psophi-
dium esse feliciorem. senior hic in angustissimo
Arcadiae angulo parvum sed annuis victibus large
sufficiens praedium colebat, numquam ex eo egressus
atque, ut e vitae genere manifestum est, minima
cupidine minimum in vita mali expertus.

[1] *V.l.* consulti.

---

[a] Tiberius Claudius Nero, afterwards the emperor Tiberius,
son of Livia by her first marriage and so stepson of Augustus;
and he also became his son-in-law by marrying Julia after the
death of Agrippa. He lived in retirement at Rhodes for
seven years.

against her father's life, the insolent withdrawal of his stepson Nero,[a] another adultery, that of his grand-daughter[b]; then the long series of misfortunes—lack of army funds, rebellion of Illyria, enlistment of slaves, shortage of man power, plague at Rome, famine in Italy, resolve on suicide and death more than half achieved by four days' starvation; next the disaster of Varus[c] and the foul slur upon his dignity; the disowning of Postumius Agrippa after his adoption as heir, and the sense of loss that followed his banishment; then his suspicion in regard to Fabius and the betrayal of secrets; afterwards the intrigues of his wife and Tiberius that tormented his latest days. In fine, this god—whether deified more by his own action or by his merits I know not—departed from life leaving his enemy's son his heir.

XLVI. In this review there come to mind the Delphic oracles sent forth by the god as if for the purpose of chastising the vanity of mankind. Here are two: 'The happiest of men is Pedius, who lately fell in battle for his country'; and secondly, when the oracle was consulted by Gyges, then the wealthiest king in the world, 'Aglaus of Psophis is happier.' This was an elderly man who cultivated an estate, small but amply sufficient for his yearly provision, in a very shut in corner of Arcadia, and who had never left it, and being (as his kind of life showed) a man of very small desires experienced a very small amount of misfortune in life.

Oracular judgement of happiness.

[b] Julia, daughter of Julia and Agrippa, wife of L. Aemilius Paulus; banished by Augustus for adultery with D. Silanus.

[c] Quintilius Varus and his army annihilated at Saltus Teutoburgensis by German rebels under Arminius, 9 B.C.

152   XLVII. Consecratus est vivus sentiensque eiusdem
oraculi iussu et Iovis deorum summi adstipulatu
Euthymus pycta, semper Olympiae victor et semel
victus. patria ei Locri in Italia; imaginem eius ibi [1] et
Olympiae alteram eodem die tactas [2] fulmine Callimachum ut nihil aliud miratum video oraculumque [3]
iussisse [4] sacrificari, quod et vivo factitatum et
mortuo, nihilque de eo mirum aliud quam hoc
placuisse dis.

153   XLVIII. De spatio atque longinquitate vitae hominum non locorum modo situs verum et tempora ac [5]
sua cuique sors nascendi incertum [6] fecere. Hesiodus,
qui primus aliqua de hoc prodidit, fabulose, ut reor,
multa hominum aevo praeferens [7] cornici novem
nostras adtribuit aetates, quadruplum eius cervis, id
triplicatum corvis, et reliqua fabulosius in phoenice ac

154 Nymphis.   Anacreon poeta Arganthonio Tartesiorum
regi CL tribuit annos, Cinyrae Cypriorum decem
annis amplius, Aegimio CC. Theopompus Epimenidi
Gnosio CLVII, Hellanicus quosdam in Aetolia
Epiorum gentis ducentos [8] explere, cui adstipulatur
Damastes memorans Pictoreum ex his praecipuum

155 corpore viribusque etiam CCC vixisse, Ephorus
Arcadum reges tricenis annis, Alexander Cornelius

---

[1] *Sic ?* *Mayhoff*: ibi imaginem eius *aut* ibi imaginem eius ibi.
[2] *Rackham*: tactam.
[3] *Mayhoff ?* : ad eumque *aut* deumque.
[4] iussisse ⟨ei⟩? *Rackham*.
[5] *Detlefsen*: verum exempla ac.
[6] incertum ⟨iudicium⟩ ? *Mayhoff*.
[7] *Mayhoff*: referens.
[8] *Mayhoff*: ducenta.

---

[a] Not in the extant works of Hesiod.

XLVII. By the command of the same oracle and with the assent of Jupiter the supreme deity, Euthymus the boxer, who won all his matches at Olympia and was only once beaten, was made a saint in his lifetime and to his own knowledge. His native place was Locri in Italy; I noticed that Callimachus records as an unparalleled marvel that a statue of him there and another at Olympia were struck by lightning on the same day, and that the oracle commanded that sacrifice should be offered to him; this was repeatedly done both during his lifetime and when he was dead, and nothing about it is surprising except that the gods so decreed.

XLVIII. As to the length and duration of men's life, not only geographical position but also dates and the various fortunes allotted at birth to each individual have made it uncertain. Hesiod, who first put forth some observations [a] on this matter, placing many creatures above man in respect of longevity, fictitiously as I think, assigns nine of our lifetimes to the crow, four times a crow's life to stags, three times a stag's to ravens, and for the rest in a more fictitious style in the case of the phoenix and the nymphs. The poet Anacreon attributes 150 years to Arganthonius king of the Tartesii, 10 years more to Cinyras king of Cyprus, and 200 to Aegimius. Theopompus gives 157 to Epimenides of Cnossus. Hellanicus says that some members of the clan of the Epii in Aetolia complete 200 years, and he is supported by Damastes who records that one of them, Pictoreus, a man of outstanding stature and strength, even lived 300 years; Ephorus records Arcadian kings of 300 years; Alexander Cornelius says that a certain Dando in

Human longevity in legend and history.

609

Dandonem quendam in Illyrico D vixisse, Xenophon in periplo Lutmiorum insulae regem DC, atque ut parce mentitus filium eius DCCC. quae omnia inscitia temporum acciderunt; annum enim alii aestate determinabant et alterum hieme, alii quadripertitis temporibus, sicut Arcades quorum anni trimenstres fuere, quidam lunae senio ut Aegyptii. itaque apud eos et singuli milia annorum vixisse produntur.

156 Sed ut ad confessa transeamus, Arganthonium Gaditanum LXXX annis regnasse prope certum est; putant quadragensimo coepisse. Masinissam LX annis regnasse indubitatum est, Gorgian Siculum CVIII vixisse. Q. Fabius Maximus LXIII annis augur fuit. M. Perperna et nuper L. Volusius Saturninus omnium quos in consulatu sententiam rogaverant superstites fuere, Perperna VIII reliquit ex iis quos

157 censor legerat: vixit annos LXXXXVIII. qua in re et illud adnotare succurrit, unum omnino quinquennium fuisse quo senator nullus moreretur, cum Flaccus et Albinus censores lustrum condidere, usque ad proxumos censores, ab anno urbis DLXXIX. M. Valerius Corvinus centum annos implevit, cuius inter primum et sextum consulatum XLVI anni fuere. idem sella curuli semel ac viciens sedit, quotiens nemo alius; aequavit eius vitae spatia Metellus pontifex.

---

^a *I.e.* who had been members of the Senate during their consulships.

Illyria lived 500 years. Xenophon in his Coasting Voyage says that a king of the island of the Lutmii lived to 600, and—as though that were only a modest fabrication—that his son lived to 800. All of these exaggerations were due to ignorance of chronology, because some people made the year coincide with the summer, the winter being a second year, others marked it by the periods of the four seasons, for example the Arcadians whose years were three months long, and some by the waning of the moon, as do the Egyptians. Consequently with them even individuals are recorded to have lived a thousand years.

But to pass to admitted facts, it is almost certain that Argathonius of Cadiz reigned for 80 years; his reign is thought to have begun in his fortieth year. It is not questioned that Masinissa reigned 60 years and that the Sicilian Gorgias lived 108 years. Quintus Fabius Maximus was augur for 63 years. Marcus Perperna and recently Lucius Volusius Saturninus outlived all the persons whose votes in debate they had taken as consuls *a*; Perperna left only seven of those whom as censor he had elected— he lived to 98. In this matter it occurs to me to note also that there has only been a single five-year period in which no senator has died, from when Flaccus and Albinus as censors performed the purification ceremony to the next censors—beginning 175 B.C. Marcus Valerius Corvinus completed 100 years, and there was an interval of 46 years between his first and sixth consulships. He also took his seat in the curule chair 21 times, which is a record; but his length of life was equalled by the pontifex Metellus.

158   Et ex feminis Livia Rutili LXXXXVII annos excessit,
Statilia Claudio principe ex nobili domo LXXXXIX,
Terentia Ciceronis CIII, Clodia Ofili CXV, haec
quidem etiam enixa quindeciens. Lucceia mima c
annis in scaena pronuntiavit. Galeria Copiola embo-
liaria reducta est in scaenam C. Poppaeo Q. Sulpicio
coss. ludis pro salute divi Augusti votivis annum CIV
agens ; producta fuerat tirocinio a M. Pomponio
aedile plebis C. Mario Cn. Carbone coss. ante annos
XCI, a Magno Pompeio magni theatri dedicatione
159 anus pro miraculo reducta. Sammulam quoque CX
annis vixisse auctor est Pedianus Asconius. Minus
miror Stephanionem, qui primus togatus[1] saltare
instituit, utrisque saecularibus ludis saltavisse, et
divi Augusti et quos Claudius Caesar consulatu suo
quarto fecit, quando LXIII non amplius anni inter-
fuere, quamquam et postea diu vixit. in Tmoli
Montis Cacumine quod vocant Tempsin CL annis
vivere Mucianus auctor est, totidem annorum[2]
censum Claudi Caesaris censura T. Fullonium Bono-
niensem, idque collatis censibus quos ante detulerat
vitaeque argumentis—etenim curae principi id
erat—verum apparuit.
160   XLIX. Poscere videtur locus ipse sideralis scientiae
sententiam. Epigenes CXII annos inpleri negavit

---

[1] togatas *Sabellius.*
[2] *Mayhoff* (cf. 164): annos.

---

^a Or possibly 'had a stage-career of a hundred years.'
^b A.D. 8.   ^c 82 B.C.

Also among women Livia wife of Rutilius ex- *Longevity of* ceeded 97 years, Statilia a lady of noble family *women.* under the Emperor Claudius 99, Terentia Cicero's wife 103, Clodia Ofilius's wife 115; the latter also bore 15 children. The actress Lucceia delivered a recitation on the stage at 100.[a] Galeria Copiola the actress of interludes was brought back to the stage in the consulship of Gaius Poppaeus and Quintus Sulpicius,[b] at the votive games celebrated for the recovery of his late Majesty Augustus, when in her 104th year; she had been brought out at her first appearance by Marcus Pomponius, aedile of the plebs, in the consulship[c] of Gaius Marius and Gnaeus Carbo, 91 years before, and she was brought back to the stage when an old woman by Pompey the Great as a marvel at the dedication of the big theatre. Also Pedianus Asconius states that Sammula lived 110 years. I am less surprised that Stephanio, who first introduced dancing in national costume, danced at both secular games, both those of his late Majesty Augustus and those celebrated by Claudius Caesar in his fourth consulship, as the interval was only 63 years, although he also lived a long time afterwards. Mucianus is the authority for one Tempsis having lived 150 years at the place called Mount Tmolus Heights; and the census of Claudius Caesar gives the same number of years for Titus Fullonius of Bologna, which has been verified by comparing the census returns he had made previously and by the facts of his career—for the emperor gave his attention to this matter.

XLIX. The topic seems of itself to call for the view *Scientific* held by astronomical science. Epigenes declared that *views as to* it is impossible to live 112 years; Berosus said that *longevity.*

posse, Berosus excedi xcvi. durat et ea ratio quam
Petosiris ac Necepsos tradidere (tetartemorion
appellant a trium signorum portione) qua posse
in Italiae tractu cxxiv annos vitae contingere
apparet. negavere illi quemquam xc partium
exortivam mensuram (quod anaphoras vocant) trans-
gredi, et has ipsas incidi occursu maleficorum siderum
aut etiam radiis eorum ˙solisque. Aesculapi rursus
secta, quae stata vitae spatia a stellis accipi dicit,
161 quantum plurimum tribuat incertum est; rara autem
esse dicunt longiora tempora, quandoquidem momentis horarum insignibus lunae dierum, ut vii
atque xv quae nocte ac die observantur, ingens
turba nascatur scansili annorum lege occidua, quam
climacteras appellant, non fere ita genitis liv annum
excedentibus.

162 Primum ergo ipsius artis inconstantia declarat
quam incerta res sit. accedunt experimenta [1]
recentissimi census quem intra quadriennium Imperatores Caesares Vespasiani pater filiusque censores egerunt. nec sunt omnia vasaria excutienda:
mediae tantum partis inter Apenninum Padumque
ponemus exempla, cxx annos Parmae tres edidere,
163 Brixilli unus, cxxv Parmae duo, cxxx Placentiae
unus, Faventiae una mulier, cxxxv Bononiae L.
Terentius M. filius, Arimini vero M. Aponius cxl,
Tertulla cxxxvii. citra Placentiam in collibus

---

[1] *V.ll. add.* exempla *aut* et exempla.

---

[a] *I.e.* Titus. The date was A.D. 74.

116 years can be exceeded. Also the theory handed down by Petosiris and Necepsos is still extant (it is called the Theory of Quarters, from its dividing up the Zodiac into groups of three signs); this theory shows it possible to attain 124 years of life in the region of Italy. These thinkers declared that nobody exceeds the ascendant measure of 90 degrees (what is called 'risings'), and stated that this period itself may be cut short by the encounter of maleficent stars, or even by their rays and by those of the sun. Again it is uncertain what is the greatest longevity allowed by the school of Aesculapius, which says that fixed periods of life are received from the stars; however, they say that longer periods of life are rare, inasmuch as vast crowds of men are born at critical moments in the hours of the lunar days, for example the 7th and the 15th hour counting by night and day, who are liable to die under the law of the ascending scale of years, called 'gradations,' persons so born rarely exceeding their fifty-fourth year.

At the outset therefore the variations in the science itself show how uncertain the matter is. *Census-cases of longevity.* In addition there are the experiences of the last census, held within the last four years by the Emperors Caesar Vespasian father and son[a] as Censors. Nor is it necessary to ransack all the records: we will only produce cases from the middle region between the Apennines and the Po. Three persons declared 120 years at Parma and one at Brescello; two at Parma 125; one man at Piacenza and one woman at Faenza 130; Lucius Terentius son of Marcus at Bologna 135; Marcus Aponius 140 and Tertulla 137 at Rimini. In the hills this side of

oppidum est Veleiatium, in quo cx annos sex
detulere, quattuor vero centenos vicenos, unus CL,
164 M. Mucius M. filius Galeria Felix. ac ne pluribus
moremur in re confessa, in regione Italiae octava
centenum annorum censi sunt homines LIV, centenum denum homines XIV, centenum vicenum
quinum homines duo, centenum tricenum homines
quattuor, centenum tricenum quinum aut septenum
totidem, centenum quadragenum homines tres.
165 Alia mortalitatis inconstantia: Homerus eadem
nocte natos Hectorem et Polydamanta tradidit,
tam diversae sortis viros; C. Mario Cn. Carbone III
coss. a. d. v. kal. Iunias M. Caelius Rufus et C. Licinius
Calvus eadem die geniti sunt, oratores quidem
ambo, sed tam dispari eventu. hoc etiam iisdem
horis nascentibus in toto mundo cotidie evenit,
pariterque domini ac servi gignuntur, reges et
inopes.
166 L. P. Cornelius Rufus, qui consul cum M'. Curio
fuit, dormiens oculorum visum amisit, cum id sibi
accidere somniaret. e diverso Pheraeus Iason de-
ploratus a medicis vomicae morbo, cum mortem in
acie quaereret, vulnerato pectore medicinam invenit
ex hoste. Q. Fabius Maximus consul apud flumen
Isaram proelio commisso adversus Allobrogum
Arvernorumque gentes a. d. VI. id. Augustas, c̄xxx
perduellium caesis, febri quartana liberatus est in
167 acie. incertum ac fragile nimirum est hoc munus
naturae, quicquid datur nobis, malignum vero et
breve etiam in his quibus largissime contigit, uni-

ᵃ *Iliad* xviii. 249 ff.
ᵇ 82 B.C.   ᶜ 121 B.C.

Piacenza is the township of Veleia, where six declared
110 years, four 120, one (Marcus Mucius Felix, son
of Marcus, of the Galerian tribe) 150. And, not to
delay with further instances in a matter of admitted
fact, the census registered in the eighth region of
Italy 54 persons of 100 years of age, 14 of 110, 2 of
125, 4 of 130, the same number of 135 or 137, 3 of
140.

Other instances of the fickleness of mortal fortunes *Striking*
are these: Homer[a] has recorded that men of such *cases of*
diverse fates as Hector and Polydamas were born on *fortune's*
the same night; Marcus Caelius Rufus and Gaius *vicissitudes.*
Licinius Calvus, both orators but with such different
success, were born on the same day, May 28 in the
consulship[b] of Gaius Marius and Gnaeus Carbo—
the latter's third. Taking the entire world, this
happens daily even to persons born at the same hours
—masters and slaves, kings and paupers come into
existence simultaneously.

L. Publius Cornelius Rufus, who was consul with
Manius Curius, lost his sight while asleep, when
dreaming that it was happening to him. In the
opposite way, Jason of Pherae being ill with a tumour
and given up by the doctors sought death in battle,
but was wounded in the chest and so obtained a cure
from the enemy. In the battle against the clans of
the Allobroges and Arverni on the river Isère, on
August 8, when 130,000 of the foe were killed, the
consul[c] Quintus Fabius Maximus got rid of a
quartan ague in action. In fact whatever be this
gift of nature that is bestowed upon us, it is uncertain
and insecure, indeed sinister and of brief duration
even in the case of those to whose lot it has fallen
in most bounteous measure, at all events when we

versum utique aevi tempus intuentibus. quid quod
aestimatione nocturnae quietis dimidio quisque spatio
vitae suae vivit, pars aequa morti similis exigitur aut
poenae, nisi contigit quies? nec reputantur infantiae
anni qui sensu carent, non senectae in poenam vivacis,
tot periculorum genera, tot morbi, tot metus, tot
curae, totiens invocata morte ut nullum frequentius
168 sit votum. natura vero nihil hominibus brevitate
vitae praestitit melius. hebescunt sensus, membra
torpent, praemoritur visus, auditus, incessus, dentis
etiam ac ciborum instrumenta, et tamen vitae hoc
tempus adnumeratur. est[1] ergo pro miraculo, et id
solitarium reperitur exemplum Xenophili musici,
centum et quinque annis vixisse sine ullo corporis in-
169 commodo. at, Hercule, reliquis omnibus per singulas
membrorum partes qualiter nullis aliis animalibus
certis pestifer calor remeat horis aut rigor, neque
horis modo sed et diebus noctibusque trinis quadri-
nisve, etiam anno toto. atque etiam morbus est
aliquantisper[2] sapientiam mori. morbis quoque
170 enim quasdam leges natura inposuit: quadrini
circuitus febrem numquam bruma, numquam hibernis
mensibus incipere, quosdam post sexagensimum
vitae spatium non accedere, aliis[3] pubertate deponi,
feminis praecipue; senes minime sentire pestilentiam.
namque et universis gentibus ingruunt morbi et
generatim modo servitiis modo procerum ordini
aliosque per gradus. qua in re observatum a meri-

---

[1] est *add. Rackham.*
[2] *Alciatus :* aliquis per.
[3] *Mayhoff :* alios.

regard the whole extent of time. What of the fact that, if we take into account our nightly period of slumber, everybody is alive for only a half of his life, whereas an equal portion is passed in a manner that resembles death, or, in default of slumber, torture. And we are not counting in the years of infancy that lack sensation, nor those of old age that remains alive to be tormented, nor all the kinds of dangers, all the diseases, all the fears, all the anxieties, with death so often invoked that this is the commonest of prayers. But nature has granted man no better *Brevity of* gift than the shortness of life. The senses grow dull, *full vitality.* the limbs are numb, sight, hearing, gait, even the teeth and alimentary organs die before we do, and yet this period is reckoned a portion of life. Consequently it is virtually a miracle—and this is the solitary instance of it found—that the musician Xenophilus lived to 105 without any bodily disablement. But assuredly with all the rest of men, as in the case of none of the other animals, morbid heat or else stiffness returns through the several portions of the limbs at fixed hours, and not only at certain hours but also every three or four days or nights, even all the year round. And moreover the death of the intellect in some measure is a disease. For nature has imposed certain laws even upon diseases : a four-day-period fever never begins at mid-winter or in the winter months, and some people are not attacked by it when over the age of 60, while with others, particularly women, it is discarded at puberty ; and old men are least susceptible to plague. For diseases attack not only entire nations but also particular classes, sometimes the slaves, sometimes the nobility, and so through other grades. In this respect it has been

dianis partibus ad occasum solis pestilentiam semper
ire nec umquam aliter fere, non hieme, nec ut ternos
excedat menses.

171   LI. Iam signa letalia: in furoris morbo risum,
sapientiae vero aegritudine fimbriarum curam et
stragulae vestis plicateras, a somno moventium
neglectum, praefandi umoris e corpore effluvium,
in oculorum quidem et narium aspectu indubitata
maxime, atque etiam supino adsidue cubitu,
venarum inaequabili aut formicante percussu, quaeque alia Hippocrati principi medicinae observata
sunt. et cum innumerabilia sint mortis signa,
salutis securitatisque nulla sunt, quippe cum
censorius Cato ad filium de validis quoque observationem ut ex oraculo aliquo prodiderit senilem
172 iuventam praematurae mortis esse signum. morborum vero tam infinita est multitudo ut Pherecydes
Syrius serpentium multitudine ex corpore eius erum-
pente expiraverit. quibusdam perpetua febris est,
sicut C. Maecenati; eidem triennio supremo nullo
horae momento contigit somnus. Antipater Sidonius
poeta omnibus annis uno die tantum natali corripie-
batur febre et eo consumptus est satis longa senecta.
173   LII. Aviola consularis in rogo revixit et, quoniam
subveniri non potuerat praevalente flamma, vivus
crematus est. similis causa in L. Lamia praetorio
viro traditur; nam C. Aelium Tuberonem praetura
functum a rogo relatum Messala Rufus et plerique

observed that plague always travels from southern quarters westward and almost never otherwise, and that it does not spread in winter, nor during a period exceeding three months.

LI. Again, signs of approaching death are: in a case of insanity laughter, but in delirium toying with fringes and making folds in the bed-clothes, disregard of persons trying to keep the patient awake, making water, while the most unmistakable signs are in the appearance of the eyes and nostrils, and also in lying constantly on the back, in an irregular and excessively slow pulse, and the other symptoms noted by that prince of medicine Hippocrates. And whereas the signs of death are innumerable, there are no signs of health being secure; inasmuch as the ex-censor Cato gave an as it were oracular utterance addressed to his son about healthy persons also, to the effect that senile characteristics in youth are a sign of premature death. But so unlimited is the number of diseases that the Syrian Pherecydes expired with a swarm of maggots bursting out of his body. Some people suffer from perpetual fever, for instance Gaius Maecenas: the same had not an hour's sleep in the last three years of his life. The poet Antipater of Sidon used to have a yearly attack of fever on one day only, his birthday, and this at a fairly advanced age carried him off. *Signs of approach of death.*

LII. The ex-consul Aviola came to life again on the funeral pyre, and as the flame was too powerful for it to be possible to come to his assistance, was burnt alive. A similar cause of death is recorded in the case of the ex-praetor Lucius Lamia, while Gaius Aelius Tubero, a former praetor, is recorded by Messala Rufus and most authorities to have been

PLINY: NATURAL HISTORY

tradunt. haec est conditio mortalium: ad has et
eiusmodi occasiones fortunae gignimur, ut de homine
174 ne morti quidem debeat credi. reperimus inter
exempla Hermotimi Clazomenii animam relicto
corpore errare solitam vagamque e longinquo multa
adnuntiare quae nisi a praesente nosci non possent,
corpore interim semianimi, donec cremato eo inimici
qui Cantharidae vocabantur remeanti animae veluti
vaginam ademerint; Aristeae etiam visam evolantem
ex ore in Proconneso corvi effigie, cum [1] magna quae
175 sequitur hanc [2] fabulositate. quam equidem et
in Gnosio Epimenide simili modo accipio, puerum
aestu et itinere fessum in specu septem et quinquaginta dormisse annis, rerum faciem mutationemque
mirantem velut postero die experrectum, hinc pari
numero dierum senio ingruente, ut tamen in septimum et quinquagesimum atque centesimum vitae
duraret annum. feminarum sexus huic malo videtur
maxime opportunus conversione volvae, quae si
corrigatur, spiritus restituitur. huc pertinet nobile
illud apud Graecos volumen Heraclidis septem diebus
feminae exanimis ad vitam revocatae.
176   Varro quoque auctor est xx viro se agros dividente
Capuae quendam qui efferretur feretro [3] domum

---

[1] *Rackham* : quae *aut* que *aut om.*
[2] *Mayhoff* : hac.   *Ammon* (*vel* toro): foro.

622

recovered from the pyre. This is the law of mortals: we are born for these and similar accidents of fortune, so that in the case of a human being no confidence must be placed even in death. Among other instances we find that the soul of Hermotimus *Disembodied* of Clazomenae used to leave his body and roam *souls.* abroad, and in its wanderings report to him from a distance many things that only one present at them could know of—his body in the meantime being only half-conscious; till finally some enemies of his named the Cantharidae burned his body and so deprived his soul on its return of what may be called its sheath. We also read that the soul of Aristeas at Proconnesus was seen flying out of his mouth in the shape of a raven, with a great deal of fabulous invention that follows this. This inventiveness I for my part also receive in a similar way in the case of Epimenides of Cnossus—that when a boy, being weary with the heat and with travel, he slept in a cave 57 years, and when he woke, just as if it had been on the following day, was surprised at the appearance of things and the change in them; and afterwards old age came on him in the same number of days as he had slept years, though nevertheless he lived to the age of 157. The female sex seems specially liable to this malady, caused by distortion of the womb; if this is set right, the breathing is restored. To this subject belongs the essay of Heraclides, well known in Greece, about the woman recalled to life after being dead for seven days.

Also Varro records that when he was acting as one *Recovery of* of the Twenty Commissioners and apportioning lands *persons* *apparently* at Capua a person being carried out on a bier to burial *dead.*

remeasse pedibus; hoc idem Aquini accidisse; Romae
quoque Corfidium materterae suae maritum funere
locato revixisse et locatorem funeris ab eo elatum.
177 adicit miracula quae tota indicasse conveniat:
e duobus fratribus equestris ordinis Corfidiis maiori
accidisse ut videretur expirasse, apertoque testa-
mento recitatum heredem minorem funeri institisse,
interim eum qui videbatur extinctus plaudendo
concivisse ministeria et narrasse a fratre se venisse,
commendatam sibi filiam ab eo, demonstratum
praeterea quo in loco defodisset aurum nullo conscio,
et rogasse ut his funebribus quae comparasset
efferretur. hoc eo narrante fratris domestici propere
adnuntiavere examinatum illum; et aurum ubi
178 dixerat repertum est. plena praeterea vita est his
vaticiniis, sed non conferenda, cum saepius falsa sint,
sicut ingenti exemplo docebimus. Bello Siculo
Gabienus Caesaris classium[1] fortissimus captus a
Sexto Pompeio iussu eius incisa cervice et vix co-
haerente iacuit in litore toto die. deinde, cum
advesperavisset, gemitu precibusque congregata
multitudine petiit uti Pompeius ad se veniret aut

---

[1] classiarius *Caesarius.*

---

[a] Between Sextus Pompeius and Octavian 38–36 B.C.
Gabienus is only known from this passage.

returned home on foot; and that the same thing
occurred at Aquino; and that also at Rome his
maternal aunt's husband Corfidius came to life again
after his funeral had been arranged for with an under-
taker, and that he himself superintended the funeral
of the relative who had made the arrangement. He
adds some marvellous occurrences that it would be
suitable to have set out in their entirety: that there
were two brothers Corfidius, of the rank of knights,
to the elder of whom it happened that he appeared
to have expired, and when his will was opened the
younger brother was read out as his heir, and set
about arranging his funeral; in the meantime the
brother who appeared to be dead summoned the
servants by clapping his hands and told them that
he had come from his brother, who had entrusted his
daughter to his care, and had also shown him where he
had without anybody's knowledge hidden some gold
in a hole dug in the ground, and had asked that the
preparations that he had made for his brother's
funeral might be used for himself. While he was
telling this story his brother's servants hurriedly came
with the news that their master was dead; and the
gold was found in the place where he had said. Moreover life is full of these prophecies, but they are not
worth collecting, because more often than not they
are false, as we will prove by an outstanding example.
In the Sicilian War[a] the bravest man in Caesar's navies
Gabienus was taken prisoner by Sextus Pompeius,
by whose order his throat was cut and almost severed,
and so he lay a whole day on the shore. Then on
the arrival of evening, a crowd having been gathered
to the spot by his groans and entreaties, he besought
that Pompey should come to him, or send one of his

aliquem ex arcanis mitteret, se enim ab inferis
179 remissum habere quae nuntiaret. misit plures
Pompeius ex amicis, quibus Gabienus dixit inferis dis
placere Pompei causas et partes pias : proinde even-
tum futurum quem optaret ; hoc se nuntiare iussum ;
argumentum fore veritatis quod peractis mandatis
protinus exspiraturus esset. idque ita evenit. post
sepulturam quoque visorum exempla sunt, nisi quod
naturae opera, non prodigia, consectamur.

180   LIII. In primis autem miraculo sunt atque
frequentes [1] mortes repentinae (hoc est summa vitae
felicitas) quas esse naturales docebimus. plurimas prodidit Verrius, nos cum delectu modum servabimus.
gaudio obiere praeter Chilonem, de quo diximus,
Sophocles et Dionysius Siciliae tyrannus, uterque accepto tragicae victoriae nuntio, mater illa Cannensi
filio incolumi reviso contra nuntium falsum, pudore
Diodorus sapientiae dialecticae professor, lusoria
quaestione non protinus ad interrogationem [2]
181 Stilponis dissoluta. nullis evidentibus causis obiere :
dum calciantur matutino, duo Caesares, praetor et
praetura perfunctus dictatoris Caesaris pater, hic
Pisis exanimatus, ille Romae, Q. Fabius Maximus
in consulatu suo pridie kal. Ian., in cuius locum C.
Rebilus paucissimarum horarum consulatum petiit,
item C. Volcatius Gurges senator, omnes adeo sani
atque tempestivi ut de progrediendo cogitarent ; Q.
Aemilius Lepidus iam egrediens incusso pollice limini

---

[1] *Rackham* : frequenter *aut* frequentia.
[2] *V.l.* ab interrogatione.

ᵃ § 119.

personal staff, as he had come back from the lower
world and had some news to tell him. Pompey sent
several of his friends, who were told by Gabienus that
the gods below approved Pompey's cause and the
righteous party, so that the issue would be what
Pompey desired; that he had had orders to bring this
news, and that a proof of its truth would be that as
soon as his errand was accomplished he would expire.
And this so happened. There are also cases of
persons appearing after burial—save that our
subject is the works of nature, not prodigies.

LIII. But most miraculous and also frequent, are *Sudden*
sudden deaths (this is life's supreme happiness), *death: a*
which we shall show to be natural. Verrius has *variety of*
reported a great many, but we will preserve modera- *cases.*
tion with a selection. Cases of people who died of
joy are (besides Chilo about whom we have spoken)[a]
Sophocles and Dionysius the tyrant of Sicily, in both
cases after receiving news of a victory with a tragedy:
also the mother who saw her son back safe from
Cannae in contradiction of a false message; Diodorus
the professor of logic died of shame because he could
not at once solve a problem put to him in jest by
Stilpo. Cases of men dying from no obvious causes
are: while putting on their shoes in the morning,
the two Caesars, the praetor and the ex-praetor,
father of the dictator Caesar, the latter dying at
Pisa and the former at Rome; Quintus Fabius
Maximus on 31 December in the year of his consulship, in whose place Gaius Rebilus obtained the
office for only a few hours; also the senator
Gaius Volcatius Gurges—all of these men so healthy
and fit that they were thinking of going out for a
walk; Quintus Aemilius Lepidus who bruised his great

PLINY: NATURAL HISTORY

cubiculi; C. Aufustius egressus cum in senatum iret
182 offenso pede in comitio. legatus quoque qui Rhodiorum causam in senatu magna cum admiratione
oraverat in limine curiae protinus expiravit progredi
volens, Cn. Baebius Tamphilus praetura et ipse
functus cum a puero quaesisset horas, Aulus Pompeius
in Capitolio cum deos salutasset, M'. Iuventius Thalna
consul cum sacrificaret, C. Servilius Pansa cum staret
in foro ad tabernam hora diei secunda in P. fratrem
innixus, Baebius iudex dum vadimonium differri
183 iubet, M. Terentius Corax dum tabellas scribit in
foro; nec non et proximo anno, dum consulari viro
in aurem dicit, Eques Romanus ante Apollinem
eboreum qui est in foro Augusti, super omnes C.
Iulius medicus dum inunguit specillum per oculum
trahens, A. Manlius Torquatus consularis cum in
cena placentam adpeteret, L. Tuccius medicus
Sullae[1] dum mulsi potionem haurit, Appius Saufeius e
balineo reversus cum mulsum bibisset ovumque sor-
beret, P. Quintius Scapula cum apud Aquilium
Gallum cenaret, Decimus Saufeius scriba cum domi
184 suae pranderet. Cornelius Gallus praetorius et T.
Hetereius Eques Romanus in venere obiere, et quos
nostra adnotavit aetas duo equestris ordinis in eodem

Detlefsen: Valla.

628

toe in the doorway of his bedroom just as he was
going out; Gaius Aufidius who after he had gone out
hit his foot against something in the Comitium when
he was on his way to the senate.   Also an envoy who
had pleaded the cause of Rhodes in the senate to
the general admiration, just as he wanted to leave
the senate-house expired on the threshold; Gnaeus
Baebius Tamphilus, who had himself also held the
praetorship, died just after asking his footman the
time; Aulus Pompeius died on the Capitol after
paying reverence to the gods, Manius Juventius
Thalna the consul while offering sacrifice, Gaius
Servilius Pansa while standing at a shop in the
market-place, leaning on his brother Publius's arm,
at seven o'clock in the morning, Baebius the judge
while in the act of giving an order for enlargement
of bail, Marcus Terentius Corax while writing a note
in the market-place; and moreover last year, a Knight
of Rome died while saying something in the ear of
an ex-consul, just in front of the ivory statue of Apollo
in the Forum of Augustus; and, most remarkable of
all, the doctor Gaius Julius died from passing the
probe through his eye while pouring in ointment,
the ex-consul Aulus Manlius Torquatus while helping
himself to a cake at dinner, Lucius Tuccius, Sulla's
doctor, while drinking a draught of mead, Appius
Saufeius when he had drunk some mead and was
sucking an egg after coming back from the bath-
house, Publius Quintius Scapula when out to dinner
with Aquilius Gallus, Decimus Saufeius the clerk
when lunching at home.   Cornelius Gallus, ex-
praetor, and Titus Hetereius Knight of Rome died
while with women; and, cases remarked on by our
own generation, two members of the Order of Knight-

pantomimo Mystico tum forma praecellente. optatissima tamen securitas mortis in M. Ofilio Hilaro
185 ab antiquis traditur: comoediarum histrio is, cum populo admodum placuisset natali die suo conviviumque haberet, edita cena calidam potionem in pultario poposcit, simulque personam eius diei acceptam intuens coronam e capite suo in eam transtulit, tali habitu rigens nullo sentiente, donec adcubantium proxumus tepescere potionem admoneret.

186 Haec felicia exempla, at contra miserorum innumera: L. Domitius clarissimae gentis apud Massiliam victus, Corfinii captus ab eodem Caesare, veneno poto propter taedium vitae, postquam biberat, omni ope ut viveret adnisus est. invenitur in actis Felice russei auriga elato in rogum eius unum e faventibus iecisse se, frivolum dictu, ne hoc gloriae artificis [1] daretur, adversis studiis copia odorum corruptum criminantibus. cum ante non multo M. Lepidus nobilissimae stirpis, quem divorti anxietate diximus mortuum, flammae vi e rogo eiectus recondi propter ardorem non potuisset, iuxta sarmentis aliis nudus crematus est.

---

[1] aurigis *Detlefsen.*

---

hood died when with the same ballet-dancer Mysticus, the leading beauty of the day. However, the most enviable case of a peaceful end is one recorded by our forefathers, that of Marcus Ofilius Hilarus: he was an actor in comedy, and having had a considerable success with the public on his birthday and while giving a party, when dinner was served called for a hot drink in a tankard, and at the same time picked up the mask that he had worn on that day and while gazing at it transferred the wreath from his own head to it, and in this attitude lay quite stiff without anybody noticing, until the guest on the next couch warned him that his drink was getting cold.

These are happy instances, but there are countless *Suicide.* numbers of unhappy ones. Lucius Domitius, a man of very distinguished family, who was defeated at Marseilles and was taken prisoner, also by Caesar, at Corfinium,[a] grew tired of life and drank poison, but afterwards made every effort to save his life. It is found in the official records that at the funeral of Felix the charioteer of the Reds one of his backers threw himself upon the pyre—a pitiful story—and the opposing backers tried to prevent this score to the record of a professional by asserting that the man had fainted owing to the quantity of scents! Not long before, the corpse of Marcus Lepidus, the man of distinguished family whose death from anxiety about his divorce we have recorded above,[b] had been dislodged from the pyre by the violence of the flame, and as it was impossible to put it back again because of the heat, it was burnt naked with a fresh supply of faggots at the side of the pyre.

631

187 LIV. Ipsum cremare apud Romanos non fuit veteris instituti; terra condebantur. at postquam longinquis bellis obrutos erui eognovere, tunc institutum. et tamen multae familiae priscos servavere ritus, sicut in Cornelia nemo ante Sullam dictatorem traditur crematus, idque voluisse veritum talionem eruto C. Mari cadavere. [sepultus vero intellegitur quoquo modo conditus, humatus vero humo contectus.][1]

188 LV. Post sepulturam variae [2] manium ambages. omnibus a supremo die eadem quae ante primum, nec magis a morte sensus ullus aut corpori aut animae quam ante natalem—eadem enim vanitas in futurum etiam se propagat et in mortis quoque tempora ipsa sibi vitam mentitur, alias inmortalitatem animae, alias transfigurationem, alias sensum inferis dando et manes colendo deumque faciendo qui iam etiam homo esse desierit—ceu vero ullo modo spirandi ratio ceteris animalibus distet, aut non diuturniora in vita multa reperiantur quibus nemo similem divinat

189 inmortalitatem. quod autem corpus animae per se? quae materia? ubi cogitatio illi? quomodo visus, auditus, aut qui tangit? quis usus ex iis [3] aut quod sine iis bonum? quae deinde sedes quantave multi-

---

[1] *Secl. Mayhoff.*
[2] vanae *Detlefsen.*
[3] *Mayhoff:* usus eius.

---

[a] This sentence reads like an interpolated note on vocabulary.

632

LIV. Cremation was not actually an old practice at *Cremation,* Rome: the dead used to be buried. But cremation *history of.* was instituted after it became known that the bodies of those fallen in wars abroad were dug up again. All the same many families kept on the old ritual, for instance it is recorded that nobody in the family of the Cornelii was cremated before Sulla the dictator, and that he had desired it because he was afraid of reprisals for having dug up the corpse of Gaius Marius. [But burial is understood to denote any mode of disposal of a corpse, but interment means covering up with earth *a*.]

LV. There are various problems concerning the *Belief in* spirits of the departed after burial. All men are in *after-life.* the same state from their last day onward as they were before their first day, and neither body nor mind possesses any sensation after death, any more than it did before birth—for the same vanity prolongs itself also into the future and fabricates for itself a life lasting even into the period of death, sometimes bestowing on the soul immortality, sometimes trans-figuration, sometimes giving sensation to those below, and worshipping ghosts and making a god of one who has already ceased to be even a man—just as if man's mode of breathing were in any way different from that of the other animals, or as if there were not many animals found of greater longevity, for which nobody prophesies a similar immortality! But what is the substance of the soul taken by itself? what is its material? where is its thought located? how does it see and hear, and with what does it touch? what use does it get from these senses, or what good can it experience without them? Next, what is the abode, or how great is the multitude,

633

tudo tot saeculis animarum vel[1] umbrarum? pueri-
lium ista deliramentorum avidaeque numquam de-
sinere mortalitatis commenta sunt. similis et de
adservandis corporibus hominum ac reviviscendi
promisso Democriti vanitas, qui non revixit ipse.
190 quae malum ista dementia est iterari vitam morte?
quaeve genitis quies umquam si in sublimi sensus
animae manet, inter inferos umbrae? perdit profecto ista dulcedo credulitasque praecipuum naturae
bonum, mortem, ac duplicat obituri dolorem etiam
post futuri aestimatione; etenim si dulce vivere est,
cui potest esse vixisse? at quanto facilius cer-
tiusque sibi quemque credere, specimen securitatis
futurae[2] antegenitali sumere experimento!

191   LVI. Consentaneum videtur, priusquam di-
grediamur a natura hominum, indicare quae cuiusque
inventa sint. emere ac vendere[3] instituit Liber pater,
idem diadema, regium insigne, et triumphum invenit,
Ceres frumenta, cum antea glande vescerentur, eadem
molere et conficere in Attica (ut alii,[4] in Sicilia), ob
id dea iudicata. eadem prima leges dedit, aut[5] ut
alii putavere Rhadamanthus.

192   Litteras semper arbitror Assyriis fuisse, sed alii
apud Aegyptios a Mercurio, ut Gellius, alii apud

---

[1] vel? *Mayhoff*: velut.
[2] futurae add. *Rackham*.
[3] vendere ⟨Mercurius, vindemiare⟩ *Mayhoff*.
[4] *Rackham* (ut alii et *Mayhoff*): aut alia, *aut* et alia.
[5] aut add. *Rackham*.

of the souls or shadows in all these ages? These are
fictions of childish absurdity, and belong to a mortality greedy for life unceasing. Similar also is the
vanity about preserving men's bodies, and about
Democritus's promise of our coming to life again—
who did not come to life again himself! Plague
take it, what is this mad idea that life is renewed by
death? what repose are the generations ever to have
if the soul retains permanent sensation in the upper
world and the ghost in the lower? Assuredly this
sweet but credulous fancy ruins nature's chief
blessing, death, and doubles the sorrow of one about
to die by the thought of sorrow to come hereafter
also; for if to live is sweet, who can find it sweet to
have done living? But how much easier and safer
for each to trust in himself, and for us to derive our
idea of future tranquillity from our experience of it
before birth!

LVI. Before we quit the subject of man's nature it *Arts and*
seems suitable to point out the various discoveries of *sciences,*
different persons. Father Liber instituted buying *by whom*
and selling,[a] and also invented the emblem of *discovered.*
royalty, the crown, and the triumphal procession.
Ceres discovered corn, men having hitherto lived on
acorns; she also invented grinding corn and making
flour in Attica (or, as others say, in Sicily), and
for this was deemed a goddess. Also she first gave
laws, though others have thought this was done by
Rhadamanthus.

I am of opinion that the Assyrians have always had
writing, but others, e.g. Gellius, hold that it was
invented in Egypt by Mercury, while others think it

---

[a] The text should probably be filled out to give 'Mercury
instituted buying and selling, and Father Liber the vintage.'

Syros repertas volunt ; utrique [1] in Graeciam attulisse e Phoenice Cadmum sedecim numero, quibus Troiano bello Palameden adiecisse quattuor hac figura ZΨΦX, totidem post eum Simonidem melicum, ΥΞΩΘ, quarum omnium vis in nostris recognoscitur. Aristoteles decem et octo priscas fuisse et duas ab Epicharmo additas ΨZ quam a Palamede mavolt.

193 Anticlides in Aegypto invenisse quendam nomine Menon tradit, xv annorum ante Phoronea antiquissimum Graeciae regem, idque monumentis adprobare conatur. e diverso Epigenes apud Babylonios DCCXXX annorum observationes siderum coctilibus laterculis inscriptas docet, gravis auctor in primis, qui minimum, Berosus et Critodemus, CCCCXC ex quo apparet aeternus litterarum usus. in Latium eas attulerunt Pelasgi.

194 Laterarias ac domos constituerunt primi Euryalus et Hyperbius fratres Athenis ; antea specus erant pro domibus. Gellio Toxius Caeli filius lutei aedificii inventor placet, exemplo sumpto ab hirundinum nidis. oppidum primum [2] Cecrops a se appellavit Cecropiam quae nunc est arx Athenis ; aliqui Argos a Phoroneo rege ante conditum volunt, quidam et Sicyonem, Aegypti vero multo ante apud ipsos

195 Diospolin. tegulas invenit Cinyra Agriopae filius

---

[1] V.l. utique.   [2] primum ? add. Mayhoff.

was discovered in Syria; both schools of thought believe that Cadmus imported an alphabet of 16 letters into Greece from Phoenicia and that to these Palamedes at the time of the Trojan war added the four characters ZΨΦX, and after him Simonides the lyric poet added another four ΥΞΩΘ, all representing sounds recognized also in the Roman alphabet. Aristotle holds that the primitive alphabet contained 18 letters, and that Ψ and Z were added by Epicharmus more probably than Palamedes. Anticlides records that a person named Menos invented the alphabet in Egypt 15,000 years before Phoroneus, the most ancient king of Greece, and he attempts to prove this by the monuments. On the other side Epigenes, an authority of the first rank, teaches that the Babylonians had astronomical observations for 730,000 years inscribed on baked bricks; and those who give the shortest period, Berosus and Critodemus, make it 490,000 years; from which it appears that the alphabet has been in use from very ancient times. It was brought to Latium by the Pelasgi.

Brick-kilns and houses were first introduced by the brothers Euryalus and Hyperbius at Athens; previously caves had served for dwellings. Gellius accepts Toxius son of Uranus as the inventor of building with clay, the example having been taken from swallows' nests. Cecrops named after himself the first town, Cecropia, which is now the Acropolis at Athens; though some hold that Argos had been founded before by King Phoroneus, and certain authorities say Sicyon also, but the Egyptians hold that Diospolis was founded in their country long before. Tiles were invented by Cinyra, son of Agriopa, as well as mining for copper, both in the

et metalla aeris, utrumque in insula Cypro, item
forcipem, martulum, vectem, incudem; puteos
Danaus ex Aegypto advectus in Graeciam quae
vocabatur Argos Dipsion; lapicidinas Cadmus
Thebis, aut ut Theophrastus in Phoenice; Thrason muros, turres ut Aristoteles Cyclopes, Tirynthii
ut Theophrastus; Aegyptii textilia, inficere lanas
196 Sardibus Lydi, fusos in lanificio Closter filius Ara-
chnae, linum et retia Arachne, fulloniam artem Nicias
Megarensis, sutrinam Tychius Boeotius; medicinam
Aegyptii apud ipsos volunt repertam, alii per Arabum
Babylonis et Apollinis filium, herbariam et medica-
197 mentariam a Chirone Saturni et Philyrae filio. aes
conflare et temperare Aristoteles Lydum Scythen
monstrasse, Theophrastus Delam Phrygem putant,
aerariam fabricam alii Chalybas alii Cyclopas, ferrum
Hesiodus in Creta eos qui vocati sunt Dactyli Idaei.
argentum invenit Erichthonius Atheniensis, ut alii
Aeacus, auri metalla et flaturam Cadmus Phoenix ad
Pangaeum montem, ut alii Thoas aut Aeacus in
Panchaia aut Sol Oceani filius cui Gellius medicinae
quoque inventionem ex metallis assignat. plumbum
album [1] ex Cassiteride insula primus adportavit Mida-
198 critus. fabricam ferrariam [2] invenerunt Cyclopes, fig-
linas Coroebus [3] Atheniensis, in iis orbem Anacharsis Scythes, ut alii Hyperbius Corinthius; fabricam

---

[1] album *add. Warmington.*
[2] *Gelenius:* ferream.
[3] Ceramus *Wilamowitz.*

---

[a] *I.e.,* Spinner, son of Spider.
[b] An imaginary island in the Indian Ocean.
[c] Cornwall and the Scillies. The MSS. give 'lead.'

island of Cyprus, and also the tongs, hammer, crow-
bar and anvil; wells by Danaus who came from
Egypt to Greece to the region that used to be called
Dry Argos; stone quarrying by Cadmus at Thebes,
or according to Theophrastus, in Phoenicia; walls
were introduced by Thrason, towers by the Cyclopes
according to Aristotle but according to Theophrastus
by the Tirynthians; woven fabrics by the Egyptians,
dyeing woollen stuffs by the Lydians at Sardis, the
use of the spindle in the manufacture of woollen by
Closter son of Arachne,[a] linen and nets by Arachne,
the fuller's craft by Nicias of Megara, the shoemaker's
by Tychius of Boeotia; medicine according to the
Egyptians was discovered among themselves, but
according to others through the agency of Arabus son
of Babylon and Apollo; and the science of herbs and
drugs was discovered by Chiron the son of Saturn and
Philyra. Aristotle thinks that Lydus the Scythian
showed how to melt and work copper, but Theophrastus holds that it was the Phrygian Delas;
manufactures of bronze some ascribe to the Chalybes
and others to the Cyclopes; the forging of iron Hesiod
ascribes to the people called the Dactyli of Ida in
Crete. Erichthonius of Athens, or according to others
Aeacus, discovered silver; mining and smelting gold
was invented by Cadmus the Phoenician at Mount
Pangaeus, or according to others by Thoas or Aeacus
in Panchaia,[b] or by the Sun, son of Oceanus, to whom
Gellius also assigns the discovery of medicine derived
from minerals. Tin was first imported by Midacri-
tus from the island of Cassiteris.[c] Working in iron
was invented by the Cyclopes, potteries by Coroebus
of Athens, the potter's wheel by the Scythian
Anacharsis, or according to others by Hyperbius of

PLINY: NATURAL HISTORY

materiariam Daedalus, et in ea serram, asciam,
perpendiculum, terebram, glutinum, ichthyocollam;
normam autem et libellam et tornum et clavem
Theodorus Samius, mensuras et pondera Phidon
Argivus, aut Palamedes ut maluit Gellius; ignem e
silice Pyrodes Cilicis filius, eundem adservare ferula
199 Prometheus, vehiculum cum quattuor rotis Phryges,
mercaturas Poeni, culturam vitium et arborum
Eumolpus Atheniensis, vinum aquae miscere [1] Staphylus Sileni filius, oleum et trapetas Aristaeus Atheniensis, idem mella; bovem et aratrum Buzyges
Atheniensis, ut alii Triptolemus; regiam civitatem
200 Aegyptii, popularem Attici post Theseum. tyrannus
primus fuit Phalaris Agraganti. servitium invenere
Lacedaemonii. iudicium capitis in Areopago primum actum est.

Proelium Afri contra Aegyptios primi fecere fusti-
bus, quos vocant phalangas. clupeos invenerunt
Proetus et Acrisius inter se bellantes, sive Chalcus
Athamantis filius, loricam Midias Messenius, galeam,
gladium, hastam Lacedaemonii, ocreas et cristas
201 Cares. arcum et sagittam Scythem Iovis filium,
alii sagittas Persen Persei filium invenisse dicunt,
lanceas Aetolos, iaculum cum ammento Aetolum
Martis filium, hastas velitares Tyrrenum, eundem [2]
pilum, Penthesileam Amazonem securim, Pisaeum,
venabula et in tormentis scorpionem, Cretas cata-
pultam, Syrophoenicas ballistam et fundam, aeneam

---

[1] miscere? *Mayhoff*: misceri.
[2] eundem *add. Mayhoff*.

---

a I.e. Ox-yoker.

640

Corinth. Carpentry was invented by Daedalus, and with it the saw, axe, plumb-line, gimlet, glue, isinglass; but the square, the plummet, the lathe and the lever by Theodorus of Samos, measures and weights by Phidon of Argos, or, as Gellius preferred, Palamedes; fire from flint by Pyrodes son of Cilix, the storing of fire in a fennel-stalk by Prometheus; a vehicle with four wheels by the Phrygians, trade by the Phoenicians, viticulture and arboriculture by Eumolpus of Athens, diluting wine with water by Staphylus son of Silenus, oil and oil-mills by Aristaeus of Athens, honey by the same; the ox and the plough by Buzyges *a* of Athens, or, as others say, by Triptolemus; monarchical government by the Egyptians, republican by the Athenians after Theseus. The first tyrant was Phalaris at Girgenti. Slavery was invented by the Spartans. Capital trials were first carried on in the Areopagus.

The Africans first fought with clubs (called poles) *Weapons of war, invention of.* in a war against the Egyptians. Shields were invented by Proetus and Acrisius in making war against each other, or else by Chalcus son of Athamas; the breastplate by Midias of Messene, the helmet, sword and spear by the Spartans, greaves and helmet-plumes by the Carians. The bow and arrow is said by some to have been invented by Scythes son of Jove; others say that arrows were invented by Perses son of Perseus, lances by the Aetolians, the spear slung with a thong by Aetolus son of Mars, spears for skirmishing by Tyrrhenus, the javelin by the same, the battle-axe by Penthesilea the Amazon, hunting-spears and among missile engines the scorpion by Pisaeus, the catapult by the Cretans, the ballista and the sling by the Syrophoenicians, the

tubam Pisaeum Tyrreni, testudines Artemonem
202 Clazomenium, equom (qui nunc aries appellatur)
in muralibus machinis Epium ad Troiam; equo vehi
Bellorophontem, frenos et strata equorum Pele-
thronium, pugnare ex equo Thessalos qui Centauri
appellati sunt habitantes secundum Pelium montem.
bigas prima iunxit Phrygum natio, quadrigas Erichthonius. ordinem exercitus, signi dationem, tes-
seras, vigilias Palamedes invenit Troiano bello,
specularum significationem eodem Sinon, inducias
Lycaon, foedera Theseus.

203   Auguria ex avibus Car a quo Caria appellata;
adiecit ex ceteris animalibus Orpheus, haruspicia
Delphus, ignispicia Amphiaraus, extispicia avium
Tiresias Thebanus, interpretationem ostentorum
et somniorum Amphictyon, astrologiam Atlans
Libyae filius, ut alii Aegyptii, ut alii Assyrii, sphaeram
in ea Milesius Anaximander, ventorum rationem
204 Aeolus Hellenis filius; musicam Amphion, fistulam
et monaulum Pan Mercuri, obliquam tibiam Midas
in Phrygia, geminas tibias Marsyas in eadem gente,
Lydios modulos Amphion, Dorios Thamyras Thrax,
Phrygios Marsyas Phryx, citharam Amphion, ut alii
Orpheus, ut alii Linus. septem chordis primum
cecinit III ad IV primas additis Terpander, octavam Simonides addidit, nonam Timotheus. cithara
sine voce cecinit Thamyris primus, cum cantu
Amphion, ut alii Linus. citharoedica carmina con-
posuit Terpander. cum tibiis canere voce Troeze-

bronze trumpet by Pysaeus son of Tyrrhenus,
tortoise-screens by Artemo of Clazomenae, among
siege-engines the horse (now called the ram) by
Epius at Troy; horse-riding by Bellerophon, reins
and saddles by Pelethronius, fighting on horse-
back by the Thessalians called Centaurs, who dwelt
along Mount Pelion. The Phrygian race first
harnessed pairs, Erichthonius four-in-hands. Military formation, the use of pass-words, tokens and
sentries were invented by Palamedes in the Trojan
war, signalling from watch-towers by Sinon in the
same war, truces by Lycaon, treaties by Theseus.

Auguries from birds were invented by Car, from *Augury, etc.,*
whom Caria got its name; Orpheus added auspices *discovery of.*
derived from the other animals, Delphus divination
from victims, Amphiaraus divination from fire,
Tiresias of Thebes divination by inspecting birds'
entrails, Amphictyon the interpretation of portents
and dreams; Atlans son of Libya, or as others say
the Egyptians and others the Assyrians, astronomy,
Anaximander of Miletus the use of a globe in astronomy, Aeolus son of Hellen the theory of winds;
Amphion music, Pan son of Mercury the pipe and
single flute, Midas in Phrygia the slanting flute,
Marsyas in the same nation the double flute, Amphion
the Lydian modes, the Thracian Thamyras the Dorian,
Marsyas of Phrygia the Phrygian, Amphion, or
others say Orpheus and others Linus, the harp.
Terpander first sang with seven strings, adding three
to the original four, Simonides added an eighth,
Timotheus a ninth. Thamyris first played the harp
without using the voice, Amphion, or according to
others Linus, accompanied the harp with singing;
Terpander composed songs for harp and voice.

nius Ardalus instituit. saltationem armatam Curetes
docuere, pyrrichen Pyrrus, utramque in Creta.
205 versum heroum Pythio oraculo debemus; de poe-
matum origine magna quaestio; ante Troianum
bellum probantur fuisse. prosam orationem condere Pherecydes Syrius instituit Cyri regis aetate,
historiam Cadmus Milesius, ludos gymnicos in
Arcadia Lycaon, funebres Acastus in Iolco, post eum
Theseus in Isthmo, Hercules Olympiae; athleticam
Pytheus, pilam lusoriam Gyges Lydus; picturam
Aegypti et in Graecia Euchir Daedali cognatus ut
Aristoteli placet, ut Theophrasto Polygnotus
Atheniensis.

206   Nave primus in Graeciam ex Aegypto Danaus
advenit; antea ratibus navigabatur inventis in Mari
Rubro inter insulas a rege Erythra. reperiuntur
qui Mysos et Troianos priores excogitasse in Hellesponto putent cum transirent adversus Thracas.
etiamnunc in Britannico oceano vitilis corio circum-
sutae fiunt, in Nilo ex papyro ac scirpo et harundine.
207 longa nave Iasonem primum navigasse Philostephanus auctor est, Hegesias Parhalum, Ctesias Samira-
min, Archemachus Aegaeonem, biremem Damastes
Erythraeos fecisse, triremem Thucydides Aminoclen

Ardalus of Troezen instituted singing to the flute.
The Curetes taught dancing in armour, Pyrrhus the
Pyrrhic dance; both of there were in Crete. Hexa-
meter verse we owe to the Pythian oracle, but as
to the origin of poetry there is much debate, though
it is proved to have existed before the Trojan War.
Pherecydes of Syria instituted prose composition in
the period of King Cyrus, Cadmus of Miletus history;
gymnastic games were started by Lycaon in Arcadia,
funeral games by Acastus in Iolcus, and subsequently
by Theseus at the Isthmus and by Hercules at
Olympia; wrestling by Pytheus, the sport of ball-
throwing by Gyges of Lydia; painting by the
Egyptians, and in Greece by Euchir the kinsman of
Daedalus according to Aristotle, but according to
Theophrastus by Polygnotus of Athens.

Danaus first came from Egypt to Greece by ship; *Navigation, development of.*
before that time rafts were used for navigation,
having been invented by King Erythras for use
between the islands in the Red Sea. Persons are
found who think that vessels were devised earlier on
the Hellespont by the Mysians and Trojans when they
crossed to war against the Thracians. Even now in
the British ocean coracles are made of wicker with
hide sown round it, and on the Nile canoes are made
of papyrus, rushes and reeds. The first voyage made
in a long ship is attributed by Philostephanus to
Jason, by Hegesias to Parhalus, by Ctesias to
Samiramis, and by Archemachus to Aegaeo. Further
advances were as follows :—

Vessel	*Inventor*	*Authority*
double-banked galley	the Erythraeans	Damastes
trireme	Aminocles of Corinth	Thucydides

Corinthium, quadriremem Aristoteles Carthaginien-
208 sis, quinqueremem Mnesigiton Salaminios, sex
ordinum Xenagoras Syracusios, ab ea ad decemremem
Mnesigiton Alexandrum Magnum, ad duodecim
ordines Philostephanus Ptolomaeum Soterem, ad
quindecim Demetrium Antigoni, ad triginta Ptolomaeum Philadelphum, ad xl Ptolomaeum Phi-
lopatorem qui Tryphon cognominatus est. onera-
riam Hippus Tyrius invenit, lembum Cyrenenses,
cumbam Phoenices, celetem Rhodii, cercyrum Cyprii ;
209 siderum observationem in navigando Phoenices,
remum Copae, latitudinem eius Plataeae, vela
Icarus, malum et antennam Daedalus, hippegum
Samii aut Pericles Atheniensis, tectas longas Thasii—
antea ex prora tantum et puppi pugnabatur. rostra
addidit Pisaeus Tyrreni, ancoram Eupalamus, eandem
bidentem Anarcharsis, harpagones et manus Pericles
Atheniensis, adminicula gubernandi Tiphys. classe
princeps depugnavit Minos.

Animal occidit primus Hyperbius Martis filius,
Prometheus bovem.

210 LVII. Gentium consensus tacitus primus omnium
conspiravit ut Ionum litteris uterentur. LVIII.
veteres Graecas fuisse easdem paene quae nunc
sunt[1] Latinae indicio erit Delphica antiqui aeris (quae
est hodie in Palatio dono principum) Minervae dicata

---

[1] *Gelenius*: sint.

Vessel	Inventor	Authority
quadrireme	the Carthaginians	Aristotle
quinquereme	the Salaminians	Mnesigiton
galleys of six banks	the Syracusans	Xenagoras
up to ten banks	Alexander the Great	Mnesigiton
up to twelve	Ptolemy Soter	Philostephanus
up to fifteen	Demetrius son of Antigonus	ditto
up to thirty	Ptolemy Philadelphus	ditto
up to forty	Ptolemy Philopator surnamed Tryphon.	ditto

The freight-ship was invented by Hippus of Tyre, the cutter by the Cyrenians, the skiff by the Phoenicians, the yacht by the Rhodians, the yawl by the Cyprians; the Phoenicians invented observing the stars in sailing, the town of Copae invented the oar, the city of Plataea the oar-blade, Icarus sails, Daedalus mast and yard, the Samians or Pericles of Athens the cavalry transport, the Thasians decked longships—previously the marines had fought from the bows and stern only. Pisaeus son of Tyrrenus added beaks, Eupalamus the anchor, Anacharsis the double-fluked anchor, Pericles of Athens grappling-irons and claws, Tiphys the tiller. Minos was the first who fought a battle with a fleet.

Hyperbius son of Mars first killed an animal, Prometheus an ox.

LVII. The first of all cases of tacit agreement between the nations was the convention to employ the alphabet of the Ionians. LVIII. The practical identity of the old Greek alphabet with the present Latin one will be proved by an ancient Delphic tablet of bronze (at the present day in the Palace, a gift of the

Invention of writing.

647

[in bibliotheca][1] cum inscriptione tali: ΝΑΥΣΙΚ-
ΡΑΤΗΣ ΑΝΕΘΕΤΟ ΤΑΙ ΔΙΟΣ ΚΟΡΑΙ ΤΑΝ ΔΕΚΑ-
ΤΑΝ . . .

211   LIX. Sequens gentium consensus in tonsoribus
fuit, sed Romanis tardior. in Italiam ex Sicilia venere
post Romam conditam anno ccccliv adducente P.
Titinio Mena, ut auctor est Varro; antea intonsi
fuere. primus omnium radi cotidie instituit Africanus sequens. divos Augustus cultris semper usus
est.

212   LX. Tertius consensus fuit in horarum observatione,
iam hic[2] ratione[3] accedens, quando et a quo in Graecia
reperta, diximus secundo volumine. serius etiam hoc
Romae contigit: xii tabulis ortus tantum et occasus
nominantur, post aliquot annos adiectus est et
meridies, accenso consulum id pronuntiante cum a
curia inter Rostra et Graecostasim proxpexisset
solem. a columna Maenia ad carcerem inclinato
sidere supremam pronuntiavit, sed hoc serenis tantum
213 diebus, usque ad primum Punicum bellum. princeps
Romanis solarium horologium statuisse ante undecim
annos quam cum Pyrro bellatum est ad aedem Quirini
L. Papirius Cursor, cum eam dedicaret a patre suo
votam, a Fabio Vestale proditur; sed neque facti
horologi rationem vel artificem significat nec unde
translatum sit aut apud quem scriptum id invenerit.
214 M. Varro primum statutum in publico secundum

---

[1] *Secl. Mayhoff.*   [2] *V.l.* hinc.
[3] *V.l.* rationem.

---

[a] Text and meaning are doubtful.
[b] II. 187.
[c] Begun 281 B.C.

emperors) dedicated to Minerva, with the following inscription: *Tithe dedicated by Nausicrates to the Daughter of Zeus. . . .*

LIX. The next agreement between nations was in the matter of shaving the beard, but with the Romans *Introduction* this was later. Barbers came to Rome from Sicily in *of shaving.* 300 B.C., according to Varro being brought there by Publius Titinius Mena; before then the Romans had been unshaved. The second Africanus first introduced a daily shave. His late Majesty Augustus never neglected the razor.

LX. The third agreement was in the observation of the hours (this now being an addition made by *Systems of* theory),[a] the date and inventor of which we have stated *time-keeping:* in Book II.[b] This also happened later at Rome: in *sun-dials.* the Twelve Tables only sunrise and sunset are specified; a few years later noon was also added, the consuls' apparitor announcing it when from the Senate-house he saw the sun between the Beaks and the Greek Lodging. When the sun sloped from the Maenian Column to the Prison he announced the last hour, but this only on clear days, down to the First Punic War. We have it on the authority of Fabius Vestalis that the first sundial was erected 11 years before the war[c] with Pyrrhus at the Temple of Quirinus by Lucius Papirius Cursor when dedicating that temple, which had been vowed by his father; but Fabius does not indicate the principle of the sun-dial's construction or the maker, nor where it was brought from or the name of the writer who is his authority for the statement. Marcus Varro records that the first public sun-dial was set up on a column along by the Beaks during the First Punic War after

649

Rostra in columna tradit bello Punico primo a M'.
Valerio Messala cos. Catina capta in Sicilia, deportatum inde post xxx annos quam de Papiriano horo.
logio traditur, anno urbis ccccLxxxxı. nec con-
gruebant ad horas eius liniae, paruerunt tamen
ei annis undecentum, donec Q. Marcius Philippus qui
cum L. Paullo fuit censor diligentius ordinatum iuxta
posuit; idque munus inter censoria opera gratissime
215 acceptum est. etiam tum tamen nubilo incertae
fuere horae usque ad proximum lustrum; tunc
Scipio Nasica collega Laenatis primus aqua divisit
horas aeque noctium ac dierum, idque horologium
sub tecto dicavit anno urbis DXCV: tamdiu populo
Romano indiscreta lux fuit.

Nunc praevertemur[1] ad reliqua animalia, primumque terrestria.

---

[1] *Mayhoff*: revertemur *aut* revertamur.

Catania in Sicily had been taken [a] by the consul Manius Valerius Messala, and that it was brought from Sicily thirty years later than the traditional date of Papirius's sundial, B.C. 264. The lines of this sundial did not agree with the hours, but all the same they followed it for 99 years, till Quintus Marcius Philippus who was Censor with Lucius Paulus placed a more carefully designed one next to it, and this gift was received as one of the most welcome of the censor's undertakings. Even then however the hours were uncertain in cloudy weather, until the next lustrum, when Scipio Nasica the colleague of Laenas instituted the first water-clock dividing the hours of the nights and the days equally, and dedicated this time-piece in a roofed building, B.C. 159. For so long a period the divisions of daylight had not been marked for the Roman public.

We will now turn to the rest of the animals, beginning with land-animals.

[a] 263 B.C.

INDEX OF PEOPLE

653

INDEX OF PEOPLE

654

INDEX OF PEOPLE

655

INDEX OF PEOPLE

INDEX OF PEOPLE

657

INDEX OF PEOPLE

INDEX OF PEOPLE

INDEX OF PEOPLE

GEOGRAPHICAL INDEX

Tiresias, legendary augur, blind, VII 203
Tiridates, king of Parthia, VII 129
Titinius, VII 211
Toranius, VII 56
Triarius, defeated by Mithridates in Pontus 68 B.C., VI 10
Triptolemus, mythical hero of Eleusis, VII 199
Trispithami, VII 26
Tritanus, VII 81
Trogus Pompeius, temp. Augustus, wrote universal history, VII 33
Tuditanus, consul 129 B.C., III 129
Tullius, VII 75
Turduli, III 8, 13, VII 71
Turranius Gracilis, African geographer, III 3
Tusci, III 51, 60, 70
Tyrrheni, III 50
Tyrrhenus, VII 201

Valeria, VII 68
Valerius Corvinus, commanded against Gauls, Etruscans and Samnites, 4th c. B.C., VII 157
Valerius Messala, VII 214
Valerius Soranus, poet, *fl.* 100 B.C., III 65
Varro, M. Terentius, 116–28 B.C., encyclopaedic author, III 8, 45, 95,

101, 109, 142, IV 62, 65, 77, 115, VI 38, 51, VII 13, 75, 80, 83, 114, 175, 211, 214
Ventidius, served under Caesar in Gaul and for Antony in Parthia, VII 135
Vergilius, VII 114
Verrius, VII 180
Vespasianus, III 30, 66, V 69
Vesta, VII 141
Vibius, VII 53
Vinnius, VII 82
Vipstanus, VII 84
Vistilia, VII 39
Volcanus, III 93, VI 187
Volcatius, VII 181
Volsci, III 59, V 129
Volusius, *d.* A.D. 56, aged 93, VII 62, 156
Vopisci, VII 47

Xenagoras, historian, early 2nd c. B.C., V 129
Xenophilus, VII 168
Xenophon, IV 95, VI 200, VII 155
Xerxes, IV 37, 46

Zoroaster, Persian, reformer of Magian religion, extant oracles spurious, VII 72

GEOGRAPHICAL INDEX

Abila, III 4
Achaia, IV 12
Actium, IV 5
Adriatic, III 150
Aegean, IV 1, 51
Aeolis, V 121
Aetolia, IV 6
Africa, V 1
Alexandria, V 62, 128
Algeria, V 17
Alps, III 132
Anglesea, IV 103
Apulia, III 103
Aquitania, IV 107
Arabian Gulf, VI 147
Argos, Gulf of, IV 18
Armenia, VI 25, 129
Armorica, IV 105

Asia, V 27
Asia Minor, V 91
Athos, IV 73
Attica, IV 23
Atlas, V 5, 11
Azov, IV 75, 78, VI 3, etc.

Babylon, VI 124
Baetica, III 7, 17
Balaklava, IV 86
Balearics, III 76
Balkh, VI 45
Barca, V 31
Bardsey, IV 103
Belgium, IV 106
Bithynia, V 148
Black Sea, IV 44, 75, 92, VI, 1, *sqq.*
Boeotia, IV 25

GEOGRAPHICAL INDEX

662

GEOGRAPHICAL INDEX

GEOGRAPHICAL INDEX

PRINTED IN GREAT BRITAIN BY RICHARD CLAY AND COMPANY, LTD.,
BUNGAY, SUFFOLK.

THE LOEB CLASSICAL LIBRARY

VOLUMES ALREADY PUBLISHED

Latin Authors

AMMIANUS MARCELLINUS. Translated by J. C. Rolfe. 3 Vols. (Vols. I. and II. *2nd Imp. revised.*)

APULEIUS: THE GOLDEN ASS (METAMORPHOSES). W. Adlington (1566). Revised by S. Gaselee. (*7th Imp.*)

ST. AUGUSTINE, CONFESSIONS OF. W. Watts (1631). 2 Vols. (*5th Imp.*)

ST. AUGUSTINE, SELECT LETTERS. J. H. Baxter.

AUSONIUS. H. G. Evelyn White. 2 Vols.

BEDE. J. E. King. 2 Vols.

BOETHIUS: TRACTS AND DE CONSOLATIONE PHILO-SOPHIAE. Rev. H. F. Stewart and E. K. Rand. (*4th Imp.*)

CAESAR: CIVIL WARS. A. G. Peskett. (*4th Imp.*)

CAESAR: GALLIC WAR. H. J. Edwards. (*9th Imp.*)

CATO AND VARRO: DE RE RUSTICA. H. B. Ash and W. D. Hooper. (*2nd Imp.*)

CATULLUS. F. W. Cornish; TIBULLUS. J. B. Postgate; AND PERVIGILIUM VENERIS. J. W. Mackail. (*11th Imp.*)

CELSUS: DE MEDICINA. W. G. Spencer. 3 Vols. (Vol. I. *2nd Imp. revised.*)

CICERO: BRUTUS, AND ORATOR. G. L. Hendrickson and H. M. Hubbell. (*2nd Imp.*)

CICERO: DE FINIBUS. H. Rackham. (*3rd Imp. revised.*)

CICERO: DE NATURA DEORUM AND ACADEMICA. H. Rackham.

CICERO: DE OFFICIIS. Walter Miller. (*4th Imp.*)

CICERO: DE ORATORE. 2 Vols. E. W. Sutton and H. Rackham.

CICERO: DE REPUBLICA AND DE LEGIBUS. Clinton W. Keyes. (*2nd Imp.*)

CICERO: DE SENECTUTE, DE AMICITIA, DE DIVI-NATIONE. W. A. Falconer. (*5th Imp.*)

CICERO: IN CATILINAM, PRO FLACCO, PRO MURENA, PRO SULLA. Louis E. Lord. (*2nd Imp. revised.*)

CICERO: LETTERS TO ATTICUS. E. O. Winstedt. 3 Vols. (Vol. I. *6th Imp.*, Vol. II. *3rd Imp.* and Vol. III. *3rd Imp.*)

CICERO : LETTERS TO HIS FRIENDS. W. Glynn Williams. 3 Vols. (Vols. I. and II. *2nd Imp. revised.*)
CICERO : PHILIPPICS. W. C. A. Ker. (*2nd Imp. revised.*)
CICERO : PRO ARCHIA, POST REDITUM, DE DOMO, DE HARUSPICUM RESPONSIS, PRO PLANCIO. N. H. Watts. (*2nd Imp.*)
CICERO : PRO CAECINA, PRO LEGE MANILIA, PRO CLUENTIO, PRO RABIRIO. H. Grose Hodge. (*2nd Imp.*)
CICERO : PRO MILONE, IN PISONEM, PRO SCAURO, PRO FONTEIO, PRO RABIRIO POSTUMO, PRO MARCELLO, PRO LIGARIO, PRO REGE DEIOTARO. N. H. Watts.
CICERO : PRO QUINCTIO, PRO ROSCIO AMERINO, PRO ROSCIO COMOEDO, CONTRA RULLUM. J. H. Freese. (*2nd Imp. revised.*)
CICERO : TUSCULAN DISPUTATIONS. J. E. King. (*2nd Imp.*)
CICERO : VERRINE ORATIONS. L. H. G. Greenwood. 2 Vols.
CLAUDIAN. M. Platnauer. 2 Vols.
COLUMELLA : DE RE RUSTICA. H. B. Ash. 3 Vols. Vol. I.
CURTIUS, QUINTUS : HISTORY OF ALEXANDER. Translated by J. C. Rolfe. 2 Vols.
FLORUS. E. S. Forster, and CORNELIUS NEPOS. J. C. Rolfe. (*2nd Imp.*)
FRONTINUS : STRATAGEMS and AQUEDUCTS. C. E. Bennett and M. B. McElwain.
FRONTO : CORRESPONDENCE. C. R. Haines. 2 Vols.
GELLIUS. J. C. Rolfe. 3 Vols. (Vols. I and II. *2nd Imp.*)
HORACE : ODES and EPODES. C. E. Bennett. (*12th Imp. revised.*)
HORACE : SATIRES, EPISTLES, ARS POETICA. H. R. Fairclough. (*7th Imp. revised.*)
JEROME : SELECTED LETTERS. F. A. Wright.
JUVENAL and PERSIUS. G. G. Ramsay. (*6th Imp.*)
LIVY. B. O. Foster, F. G. Moore, Evan T. Sage, and A. C. Schlesinger. 13 Vols. Vols. I.–VII., IX.–XII. (Vol. I. *3rd Imp.*, Vols. II., III. and IX. *2nd Imp. revised.*)
LUCAN. J. D. Duff. (*2nd Imp.*)
LUCRETIUS. W. H. D. Rouse. (*6th Imp. revised.*)
MARTIAL. W. C. A. Ker. 2 Vols. (Vol. I. *5th Imp.*, Vol. II. *3rd Imp. revised.*)
MINOR LATIN POETS : from PUBLILIUS SYRUS to RUTILIUS NAMATIANUS, including GRATTIUS, CALPURNIUS SICULUS, NEMESIANUS, AVIANUS, and others with " Aetna " and the " Phoenix." J. Wight Duff and Arnold M. Duff. (*2nd Imp.*)
OVID : THE ART OF LOVE and OTHER POEMS. J. H. Mozley. (*3rd Imp.*)
OVID : FASTI. Sir James G. Frazer.
OVID : HEROIDES and AMORES. Grant Showerman. (*4th Imp.*)

2

OVID : METAMORPHOSES. F. J. Miller. 2 Vols. (Vol.
I. 9th Imp., Vol. II. 7th Imp.)
OVID : TRISTIA and EX PONTO. A. L. Wheeler. (2nd Imp.)
PERSIUS. Cf. JUVENAL.
PETRONIUS. M. Heseltine; SENECA : APOCOLOCYN-
TOSIS. W. H. D. Rouse. (7th Imp. revised.)
PLAUTUS. Paul Nixon. 5 Vols. (Vols. I. and II. 4th Imp.,
Vol. III. 3rd Imp.)
PLINY : LETTERS. Melmoth's Translation revised by
W. M. L. Hutchinson. 2 Vols. (5th Imp.)
PLINY : NATURAL HISTORY. H. Rackham and W. H. S.
Jones. 10 Vols. Vols. I–V. H. Rackham. (Vol. I. 3rd Imp.
Vols. II. and III. 2nd Imp.)
PROPERTIUS. H. E. Butler. (5th Imp.)
QUINTILIAN. H. E. Butler. 4 Vols. (2nd Imp.)
REMAINS OF OLD LATIN. E. H. Warmington. 4 Vols.
Vol. I. (ENNIUS AND CAECILIUS.) Vol. II. (LIVIUS,
NAEVIUS, PACUVIUS, ACCIUS.) Vol. III. (LUCILIUS
and LAWS OF XII TABLES). Vol. IV. (ARCHAIC
INSCRIPTIONS.)
SALLUST. J. C. Rolfe. (3rd Imp. revised.)
SCRIPTORES HISTORIAE AUGUSTAE. D. Magie. 3
Vols. (Vol. I. 2nd Imp. revised.)
SENECA : APOCOLOCYNTOSIS. Cf. PETRONIUS.
SENECA : EPISTULAE MORALES. R. M. Gummere. 3
Vols. (Vol. I. 3rd Imp., Vols. II. and III. 2nd Imp. revised.)
SENECA : MORAL ESSAYS. J. W. Basore. 3 Vols. (Vols.
II. and III. 2nd Imp. revised.)
SENECA : TRAGEDIES. F. J. Miller. 2 Vols. (Vol. I.
3rd Imp., Vol. II. 2nd Imp. revised.)
SIDONIUS : POEMS and LETTERS. W. B. Anderson.
2 Vols. Vol. I.
SILIUS ITALICUS. J. D. Duff. 2 Vols. (Vol. II. 2nd Imp.)
STATIUS. J. H. Mozley. 2 Vols.
SUETONIUS. J. C. Rolfe. 2 Vols. (Vol. I. 6th Imp., Vol. II.
5th Imp. revised.)
TACITUS : DIALOGUS. Sir Wm. Peterson. AGRICOLA
and GERMANIA. Maurice Hutton. (6th Imp.)
TACITUS : HISTORIES and ANNALS. C. H. Moore and
J. Jackson. 4 Vols. (Vols. I. and II. 2nd Imp.)
TERENCE. John Sargeaunt. 2 Vols. (Vol. I. 6th Imp.,
Vol. II. 5th Imp.)
TERTULLIAN : APOLOGIA and DE SPECTACULIS.
T. R. Glover. MINUCIUS FELIX. G. H. Rendall.
VALERIUS FLACCUS. J. H. Mozley. (2nd Imp. revised.)
VARRO : DE LINGUA LATINA. R. G. Kent. 2 Vols.
(2nd Imp.)
VELLEIUS PATERCULUS and RES GESTAE DIVI
AUGUSTI. F. W. Shipley.
VIRGIL. H. R. Fairclough. 2 Vols. (Vol. I. 16th Imp.,
Vol. II. 13th Imp. revised.)

3

VITRUVIUS : DE ARCHITECTURA. F. Granger. 2 Vols. (Vol. I. *2nd Imp.*)

Greek Authors

ACHILLES TATIUS. S. Gaselee. (*2nd Imp.*)
AENEAS TACTICUS, ASCLEPIODOTUS AND ONASANDER. The Illinois Greek Club.
AESCHINES. C. D. Adams. (*2nd Imp.*)
AESCHYLUS. H. Weir Smyth. 2 Vols. (Vol. I. *5th Imp.*, Vol. II. *4th Imp.*)
ANDOCIDES, ANTIPHON. Cf. MINOR ATTIC ORATORS.
APOLLODORUS. Sir James G. Frazer. 2 Vols. (*2nd Imp.*)
APOLLONIUS RHODIUS. R. C. Seaton. (*4th Imp.*)
THE APOSTOLIC FATHERS. Kirsopp Lake. 2 Vols. (Vol. I. *6th Imp.*, Vol. II. *5th Imp.*)
APPIAN'S ROMAN HISTORY. Horace White. 4 Vols. (Vol. I. *3rd Imp.*, Vols. II., III. and IV. *2nd Imp.*)
ARATUS. Cf. CALLIMACHUS.
ARISTOPHANES. Benjamin Bickley Rogers. 3 Vols. Verse trans. (*4th Imp.*)
ARISTOTLE : ART OF RHETORIC. J. H. Freese. (*3rd Imp.*)
ARISTOTLE : ATHENIAN CONSTITUTION, EUDEMIAN ETHICS, VICES AND VIRTUES. H. Rackham. (*2nd Imp.*)
ARISTOTLE : GENERATION OF ANIMALS. A. L. Peck. (*3rd Imp.*)
ARISTOTLE : METAPHYSICS. H. Tredennick. 2 Vols. (*3rd Imp.*)
ARISTOTLE : MINOR WORKS. W. S. Hett. On Colours, On Things Heard, On Physiognomies, On Plants, On Marvellous Things Heard, Mechanical Problems, On Indivisible Lines, On Position and Names of Winds.
ARISTOTLE : NICOMACHEAN ETHICS. H. Rackham. (*5th Imp. revised.*)
ARISTOTLE : OECONOMICA AND MAGNA MORALIA. G. C. Armstrong; (with Metaphysics, Vol. II.). (*3rd Imp.*)
ARISTOTLE : ON THE HEAVENS. W. K. C. Guthrie. (*2nd Imp. revised.*)
ARISTOTLE : ON THE SOUL, PARVA NATURALIA, ON BREATH. W. S. Hett. (*2nd Imp. revised.*)
ARISTOTLE : ORGANON. H. P. Cooke and H. Tredennick. 2 Vols. Vol. I.
ARISTOTLE : PARTS OF ANIMALS. A. L. Peck; MOTION AND PROGRESSION OF ANIMALS. E. S. Forster. (*2nd Imp. revised.*)
ARISTOTLE : PHYSICS. Rev. P. Wicksteed and F. M. Cornford. 2 Vols. (Vol. II. *2nd Imp.*)
ARISTOTLE : POETICS AND LONGINUS. W. Hamilton Fyfe; DEMETRIUS ON STYLE. W. Rhys Roberts. (*4th Imp. revised.*)
ARISTOTLE : POLITICS. H. Rackham. (*3rd Imp. revised.*)
ARISTOTLE : PROBLEMS. W. S. Hett. 2 Vols.

4

ARISTOTLE: RHETORICA AD ALEXANDRUM (with
PROBLEMS, Vol. II.). H. Rackham.
ARRIAN: HISTORY OF ALEXANDER AND INDICA.
Rev. E. Iliffe Robson. 2 Vols. (Vol. I. *2nd Imp.*)
ATHENAEUS: DEIPNOSOPHISTAE. C. B. Gulick. 7
Vols. (Vols. V. and VI. *2nd Imp.*)
ST. BASIL: LETTERS. R. J. Deferrari. 4 Vols.
CALLIMACHUS AND LYCOPHRON. A. W. Mair; ARA-
TUS. G. R. Mair.
CLEMENT OF ALEXANDRIA. Rev. G. W. Butterworth.
(*2nd Imp.*)
COLLUTHUS. Cf. OPPIAN.
DAPHNIS AND CHLOE. Thornley's Translation revised by
J. M. Edmonds; AND PARTHENIUS. S. Gaselee. (*3rd
Imp.*)
DEMOSTHENES: DE CORONA AND DE FALSA LEGA-
TIONE. C. A. Vince and J. H. Vince. (*2nd Imp. revised.*)
DEMOSTHENES: MEIDIAS, ANDROTION, ARISTO-
CRATES, TIMOCRATES AND ARISTOGEITON, I. AND
II. Translated by J. H. Vince.
DEMOSTHENES: OLYNTHIACS, PHILIPPICS AND MINOR
ORATIONS: I.–XVII. AND XX. J. H. Vince.
DEMOSTHENES: PRIVATE ORATIONS. A. T. Murray.
3 Vols. (Vol. I. *2nd Imp.*)
DIO CASSIUS: ROMAN HISTORY. E. Cary. 9 Vols.
(Vols. I. and II. *2nd Imp.*)
DIO CHRYSOSTOM. J. W. Cohoon and H. Lamar Crosby.
5 Vols. Vols. I.–IV.
DIODORUS SICULUS: THE LIBRARY. 12 Vols. Vols.
I.–IV. translated by C. H. Oldfather. Vol. IX. translated
by C. H. Geer.
DIOGENES LAERTIUS. R. D. Hicks. 2 Vols. (Vol. I.
3rd Imp., Vol. II. *2nd Imp.*)
DIONYSIUS OF HALICARNASSUS: ROMAN ANTI-
QUITIES. Spelman's translation revised by E. Cary. 7
Vols. Vols. I.–VI. (Vol. I. *2nd Imp.*)
EPICTETUS. W. A. Oldfather. 2 Vols. (Vol. I. *2nd Imp.*)
EURIPIDES. A. S. Way. 4 Vols. (Vols. I., II. and IV. *6th
Imp.*, Vol. III. *5th Imp.*) Verse trans.
EUSEBIUS: ECCLESIASTICAL HISTORY. Kirsopp Lake
and J. E. L. Oulton. 2 Vols. (Vol. I. *2nd Imp.*, Vol. II.
3rd Imp.)
GALEN: ON THE NATURAL FACULTIES. A. J. Brock.
(*3rd Imp.*)
THE GREEK ANTHOLOGY. W. R. Paton. 5 Vols. (Vols.
I. and II. *4th Imp.*, Vols. III. and IV. *3rd Imp.*)
GREEK ELEGY AND IAMBUS WITH THE ANACREONTEA.
J. M. Edmonds. 2 Vols. (Vol. I. *2nd Imp.*)
THE GREEK BUCOLIC POETS (THEOCRITUS, BION,
MOSCHUS). J. M. Edmonds. (*6th Imp. revised.*)
GREEK MATHEMATICAL WORKS. Ivor Thomas. 2 Vols.

HERODES. Cf. THEOPHRASTUS : CHARACTERS.
HERODOTUS. A. D. Godley. 4 Vols. (Vol. I. 4th Imp.,
Vols. II. IV. 3rd Imp.)
HESIOD AND THE HOMERIC HYMNS. H. G. Evelyn
White. (6th Imp., revised and enlarged.)
HIPPOCRATES AND THE FRAGMENTS OF HERACLEITUS.
W. H. S. Jones and E. T. Withington. 4 Vols. (Vols. I., II.
and IV. 2nd Imp., Vol. III. 3rd Imp.)
HOMER : ILIAD. A. T. Murray. 2 Vols. (5th Imp.)
HOMER : ODYSSEY. A. T. Murray. 2 Vols. (7th Imp.)
ISAEUS. E. W. Forster. (2nd Imp.)
ISOCRATES. George Norlin. 3 Vols.
ST. JOHN DAMASCENE : BARLAAM AND IOASAPH.
Rev. G. R. Woodward and Harold Mattingly. (2nd Imp.
revised.)
JOSEPHUS. H. St. J. Thackeray and Ralph Marcus. 9 Vols.
Vols. I.–VII. (Vol. V. 2nd Imp.)
JULIAN. Wilmer Cave Wright. 3 Vols. (Vols. I. and II.
2nd Imp.)
LUCIAN. A. M. Harmon. 8 Vols. Vols. I.–V. (Vols. I.
and II. 3rd Imp., Vol. III. 2nd Imp.)
LYCOPHRON. Cf. CALLIMACHUS.
LYRA GRAECA. J. M. Edmonds. 3 Vols. (Vol. I. and III.
3rd Imp., Vol. II. 2nd Ed. revised and enlarged.)
LYSIAS. W. R. M. Lamb. (2nd Imp.)
MANETHO. W. G. Waddell : PTOLEMY : TETRABIBLOS.
F. E. Robbins. (2nd Imp.)
MARCUS AURELIUS. C. R. Haines. (3rd Imp. revised.)
MENANDER. F. G. Allinson. (2nd Imp. revised.)
MINOR ATTIC ORATORS (ANTIPHON, ANDOCIDES,
DEMADES, DEINARCHUS, HYPEREIDES). K. J. Maid-
ment and J. O. Burtt. 2 Vols. Vol. I. K. J. Maidment.
NONNOS. W. H. D. Rouse. 3 Vols. (Vol. III. 2nd Imp.)
OPPIAN, COLLUTHUS, TRYPHIODORUS. A. W. Mair.
PAPYRI. NON-LITERARY SELECTIONS. A. S. Hunt and
C. C. Edgar. 2 Vols. LITERARY SELECTIONS. Vol. I.
(Poetry). D. L. Page. (2nd Imp.)
PARTHENIUS. Cf. DAPHNIS AND CHLOE.
PAUSANIAS : DESCRIPTION OF GREECE. W. H. S.
Jones. 5 Vols. and Companion Vol. (Vols. I. and III. 2nd
Imp.)
PHILO. 10 Vols. Vols. I.–V.; F. H. Colson and Rev. G. H.
Whitaker. Vols. VI.–IX.; F. H. Colson. (Vol. IV. 2nd Imp.)
PHILOSTRATUS : THE LIFE OF APOLLONIUS OF
TYANA. F. C. Conybeare. 2 Vols. (Vol. I. 3rd Imp.,
Vol. II. 2nd Imp.)
PHILOSTRATUS : IMAGINES; CALLISTRATUS : DE-
SCRIPTIONS. A. Fairbanks.
PHILOSTRATUS AND EUNAPIUS : LIVES OF THE
SOPHISTS. Wilmer Cave Wright.
PINDAR. Sir J. E. Sandys. (7th Imp. revised.)

PLATO: CHARMIDES, ALCIBIADES, HIPPARCHUS, THE LOVERS, THEAGES, MINOS AND EPINOMIS. W. R. M. Lamb.

PLATO: CRATYLUS, PARMENIDES, GREATER HIPPIAS, LESSER HIPPIAS. H. N. Fowler. (*3rd Imp.*)

PLATO: EUTHYPHRO, APOLOGY, CRITO, PHAEDO, PHAEDRUS. H. N. Fowler. (*9th Imp.*)

PLATO: LACHES, PROTAGORAS, MENO, EUTHYDEMUS. W. R. M. Lamb. (*2nd Imp. revised.*)

PLATO: LAWS. Rev. R. G. Bury. 2 Vols. (*2nd Imp.*)

PLATO: LYSIS, SYMPOSIUM, GORGIAS. W. R. M. Lamb. (*4th Imp. revised.*)

PLATO: REPUBLIC. Paul Shorey. 2 Vols. (Vol. I. *4th Imp.*, Vol. II. *3rd Imp.*)

PLATO: STATESMAN, PHILEBUS. H. N. Fowler; ION. W. R. M. Lamb. (*3rd Imp.*)

PLATO: THEAETETUS AND SOPHIST. H. N. Fowler. (*3rd Imp.*)

PLATO: TIMAEUS, CRITIAS, CLITOPHO, MENEXENUS, EPISTULAE. Rev. R. G. Bury. (*2nd Imp.*)

PLUTARCH: MORALIA. 14 Vols. Vols. I.–V. F. C. Babbitt; Vol. VI. W. C. Helmbold; Vol. X. H. N. Fowler.

PLUTARCH: THE PARALLEL LIVES. B. Perrin. 11 Vols. (Vols. I., II., III., VI., VII., and XI. *2nd Imp.*)

POLYBIUS. W. R. Paton. 6 Vols.

PROCOPIUS: HISTORY OF THE WARS. H. B. Dewing. 7 Vols. (Vol. I. *2nd Imp.*)

PTOLEMY: TETRABIBLOS. Cf. MANETHO.

QUINTUS SMYRNAEUS. A. S. Way. Verse trans. (*2nd Imp.*)

SEXTUS EMPIRICUS. Rev. R. G. Bury. 4 Vols. (Vol. I. *2nd Imp.*)

SOPHOCLES. F. Storr. 2 Vols. (Vol. I. *8th Imp.*, Vol. II. *5th Imp.*) Verse trans.

STRABO: GEOGRAPHY. Horace L. Jones. 8 Vols. (Vols. I., V. and VIII. *2nd Imp.*)

THEOPHRASTUS: CHARACTERS. J. M. Edmonds; HERODES, etc. A. D. Knox. (*2nd Imp.*)

THEOPHRASTUS: ENQUIRY INTO PLANTS. Sir Arthur Hort, Bart. 2 Vols.

THUCYDIDES. C. F. Smith. 4 Vols. (Vol. I. *3rd Imp.*, Vols. II., III. and IV. *2nd Imp. revised.*)

TRYPHIODORUS. Cf. OPPIAN.

XENOPHON: CYROPAEDIA. Walter Miller. 2 Vols. (Vol. I. *2nd Imp.*, Vol. II. *3rd Imp.*)

XENOPHON: HELLENICA, ANABASIS, APOLOGY, AND SYMPOSIUM. C. L. Brownson and O. J. Todd. 3 Vols. (*3rd Imp.*)

XENOPHON: MEMORABILIA AND OECONOMICUS. E. C. Marchant. (*2nd Imp.*)

XENOPHON: SCRIPTAMINORA. E. C. Marchant. (*2nd Imp.*)

IN PREPARATION

Greek Authors

ALCIPHRON. A. R. Benner and F. Fobes.
ARISTOTLE : DE MUNDO.
ARISTOTLE : HISTORY OF ANIMALS. A. L. Peck.
ARISTOTLE : METEOROLOGICA. H. P. Lee.
DEMOSTHENES : EPISTLES, etc. N. W. and N. J. De Witt.
PLOTINUS.

Latin Authors

ST. AUGUSTINE : CITY OF GOD. W. S. Maguinness.
[CICERO] : AD HERENNIUM. H. Caplan.
CICERO : DE INVENTIONE, etc. H. M. Hubbell.
CICERO : PRO SESTIO, IN VATINIUM, PRO CAELIO,
    DE PROVINCIIS CONSULARIBUS, PRO BALBO. J. H.
    Freese and R. Gardner.
PHAEDRUS AND OTHER FABULISTS. B. E. Perry.
PRUDENTIUS. J. H. Thomson.

DESCRIPTIVE PROSPECTUS ON APPLICATION

London   -   WILLIAM HEINEMANN LTD
Cambridge, Mass.   HARVARD UNIVERSITY PRESS